George Petrie (1790-1866)

The Rediscovery of Ireland's Past

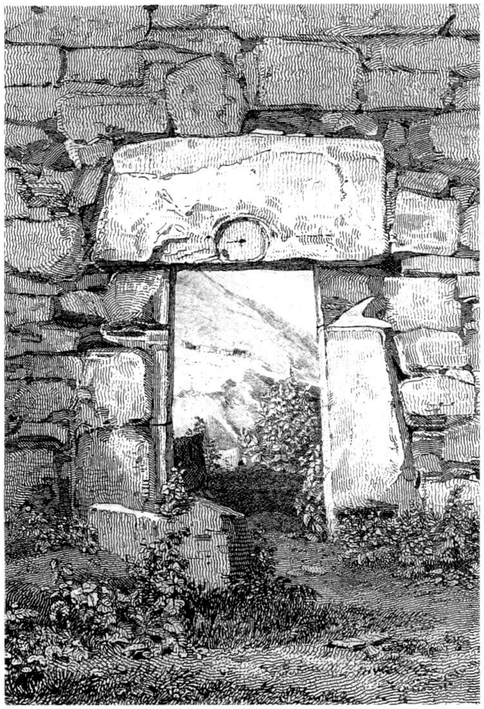

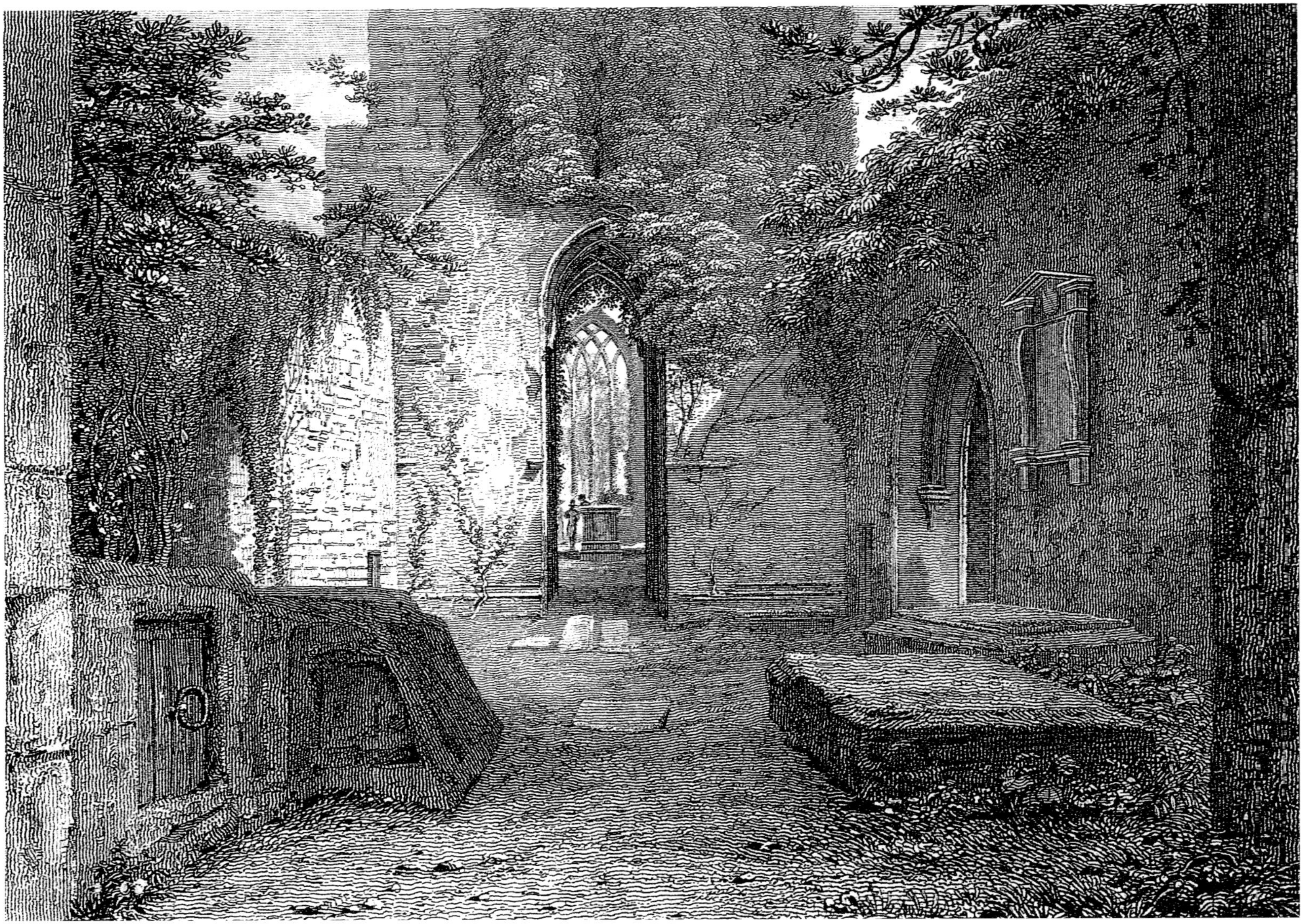

Interior of Mucruss Abbey

engraving after Petrie from G.N. Wright, *A Guide to the Lakes of Killarney*, 1823

preceding page: *The Door of St. Fechin's Church, Fore, Co. of Westmeath*, engraving after Petrie from T. Cromwell, *Excursions through Ireland*, vol. ii, 1820

George Petrie

(1790-1866)

THE REDISCOVERY OF IRELAND'S PAST

CRAWFORD MUNICIPAL ART GALLERY, CORK
GANDON EDITIONS, KINSALEGEORGE PETRIE (1790-1866) – THE REDISCOVERY OF IRELAND'S PAST

GEORGE PETRIE (1790-1866) – THE REDISCOVERY OF IRELAND'S PAST
by Peter Murray
with essays by Joep Leerssen and Tom Dunne

Published by the Crawford Municipal Art Gallery and Gandon Editions to coincide with the exhibition
of the same name at the Crawford Municipal Art Gallery, March-April 2004,
and subsequently at the National Gallery of Ireland.

ISBN 0948037 091 hb / ISBN 0948037 105 pb

Produced by Gandon Editions for the Crawford Municipal Art Gallery
Designed by John O'Regan (© Gandon, 2004)
Produced by Nicola Dearey
Printed by Nicholson & Bass, Belfast

Crawford Municipal Art Gallery
Emmet Place, Cork, Ireland
tel +353 (0)21-4273377 / fax 021-4805043 / e-mail crawfordgallery@eircom.net
www.crawfordartgallery.com

Gandon Editions
Oysterhaven, Kinsale, Co Cork, Ireland
tel +353 (0)21-4770830 / fax 021-4770755 / e-mail gandon@eircom.net
www.gandon-editions.com
Gandon Editions is grant-aided by The Arts Council / An Chomhairle Ealaíon

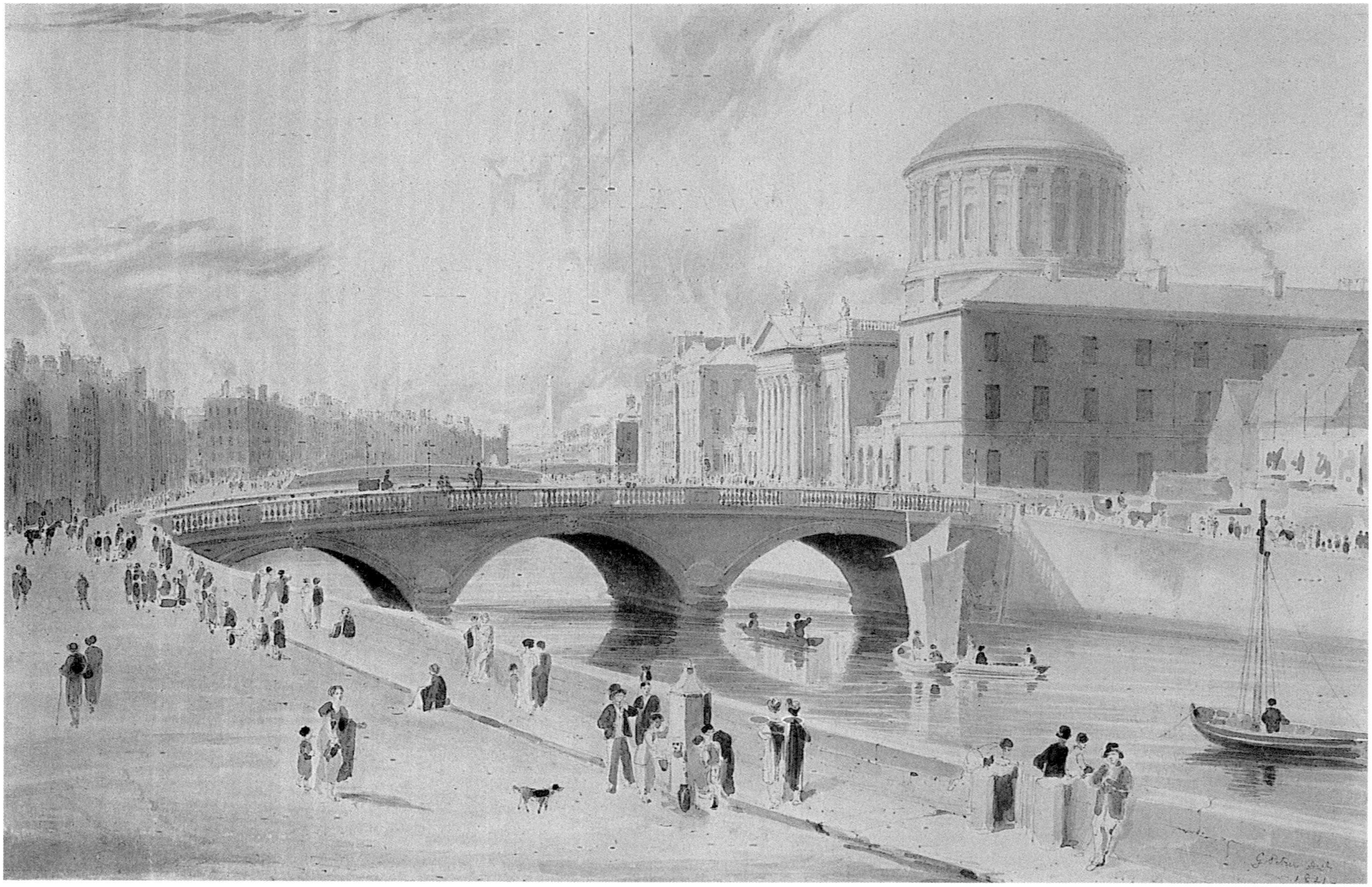

The Law Courts
c.1820-21, Indian ink on paper, 16 x 24 cm (coll: RIA)

opposite: James Petrie, *Portrait of George Petrie*
watercolour on ivory, 6.5 x 5.5 cm (coll: National Gallery of Ireland, cat. no. 3036)

Introduction

Petrie: Polymath and Innovator

JOEP LEERSSEN

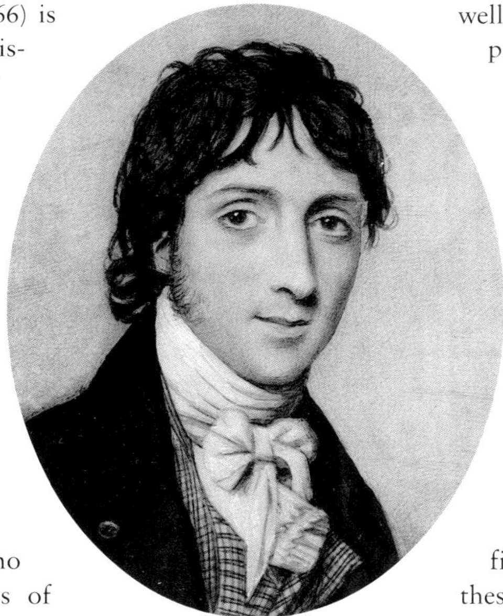

The genius of George Petrie (1790-1866) is perhaps obscured by having been dispersed over so many fields. In many areas of cultural history, people come across his name; in each case, they only come across a partial aspect of his work. Painter, antiquary, ethnographer, scholar, academician, archaeologist, musician: in each of these areas we encounter his achievements.

Petrie, more than any other single individual in the 19th century, traced the cultural profile by which Ireland is still identified today. His view of the Irish landscape is still with us, not only pictorially, but also iconographically. It was Petrie who began to explore the Irish space and landscape as an echo chamber informed by the lingering memories of native cultural traditions and antiquities; it was Petrie who began the exploration of this repository for its cultural riches; it was he who, practically the first among the English-oriented, educated elite, began to see the living peasantry, not just as menial rustics, but as the living heirs and continuance of Gaelic antiquity.

PAINTING, MUSIC

The beginnings of Petrie's culture-historical concerns were visual and aural, pictorial and musical. His career as a landscape artist is well known, born as he was a son of a Dublin portrait painter of Scottish descent. His talent was precocious: at age fourteen he received a silver medal from the Dublin Society, and as early as 1816 he established himself on the Irish artistic scene with his exhibition of Wicklow landscapes at Somerset House, London. From that moment onwards he was to remain the foremost Irish landscape artist, and much in demand as an illustrator. He was associated from its beginning with the Royal Hibernian Academy, became its librarian in 1830, and eventually (until 1859) its president. But even at the early stages of his career as a painter, the Irish landscape for him was more than just a sublime panoramic vista: it was filled, informed, with cultural resonances. One of these was music. Petrie was also a gifted violinist, and from boyhood onwards had noted down folk airs.

'From my very boy-days, whenever I heard an air which in any degree touched my feelings, or appeared to me to be either an unpublished one, or a better version of an air than what had already been printed, I never neglected to note it down.' Petrie had furnished Tom Moore (an old schoolmate) with airs for that poet's collection of Irish melodies, which began to be published from 1808 onwards. He was friendly with Edward Bunting, the premier music collector of Ireland, who had co-organised the Harpers' Festival in Belfast in 1792; and in the year of his Somerset House exhibition, 1816, Petrie also published an 'Essay on Irish Music'.

Painting and music were to run in tandem for the rest of his life. Seventeen airs collected by him were included in Bunting's 1840 collection *The Ancient Music of Ireland*, which also had a chapter by Petrie on, tellingly, a link between music and antiquity – the so-styled 'harp of Brian Ború', now kept in Trinity College Dublin. Petrie brought out some specimens from his own collection (which in total numbered more than 2,000 airs) in 1855 as *The Ancient Music of Ireland*, better known – to distinguish it from Bunting's – as *The Petrie Collection*. Petrie had set up, towards the end of 1851, the Society for the Preservation and Publication of the Melodies of Ireland; his entire collection was passed on after his death to Charles Villiers Stanford, godfather of Irish and English national schools of classical composition, who brought out a complete edition between 1902 and 1905 with the assistance of the Irish Literary Society of London.

ANTIQUITIES: JOURNALISM, ORDNANCE SURVEY

Petrie was a true romantic. His appreciation of landscape was deeply indebted to Wordsworth, whom he revered, and he was romantic also in his constant awareness of the continuity between living folk art and antiquity. Much as the Grimm Brothers revolutionised the collecting of folk tales – they saw folk and fairy tales as the repository of a watered-down ethnic mythology, rather than as amusing, demotic pastimes, as they had been seen before – so too Petrie read the Irish social landscape as a record of the country's ancient Gaelic culture. He pursued this vision in a multitude of directions, and publicised it in a variety of ways. He was among the very first to turn to the new, cheap medium of the printed press as a means of expression. The *Dublin Penny Journal* (which he edited in 1832, together with Caesar Otway) in its very title reflected the new realisation that print was becoming cheap following the invention of the rotary printing press and woodpulp-based paper. As a result of this, printed matter was to obtain a social penetration which revolutionised the media and its role in public life. More than a decade before the Young Irelanders were to found *The Nation* as their platform for nationalist politics, Petrie proclaimed his cultural view of the Irish landscape as a repository for Irish antiquity by way of the *Dublin Penny Journal*. Round towers, high crosses, abbey ruins and Norman towers – these romantic, picturesque traces of Irish history in Irish space he inventoried and disseminated among a large urban readership.

By then he was more than a painter-journalist. His studies of the Irish landscape had taken him first into government service, and then into academic circles. First came the Ordnance Survey, a government-sponsored Irish mapping project entrusted to army engineers. It was more than merely cartographical, but was also intended to include a gazetteer and description of Irish geographical features, including cultural and archaeological ones. Such projects were common in Europe, following the pattern of the enormous and all-encompassing *Description de l'Egypte* (1809) which Napoleon had ordered after his conquest of that land. In many cases, ethnographic data on dress, architecture, manners and customs were part of the inventory. The Russian geographic service, run by the army, noted down folk tales which were to be used gratefully by the Russian Grimm – the fairy tales collector Aleksander Afanas'ev. Folklore investigations and questionnaires were attached to geographic surveys in Italy and France around the same period.

The Irish Ordnance Survey has come to enjoy a poor reputation (as yet another Anglocentric nail in the coffin of native culture), which is undeserved and probably due to some unguarded remarks by Douglas Hyde (in his lecture 'On the necessity for de-Anglicising Ireland', 1891) and Brian Friel's misguided and misleading play *Translations*. In point of fact, the Ordnance Survey, and especially the part played in it by Petrie, was an enormous salvage operation to collect and preserve the broken remains of Ireland's native culture on the very eve of the further devastations caused by the Great Famine of 1845-48. Petrie and his collaborators (including those giants of Irish learning, Eugene O'Curry and John O'Donovan) painstakingly retrieved the Irish roots of place-names, carefully transliterated them into English spelling, and in the process recorded archaeological remains and ethnographic customs and traditions from all 32 counties. Although the Ordnance Survey was stopped mid-track and never led to any full-scale publication, it is not too much to say that all 'sense of place' in Ireland, all knowledge concerning the ways Irish places and place-names were informed with the country's native culture, stands deeply indebted to the work of Petrie and his protégés O'Donovan and O'Curry. Their heritage can be found in every place-name, on every bilingual road sign in the Irish countryside.

Work on the Ordnance Survey occupied Petrie throughout the 1830s. It turned him into an archaeologist, and as such he was invited to join the Royal Irish Academy, a learned body which he helped to revitalise and transform.

ARCHAEOLOGY: ACADEMY, MUSEUM, ARCHIVE

The Royal Irish Academy had been established in the 1780s as a learned society for erudite Ascendancy gentlemen of leisure. Although it had provided a platform for the study of Gaelic antiquity in the pre-Union decades, the repercussions of the 1798 Rebellion and the 1801 Act of Union had sent the Academy into a cramped stupor. Only in the 1820s, when Petrie and the mathematical genius William Rowan Hamilton were appointed members, did a period of recuperation set in. Petrie sat on numerous committees, and he submitted lectures and prize essays to the Academy which may safely count as the beginning of scientific archaeology in Ireland. The two most important landmarks in this respect were his essays on the round towers, and on the Hill of Tara. That last was intended to showcase the achievements of the Ordnance Survey and its interdisciplinary approach involving the use of native, bardic descriptions alongside a meticulously descriptive survey of the physical site. In addition, Petrie evinced a marked reluctance to go beyond the firm evidence, and eschewed the type of freewheeling speculation which had until then been the hallmark of Irish antiquaries. The preceding generation had revelled in conjectures about the mystical, Oriental origin of Irish antiquities, invoking Etruscans and Phoenicians on the slightest pretext, and interpreting obscure texts with great inventiveness and little understanding. Petrie sternly advocated an approach that rested on solid evidence alone. This new type of approach led to a huge and often scurrilous controversy concerning the origin of the round towers, which divided learned opinion and the Academy's membership, and which may, in hindsight, be seen as the crisis marking the transition of amateur antiquarianism into scholarly archaeology. Petrie's scholarly sobriety eventually carried the day.

Meanwhile Petrie worked hard at committee level to expand the Royal Irish Academy's collections of artefacts and manuscripts. He assiduously eyed auctions to see what came onto the market, and proposed the allocation of Academy funds to acquire important cultural heirlooms before they would disappear out of the country or into private collections. Among the most important acquisitions of Petrie's committee tenure are the manuscript copy of the Annals of the Four Masters, the Cross of Cong, the *Domhnach airgid* book shrine, and other antiquities known collectively as the Dawson collection. Indeed the Academy's collection became so important that Petrie instigated a museum for their display – eventually merging into what now is the National Museum of Ireland. Meanwhile, John O'Donovan, still one of Petrie's most trusted fellow-workers in the philological field, edited the Annals of the Four Masters for the Academy and thereby transformed the 19th-century historiography of Gaelic Ireland. Petrie and O'Donovan founded a society particularly aimed at preserving and editing ancient Irish manuscripts – the Irish Archaeological Society – which was to maintain in the field of text-editing the scholarly rigour that Petrie had championed in archaeology.

PETRIE AS AN IRISH SCHOLAR

Petrie's achievement in Irish learning and culture can be grouped under four headings. He was a hard worker combining large enterprises with a meticulous sense of detail; a publicist with a keen sense of how to promulgate his insights and findings; a team worker who not only pursued his own interests, but organised like-minded fellow-workers into collective efforts; and most importantly, he was an all-round cultural historian, even by today's standards.

Petrie's work ethic was daunting. He undertook enormous tasks and pursued them with relentless attention to detail. That combination was, and is, unusual: specialists mostly work on small topics, generalists usually work on the 'great outline' of things. In Petrie's case, pursuits, once begun, would occupy him for the rest of his life – his collection of music, his study of Ireland's ancient architecture. At times it was almost self-defeating: the public would impatiently wait for the result of his inquiries, but Petrie would put off a definitive publication year after year, because he was not yet satisfied in his own mind that he had exhaustively covered the topic. This sorely tried people's patience, and on occasion could backfire on him (the failure of the Ordnance Survey may be due in part to his tendency to combine huge scale with minute detail), but it gave his publications, once (reluctantly!) delivered, an unequalled prestige, reliability, influence, and shelf-life.

At the same time, he was no ivory-tower-closeted don. His ventures into the field of journalism, and his sense that the Academy should develop a museum-style collection of antiquities, evince a notion that the fruits of scholarship should be spread throughout society, and that popular education was the natural attendant of scholarly research. Tellingly, one of the conflicts which he faced as president of the Royal Hibernian Academy was his insistence on cheap late-evening openings (the so-called 'Gaslight' exhibitions, with an entrance fee of one penny instead of the usual shilling) for the benefit of the working classes. At the same time, he was canny in obtaining the patronage and sponsorship of aristocrats and notables, who were always very well represented on the boards of his societies and ventures. Nor was he a soloist; his best work was done in collaboration with others, in the context of the Ordnance Survey, the Academy, and the bodies that he founded, such as the Irish Archaeological Society and the Society for the Preservation and Publication of the Melodies of Ireland.

As an all-round cultural historian, Petrie drew on the evidence of landscape, antiquities, cultural practices and ancient texts to penetrate Ireland's lost antiquity. These sources he collated, bringing together bardic writings, oral tradition and place-names in order to give archaeological interpretations of ancient sites and remains. His command of Irish was limited, but this was obviated by the excellent working relation he had with the great John O'Donovan. In the process, Petrie lifted the heritage of Gaelic antiquity from the ruins of the colonised countryside and its pauperised peasantry, and enshrined it into the self-image of learned, urban circles in post-Union Ireland. Before Petrie, the reputation of Gaelic antiquity had been shadowy, seen as the self-aggrandising myths of a boastful, oppressed peasantry or the shadowy preserve of enthusiasts. With Petrie, archaeology was winnowed from legend, and the notion that Ireland had ancient and admirable roots in Gaelic antiquity became a point of pride, of self-identification even, even for English-speaking urban, Protestant Irishmen and women. What Walter Scott did for Scotland was done for Ireland, not by a novelist, but by this painter-musician-archaeologist-academician.

THE EUROPEAN CONTEXT

In all respects, Petrie was one of the earliest exemplars within Ireland of a new European attitude to the study of culture and antiquity. Giambattista Vico had, in the 1720s, given a philosophical basis for the study of national languages, myth, and folklore; Johann Gottfried Herder had argued in the 1760s and 1770s that culture was, first and foremost, always particular to ethnic and national traditions. While on the European continent this was, from 1810 onwards, applied in the study of linguistics, mythology, antiquities, manners and customs (the foremost representative of this new learning being probably Jacob Grimm), intellectuals in the British Isles on the whole were still erudite amateur gentlemen in the tradition of Bishop Percy, Charles O'Conor or Sir William Betham – antiquarians who pursued the study of antiquity on an unsystematic ad-hoc basis, going by whatever sources they happened to find in their (often considerable) private collections and networks, often with a good deal of self-taught lore, hearsay information, ingenuity and credulity, but occasionally rather short on solid factual information.

Petrie was the herald of a new dispensation. He was no gentleman of leisure, his scholarly reputation depended on his reliability rather than on his social standing. His source material was no longer that of private collections or private acquaintances, and indeed most of his activities were indicative of a trend (widespread also elsewhere in Europe) to relocate private collections into the ownership of public bodies. Petrie's assiduous acquisition policy on behalf of the Royal Academy, buying up privately held collectibles for their scholarly interest, was indicative of a long-term, ongoing transfer of cultural heirlooms from the private to the public domain, noticeable (again) all over Europe. The 19th century was the century when Europe's great archives, libraries and museums were founded, gobbled up private sub-collections, or else were transmuted from royal into 'national' institutions, accessible to the public at large, and indeed functioning on their behalf. At the same time, we see the decline of private networks among gentleman-scholars (such as had dominated the 18th century), and the rise of professional or scholarly networks among fellow-workers. Petrie's tendency to form clubs and societies was, in this respects, characteristic of a time which has been called the century of 'sociability'. His use of the new, cheap, periodical print media was, likewise, an echo of similar developments elsewhere in Europe.

Most of all, Petrie's historicism – his belief that explanations of cultural phenomena have to trace their historical roots and be themselves founded on historical fact – stands in shrill contrast to the method of his immediate predecessors like Betham, and was very close to that of European contemporaries like the Grimm Brothers. There is no better indication to this effect, perhaps, than his attitude to music collection. Whereas most of his contemporaries were content to reconcile different variants of a given air into a 'correct' master-version, Petrie gave equal weight to all different versions. His predecessor Bunting felt that 'a strain of music, once impressed on the popular ear, never varies'; Petrie noted as many as fifty variants of a single melody, and grouped these into what musicologists now call 'tune families'. That method is a close analogy to the folklore and philology of the Grimm Brothers, and anticipated the structuralist method in folklore research.

Was Petrie a conscious and deliberate adept in the new European learning? There are some indications to that effect. In voicing his exasperation with his vain, credulous and speculative predecessor Betham, he evinced some awareness that archaeology and philology were conducted on a more solid basis on the Continent. He must have been aware of the new historical approach that in Britain led to the County Histories. The Ordnance Survey cannot have functioned in ignorance of similar government initiatives elsewhere in Europe, and some other Ascendancy scholars, like Thomas Crofton Croker and Samuel Ferguson, had also a notion of what was going on in Europe-beyond-Britain. Croker sent his collection of Irish fairy tales to the Grimm Brothers, Ferguson made Jacob Grimm, as well as a number of other continental scholars, honorary members of the Royal Irish Academy in 1854. However, although Petrie himself was associated with learned bodies in Paris, Rome, and Copenhagen, he never travelled further than England and Scotland.

Existing studies on Petrie emphasise only his importance in his own country, and within the Irish context. Research into Petrie's letters and archive is still needed to establish precisely which Continental contacts he maintained, and by which conduits the inspiration of the new, romantic-historicist learning in Europe reached him. His international contacts have been obscured by his national importance, much as the very width and expansiveness of his achievement has tended to impede our full appreciation of it.

JOEP LEERSSEN is Professor of Modern European Literature at the University of Amsterdam, and director of the Huizinga-Instituut (Dutch Research Institute for Cultural History). His publications on Irish literacy and cultural history include *Mere Irish and Fíor-Ghael* (1986), *Remembrance and Imagination* (1996), and *Hidden Ireland, Public Space* (2002).

BIBLIOGRAPHY

David Cooper, 'Petrie, George', *Grove Music Online*, L. Macy (ed.) (accessed 19 January 2004), www.grovemusic.com

Roman Jakobson & Pyotr Bogatyrev, 'Die Folklore als eine besondere Form des Schaffens', in *Donum Natalicum Schrijnen* (Dekker & Van de Vegt, Nijmegen and Utrecht, 1929) pp.900-913

Joep Leerssen, *Remembrance and Imagination: Patterns in the historical and literary representation of Ireland in the nineteenth century* (Cork University Press, 1996)

Joep Leerssen, *Hidden Ireland, Public Space* (Arlen House / Centre for Irish Studies, Galway, 2002)

Joep Leerssen, 'Literary Historicism: Romanticism, Philologists, and the Presence of the Past', *Modern Language Quarterly*, 65, no. 2 (forthcoming, 2004)

Philippa Levine, *The Amateur and the Professional: Antiquarians, Historians and Archaeologists in Victorian England, 1838-1886* (Cambridge University Press, 1986)

Damien Murray, *Romanticism, Nationalism and Irish Antiquarian Societies 1840-80* (Dept of Old & Middle Irish, NUI Maynooth, 2000)

Peter Murray, 'Trouble at the Mill: George Petrie and the Royal Hibernian Academy', in Maureen Charlton (ed.), *Martello Arts Review*, Royal Hibernian Academy of Arts Special Issue (Dublin, 1991) pp.14-22

Diarmuid Ó Giolláin, *Locating Irish Folklore: Tradition, Modernity, Identity* (Cork University Press, 2000)

William Stokes, *The Life and Labours in Art and Archaeology of George Petrie, LL.D., MRIA* (Longman Green & Co, London, 1868).

Colour Plates

The Upper Lake at Glendalough
watercolour on paper, 28 x 37

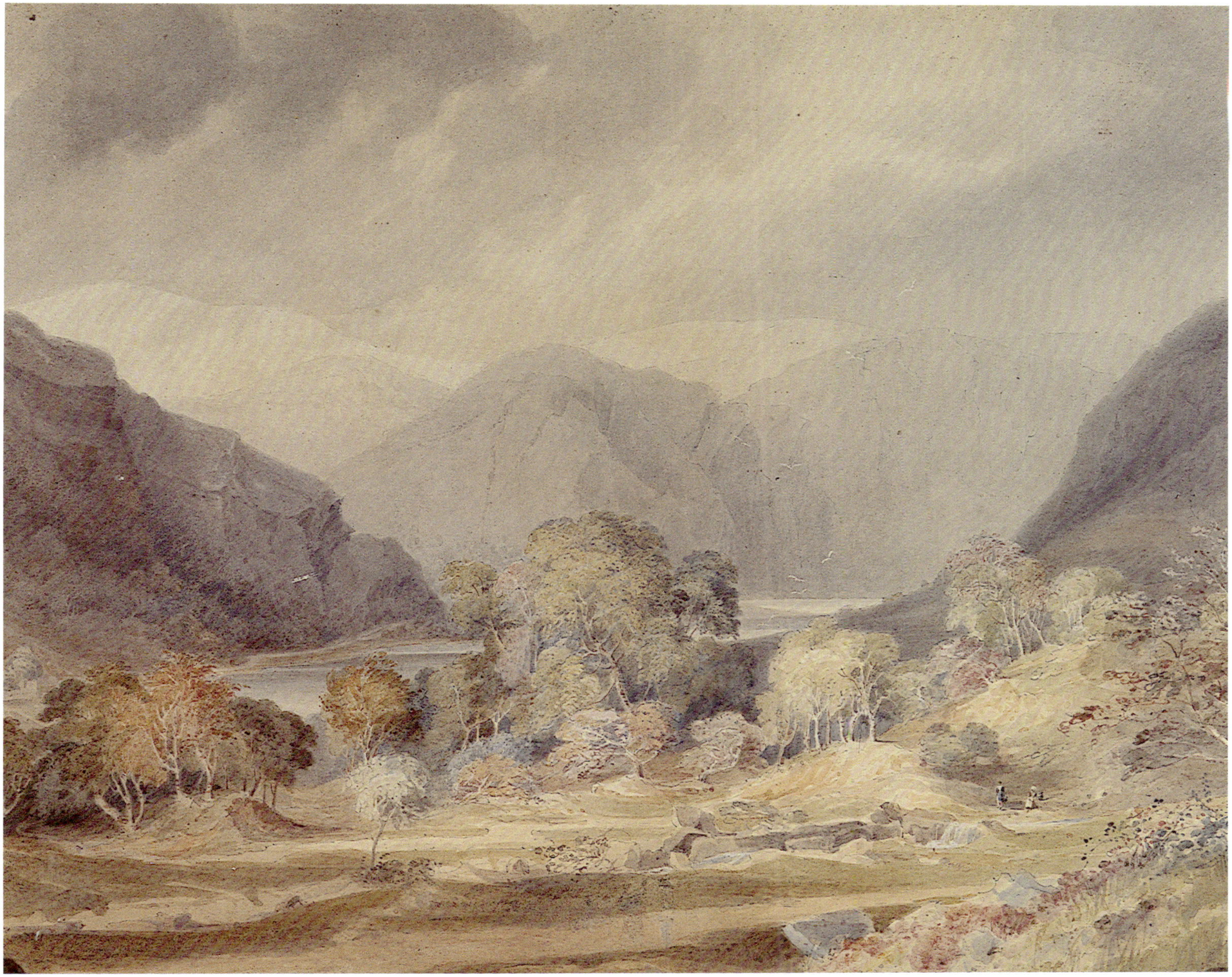

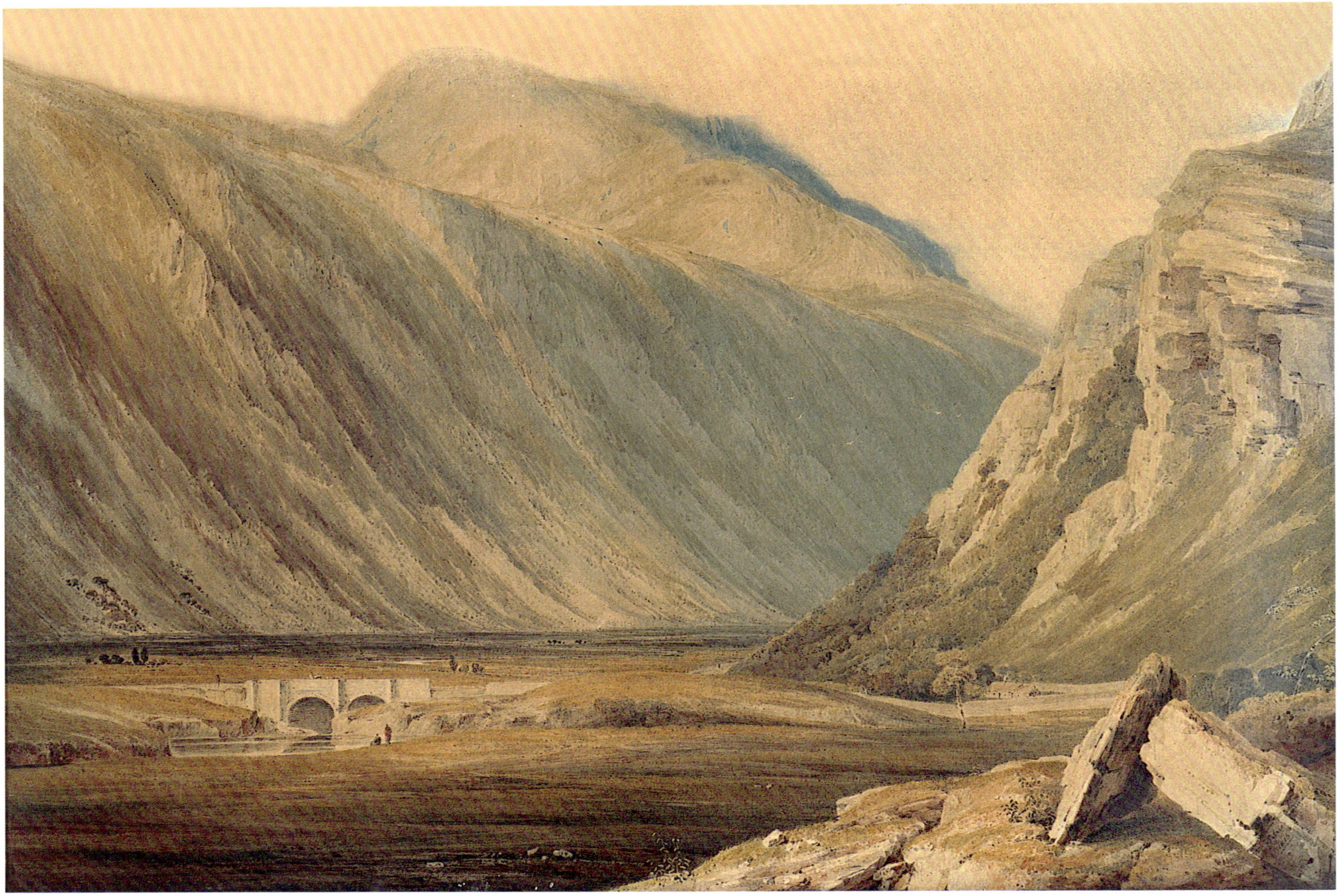

Glenmalure in the County Wicklow
1815, watercolour on paper laid on canvas, 66 x 96.5 (visible size)

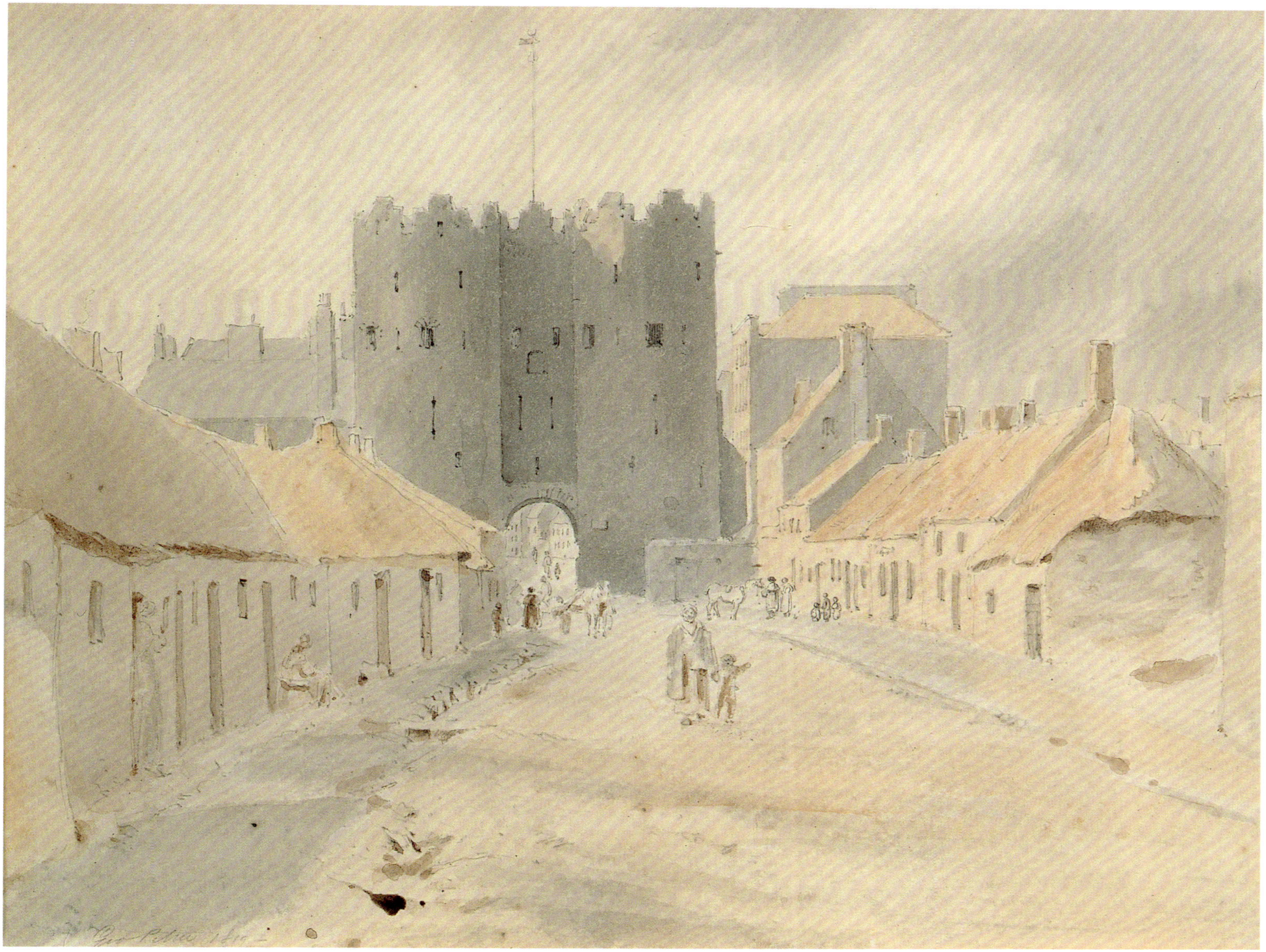

St. Lawrence's Gate, Drogheda
1819, watercolour on paper, 17.8 x 23.4 (coll: NGI, cat. no. 2374)

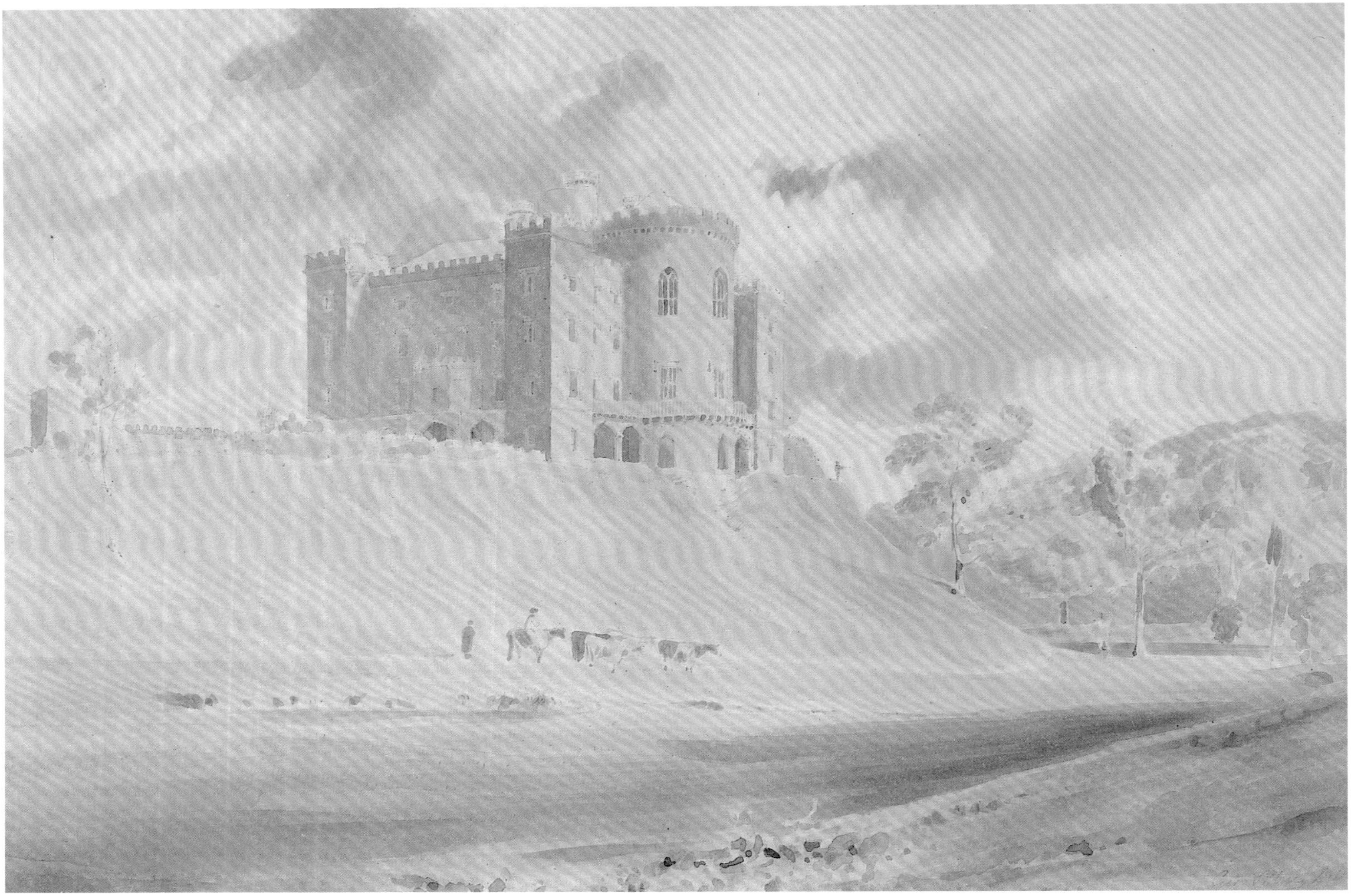

Slane Castle, Co. *Meath*
c.1819, watercolour on paper, 18 x 26.7 (coll: NGI, cat. no. 2367)

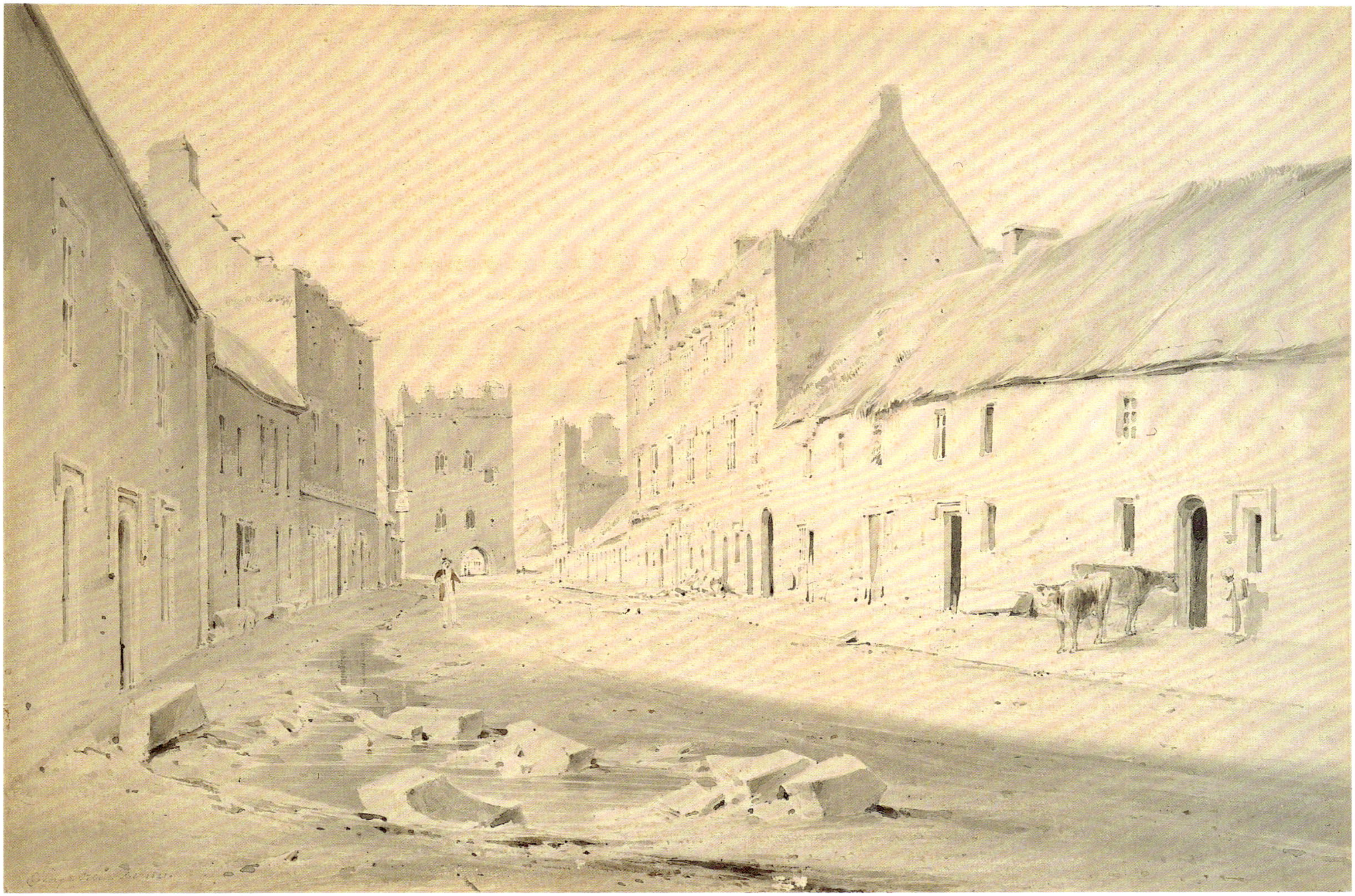

Kilmallock High Street, Co. Limerick
1821, sepia on paper, 26.7 x 39.7 (coll: NGI, cat. no. 2375)

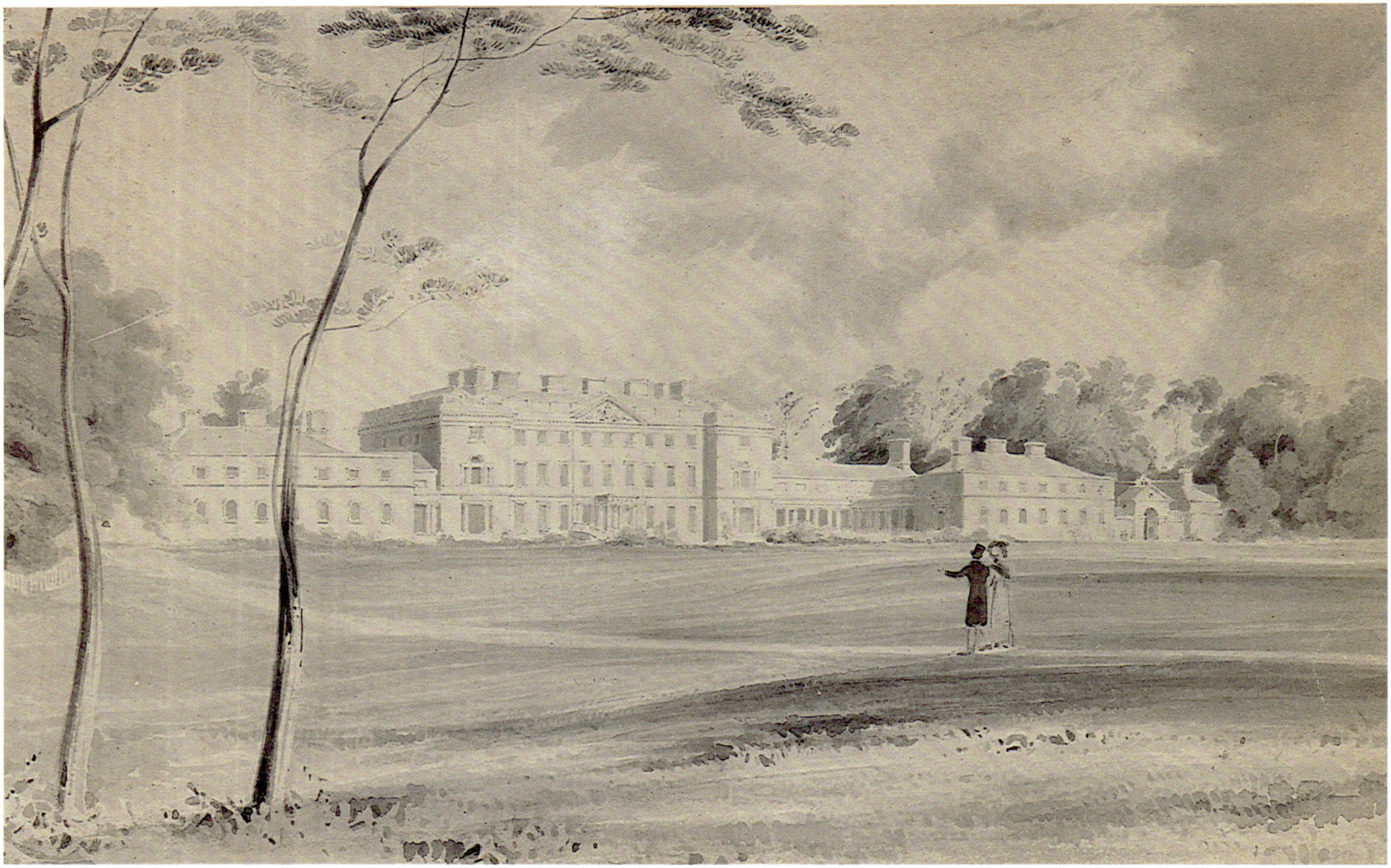

View of Carton
1824-25, sepia ink on paper, 21 x 30

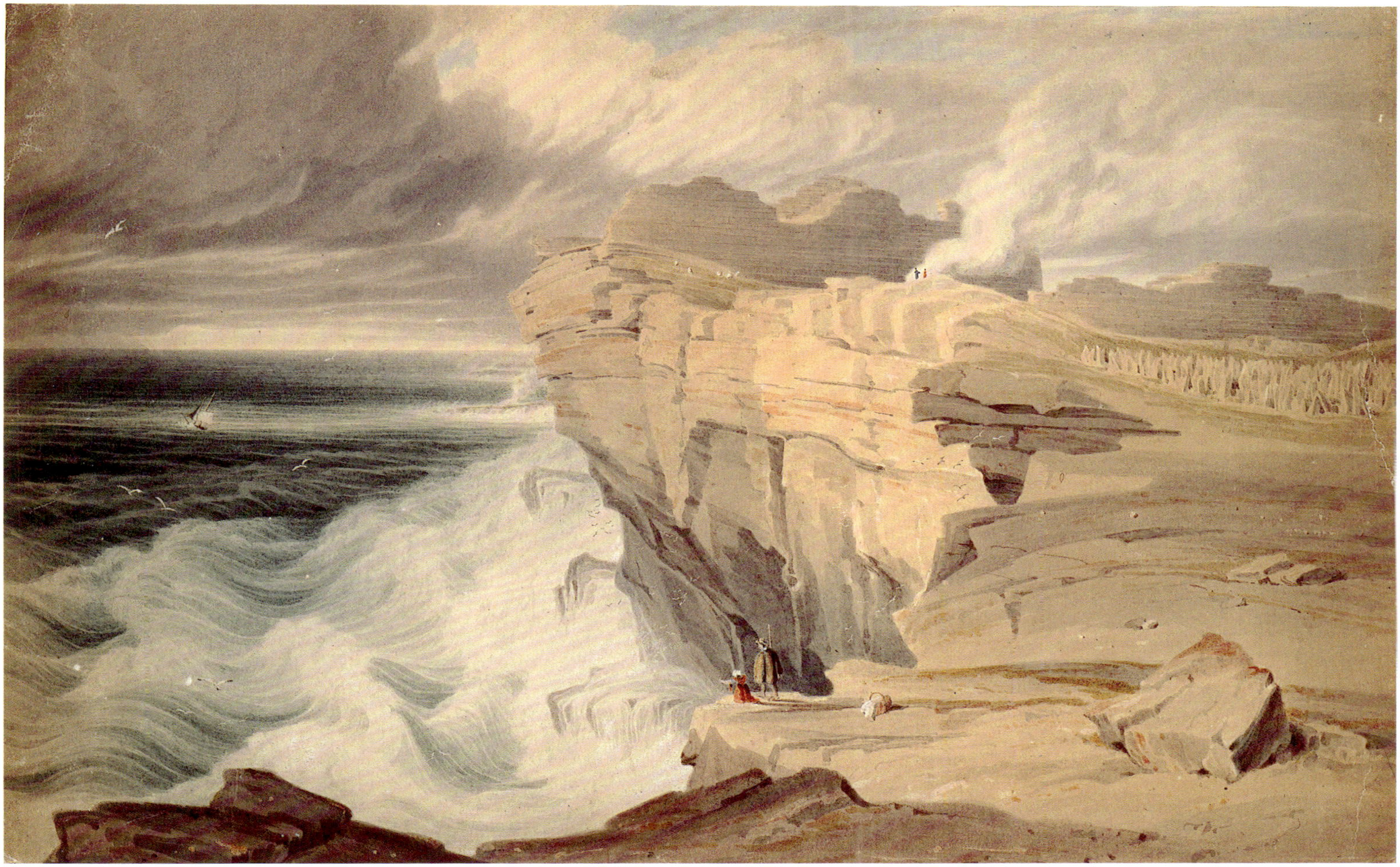

Dun Aengus Fort, Inismore, Aran Islands
c.1827, watercolour on paper, 29.8 x 46.4 (coll: NGI, cat. no. 7481)

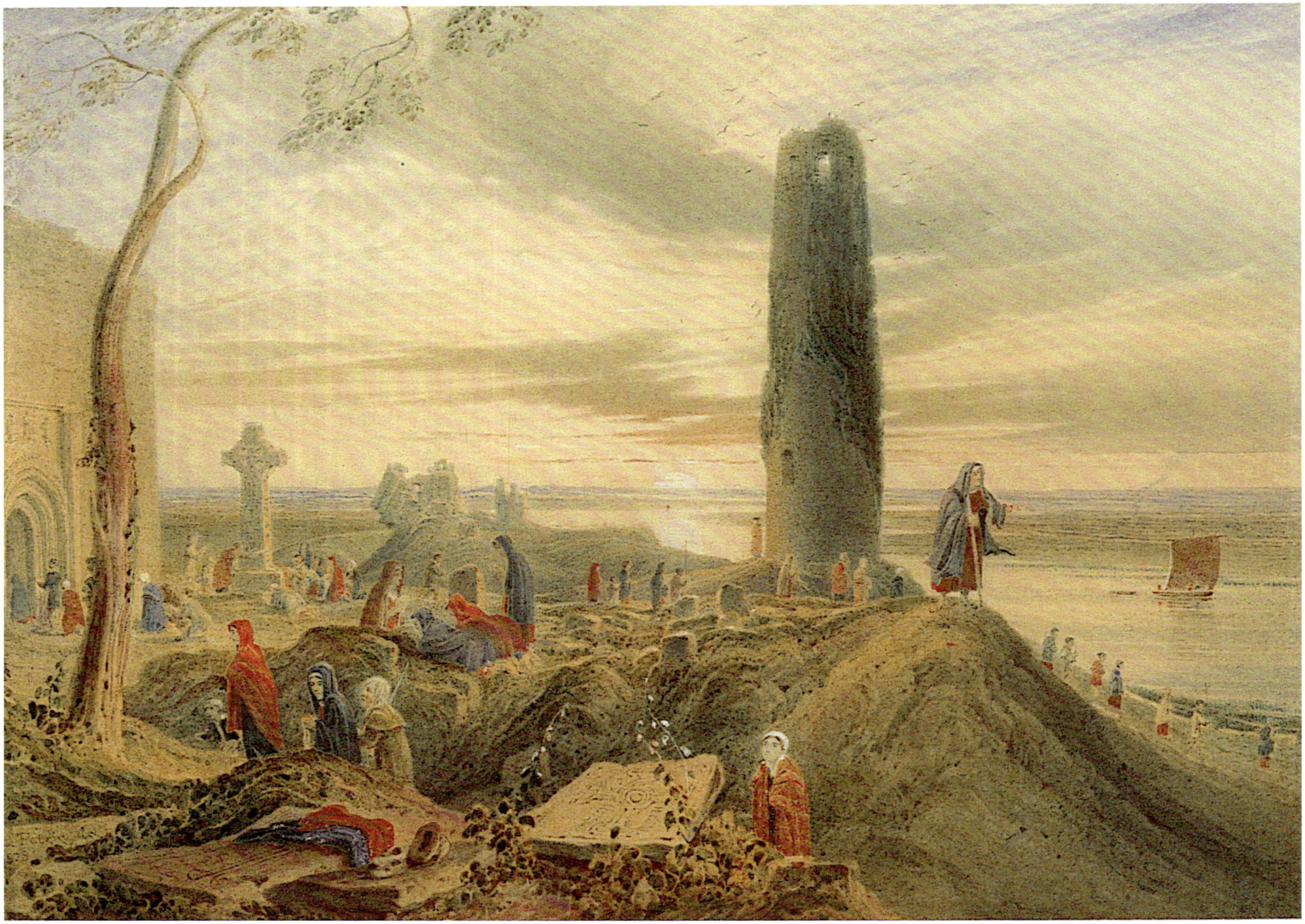

The Last Circuit of the Pilgrims at Clonmacnoise
*c.*1828, watercolour on paper (coll: Richard Wood collection, University of Limerick)

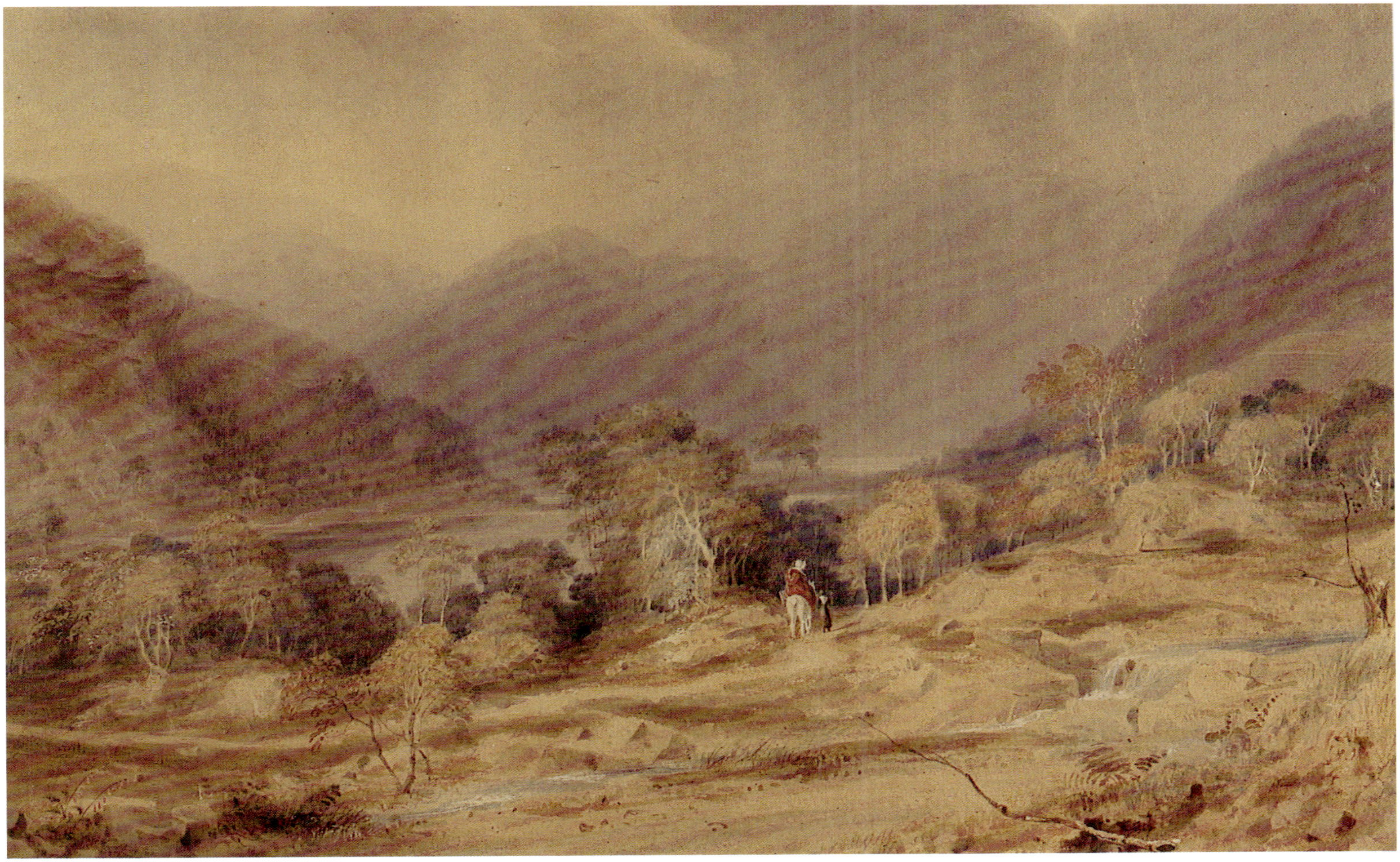

The Knight and the Lady
*c.*1828, watercolour on paper

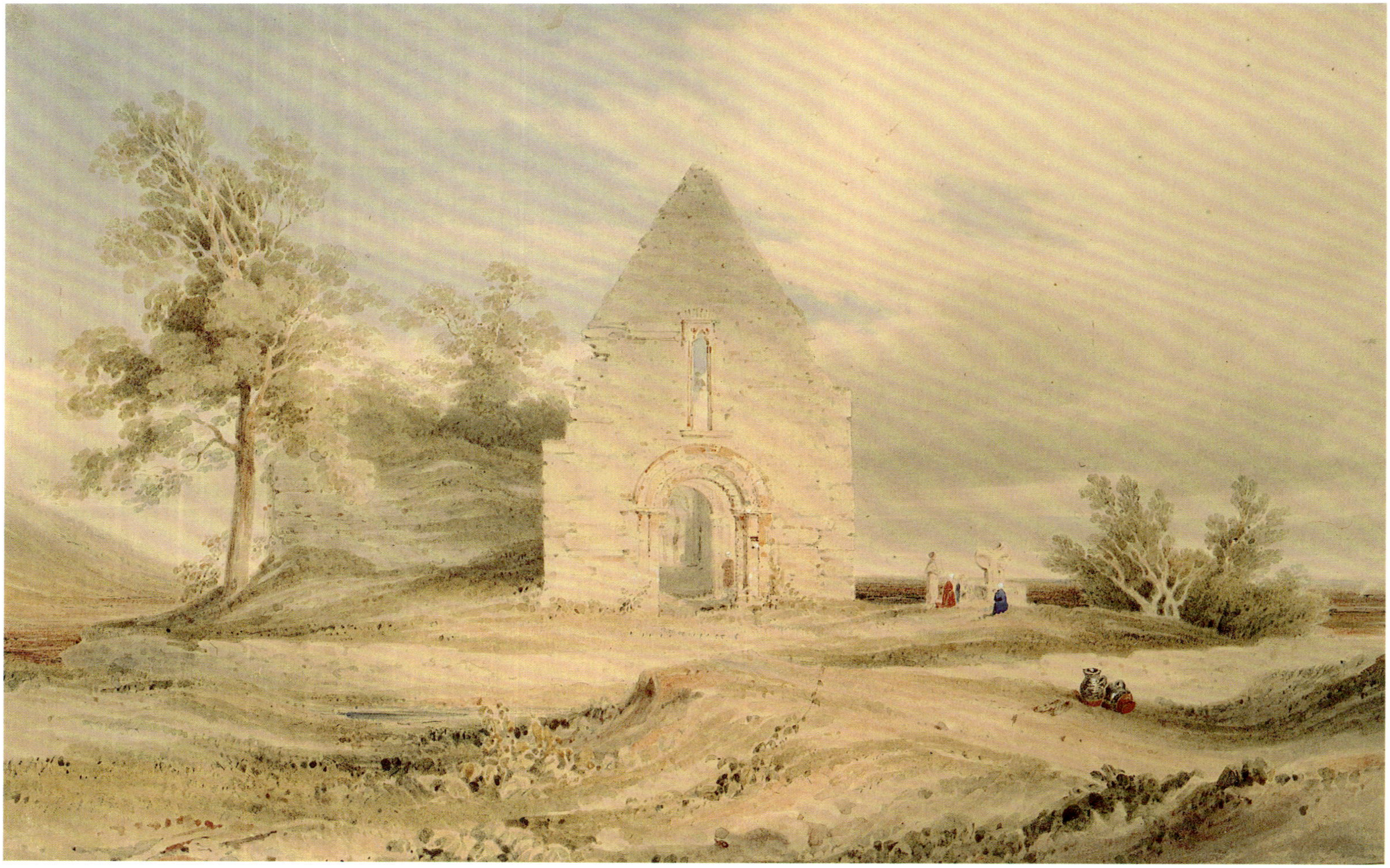

Culdean Abbey or Mona Incha Abbey, Co. Tipperary
1829, watercolour on paper, 23.8 x 36.3 (coll: NGI, cat. no. 2377)

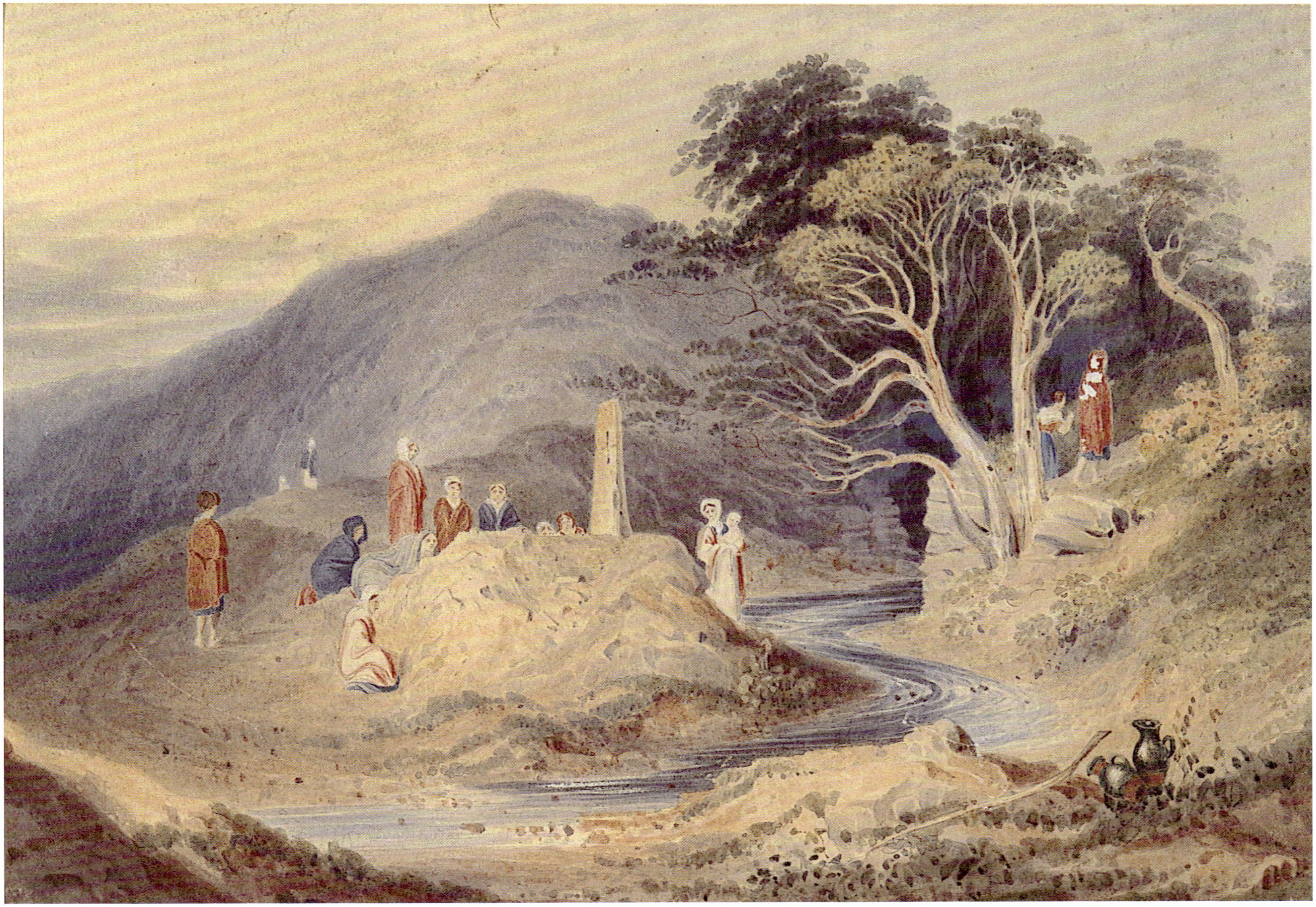

St. Brigid's Well
*c.*1829, watercolour on paper

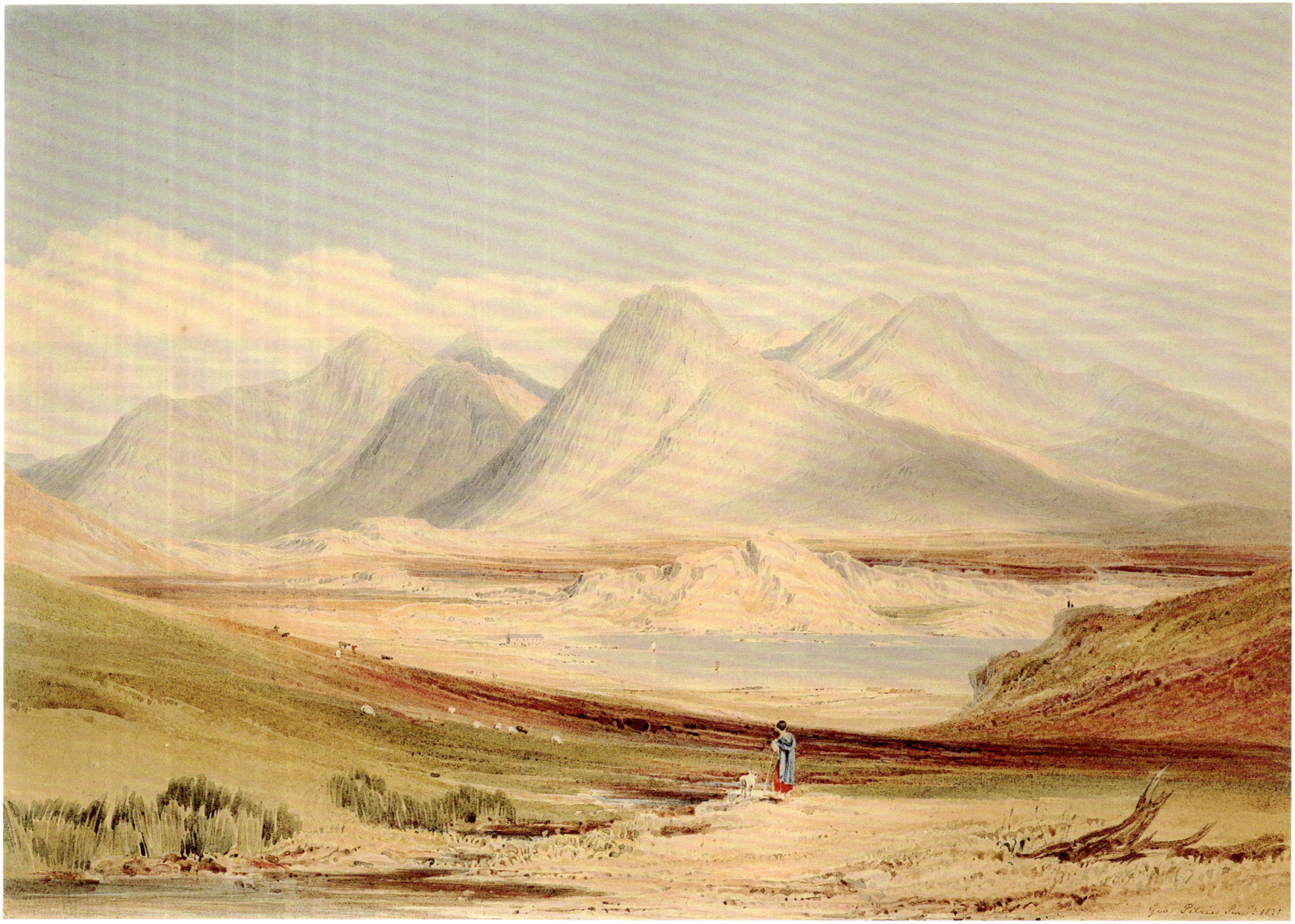

The Twelve Pins, Connemara, from the north head of Ballinakill Bay
1831, watercolour on paper, 29.4 x 41.1 (coll: NGI, cat. no. 6027)

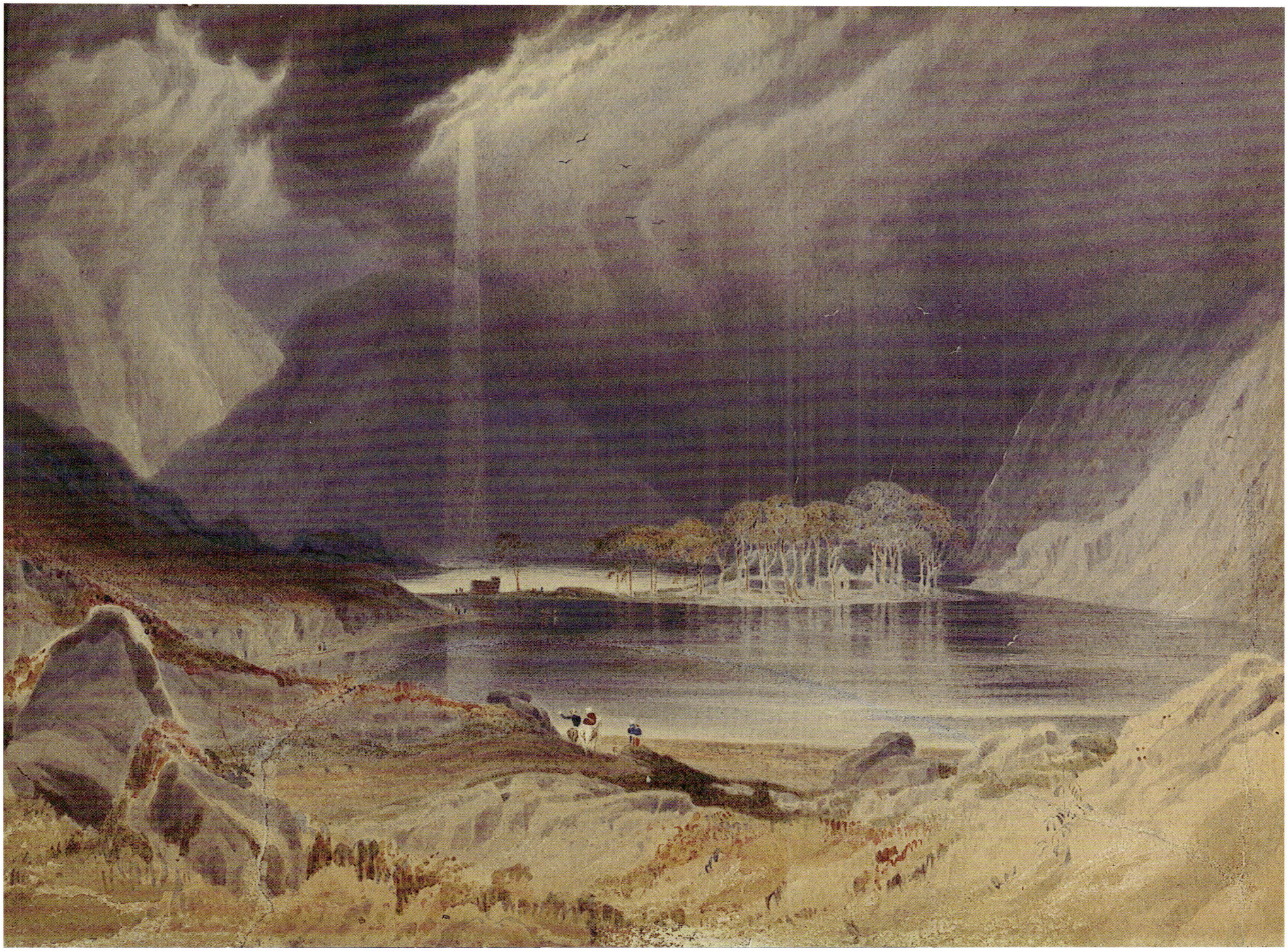

Gougane Barra
c.1831, watercolour on paper, 28 x 38 (visible size)

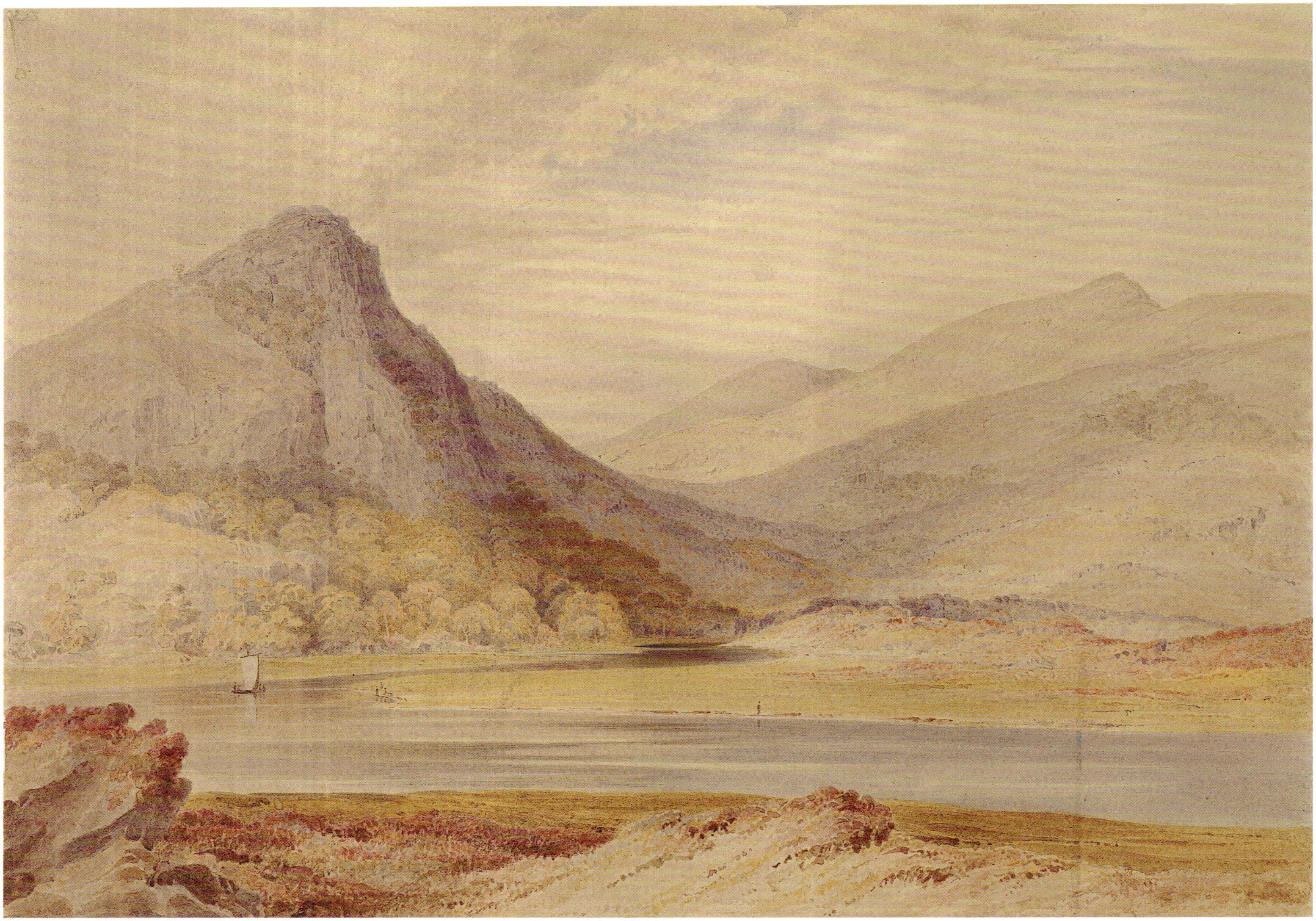

The Eagle's Nest at Killarney
*c.*1831, pencil and watercolour on paper, 26.2 x 36.4 (coll: Ulster Museum, cat. no. 1119)

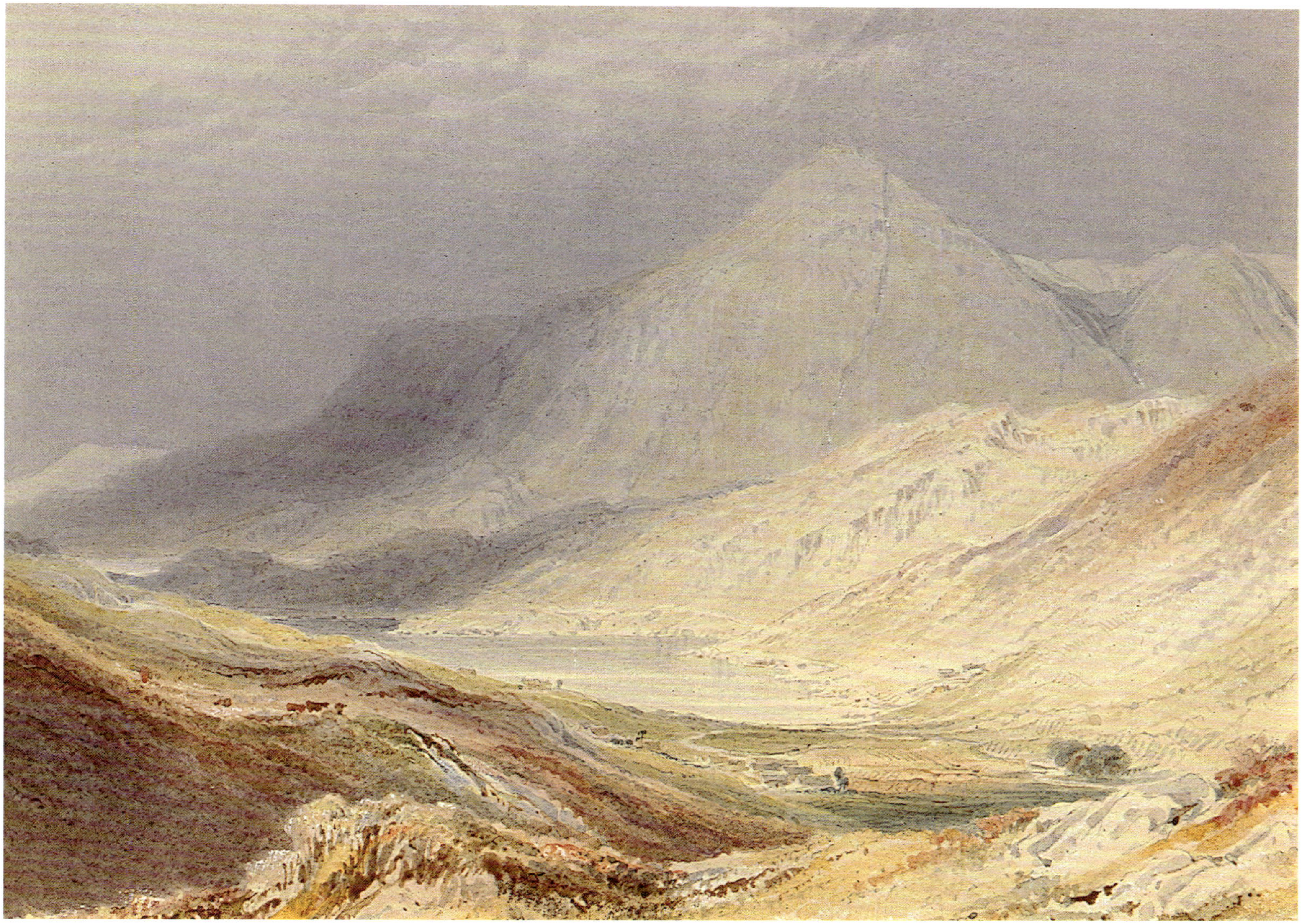

Connemara Mountain Landscape
*c.*1833, watercolour on paper, 15.5 x 22

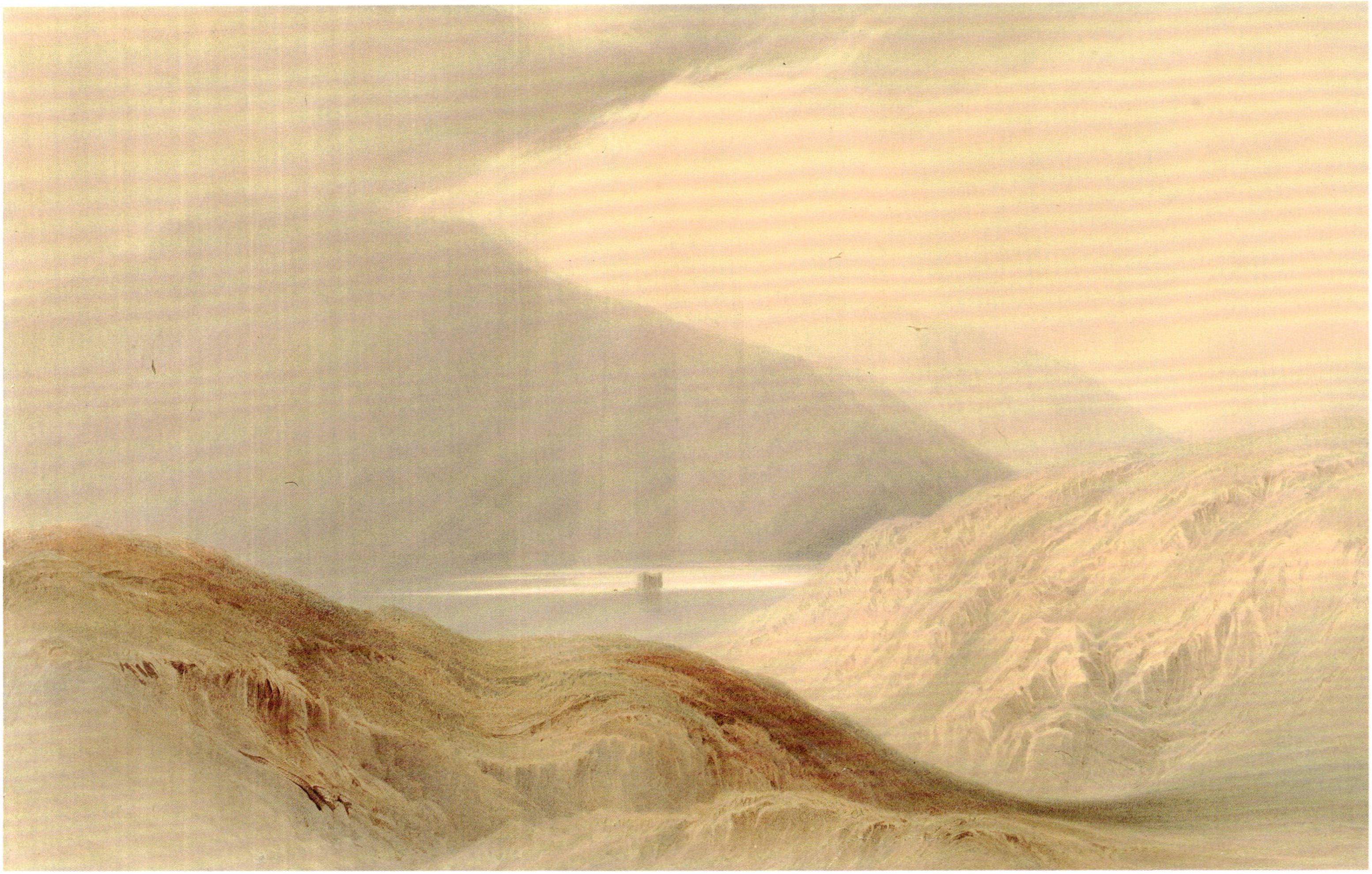

Hen's Castle on Lough Corrib, Co. Galway
*c.*1833-34, watercolour on paper, 32.5 x 50 (coll: NGI, cat. no. 6032)

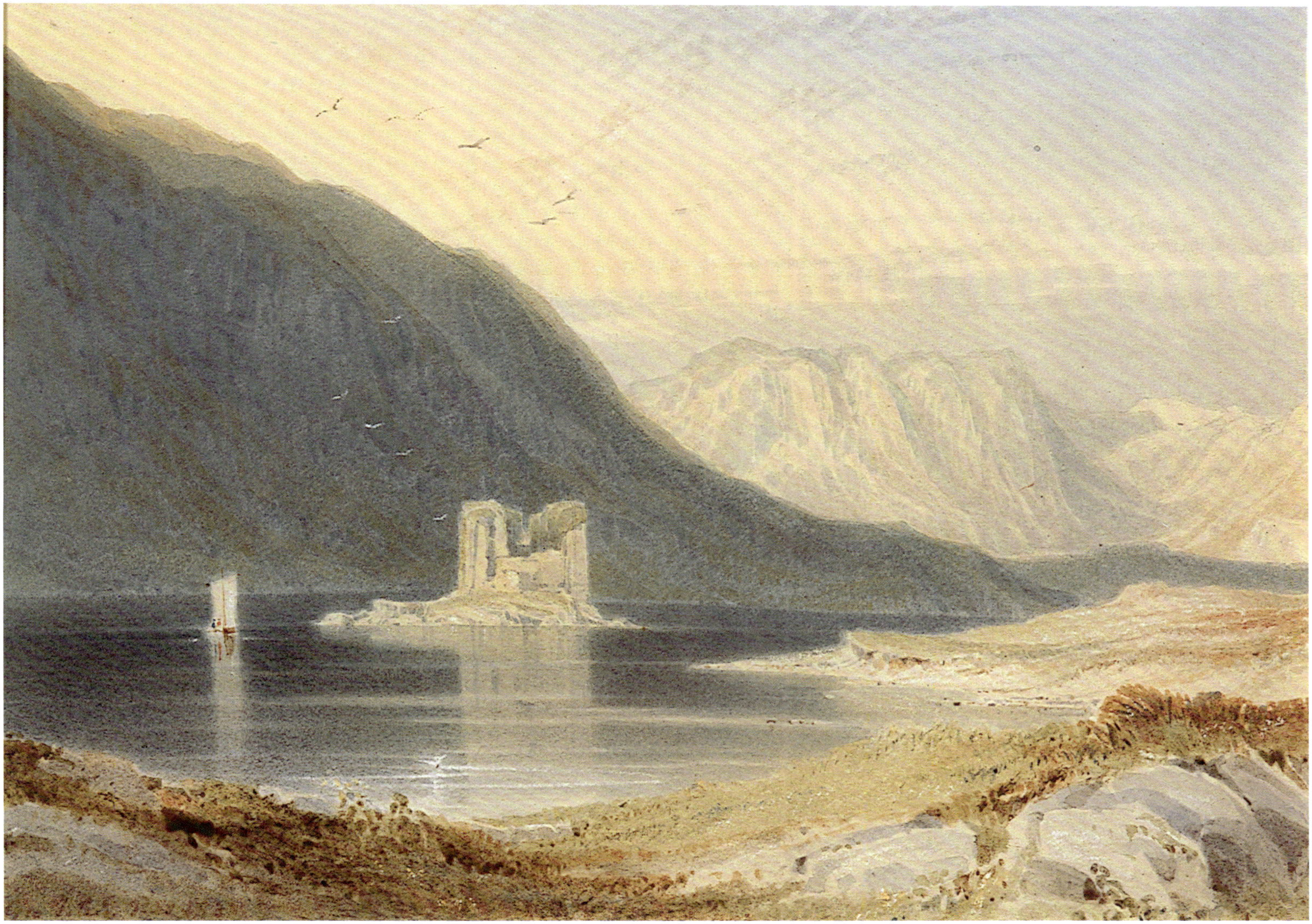

Hen's Castle, Loch Corrib, Connemara
c.1834, watercolour on paper, 32.5 x 50

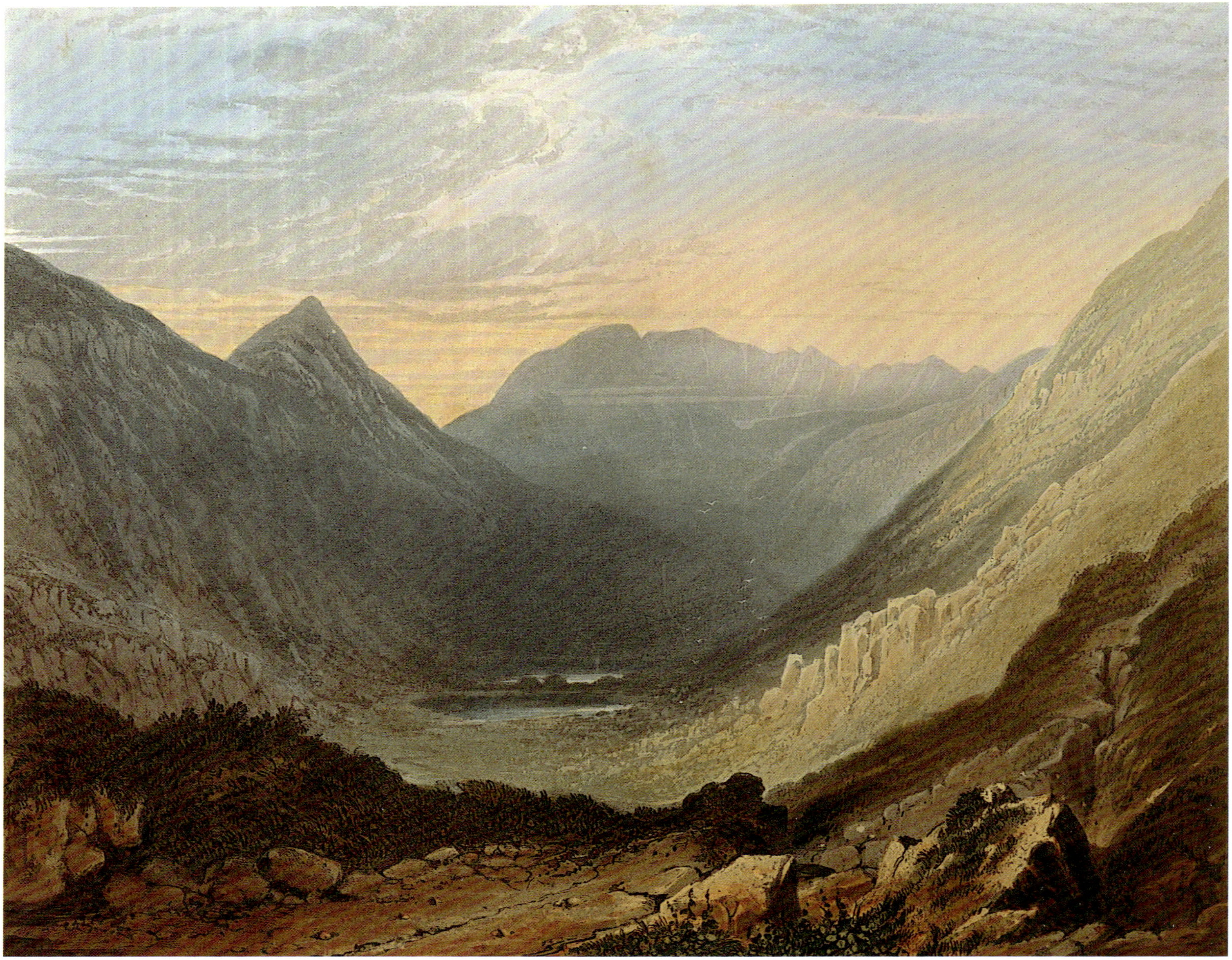

Comeen Duff or Black Valley, Killarney
c.1835, coloured aquatint, 23 x 27 (the original painting on which this aquatint is based has not been traced)

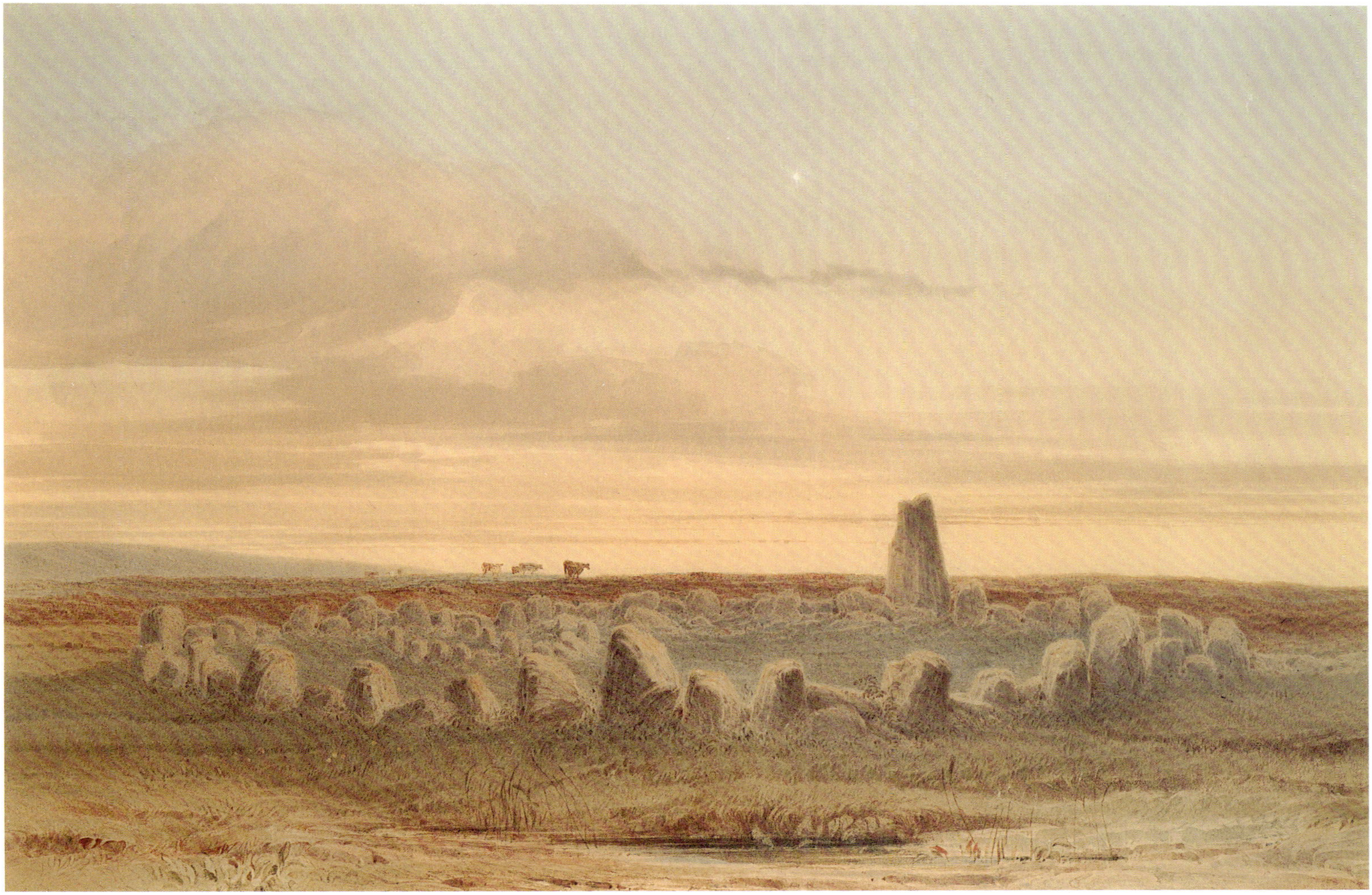

Pagan Sepulchral Monument on the Caugh Hill, a mountain in the parish of Bannagher, County of Londonderry – Twilight
or *The Stone Circle on Caan Hill, Derry*
c.1839-40, watercolour on paper, 33.1 x 51.4 (coll: NGI, cat. no. 6033)

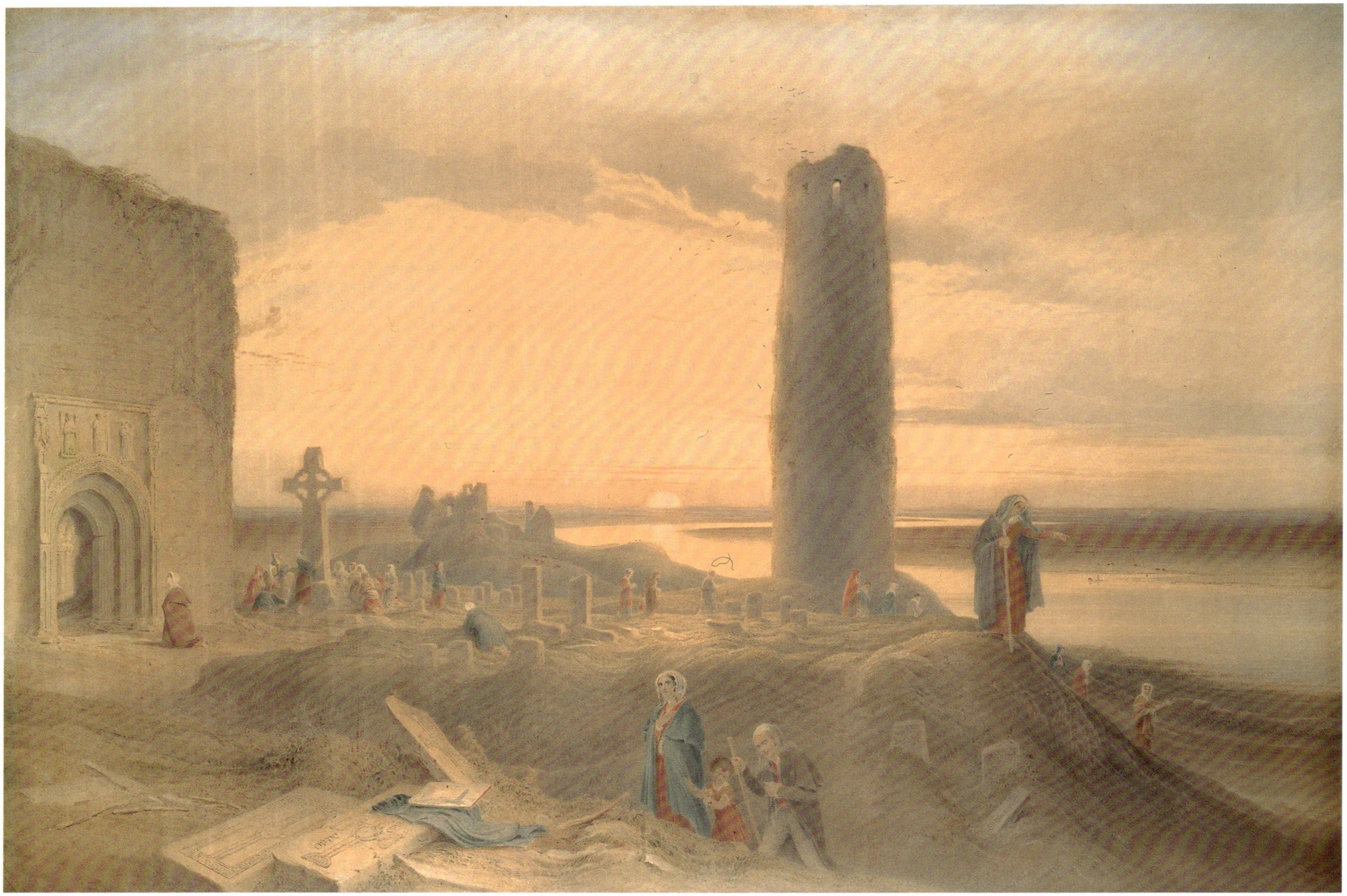

The Last Circuit of the Pilgrims at Clonmacnoise, Co. Offaly
*c.*1842, watercolour on paper, 67.2 x 98 (coll: NGI, cat. no. 2230)

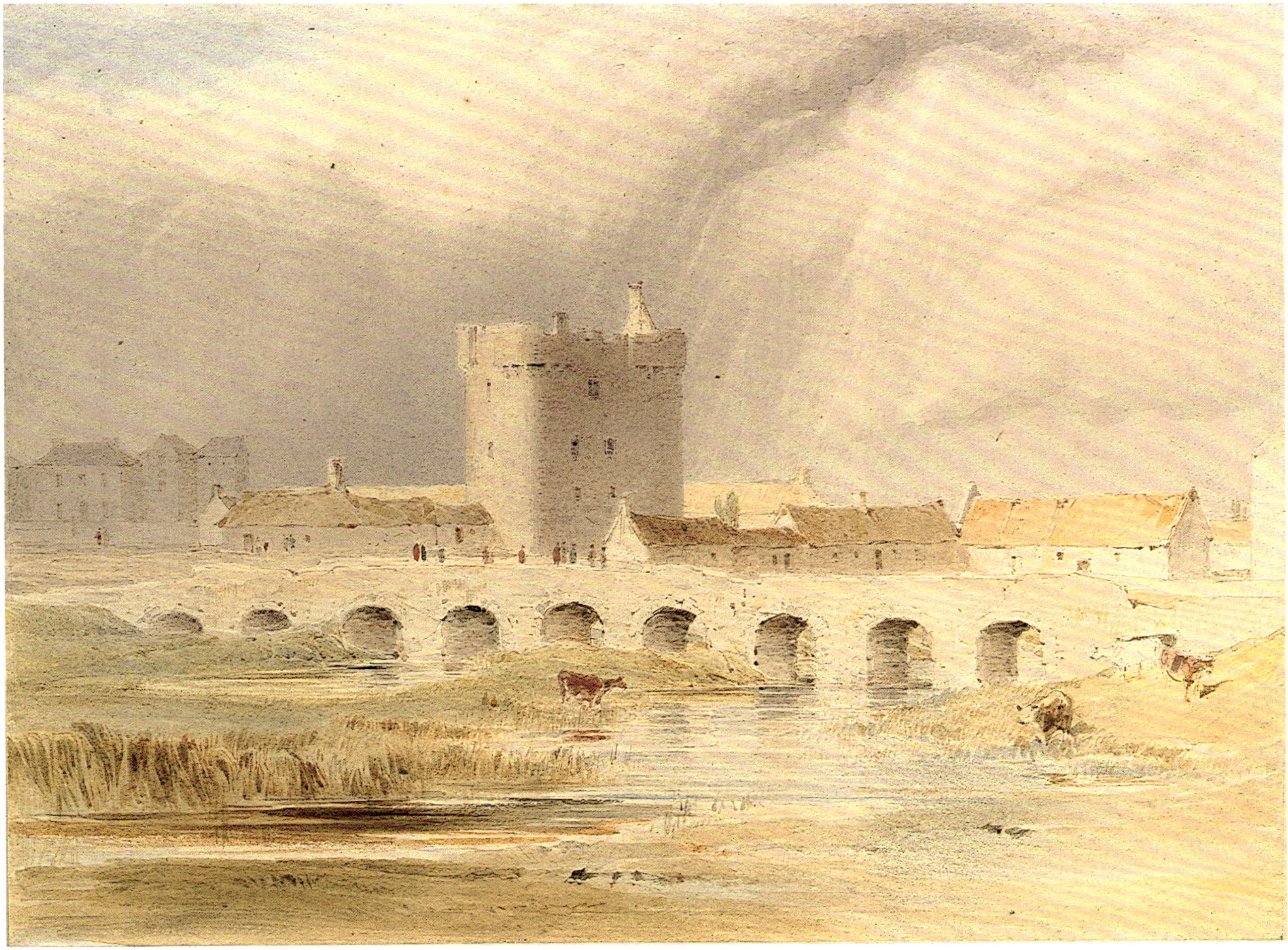

Bridge and Castle of Shrule, Co. Mayo
c.1843, watercolour on paper

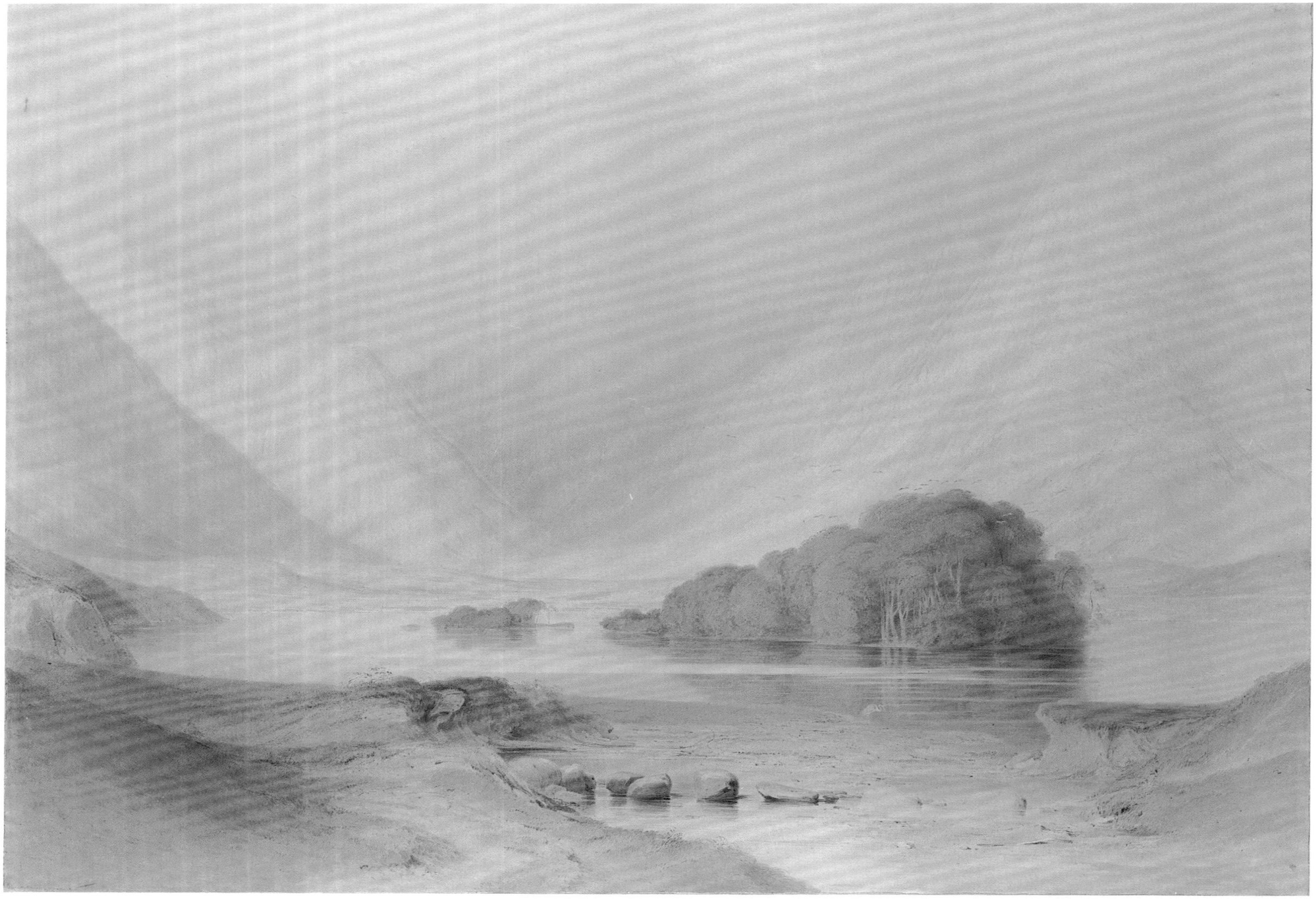

The Home of the Heron, Lough Atri, Looking into Glen Hoghan, Connemara – Evening
*c.*1845, watercolour on paper laid on canvas, 67 x 96 (coll: NGI, cat. no. 6871)

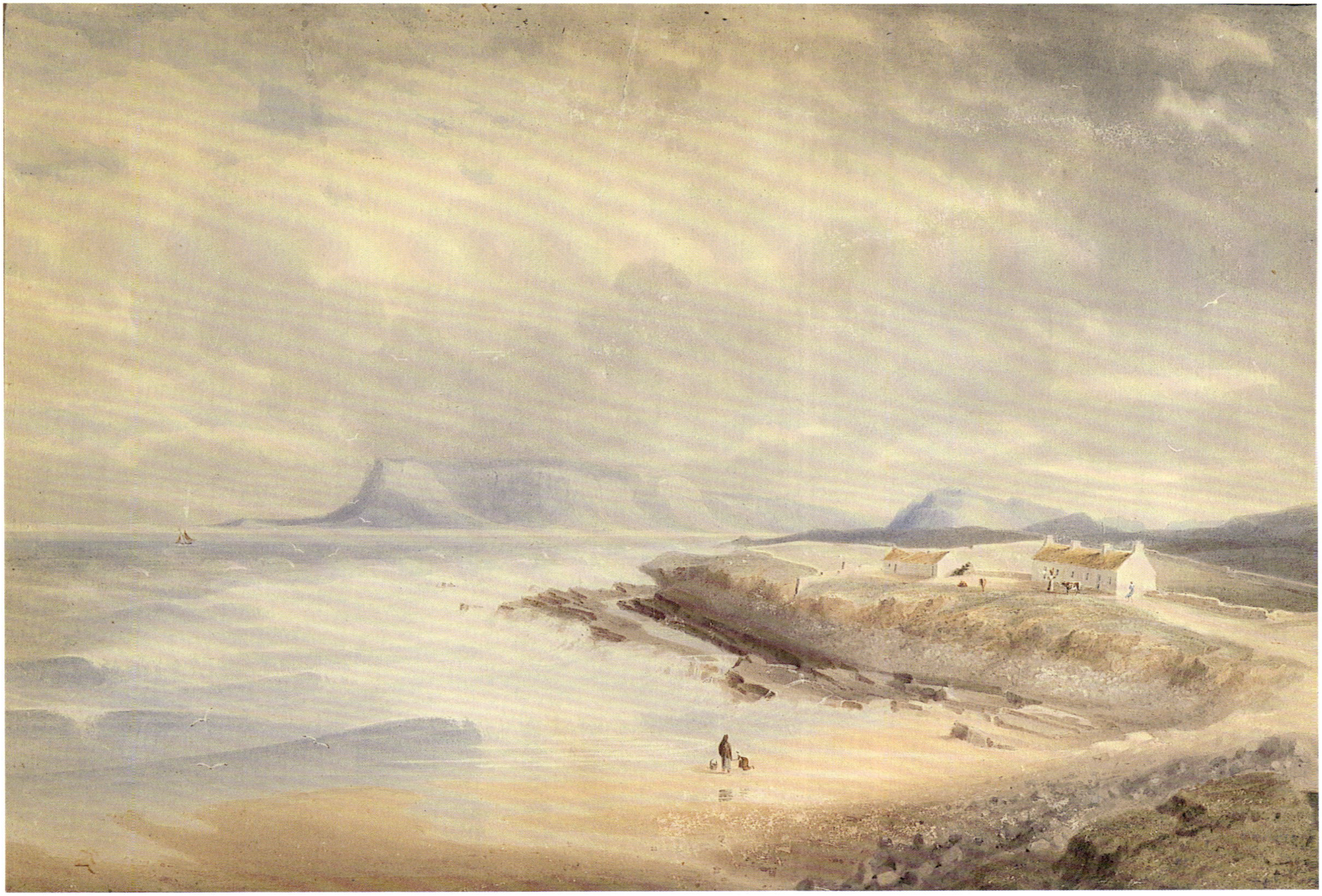

Achill
watercolour on paper, 33.5 x 49 (visible size)

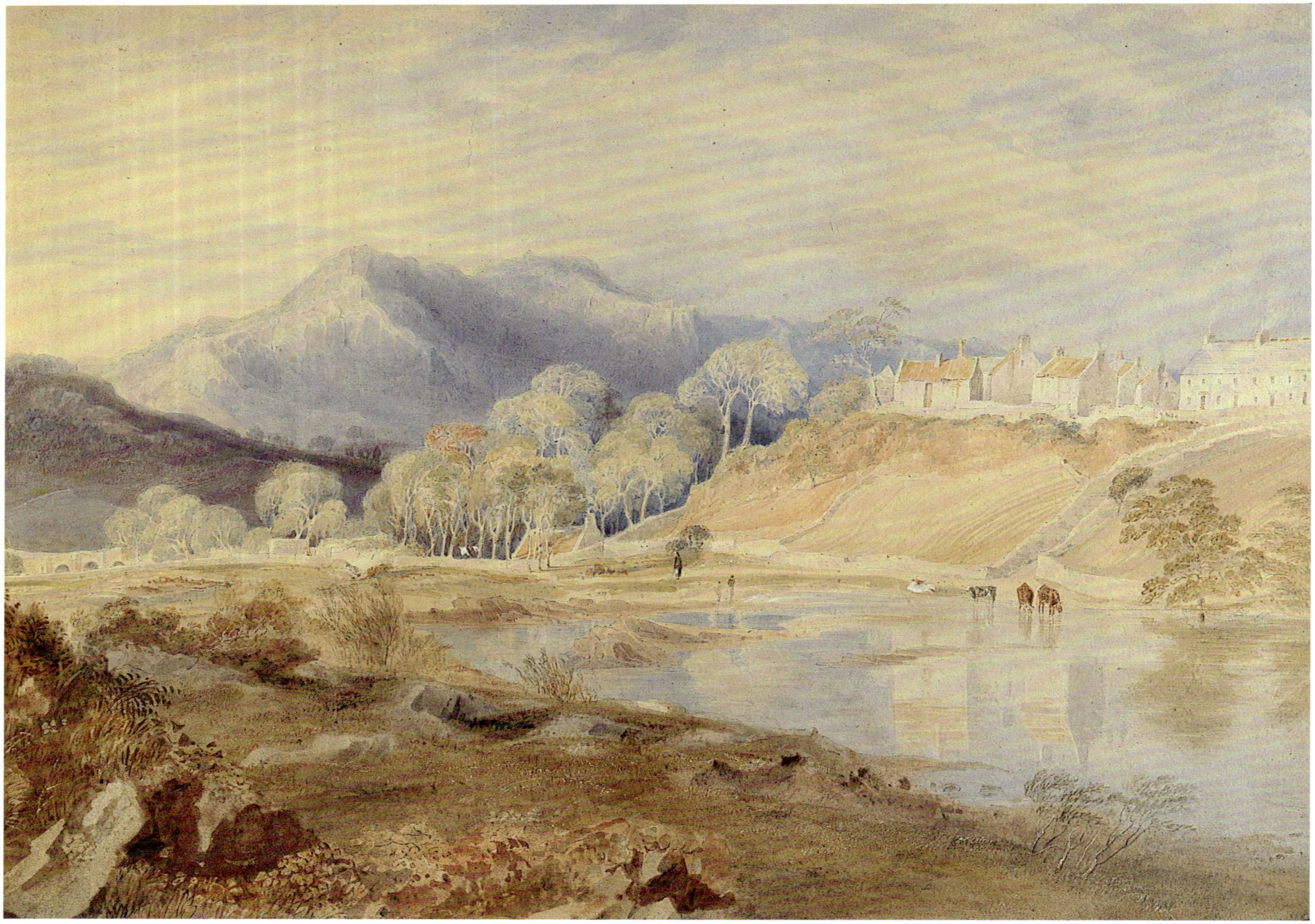

Landscape, The Reeks
Watercolour on paper, 30.5 x 43

George Petrie (1790-1866) – The Rediscovery of Ireland's Past

by Peter Murray

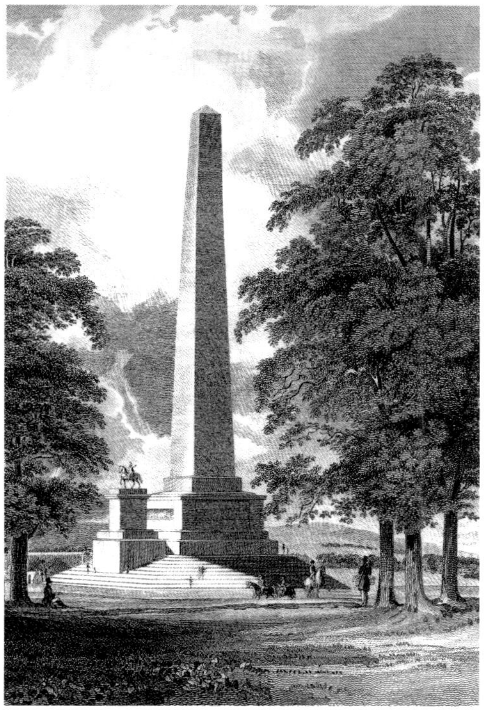

The Wellington Testimonial, Phœnix Park
engraving after Petrie from G.N. Wright, *Ireland Illustrated*, 1832

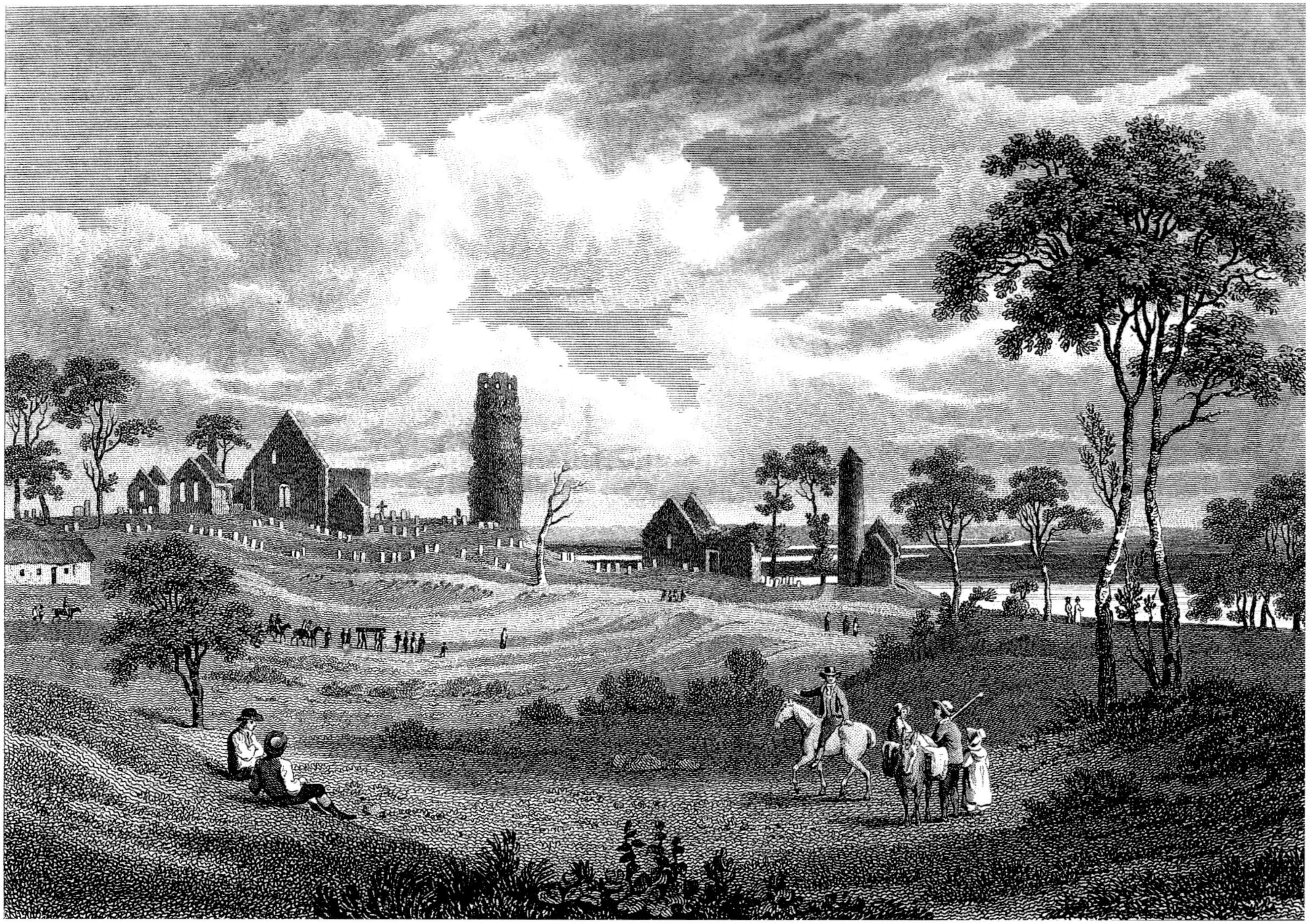

Ruins of Clonmacnois, Kings Co.
engraving after Petrie from J.N. Brewer, *The Beauties of Ireland,* vol. ii, 1826

opposite: *Doorway of the stone-roofed Church at Killaloe,* from G. Petrie, *The Ecclesiastical Architecture of Ireland,* 1845

George Petrie
The Rediscovery of Ireland's Past

PETER MURRAY

The principal source for information on the artist and antiquarian George Petrie is William Stokes' *The Life and Labours in Art and Archaeology of George Petrie LL.D, MRIA*. Written in the years immediately following Petrie's death, and published in 1868, it is a comprehensive account of the artist's career and achievements, written by one of his closest friends.[1] Most subsequent articles on Petrie are largely based on the *Life*, for besides his own wealth of personal experience, the author had access to Petrie's papers, both during and after the artist's life. When Petrie died, intestate, on 12 January 1866, his daughter Mary Ann was appointed executrix of his estate, and it can be assumed that she gave Stokes almost complete freedom to search through her father's papers for material for the biography.[2]

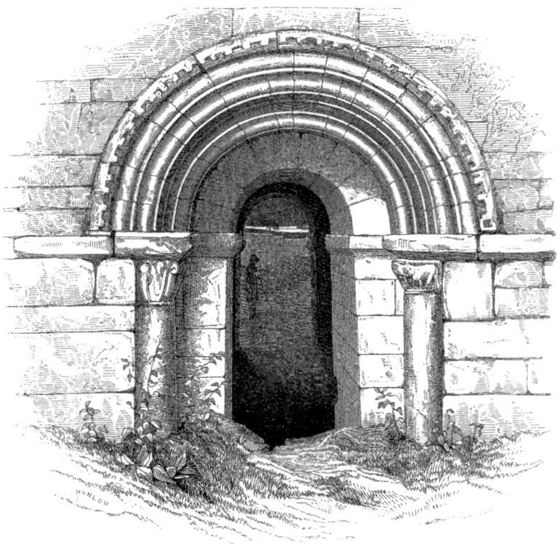

The *Life* was an ambitious undertaking. Its subject was a prolific polymath; apart from being an accomplished painter in watercolours, Petrie was a writer, musicologist, archaeologist and historian, dominating the newly emergent field of Irish studies in the first half of the 19th century. Contributing no less than twenty-seven articles to the *Transactions of the Royal Irish Academy*, he was also curator of RIA's museum of antiquities, securing for the Academy such items as the autograph 17th-century Annals of the Four Masters and the 17th-century O'Cleirigh manuscripts, *The Book of Invasions* and *The Book of Genealogies*. To assist in the publication of John O'Donovan's 1848 translations of the Annals, Petrie even designed a new typeface, based on Gaelic uncial scripts.

Petrie's essay on the antiquities of the Hill of Tara was published by the RIA, as was his monumental *Ecclesiastical Architecture of Ireland*, a survey of Irish churches and monasteries before the Norman invasion, in which he dismissed the fanciful theories of Charles Vallancey and Miss Beaufort concerning the origins of the round towers.[3] His writings, and the engravings which illustrated them, influenced the Hiberno-Romanesque Revival (including such buildings as St Enda's church in Spiddal and the Honan Chapel in Cork). Petrie's accounts of his visits to the Aran Islands influenced John Millington Synge, according the islands and their inhabitants an iconic status in the development of Irish national consciousness.

As well as writing highly academic papers, Petrie also worked hard to popularise his ideas on art and architecture. Aged 26, he contributed essays to the *Dublin Examiner* in which he detailed attempts to found an Academy of Arts in Dublin between 1809-16.[4] When the Rev Caesar Otway founded the *Dublin Penny Journal* in 1832, in an attempt to educate people away from what he regarded as superstitious beliefs, Petrie joined him as editor for a year, before the publication was taken over by the distinctly less high-minded Philip Dixon Hardy. Petrie contributed many articles to the 56 weekly issues during his period as editor. He was sole editor of the short-lived *Irish Penny Journal* in 1842.[5] From 1833 to 1841, he was employed by the government, leading the Topographical Department of the Ordnance Survey in compiling an ambitious survey of Irish topographical, natural and cultural history. In this capacity he employed scholars, writers and artists such as Eugene O'Curry, John O'Donovan, James Clarence Mangan, William Frederick Wakeman and George Du Noyer in carrying out the work. A member of the Royal Hibernian Academy from its foundation in 1826, Petrie exhibited topographical watercolours at the annual exhibitions until 1858. He was elected president in 1856, although his term of office was marred by controversy. The following year, disagreement also attended his designs for the tomb of Daniel O'Connell in Glasnevin Cemetery, the round tower being the only element eventually, and incorrectly, completed.[6] From an early age, Petrie, who played the violin, collected traditional Irish songs and tunes on his travels in Wicklow and in the west of Ireland. His book *The Ancient Music of Ireland* containing 147 airs, was published in 1855. He is credited with being the first person to write down the traditional *Derry Air.*

The Earl of Dunraven, who published his own antiquarian *Notes on Irish Architecture* in 1875, assisted Stokes in compiling the *Life*, and when it was completed, not wishing to take responsibility for destroying the letters and sketches, by his own account Stokes entrusted at least some of them to the care of the Royal Irish Academy, where they have remained since.[7] But none of these papers, nor any of those preserved in the National Library of Ireland, the other main repository for Petrie manuscripts, casts much light on the artist's personal life; they are almost totally concerned with his professional work in antiquarian matters. Grace Calder writes in her book *Petrie and the Ancient Music of Ireland*, that it is generally believed that Petrie left more manuscripts than have been published.[8] That Stokes retained some of the papers that he worked from we may be sure, for in 1900 his daughter Margaret bequeathed several portfolios of Petrie sketches to the National Gallery of Ireland,[9] and Stokes himself quotes extensively from manuscript sources that are now lost, including an account of a journey through Co Wicklow, written by Petrie in 1808.[10] This appears to be no longer extant; it is certainly not amongst the papers preserved in the Royal Irish Academy or the National Library.

In any case, Stokes made good use of his sources and anyone misled by the romantic prose style of the book or its lack of footnotes, need only refer to the original sources to realise how expertly the author used his material to enhance the reputation and standing of his subject. The biography was dedicated to Dunraven, Henry Wentworth Acland and James Henthorn Todd. Like Stokes, Acland, Regius Professor of Medicine at Oxford, was a medical doctor with a keen interest in history and the sciences. More pertinently, he was a close friend of John Ruskin, whose theories on art as a language were central to Stokes' interpretation of Petrie's work. When the biography was published, as Lady Ferguson relates,[11] Stokes called on the home of Sir Samuel Ferguson at 20 North Great Georges Street, on Christmas Day 1868, to present him with a copy and ask his opinion of the work, for as he put it:

> I know so little of the literary world that I have none to consult but yourself in this matter ... I could have easily made the book larger and am almost sorry I did not do so, yet I was anxious to keep it within moderate bounds. But I have done my best under difficulties and they say that what a man does do is his best.[12]

This last rather neatly describes both the aims and limitation of the present work. It is an extension of Stokes, filling out those areas that he treated lightly; providing a more complete catalogue of Petrie's watercolours and drawings, and detailing the engravings of Petrie's works that appeared in guide books in the second quarter of the 19th century. It also explores the few details of the artist's private life that are available to the researcher, examining areas of aesthetic and antiquarian theory that throw light on his achievements.

Although Petrie's interests were wide-ranging, in assessing his life, it is important to remember that he regarded these interests not as separate and distinct disciplines, but rather as reflections, or facets, of the single overriding passion that dominated his life's endeavours – a love of his native land; its people, history and landscape. He believed that by opening people's eyes – particularly his people, the wealthy and literate middle classes – to the beauties of Ireland, to the wealth of its history and culture, and to the inherent qualities of the native population, that the root cause of the social unrest that was plaguing Ireland at that time – which he identified as ignorance – would be swept away and replaced by a new age of high civilisation.

Chapter 1

The Early Years: Ireland Discovered

The Petrie family came originally from Scotland. The name is a patronymic – Petri, son of Peter. It has been spelt in several different ways down through the years. The original Petries hailed from Aberdeen and Kincardine, and one of them is said to have fought at Bannockburn, where Robert the Bruce defeated the English in 1314. There are fifteen members of the family on the burgess-roll of Aberdeen between 1399 and 1631, and in the early years of the reign of Charles II, one Robert Petrie was Provost of Aberdeen and MP for that city. Supporting the Stuarts after the Glorious Revolution of 1688 resulted in the family fortunes declining and probably led to the decision by George Petrie's grandfather, along with other dissenting Scots, to quit Aberdeen and settle in Ireland.[13]

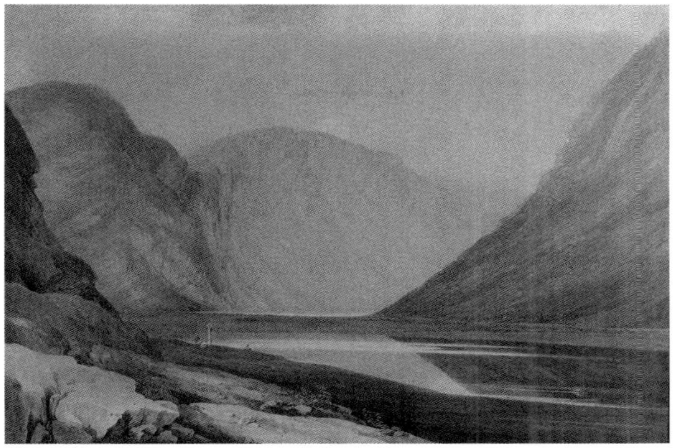

Glendalough
1815, watercolour on paper laid on canvas, 66 x 96.5 (visible size)

While George Petrie's paternal grandfather was a native of Aberdeen, his grandmother was the daughter of a Mr Robinson of Edinburgh, a wine merchant. George Petrie's father, James, was thus first-generation Irish but he reinforced the Scottish connection by marrying the daughter of Sacheverel Simpson of Edinburgh; her name was Elizabeth. She died on 8 April 1793, three years after giving birth to their only child, George.[14] Stokes refers to her 'extreme beauty', citing the evidence of a portrait – probably one of the two extant portraits of her, in the National Gallery of Ireland. One of these is by James himself, for he was a noted miniature portrait painter. In the same collection there is another portrait by him, that of his son George.[15]

George Petrie, according to Strickland's *Dictionary of Irish Artists*, was born on 1 January 1790, although his dates are commonly given as 1789 to 1866. He was an only child, growing up in an atmosphere imbued with the love of art and the antique. His father James had studied at the Dublin Society's Drawing Schools, and afterwards practised as a miniature painter, jeweller and dealer in coins and medals at 82 Dame Street. However, James Petrie's interests extended beyond coins and medals; following the dissenting tradition, his best-known portraits are not of members of the establishment, but of rebels.[16] While William Stokes describes James Petrie as loyal to the Crown, Strickland paints a different picture: 'In the troublous time of the Rebellion, Petrie was arrested on suspicion of being connected with the United Irishmen, and spent a short time in the Provost prison.'[17] Strickland goes on to relate that Petrie owed his release to striking up a friendship with the notorious officer in charge of the prison, Major Sandys, whose portrait he painted. Although most of James Petrie's original portraits are lost, engravings survive. A print of Napper Tandy in the British Museum was engraved by James Heath, as was the romanticised portrait of Robert Emmet in the National Library of Ireland – the head thrown back, the eyes full of passionate expression.[18] Emmet's biographer Ruan O'Donnell describes how this portrait was made after the failed 1803 rebellion:

> James Petrie, a suspected United Irishman and ex-political prisoner, attended Emmet's trial and drew the defendant on the back of an envelope and other loose papers. This work formed the basis of a portrait obtained by Sir Jonah Barrington and produced the best frontal image of the Dubliner. Petrie subsequently engraved a left profile of Emmet.[19]

In the National Gallery of Ireland are preserved the faded drawings showing Emmet's trial. In the recently opened Kilmainham Gaol, James Petrie drew portraits of the imprisoned leaders. A stipple engraving of Michael Dwyer is in the National Library of Ireland, along with portraits *Henry Howley*, *Felix Rourke* and (crudely engraved by 'Maguire') *Denis Lambert Redmond*.[20] After the rebellion of 1803, Howley, a carpenter, was condemned to death for shooting Colonel Lyde Brown in Bridgefoot Street, while Rourke, the son of a farmer from Rathcoole, was also executed. Also in the NLI is a portrait by James Petrie, *The Rev. John Austin (1717-1784), S.J.*, a Dublin preacher famed for his charitable works. Engraved by Henry Brocas Senior, it was published in 1792.

It is unlikely that George Petrie, who would have been nine at the time of the 1798 United Irishmen rebellion, and fourteen at the time of the trial and public execution of Robert Emmet, could have failed to be influenced by these events. Stokes relates an incident when young George was sitting alone reading in the drawing room of the Petrie household. The door opened and a heavily veiled woman entered the room. There was a portrait of Emmet on an easel which, when the woman saw it, reduced her to floods of tears while the terrified George, unnoticed, looked on. The woman was Sarah Curran, to whom Emmet was engaged at the time of his death.[21] Sarah Curran's father was the advocate John Philpot Curran, who defended many of the United Irishmen during their trials.

At the age of nine or ten, George was sent to the English Grammar School, run by Dr Samuel Whyte, at 75 Grafton Street (where Bewley's Café now stands). Whyte was a popular poet in late 18th-century Ireland. His collection of poetry and songs, *The Shamrock*, or *Hibernian Cresses* (1772)[22] marked a change in attitude towards the traditional songs and culture of Ireland. Whyte's literary patriotism was an inspiration to his pupils, who included Richard Brinsley Sheridan, Robert Emmet and Thomas Moore. At his academy, Emmet and Moore formed the friendship that was to endure through their undergraduate days at Trinity College. However, there was also a political side to Whyte, who was an educational reformer and progressive teacher. He used drama in education, bringing his students to Crowe Street Theatre where they performed as extras. Students who excelled in their scholastic endeavours were given, as prizes, neatly framed pictures of their headmaster. Close to Trinity College, Grafton Street was a centre for radicals. It was at the bookshop on Grafton Street run by United Irishman Byrne that Henry and John Sheares met their betrayer Armstrong. Their execution and the traumatic events of 1798 formed a backdrop to the early school days of Petrie. However, after a number of years at Whyte's, he went on to attend a school in the less revolutionary environs of Monkstown.[23]

After spending five or six years in these schools, the question of a career began to arise. Petrie's father wished him to become a surgeon, but his delicate health prevented this; also his natural inclination lay in the direction of art.[24] Accordingly he enrolled in the Drawing Schools of the Dublin Society, which had been transferred in 1796 from their rather dingy quarters in Grafton Street to a somewhat better building in Hawkins Street, not far from the Petrie household at 82 Dame Street.[25] The Drawing Schools made a major contribution to the arts in Ireland at that time, for they were free and open to both the sons of the wealthy and to apprentices in the building and architectural trades (although in later years a division was established whereby the sons of the wealthy paid one guinea a year in fees so that they would not bear the social stigma of having received a charity education).[26] The Drawings Schools remained in Hawkins Street until 1818, when they were transferred to the converted coachhouse of the Society's new home in Kildare House (Leinster House) in Kildare Street.

As was the case in most European art schools of this period, emphasis was placed on learning to depict the human figure – drawing from antique sculpture casts and live models. In addition, students would copy Old Master drawings and engravings, as well as using some of the School's textbooks such as Dodsley's *Preceptor* (1749), a manual of practical instruction in art. In Lesson 10, Dodsley advocated landscape drawing as useful both 'in Business and Conversation'.[27] In early 19th-century Dublin, landscape painting was still considered a subsidiary branch of the visual arts, and was relegated at the Society's Schools to a position equal to that of 'ornament'. The technique of watercolour painting was still relatively new when Petrie enrolled as a student. In 1782 the first specimen watercolour paints had been introduced to the Dublin Society Schools by Henry Graham, Graham having modelled his watercolour box on that offered in London by 'Messrs. Reeves'.[28] At this time, the master of the 'School of Landscape and Ornament' in the Schools was Henry Brocas. His predecessors were John James Barralet and William Waldron. There was obviously little competition for the post, for Brocas held it until his death in 1837 at the age of seventy-four.[29] After his death, and in spite of the rival candidacy of Andrew Nichol, Brocas's youngest son Henry Jnr (*c*.1798-1873) was appointed to the same position, which he held until 1854. The effective director of the School was former army officer Charles Vallancey (1721-1812), a co-founder of the Royal Irish Academy in 1782 and editor of *Collectanea de Rebus Hibernicis*, which featured articles on topics such as the Druids and astronomy in ancient Ireland. Vallancey also asserted that the round towers were built by Phoenicians and that Tara Hill contained the remains of a temple of Mithras, ideas that Petrie would rebut decades later. As the records in the Royal Dublin Society for this period are scanty, little is known of the conduct or activities of Petrie. It was stated in a report at this time that 'the boys are irregular in attendance and remiss in application, displaying a want of energy'.[30] However it need not be assumed that this applies to Petrie, for in 1805 he was awarded a medal and 'a first class premium' for a group of figures,[31] and two years later, while still a student, a landscape painted by him was hung in the Society's Exhibition Room. In 1809 and in the two years following, the galleries in Hawkins Street were availed of by the Society of Artists in Ireland for their annual exhibition. In 1813, this Society split into two rival groups, Petrie joining with the breakaway Society of Artists of the City of Dublin. Other members of this group included William Sadler, George Papworth and Thomas Kirk. William Ashford and Thomas Sautell Roberts remained with the original society. In 1815, the two groups settled their differences, only to split again the following year.[32] Petrie was part of a committee formed at the request of the Dublin Society, to try and sort out the annual rival exhibitions. Throughout his career, Petrie maintained a connection with the Dublin Society; in the 1840s he served on the RDS Committee of Fine Arts, along with Richard Atkinson and Martin Cregan.[33]

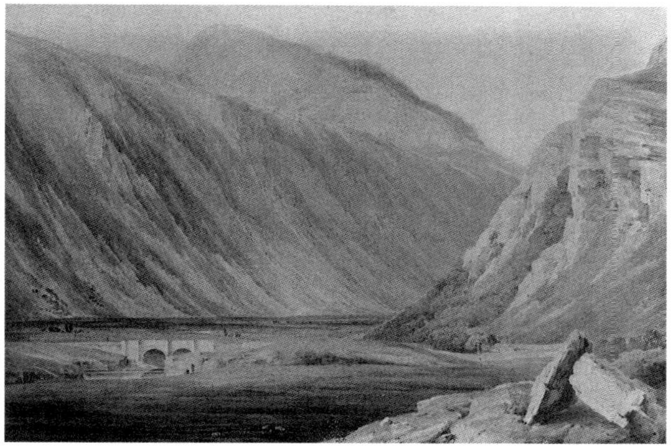

Glenmalure in the County Wicklow
1815, watercolour on paper laid on canvas, 66 x 96.5 (visible size) (colour p.14)

When George Petrie was eighteen years old, his father married again. The bride's name was Wilhelmina Bate, and the ceremony was held in St Werburgh's Church on 20 July 1808. Wilhelmina shared the family passion for collecting antiquities – presumably James and she had been brought together by this common interest. George readily accepted his stepmother; she seems to have been a popular figure with all her friends also. After James Petrie died, she carried on the jewellery and antique business in Dame Street. Wilhelmina survived until 1862, after living in Great Charles Street and Charlemont Place with George and his family.[34]

While all this was happening, George was forming his own connections. Among the young men at the Drawing Schools were two to whom he became particularly close; James Arthur O'Connor and Francis Danby. O'Connor, two years younger than Petrie, was the son of a print-selling engraver. Danby, three years younger, the son of a small landed proprietor in Co Wexford.[35] 'My family, like many others, were destroyed by political and party feeling, many of them lost their lives on both side of the unhappy question', wrote Danby of his childhood and the 1798 Rebellion. Danby tried to escape his troubles through immersing himself in art. He later settled in Bristol, commenting to a friend, 'Ireland to me is a desert without an interest'.[36] Although a prolific artist, James Arthur O'Connor also enjoyed erratic success in his subsequent career. Older and better educated, Petrie formed the natural leader of this trio of budding Romantic landscape artists; he had all his father's experience behind him and also had access to private art collections in Dublin, including those of Major Sirr and W. Harrington.[37] He gave his two friends advice and encouragement. 'Some of your early works acted on me as inducements at first to become an artist . .' Danby wrote to Petrie in 1845.[38] Both his friends later took up residence in Britain and so broke up the close friendship that existed between them, but for the present they spent their time together in the dry atmosphere of the school, laboriously copying from the antique or drawing the 'lusty male model' that sat for the classes throughout the year, or in the mountains that lie immediately to the south of Dublin city, containing some of the finest landscape in Ireland. Stokes refers to a sketchbook that Petrie had kept in the years 1808-09 that he had seen. It contained 45 drawings, 'principally of trees, studies of river scenery and cattle, and but two antiquarian drawings – the interior of Howth Abbey and an unnamed ruined arch. The style of the drawings is free and broad, but wanting in the delicacy of his after works.'[39] Several drawings in the National Gallery are evidently from this sketchbook, including *The Entrance to the Dargle River*, an ink drawing signed and dated 1807.[40]

In his wanderings around Wicklow and Dublin, Petrie also kept written journals in which he noted items that interested him; customs and manners of the people, remains of antiquity in the landscape, legends and traditional tunes that he picked up as he tramped the hills. Stokes refers to a journal (untraced) from 1808 of a trip through Wicklow, and quotes several passages from it. In this journal, Petrie describes the 'Piper's Stones', a circle of prehistoric stones near Athgreany, as being of 'prodigious size' and numbering thirty, though originally he reckoned that they numbered thirty-five or so. Today, just thirteen of these stones remain.[41] In another journal made later that year, Petrie records his interest in music and history; collecting airs from a countryman, researching the 'painful history' of the once aristocratic O'Toole and Byrne families: 'What and where are they now? Peasants, to be found in the villain hovels in the wilderness, their rank and inheritance gone and forever.'[42]

Petrie believed that the time had arrived when these ancient wrongs could be discussed openly, and a 'wise and liberal' England could bear the errors of past times to be spoken of, and not refuse admiration to men who loved their country 'not wisely but too well'. While the main object of the 1808 Wicklow trip was to draw the Poulaphuca Waterfall on the River Liffey, Petrie also visited Ballymore Eustace and the waterfall called the Gurgle: 'It is very beautiful, resembling much the Salmon Leap, but has a bad background.'[43] Stokes describes how Petrie would set out walking, at nightfall, so as to reach a chosen spot in the Wicklow mountains as dawn broke.

Although his interest clearly lay in landscape painting, the first income Petrie received was for portrait painting, and he is said to have executed many orders for the Liverpool market, but his only identified sitter from this period was Lord Manners, Lord Chancellor.[44] Since Manners was appointed to this post in 1807, the portrait may be dated to after this year. Its present whereabouts are unknown, but Strickland states it was engraved by Maguire, who had also engraved several of James Petrie's portraits. The commission must have been something of a coup for the teenage Petrie.

EARLY TRAVELS IN BRITAIN

In 1810 Petrie stayed at the home of Lord Glentworth in Gosphonage Bangor-Ferry, the first of many trips he was to make to Wales. Ten years later, Bangor-Ferry was chosen by Telford as the site for his suspension bridge over the Menai Straits. This bridge, and a second one at Conway Castle, were recorded by Petrie in drawings now preserved in the National Gallery of Ireland.[45] These drawings show Petrie's interest in the landscape was not entirely confined to the antiquarian or picturesque, and that his travels to Wales extended over a long period. Just east of the Menai Straits on the foothills of Snowdonia, Dolbadarn Castle was a favourite subject, drawn and painted by Petrie on several occasions. His favourite vantage point was Dolbadarn, seen from Llyn Padern across the lake. Stokes cites the influence of the mountains of Caernarvonshire on Petrie's aesthetic sensibility: 'In Wales he learned to love the solitude and wildness of nature, in its peaked and barren mountain scenes, and perhaps acquired an inclination to a peculiar tone of colouring which is not decidedly Irish, and which we recognise at once, when travelling through the Snowdonian range, as characteristic of Petrie's works.' There is little information on the 1810 trip, apart from a letter he wrote to his friend Charles Hanlon. Concerning his host Lord Glentworth, the *Annual Register* of 1834 speaks of him as a 'clever but imprudent young nobleman, gifted by nature with great talents, who fell a victim to a career of reckless indulgence'. The *Register* goes on to relate how Glentworth, after he had come of age, spent 'the greatest part of his time' in prison.[46] Petrie's letter to Hanlon, however, is hardly that of a profligate young rake:

> Do you practise drawing, dear Charles? Let me earnestly entreat you to do so. It will be an endless source of pleasure to you hereafter; you have, I assure you without flattery, an abundance of natural talent. The first eight days after my

> landing I spent exactly to my wishes – studying nature; but nature should be studied by months each year, not days. You will rejoice when I tell you I have some fine subjects, and two or three *grand* ones; but I must confess that for colour I saw nothing equal to lonely Lough Bray.[47]

Today, Lough Bray is as unspoilt as in Petrie's time, and anyone who has climbed up to it can readily appreciate his feelings. Years later, when Stokes set out to write his biography, he enlisted the aid of Charles Hanlon's son. When Hanlon called on his elderly father, in February 1866, he found him very ill, and his memory much impaired. The old man struggled to recall the events of half a century before; he remembered Petrie as being a good-natured person with charming manners, who, as a little boy, was so fond of coins that he used spend all his money in the purchase of them. He remembered that Petrie was also passionately fond of music and would walk miles and miles to listen to the Militia Bands when they were out marching. One event stood out in Charles Hanlon's mind, which he recounted to his son:

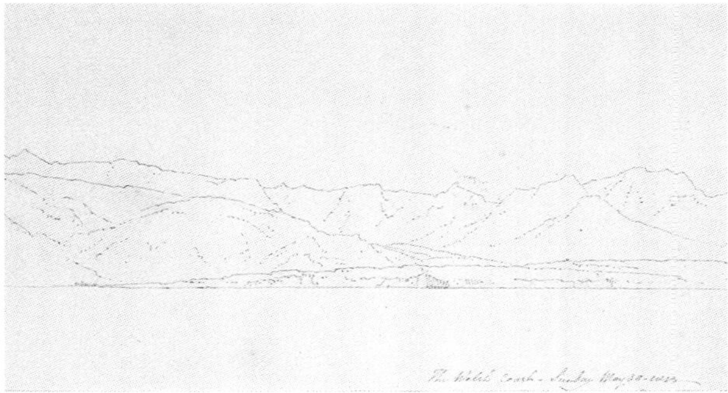

The Welsh Coast, dated Sunday May 30th 1813
Ink on paper, 14.3 x 26.5 (coll: NGI, cat. no. 6742)

> On the occasion of Mozart's 'Don Giovanni' first being played in Ireland, the part of the 'Don' was performed by Ambrogetti for whom the music was written and whose performance of it will in all probability never be equalled. Such was Petrie's admiration of the music that for the forty nights that the opera was played consecutively he went every night to hear it.
>
> He used to say that he would make up his mind each day not to go *that night* and after dinner he would settle himself to some useful employment, but as the hour would draw near for the opening of the Theatre he would begin to get fidgety and unhappy and at last he would fling aside whatever he was employed on and rush off to be in time to hear the first grand chords of the overture.[48]

This seemed an incredible claim to Stokes, who set a researcher to work on the Dublin papers of the period to check if it was possible for Petrie to have attended forty nights of *Don Giovanni*, as Hanlon asserted. The researcher, R. M. Leary, came up with the information that the opera in question had only run in Dublin from 27 September 1819 until 12 October of that same year. ' it would be a pity that anything not critically correct should appear in connection with Dear Dr. Petrie', he wrote.[49] Yet Hanlon's story is so circumstantial that it is possible that Petrie did in fact see almost the full run of the opera at the Crowe Street Theatre.

In 1813 the three friends, Danby, O'Connor and Petrie, had finished their courses in the Drawing Schools and they decided to go to London to complete their artistic education. Petrie's father provided the funds for his expenses, but the other two were not so fortunate; they had to sell some of their paintings by lottery to raise the money for their journey.[50] It was a policy of the Dublin Society to buy students' paintings to help them on their way, but they do not seem to have done so in this case; nor did they provide any money in the way of grants.[51] Nevertheless the three artists managed to accumulate sufficient funds for the trip, and, perhaps more importantly, Petrie was able to obtain a letter of introduction to Sir Benjamin West, president of the Royal Academy, that would also ensure access to art collections in private houses in London. The trio arrived, travelling via Bristol, in the first week of June 1813, and set up in some style in an hotel. Petrie made some sketches on the journey, five of which are preserved in the National Gallery of Ireland. They are all dated 30 May 1813, and they depict the Welsh coast as seen from the ship on which he was travelling, as they approached Bristol.[52] He wrote to Eliza Mills, the woman who was to become his wife, a few days after their arrival:

June 10th, 1813

> Eight days have passed since I arrived in this magnificent seat of arts and learning, the entire of which has been busily employed in seeing and admiring the various interesting objects which this vast and truly wonderful city presents to the astonished mind of a stranger. I would fain give you an

account of the points in which London and Dublin most differ, and of the superiority of the former, but such would be impossible in the form of an epistle. That which amazed me most of all things here is the knowledge in the arts which the people possess. There is not an artist of any rank whose merits they are not acquainted with, even in the middle ranks. I never go through an obscure lane or street in which I do not meet shops where coins, antiquities, books, prints, pictures, &c., are the only things they sell, and I always found that they knew the rarity and value of every article they had. This evening my heart leaped at the sight of two beautiful Etruscan vases in a little miserable, old furniture shop. I already anticipated the joy of carrying them home, but on inquiring of the very young woman the price she replied, 'Three guineas and a half'. She also observed, on marking my astonishment, that they were genuine Etruscan vases, and very cheap.

> In the same lane, in a hole which I could scarce turn in, I found a poor sick-looking woman, who to my astonishment had all the information of a complete print connoisseur; the works of the different ages and classes of engravers were arranged in the most systematic manner, and the prices marked on each with the most perfect knowledge of their value. She could hand me the work of any particular master, and speak at length of its merits.

> I have been with Mr. West, the President of the Royal Academy, who received me with kindness and attention. I have had the honour and felicity of his conversation and advice, two separate times and upwards of an hour each, an incident, which I shall ever remember with peculiar pride and delight. He explained to me the several figures in the large picture ('Christ before Pilate'), which he is at present employed at, and for which he has been offered a thousand guineas.[53]

It is not certain whether his two friends accompanied Petrie on these interviews. The *Art Journal* obituary of Danby stated that he and O'Connor also had letters of introduction to West.[54] Charles Hanlon recalled that Petrie alone had a letter of introduction to West, but that he resolved to use it to bring his friends before the great man. 'The three young men were civilly received by the President; but he took an opportunity when parting to tell Petrie that he would be at all times happy to see him provided he came without his companions, as he did not wish to see them again'.[55] The three young men stayed less than a month in the capital; they saw, amongst many other things, Turner's *Frosty Morning*, which Danby later described as 'a beautiful and wonderful picture'.[56] William Frederick Wakeman (who in later years was to work with Petrie in the Ordnance Survey) describes their position at this time:

> Petrie has often related, in the presence of the writer of this paper, an account of the adventure of the youthful trio in the English capital. How, as their bullion evaporated – as bullion will in London – they gradually descended from their high estate in a hotel, and sought furnished lodgings and restaurants – for even poetical young artists cannot choose but eat. Their last dinner in London was in one of those mysterious dens where gentlemen pay in advance, are furnished with knives and forks chained to the table, and are not supposed to object to having their viands peppered with flies, or other little animals, which we refrain from naming.[57]

Stokes relates that, in the time of their distress, Petrie's father sent over a picture to him with instructions to sell it and return home:

> I could wish it was disposed of, that you might return home; your presence would cheer me. However, it can't be long till I have that happiness. Of your friendship and affection, my dear George, I have had many instances. You have ever been the idol of my heart, under all the pressure of my life, you it was who buoyed me, therefore it is not a weakness to express to you how much I long for your presence.

> How are Danby and O'Connor? What are they doing? Have they stolen any of the great men's works? I mean, have they lodged in their brains all their excellences?[58]

But whether Petrie did in fact return home directly is uncertain. Stokes says that Danby, in a conversation with Rothwell many years later, recalled Petrie's generosity on leaving London, in giving Danby and O'Connor two valuable rings which they were to sell if they found themselves in acute difficulties – the implication being that Petrie left the others and went home alone. Wakeman, on the other hand, says he had it from Petrie himself that when the trio found their stock of cash was not sufficient for the coach-fare, they decided to walk to Bristol and catch the ship to Dublin there:

Upon this road, in the country of the barbarous English or Welsh – it matters not which, they arrived in a half-famished state at a farmhouse, and showing a piece of coin, asked imploringly for something wherewith to stay heir hunger. Nothing was to be had. 'Stop a moment,' said a Saxon in frock and highlows to the last who was retiring; 'Oi think thoult relish a bit o'meat.' They joyfully returned and waited. A frizzing sound soon commenced in an adjoining room, and when it eased expectation had given such a whet, that they declared they could devour anything. It was a steak – but of an eccentric colour, strong-smelling, and oh! How tough! But the hungry teeth pierced its fibres; and the landlord being paid, each party was satisfied. Petrie was wont to declare, years later, that on leaving the place they saw, in a yard adjoining the kitchen, the carcass of a colt, a victim apparently of consumption, from the attenuated flank of which had been cut a piece that exactly corresponded in length, breadth and thickness, with the dimensions of their tough and odoriferous steak.[59]

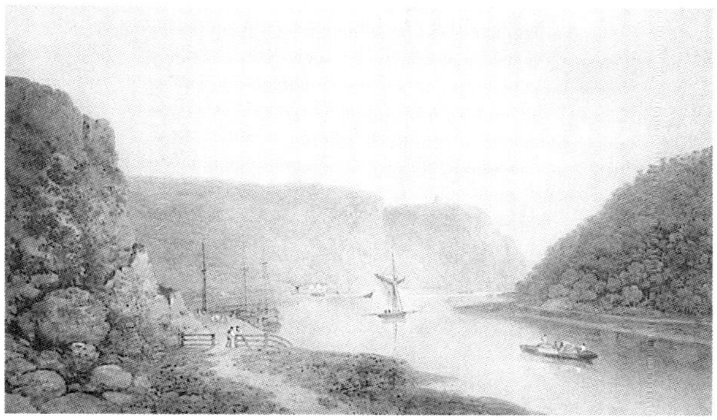

Francis Danby, *View of Avon Bridge, Bristol*
Watercolour

Wakeman states that it was from Bristol that Petrie departed for Dublin, after receiving help from his father; but in the meantime, being penniless, they decided to make use of their talents and avail of the celebrated scenery around Bristol, by painting views of the area and selling them. Danby went to the shop of a stationer and print-seller called Minthorn, on College Green, to show him some of their drawings. Adams, in his biography of Danby, cites a letter that John Minthorn, son of the print-seller, wrote to the *Western Daily Press* after Danby's death, when he recalled how he had been present in the shop when Danby had entered it. (He does not mention whether Petrie was present.)[60] Minthorn was delighted with the drawings and bought the three works Danby had with him, promising to buy any others that he supplied. Wakeman corroborates this, stating that the three artists lived in Bristol by making and selling little watercolour sketches at 3s 6d each. Through this newly found patron, Danby secured a commission to paint a picture in oils for a nobleman living near Bristol, which he executed. A letter from Danby to J. Gibbons, written twenty-three years later, and quoted in John Hutchinson's monograph on James Arthur O'Connor, asserts that when they sold the drawings they could raise only enough funds to pay for the passage of one of them, and O'Connor was forced to take advantage of this as his orphan sisters were depending on his return.[61]

In his biography of that other famous 19th-century Irish artist, Daniel Maclise, author Justin O'Driscoll recounts a story which he says Petrie 'was often heard to relate'; of how the three artists decided to paint a 'joint-stock' picture – that is, each artist executing the part he was best at. O'Connor did the landscape and background; Petrie added some architectural ruins and Danby dealt with the figures and foreground. Such a division of work would certainly accord with their respective talents. According to O'Driscoll, the picture was sold and the proceeds divided between the three.[62]

It seems likely that it was in Bristol that the three friends finally split up, Danby remaining to paint views of the Avon Gorge, Petrie returning to Ireland, and O'Connor embarking on a career marred by tragic episodes. Stokes states that they all visited Wales later in that same year, but gives no additional information. Charles Hanlon stated that O'Connor and Danby had remained in England for want of money to return home, and that although Petrie only had sufficient money to reach Ireland with, his friends often thought it would have been better for him if he had, like his companions, been compelled to remain in 'the Sister Kingdom'.[63]

Chapter II

Ireland Delineated I: Petrie's Artistic Development

Apart from his adventures in England in 1813, there is little information on Petrie's life at this time. It is clear that unlike most of his artistic peers, he did not look to London as a natural destination, but regarded his future as being closely bound up with that of Ireland. However, the degree to which artists moved back and forth between Ireland and Britain during this period has perhaps been underestimated. Apart from Petrie, Danby and O'Connor, Dublin artists William Brocas and James Henry Brocas also made trips to Wales and England during these years; a sketchbook in the National Library dated to 1823-24 contains views of London by the latter.[64] Through travel, correspondence and reading, Petrie was familiar with new developments and theories in art. During his formative years, the events of the French Revolution – and in Ireland the 1798 Rebellion – had undermined conventional views on society; when Petrie embarked on his career, imagination and subjective experience were beginning to hold sway in the world of art and literature. This shift of concern from general to particular conceptions of truth was promoted later in the 19th century by John Ruskin, who emphasised the role of painting as a language, invaluable as a means of communicating ideas, but of itself of little importance. Through his watercolour paintings with researches in archaeology, Petrie combined the Romanticism of the age with a belief in science and reason.

Petrie painted exclusively in watercolour rather than oils, a reluctance that ultimately brought him into conflict with other members of the Royal Hibernian Academy. Up to the end of the 18th century watercolours were regarded as being inferior in every respect to oil paintings, being rarely worked up fully or exhibited separately. They were used either to provide studies for oil paintings, or pictures that could be readily reproduced by engravers. Edward Dayes, in his *Instructions for Drawing and Colouring Landscapes* (1805), gives an account of these traditional techniques:

> Supposing the outline complete, and ready to work on, there are two ways of working it up. The first and most easy way, is to make all the shadows and middle tints, with Prussian blue and brown Indian ink. The other is, by dead colouring it all over, making light shade and middle tint as is done in oil painting (only preserving the lights), and so proceed, strengthening each part, till the whole is finished.[65]

While Turner and Girtin broke away from this approach and began to paint more directly, applying broad washes and local colour directly onto paper with no previous underpainting, Petrie, often referred to as 'the Irish Turner', was not so revolutionary in his approach; his qualities as an artist reside in his masterly use of underpainting to create effect of mood, and building up the painting using low-key colours. The final effect, in his major works, is one of controlled excitement. It raises them from being picturesque to something a great deal more. His pencil drawings, made on the spot during his sketching tours, are precise and delicate. Although sometimes barely visible on the Whatman paper he preferred to use, these drawings are very fine indeed. Petrie's achievement, within the watercolour tradition, was to blend the topographical styles of Francis Place, Wenceslaus Hollar and Paul Sandby with the new emotional sensibility of the Romantic era. In books such as David Cox's *Treatise on Landscape Painting and Effect in Watercolour* (1814) and William Gilpin's *Three Essays: On Picturesque Beauty, On Picturesque Travel, and On Picturesque Landscape* (1792), the new status of landscape painting was defined and codified.[66] Petrie was not a 'picturesque' artist; indeed his Connemara and Wicklow landscapes with their bare hillsides could well have been used by Gilpin as illustrations in his 'Three Essays of Non-Picturesque Mountain Landscapes'.

When the Government took over the Royal Dublin Society's schools in 1877, a collection of over one hundred drawings and watercolours was transferred to the National Museum and from there to the National Library. This collection, which includes works by and after John Varley, Francis Nicholson, Samuel Prout and Copley Fielding, gives an insight into the teaching of landscape painting at the Society's Schools the early 19th century, with the emphasis being clearly on the 'picturesque', a term popularised by Uvedale Price in his *Essay on the Picturesque*, published in 1792. The English artist Paul Sandby had accompanied Sir Watkins Williams-Wynn on his pioneering 'picturesque' tour of Wales in 1771.[67] Sandby also visited Ireland, and his view of Glendalough was published as an engraving. The increased opportunities for travel and appreciation of local scenery resulted in a great expansion in the production of engravings. In Ireland, Jonathan Fisher (d.1809) was one of the most important topographical artists who also produced his own engravings, and there is no doubt that, in his precise and accurate manner of delineating landscape, he greatly influenced Petrie. Francis Nicholson, one of the artists represented in the Drawings School's collection, had travelled and worked in Ireland; his daughter Marianne married Crofton Croker. John Varley was a popular drawing master, whose *Treatise* (1816-21) was widely respected. He also visited Ireland; a drawing by him of Kerry is preserved in the Ashmolean Museum.

Petrie followed the example of his fellow students and his teacher Henry Brocas in making sketching tours to beauty spots around Dublin. The invention of the small portable Reeves watercolour boxes, and the availability of high-quality Whatman paper, had liberated artists from the studio and enabled them to travel widely in search of inspiration. Another device often employed by artists was a 'Claude glass', a smoked mirror that unfolded from a small case. When landscapes were viewed reflected in the glass, contrasts of light and shade were reduced and the landscape and sky framed in a harmonious pictorial composition. (The effect not dissimilar to viewing a landscape through Polaroid sunglasses.) Finished paintings were worked up in the studio from these sketches, where nature, according to the principles of Claude or Poussin, was 'improved' or idealised. This 17th-century idea, based on the *Poetics* of Aristotle, held that the particular or actual was imperfect, whereas the general or idealised could be used to express high ideals in painting. This idealisation of landscape was in contrast to the topographical tradition which had its origins in map-making and military draughtsmanship, and revelled in the detailed depiction of actual places.

The early 19th-century craze for sketching tours in England, Scotland, Wales and Ireland was summed up by Robert Southey: 'Within the last thirty years a taste for the picturesque has sprung up; and a course of summer travelling is now looked upon to be as essential as ever a course of spring physic was in old times. While one of the flocks of fashion migrates to the sea-coast, another flies off to the mountains of Wales, to the lakes in the northern provinces, or to Scotland; some to mineralogise, some to botanise, some to take views of the country – all to study the picturesque, a new science for which a new language has been formed.'[68] However, the passion for the picturesque was not quite as new as Southey asserted. Around 1760, inspired by Edmund Burke's call to artists to incorporate the awesome power of mountains and chasms in their work, artists had begun to explore areas such as the Lake District, Snowdonia and Killarney. As well as being one of the first artists to explore north Wales, the Irish artist George Barret had produced several dramatic paintings of the waterfall at Powerscourt. The best known of these, in the National Gallery of Ireland, prefigures 19th-century interest in the sublime. Burke proposed that the idea of the sublime lay in the struggle for individual survival in a potentially hostile landscape, while he associated 'the beautiful' with forms of social interaction necessary for the survival of humanity in a more collective sense. Burke proposed a graduated scale of the sublime, in which 'astonishment' lies halfway between 'respect' and 'terror'. Burke understood that certain colours, forms and textures trigger intuitive responses within the onlooker. He associated curving lines with gentleness of form and femininity; the sublime, with its precipices and chasms, he considered more masculine territory. With these leaps of association, Burke invested nature with a gendered construct based on the social mores of his time. It was a philosophy that found a ready audience amongst intellectuals anxious to consolidate a sense of nationhood and establish a meaningful relationship between city dwellers and the land. People were now being taught how to look at landscapes, and to grade them according to a series of standards. Landscapes and buildings were viewed critically in terms of their Picturesque qualities. The gables at Tintern Abbey caused problems to artists seeking an idealised Romantic image: they were not ruinous enough. The regularity of canals was also a problem; Gilpin found them 'disgusting'.The tension between an idealised 'imagined' nature, whether sublime or beautiful, and empirical observation, with its jagged lines and abrupt changes in tone, underlies most Romantic landscape painting. However, the essence of the Romantic landscape was that it anticipated an emotional rather than an intellectual response from the viewer.

'The pictures of the elder Barrett, in Ireland, and of Wilson, in England, were objects of great admiration to the mind of Petrie,' wrote Stokes, adding that one of Petrie's early works, *Dolbaddern Castle*, exhibited at the RHA in 1832, was later sold as a Richard Wilson. George Barret had also visited Wilson's favourite haunts in Wales, painting *Llanberis with the early morning mists dispersing*.[69] Stokes mentions that Turner had also painted this same subject, in the style of Wilson.[70] Although Petrie's version has not been traced, several drawings by him, of *Dolbaddern Castle* and the *Upper Lake at Llanberis in Carnarvonshire*, where Wilson died in 1782, are preserved in the National Gallery of Ireland and the Crawford Art Gallery in Cork. Other parallels can be found in the work of the English artist John Varley (1778-1842), whose watercolours the *Pass at Llanberis* or *Dolbaddern Castle* could well have been painted by Petrie and whose early views of Bristol were engraved in John Britton's *The Beauties of England and Wales*, anticipating Petrie's own career.[71] Two years older than Petrie, the watercolourist Anthony Vandyke Copley Fielding (1787-1855) also visited Wales. His version of the oft-depicted *Llanberis Lake with Dolbadern Castle* captures the moist atmosphere of the mountains of Wales in a low-key colour range reminiscent of the Irish artist and quite different from the gusting wind and driving rains so beloved of Turner or David Cox.[72] Petrie's watercolours may lack some of the sparkle of Peter de Wint, another contemporary who trudged through North Wales with his folio of paper and watercolour box, but the Irish artist's technique was more studied and conservative. His style was more firmly rooted in the 18th-century aesthetic of Thomas Girtin, who painted Conway Castle in 1800, or with the Bristol artist Samuel Jackson (1794-1869) whose views of the Avon Gorge and indeed of *The Eagle's Nest, Killarney* are tranquil and limpid.[73]

Although Wilson flooded his Welsh landscapes such as *Llyn Peris and Dolbadarn Castle* (1764), with the clear Italian light he had absorbed during his years in Rome, his classical restraint failed to find favour in the Romantic age, with its hunger for feeling and emotion.[74] Petrie, who never visited Italy, used the mists and sun-drenched haze of Irish and Welsh landscapes to evoke these same profound feelings. He pared back the theatrical conventions, the framing trees and gesturing figures of Nicolas Poussin and Claude Lorrain, but retained the former's fondness for funereal visions and the latter's golden autumnal sunsets. Although he rarely if ever painted in oils, Petrie emulates Wilson in the use of delicate tonal values, the distortion of vertical proportions and in the 'discovery' of Irish monasteries and landscapes as suitable subject matter for idealised paintings. In substituting the broken traceries of Gothic windows and heather-clad mountains for the more formal classical temples, cypress trees and the Roman Campagna, he tried to evoke the 'soul' of his native country. Where his 18th-century predecessor would have placed an obelisk or urn, Petrie, with equal reverence, placed a high cross or round tower. Within the wider European Romantic art tradition, his work contains echoes of Caspar David Friedrich, who often depicted ruined monasteries. A favourite was Oybin, the setting for *The Dreamer (Ruins of a Monastery at Oybin)*.[75] For Friedrich and his contemporaries, this historic religious site occupied the same position as did Clonmacnoise for Petrie. In Saxony, monastic ruins symbolised a decline from the glories of the Middle Age to the ignominy of occupation by Napoleon. In Ireland, they were also beginning to form an important part of the jigsaw of emerging nationalism.

From the outset, Petrie's style of drawing and painting was characterised by its low key, precision and delicacy. His draughtsmanship was greatly admired and, according to his biographer Stokes, he was considered by his contemporaries to have discarded 'all conventional tricks' of art:

> But he was more than a draughtsman; his drawings and pictures were peculiarly imbued with that indescribable charm which, for want of a better word, has been styled feeling, and which only genius of the highest order can convey. His simplest sketch assumed the character of a painted poem; a green hillside, a shattered cross, a ruined watch-tower, as treated by his genius, become the subject of a picture...[76]

Stokes emphasised how Petrie, while adhering to 'perfect truthfulness of detail' strove to make his art 'subservient to a higher aim' and went on to quote the artist's own words: 'We cannot get the full effect and beauty of nature; but we can paint her so as to convey her spiritual lessons in however faint a degree.'[77] Stokes repeatedly defends Petrie's style as 'faithful to the most minute particular', and praises the degree to which the artist held 'communion with his subjects', virtually establishing the stereotypical image of the 'Celtic Twilight', complete with round towers and dramatic sunsets, that was to so dominate Irish cultural history over the following century. 'And so over all his works, a sad and sunset gold is made to shine.' He cites Petrie's love of the poetry of William Wordsworth, comparing the poet's descriptions of nature with the artist's treatment of similar subject matter in his paintings, a delicate approach, in contrast to the vivid and passionate verses of Keats, Shelley or Byron.

In Wordsworth, Petrie found an echo of his own quasi-religious beliefs in nature as an arbiter and teacher of human morality and ethics. Stokes himself promotes this Ruskinian doctrine: 'Into the heart of such a man her lessons sink silently; he finds the workings of the law of love everywhere; sees God's beauty poured forth over the whole world, and feels his own mind advancing on the path which is to end in light.' Stokes addresses criticisms of Petrie's work, including a perceived deficiency of colour, by stressing that the artist did not set out to represent accurately what he saw, but to translate:

> We may use the word translate, as the mere effort to copy nature should not be, in his opinion, the landscape painter's object. Nor was painting with him ever a mere mimetic art; one good reason for this, being, simply, that absolute reproduction of effect is impossible. Take, for example, any one scene in nature: the landscape painter cannot give its brightest light or deepest shade.
>
> There may be medium tints which are within his power to attain; but if such are given by the hand which fails to reach the fuller tones, to which they form the intermediate passages, the work is at once thrown out of harmony; the tones which should be secondary strike on the eye as vividly as those of primary importance, for want of proportionate strength in those which are beyond the painter's power to reach; so that a certain portion of truth must be sacrificed in these medium tints. Partial truth must yield to general truth, and the painter must think of his work as an instrument to be attuned by him to a key of a certain pitch, to which every note must be brought into subjection and harmony.[78]

In Petrie's paintings, his figures, be they pilgrims or tourists, seem dwarfed by awe-inspiring landscapes, as they contemplate the infinite. However, notwithstanding Stokes' valiant defence, there are characteristics of Petrie's paintings which come close to mannerism, but these do not detract from his overall achievement in uniting the landscapes and ancient historic sites of Ireland within a strongly Romantic and yet topographically accurate tradition.

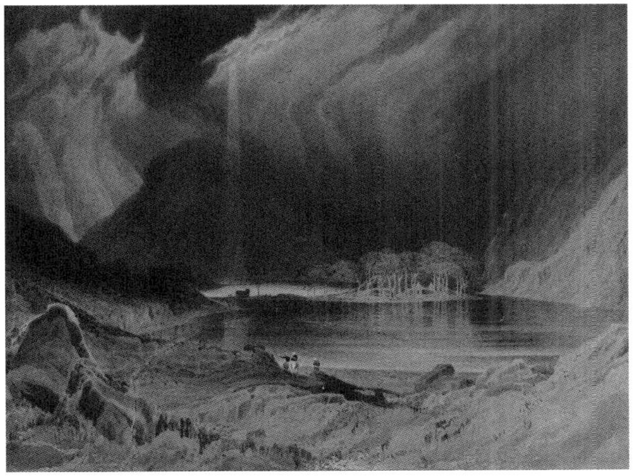

Gougane Barra
*c.*1831, watercolour on paper, 28 x 38 (visible size)
(see colour plate p.25)

Chapter III

Ireland Delineated II: Petrie's Involvement with Engravers and Publishers

The five years that followed Petrie's return from London remain an almost total blank. There is very little material from this period that can be used to glean information about his life and travels. The few paintings dating from this time indicate that Petrie continued his sketching trips into the Wicklow mountains. Strickland refers to a Crucifixion that Petrie painted for the Roman Catholic Chapel at Kinnegad in 1815, that was also exhibited in Dublin.[79] The following year, 1816, he exhibited two paintings at the Royal Academy in London, the only time he showed at Somerset House. The two paintings – *Glendalough* and *Glenmalure* – are among the largest paintings he did, both measuring over two feet by three feet.[80] Signed and dated, they are mentioned by Stokes as being the property of Lord Whitworth, who was Viceroy of Ireland (as Lord Lieutenant) at this time. The only other paintings that can be certainly dated to 1816 are two very much smaller sepia sketches – *Dalkey Castle* and *Luggelaw*.[81] It is well documented that Petrie painted miniature portraits, although none has been identified. Strickland relates how Petrie's first introduction to art was helping his father, and also notes a portrait of Lord Manners by Petrie, probably painted before 1808 and subsequently engraved by Maguire.[82] He was obviously not attracted to portraiture, and did not practise it for long, but was occasionally prevailed upon to produce a portrait. In 1826 his friend Levinge asked him to execute a likeness of his nephew Jack Somers, but whether Petrie actually carried out this commission is unknown.[83] In that same year, Olivia Bellew, wife of Christopher Bellew, with whom Petrie had stayed on his tours of the west, wrote to Petrie and asked him to execute a miniature of her recently deceased husband:

> I so anxiously hope that the miniature is a perfect resemblance – coming from you the drawing will be beautiful, yet you will excuse me to say that a *resemblance* is what will console me in some way for my insuperable loss. I trust you have not made the likeness *too young* or *handsome*. At his age kindness and goodness were what he possessed, his features were large and the face short.[84]

Petrie complied as best he could with the request, working as he was from memory and a bad likeness of the late Christopher, and he dispatched the completed miniature, nicely framed, to Olivia in July 1827. She was please with it, and felt that Petrie's 'feeling heart' had made it a perfect resemblance in almost every respect:

> ...you have desired me sincerely to say if any change would be necessary – *very little* would make it more like – as you observe – about the eyebrows and eyes – and the upper part of the face rather pale. The Slightest touch. Any other might change it too much.[85]

She dispatched the miniature back to Petrie in Dublin, so that he could take care of the rather vague improvements she had detailed: 'A few changes will make it so like so dear a resemblance to me whose only consolation it is.'

While portraiture held little attraction for Petrie, the responsibility of having to support a wife and household of his own spurred him on to greater efforts in earning money by his pen and brush. Immediately after his father's death in 1819, Petrie and Eliza

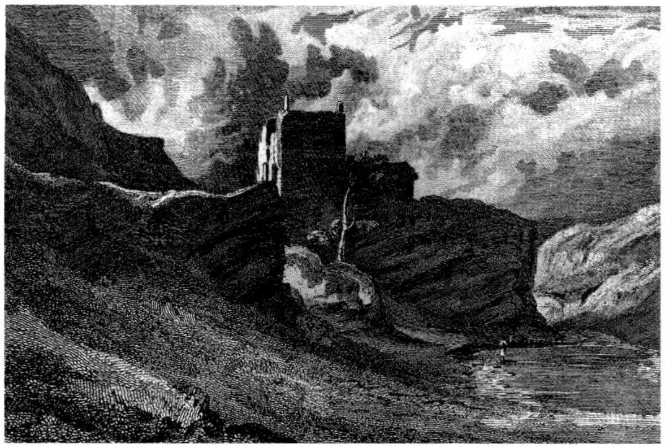

The Black Castle of the Naul, Co. of Dublin
engraving after Petrie from T. Cromwell, *Excursions through Ireland*, vol. ii, 1820

Interior of Mucruss Abbey
engraving after Petrie from G.N. Wright, *A Guide to the Lakes of Killarney*, 1823

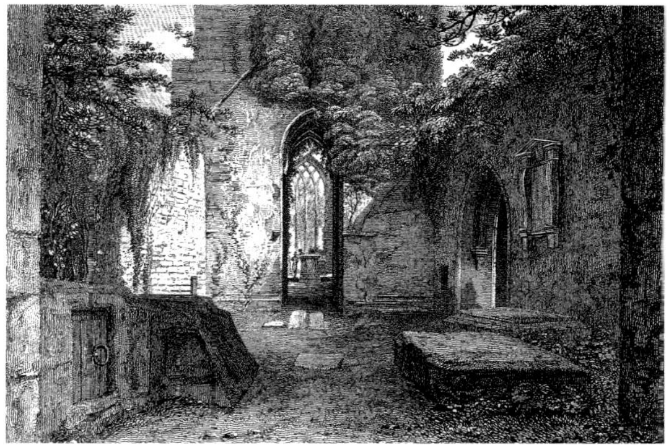

Mills were married and the couple moved to a house at 5 Essex Quay. Petrie travelled extensively that year, painting views of Irish scenery, among them the signed and dated works *St Lawrence's Gate, Drogheda*, *View of Kells*, *Howth Castle*, *Kildare Cathedral*,[86] and *Clondalkin Round Tower*. All five works are in monochrome. In the Ulster Museum there is a view of *Black Castle, Co. Wicklow*,[87] also dated 1819. On the basis of these dated works, other watercolours can be assigned to this period: *View at Mount Usher*, *Old Kilcullen Bridge*, *Slane Castle*, and *Rathmichael Church*.[88] The existence of this group of connected views raises the obvious question: for whom were they produced? The answer is to be found in a new type of publication appearing at this time, mass-produced guidebooks illustrated with steel engravings, describing and illustrating the beauties of the Irish landscape.

The growth of tourism and increasing literacy in the early 19th century created a market for guidebooks illustrated with topographical engravings. During the Napoleonic Wars, with the Continent off-limits to tourists from Britain or Ireland, the affluent middle-class and aristocracy began to explore scenic areas such as the Lake District, the Scottish highlands, Wales and the west of Ireland. The first three decades of the 19th century saw an enormous growth in the publication of guidebooks, most illustrated with steel engravings. These guidebooks differed from their 18th-century predecessors in that they were smaller in scale and less expensive. The use of steel rather than copper plates for printing the engravings meant that the books could be mass-produced. Jonathan Fisher's *A Picturesque Tour of Killarney*, published in a limited edition in 1789, contained twenty large aquatint plates of views such as O'Sullivan's Cascade, Ross Castle, the Old Weir Bridge, and the Eagle's Nest. Thirty-four years later, the Rev G.N. Wright's *Guide to Killarney*, illustrated by Petrie, was in the bookshops, selling to a much wider audience. The views selected by Petrie were virtually the same as those depicted by Fisher, but the scale of the plates is minute by comparison with the 18th-century publication. Wright's Guide to Killarney was a practical guidebook designed to be carried in the pocket; Fisher's aquatints were intended to be appreciated in the drawing room. One of the earliest of the new-style guidebooks was John Britton and Edward Brayley's *Beauties of England and Wales*, a massive undertaking begun in 1801 that would eventually contain over 700 engravings, published in many volumes. In 1805, after the publication of the fifth volume, Britton and his partner withdrew, protesting that the publishers were less interested in antiquities than in describing the homes and estates of the gentry – a divergence of views that would later feature in Petrie's career. Britton's 'scientific artists' were trained to produce views of buildings and topography which were both accurate and picturesque. Britton himself illustrated the *Architectural Antiquities of Great Britain* (1804-14), as well as works on the architecture of the Middle Ages. Even Turner reached a wide public through engravings of his paintings, which he often personally supervised. Cooke's *Picturesque Views on the Southern Coast of England*, *Views in Sussex* and *Provincial Antiquities of Scotland* were just three of the dozen or so guidebooks featuring Turner engravings. (Cooke would also work with Petrie on some of the Irish books.) Other artists in this field included Frederick Nash, who contributed to *Twelve Views of the Antiquities of London* (1805-10), Samuel Prout, who contributed

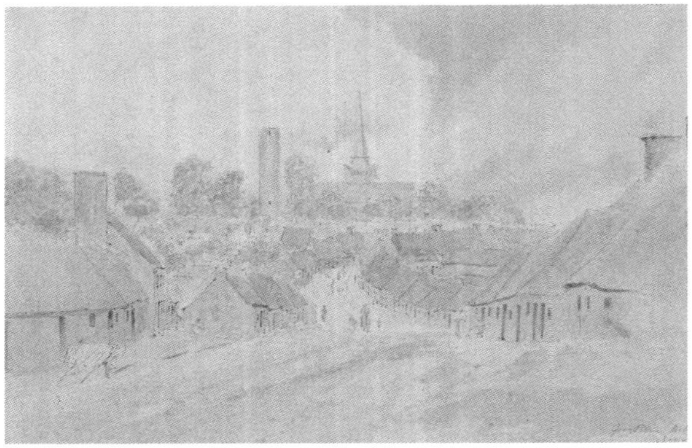

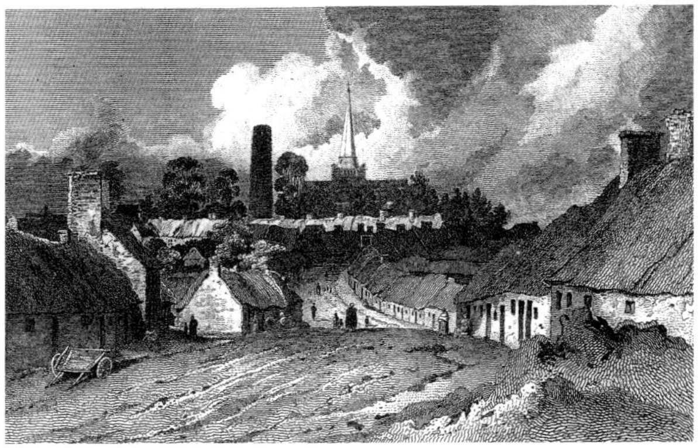

View of Kells, High Street, Co. Meath
1819, watercolour on paper, 20 x 29.3 (coll: NGI, cat. no. 2369)

Kells, Co. of Eastmeath
engraving after Petrie from T. Cromwell, *Excursions through Ireland,* vol. ii, 1820

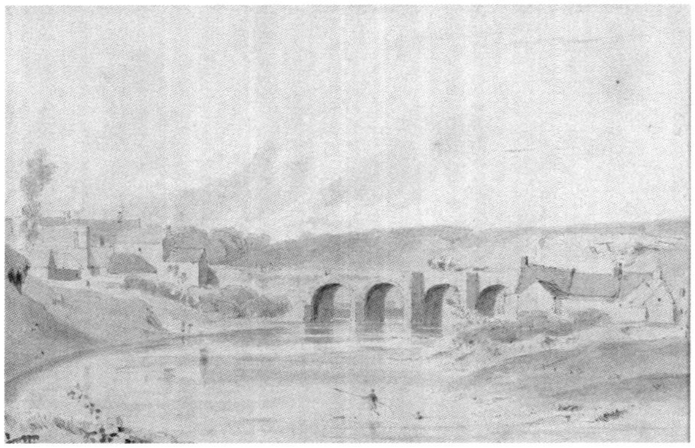

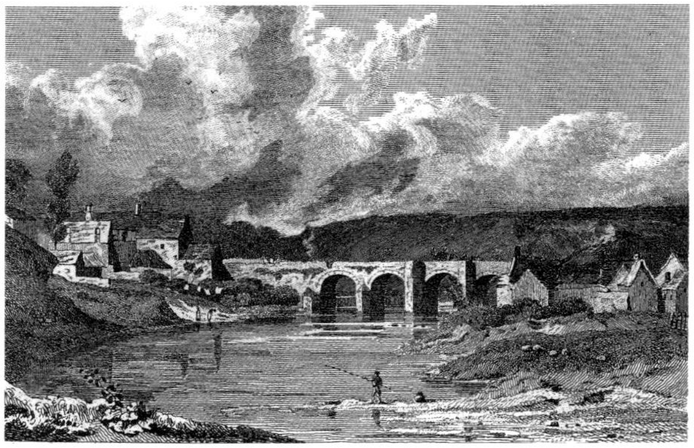

Old Kilcullen Bridge, Co. Kildare
*c.*1819, watercolour on paper, 14.8 x 22.5 (coll: NGI, cat. no. 2368)

Kilcullen Bridge, Co. of Kildare
engraving after Petrie from T. Cromwell, *Excursions through Ireland,* vol. ii, 1820

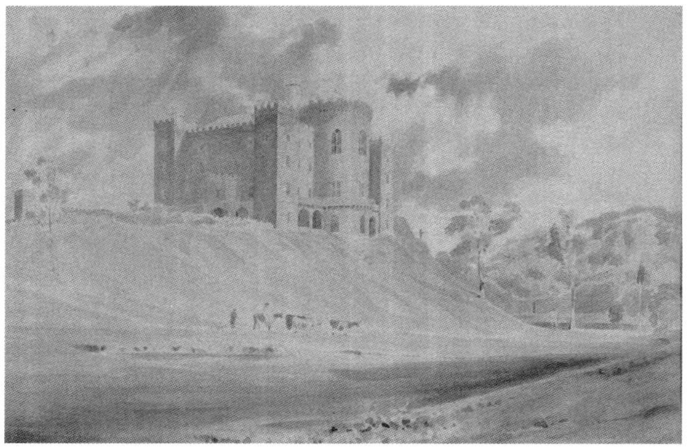

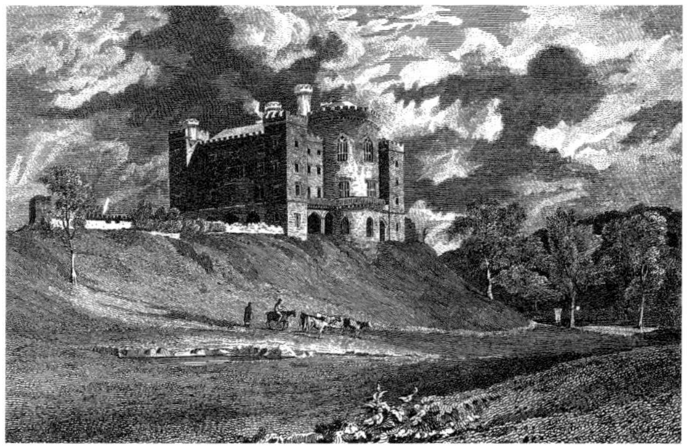

Slane Castle, Co. Meath
*c.*1819, watercolour on paper, 18 x 26.7 (coll: NGI, cat. no. 2367) (see colour plate p.16)

Slane Castle, The Seat of the Marquis of Cunningham, Co. of Eastmeath
engraving after Petrie from T. Cromwell, *Excursions through Ireland,* vol. ii, 1820

opposite

The Church of Duleek, Co. of Eastmeath
engraving after Petrie from T. Cromwell, *Excursions through Ireland,* vol. ii, 1820

views to *The Beauties of England and Wales*, Thomas Shepherd who worked on the 1822 *Excursions in the County of Kent*, while in Scotland, the landscape painter Horatio McCulloch contributed to *Scotland Illustrated*, published around 1838. A pupil of John Britton's, William Henry Bartlett's views were engraved, along with Petrie's, for *Ireland Illustrated* in 1841. Previously Bartlett (1809-1854) had engraved views of scenery in England, Switzerland Turkey and America. It was into this competitive field that Petrie threw himself in 1819.

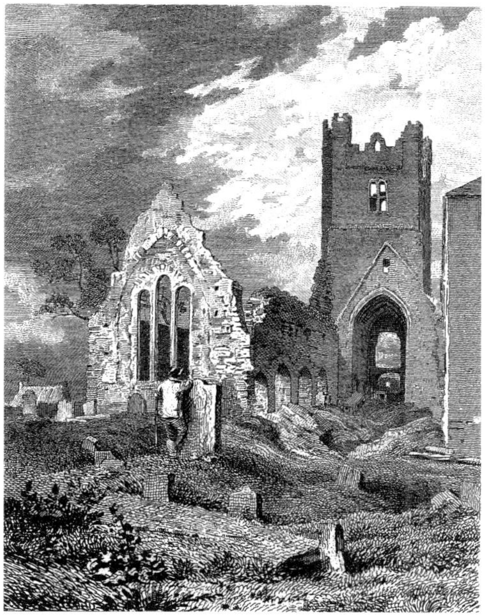

Petrie's involvement with the engravers and publishers of these guide-books was not without trouble and dissent, but it was profitable and it obliged him to produce drawings by the dozen; illustrations of Irish scenery that were precise and truthful depictions, and yet had 'interest'. This last was probably the most difficult prerequisite for a Romantic painter like Petrie, as it involved selecting views that inclined towards the picturesque rather than the sublime, views that pandered to popular public taste rather than high-brow connoisseurship in terms of subject matter and treatment. The story of how Petrie coped with these conflicting pressures is interesting, especially in view of his later career. His work appeared in several publications, most notably T.K. Cromwell's *Excursions through Ireland* (1820-21), *The New Picture of Dublin* (1821), G.N. Wright's *Historical Guide to Ancient and Modern Dublin* (1821-25), G.N. Wright's *Guide to the Giant's Causeway, Guide to Wicklow* and *Guide to Killarney* (1823), James Norris Brewer's *Beauties of Ireland* (1825-26) and G.N. Wright's *Ireland Illustrated* (*c.*1842), published by Fisher, Son & Jackson.

THOMAS KITSON CROMWELL'S *EXCURSIONS THROUGH IRELAND* (1820-21)

The first major work for which Petrie produced drawings was Thomas Kitson Cromwell's *Excursions through Ireland*,[89] published in three volumes. The publication date on the original cardboard bindings is 1820, but this can hardly be correct, for the engravings themselves are dated individually, and the dates run from 1 July 1819 to 1 October 1821. There are one hundred and nineteen engravings in Cromwell's *Excursions through Ireland*, of which no less than ninety-seven are after drawings by Petrie. The engravings, with just two exceptions, were published in lots, on the first day of the month. Petrie was slow in meeting the deadlines set by the publishers. He was methodical and precise in his execution of scenes, but had to be constantly harried by the engravers and publishers to produce the drawings on time. 'Delay', a friend wrote rather tartly, was 'a handmaid' of Petrie's.[90] As soon as Petrie's ink wash drawings reached the publishers, they were put in the hands of the engravers who set to work, transposing the images onto steel plates from which thousands of impressions could be taken. Different craftsmen were responsible for the engraving; in charge was John Greig, who along with Thomas Higham (1796-1844) undertook the lion's share of the work. The third main engraver was James Sargant Storer (1771-1853). Born in Cambridge, Storer specialised in views of cathedrals and other medieval buildings. Greig, a lithographer, engraver and painter, had also worked with Storer on *The Antiquarian Cabinet*. Greig's engravings can be found in *Promenades Across London* (1817), *The New British Traveller* (1819), *Tours in Cornwall* (1824), and Britton's *Beauties of England and Wales* (1801-15). These engravers were generally also artists in their own right. Thomas Higham exhibited at the Royal Academy from 1824 to 1830; his engravings can be found in *The Antiquarian Itinerary* and *Excursions in the County of Kent* (1822). Other engravers who worked on Cromwell's *Excursions through Ireland* included Thomas Barber, T. Ranson, W. Deeble, T.A. Dale, J.C. Varrall, W. Wallis and R. Acon. Several of these engravers, including Higham and Barber, were to work with Petrie on later publications.

Sources for information on the progress of *Excursions through Ireland* are sparse. There is little to go on save the engravings themselves, which are dated. Taking them in groups according to date of publication (which does not necessarily correspond to

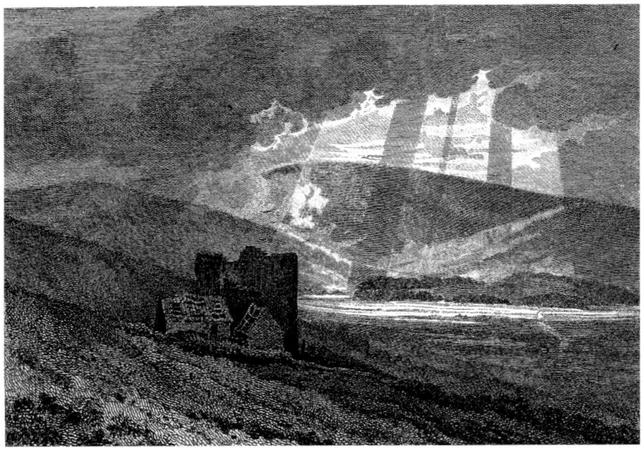

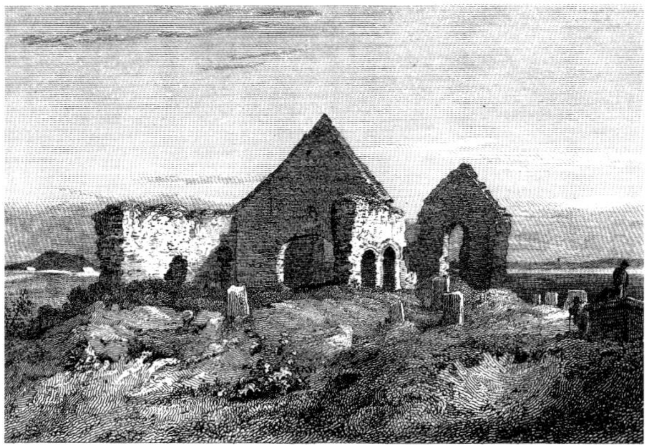

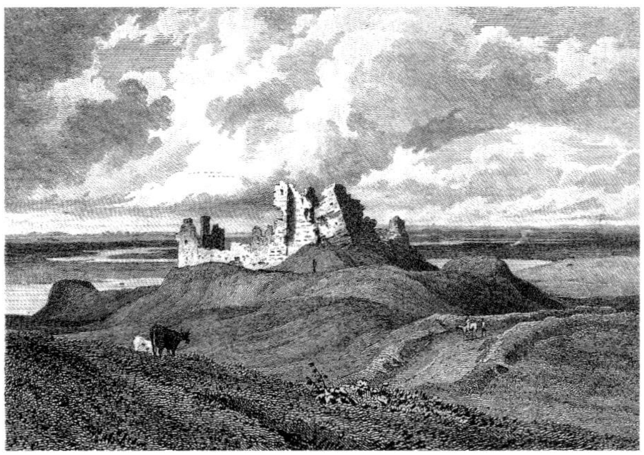

left

Puck's Castle, Co of Dublin
engraving after Petrie from
T. Cromwell, *Excursions through Ireland*, vol. i, 1820

Remains of the Abbey of Kilbarrick, Co. of Dublin
engraving after Petrie from
T. Cromwell, *Excursions through Ireland*, vol. i, 1820

The Castle at Clonmacnois, King's County
engraving after Petrie from
T. Cromwell, *Excursions through Ireland*, vol. ii, 1820

right

Deralossory Church, Co. of Wicklow
engraving after Petrie from
T. Cromwell, *Excursions through Ireland*, vol. i, 1820

The Franciscan Abbey, Kilkenny
engraving after Petrie from
T. Cromwell, *Excursions through Ireland*, vol. ii, 1820

North Gate, Athlone
engraving after Petrie from
T. Cromwell, *Excursions through Ireland*, vol. i, 1820

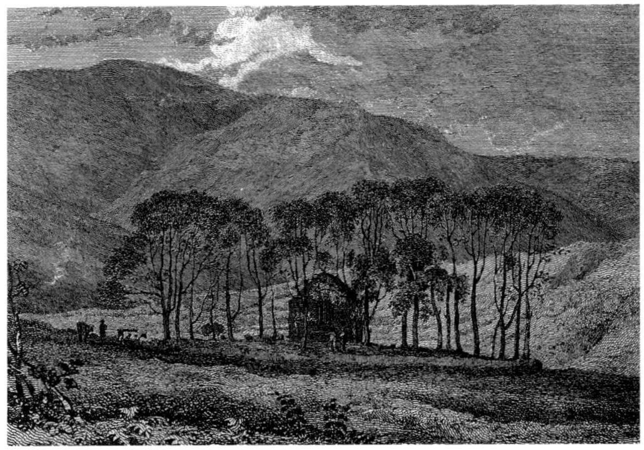

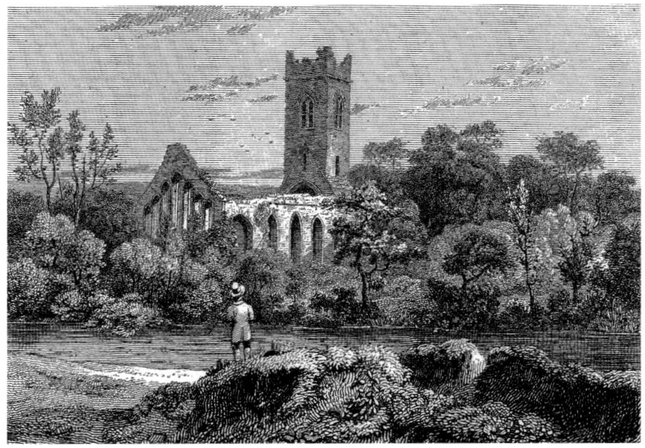

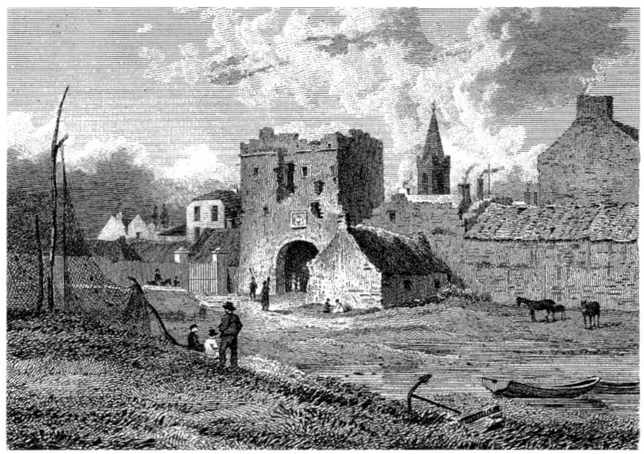

opposite

Dublin, from the Phoenix Park
engraving after Petrie from
J.N. Brewer, *The Beauties of Ireland*, vol. i, 1826

their distribution throughout the published work), some patterns emerge. As stated above, the earliest engravings are dated 1 July 1819. These, and the next three groups published, consist exclusively of views taken in and around Dublin. An example of this early group is *Puck's Castle in the County of Dublin*, the engraving of which is dated 1 September 1819 (engraved by Grieg), and the preparatory drawing for which survives.[91] The engraving is small in scale, but rich in contrasts, with the ruined castle silhouetted on a gently sloping hillside with shafts of sunlight breaking through the clouds and illuminating the Wicklow hills in the distance. The next seven groups, published in the months between November 1819 and June 1820, take the bridges, churches and beauty spots of counties immediately outside Dublin as their subject. It is difficult to trace a definite pattern, or to establish the route of the tours that Petrie would have made in order to make these drawings; they shift randomly from Kildare to Wicklow to Westmeath (and Eastmeath). Subjects include *The Old Church of Deral-Ossory, Co. Wicklow* and *The Church of Kilbarrack*. There is only one from further afield, that of *The Franciscan Abbey at Kilkenny*, published in April 1820. After a break in the production of engravings over the summer of 1820, Greig, Barber and Higham took the task of engraving the views entirely to themselves. These later engravings cover the same areas, with one notable addition: Petrie's tour of the River Shannon in 1820 yielded drawings from King's County (as Offaly then was), the ancient monastic city of Clonmacnoise, and the town of Athlone. Among these engravings are *The Church of St Fechin le Fore*, engraved in November 1820. Production continued through the winter of 1820 and the spring of 1821, at which point Greig assumed full control, engraving the last three groups himself – eleven views in Meath, Westmeath, Dublin and Wicklow. The last group was published on 1 October 1821, and the entire work came into the bookshops shortly afterwards. It sold for £2.5s. In November, Greig wrote to Petrie regretting that he could not come to Ireland that autumn because of illness in the family, and promising to transmit to him as soon as possible a Bank of England note to the full amount due to Petrie for his drawings.[92] Two years later the money still had not been paid, and Petrie had obviously become so exasperated with the whole business that in June 1823 he went over to London, mainly, it seems, to sort out his financial affairs. However, Greig forestalled him by a few days, and Petrie was informed in London by a friend of his in Dublin, John Smith, that a bill for £100 had just been received at Great Charles Street by Petrie's wife:

> Bess received a letter on Wednesday enclosing a bill for £100, from Gregg [sic], on Mr P. Youngman, Bookseller, Witham, Essex, and accepted by him & payable at Messrs. Barclay & Co. Bankers, London & that he would send you the remd. In Post Bills when he had heard of the receipt of this.[93]

Smith asked Petrie to check that the bill was good and to get a similar bill from Grieg for the remainder owed to him and so put an end to the matter while he was on the spot.

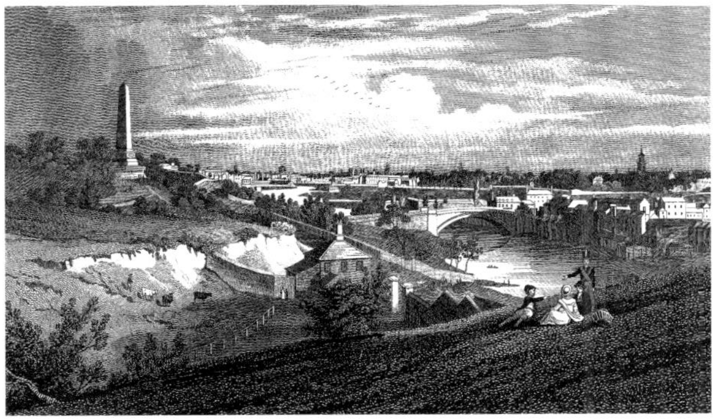

JAMES NORRIS BREWER'S *THE BEAUTIES OF IRELAND* (1825-26)

Petrie was not left idle for long; as soon as he had completed the drawings for Cromwell's *Excursions* he was engaged by James Norris Brewer for a similar task. The energetic Brewer had already produced copious historical and topographical notes for *The Beauties of England and Wales*, and was now preparing a series of books on Ireland that he hoped would become a standard work of reference on the subject.[94] Unfortunately this was not to be so. *The Beauties of Ireland* was to have been published in three volumes, the first of these appearing in October 1821; however this volume did not reach the bookshops until 1825. The second volume followed the next year, but the publishers were clearly dissatisfied with the success of the work and the printing of volume three was halted. The publishers, Sherwood, Jones and Co, of Paternoster Row in London, seem to have exercised a great deal of control over the venture; Brewer refers to them as 'The Proprietors'.[95]

Petrie was not the only artist to

work on the *Beauties*. While he did the frontispiece, *Dublin from the Phoenix Park*, along with views of Carton, Kilmallock, Parsonstown Castle, Slane Castle and Glendalough, other engravings in the book include views of Blarney Castle and St John's Abbey after G. Holmes, two battlemented castles, Ballyheigue in Co Kerry and Thomastown in Co Tipperary after drawings by architect Richard Morrison, *Gracefield Lodge in Queen's County* by P. Duggan, and *Boyle Abbey* by J. Peacock. Petrie's *Dublin from the Phoenix Park* is a fine engraving, depicting the city from the same vantage point employed in the 18th century by several artists. The foreground, with its picnic group, is crude and was evidently added by the engraver. However, the background, with the Wellington Testimonial, Islandbridge and the Royal Hospital, is finer work. This engraving is dated September 1824. *Kilmallock*, perhaps the finest of all Petrie's prints, was published in volume I of *The Beauties of Ireland*, the original sepia drawing for which is in the National Gallery of Ireland, signed and dated 1821.[96] The engraving preserves the quality of the sepia drawing, and provides a poignant record of a once-proud ecclesiastical centre, its main street lined with Tudor stone houses and a castle, reduced to penury, with piles of rubble and wandering cattle. Slane Castle, at that time a relatively new mansion, designed in the Neo-Gothic style by Richard Morrison, is shown perched on a bluff overlooking the river Boyne. Perhaps the engraving most characteristic of Petrie is *Glendalough*, with its shafts of sunlight illuminating the round tower and ruined church of St Kevin. Clouds sweep across the mountains surrounding the lake, while the round tower and ruined churches are in shadow, silhouetted against the brightly lit lake. During the long years of the book's gestation, Brewer and Petrie corresponded frequently, so a good impression of the progress of the work can be gained, though all the extant correspondence is from Brewer to Petrie.

This correspondence consists mainly of advice on which subjects to choose for illustration, and which to avoid; requests for information on various aspects of Irish life, and pleas for more speed and punctuality on Petrie's part. Brewer was initially extremely sympathetic towards Petrie's desires about the subject matter of the engravings: Petrie wanted to illustrate the book with views that had both a romantic and an antiquarian flavour. Brewer assured him, 'my feeling, as well I believe as your own, would rather incline highly to ruins; interesting from architectural character or picturesque features'.[97] And elsewhere he wrote to assure Petrie that he would do everything 'to serve that estimable love of reputation that forms the groundwork of your exertions'.[98] Sympathetic Brewer may have been, but the publishers were not. They insisted that views of a large number of 'seats' be included – that is, the residences of gentlemen and the nobility. Petrie felt that such work was on a rather pedestrian level, but Brewer was forced to call the tune in this case:

> With any views you may be preparing of Dublin, be so good as otherwise to make drawings of one or two seats of nobility or gentry. I should think the county in which they are situated would be no object. There must be a proportionate quantity of seats...[99]

This point is repeatedly made during the course of their correspondence. Brewer suggests houses that Petrie might consider drawing –

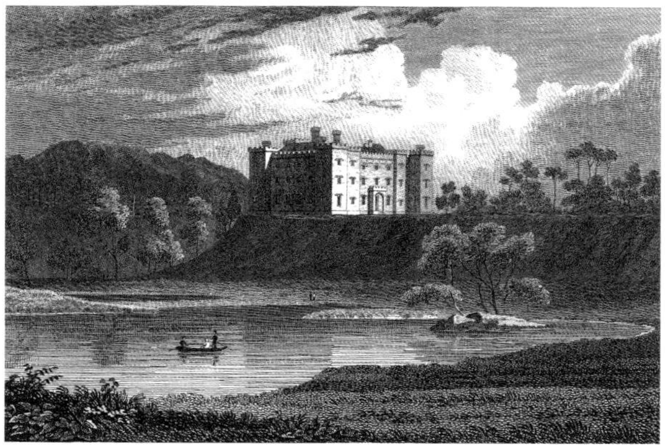

Slane Castle, The Seat of Marquis Conyngham, Co. of Meath

Glendalough, Co. of Wicklow

both engravings after Petrie from J.N. Brewer, *The Beauties of Ireland*, vol. i, 1826

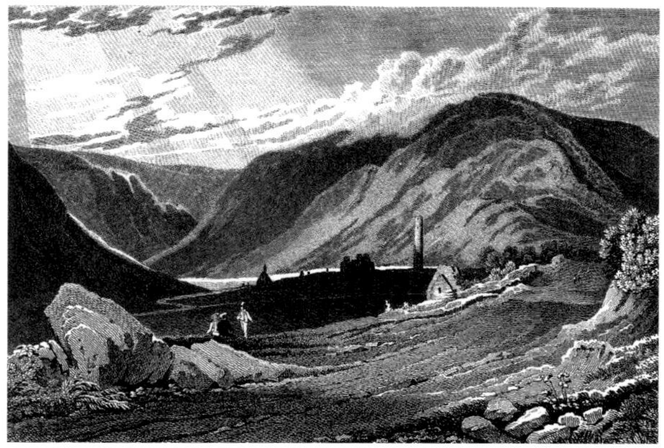

Kilmallock High Street, Co. Limerick
1821, sepia on paper, 26.7 x 39.7
(coll: NGI, cat. no. 2375)
(see colour plate p.17)

Kilmallock, Co. of Limerick
engraving after Petrie from J.N. Brewer, *The Beauties of Ireland*, vol. i, 1826

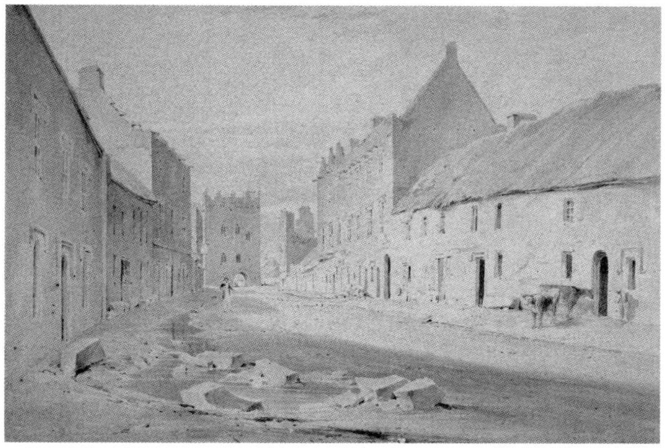

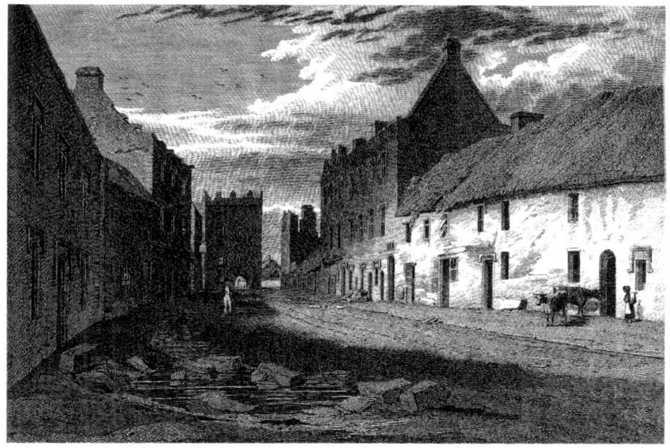

Shelton Abbey, for instance, or Carton House in Co Kildare: 'Carton is ugly enough, but the Duke's name is "a tower of strength."'[100] Petrie's view of the 'seat' of the Duke of Leinster translated into a fine engraving. A tree frames the foreground, while an elegant couple promenade amongst sheep grazing in front of the Palladian house. On occasion, Petrie chose the house; Parsonstown Castle, the seat of the Earl of Rosse, was one instance where Brewer waived any objections he might have had.[101] Stokes quotes a letter from Petrie to his newly married wife, written from Birr in August 1820:

> To-day I have been till now (four o'clock), sketching a nobleman's seat here (Lord Rosse's) which, though very fine, cost me a great deal too much time; but, in fact, it has been the same with all the subjects of that character which I have hitherto done; less than four or five hours will not suffice for one sketch. The weather continues broken and windy. I should not have been able to sketch today but for the leeward side of haycock, which I had the good fortune to meet with. Notwithstanding the very bad weather we have had, I have made a considerable number of sketches for the time.[102]

In a work of such a nature, there was always the prospect of the occasional perquisite for the writer and the illustrator. Christopher Bellew of Mount Bellew in Co Galway, wrote to Brewer when he heard of the forthcoming work and offered to help and accommodate Brewer and Petrie in their travels. Brewer was flattered:

> The spirit of literary liberality evinced by this gentleman is

View of Carton
Sepia ink on paper, 21 x 30
(see colour plate p.18)

Carton, The Seat of His Grace the Duke of Leinster, Co. of Kildare
engraving after Petrie from J.N. Brewer, *The Beauties of Ireland*, vol. i, 1826

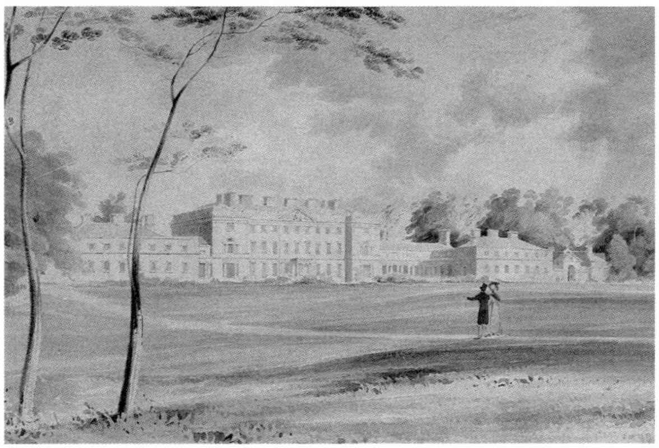

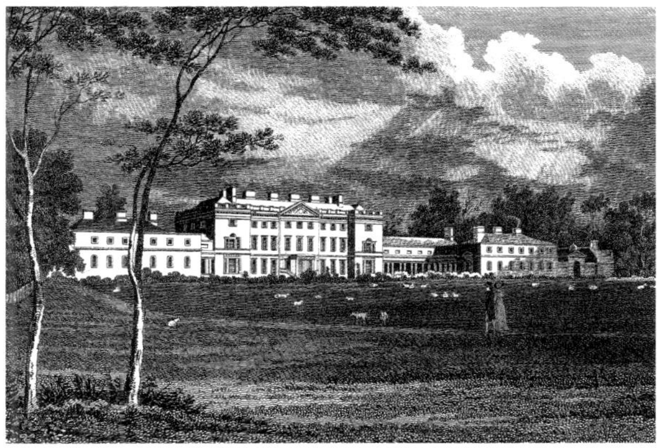

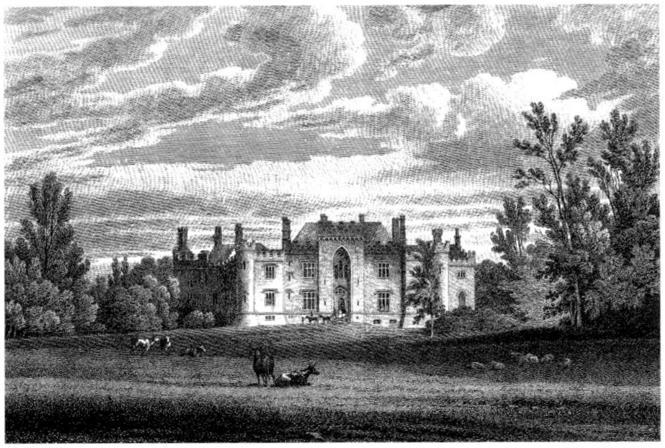

Parson's Town Castle, Seat of the Earl of Ross, Co. of Kings

Mount Bellew, Seat of Christopher Dillon Bellow, Esqr., Co. Galway

both engravings after Petrie from J.N. Brewer, *The Beauties of Ireland*, vol. ii, 1826

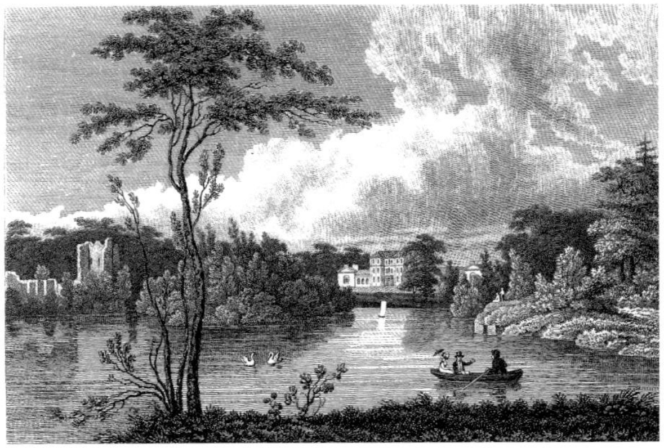

> just what is too much wanting among the gentry of Ireland and I am equally gratified and obliged by his attentions ... if his house (the avenue of which I passed, compulsorily without stopping, as I was in the stage) is a good subject, it would be very desirable to draw and engrave a view of it.[103]

Bellew was indeed anxious to have his house included, even offering to have the engravings done at his own expense. He wrote to Brewer:

> I have not heard from Mr Petrie. He is one of our best artists. I left a message for him at Mrs. Petrie's, Dame St, last summer. I am well aware of the expense of plates and trust he would have no occasion to complain of illiberality in that particular. Should the undertaking bring him to this part of the country I shall be happy to afford him every attention, welcome and hospitality. A line mentioning the day on which he would arrive would prevent my absence. My post town is Castle Blakeney. A daily mail coach passes from Dublin, and a carriage from hence should meet him.[104]

Other proprietors did not have to try so hard: 'If any building connected with the Duke of Buckingham's estates in Ireland is deserving of an engraving I have particular motives for wishing a drawing to be made for our work, if agreeable to you.' Brewer wrote to Petrie in 1823,[105] and when the second volume was eventually published it was dedicated to this same man, Richard Grenville-Brydges-Chandos Temple,[106] as an appreciation of the help he had given in making his large collection of ancient Irish manuscripts available for Brewer's use. As time wore on and the publication date was deferred again and again, the sympathy that Brewer held for Petrie's Romantic idealism began to wear a little thin; 'Bective Abbey would be a good subject, but we have enough ruins in that area – concentrate on seats' he wrote shortly in 1824.[107]

Brewer was not the only person that Petrie had to contend with in the preparation of the illustrations; the engravers themselves, James Sargent Storer and his son Henry, also corresponded with Petrie, who found them rather difficult to deal with.[108] Yet he could do little, for the engravers were powerful men in the publishing world, uncompromising and independent in their attitudes. Brewer was continually apologising to Petrie for Storer's manners. He described him as 'a man who mixes little with the world and has some peculiarities, but all of an inoffensive kind and such as his friends readily tolerate',[109] and later, when he was forwarding a letter from Storer to Petrie, he remarked that it resembles Storer in that it was 'not very scrupulously attended to on the exterior',[110] but he reassured him that it meant to be 'very civil'. Brewer was thus continually playing the diplomat between Petrie, who had a low regard for Storer's talents as an engraver, and Storer himself, with his blunt and offensive manner. He wrote to Petrie in 1821: 'Your general view of Dublin is admired by every person who has seen it. Mr. Storer spoke loudly of the taste displayed in it...'[111] And later in the same letter he assured Petrie that the Storers were well-intentioned men of whom Petrie would approve when he personally knew them, and that they would endeavour to do justice to the drawings. Petrie had been concerned at criticisms of the Storers' engravings, in the *London Magazine*, but Brewer attributed this to 'party malevolence' and added: 'No man's reputation is safe if such criticisms are to be taken as the test of a man's character.'[112] Petrie criticised the engravings in *The Beauties of England*, an earlier work of Brewer's, but Brewer answered the accusation by blaming them on 'a very insufficient draughtsman named J.P. Neale, who had an entire rule over the engravings',[113] and he claimed that the engravings in the earlier part of that work were creditable and had led to the adoption of 'a memorable national improvement' in the style of decorating topographical works. Whether he succeeded in allaying Petrie's fear with these grandiose statements is not known, but Petrie's whole attitude toward the work was less than enthusiastic, and he was continually being cajoled by Brewer to speed up in the production of drawings. But not alone was Petrie being interfered with in the matter of the subjects he was to choose; his *style* of executing the drawings was questioned by the engravers; Storer demanded that Petrie introduce figures of all descriptions, carriages and the like, in order to impart animation to the scenery.[114] It can be imagined how Petrie must have shuddered at this request, when his whole being inclined towards the introduction of sublimity into the scenery, a feeling of mystery perhaps, a sense of great antiquity maybe; but animation, no.

Not alone did Petrie have his arguments with the engravers, he also differed with the publisher of the book, Mr Sherwood, on the matter of the engravings. What the exact nature of the dispute was is not known. Brewer took care to keep well out of it, and offered no support or encouragement: 'I do all I can but I live shut off from the world of booksellers and publishers and have nothing to do with the engraving of the work.'[115]

When the first volume was published in 1825, the plates were bound together at the beginning of the book, before the preface. Although they were on a larger scale than those in Cromwell or Wright, they were more disparate and the execution was rather coarse. Petrie seems to have been bitterly disappointed with the outcome of the work, after he had been obliged to put so much personal effort into it – not only in terms of drawing, but also in duties that went 'beyond the pale', supplying descriptions and information, checking details and even reading the proofs of the work.[116] Brewer had promised payment for these services from his own pocket, but Petrie was far too much the gentleman to bring up the subject of money in their correspondence. He described to Brewer how gentlemen in Dublin were picking up the book in the shops, and finding the plates coarsely executed, were refusing to buy it. It finally begins to dawn on Brewer that Petrie's complaints about the engravers were well founded but he can only ask Petrie to stop and think for a moment:

> This was a book of literary work, presented to their [the public's] consideration, and was yet rejected (whether intended to do honour to their country or otherwise they knew not) without the inspection of any of its pages, because the engravings were coarse. I have heard of children refusing to buy a book 'because the pictures were not pretty' but I have yet to learn that such practice is the usual conduct of men.[117]

Small consolation for Petrie, but Brewer at least promised to interfere so far as to insist on the engravings being better in the remainder of the work. Unluckily there were still several unpublished plates

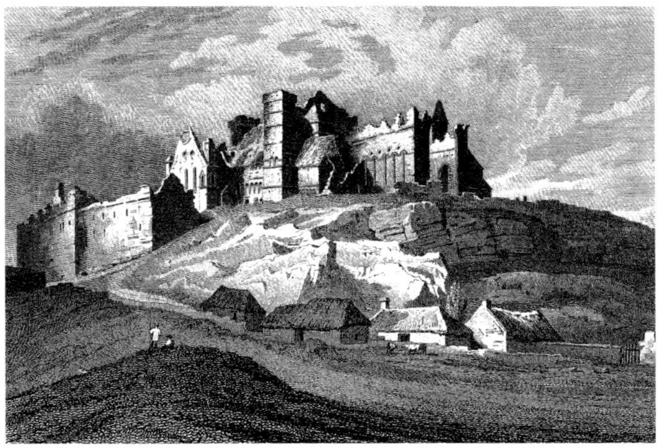

Mount Cashell, Co. of Tipperary

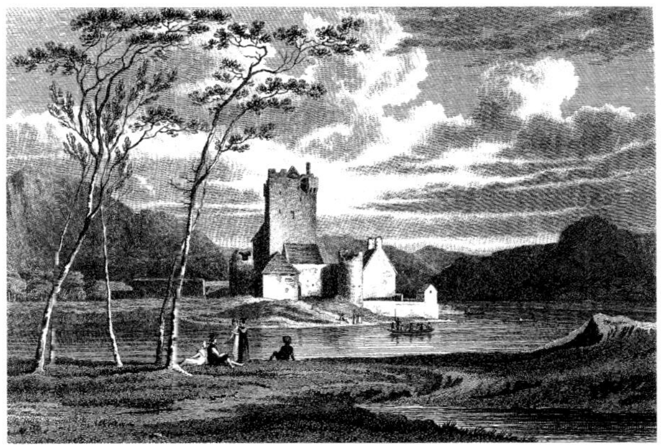

Ross Castle, Co. of Kerry

both engravings after Petrie from J.N. Brewer, *The Beauties of Ireland*, vol. ii, 1826

of the same low standard. Brewer eventually stated that he was 'disgusted with Storer'. The second volume followed in 1826, and the third was largely printed by the spring of 1827. This last volume was to include Limerick, Waterford, Clare, Galway, Kerry and Roscommon, but it was never published – the date was deferred again and again, because of 'troubles in the publishing world'. Brewer remained optimistic right up to the last, and his election as a member of the Royal Irish Academy he saw as a public recognition of the quality of the work. All the engravings from the two published volumes are reproduced in the illustrations accompanying the present work. It is not known whether any plates were prepared for the projected third volume.

G.N. WRIGHT'S GUIDES TO IRELAND (1821-25)

Another book for which Petrie provided topographical drawings at this time was George Newham Wright's *Historical Guide to Ancient and Modern Dublin*.[118] It was published in London in 1821, with a second edition appearing in 1825, and its preparation seems to have been attended by none of the difficulties that beset *The Beauties of Ireland*, though there is very little information on the background to its publication. The drawings that Petrie sent to the engravers are preserved in the Royal Irish Academy. They are all in Indian ink over pencil, and they form a unique and distinct portion of Petrie's extant works. The Marquis of Kildare presented them to the Academy in 1866, the year of Petrie's death. Wright published several other such guides, or *Tours in Ireland*, as they were called: *The Lakes of Killarney*, *The County of Wicklow* and *The Giant's Causeway* (on the coast of Antrim).[119] They appeared in 1823, and were all illustrated with engravings after Petrie. The engravers of these guides were Barber and Higham (these two had also worked on Cromwell's *Excursions*), along with George Cooke and Thomas Ransom. Barber and Higham engraved the Killarney and Wicklow plates, Ransom was responsible for the Glendalough plate alone, while Cooke had a sole hand in the engraving of the four plates for the third of the volumes – *The Giant's Causeway*. Among the Wicklow plates, *Drumgoff Barracks* is of interest in that the bridge depicted in the left middle-distance does not appear in the original painting,[120] while both a drawing and preparatory watercolour survive for the Glendalough plate.[121] A sepia drawing for the Killarney plate, *The Reeks from Aghadowey*, also survives.[122] The engravers again felt that Petrie's drawings were somewhat dry and lacked animation, and he was asked to insert figures into the views, especially that of *The Great Courtyard of Dublin Castle*. As he had already sent this view to Thomas Higham, Petrie had to write to ask for a proof engraved with the outline only. Higham explained that he would then have difficulty in removing the outline where the figures crossed it so instead he sent a reduced drawing, the size of the plate, for Petrie to work on. He thanked Petrie for recommending himself and Barber to the publishers, Baldwin & Co, and adds: 'Mr. Barber and myself are much gratified by the kind manner in which you are pleased to commend our plates.'[123]

George Cooke wrote to Petrie in August 1823 and sent him two proofs of the first plates to be completed, with apologies for the

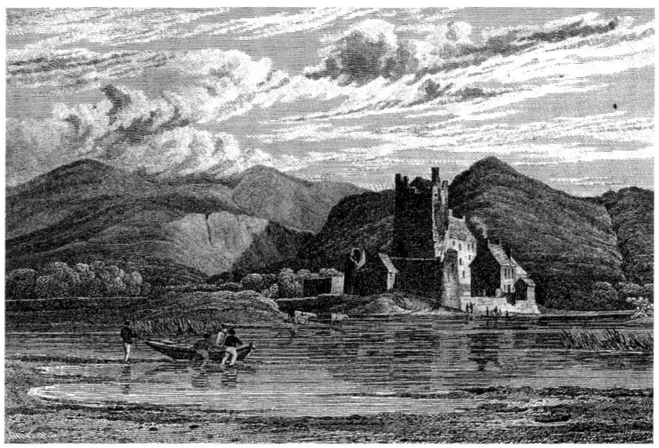

Ross Castle
engraving after Petrie from G.N. Wright, *A Guide to the Lakes of Killarney*, 1823

Dunluce Castle, County of Antrim
engraving after Petrie from G.N. Wright, *A Guide to the Giant's Causeway*, 1823

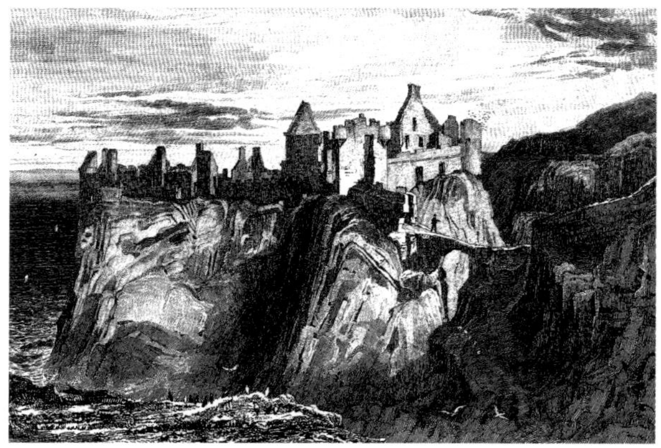

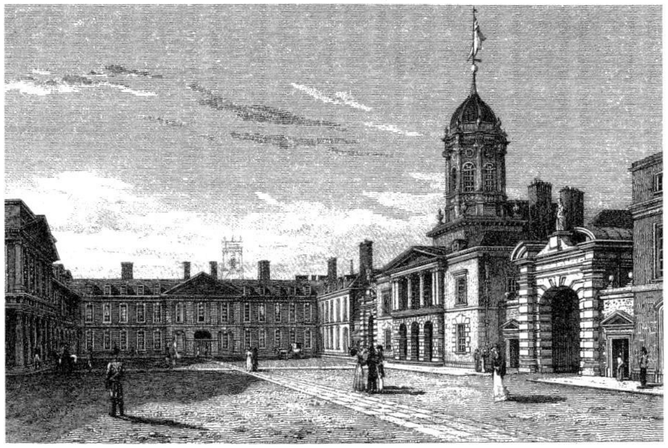

The Castle
engraving after Petrie from G.N. Wright, *Historical Guide to Ancient and Modern Dublin*, 1821

The Giant's Causeway, County of Antrim
engraving after Petrie from G.N. Wright, *A Guide to the Giant's Causeway*, 1823

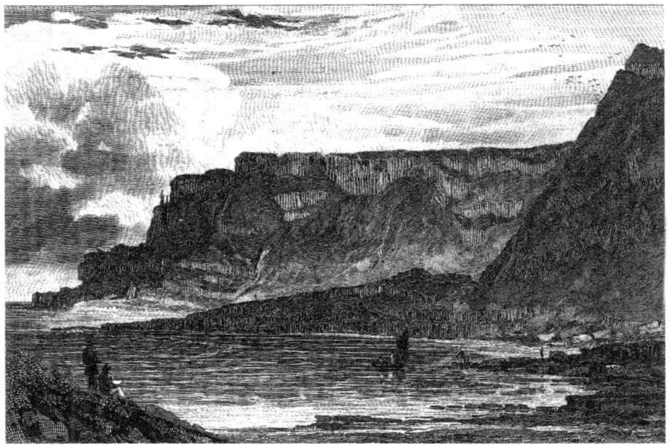

delay. Petrie had been anxious to see them in order to voice any criticisms he might have at an early stage. The two plates in question were probably those of *The Giant's Causeway* and *Dunluce Castle*, for nine days later Cooke sent proofs of the views in Antrim – *Carrick-a-Rede* and *Fairhead*. The book must have been just published at this stage, for again Cooke apologises to Petrie for not getting the proofs to him in time for him to make any constructive criticisms. He trusts that Petrie will not see 'any glaring deformities'. Cooke himself did not seem to be doing too well; he was intending to engrave some works by another artist, which were to be on a very large scale: 'I hope it will be a prosperous undertaking or I am done for.'[124] William Wakeman had been to see Cooke in Hackney (Cooke describes him as 'a very pleasant genteel man') and had told him of Petrie's desire to see the proofs immediately, but it had taken Cooke two weeks to finish them off and send them over to Petrie.[125] Wakeman had some connection with the guides; in 1821 he had been responsible for seeing the guide to Dublin delivered from the printers to Dublin, in 'five immense cases'.[126]

The engravings in the guides are amongst the finest that were made of Petrie's works. The lines graven in the copper plates preserve almost exactly the light tonality and feeling of airiness characteristic of Petrie's watercolours (Plates 194-207). However, Petrie's satisfaction must have been mitigated by the fact that he was never paid the full amount due to him, for in 1830, when Edward Johnston was returning from the Continent, he stopped off in London to attend to some affairs of Petrie's. Baldwin Cradock & Joy had gone bankrupt, leaving a lot of unpaid debts, including Petrie's payment for his drawings for the guides, of which they had been the publishers. The actual drawings were in the hands of Mr Joy. The affairs of the firm had been put in the hands of the receiver, a Mr Rees, who could promise Petrie a payment of only ten shillings in the pound; and that spread over two years, with only the last payment guaranteed. Johnston advised Petrie that he had the option of taking back the drawings and writing off the debt or claiming as a creditor on the Estate but as Joy's affairs were in 'such a bad way', Petrie was not likely to derive much satisfaction from the latter course. Rees offered to sell the drawings in London, which he reckoned would be to Petrie's advantage. Rees also mentioned something rather ambiguous:

> ...and he also said that they (Longman & Co.) have now a work on Wales in progress for which he had some hope they or some of them might be rendered available – what the nature of the work was he did not tell me...[127]

Was Petrie supplying drawing of Wales to the publishers for a projected work on that country? The question will have to be left open for the moment.

A short time before August 1828, Petrie paid a second visit to London, accompanied by a friend, the artist Richard Rothwell. Petrie made his way back to Ireland alone, Rothwell following later. After his return, Rothwell wrote to Petrie from Castle Antrim, recounting the story of an accident that had befallen him on the journey from London. The leading horses of the coach in which he was travelling had taken fright and made a plunge across a drain at the side of the road, dragging the coach after them. Rothwell was on top of the coach with twelve other passengers, and as it careered

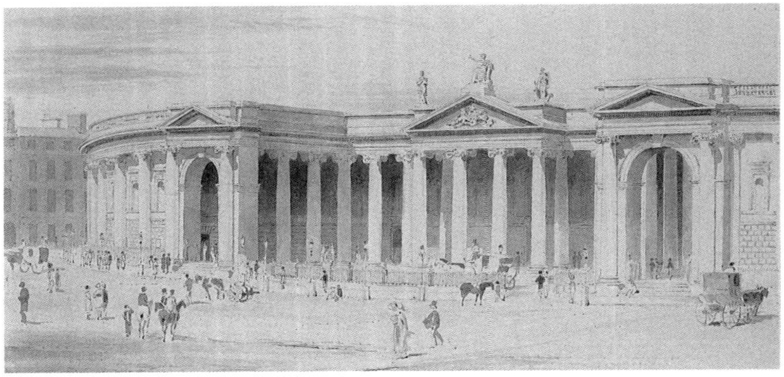

The Bank of Ireland
*c.*1820-21, Indian ink on paper, 12 x 24 (coll: RIA)

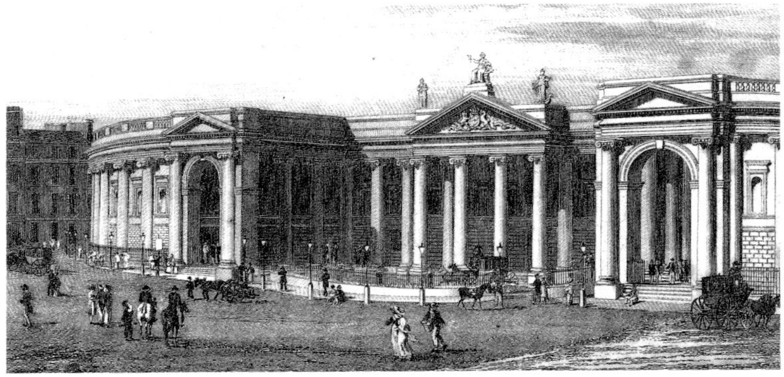

The Bank (detail)
engraving after Petrie from G.N. Wright, *Historical Guide to Ancient and Modern Dublin*, 1821

across the road some of them were about to throw themselves off, but Rothwell kept his head and restrained them from doing so until the coach came to a standstill and toppled over, precipitating them all into the mud. For this quick thinking, he received he 'blessing of half a dozen Catholics with a promise to mention me in their Parish Chapel'. What could have been a tragedy turned to amusement as they lay in the mud and watched desperate struggles of a white-haired old man squeezing himself out through the window of the coach and shouting for assistance, 'with an unfortunate lady and two children' clinging to him. The coach was righted eventually and they proceeded on their journey. It was a stroke of luck that had prevented Petrie from leaving London on the same coach as Rothwell; a fact, he says, that Petrie should appreciate, 'as it generally happens the lightest or rather those of least consequence swim through perils that those of more consequence fall victim to'.[128] Rothwell had a high regard for Petrie's talents, and he expressed the hope that the next time they visited London, he would be able to introduce him as 'The Petrie', and not, as he had been doing, as 'The Irish Turner'. He exhorted Petrie not to forget their common determination to succeed as artists. Petrie had shown a drawing to Robson, for his opinion, and Rothwell reassures him: 'if you have been disappointed in the least, it will make us desperate in our struggle for the promi-

The Law Courts
*c.*1820-21, Indian ink on paper, 16 x 24 (coll: RIA) (detail)

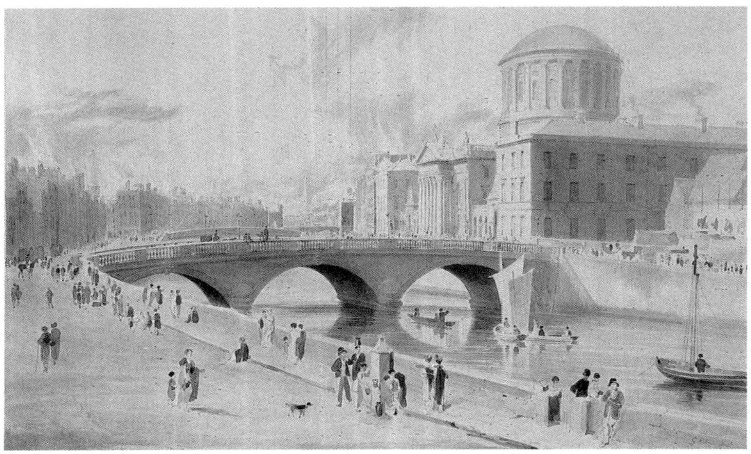

The Law Courts
engraving after Petrie from G.N. Wright, *Historical Guide to Ancient and Modern Dublin*, 1821

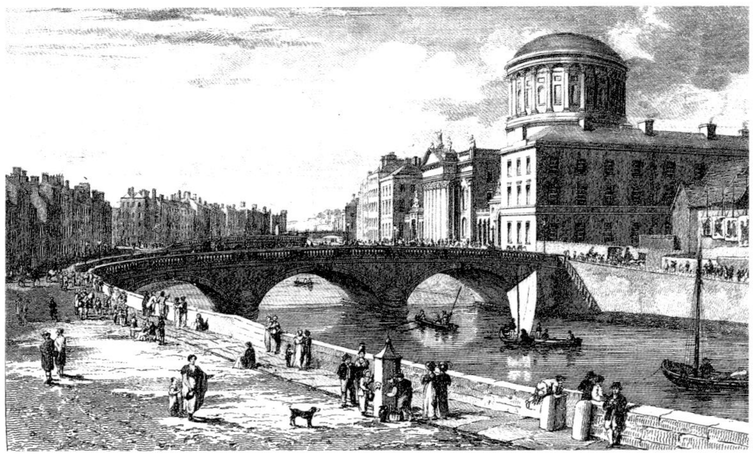

nence.' And elsewhere he entreats his friend 'Look, that nature may unfold brighter days than were ever sketched by Claude...' [129] Rothwell himself had spent the last six days experimenting with the lakes (watercolours) that he had bought in London, painting closely from flowers, and he thought it had given him a carefulness of touch that he had not had before. The last studies, painted at one sitting, he felt were better than previous ones on which he had spent two days. Now at last he was in a position to anticipate his 'chef d'oeuvre', having gotten rid of the 'brick-dust' in his eyes that Vandyke had bequeathed him. Rothwell was determined to make something worthy of himself as a serious artist. He did not approve of Petrie's dabblings in the world of antiquities:

> Plague on your Round Towers, it robs the world of your fine perception of the beautiful. Nature ever young and beautiful should for the world's sake engross you. But we are creatures of feeling and we are not to be turned from our hobby I suppose.[130]

'TRUST THE WIND', THEY SAY, 'AS SOON AS PETRIE' – G.N. WRIGHT'S *IRELAND ILLUSTRATED* (1828-39)

The first Petrie heard of Robert Fisher was in August 1828, after the latter had become the purchaser of the *Excursions through Ireland*. Fisher was a member of a London publishing company – Fisher, Son & Jackson (Robert was the 'Son'). John Greig, one of the engravers of the *Excursions*, did Petrie the service of recommending him strongly to Fisher, who got in touch with the artist and asked him if he would consider taking a series of views for them around Dublin and in other parts of Ireland, for a forthcoming publication of theirs.[131] Fisher also wanted to know whether Petrie would be willing to engage in similar work in England and elsewhere. The matter of style was raised almost immediately. Would Petrie be able or willing to follow the style of Jones' *Views of London Buildings*? Would he supply them with a sample drawing of a new public building in Dublin, along the lines of Jones' views? Whether Petrie did this is not known, but certainly his new employers were impressed with and anxious to proceed with a new 'Dublin', for within three weeks he was back into the fray with a vengeance. Fisher, whose letters are brisk and to the point, informed him:

> We have heard a rumour that others are about to commence Dublin – I feel confidant the mention of this will stimulate you to every possible exertion & to let us have some drawings, at *least* 4 by the end of another week – It is a speculation of some moment & unless we can get into the field soon, will be one of almost ruin to us – but I am sure from what I saw you will not allow this.[132]

Petrie was asked to employ someone to take drawings under his supervision, in order to speed up the production of engravings. Fisher was intent on keeping up the pressure on Petrie, for the next day, 18 September, he wrote to him again enclosing a notice about the proposed rival to their book, taking care to assure him that 'they do not pay above half what we have agreed to give you for drawings...' [133] And what was Petrie being paid for his work? Because of the nature of the book, the publishers looked for their profits in the long term sales, rather than making a quick killing. Fisher put forward a couple of his proposals for remuneration. The first involved Petrie being paid two guineas for each thousand copies sold of any of the numbers. (The work was apparently being published in several 'numbers'.) But this did not come into effect until the first 5,000 had been sold to cover the expenses of the publication, so it would have required a great deal of confidence on Petrie's part concerning the eventual success of the work. This indeed was Fisher's intention; he felt that the drawings would be of higher quality if the artist had an 'interested anxiety' in the work. His second proposal, to avoid 'ultimate dispute and litigation', was to give Petrie a sixth share of the profits, after all the expenses had been cleared. This would certainly seem a more advantageous arrangement from Petrie's point of view, until Fisher proceeds to detail the expenses. The letter press and plates would be composed and printed by them, and they would debit this against the work at the rate which would be charged by a 'respectable house'. The paper they would buy on the best terms possible, and the cost of the engraving would be what they were currently paying R. Wallis for the 'Lancashire work'. The folding and stitching would be done by themselves, again at the standard rate. But the expenses do not stop there:

> ...there are five or six items, which though regularly charged, by the Bookseller would be entirely borne by ourselves in order to simplify the thing ... *1st* 10 per cent commission as agents beyond the 25 per cent as Booksellers. *2ndly* the 25th

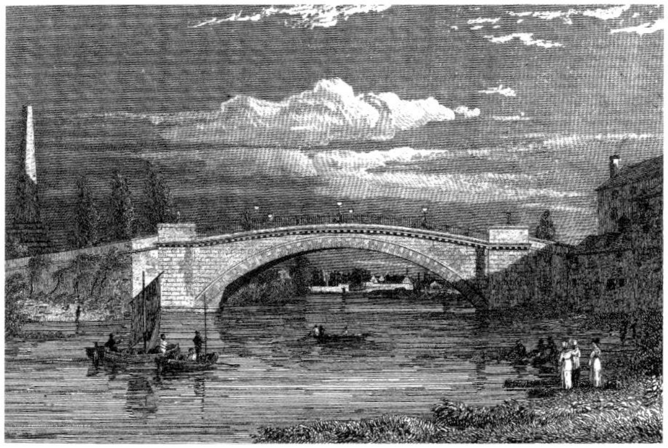

Sarah Bridge, on the River Anna Liffey

Dublin, from Blaquiere Bridge, Royal Canal

both engravings after Petrie from G.N. Wright, *Ireland Illustrated*, 1832

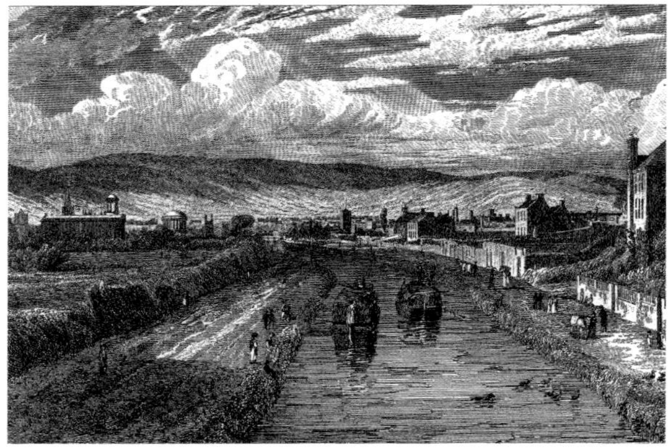

> of each number (where 25 or more are taken) which are allowed to the trade. *3rd* Advertisements, which will be something considerable. *4th* Bills and Prospectuses. *5th* the circulation of our own catalogue to the amount of about a million yearly & *6th* (a most important point indeed) you will have to run no risks of failure, bad debts &c &c as we shall pay the expense of the number whether we lose all or none.[134]

Besides whatever portion of the profits might accrue to Petrie, he was also to be paid a flat rate for his drawings; £4 and six impressions of each plate. This was to be paid one month after each drawing had been approved. The drawings were to be forwarded to London at the rate of three per week for the first four weeks, and two per week after that. Fisher felt that they could not start until they had at least twelve drawings in hand. Petrie accepted these conditions, and ten days later the first parcel arrived at Newgate Street containing three drawings: *The Sarah Bridge* (incorrectly inscribed on the engraving 'Sarah's Bridge'), *The Wellington Testimonial* and *The R.C. Chapel at Phibsboro*. The engravers of these were to be E. Goodall, J. Archer and B. Winkles respectively. The first two of these were regarded as being 'satisfactory', but the RC chapel was not thought to be a suitable subject for a first, or even a second number, and Petrie's treatment of it was criticised because he had made the view tall rather than wide. He was asked to supply a companion drawing so that the engravers could make the necessary alterations. The engravers were also critical of the style of the drawings. They thought them 'feeble', and Petrie was asked to introduce greater 'effect' into the scenes, for they wanted the street scenes full of life and bustle. The drawings were to be engraved on steel plates in two forms; tall and wide. The dimensions of the tall plates were to be 6 x $3^7/_8$ inches, those of the wide plates were to be $3^7/_8$ x $6^1/_8$ inches, and Petrie was to keep to these dimensions as closely as possible and to avoid the tall format except where the subject demanded it, as in the case of the Wellington Testimonial, or church steeples.

Fisher was paranoid about some rival stealing the march on them and he bound Petrie to total secrecy, even going so far as to ask Petrie not to put his name or initials on the outside of the packages he sent over, as Fisher did not trust even his own employees, let alone his rivals, of whom he wrote:

> ...we must put competition out of reach or we shall fail & pray do not let the supposition that no one has yet commenced in Dublin slacken your exertions, you can hardly guess what active and persevering opponents we have to deal with on every side & once they know our design will stir heaven and earth to get the start of us.[135]

Their main rival was Thomas Hosmer Shepherd, who had worked on *Excursions in the County of Kent* in 1822. Shepherd was known to be preparing a work on Dublin. Fisher's contacts in the publishing world had informed him that Shepherd had returned to Dublin in the middle of October, having completed his list of drawings. He was also understood to have sent some drawings over to London before his return. Fisher asked Petrie to 'take pains' to find out anything he could about Shepherd's plans.[136]

Early in October Petrie forwarded the *View of Dublin from*

Blaquire Bridge, Royal Canal, which he was so pleased with that he proposed that it be engraved on a larger scale than the others. Fisher praised it highly but was reluctant to alter the format of the engravings and he gave it to E. Goodall to be engraved immediately. Goodall, an engraver of high repute, had taken over the job of engraving and Fisher assured Petrie that all the subsequent engravings would be either done by him, or directly under his supervision. Goodall had been connected with the publishers for a long time, but he worked independently, in his own house. The early engravings had all been cut on large plates, the intention being to have two engravings per plate, but, as usual, Petrie's slowness in producing drawings held up the completion of these, and consequently the printing of the work, much to the irritation of Fisher: 'One week lost and the success of the work is lost beyond redemption & that others are preparing we have no doubt.'[137] At the end of the first week in October, Petrie dispatched the view of *The Memorial of the King's Visit to Ireland, Kingstown*, which had been intended for a vignette on the wrapper or the title page, but which was eventually set in the same plate as *The Wellington Testimonial*. Along with it, he sent *The Phoenix Lodge*, the residence of the Viceroy of Ireland. This last was felt by the engravers to be lacking in animation and interest. Fisher advised the inclusion of figures:

> In order to have given it life and bustle, the Lord Lieutenant's Carriage & Four with an escort of soldiers behind it (as is the case I suppose) might have been dashing up the Park – or the ladies Paget & some friends prancing about on horseback – I think also you do not give the buildings large enough, for the kind of work ours is meant to be – a work of *Public Buildings* – though perhaps the subjects yet given are not to be judged of as of that peculiar kind.[138]

Again, Fisher refers to Jones' 'London' as an example of the broad, bold style he wanted; in contrast to Jennings' 'Paris' which he describes as 'niggardly & diminutive'. Then, in perhaps the unkindest cut of all, Fisher recommends Petrie to use the camera obscura in order to get the views 'strictly correct', saying that it was commonly used in works of this kind. The list of artists who have used the camera obscura is surprisingly extensive, among them Paul Sandby, John Crome and Thomas Girtin – watercolour painters who had revolutionised the use of this medium in Petrie's time – but for Petrie, who prided himself rightly on his painstaking exactitude and topographical accuracy, it must have hurt to have the use of such mechanical means of reproducing scenes recommended. But not content with this, Fisher then advises Petrie to 'meet' an architectural draughtsman, to expedite the work. It was difficult nonetheless, for Fisher to convey to Petrie the idea of the type of view he wanted, being no artist himself and being restricted to letters. He expresses himself clumsily:

> I would instance as what I wish – if the Post Office were being taken, that it alone should be represented as large as it possibly could & the houses beyond brought in small to fill up – not the Post office given in a group, if I may use that expression. A street view of course would be different. The upper part of Sackville Street might begin the picture & the Post

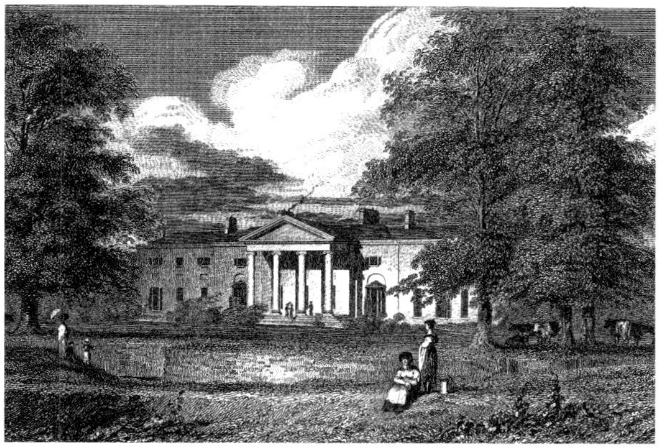

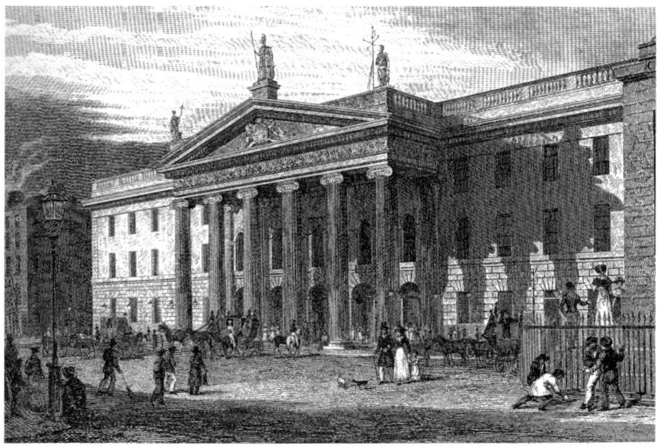

The Vice Regal Lodge, Phœnix Park, Near Dublin

Post Office, Dublin

both engravings after Petrie from G.N. Wright, *Ireland Illustrated*, 1832

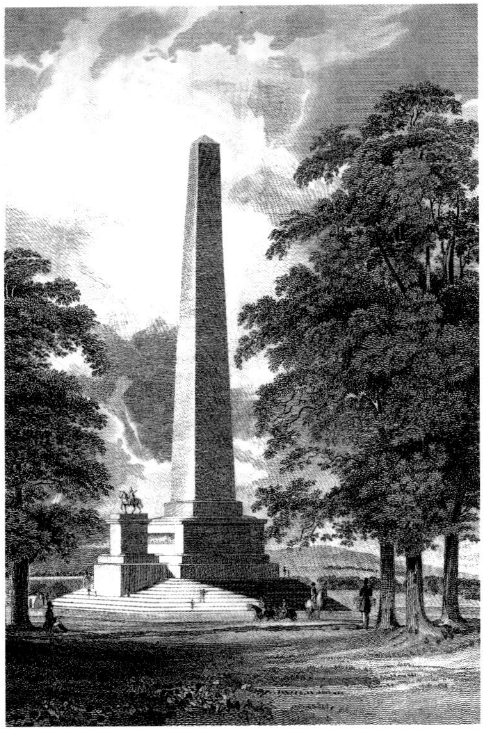

The Wellington Testimonial, Phœnix Park

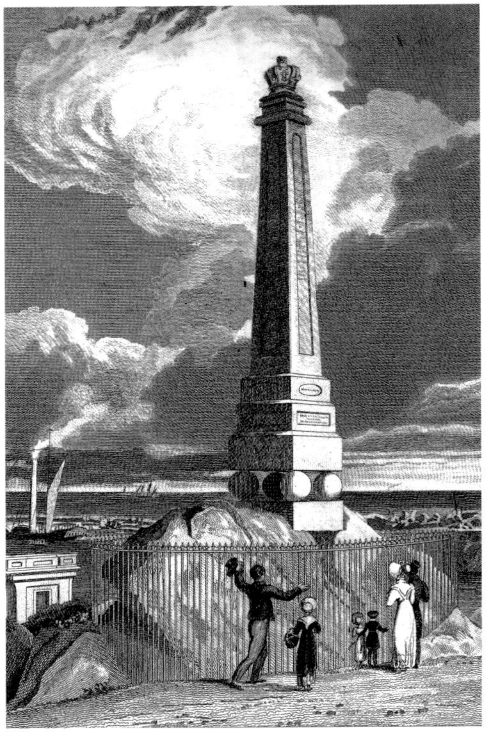

Memorial of the King's Visit to Ireland, Kingstown

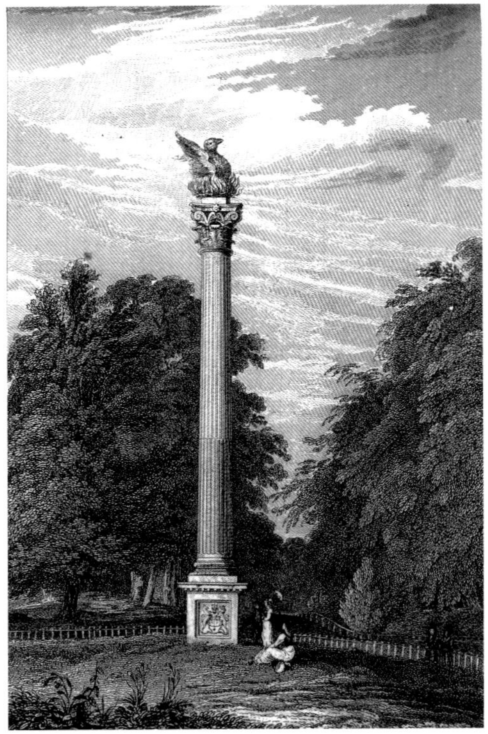

The Phœnix Pillar, Phœnix Park
all after Petrie from G.N. Wright, *Ireland Illustrated*, 1832

> Office fall in the distance – but when the drawing is called, for instance, 'The Bank', 'The Post Office' &c &c, that building to be the building in the drawing.[139]

Later, he exhorts him not to lose sight of 'the bright sunshine effect', which was so particularly noticeable in Shepherd's 'London', and he presents him with a series of guideline on the selection and execution of the views:

> *1st* A series of views of the city or town from 2 to 4 distant points showing the commanding & exterior features & forms of the buildings & the surrounding countryside being very scrupulous in drawing the outlines of the hills and buildings.
> *2nd* The popular entrances or approaches to the place taking in each view some *leading object* near the foreground to come as a principal feature.
> *3rd* Show some of the finest & best streets, squares, terraces, etc.
> *4th* The most interesting buildings internally and externally.
> *5th* Monuments of very eminent persons, local processions, ceremonies, customs.
> *6th* In street views, where practible, give the *names distinctly* over the various shops – it interests the parties in the work.[140]

Not a very adventurous set of guidelines, but the last one is interesting inasmuch as it highlights the commercial nature of the work.

In November, Petrie dispatched *The Post Office*. It arrived in London on the third day of that month. Petrie had obviously taken note of Fisher's instructions, and the publishers were pleased with it, although they insisted that they wanted more drawings in a short space of time; for Petrie had again been falling behind in his promised rate of six drawings a month – they had only received three the previous month, and both *The Phoenix Lodge* and *The Phoenix Column* were still awaiting their mates. The engravers, as has been pointed out, worked independently, and as they usually had so much work in hand, were not prone to sitting around waiting for drawings which were possibly not going to arrive. This was a far cry from the situation as it had been three or four years previously, when the engravers had to go out begging for work. In 1828 they were a far more intractable group of men, and their demands reflect this. Fisher told Petrie to make sure that he finished the drawings exactly as they were to be engraved, concentrating especially on the figures, and he added, by way of spurring the artist on to greater efforts, that their great rival Shepherd would not allow any alterations in his drawings in terms of effect or anything else. Speed was essential:

> If the work is to succeed you must never be below the mark of 4 per month; Make up your mind to do this, My Dear Sir – it is indispensable & I am sure you will not voluntarily plunge us into ruinous difficulties.[141]

Although the engravers regarded Petrie's drawings as sketchy, and resented having to spend time deciphering indistinct figures or filling in areas that had been left incomplete, Fisher thought that they were 'infinitely better' than Shepherd's drawings.

> All make the same complaints as to your drawings – 'beautifully outlined' – 'milk and water effects' Barber, Higham, Goodall, Winkles – Brewer &c &c, – as to the skies do take our advice and make them as quiet as possible with a light flickering cloud or two hovering about – this in a general way would add much to the engravings.[142]

He then asks Petrie if he would agree to just taking the outlines and letting the publishers have the effects and figures filled in by their own artists. He recommends the use of sepia rather that Indian ink, adding that not more than two colours should be used. He reminded Petrie of the importance of ensuring that the drawings were made to the exact size that they were to be engraved. Detailed parts should be drawn on a separate piece of paper on a larger scale.

As to what the engravers themselves were being paid for their work, it seems that fifteen guineas was the standard rate for engraving a drawing. At least that was what Barber, Higham and Varrel were to be paid. A more exceptional engraver could command higher wages: Goodall, for instance, was paid £20 for the engraving of *Dublin from the Phoenix Park*, although this was such exceptional remuneration that Petrie was asked not to 'whisper it' to anyone. Mr Woolnott, another engraver of high repute, had promised to do two views within six months for fifty guineas; Fisher was so pushed for time that he had no choice but to accept these exorbitant terms, but he asked Petrie to send two 'down-right heavy' subjects, so that at least he would get his money's worth. However, due to Petrie's dilatoriness, Woolnott never received any drawings. Petrie's view of *Dublin from the Phoenix Park* is virtually identical to an engraving in the National Library of Ireland after a view by Samuel Frederick Brocas, which can be dated to this period. Petrie's rivalry with the Brocas family must have been intense. Samuel Brocas's twelve views of Dublin, engraved by his younger brother Henry Junior, had been published by J. Le Petit in the early 1820s as *Select Views in the City of Dublin*, the first part of an intended publication, *A Book of Views of Ireland*, that never materialised. Although crude and awkward in terms of perspective, the Brocas views are crowded and animated.

Nelson's Pillar, Sackville-Street, Dublin

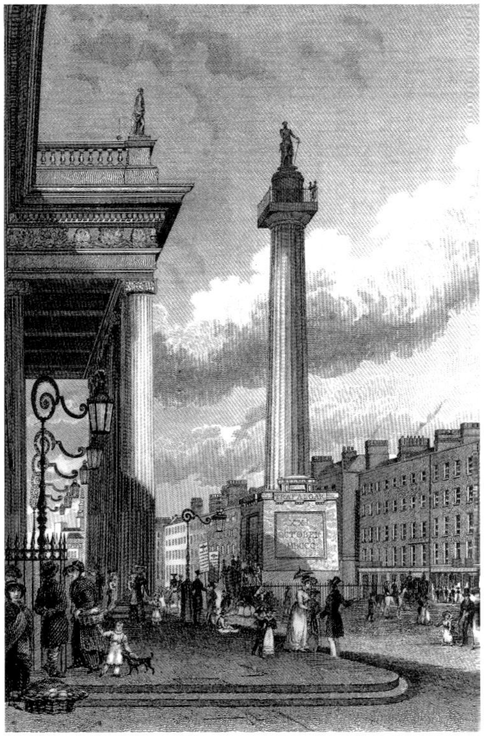

As 1828 drew to a close, the prospectuses for the work were distributed amongst the booksellers and the date of publication approached rapidly. The engraving of the Vice-Regal Lodge was at an advanced state, but was wanting a companion view, as was *The Phoenix Column*. Goodall had sketched in the *View of Dublin from The Phoenix Park*, and *Nelson's Pillar* was due to go to the engraver as soon as

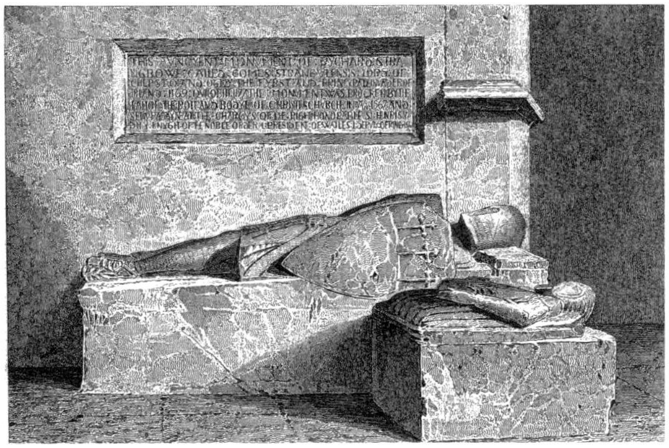

Strongbow's Monument

Interior of the Church of the Carmelite Friary

below

Howth Light House, from the Needles

all after Petrie from G.N. Wright, *Ireland Illustrated*, 1832

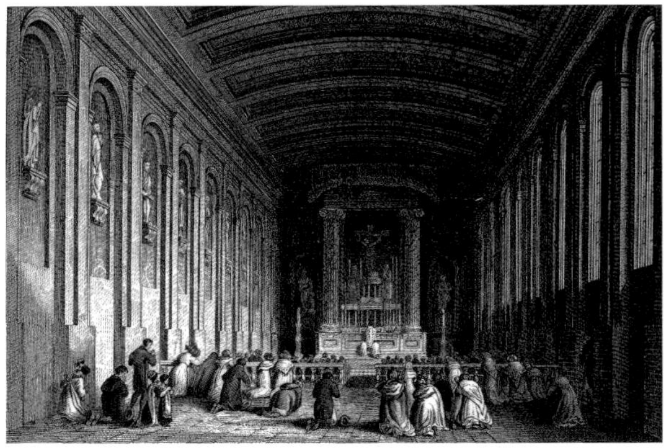

work commenced after Christmas. (The latest word on Shepherd was that he had not yet commenced engraving, so Fisher felt that he could breath easier.) *The Post Office* and *Strongbow's Monument* had been engraved on one plate by Richard Winkles and was thought to be a superior plate. By March of 1829, Goodall had completed the view of Dublin and was working on the vignette, *Howth Lighthouse*. Barber was offered *The Interior of the Church of the Carmelite Friary*, which he 'boggled at' and refused to do, although Fisher offered him eighteen guineas for it, and *The Vice-Regal Lodge* was completed. This last had been engraved by J. McGahey, an Irish lad who had completed his apprenticeship at the Caxton office. Fisher claimed that his was the only House to have 'patronised' the Irish by taking their boy apprentices. Petrie was asked to forward a 'shewey piece' to accompany McGahey's engraving, and he did so. His view of *Terenure, Co. Dublin* (the home of Frederick Bourne), arrived shortly afterwards but was felt to be too slight and unfinished, and as Fisher did not have time to return it to Petrie for completion, he employed an artist to fill in 'effect' before it was handed to McGahey for engraving. The engravers at this stage were thoroughly tired of the numerous delays in receiving drawings:

> ...but engravers get tired of being 'Humbugged' in calling about drawings & they turn up the nose about our 'promise of Dublin drawings.' 'Trust the wind' say they 'as soon as Petrie.'[143]

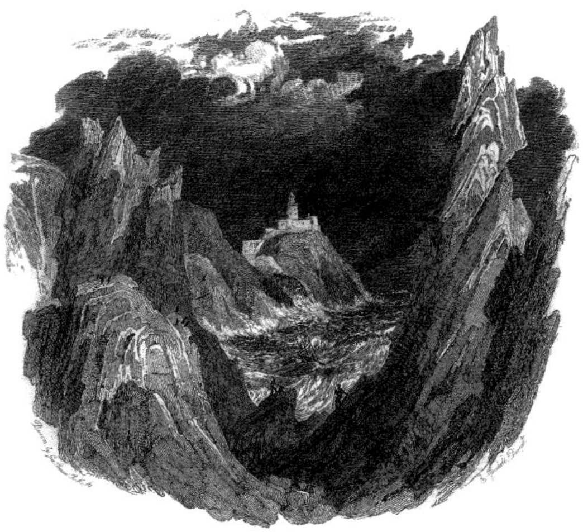

On Petrie's recommendation, George Wright had been requested to write the historical and topographical descriptions for the forthcoming work, a job he was well qualified to do after the several books he had already written on Ireland, especially the *Historical Guide to Ancient and Modern Dublin*, which had been published several years earlier and for which Petrie had also supplied drawings.[144] Fisher met Wright early in September 1828 to discuss the projected work, and everything was arranged 'most amicably' between them – Wright was to get five guineas a sheet for editing the text. He suggested to Fisher that engravings that were likely to require a lot of letter-press should be cut on the same steel as those that would require very little, so that the plates would be evenly distributed throughout the book, and this course was adopted. He was asked to write the prospectus for the work, a task which he completed in less than two weeks; he sent it off to the publishers at the end of September for their approval. They felt that he had misunderstood the nature of the work because of the emphasis he gave to the word 'antiquity'. Their intention was to concentrate on the more modern buildings, in an effort to bring it into the same league as Jones'

Metropolitan Improvements.[145]

The fine title page that had been prepared for the work and which included a view of *Howth Lighthouse from the Needles* as a vignette (the preparatory sketch for which is in the National Gallery of Ireland)[146] was rendered slightly obsolete, as the date of publication which had been inscribed on it, slipped past. In the finally published work it was immediately followed by another title page, which was simpler and truer, in that it gave the date of publication as 1831, and included the names of other artists who had illustrated the book; namely, W.H. Bartlett and T.M. Baynes. To these should be added Henry Kirchhoffer, who contributed several views. The book was re-issued on several occasions, the plates being re-cut. In one edition of *Ireland Illustrated*, the plates are dated up to 1839.

TEN VIEWS OF THE NORTH AND NORTH-WEST (1829-30)

In 1829, after finishing the engravings for Fisher, Petrie became immediately involved in yet another publishing venture. This time it was with the firms of William Curry Jnr & Co, and the book was to be simply entitled *Ten Views of the North and North-West*. Petrie's illustrations were to be the central feature of the book, with short descriptions of the views appended. William Millar was the engraver; he lived and worked in Edinburgh. By November of that same year, the work on the plates appears to have been far advanced, as Millar was in a position to send the publishers an impression of the plate of *Dunluce Castle*, and etchings of it and the view of *The Giant's Causeway*, the engraving of which was also in a forward state. He intended to work some more on the view of Dunluce Castle, 'to improve the effect'. The plate of *Lough Gill*, he assured them, was also well under way.[147]

William Curry was a Dublin publisher, so presumably there was a high degree of contact between him and Petrie, thus avoiding the continual irritation of correspondence across the Irish Sea. In the spring of 1830, Petrie exhibited four of the watercolour sketches that he had done for the *Northern Tourist*, as it was more colloquially referred to, in the Royal Hibernian Academy's annual exhibition. These were *Lough Gill*, *Narrow-Water Castle*, *Carrick-a-Rede* and *The Long Bridge and Cave Hill, Belfast*.[148] Pencil sketches for these paintings are in the National Gallery of Ireland.[149] Sketches for another three that were not exhibited are also in the NGI: *Rostrevor*, *The Giant's Causeway* and *Dunluce Castle*.[150] In the Ulster Museum there is a sketch of *Belfast from Turf Lodge*,[151] which Petrie completed as a watercolour, and which closely resembles the published engraving. It is likely that similar highly finished watercolours were supplied by Petrie for the other nine engravings, and indeed *Dunluce Castle* is another such finished watercolour[152] which provides positive evidence, it any be needed, that it was from this sort of painting that Millar made his engravings, for it contains the figure of a woman that appears in the published engraving but that does not feature in the preparatory sketch in the portfolio of Petrie drawings in the NGI.[153]

From little clues such as these an idea can be formed of Petrie's methods of working. A highly detailed pencil sketch would be prepared on the spot from the actual landscape or monument, but it would include no details of sky or vegetation or sea – just the pure but precise outline of whatever object was being depicted. Petrie himself said that he would often spend as much as four or five hours on a drawing,[154] and as the many extant sketches in the NGI display a painstaking attention to detail and accuracy, this is not hard to believe. The colour would be added at a later stage, when Petrie had returned to his studio from his sketching tour. This accounts for the rather mannered appearance of the paintings in such areas as foreground vegetation or landscape, while the main subject, if there be one, is lucidly and objectively rendered. In many cases, Petrie would preserve the original pencil sketch and make a duplicate drawing, which would then be coloured in. The only exceptions to this are the monochrome Indian ink drawings that he supplied for *The Picture of Dublin*, now in the Royal Irish Academy.[155]

The engravers in almost every case adhered scrupulously to the painting with which they were presented, and it is a measure of their fidelity to the originals that their engravings can be compared quite favourably with photographs of the same paintings. It is also of great benefit to the present-day researcher; for the complete corpus of engravings runs to over two hundred pictures, and they consequently form an effective 'liber veritatis' of Petrie paintings.

Chapter IV

Ireland Described: Tours of the West 1821-22

When discussing Petrie's tours in the west of Ireland, two things should be borne in mind. Firstly, the accounts that Petrie himself wrote of his travels during the 1820s were written many years later, and he paid little heed to getting dates correct. Secondly, the accounts that Stokes wrote in his *Life* were culled from different sources, including Petrie's writings and Stokes' own memory, and they are just as inaccurate as regards dating. The present work being more pernickety about such matters, an attempt will be made to establish, with some degree of certainty, the different tours that Petrie made in the West and in other places.

On 20 July 1821 Petrie set out on a tour that he intended to last at least three weeks.[156] The watercolour of *Kilmallock*, signed and dated to this year, suggests that he may have visited this historic Co Limerick town during this trip.[157] The ultimate purpose was to visit the Aran Islands, at that time considered to be extremely remote and inaccessible. It is not known if he was accompanied on this trip, but it is unlikely that he would set out on such a venture alone. A sketchbook from this period survives. It is inscribed '1821', but not in Petrie's hand, and all the sketches have been removed, so the book can do little more than provide a dumb record of Petrie's travels on the islands. The book was probably compiled by Margaret Stokes, for the captions beneath the (missing) sketches are in the same handwriting that may be seen in the Margaret Stokes bequest of drawings by Petrie to the National Gallery of Ireland, and they would appear to have been transcribed from Petrie's original notes on the drawings. This sketchbook is now preserved in the Royal Irish Academy.[158] In another (undated) sketchbook in the same archive, there are eight sketches by Petrie of antiquities on the Aran Islands. (A list of the many other drawings in this book will be found in the catalogue of drawings.) Stokes mention this trip and states that on this visit, Petrie made studies for his picture of Teampull Brecan, which he did not complete until many years later, in 1857. Stokes describes the islands and the picture:

> These islands lie low and flat, and except at the western side, are devoid of anything like cliff scenery. Vast slabs of rock form the surface of the islands, and no tree is to be found, save here and there the mystic elder overshadowing the bed of some early saint. The growth of timber is rendered impossible by the absence of soil, and by the masses of spray drifting across from the stormy Atlantic. Yet these islands cannot be called barren. In the deep fissures dividing these great masses of grey rock the forms of the 'Maiden-hair fern' rise in luxuriance like a fringe of delicate green around them, mingled with wild flowers of every hue. The picture represents the Seven Churches or the College of St Brecan. They stand in a little hollow, apparently produced by the sinking of the strata, and form, with their picturesque group. Beyond them the rocky expanse falls towards the deep blue sea, while in the distance rise the high mountains of Connemara.[159]

When Petrie returned from Connemara to Dublin, he informed Brewer of his intention to write an account of the Aran Islands. Brewer was guarded in his response, stating that the obscurity and comparative insignificance of the islands were arguments against attempting such a work:

> On the other hand the very circumstance of obscurity as related to insulated tracts so near home – the entire ignorance

> of the polished and reading part of the world concerning the natural features and (as I was taught to believe when at Galway) the very curious traces of ancient manners – unite in rendering the subject worthy of attention. The hand of taste may elicit charms from any soil.[160]

Petrie made a second tour of the west of Ireland in 1822. In an autograph manuscript in the Royal Irish Academy, Petrie describes how, in July of that year, he left Dublin with a few weeks at his command and the notion that he would like to explore the wilder parts of counties Clare and Galway. He also mentions his particular desire to visit the Aran Islands, and this might indicate that the date on this manuscript is incorrect, as he certainly visited these islands in 1821. For the time being, however, the date can be accepted. He was accompanied by a 'Major P' – [Patrickson], a seasoned traveller. On the afternoon of 10 July 1822, at two o'clock, the Grand Canal packet left Portobello for Shannon Harbour with Petrie and friend on board. The day was bright and showery – 'characteristic Irish weather', Petrie remarks.[161] In another draft of the same account, Petrie expands on this subject:

> It may be of use to future tourists in Ireland to be informed that if they would desire to be accompanied by dry weather they should choose an earlier or much later period of the summer for their journey ... The climate of Ireland has not changed for the last century when Doctor Gerald Boate remarked that 'It raineth very much all the summer long, so as it is a rare thing to see a whole summer pass without it and many summers it is never dry weather two or three days together. In the Spring and the latter part of Autumn there is usually clear dry weather. 'The legend of St Swithin and the forty days rain is in Ireland more than annually verified.[162]

At Shannon Harbour, the western terminus of the Grand Canal, travellers transferred to a steam packet to continue their journey up the Shannon as far as Athlone. This was Petrie's first experience of inland navigation in Ireland, 'a mode of travelling tedious and insipid to the man of business'. As the steamer approached the town of Athlone, the day was drawing to a close and the broad sweep of the Shannon reflected the glory of the setting sun. His first impression of the town was a favourable one; the inhabitants were abroad enjoying the evening, promenading in their gayest attire. There was a sprinkling of military finery and the band of the garrison was playing the tattoo through the town:

> There was a promise of picturesqueness too, in its narrow streets and lanes, its bridge, abbey, ancient gateway and castle – and in some instances they really are so, but truth obliges me to own that Athlone, in its everyday dress, is but a sorry Irish town, with little to boast of, except the noble river on whose banks it is placed ... But Athlone is rich in ancient recollections – and the Annals of the ancient King of the West of Ireland would furnish an interesting slice of social history.[163]

An engraving of Athlone, after Petrie, is in Cromwell's *Excursions through Ireland*. This view was engraved before March 1821 – so it

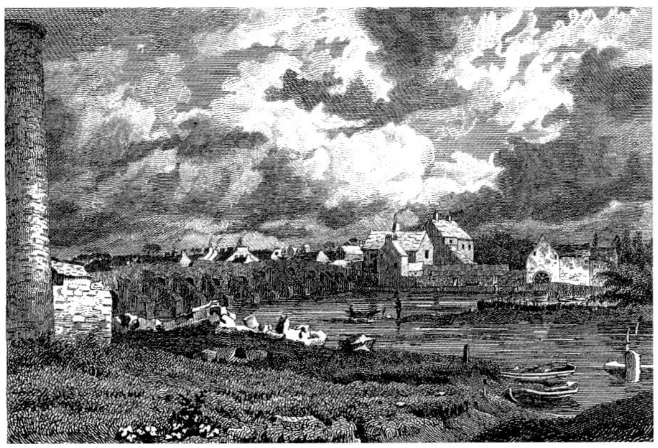

Banagher, King's County
engraving after Petrie from T. Cromwell, *Excursions through Ireland*, vol. iii, 1820

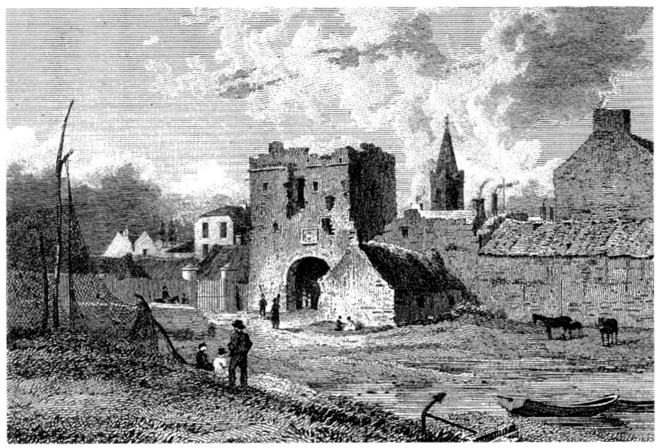

North Gate, Athlone
engraving after Petrie from T. Cromwell, *Excursions through Ireland*, vol. i, 1820

is not from this trip – but it may be compared nonetheless with Petrie's written description of the town. From Athlone the travellers proceeded westwards into Connaught. Petrie describes their progress, seated on a gig lumbered with sketching chairs, umbrellas, fishing rods (the last were not Petrie's) in front; two large valises strapped behind; and the well, the box-seat etc., filled with books and measuring tapes and other necessary apparatus. Thus equipped and wrapped up in great coats,

> ...and our sallow physiognomies and looking very knowing under the shade of our light skimming dish hats, we entered the city of Tuam on the evening of the July, to the no small wonder and puzzleification of the lounging and gossiping half-dandies of the place, who judging by their looks had certainly never seen anything of this kind before.[164]

In Tuam, they stayed at the house of a Mr M— , a professional gentleman, whom they had met while staying at Mount Bellew, the home of Christopher Bellew, where they had passed a fortnight. Petrie refers to Bellew as 'my honoured and beloved friend', which is rather puzzling. In the letter from Brewer to Petrie written in April 1823 quoted earlier it would appear that Bellew had left a message at Mrs. Petrie's in the summer of 1822, inviting Petrie to stay at Mount Bellew should his travels bring him to that part of the country. Brewer, writing in 1823, encouraged Petrie to take up that offer, the implication being that in 1823, Petrie had not yet stayed at Mount Bellew. This inconsistency casts doubt on the accuracy of the journal that Petrie wrote. It is probable that Petrie was writing it not as a personal diary, but as the basis of a book of his travels, which would include pieces on the history and topography of the country. This is confirmed by Stokes.[165] In a piece already quoted, Petrie describes his first impressions of Athlone, in the summer of 1822. This is hard to reconcile with another extract quoted in Stokes, which begins: 'It was in the year 1820, when, standing on the bridge of Athlone, I first saw the Shannon...'[166]

Yet these draft journals, extracts from essays and other pieces, collected together in the Royal Irish Academy, are the only source material there is, and so they may be taken at face value as regards dating, unless there is contradictory evidence. Stokes had access to these manuscripts and evidently to others for he quotes some passages that do not exist in the journals as they now stand, but that tie in perfectly with them. Evidently he was using a more complete version of the projected book on Petrie's western travels, which is now lost or destroyed. Comparing Stokes' quotations with the originals, where this can be done, reveals that he took certain liberties with Petrie's text, but there are very few actual misquotes and the sense of the passage is never affected.

The two travellers spent several days in Tuam. Petrie was not impressed by this town any more than he was by Athlone:

> Tuam, or the city, as the name signifies – anciently the capital of this kingdom of Connaught – is at present a poor looking second rate county town with little appearance of activity or prosperity. It consists of three streets and a few lanes of cabins. As usual in all country towns in Ireland, long lines of cabins stretch out on either side. It has a market house in the centre of the town built about a century ago by Timothy Dunne, Esq., sovereign of the town ... There is a small and picturesque demesne attached to the Palace of the Protestant Prelate to which the respectable inhabitants of the town have access, and there are two Inns of tolerably respectable appearance. The Rival Religions, as they may now be called, each have a place of worship. The Cathedral is a respectable edifice for an Irish country church but it is a paltry building for the chief temple dedicated to God for the province. It was in a ruinous state until repaired by the present archbishop. The Catholic Chapel is as usual a humble structure without any architectural pretension but the Catholic inhabitants of Tuam and its vicinity are at present raising funds to create a bigger one. Each religion also has a school for educating the children of the poor – that belonging to the Catholics is very numerously attended. Tuam is a corporate town established by act of James I in 1646 (the 11th of James I). The corporation consists of a sovereign and twelve burgesses elected by the Freemen who are themselves elected to their freedom by the Sovereign and burgesses. This is a monopoly in violation of the charter according to which all inhabitants of the town are declared free.

Petrie goes on to describe the corruption of the Corporation, and how the Roman Catholics had violently possessed themselves of the corporate power, incurring the hatred of the Protestant inhabitants of the place; how the right of returning members to the Irish parliament had been sold by the Bingham family for a peerage and £23,000 at the time of the Act of Union, and how the tolls and customs had been sold by Lord Clonmorris to a Mr Morris, 'a gentleman of that exclusive establishment, the Tuam Bank', for £3,200.[167]

Moving on from this scathing account of life and politics in an average Irish town, Petrie discusses the remains of antiquity in Tuam. He gives a detailed description of the cathedral, and in the NGI there is a drawing by him of its very fine chancel arch. (In later years, Petrie praised the rebuilding of the chancel arch by the architect Benjamin Woodward.) The drawing is undated but was probably made on this trip. He also gives a description of the cross of Tuam.[168] In his *Ecclesiastical Architecture of Ireland*, Petrie described this cross, inscribed with the name of king Turlogh O'Conor, as 'the finest monument of its class and age' remaining in Ireland 'and yet, to the disgrace of the inhabitants of that ancient city, its shaft, head, and base, though all remaining, are allowed to be in different localities, detached from each other.'[169] (The base was in the market place, the shaft over the grave of Archbishop Singe in the grounds of St Mary's Cathedral; it has since been re-erected in the town centre.) Having covered almost everything of interest to be seen in Tuam, Petrie turns his attention to the inhabitants; who make

> ...a respectable and picturesque appearance, particularly the women dressed in blue cloaks and madder gowns and petticoats. The young unmarried women do not look badly with the their long black locks hanging on their shoulders or floating on the wind, for you must know it is considered immodest among the lower orders here to turn up the hair until the zone of Venus has been loosened.[170]

Of the morals of the inhabitants, Petrie had no first hand knowledge, as he (tongue in cheek) admits himself, but had to rely on hearsay evidence. He had heard that the lower orders were not remarkable for their morality, but he observed that such was the case in all crowded communities, especially when their betters did not set a good example. Of the middle classes of Tuam he had little to say. They were fond of scandal, of law and of squabbling, 'which qualities are equally characteristic of a hundred country towns of Ireland'. He did observe a lack of religious strife and bigotry, or as he put it, 'they do not much hate each other 'pour l'amour de Dieu'.' He hoped that they would preserve that feature in what he describes as 'these perilous times'. And what of the recreations and pastimes of the people of Tuam in 1822?

> You will judge of their civilisation by the fact that you could not bye [sic] a sheet almanack in the town of Tuam, nor could you find is there ever a circulating library here or I believe I might add in any other town in Connaught. How then you will ask do they pass their time? Why, the elderly people play cards and the young gentlemen who, if their fathers can keep a table are never reared to a profession or employment or anything. They lounge about the town in groups in the forenoon, querying the passers-by, or lolling on the counters of the shop-keepers – and their evenings are spent in occupations which I leave you to guess, less creditable to themselves and more baneful to society – corrupting the morals of the country girls; and this being the case it is no wonder the said girls are corrupted.[171]

Continuing this dissection of Irish rural society in the early 19th century, Petrie moves on to the question of family pride, noting that the inhabitants were classed into various ranks according to the purity and antiquity of their blood. He cites a recent instance when the only son of a respectable apothecary married the daughter of another apothecary of equal professional standing:

Base of the great Stone Cross in the Market-place of Tuam
from G. Petrie, *The Ecclesiastical Architecture of Ireland*, 1845

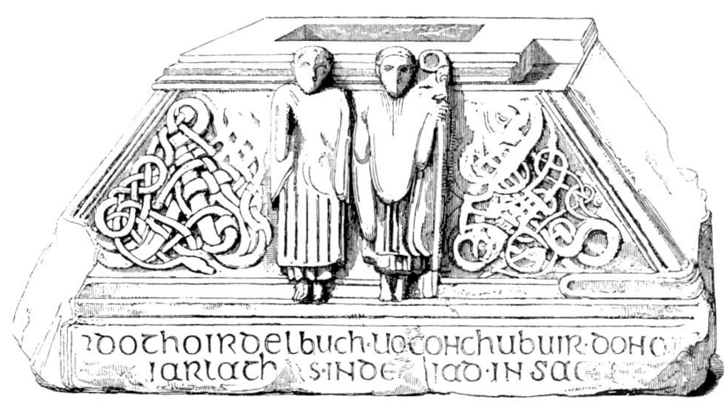

> The father and mother of the young man were so enraged, on the grounds solely of his uniting himself with a person of inferior blood, for the lady it was acknowledged was virtuous and accomplished, that they declared their fixed determination to banish him from their sight for ever.

From Tuam, Petrie and Major Patrickson set off for the wild regions of Connemara, accompanied by their host, Mr M— [Richard Martin?], who

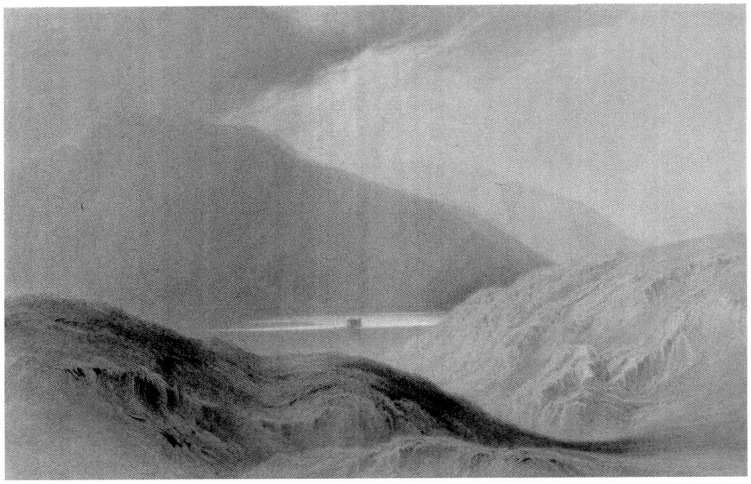

Hen's Castle on Lough Corrib, Co. Galway
*c.*1833-34, watercolour on paper, 32.5 x 50 (coll: NGI, cat. no. 6032) (see colour plate p.28)

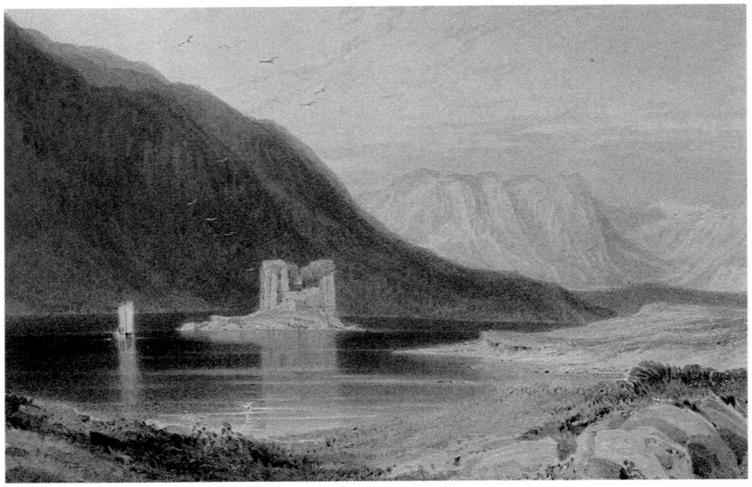

Hen's Castle, Lough Corrib
*c.*1833-34, watercolour on paper, 32.5 x 50 (see colour plate p.29)

had decided to join their party for the remainder of the journey.[172] They took the road to Headford, close by Lough Corrib, and spent some days exploring the shores and islands of that lake, Petrie taking sketches as they went along. In the Petrie Portfolio in the NGI there are some drawings of Lough Corrib, which may be assigned to this period,[173] and the large watercolour of *The Hen's Castle, Lough Corrib* in the NGI was probably based on sketches at this time.[174]

There is, in the National Library of Ireland, a written description of Lough Corrib and its island. Extending to fourteen pages, it is in Petrie's own handwriting.[175] The travellers visited several of the islands on the lake, notably Inchnagoill, 'Island of the Foreigners', on which are the remains of an early monastery. It was nearly sunset before they thought of leaving this beautiful island, but before they departed they ascended to the highest promontory on the island, which shelters a little sandy bay, to take a farewell view of Doon Hill on the eastern shore of Lough Corrib, with the mountains of the west behind, illuminated by the rays of the setting sun. They then embarked for Cong, a small village at the northern end of the lake: 'Our voyage was as delightful as could be imagined. The wind abated as the sun sank and the moon streaming along the silent lake, arose in harmony with our feelings'.[176] And when they landed in Cong and entered the dark and silent village, they felt '...as if in a land of fairy romance rather than seeking a night's lodgings amongst a few poor cottages in the west of Ireland.' Petrie's account of Cong, which Stokes quotes from extensively, is also contained in the Petrie manuscripts in the Royal Irish Academy.

> Cong is situated near the eastern extremity of Lough Corrib, in a wild region of rugged limestone rocks with grassy valleys intervening, which separate that lake from Lough Mask, and through which the waters of one find their way to the other by subterranean streams, occasionally receiving in their course a dim gleam of sunlight, and again sinking into darkness, until they finally burst out into broad daylight a little above the town, surrounding and embracing it with a joyful and unceasing babble, then uniting to form a rapid but silent and beautiful river, flowing into the lake.
>
> This little island town, thus encircled by crystal streams, and full of romantic beauty, contains within its circle about forty houses; the ruins of a noble monastery, a new church, a chapel, and a barrack, and it has three small bridges thrown across the surrounding streams.[177]

Describing the new Protestant church as 'a small, tasteless, modern fabric', Petrie goes on to excoriate the Church of Ireland for its neglect of the fine arts.

> The fact is, that however lukewarm may have been the piety

> of the Church Establishment, and the manner in which its great wealth is appropriated contributes to make it so, it is still more characterised by neglect of the cultivation of those arts which refine and give dignity to civilised life.[178]

The removal, by the local clergyman, of the old Market Cross, was also condemned by Petrie; happily a legal action threatened against the rector, led to its restoration. Searching amongst the large monumental flagstones in Cong Abbey for any of historical interest, he was told that two lay buried in the choir, near the high altar. As time was pressing, and night was falling, Petrie employed some men to conduct an excavation in search of the ancient monuments.

> While the excavation proceeded, I stood removed from the crowd to enjoy the scene. The figure of the man who was digging was thrown into strong light, from the candles held by those who immediately surrounded him, while, behind, a crowd of shadowy spectators, with outstretched necks and anxious looks, watched in silence the progress of the work ... The strong effect of light and shade on the crowd, and the mystery of the scene, were greatly heightened by the solemn stillness of the background, formed of the ivied wall of the church, while a tranquil moonlit sky was seen through its lofty windows.[179]

The results of the excavation were, however, disappointing. Petrie also found time to explore the limestone caverns near Cong, finding them 'gloomy and terrific'. From the village of Cong, they set off into what Petrie describes as 'one of the wildest and most unknown districts of the old world'.[180] Petrie had intended his tour to last only two or three weeks, but he extended his stay to several months and when he finally returned to Dublin he had two volumes of notes and many sketches. (It is from these notes that this account is derived.) Two miles from Cong, on the Ballinrobe Road, they stopped off to visit 'the last mitred abbot in Ireland', the Reverend Mr Prendergast. Petrie had been given a letter of introduction to him by the Reverend Mr Swiney:

> The object of my visit was to see some interesting remains of antiquity, formerly the property of the abbey, and still in the possession its last mitred abbot; but the singularly picturesque and romantic situation of the abbot's humble retreat would in itself have been one worthy of attention. It is a small but neat thatched cottage, almost buried in a little wooded dell, a perfect wilderness of rocks and trees, through which we must wind along a little wooded path, barely wide enough to permit a horse to force his way, and presenting in several elevated points most romantic vistas of Lough Corrib, with its many islands, and the long line of distant mountains that constitute its background.
>
> The venerable clergyman received us at the door with easy politeness, which warmed into cordiality on perusing his friend's letter of introduction, and after some general conversation relative to the object of my visit to that unfrequented part of Ireland, favoured us with a sight of this wonderful relic, the Cross of Cong.[181]

This passage, culled from Stokes, is one of the many instances where Stokes is quoting from a Petrie manuscript that is no longer available or extant, and one begins to get the impression that the material that remains, even supplemented by those extracts given in Stokes, is but a fraction of the original collection of essays and accounts of Petrie's tours in Ireland, a fact to be regretted in view of their clarity and objectivity. Stokes gives a description of the Cross of Cong (now in the National Museum of Ireland) and of the background to its creation, and them quotes a further passage from the same essay.

> This reliquary was found by the Reverend Mr. Prendergast, P.P., in an oaken chest kept in a cottage of the town where it and other remains of antiquity had probably been concealed since the Reformation, or at least subsequent to the rebellion of 1641. A great portion of the valuables thus hidden consisted of deeds of grants of land to the abbey, and of Irish manuscripts in vellum splendidly illuminated! It grieves me to say that these no longer exist. The abbot, as he confesses, being at the time ignorant of the value of such remains, thought little about them; and on going to the Continent shortly after to improve his education, carelessly left them in the charge of a young priest whom he appointed to do his duty during his absence. He remained abroad for eleven years during which time he found that the most ancient and valuable manuscripts which he saw on the Continent, appeared to resemble, but not equal in beauty, those he had left at home. Thus awakened to a sense of their value, we may imagine,

> what at least ought to have been, his astonishment and horror, on finding on his return home, that his deputy had during his absence lost or destroyed all those curious and valuable remains – the cross excepted; and that, unfortunately, the very beauty of the manuscripts had been a chief cause of their destruction, the ignorant young man having cut them up, to decorate his breviaries, &c., with the illuminated letters which they contained![182]

Following Petrie's movements after he left Cong requires a little detective work. There is a letter amongst the Petrie papers in the National Library that is dated 'Clifden, 9th August 1822'. It is not known who wrote it, or to whom it was addressed, but it is reasonable to assume that Petrie was the latter, for the writer of the letter has settled that his correspondent will come and he will meet him at Oughterard. They were then to stay with a Mr Martin of Ballinahinch. The writer then goes on to talk of O'Flaherty of Aran (a good friend of Petrie's from his visit there), and pins, crosses and inscriptions.[183] It is this letter that enables us to date tentatively a manuscript in the Royal Irish Academy, which concerns the visit that Petrie made to MacDara's Island, with this Mr Martin. The manuscript is in Petrie's hand, and is dated August, but no year is given. He describes how they left Ballinahinch Castle on horseback about noon, 'a pleasant party of five'. St MacDara's Island is about a mile off the Connemara coast. There is an ancient church on the eastern shore, on the site of a monastery founded by a 6th-century saint named MacDara, or 'son of the fox'. Traditionally, pilgrims visit the island on the saint's festival, on 16 July and 28 September. St MacDara was so venerated by local sailors that they would lower their sails in his honour as they passed the island. There are the remains of several pilgrimage stations on the island, with Early Christian decorated slabs. Stokes did not include Petrie's account in his book, which is surprising, for it is a vivid and memorable description of the island and its inhabitant, as well as the nearby mainland:

> This sacred island is not much more than a mile distant from a promontory of the Connemara coast called Misanna [not clear in the manuscript; the promontory is called in English, Mace Head], but from Roundstone Bay, a harbour which takes its name from the innumerable rocky tumblers which are tossed in wild confusion on its shores, it is distant between two and three leagues, and the bay is about the same distance from Ballynahinch Castle. The road follows at a little distance the windings of the Ballynahinch river, as it rushes to the Atlantic, and whether we look forward, or backward on the mountain region of Benabeola, it presents a series of scenes, differing in their picturesque features, but equally wild and magnificent. The shore of Roundstone Bay is broken at high tide into a number of little rocky islands, forming a considerable line of relk-shore [seaweed?] whose rich brown tints at low water finely harmonise with the broken surface of grassy verdure and rock with which they commingle. Here and there, sheltered from the west wind by some huge rocky tumbler, a fisherman's hut may be discovered by the curling smoke which it send up.[184]

Petrie praises the Connemara granite with its large crystals of red feldspar, quartz and black mica, and compares it to the finest Egyptian specimens: 'It receives a high polish and would be a beautiful material for various architectural and other ornamental purposes.' At a spot not far away, the sea had, thirty years before, washed away a bank of sand forty to fifty feet high, in a storm, and exposed seven or eight houses of circular plan. They were built of stone without cement, and the people who had seen them told Petrie that they were in a perfect state of preservation and admirable for the skill displayed in their construction: 'They suffered a partial demolition from the peasantry before a fresh accumulation of sand preserved their ruins for some future convulsion of the elements to exhibit them to the wonder of a new generation.' It is unfortunate that Petrie does not give more details of the houses and their situations, although it is difficult to say whether they would be of great archaeological interest; all along the west coast of Ireland there are small settlements of stone, and wattle-and-daub, thatched huts, mostly dating from the first millennium A.D., and such structures were built right up to the end of the 19th century.

Petrie describes the people of Roundstone Bay as being a healthy, handsome and robust race; richer than the inhabitants of the inland districts, and indefatigable in their industry.

> As an instance of their active warm heartedness and frankness of manner, I owe to them to mention that as I lingered behind my companions, attracted by the beauty and novelty of the scenery, I was frequently addressed by the peasantry in terms of ardent entreaty that I would not trust myself that

day to the dangerous elements we were about to encounter. 'For the love of God, Sir, do not venture one inch a day as this, but make the gentlemen return; the sea looks bad enough even now, bit if it grows worse as it is likely to do, it would be impossible to get back from any of the islands.' 'Surely' said I 'if there were any danger Mr. Martin would not think of proceeding.' 'Mr. Martin does not know the danger as well as we, but even if he *did* Sir, he would not mend it, Mr. Martin, Sir, would face the Divil, God bless him!'

> These entreaties of the moment made but little impression on me though the day was blustery and the wind was blowing from the north-west, as I understood from Mr. Martin that we should have a stout sail-boat, or, if not, the oared boat of the waterguard. I was even pleased in the anticipation of seeing again the great Atlantic. But when, on reaching the shore I found my companions seating themselves not in the sail-boat or even the barge of the waterguard (neither of which it appeared could be had), but in a small and clumsy fishing boat, ill provided with oars, I began to think that Mr. Martin really would, as my friend had told me, 'face the divil', and could not help acquainting him with the friendly caution I had received. A council was held, and the opinion of our crew asked and received, who, recommending a second boat to proceed in company to be of use in case of accident, a second boat was quickly procured and thus attended we boldly set forward.

However, before they left the bay, the sail-boat from Galway hove in sight and they transferred themselves onto it and set off again:

> Never shall I forget the magnificent spectacle which the mighty swell of the Atlantic presented that day. The island we were journeying to alternatively sank from our sight and rose again as we ascended and descended each mountain of water that with a stately motion met us in our progress; and as we followed with our eyes their progress towards the land we had left, they seemed like a deluge to envelop even the lofty peaks of Benabeola which but a moment before gave out their jagged precipices to the sunshine.

They had intended to land at Crugha na Keela, but the roughness of the sea prevented this. Crugha na Keela is an island about two miles north-west of MacDara's Island. Petrie says that it had a cross on it which had been made by a hermit monk called St Killan, whose will was still extant in 1822 and was venerated by the people. The island was the home of numerous rabbits and Mr Martin had one hundred deer grazing there. After an hour's voyage, they landed on MacDara's Island. A bleak granite outcrop, it could support only four families in constant residency due to the meagre soil:

> For this privilege they pay £20 a year to a middleman who holds it from Mr. Martin – which rent they make out of the kelp thrown on its shore. Mr. Martin had never been on the island before and did not know that it was inhabited. These people are so wretchedly poor as not to possess fishing nets or even a boat to enable them to visit the neighbouring shore but are dependant solely on accident for their opportunity of doing so. Their habitations, which are built of stone without cement and covered with sods, are scarcely large enough to sleep in and not high enough to allow the inhabitants to stand upright in. They have neither door, window or chimney and the rain and wind comes in through the apertures in the walls and roof! And yet these people were healthy and robust, courteous and hospitable and apparently cheerful and contented with their situation.

Petrie goes on to discuss the remains of antiquity on the island, principally the saint's oratory and cell. He gives detailed measurements of the oratory, or Teampull MacDara, as it is called, and notices the 'antae' or buttresses on the gable end of the walls that make it such a distinctive building. He was told by the inhabitants of the various legends surrounding the saint's miraculous powers, and how his cross was regarded as a sacred relic of the highest order. Until recently, Petrie was told, they had his bell on the island also, but it was lost by sending it to Galway for some necessary repairs.

Towards evening they set out to return to Roundstone Bay: 'The wind had nearly died away, but the sea retained all its magnificent grandeur and the long line of the mountains catching the last rays of the sun, shone out in greater glory.' The crew provided them with something to make them more social, and entertained them with tales of their perilous adventures. They were shown an island where several of them had been driven a few years before and stranded for a fortnight, living on what Petrie calls 'delisk water' (water formed by condensation or deliquescence). Further on, the steers-

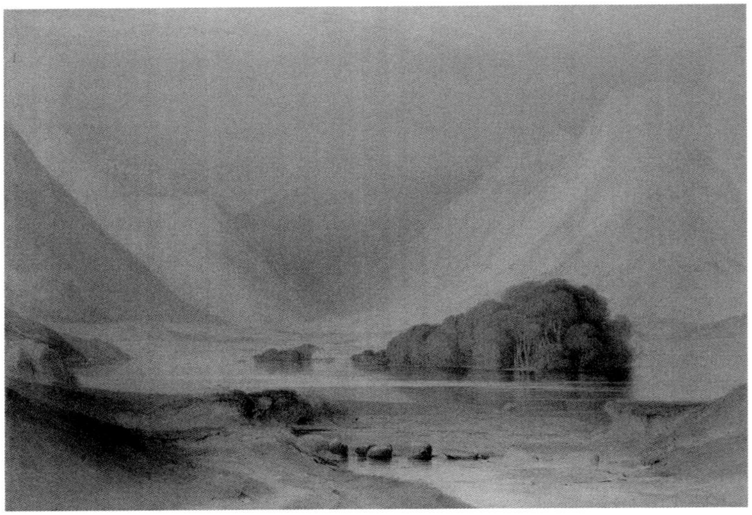

The Home of the Heron, Lough Atri ... Connemara – Evening
c.1845, watercolour on paper, 67 x 96 (coll: NGI, cat. no. 6871) (see colour plate p.34)

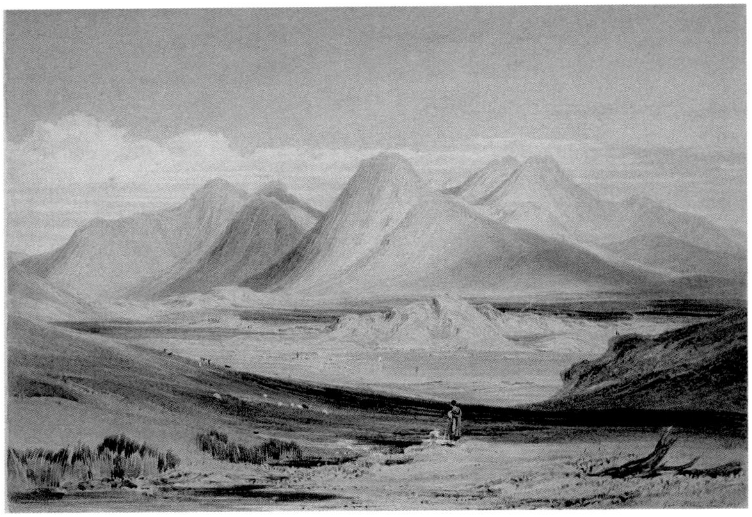

The Twelve Pins, Connemara, from the north head of Ballinakill Bay
1831, watercolour on paper, 29.4 x 41.1 (coll: NGI, cat. no. 6027)(see colour plate p.24)

man, who was the owner of the boat, pointed out the place where on the preceding summer, going with turf to Galway in company with another boar belonging to his friend, he saw it suddenly swallowed up by the breaker which he himself had just passed over. They were told that accidents of this kind were frequent in the perilous navigation of the Connemara coast. The sun sank beneath the horizon:

> As night closed in and conversation sank, the Captain's brother, as fine a Milesian looking fellow as himself, lulled with some of the most beautiful melodies of his country, which he murmured with a pathos that delighted all his listeners. While we were indulging ourselves in this pleasing tranquillity and admiring the crescent moon, which had lately got up, we were suddenly alarmed with a shot fired at us, which came, whirring across the water from we knew not where. 'Is there anyone killed or wounded?' was our first enquiry, naturally. None! Are we attacked by pirates? Or is it only an assault by water of Captain Rock? Alas, not so romantic – it was only a signal to lie to, sent by the water-guard, who, knowing that we had the king of Connemara on board, were making a vain display of vigilance by pretending to mistake us for smugglers! Except for this fright they gave us however, we had reason to be obliged to them, as by rowing us to shore they enabled us to get home some hours earlier than we should otherwise have done. Here we found our horses in readiness, and Mr. Martin, who was last mounted but best acquainted with the road, dashed off alone to remove any apprehension which our delay might cause at B. Castle, leaving us to tumble along in the dark among rocks and bog-holes, in which way we reached home about midnight.[185]

During his stay with the Martins at Ballinahinch, Petrie sketched the house and the surrounding countryside. These drawings are in the National Gallery of Ireland, as is one of his most ambitious later paintings, *The Home of the Heron*, the setting of which is Lough Atri and Glen Hoghan, on the far side of Ballinahinch Lake.[186] From Ballinahinch, Petrie and his friends struck northwards to Clifden and Renvyle. There is a pencil sketch in the NGI of *Clifden from the Road to the Castle*, probably taken at this time.[187] It is one of a large group of pencil sketches which were bequeathed to the gallery by Margaret Stokes in 1900. Very few are dated, but most of them are of identified scenes. Amongst the sketches are several views of the Twelve Pins or Beanna Beola, taken from various points along the coast,[188] and there is one finished watercolour showing a panoramic view of these beautiful mountains. Its restoration by the conservation department of the National Gallery in recent years shows that

Petrie's colouration is not so dull as is commonly believed; the purity and clarity of the colours is stunning. In Renvyle, the travellers continued their explorations of the islands off the coast, and one of their journeys, to the Crump Islands, is recorded in Stokes in another extract from the journals.[189] Apart from this, there is no further information on Petrie's tour of 1822.

There is yet another problem concerning the dates of Petrie's tours in the early 1820s. Uniacke, who had written to Petrie in 1822 arranging to meet him at Oughterard and informing him that they would be staying with Mr Martin of Ballinahinch, features again in the Petrie correspondence, this time in February of 1823. (The Uniacke family were from Mount Uniacke, in Co Waterford.) In the first of these later letters, dated 10 February 1823, Uniacke informs Petrie of his visit to High Island, off the coast of Connemara, and of his failure to find any inscriptions. He had learned from a 'gentleman who professes to have considerable information on the antiquities of this country' that it was inhabited by monks in the 6th century who were driven there by religious persecution. Uniacke hopes to visit it again with Petrie this summer, as well as many other such places, 'but should I happen to leave the country before your arrival I will direct you as far as I am able to what is best worth your attention, for, unlike Arran, you will get but little information here on the subject of antiquities.'[190] From this it would appear that Petrie was intending to visit the West again, for the third year running, and save for the fact that Uniacke's first letter to him is very definitely dated 1822, it would seem natural to assume that the tour of Connemara described in the preceding section in fact took place in 1823. Uniacke goes on to state that there were the remains of many churches along the coast, but that usually little more than the foundations were left, as the stones had been mostly carried away by the O'Flaherty's to build their castles. Two friends of the famous Mr O'Flaherty of Aran had been to see him and reported that the gentleman in question was in good health. They mentioned his having received a present from Petrie of a book by O'Mara, and how he was highly delighted with it. O'Flaherty, at Petrie's request, had commissioned a Mr French to write an account of the natural history of Aran, and this had been dispatched to Dublin. Uniacke rounds off his letter with a plea to Petrie for books and newspapers, even old ones, an appeal which bears out Petrie's comments on the scarcity of reading matter west of the Shannon.

> ...indeed you can have no conception what a treat a book is to me at present as the nearest conversable person is four miles from me & if you can occasionally send me an old newspaper when they happen to contain anything worth reading, you will lay me under great obligation.

Eleven days later, Uniacke wrote to Petrie to inform him that he was going to London, but he had arranged for Mr Martin of Ballinahinch to take care of Petrie if he came down to Connemara, and to offer him his house as his headquarters. Whether or not Petrie did make the journey is not known.[191]

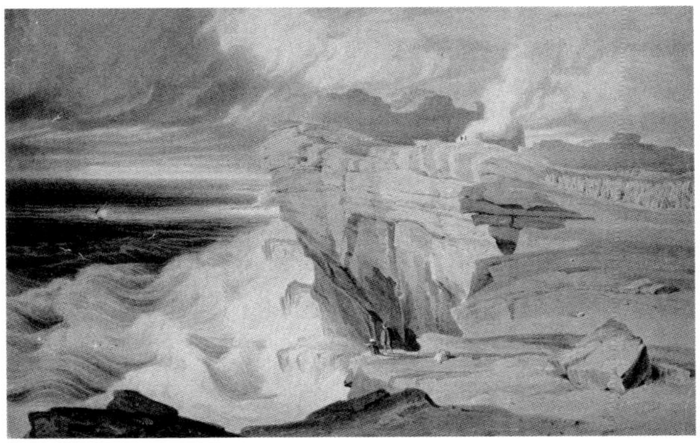

Dun Aengus Fort, Inismore, Aran Islands
*c.*1827, watercolour on paper, 29.8 x 46.4
(coll: NGI, cat. no. 7481) (see colour plate p.19)

Chapter V

The Accomplished Antiquary: Petrie and the Royal Irish Academy

Throughout his career, Petrie's interest in collecting antiquities ran parallel with his other pursuits. He rarely passed up the opportunity of acquiring anything that had the patina of age, and his tastes were catholic; his collection, at the time of his death, was one of the finest in Ireland. It included implements such as flint arrowheads, funerary urns from the Bronze Age and was particularly strong in material from the Early Christian and Medieval times, such as bells, chalices and crosses. One of the finest objects was the shrine of St Mogue, with its metalwork portrait of King David playing the harp. Petrie was fond of associating objects with particular saints, as attested by his 'Crozier of Cormac' or 'Staff of Murus'; he read a paper before the Academy, setting out the case for his assertion that a bell in his collection had actually belonged to St Patrick. The *Dublin University Magazine* described the scene:

> After the proofs had been given, and the antiquity and genuineness of the bell established, it was placed upon the table. 'And now, Mr. President,' said the owner, 'The Academy have the opportunity of hearing the very sounds which heralded the advent of Christianity to the Isle of Saints.' So saying, he struck the bell, which has a peculiarly sweet and silvery tone. The effect was electrical.[192]

During the early 1800s it was becoming more and more fashionable to form collections of antiquities; collections that would consist, in the main, of 'Danish stone hammers', bronze arrowheads, beads and the occasional urn. Gold ornaments were reserved for those who could afford them, and the trade in them was carried on to a great extent by jewellers. The great pity about these collections was that their owners were mainly concerned with acquiring objects that would form suitable exhibits for glass cases that stood in their libraries and studies, and they were uninterested in where the objects came from. Petrie himself played an important role in developing this interest, curating and commencing the cataloguing of the collection of antiquities at the Academy. Although Petrie was also compiling a catalogue of his own collection in the 1860s, this was never completed. After his death, his collection was acquired by the Royal Irish Academy. The bulk of these two collections is now in the National Museum of Ireland.

One of the most important items in Petrie's collection was the so-called 'Petrie Crown', now in the National Museum. Its origins are a mystery, which is a great pity, for it is probably the most significant piece of Iron Age La Tène metalwork, in artistic terms, to have been found in Ireland, but as it was never given the vaguest provenance by Petrie, it can form no part of discussions on the development of Celtic art, save as an object in its own right. This is common to nearly all the pieces in Petrie's collection; that he failed to record any details of their origin, or if he did, such records are lost. Considering the extremely high standard of his instructions to the Shannon Commissioners on the recording and treatment of objects found during their land drainages, it is odd that he did not follow such advice himself.[193] But, as will be seen, his collection was drawn from such diverse sources that it is probable that in many cases he himself was not aware of the circumstances of discovery of many of the artefacts. He bought indiscriminately from amateurs, jewellers, tinkers and antiquarians. He frequently exchanged articles with others, and was not reluctant to break up a collection of, say, coins, that had come into his hands from an original source.

Petrie kept in contact with an extended network of other private collectors, among them Edwin Wyndham-Quin (1812-1871), Viscount Adare, later 3rd Earl of Dunraven, who maintained estates in both Ireland and Wales and who became something of a disciple of Petrie's. At a conference of Welsh and Irish archaeologists held at Dunraven Castle at Bridgend in 1849, Petrie defended his assertion that cromlechs (dolmens) were funerary monuments, and not 'altars of the Druids', as was popularly believed.[194] Although the Dunraven title was Welsh, Wyndham-Quin was no absentee landlord. In addition to rebuilding Adare Manor in the Gothick style, he restored Adare village and several local churches. A keen archaeologist, he was not averse to removing to his museum at Adare interesting remains that took his fancy, including an ancient cross from Inis Cealtra (also known as Holy Island), on Lough Derg, Dunraven erroneously believed its inscription 'Oroit do Chunn' referred to a Quin ancestor. Years later, Petrie wrote to Adare: 'I should have written the Inis Ealtra inscription thus ... OROIT DO CHUNN meaning, a prayer for (the soul) of Choonn. I – think – the bungling way I wrote it is pretty conclusive evidence of that decay of mind to which I alluded?!'[195]

Another regular correspondent on the subject of antiquities was Levinge, who wrote to Petrie in 1826 on the matter of antiquities, offering to make them 'fair and square' by returning Greek and Roman coins, a bronze of the Last Supper and a ring which Petrie had got from John Daly, 'and, best of all, to be exempted from your importunity, would I believe tempt me to sign, seal and deliver the Seal'.[196] This seal was presumably the great seal of Henry II that Petrie had in his collection in 1839.[197] In return, Levinge asked that Petrie execute a likeness of his nephew, Jack Somers, of whom he had a good cast: 'You will undertake it, and not as a thank 'ye matter.' Levinge rounds off in his usual style:

> 'Show me your Ultimatum madam', said the man in the play; 'I show you my ultimatum!' declared the indignant lady, 'What do you take me for, Sir?' – Dear fellow worshipper of ant(in)iquity, [sic] you have seen mine, and so, that it may not seem that I wish to whet you, I shall conclude without saying a word of how good a bargain it appears to me is offered you; of how much more I would exact from any other person than you (excepting one); or of what is to be the fate of the Seal should you say 'No' in answer to my proposal, and thus agreeably disappoint me, for really, I fear you may accept it; but being bound to give you a preference I must run the risk.[198]

Coins, medals and seals formed only a part of Petrie's interest in antiquities. Nine months earlier, the collector J. Bell of Dungannon had written to him and sent him, along with two 'rude arrowheads' and the inscription from an old bell, the pattern from an ancient shoe. Bell transcribes a description of the shoes written by the Reverend Dr Malcolm of Newry.[199] Bell had several such shoes in his possession, they were usually found in turf-cutting. In 1840, an R.H. Gordon wrote to Petrie to tell him of a slipper found in a bog near Bellaghly, at a depth of twelve feet. The man who discovered it would not touch it at other than spade's length, and the other inhabitants fled on seeing it, saying that it was the fairies' property. 'The article is at present in the possession of a foolish pedantical little fellow – a kind of hedge schoolmaster, who holds onto it like a vice – or as he says himself, is "resolved" to keep it – nothing else.'[200] The shoe was tattooed all over with what looked like legible characters, but Gordon was ignorant of the Irish language and was unable to say. The schoolmaster obviously realised its true value.

Elected a member of the Royal Irish Academy in 1828, Petrie was appointed to its Council two years later, as a member of the Committee of Antiquities. His first move was to collect together the antiquities, presented by various donors (including the King of Denmark) and place them in glass cases in the Round Room of the Academy house. These antiquities had previously been stored on the floor of room in the upper storey of the building. Petrie reckoned that nearly one half of them, and the best at that, had disappeared since he had first seen them a few years previously. Petrie also at this time initiated the formation of a library and organised glass cases for books to be placed in one of the council rooms, to receive the valuable manuscripts that the Academy possessed.[201]

The story of how the Academy came into possession of these manuscripts is a record, in many cases, of triumph against the odds, and selflessness on the part of its members. In 1831 the library of Mr Austin Cooper which had originally belonged to Colonel Burton Conyngham, was offered for sale. At his request, the sum of £50 was placed at the disposal of Petrie and Mr D'Alton for the purpose of buying several works for the Academy's manuscript collection. Stokes' account of this auction, and of Petrie's coup at the end of the sale in procuring at a very low price the Annals of the Four Masters is recounted in a history of the Royal Irish Academy, which he (Stokes) was writing in 1852.[202] In his own words:

> Further, Dr Petrie, having at the same sale purchased on his

> own account, the autograph copy of the second half of the Annals of the Four Masters, which he was enabled to do owing to the ignorance of the English agents sent over with unlimited authority to buy all the manuscripts in that collection ... though immediately on its becoming known in the sale room what the MS was, he was offered, in the first instance, one hundred pounds over the purchase money by Mr. Cochrane the agent of Mr. Thos Phillips, and subsequently pressed to name any sum that would induce him to resign it.[203]

Petrie declined these approaches and offered the Annals of the Four Masters to the RIA, for the price he had paid. On the motion of Dr William West, Petrie was subsequently made a life member of the Academy in recognition of this act of altruism. Other manuscripts were acquired in rapid succession – the collection of the Chevalier O'Gorman, the state papers of James II in the Southwell collection, the collection of Sir William Betham, and lastly, in 1844, the fine collection of Hodges & Smith, the publishers. Among the manuscripts in the Hodges & Smith collection was the 11th to 13th century *Book of the Dun Cow* (*Lebor na hUidhre*). Stokes, in his manuscript history of the Academy, goes on to relate how the Academy began to build up a large collection of printed books through mutual exchange with other societies and through purchase. An allowance of £1,000 was placed at the disposal of the Council, half of which was spent on books on science, £350 on literature, and the remainder, £150, on books relating to the history and antiquities of Ireland. On Petrie's motion this latter grant was raised by £200.

Stokes records how Petrie induced Mr Underwood to place a small but valuable collection of antiquities for sale to the Academy in 1837. This was the first material addition to the museum since the King of Denmark had donated the small collection of stone weapons and implements, which Petrie had gathered together. Underwood was paid £73.10s for his collection. But a letter in the Adare Papers written by Underwood almost twenty years later hints that all was not plain sailing:

> Dr. Petrie, I regret to say that on many occasions you have opposed whenever I troubled you to offer many objects of antiquarian interest to the council of the Royal Irish Academy and as I always was of opinion that you were the only member of that council who really took an interest in the possessing and saving from destruction the neglected mementoes of the fallen greatness I am therefore indebted to you and most heartily sorry for having ... incurred your displeasure. But I am a very poor man and anxious to seek some market where these relics will be more thought of and appreciated...'[204]

In 1839 Professor MacCullagh proposed that Petrie should be sent down to Cong to negotiate the purchase of the Cross of Cong on behalf of the Academy. Petrie's account of his seeing the cross on his journey in the West in 1822 has already been given. For some reason, however, Petrie felt afraid of entering into negotiations, and he suggested that George Smith should go instead. Smith was often sent on missions of this kind, and it comes as no surprise to learn that he secured it for £100.

In February of that same year, Petrie exhibited the 'Tara Torques' to the Academy at a meeting and proposed that they should be purchased by subscription. To this end, the inimitable George Smith held a social evening in his home, to which members of the Academy were invited; most of them not realising the true purpose of the event. The subject of the subscription was brought up and it was proposed that the gentlemen present should take the initiative. MacCullagh headed the list by putting in £10; Callwell followed with a similar sum, and all the gentlemen, realising the trap into which they had been led, could do nothing but cough up their contributions. On 24 June, the torques were presented by Petrie to the Academy, along with the names of those who had been present at what must have proved a most expensive night out. The Cross of Cong was presented that same evening. Some artefacts Petrie kept; the Cashel Crozier, in the form of a serpent's head curving around a man fighting a dragon, was discovered in the tomb of Cormac McCarthy in Cormac's Chapel. After years in the possession of Austin Cooper, it was passed on to Joseph Cooper Walker, author of *Memoirs of the Irish Bards*. Dr Tuke then acquired it for his museum and from there it entered Petrie's collection.[205] Petrie also had 'in my own cabinet' the crozier of the 'virgin and martyr Damhnad Ochene'.[206]

Stokes gives some interesting background information on the acquisition of the superb museum of Dean Dawson. Petrie and the dean were good friends; in 1833 they went together on a steamer excursion to Iona.[207] Dawson had formed his collection with the help and advice of Petrie, with the ultimate intention of presenting it to the Academy – in fact, he had several times advised Petrie to get glass cases into the Academy house in order to receive the exhibits.[208] Caesar Otway, however, advised Petrie not to rush the matter too much as the Dean was collecting at such a rate that any delay could only prove of benefit to the Academy; as the Dean would not have such an interest in enlarging the collection once it was out of his hands. This little plan misfired badly when the good Dean died in the summer of 1840, intestate; without having presented the collection, leaving the Academy with no claim other than that which they could put to the Dean's wife on the grounds of her husband's intentions. She and her family, however, seem to have been neglected at the expense of the Dean's museum, and as Stokes puts it, they were in 'circumstances which did not justify their making so great a sacrifice as the gift of the museum would be'.[209] Nevertheless, the 'high-minded widow' did wish that her husband's intentions would come to fruition, and she resisted some of her husband's relations who were proposing that the collection be sent to London and sold, where they believed it would fetch better prices than in Ireland. She offered to sell it to the Academy at their valuation, which duty she entrusted to Aguilla Smith and Petrie. There was a delay of several months before proceeding as she was away on the Continent and was unavailable. Smith valued the coins in the collection; Petrie the other antiquities, and their final tally came to £1,060. On 27 March 1841, the Committee authorised Petrie and Smith to offer £1,000 (the 6% reduction, they explained, was just that which would have been expended in a public auction on expenses). Mrs Dawson accepted the offer on 26 June. The subscription that the Committee had raised was moving too slowly, however, and Petrie was requested by Mr Carr (who was acting on the Committee of Antiquities as Mrs Dawson's personal friend) to take over the raising of the money. Petrie recircularised the members and others, and was successful in getting them to pay up, so much so, that when the deal was concluded, there was over £24 left in the fund. The first installment of £500 was paid on 9 April 1842, and the collection was brought soon afterwards to the Academy house. On 31 May the remainder was paid.[210]

In the course of formulating a systematic approach to the study of the antiquities of Europe during the Stone, Bronze and Iron Ages, Jens Jacob Asmussen Worsaae (1821-1885), the famous Danish archaeologist, travelled extensively around Europe, visiting sites and excavations. Stokes mentions the visit of Worsaae to the home of the MacDonalds on the Isle of Skye, which took place a few years before Petrie himself visited the same house in 1846. Worsaae did not know Petrie personally at that stage, but the two men were familiar with each other's work.[211] Worsaae was back in Scotland himself that year, staying as the guest of Mr Chalmers (another friend of Petrie's), at Auldbar Castle in Brechin. He had been given a letter of introduction to Petrie by Thomson, curator of the National Museum of Denmark, and he wrote to him, saying that he wished to meet 'the first antiquary in Ireland'. Petrie, he knew, was planning to visit Scotland that year, and as Worsaae wished to go to Dublin in the near future he wanted to ensure that he did not miss Petrie.[212] In his reply, Petrie stated that he would be in Ireland for some time, so here was no hurry for Worsaae, who decided to stay on at Brechin at the request of Mr Chalmers. At the beginning of November, Worsaae moved to Edinburgh to continue his researches, and after spending about ten days there went on to Glasgow. He wrote to Petrie:

> If I not against my will should be detoured, I hope to be in Dublin one of the first days next week, when I soon after my arrival shall take me the liberty to call upon you. I am very anxious to see the Irish antiquities.[213]

Worsaae did in fact come to Dublin and meet Petrie, early in 1847. He spoke at the Academy and promulgated the Three Age System with Thomson had devised and which was gaining acceptance all over Europe at this time. Worsaae made Petrie promise that he would prepare all his archaeological drawings for publication in a popular work in the near future:

> I cannot too often repeat how much we antiquaries expect of you, and how much you must do for Ireland and for yourself. You know my ideas about the popular works upon the antiquities of Ireland. When will you commence? By all means do it as soon as possible. It won't cost you much trouble and it will be of the greatest value for other people. The cleverest men here commence to see that Antiquities and National History will in Ireland be a good substitute for your eternal political quarrels.[214]

Worsaae had spoken to Petrie about his plans to set up a museum in opposition to the British Museum, but he describes the idea as a 'loose' one. Evidently there was a common feeling between the two men, as antiquarians of the Northern school of archaeology. Worsaae wanted to organise a meeting of European antiquaries, and he asked Petrie to visit Denmark as soon as possible. Seven months later, in October 1847, at a general meeting of the Royal Society of Northern Antiquaries, held in Copenhagen, Petrie was unanimously elected a Fellow of this important body.

The story of how the country was scoured by clergy and antiquarians for ancient artefacts casts some interesting light on the social history of the period. The Cross of Cong, which has been mentioned, is a case in point. George Smith, who was to go down to Cong to negotiate the purchase of this magnificent reliquary, was informed by M. Waldron (who was writing from Cong) that the local inhabitants would not part with the cross under any circumstances:

> They actually got furious at the very thought of it; with all their poverty they offered to make up the sum offered for it without delay, tho' the only commodity the greater part of them have at present for market is the potato and mind not enough of that root for the year's supply, they also before they separated got into a subscription to create a fund to have it sent to Dublin to have it repaired and cleaned and to have any of the pebbles that have been lost replaced by new ones.[215]

So enthusiastic were the feelings of the population toward any relics of the Abbey at Cong that they were also proposing to buy back the 'Tooth of Patrick' (*Fiacal Pádraig*), which had been sold to William Stokes, who had deposited it in the Academy. However, in spite of all these efforts to retain the last vestiges of the splendour of Cong in olden times, George Smith does not seem to have had too much difficulty in procuring the cross the next year for £100 for the Academy.

An even more remarkable case was where Charles Ligar in 1836 tracked down an old bell to the house of the McGuirk family in Dungannon. The bell was said to have been given to the old church of Termon, in the parish of Termonnaguirk, Co Tyrone, by St Columb and afterwards to have been stolen and taken to Scotland:

> They say it was seen again in a small stream near the church with a light shining about it and that the light disappeared to everyone until a man of this McGuirk family came near and picked up the bell. Since which it has been held by that family who are now in the habit of lending it for a ten-penny piece with a pound or guinea deposited for its safe return. When a person suspects another of having stolen anything, the bell is procured and the suspected party are desired to swear by kissing he bell and it is said that great miracles and punishments have been shown on such as dared to swear false.[216]

Ligar was obviously intending to pay the fee and the deposit and abscond with the bell, but some of the McGuirks suspected as much and refused to give it to him. Others of the family disagreed and eventually a fight broke out amongst them and they came to blows. Ligar managed to break up the fight but in the confusion one of the women made off with the bell and hid it, so in the end he could not even get a drawing of it. He describes it as being half eaten away with rust, and says that in Irish it was called *Clog na Deealta*, or the Bell of the Avenging Spirit.

Another old bell that Petrie mentions was in the possession of a Major Nesbitt, an avid collector of old coins and antiquities. Lord George Hill offered to buy it from him, on behalf of the Dean of St Patrick's, for the sum of two cows! – 'quite in the old Irish style'.[217] Eight years later, in 1843, the bell is mentioned again, when Petrie advised Lord Adare, who was planning a trip to Donegal, to look in on Major Nesbitt near Glencolmcille and see the bell. The bell was called St Conald Keel's Bell, and it had been preserved on the island of Inishkeel until Nesbitt had acquired it. Also on the island was the church and holy well of the saint. Petrie advised Adare to be on the lookout for other relics; the bell of St Columba for example, which had been stolen from Tory island by a tinker at the beginning of the century; also the 'Red Stone' of St Colmcille, which was carried by the O'Rahans, the Earnachs, or hereditary keepers.[218] A month later, Petrie wrote to congratulate Adare on acquiring an ancient relic, the reliquary of St Molaise. He was at pains to assure Adare that, although he had heard of its existence before, he had not concealed the knowledge from him with a view to acquiring it himself at some later date, but merely because Walker, his informant, had asked him to remain silent about it:

> I first heard of its existence many years ago, from a curious report of a petty sessions trial in the Co. of Sligo, in which this was brought forward to swear a witness upon it, whose oath on the printed, or nay other gospels, would not be valued! After this I spoke to my friend Walker about it, and he told me that he had 'spotted it' – and begged me to be silent.

> And so from being silent for years – on his account – I actually forgot it myself.[219]

This was not the only reliquary in which Walker had an interest. A square saint's bell which was used for swearing on in the barony of Leyny had come to his notice, and he had offered the old woman who had it the sum of £5 in order to purchase it. But the old woman, who was going to accept this offer, died, and the bell was rapidly acquired by a third party. It seems that the bell had originally been borrowed by the old woman, who had paid the owner the usual deposit of thirty shillings for it. She had never returned it, and it was he that had acquired it upon her death. Although Walker was a close confidant of Petrie's in these matters, he would not tell him of the bell's whereabouts, for fear that Petrie would get it first. The bell in question was called the 'Bell of Maine', Maine being a disciple of St Patrick's.[220] The same J. Bell of Dungannon who had written to Petrie on the subject of ancient shoes in 1826, reappears over thirty years later, when Thomas Tennison wrote to Petrie on his behalf:

> Mr. Bell of Dungannon has been staying with me during the last two days. We have had much conversation on Antiquarian subjects & he has been disposing of a large portion of his collection to English and Scotch purchasers. The most valuable portion however, including The Bells are still in his possession & I should certainly much regret their being lost to the country to which they belong. I hope therefore that you will kindly excuse the liberty I take in suggesting that before it is too late, such steps as may be considered advisable should be taken, so as to secure them for the RI Academy.[221]

One of Petrie's most assiduous collector friends was a Mr Anthony, who lived in Piltown House, about seven miles south of New Ross on the river Barrow. Anthony would go to great lengths to procure antiquities for his 'private museum', and he both sent and received antiquities from Petrie, such as crescent-shaped gold gorgets, leaden coins, tea-pots, an old Irish bow – in fact anything that remotely resembled an antique was fair game. One article he sent for Petrie's inspection was a fibulae:

> ...a gentleman had bought it off a sea-faring looking man in Cork and seeing it was a curious looking thing asked its use – when the man said it passed as money – in Africa or South America or some other place, I forget, but think it the first place. However be it as it may, whether he told a lie or not I don't know. But this I know it looks from its form very like an Irish fibulae...[222]

Although Anthony over the years built up quite a considerable collection of antiquities, he did not consider himself to be a true antiquarian. He thought he had as much claim to the title as 'the fellow whom, blowing the bellows, thought he play'd the organ'.[223] He had a bog-oak case in which he kept his gold ornaments, and he describes some of the treasures he had acquired. One was what is now known as a sun-disc, which he had purchased in Cork and paid £1.10s for, at the rate of £20 per ounce, which was very expensive he thought, but he justifies the expenditure:

> The truth is one can't expect a rare article light in weight at the same rate as fibulae, collars, torques etc., which are beyond everybody's money, and few purchase, from their great weight. It's all chance when other wise. They are so shewey in any museum that he would have got his price for them.

Anthony had brought another two sun-discs in Enniscorthy, both of which weighed nearly half an ounce and were three inches across. He describes them as being ruder than other ones he had seen and thus he infers that they must be of greater antiquity. They were found 'near a great stone cross (X) within half a mile of Kilmutesioge, Co. Wexford...' He paid twelve guineas an ounce for them and said that he was lucky to get them as a Jew in Dublin named Lazarus had made an offer for them, and others had asked the vendor to name his price.

Sometimes the methods used by collectors to acquire valuable pieces were less than honest – in one or two cases it was nothing less than larceny. As will be seen, the religious nature of many of the antiquities meant that they were unlikely to be given up easily by the people in whose possession they had been for generations. When a close friend of Petrie's, William Wakeman, was in Kerry, he came up against an instance of this. While he was travelling around and sketching ancient monuments, he arrived at Ballyaughtra and enquired for a Mr Purse, with whom Burton had stayed on his travels in Kerry. But when he arrived at Purse's house, he found it in 'great disorder' and Purse told him that he would be unable to take him in. The reason for this was that the previous week Purse had been badly beaten and had one pound in silver taken from him by three men. He was certain that it had not been strangers to the area, but locals, who had attacked him, and he was sure that the attack had been prompted by revenge, as he was suspected by the neighbours of having been one of a party that 'had carried away an ancient chalice from one of the Blasquets'. Wakeman does not make any comment on the veracity of this claim.[224]

Other friends of Petrie were more practical in their approach; especially a Mr Lloyd, who describes himself as 'an old guardian friend' of Petrie's. He was writing an account of an excavation he and a friend undertook on a barrow near Roscommon, which was about twenty feet high and seventy feet in diameter. His account is interesting in as much as it reveals that while their main objective in undertaking the excavation, which had been prompted by the discovery of old armour in the area, was the uncovering of a burial rich in grave goods, and when this hope was not realised they just did not regard the project as a failure and leave it at that. Lloyd provides Petrie with a detailed account of the stratigraphy of the shaft which had been dug by six workmen in four days. They were unable to complete the excavation to their satisfaction because of the crumbly nature of the sand through which they were digging, so the shaft at the bottom measured only three feet by two.

> The few things we observed were interesting – the first two feet of the cone were without any remains, then came a layer of small stones under which about five feet of animalised material lying east to west occurred, of such a distant date that all the larger bones were perfectly decomposed, nothing except their line remaining. A prodigious number of teeth with a few flat bones, which were protected by stones from the percolation of the rain, escaped, and enabled us to ascertain that only horses and dogs were interred in this part of the mound. Among these fragments we met the long under jaw of a grey hound, also a fowl's thighbone – possibly a hawk's. Next we came down on an irregular pile of stones the lowest layer of which consisted of very large ones, requiring much labour to displace. These covered a quantity of ashes indicating a fire of excessive intensity, as the stones occurring in them were reduced to lime. Here we also met with teeth in great number, but they were those of sheep, swine and deer and if I be not mistaken, also some long bones, apparently preserved by having been boiled, and showing marks of the butcher's saw. Also several pounds weight of melted brass and nails on which the fire had produced no effect. No human bones were anywhere visible, and in the lowest part of the mound we detected nothing whatever.[225]

The antiquarians and Protestant clergy were not the only people with an interest in taking these sacred relics out of the hands of the country folk. Arthur Nugent told Petrie of a relic called 'St Patrick's hand', which the Roman Catholic bishop Dr Denvir had recently acquired:

> ...he purchased it for seven pounds and as I think he bought it more to take a superstitious bauble out of the country than for any particular fancy for it, I should think that if the Society made a pressing application for it he would fill it. If he would only have a curiosity to take a peep inside the silver case he would find, instead of the arm of our patron saint, a tough piece of beech or other hard wood.[226]

Another important antiquity that Petrie was responsible for bringing into the collection of the Academy was the reliquary called the *Domhnach airgid*. Petrie had read a paper on it to the Academy in October of 1832, and a second one in January 1837. He had become aware of its existence in Co Monaghan in 1831, and suggested to the Dean of St Patrick's that he should try and purchase it. The Dean did try, but failed. Stokes, in his account, glosses over these transactions, stating that 'it was secured, for a comparatively small sum, by a friend, who offered it to Petrie at cost price. Having discovered its great value, he generously declined the offer, and it was finally purchased by Mr Westenra, afterwards Lord Rossmore, for three hundred pounds, with the view of preserving it to the country'.[227] However, in his manuscript of this account, Stokes identifies the 'friend' as none other than George Smith, whose capabilities as a procurer of antiquities in the face of all opposition begin to seem unlimited. One can only wonder at that methods he must have used, to succeed where both Petrie and Dean Dawson had failed. However he managed it, Smith did succeed in obtaining the reliquary at a price well below its true value, which was discovered by Petrie a few days after it had come into Smith's possession. It was on Petrie's recommendation that Westenra purchased the reliquary from Smith for £300, but what the original purchase price was is not known. Westenra asked Petrie to communicate to the Academy that he would be willing to surrender it at any time for the money he had paid, but it was over fourteen years before any action was taken, and when it was, it came from an individual within the Academy. Professor MacCullagh finally decided that he would buy the *Domhnach airgid* himself and try and recoup the money from a subscription raised amongst the members of the Academy. At this stage, however, Westenra quite rightly felt no longer bound by his promise of so many years previous, and the sum that was eventually settled on is not disclosed. The folklorist Thomas Crofton Croker wrote to Petrie from Gloucester Road in London in 1835, firing off a string of questions mainly relating to beads and stone arrowheads and offering to assist Petrie in his cataloguing of the Academy's collection:

> I can only in return to these enquiries offer you any information that it is in my power to afford; merely mentioning that during his absence from Ireland Sir Edward Belcher has placed in my hands his very extraordinary Collection of Stone implements mady many years ago among the Esquimeaux, and that I possess some important illustrations from Persia, Marathon, the Cape of Good Hope, North America, the Caribbean Islands, Patagonia, the Island in the Pacific, Mexico, California, New Zealand and Scotland; particularly as to the mode of manufacture, fixing use, and even relative value as matters of barter.[228]

The last major purchase that the Academy was to make was at the close of 1843, when the Reverend J. D'A. Sirr offered his father's collection of antiquities to the Academy for £400. On 16 March in the following year it was agreed to pay £350, cancel his arrears, and make him a life member, in exchange for the collection. From this time onwards, the annual grant of £50 was used for the occasional purchase, but the Shannon Commissioners and the Commissioners of the Board of Works engaged in drainage schemes, donated massive collections of antiquities to the Academy, which more than compensated for their lack of buying power.[229]

But what became of Petrie's influence? There is, in the National Library, an undated letter from Petrie to Lord Adare, which gives an insight into his involvement in the Academy in later years. Petrie informs his lordship that he had recently moved into a new residence, which he describes as 'cheerful and salubrious'. The move was apparently only made possible through the generosity of his friends; whether this was due to his own poverty is unknown, but he reckoned that it was the saving of his daughter's life. This was probably the move from Great Charles Street to Fortesque Terrace in Rathmines (He addresses his letters 67 Rathmines Road), which took place in 1850. Petrie talks of the state of affairs in the museum of the Royal Irish Academy, a state that gave no reason for optimism. He informs Adare, 'between you and me', that he is the only person in the Academy with any interest in antiquities,

> ...and my influence, which was powerful for many a long year, when men did not make any pretension to knowledge on such matters, has been long on the wane, and is now utterly annihilated. Do I regret this? Not a jot on my own account, but I do very much deplore on account of the Academy and the Country for I see clearly what will be the end of it.[230]

He believes that only one article in fifty that comes on the market now gets into the Academy. 'Almost every man on the Committee thinks he knows more than the old teacher, whose day is gone by.' He believes that the other members now look on his ardour as folly, but they take the 'Curator's cold indifference as wisdom'. Petrie insists that ardour is as necessary as wisdom, and now that his influence has been checked, the museum will progress miserably – objects were passing out of the country daily that should have been finding their way into the museum. In fact, things are in such a bad way that Petrie goes so far as to say that he would even be prepared to welcome Betham onto the Committee, in spite of all his foolishness about the Phoenician origin of the Irish.

Chapter VI

Little Back Parlour in Great Charles St: The Ordnance Survey in Ireland

During the years 1824 and 1825, Petrie continued his work of drawing and painting, buying and selling antiquities, and settling into a family life in Great Charles Street, a life of tranquility that was to be shattered by the arrival of the entire Topographical Department of the Ordnance Survey into his house, for in 1824 a decision was made that was to profoundly influence the rest of Petrie's life. A Committee of the House of Commons made a recommendation that a townland survey of Ireland on the scale of six inches to the mile be commenced immediately by the Army Ordnance Corps. (Army Ordnance meaning in this case the stores and equipment section of the army rather than the artillery proper.) The numerous officers and men of the Ordnance were not overworked in peacetime and they had all the necessary instruments for the job, for the survey of Great Britain was at that time being undertaken under the direction of Colonel Colby, and it was generally accepted that sooner or later it would be extended to Ireland. When the Duke of Wellington consented to the recommendations of the committee, he set in motion a work that was to grow to huge proportions over the next decade, encompassing not only cartography, but also the geology, economics, history and antiquities of Ireland; a work that was to grow so large as to become a political force in its own right, and that was to be terminated prematurely, cut off at its peak amidst bitterness and acrimony. The men who were to work on this great project were mainly English. As J. H. Andrews points out in his definitive history of the early years of the Irish Ordnance Survey, *A Paper Landscape*, there was a heavy bias against the employment of Irishmen:

> The Marquis of Wellesley declared in 1824 that the proposed survey could not be carried out by Irish personnel, 'Neither science, not skill, nor diligence, not discipline, nor integrity, sufficient for such a work can be found in Ireland.'[231]

Three companies of sappers were specially raised for the purpose of providing personnel and in a short time the actual work of surveying was under way. The survey had initially been undertaken with a view to establishing a uniform valuation for county and local rates, but the maps, when completed, were found to be so accurate that the valuation could proceed by farm and holding, instead of townland. This accuracy had not been achieved without a great deal of attention to detail. The survey teams had started in the northern counties and as they moved south, their increasing expertise and experience resulted in marvellous detail and accuracy in the later maps.[232]

Andrews details the setting up of the Topographical Department, of which Petrie was to be appointed superintendent. Its original purpose was to provide correct spelling of names for the six-inch maps, but this was later extended to providing historical data from memoirs to accompany the maps. In 1826, Captain Larcom of the Royal Engineers was attached to the Irish Survey, and in 1828 he was appointed director of the central office at Mountjoy Barracks in the Phoenix Park, where the headquarters of the present Ordnance Survey are still located. He was responsible for some far-reaching reforms in the treatment of place names, though here he was hampered by the fact that much of the material came form Richard Griffith's Boundary Department, a source outside ordnance jurisdiction. Griffith was the only one of the original map-makers who succeeded in getting a part in the new survey. By December 1830 he recorded that there were nineteen young men, graduates of the Drawing Schools, employed under his supervision in the Boundary Department of the Survey.

Larcom had initially held the Engineer officers responsible for establishing the place names, but they were not trained for this sort of work. He established as official policy the practice of retaining the name closest to the original Irish descriptive name, when presented with several different versions of the same name. To achieve this, qualified linguists had to be sent into the field to hear the names pronounced and interpreted by residents, and to study them in the context of local topography and antiquities; also historical documents were to be used to supplement the place-names books. And so, the Topographical Department was created, to correlate names from the questionnaires (or 'Inquisitions', as they were called) that were sent out to landowners, the Down Survey, the books of survey and distribution and other documents. But Larcom's major innovation was the idea of compiling a memoir for each parish in Ireland. These memoirs would contain information that would complement the maps – information on the geography, natural products, history and antiquities, economic state and social conditions of the areas delineated on the six-inch map. What Stokes calls 'This great and comprehensive thought, this truly imperial idea' was the rock on which Larcom would eventually founder.

On 12 July 1833 Colonel Colby wrote to Sir William Gosset at the treasury, describing the proposal for the printing of a memoir. He explained that the maps alone would be insufficient and that the compiling of such a memoir as would show information that could not be given on the maps would give the officers employed a greater incentive to achieve perfection in their work, apart from boosting the sales of the maps. Colby had already made preliminary arrangements with Hodges & Smith for the printing and publishing of the memoir (they had already been appointed agents for the sale of the maps). Hodges & Smith were to employ competent artists to illustrate the work, and they would print it at a charge of £100 for each number. The numbers were to consist of six sheets, so that three or four numbers would make a moderate sized octavo volume. They would deliver to the Government 1,500 impressions of each number – and they would ensure that no others were printed. They would also undertake to sell the work at 2s.6d a copy; the Government would allow them the usual 35% on each sale. Colby reckoned that under this arrangement the whole of the Derry memoir (the first that was to be printed) would cost no more than £400 or £500.[233] On 8 August, this proposal was sanctioned by the Treasury – but purely on an experimental basis, and any future publications were dependant on the success of the Derry memoir. Andrews points out that this backing from the treasury was probably a result of the interest of the Chancellor of the Exchequer, Thomas Spring Rice, in the affair. Spring Rice was an Irishman, and he himself had, nine years earlier, led a campaign for a general cartographic survey of Ireland.[234]

It is difficult to date the actual commencement of Petrie's employment in the Survey. Although Larcom states at one stage that it was in 1835, there are letters from Larcom to Petrie relating to the memoir that date back to August 1833.[235] Petrie was appointed head of the Topographical Department. This department he located, not in the Phoenix Park with the rest of the Survey's offices, but in his own home in Great Charles Street, so that the staff would be closer to the libraries they needed for their researches. William Frederick Wakeman, the artist and friend of Petrie's, was employed there, describes the scene:

> How well do I recollect my first sketching journey, when employed on the intended ordnance memoir. Dr Petrie was the head of that particular department of the survey to which I was attached. In the little back parlour in Great Charles-street we used to meet daily; by we, I mean John O'Donovan, Eugene Curry, Clarence Mangan, P. O'Keeffe, J. O'Connor, besides two or three more. The duty of the office was to collect every possible information, antiquarian or topographical, about that particular portion of the country, which was at the time being surveyed. All sorts of old documents were examined, old spellings of names compared and considered. O'Donovan and Curry, even then the first Celtic scholars of the age, settled the orthography of the towns, villages, baronies, or other divisions of land, so that the ordnance maps might be as correct, in a literary sense, as they undoubtedly were as surveys. At that time Petrie's great work on the 'Ecclesiastical Architecture of Ireland' as also his admirable essay on the 'Antiquities of Tara Hill' were being completed. Indeed we lived in such an atmosphere of antiquarianism, that a thousand years ago seemed as familiar to us as the time when we first donned breeches. For my own part, I felt as if I has a personal acquaintance with Niall of the Nine Hostages, or Con of the Hundred Battles (or bottles, as poor Mangan humorously misstyled the hero), or with Loegaire, who would not mind the exhortations of Saint Patrick, but insisted on being interred, sword in hand, in his rath at Tara, with his face turned to the east, as bidding defiance to the men of

> Leinster. Petrie, as head of the office, superintended everything; and the mass of antiquarian and topographical information collected far exceeded the expectations of the most sanguine.[236]

To say that Petrie was in charge of the Topographical Department meant effectively that he was fully responsible for the work of that section. He enjoyed a great deal of autonomy and was answerable only to Larcom himself. Assisted by the scholars that Wakeman names, Petrie collected material from all over the country and drew up the sections on history, antiquities and topography that were to be included in his memoirs. In the summer, the scholars, O'Donovan, O'Curry and the others, were sent into the field to identify the names of places and correct them from pronunciations on the spot. In the winter months when fieldwork was impossible they gathered in the back-parlour in Petrie's house to collate the material. Petrie had no annual salary while he was employed on the survey; neither had any of the others. They were paid only for the days they worked, which excluded Sundays and holidays. During this time, Petrie did not entirely neglect his artistic pursuits. In a biographical notice in the *Dublin University Magazine* in 1839, the writer observes:

> Neither has the pencil been altogether abandoned; the easel may still be seen occasionally in his study, and if we are not deceived, our next exhibition will show that a recent tour into Joyce Country [Connemara] has not been without its proper fruits.[237]

However, Stokes claims that Petrie's zeal for the furtherance of such great designs 'caused him in a great measure to forsake his profession as a painter' and throw himself fully into the work of the Survey. That he did so is evident from the amount of work that was done in the years following the decision to proceed with the memoir. The summer of 1833 found Petrie in Dungiven with Larcom, collecting material and writing. Their work was impeded by Petrie having a bad fall and suffering internal bruising which left him sick and fevered in bed. O'Keeffe was meant to have accompanied them, but he never turned up, much to Larcom's annoyance, who said he was convinced O'Keeffe's mind was not right.[238] At this stage they were beginning to start work on the Antrim memoir, having completed most of the field research for the Derry volume.[239] Both William Stokes and Samuel Ferguson supplied information to the Survey on historical matters; Stokes finished a report on Dungiven in late 1833, and Ferguson wrote the history of Coleraine and its plantation.[240] Ferguson became friendly with Petrie at this time; he met the scholars working on the survey in Petrie's house, and so became acquainted with O'Donovan, Curry and Mangan.[241]

Earlier that year, in March, when O'Donovan had been in the North, walking the parishes and collecting information on place names, he had come up against some religious intolerance. Introduced by MacCaughey, the celebrated Belfast naturalist, to a Captain Garner, who lived in the townland of Ballymaghan, O'Donovan chatted away quite amicably to him on the subject of antiquities until Garner discovered in the course of the conversation that O'Donovan was a Catholic, whereupon he refused to talk to him further. O'Donovan shrugged off the incident; presumably he had come up against that sort of bigotry before.[242]

By February 1834 the maps of Derry and Antrim had been printed and Larcom was working feverishly to prepare the memoir for the printers, but it was not to appear until November 1837, during which time it had grown to a size far beyond that which had been originally envisaged. By April 1834 things were getting on rapidly. Petrie was working on the 'liberalised' city of Derry. O'Donovan was in Hillsborough collecting at a great rate. Larcom had to send him, and O'Keeffe, who was working with him, common-place books in which they could enter their findings, as they insisted on writing on any old scraps of paper they could find and sending them off to Dublin, to Larcom's distraction.[243] Petrie was working on his own, and he felt the absence of O'Donovan greatly, for he relied heavily on his scholarship and his no-nonsense approach to bureaucracy. It is difficult to understand the delay in bringing out the first memoir, that of the parish of Templemore, which contained the city of Derry.

PUBLICATION OF THE DERRY MEMOIR

The delay in publication of the memoir was probably caused mainly by the endless corrections that were needed before each sheet could go to the press. Also it was assumed that the other memoirs would be following at regular intervals, so they also had to be prepared for the printers. In the years 1835 and 1836, Petrie and his staff were occupied in working on Counties Louth, Cavan and Donegal, and Petrie himself did not entirely neglect his other interests of collecting antiquities and old Irish music. As the time of publication approached, sheets were being sent off to the printers at regular intervals. Clayton, the artist, was engaged to engrave the illustrations, but he turned out to be a great disappointment. Larcom described his views as 'barbarous cuts', and added that they were no better than Du Noyer's. Larcom railed against their 'unfortunate connection with the swindler Clayton – who neither drew them on time nor sent them to London'.[244] He insisted that he would send back any illustration that he was not satisfied with, to be re-done. Du Noyer was put under Petrie's supervision in making illustrations for the wood-cutters. These annoyances and frustrations dogged their every step, and as 1837 approached, Larcom became increasingly depressed about the progress of the work. The printers were calling for copy:

> I confess I grow very uneasy, for everything seems asleep. Each sheet is slower that the one before it – as if the work was coming to a natural death...[245]

The situation did not improve; later he wrote:

> ... to stop another week – it would be more noble to shoot oneself at once than bleed to death by degrees – and more as we are dying by mere inanimation & miserable lingering.[246]

One major reason for the slowness of the work was the difficult territory in which they found themselves, having chosen Derry as the city which would feature in the first memoir. Questions of race, religion and politics beset them at an early stage, with O'Donovan going through the census returns putting I, E or S before each name to denote their racial origin (Irish, English or Scottish). Petrie evaluated these results in a section on race and religion, which did not appeal to Larcom: 'I have no political or polemical squeamishness on that subject, but it is a mystical subject which no-one, or very few, understand.'[247] Larcom regretted that religion was the only 'enumeration' into which race could be allowed – his preference was for something more informative, such as crime, or occupation. He believed it unwise to keep religion so prominently in the public eye:

> That truth never can do harm is an axiom more in sound than in reality – for what is truth – or rather who shall say what is truth. If religion is touched at all, it must be done with extraordinary care.[248]

In the end, the results were inserted in the memoir in form of a table.

Throughout 1837, work continued on many different subjects, and judging from the correspondence between Larcom and Petrie during the course of that year, the Templemore memoir was not touched on much, save to go through it with a fine-tooth comb looking for flaws and errors, of which Larcom said: 'The misfortune of this and many similar *small* errors is that they are find-out-able by common people – and such unhappily are the majority of the public.'[249] John O'Donovan came in for some criticism from Larcom on account of his critical attitudes (probably that acerbic humour that has delighted generations of Irish scholars). Larcom reckoned that O'Donovan had no special qualities in his field but was fortunate in having so many doors opened to him, and facilities that his predecessors lacked, so that he should not be too quick to criticise other people's work. Surrounded by all these pressures, Larcom often wished, as O'Donovan would say, that 'like the people on the moon', he could take off his head 'and put it by to rest for a while'.[250]

It is often suggested that Petrie used O'Donovan rather cynically for his own end, but this is substantiated nowhere in any correspondence of the time. O'Donovan and Petrie seem to have had only the highest respect for each other's abilities and both of them are so scathing in their attacks on any form of underhand behaviour that it is unlikely that they would have tolerated it from each other; and O'Donovan was certainly not a man to be used.

While he was traversing the countryside in search of information on the history and folklore of the inhabitants, he kept in constant touch with Petrie in Dublin, sending him long letters every few weeks that describe the more humorous episodes in the life of this 'wearied wanderer and weather-beaten traveller', as he describes himself. The correspondence starts in 1831, when O'Donovan first became acquainted with Petrie, and it runs, intermittently, up to the 1860s; but the majority of the letters date from the late 30s and early 40s. Of their first meeting, O'Donovan said:

> ...you know very well that the regard I have for you amounts to more than friendship; I have looked up to you as a father since the year '31 when I first had the honor of becoming personally acquainted with you, and since that time our mutual friendship has remained perfect.[251]

O'Donovan was employed in the Ordnance Survey by Captain Larcom from October of 1830, but in 1833, after some disagreement, he left for a while.[252] The reasons for his leaving are not clear – possibly it was prompted by Larcom's anxiety to keep the expenses down by employing people at as low a rate as possible; and O'Donovan had no doubts as to his own indispensability to such a survey. When he left the Survey, Larcom had immediately employed another in his place but the replacement proved not to be up to the job. Petrie, upon his appointment to the Survey, insisted that O'Donovan be re-employed, which Larcom did with considerable reluctance. Petrie told O'Donovan afterwards that Larcom would not have taken him back, 'not on any condition', had it not been for his intercession. O'Donovan later told Lord Adare:

> This was in 1833, and my work in my own handwriting will tell how I laboured, till Jan 31st 1842 when I was disemployed. To the Survey I owe much, but *nothing* to those who employed me, because they could not get any other capable of doing my work.[253]

And it was in return for this and many other services that Petrie rendered him that O'Donovan gave his time freely and willingly to assist Petrie in his work, especially after Petrie's office broke up, and he was preparing his work on the round towers for publication.

Petrie was at this time working on inserting ancient monuments on the Survey maps; features such as the promontory fort near the Baily in Howth, or the ancient remains at Kilternan that Larcom suspected could be the Eblana of old.[254] In August, Petrie went North to Knocknarea in Sligo. He had intended to move on from there to Derry, but returned to Dublin instead. He had made valuable use of his time, however, putting the remains of the ancient battlefield of Moy Tura on the map. From this he was to move on to the completion of Kildare and the preparation of King's County (Offaly), but he was forced by illness to return home. Dr Stokes treated him and Larcom wrote to him:

> ...tho' I doubt not this eruption, when carried off, will like other eruptions, leave the mountain more quiet afterwards. Stokes is not a man to overphysic – as some doctor at Belfast has just being doing to old Portlock with a double dose of opium – but he is awake again and at work.[255]

At the end of 1837 they moved on to deal with Castledermot, investigating the origins of the people, 'nationalising' the names of the villages and townlands and trying to trace whether the names of the original settlers, whose houses were drawn by Phillips, still remained in the original locality. 'It is obvious that we here approach a subject of extraordinary value to the country – the registration of all the changes property has undergone – it will excite alarm unless well handled.'[256]

When the Templemore memoir was finally published, the newspapers of the time were enthusiastic in their reception, as were most other sections of society. Andrews comments on its impact:

> In later years, when the memoir became a national issue (and in some respects it has remained a national issue ever since), the Templemore volume was to be loyally praised by the majority of Irish writers. From a tactical viewpoint, however, it was an almost unmitigated disaster. Admittedly it has a number of merits: It is accurate, comprehensive, interesting when one gets into it, and it sold 1,250 in six years, which would be quite good for a book of similar character in present-day Ireland. But all these virtues were dwarfed by its enormous sprawling bulk.[257]

The printing of further memoirs was halted, mainly on the grounds that the expenses were out of hand. The original price of publication had been increased considerably by the adoption of quarto form instead of the intended octavo, and smaller type had been used. There were also other expenses:

> The arrangements made by Messrs. Hodges Smith embraced a payment by them of £20 or £25 a month to Mr. Petrie who was to prepare for publication the antiquarian matter which had been collected in addition to drawings and illustrations.[258]

Whether this was in addition to the ten shillings a day that Petrie was being paid by the Survey is not clear. Presumably it was, in which case it would bring his annual income while he was working on the memoir to less than £500, a considerable drop from the £700 to £800 he claimed he was earning prior to his involvement in the Ordnance Survey.[259] But since there is evidence that he kept up his drawing lessons during this period, and had other, minor, sources of income as an artist and man of letters, there is no reason to believe that he suffered that greatly financially from his involvement in the survey. Colby had reckoned that the memoir would cost the government no more than £400 to £500, but when the bill was finally presented, it amounted to £1,700. Of that, £200 was for the special copies that had been printed for the meeting of the British Association in Dublin in 1835, and a similar amount was expended in merely making corrections and alterations to the finished text, as well as the other 'inevitable failures and perplexities' of such an experimental work.[260]

And what of the reasons for the decision not to continue with the publication of further memoirs, even though much of the material from the other parishes had already been collected by the Topographical Department? The Chancellor of the Exchequer, in a letter to Lord Morpeth, explained the reasons behind the decision under three headings; expediency, justice and safety. He did not think it expedient for Engineer officers to be employed in literary work, when their duties lay in a more purely topographical area; he doubted the justice of the memoirs because they were in direct competition with private literary endeavours such as Whitelaw's, and more recently, D'Alton's histories of Dublin, and would greatly injure the sales of these and other works; and lastly, but most importantly, he did not wish to see the Government making itself responsible for the opinions expressed in the memoirs, touching, as they did, on the most sensitive areas of Irish life – history, politics and social economy. He was especially concerned about the history:

> With mere facts we may deal, but giving the history of Derry and the history of Limerick, the siege of one and the treaty of the other, open all the debatable questions in the Irish party division ... If these events had never occurred or could be buried, it would be better, but as they have occurred and are remembered & their effects continue, whether it is better for the public to take their account of them from the party writers on both sides – the Orangeman and the agitator, or take both from the same impartial disinterested source – they are facts and must be stated as such – they are local history and of neither the one nor the other are both sides yet known. Neither party has anything to fear from truth – but both have much to fear from squeamishness.[261]

The argument having thus led him around to almost disagreeing with his reasons for stopping the memoir, the Chancellor hastily concludes his letter. The halting of the publication may also have been influenced by wider political concerns. Because the Whig government depended on Daniel O'Connell's support for its survival, O'Connell was able to press for the inclusion of a survey of Irish place names and antiquities in the Ordnance Survey. When the Tory government came to power, such influence evaporated.

LATER TOURS OF IRELAND

Petrie's researches for the Survey were not confined to libraries and academies. In a cold and showery August in 1838, he travelled north along the eastern coast, through Mellifont, Monasterboice, Drogheda and then into Ulster, to Newry and Armagh. Throughout, he was constantly observing and noting details, comparing theories with actual sites. At Monasterboice he noted the presence of 'long and short masonry', which he thought fitted in with Rickman's theory as an indicator of a Saxon date. At Mellifont he was delighted with what he described as the most beautiful remains of the 12th century he had ever seen in Ireland. From Armagh, where he stayed with a Mr Bennet, he visited various sites of interest, such as Emania and Tynan. He comments on the cathedral then being re-built at Armagh:

> I had heard so much in praise of this work of Cottingham's, an English architect of high character that I had expected too much and consequently suffered a disappointment. The restorer of the cathedral of Armagh should be an Irish historical architect and antiquarian. This Mr. Cottingham is not, and in consequence he has destroyed the associations which the antiquity of the building did and should still excite, by making it a regular English parish church of Tudor architecture, the only style, it is probable, with which he is acquainted. Even the material – reddish sandstone – has an English character or look and the horizontal roof, stuccoed and painted to imitate oak, destroys the loftiness and grandeur of the interior. The screen is indeed beautiful in its way, but it is a way we never had in Ireland.[262]

The architect and medievalist Lewis N. Cottingham was a key figure in the early Gothic Revival in England and Ireland. Despite his reservations about the 'redification' of the cathedral, Petrie believed that the situation of the building was the finest in Ireland, overlooking the town from its anciently fortified position. His daughter had accompanied him on this trip, as she had done the year before, for the uncertain state of Petrie's health made a travelling companion necessary. They moved on to Dungannon, after spending about a week in Armagh, to stay with Charles Ligar and his family. Ligar's wife, a 'kind and lively creature', made the young Petrie girl feel at home while Petrie roamed the countryside in the rain.[263] On 6 August Petrie went on to Moneymore, and from there to Dungiven in the heart of Derry county, where he met up with Portlock, who was also working on the memoir. The weather continued very bad; so much so that the people were praying in the chapels for a change. After spending several days in Derry city, they returned to Dublin.

August 1839 found Petrie in Galway, meeting Wakeman, O'Donovan and the famous Galway historian, Hardiman. O'Donovan was staying at Hardiman's house, where he had a little room in which he worked from morning until two o'clock every night, seven days a week – or so Petrie claims. But Petrie was very anxious to reassure Larcom, who was furious at the idea of Hardiman diverting his men from their duties, and he said that O'Donovan was writing at the rate of twenty pages a day, and had by then completed two hundred and forty pages, for which Wakeman had provided some beautiful illustrations. Petrie himself was not happy at the idea of memoir work being conducted in Hardiman's house, if only because of the great comfort there, which was a temptation to anybody, but he emphasises that he did not think that O'Donovan acted 'unfairly' by staying at Hardiman's. On his way to Galway, Petrie had stopped off at Clonmacnoise, and he comments on the state of the place:

> The churches are more dilapidated since I was last there than I thought they would be in a century. And if I had not sketched so much three years since, very little would be known hereafter of the antiquities of the place. Even the Irish inscriptions have been destroyed or the flags carried away. And this shows the necessity of having a draughtsman with the topographer. The antiquities of Arran are also fast disappearing.[264]

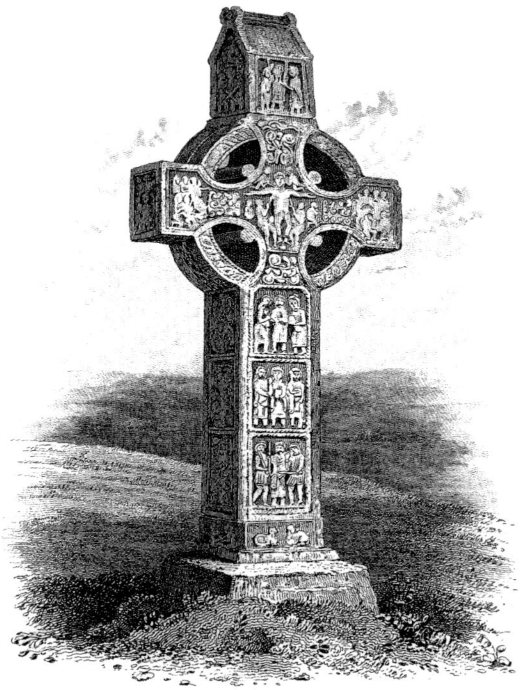

St. Patrick's Cross, Monasterboice, Co. of Louth
engraving after Petrie from T. Cromwell, *Excursions through Ireland*, 1820

opposite: *Ruins of Clonmacnois, Kings Co.*
engraving after Petrie from J.N. Brewer, *The Beauties of Ireland*, 1826

Although Petrie was prone to exaggerate the rate of destruction of Ireland's antiquities, in this case he had good cause for concern. The east wall of the cathedral at Clonmacnoise, with its two-light window, which he had seen on his first visits, subsequently collapsed and is now known only through the Petrie engraving in Brewer's *The Beauties of Ireland* in 1825-26.[265] Petrie, in his 1845 essay on round towers, also refers to the damage done to the cathedral's west door since his first visit.

After spending several days at Galway, Petrie set off for the West, and on 24 August 1839 he wrote to Larcom from Oughterard giving his impressions of the country. He thought that the whole of the western part of Connaught was still a region of romance, but it was destined to be so not much longer – the progress of civilisation would soon convert its wild beauties into cornfields or gentlemen's walled parks 'and adieu then to its solitary lakes and mountains – its "Desert isles and fairy lands forlorn".' The antiquities of every kind would soon disappear, as would the simplicity and honesty of its inhabitants:

> ...the costume of the women, so exquisitely beautiful and simple – exactly as if they had stepped out of the pictures of Raphael or Murillo. We shall soon have in their place cheap cotton gowns so odious to the lover of the picturesque, stays to destroy the grace and freedom of attitude that delight us every moment, and shoes and stockings to cramp the feet and give them corns and bunions and deprive their Grecian long toes of the classical proportions. By the bye, I never saw so much beauty of female form in a wild district before, as I have met in this; and what is very remarkable their hands are quite

> aristocratic and elegantly formed in the highest degree. Burton, the artist, who is one of our party, is almost mad with delight. He is a charming fellow and his company adds greatly to the pleasure of my journey.[266]

Petrie was living life to the full in this wild region, delighting, as he puts it himself, in a mere animal-like existence; eating, drinking, laughing and sleeping as much as he liked. His head and whiskers had been restored to their original brownish-black and he expected to go back to Dublin a stone or two heavier than when he left. His breakfast on 24 August was, in addition to the usual tea and toast, a plateful of salmon, another of ham, three or four fresh eggs, and so on. But enough of this eating and drinking and 'glasses of mountain dew to wash the solids down', there was work to be done. Petrie moved on to stay at the Maam hotel with his health and vigour restored.

The following year, 1840, Petrie returned to Galway, but the only information there is on this trip is contained in a letter from Robert Gavan to Petrie in Galway. Gavan regretted that Petrie's trip had been 'unproductive' and speaks of the delays in going to press caused by Petrie; presumably he refers to the *Irish Penny Journal*, as Ferguson had promised an article on Antrim for the same edition.

> God help and forgive me, but I have once or twice wished, when I saw all hands waiting for Antrim, that you had been caught, aye, and kept, in a Twenty-Four Hour Thunderstorm on MacGillicuddy's Reeks, or some other equally savage place. However, I find that God has been somewhat more benevolent, and compromised the matter by offering you the miserable shelter of a Country Inn. And yet – after all – it is perhaps but a refinement in cruelty.[267]

In 1841, when the work of the Topographical Department was concentrated on counties Cork and Kerry, that summer found Wakeman and O'Donovan traversing that countryside. At the beginning of July they moved on from Tralee to Dingle; Wakeman sketching, O'Donovan researching. Petrie was also in Dingle for a short period in late summer, working on an account of the Early Christian architecture of the area. He returned to Dublin in late September.[268] In November Wakeman was still in Kerry, sketching the windows of the round tower at Rattoo for Petrie.[269] O'Donovan communicated back to Petrie a detailed description of the church at Ratass, and the tower at Rattoo, which at that time was so covered in ivy that O'Donovan feared for its safety. He wrote that the silver bell of the tower was reputed to be at the bottom of a near-by river, but said that the same story was believed of every tower in Ireland.[270]

Near Dingle, Wakeman went to visit a graveyard, which contained the stone and grave of St Monaghawn, according to his guide. Below the grave (merely a mound of earth), lay the well of the saint, a clear spring. Wakeman was not lucky enough to see the blessed trout that was sometimes to be seen in its waters. The fish was supposed to be about one-and-a-half feet long, and peculiarly 'clare' and 'bright'. 'Sure it must be a holy fish' said Wakeman's guide, 'or how would it live in spring wather where it'd get nothing to ate'.[271] Wakeman visited, and sketched, Gallarus oratory, Kilmelcadar church, the round tower of Aghadoe, and the 'caves' at Dunloe, within which had been found numerous stones bearing oghams, two years previously. The stones have since been removed from the souterrains (which the caves are, in fact), and erected in a circle above ground, where they now stand. Petrie had been told by Burton of the existence of a cahir, or stone fort, near Dingle, and he asked Wakeman to have a look for it. Wakeman did eventually find one, near a place called Ballhay, but not without some difficulty:

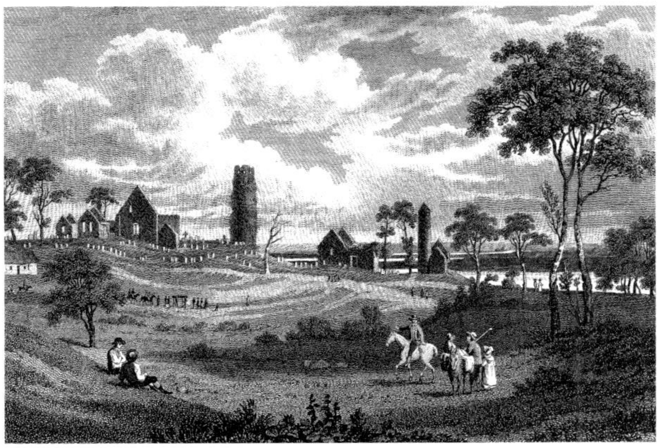

> When inquiring for this place today, I asked a man whom I met if there was any old cahir upon the road in a certain direction. He said that here was not, but that he saw the wheels of an old car in a field about half a mile off.[272]

Many times, when he was tramping the mountains of Kerry in rain, Wakeman had occasion to wish that he was back in Great Charles Street cutting the bread and butter, and not trying to make sense out of the inhabitants of the area, who would send him off on a wild goose chase, looking for a 'berrin' ground. The sense of cultural continuity that existed amongst the people of Kerry at that time, where the age of a building did not matter as much as its associations or venerability, was not helpful to an enquiring antiquary.

THE SURVEYING OF CARROWMORE, KNOCKAREA AND MOYTURA

Even before Petrie worked for the Ordnance Survey, his interest in ancient monuments extended beyond sketching and describing them. In 1828, he commissioned a friend of his, Roger Chambers Walker, of Rathcarrick House, Co Sligo to supply him with a map of the megalithic cemetery at Carrowmore, close to where Walker lived. The map was to show the exact location of the cromlechs in relation to the townland boundaries. But when Walker gained access to the County Maps, 'armed with pencil and sundry sheets of tracing paper', he discovered that the townlands were not marked on these maps, 'and the only mention made of the cromlechs is by several dabs of Indian ink along the Carrowmore Road entitled "Old Caves"'.[273] So Walker hired himself a 'regular land surveyor' and on 29 December watched him chain out the distance between the different circles. The surveyor promised to prepare a neat map, for the grand sum of one pound. The map he prepared is unfortunately lost; it would be a boon to modern archaeologists for many of the tombs have been destroyed in relatively recent times by gravel quarrying. Petrie himself witnessed several scenes of such destruction.

However, in a manuscript draft of a memoir on Carrowmore, preserved in the Royal Irish Academy, Petrie's characteristic amnesia seems to be at work when he wrote that he first noted the remains of the cromlechs at Carrowmore in 1835, when he was passing a few weeks at Rathcarrick House: 'and they were first communicated to my friend Captain Larcom, R.E. in a letter ... dated August the 12th 1837, which is now preserved amongst the collection for the Ordnance Survey of Ireland at the Establishment in the Phoenix Park'.[274] Petrie goes on to relate how, in 1837, he marked on the Ordnance maps of the townland, then nearly prepared for publication, a great number of the monuments which had escaped the notice of the Ordnance surveyors. Larcom had directed that these extra monuments be engraved on the plates, and they were revised carefully the next year by R.C. Walker on the spot. Petrie read a paper on them to the Academy at a meeting held on 28 February 1838, the purpose of which was to establish that the monuments were in fact tombs, and not, as had been commonly believed, Druidical altars and temples. Petrie did not dismiss entirely the notion that they may have been used for such a purpose but he surmised correctly that such use would have been secondary. The majority of the tombs are in fact a mixture of small passage-graves and dolmens, usually surrounded by a stone kerb.

It was in early August 1837 that Petrie had arrived in Sligo to examine the Carrowmore remains, taking a break from his tour of the West in the autumn of that year. Travelling from Roscommon to Sligo, he had caught a chill as a consequence of the bad weather and of having to travel in the mail-coach with his head uncovered because of the lowness of the roof. This kept him in bed for three days, but he 'miraculously' avoided catching a fever. He spent this time examining the tracings of the maps, and when he had recovered his strength he threw himself into the work again, staying out in the fields all day, inserting on the tracings any monuments that had been omitted, and returning to the hotel later in the evening for dinner. Afterwards he would endeavour to make himself 'agreeable' to the ladies, but the charms of the opposite sex did not distract him from his work:

> You have no idea of the astonishing assemblage of pagan remains here. It is the Carnac of the British Islands, and I have actually been bewildered in the endeavour to trace its extent and arrangement. I have little doubt now but that I shall be able to ascertain with certainty, the existence, down to a recent period, of upwards of 40 stone circles, mostly double and sometime treble – with one or more cromlechs in each. And the possibility is that there were not less than 100 originally![275]

Petrie noted that the circles were being destroyed at a frightening rate. With the month before his arrival, two fine circles with their cromlechs had been blasted by a Mr Chambers, a cousin of Petrie's friend Walker, to obtain stones for building walls. The landowners were by no means the only culprits:

> But the destruction going on daily is horrible and if I did not

> work now it would be too late to preserve a memorial of them in a short time. The peasantry generally have no reluctance to destroy them – on the contrary, are glad to get permission to clear the land of them.[276]

Another instance of the wanton destruction of the monuments was provided by a farmer called Walsh, who destroyed, according to Petrie, eight or ten of the circles.[277]

Petrie spent long hours in the field, recording and describing the monuments. On 12 August he had finished and he sent the report to Larcom in Dublin. Altogether he dealt with sixty-three monuments at Carrowmore, describing them individually, noting their position on the map, and including sketches of six. His notes have been printed several times – Stokes quotes them fully,[278] and they are included in the Sligo volume of the *O'Donovan Letters* printed under the supervision of M.J. O'Flanagan in 1927.[279] But the map, to which the numbered descriptions refer, is lost.

Petrie reckoned that at one time, over three thousand stones had been arranged in circles at Carrowmore, averaging about fifty for each circle. He also discovered that the line of circles originally extended to the sea and by keeping to this line he came upon a cairn and two remarkable circles of stone, and also a perforated boundary stone which measured nine feet by nine feet.[280]

He believed that all these tombs were those of the Belgae, who, after the battle of Moy-tuire in Mayo, retreated into this peninsula of Cuil-Irra, having been again defeated and their king slain in crossing the strand at Ballysadare Bay. He believed the monuments to be purely sepulchral and coeval – probably the tombs of the Belgae chiefs killed in the battle, the common soldiers being interred in one great circular mound nearby; a circular field which was completely filled with human bones, called Calltragh.

> As a single monument Stonehenge or Avebury is grander than anything here. But viewed as a whole there is nothing in the British Islands of pagan antiquity equal in interest or importance to the collection of monuments at Carrowmore.[281]

Getting back to Roger Walker, when he was having Carrowmore surveyed for Petrie in 1828, he did not confine his attentions to the stone circles alone, but spent some time on the nearby hill of Knocknarea, investigating the great cairn of stones where Queen Maeve is said to be buried. This cairn has never been excavated, but it probably conceals a passage grave; it is about thirty-five feet high and two hundred feet in diameter. Petrie had asked Walker to examine the outer ring around the cairn and ascertain if it was composed of round granite rocks. Walker did so, and found that it was in fact an earthen bank, which originally must have been much larger. There was only one very large granite rock on the ring, at the south-east side of the cairn, with three other smaller ones sunk in other parts of the ring, and one very large flat limestone. Walker did, however, notice something that Petrie has missed: around the great cairn are several smaller 'satellite' tombs, like those in the Boyne valley. Walker describes how; one lying to the north of the main cairn at a distance of about fifty yards, composed of clay and measuring six or seven yards in diameter; the other a similar distance beyond, had fourteen large granite stones in its circle with an oblong flat limestone in the centre. Petrie had noticed three other circles of stones to the north of the cairn on his visit (when exactly this was is unknown). Walker had made enquiries in the neighbourhood about other possible sites or monuments, but had come up with little, only that a Mr Duke who lived locally had an ancient sepulchral urn which had been found in the area, and which Walker hoped to get a 'peep' at in the near future.

Walker continued his scouting operations in the Sligo area through the years searching for antiquities and curiosities. In 1836, he summoned Petrie to meet him in Castlebar with Dr West threatening that if he did not come he would go Great Charles Street and drag him from his 'punctilia' and sacrifice him to the 'infernal Deities upon the nearest Cromlech'.[282] The purpose of this journey was to proceed in company to Sligo to witness the opening of the cairn on Knockarea. The correspondence unfortunately goes no further on this topic, but it is unlikely that any excavation did take place, for Petrie wrote to Adare in 1843:

> And this reminds me to tell you – but *seriously*, as a great secret – that he Walker is to open the Virgin Cairn of Knockna-ree next Summer. Stokes, Burton and I are to be present as commissioners on the occasion McCullagh too, – and I have insisted that there shall be a lord too, whom I shall not now name. At this proposal Walker exclaimed 'Ah, my dear fellow, if I asked one of his rank my Aunty Mary (who keeps house for his father) would be terrified out of her wits!' So we shall have to convince the simple lady beforehand that a Lord is after all not so awful a personage as she supposes.[283]

Knockarea and Carrowmore are well known today, but the third site in which Petrie was interested, in this area, called Moy-Tuire, has been largely forgotten. In July 1837, Petrie was in Boyle waiting for O'Donovan to show up so that they could go together and see this ancient battlefield. (Moy-Tuire is about ten miles from Boyle, in Co Sligo.)But after he had waited several days in vain, Petrie decided to go on without O'Donovan. His first excursion ended in failure, however, when a torrent of rain obliged him to take shelter under a 'dense umbrageous tree' for two hours, making it impossible for him to continue on that day.[284] The next day he made another, more successful, attempt and after spending some hours exploring the terrain, moved on the Rathcarrick House, where his friend Walker lived. He wrote to Larcom from here, while a fierce storm raged outside over Knockarea, telling of his researches. The field of Moy-Tuire, which takes its name from the two cyclopean towers, which once stood there, originally extended from Lough Arrow to the strand at Ballysadare. Petrie wrote that he had discovered the remains of these two towers, which he described as 'very remarkable' and he noted that he had seen two similar, in the southern Moy-Tuire, near Cong.[285] He forwarded to Larcom maps of this ancient battlefield, on which he had marked several stone circles as well as the two cyclopean towers from which the name was derived. He explained to Larcom that this name should apply to an extensive plain and not just to the one field which contained the remains of the towers, and he advised him when preparing the maps of the area, not to insert 'Moy-Tuire' but rather 'Girt Tuire'.[286] However, in the six-inch map of the Sligo area published in 1838, no such name appears. By Petrie's account, the towers measured over one hundred feet in diameter.

Concerning the actual sites of the two castles of Moy-Tuire, Sir William Wilde (who named his own house near Cong after the historic battle site) read a paper on this subject at the Royal Irish Academy in 1866, in which he indicated the locations of the two plains on which the battles are supposed to have been fought. The first the 'Southern Moy-Tura' on the borders of Galway and Mayo, Wilde states was now called Ath Readh, but it is the 'Northern Moy-Tura' with which Petrie was concerned. It is situated in the parish of Kilmacteraney in Co Sligo about fifty miles north-east of the sourthern Moy-Tuire. It was called 'Moy-Tuire of the Formorians' and it extended, as has already been stated, from Lough Arrow to the strand at Ballysadare.[287] The areas marked on the six-inch map as 'Moytirra West' and Moytirra East' constitute only a small portion of this extensive plain. Of the two towers that Petrie stated he had discovered, there is no indication given, although he had inscribed them on his tracing of the map, which he sent into the Ordnance office in September 1837. The absence of O'Donovan was felt strongly by Petrie at times like this, when he could not turn to the Irish scholar for advice on what to do. He himself was undecided as to what name should be inserted on the maps and did not share O'Donovan's prowess at seeking out the ancient names of places.

> I have dotted these northern ones on the map, but I want your advice in giving them a name, for unfortunately, I was so occupied with their construction, etc., that I did not think of making such enquiries as I ought, relative to their Irish name. The whole of the information, which I obtained, was this, that the field, or enclosure, in which they are situated, is called, in English, 'the Ture field', and that these are the only stone forts or cashels in the barony. The question then, which I propound, is should 'Ture field' be inserted on the map? Or if not what would you suggest?[288]

– he wrote to O'Donovan in 1837. What O'Donovan's answer was is not known, but Petrie came to the conclusion that the towers should be inserted on the map in the manner in which he had inscribed them on the tracing, that is, a dotted line, and it is strange that they do not appear in the published maps, as both Petrie and O'Donovan regarded them as monuments of the first importance.

THE MEMOIR FADES AWAY

It is difficult to trace the exact point when it was realised that there was no possibility of further memoirs being published. The officers of the Survey continued to collect material for the publication of further volumes through the year 1841, although an order had come from the Ordnance Office in 1840 to put an end to that part of the Survey. On the 4 July 1840, Larcom informed Petrie that the memoir had 'fallen through'.[289] *Freeman's Journal* attributed the decision to the 'West Briton' Chancellor of the Exchequer, Lord Monteagle, and went on to say:

> Let us not forget that the cost of this survey would be a sum less by £10,000 than that which was expended in one year on

> her Majesty's dog kennels at Windsor, and that year the precise one in which the English Government judged it advisable to stop the progress of the memoir on the grounds of economy.[290]

The memoir department was being steadily run down; in December 1841 most of the staff were laid off, the only ones remaining were O'Donovan, O'Curry and of course Petrie himself. By the end of 1842, many of those employed in the Survey as a whole were laid off because of the Government's reduced grants. Nearly three hundred had been made redundant in England alone.

Colby was greatly disappointed at the halting of the work on the memoirs. He had held high hopes for it from the beginning, believing it would solve many of the political ills of the country; for, with it, the future legislators would be able to make the right decisions either because they had the necessary information or because they would be forced into such a course by an informed public. Colby thought highly of Ireland:

> When I first examined Ireland, I found a country capable of producing the necessaries, the comforts and the luxuries of life in great abundance; with a people both able and willing to labour, and possessing sufficient intellectual power to be readily trained to form the successive grades of a happy and a wealthy society. Yet all these gifts of nature were paralyzed by an ignorant system of government, and the people were reduced to the verge of starvation.[291]

Colby felt it his duty to aim at dispelling this ignorance if the opportunity presented itself; this was the reasoning behind putting forward the idea of the memoir. But Colby's ambitions were to be stymied by the Inspector-General of the Ordnance Survey, who had given the order for work on it to cease. He was ordered to forward any letter that was sent to him concerning the revival of the memoir to the office of the Inspector-General, which effectively stifled any possibility of its revival. Throughout the early forties, rumours and counter-rumours flew about. Would the Royal Irish Academy take over the publication of the memoirs? Would Larcom agree to carry it on, for he was the only person who could do so; to what extent would Petrie be prepared to commit himself and abandon his other pursuits? Did anyone realise the magnitude of the task, to accomplish Derry within the year – four baronies, fifty parishes, in fifty-two weeks? Would Petrie accept a lump sum to complete Derry and re-employ O'Donovan and O'Curry? To try and follow the thread of events in the confusion is difficult. In 1840, in response to a request from the Ordnance Office, Colby submitted two estimates of the cost of completing the memoir for Co Derry. The first was from Portlock, who was engaged on the geological survey, and it included natural history and statistics. The other estimate was from Larcom and it covered the other areas, including the orthographical and topographical. Portlock's estimate was for £1,250, Larcom's was for £1,700, of which £500 was to go to Petrie who would be in charge of the whole scene.[292] Colby disagreed with the idea of having Petrie in charge of an entire department:

> I have the greatest respect for Mr. Petrie's knowledge of the history and antiquities of Ireland and of his unwearied diligence and other estimable qualities. But I cannot admit his fitness to manage a large department or the expediency of suddenly proposing to advance his pay from £156 to £500 a year.[293]

Colby's reasons for this were simple. Being an officer in the army, and employed in the Ordnance Survey – work mainly undertaken by army engineers – he did not wish to see it taken over by civilians, thereby admitting the failure of it as an 'Engineer work'. Petrie also read and pondered over the report. He realised that Larcom was working in his interest and that it would be better to leave matters in his hands. He did not think much of the money proposed: 'Five hundred will hardly be a remuneratory payment for a year's labour such as mine would be.'[294] But he decided not to say anything about it at present for fear of injuring his chances. He thought that the 'Colonel' (Colby) would let him retain his salary as topographer etc., on top of everything he was paid for completing the work, for he describes himself as 'really run low' financially by the 'desperate game' he had played. But Larcom shattered these hopes by showing him the note from Colby (which has been quoted above). Petrie reckoned that Colby

> ...will do nothing and permit nothing to be done for me. I can no more see the wisdom than the justice of this. If he really wishes this great work to go on, he neither should not expect an important and popular branch of it to be done for nothing, or by a person unknown for competence to the public.[295]

Colby was adamant. He did not feel that antiquarian research was to the taste of the time and he told Larcom that he must feel disappointed if the board rejected the proposal of £1,700 to finish the history and antiquities of Derry, although he did feel sorry for Petrie. Andrews states that Colby was indifferent to the question of antiquities and disliked 'ornamental or insubstantial knowledge', preferring to concentrate on geology, natural history and statistics. This is true to some extent, but Colby was no Philistine. He felt that the emphasis on antiquarian research as the basis for a revived memoir would not be good, only because it would cease to command interest.[296] He said that the study of antiquities was at a low ebb:

> About 30 or 40 years since, they were deemed the acme of knowledge; in later years they have fallen below their true value in the public's estimation. Voluntarily to forego the knowledge of what has been, seems to be one approach towards the level of the brute creature, which derives no experience from the records of its ancestors. And to forego all antiquarian research because some antiquaries have substituted the result of a fertile imagination for well attested facts, seems to be no wiser than giving up the use of paper money because some notes have been forged.[297]

But in spite of all the meetings held, and the resolutions passed, nothing came of the attempts to revive the memoir. Events in Ireland were overtaking the problems of Petrie and his colleagues, and it was in this decade that the worst fears of Colby were to be realised. A commission of inquiry was set up by the government to investigate the future of the Ordnance Memoir, and Petrie was called before it to give evidence, in July of 1843. Although the recommendations of the Commissioners were favourable, there was a general air of despondency about the likelihood of their being carried out. Petrie's acceptance of the end of the memoir was philosophical:

> It is to be expected. The game is up I think. I wish it had not been necessary to make the estimate for the history and antiquities so large, for it will surely never pass in these utilitarian times. And what is worse than all, I fear that D [D'Alton] or some such character will get hold of our collection to cobble for the Government at cobbler's prices.[298]

Chapter VII

The Tara Paper Controversy and the Round Towers Essay

In November 1837 Petrie read a paper before the Royal Irish Academy on the history and antiquities of Tara Hill. This essay was based on material that had been collected by the Ordnance Survey, and was originally intended to have been part of the memoir for Co Meath. The essay was later printed by the Academy, who awarded Petrie a gold medal for it. This raised some difficult questions. Was Petrie acting improperly in presenting as his own work a paper that had been prepared under the auspices of a government agency? Sir William Betham, for one, thought so, and he took grave exception (an exception, it must be admitted, exacerbated by jealousy at Petrie's success). He resigned from the Committee of Antiquities and addressed a letter of protest to the president of the Academy, Sir William Hamilton Rowan, complaining that the essay was undeserving of a medal, was unfit to be published, and, besides, was the work of the Ordnance Survey and should not be accredited to one man. He enjoyed little support from the other members of the Academy, for it was generally recognised that the essay was almost entirely the work of Petrie, be he inside the Survey or outside it, and that there would have been little chance of having it published ever, if the Academy had not accepted it. One of these who loyally supported Petrie during the 'rumpus' was Huband Smith, who assured Petrie that he would have his vote in the Academy, if it came to that, for Huband Smith thought that it was Betham's aim in getting out the circular to force Petrie and Todd off the Council of the Academy, and make way for new men.[299] Another supporter, Henry Petrie, wrote to the Irish antiquarian in July of that year, 1840:

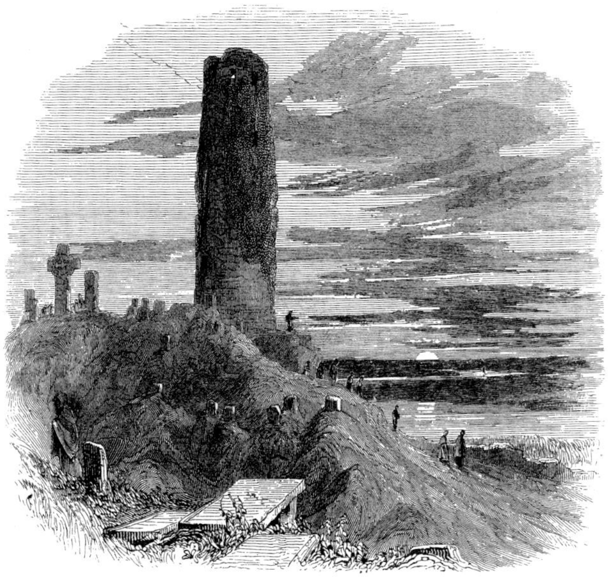

View of the greater Tower of Clonmacnoise
from G. Petrie, *The Ecclesiastical Architecture of Ireland*, 1845

> To be engaged in controversy is at all times an ungracious task; but when a man has been driven to it, it affords his friends great consolation to find him in a condition to conduct it in the manner you have done on the present occasion.[300]

But Betham's letter had sparked off more than just a struggle within the Academy; word of it had filtered into other, more dangerous areas. In May 1840, Larcom told Petrie that Colby had no authority to give permission for the publication of the Tara paper, and now that trouble was brewing, he was afraid that Colby would 'ricochet' the trouble on his head. Larcom told Petrie that he could use any of his letters if they would be of use in his defence.[301] Two days later, Larcom pointed out to Petrie an error that he had made in the Tara paper in asserting that it was a portion of the memoir of Co Meath, written to illustrate the map, and soon to be published. It was in fact the map that was soon to be published, and not the memoir; and people were asking why Petrie had claimed it as his own work, merely assisted by the officers of the Survey and O'Donovan. The memoir of that county was nowhere near publication, and Colby had allowed Petrie to put out the Tara part earlier as it was of ' peculiar interest'. Larcom compares this with the early days of the English Survey when the accounts of the early measurements, section and other parts of interest, were published by Noy and Mudge (officers of the Survey) in the *Transactions* of the Royal Society, and afterwards republished in the survey volumes. Larcom admits that the Tara paper is completely Petrie's work, but he adds:

> I think you do harm to your cause, considering it too strongly a separate and independent work of your own, merely assisted by the officers of the Survey and Mr O'Donovan.[302]

The controversy grew daily, and Petrie began to fall back on Larcom for support, which, however, was not forthcoming. Larcom reprimanded Petrie for printing, in his reply to the attacks on the Tara paper, two letters, one from Colby and one from himself, without first asking their permission, especially as he could not see what bearing they had in establishing the authorship of the paper but merely served to involve them in the controversy. Colby, in permitting the article to be read before, and printed by, the Academy, had taken on himself a 'grave responsibility' in not seeking the permission of the Government first. Petrie could look for consolation in the fact that, if the worst came to the worst, it would be Colby who would have to accept responsibility and not himself; but Larcom warned him that he would have to face Colby's ire when he returned to Ireland. He reiterates his point about Petrie's claim to authorship:

> Merely saying that some of the officers assisted you with plans & Mr. O'Donovan with translations may be construed to mean that it was composed independently of the Survey with casual assistance from individuals, instead of being the daily work of your department for a considerable time. Being the work of your department does not make it less yours – is not the Survey Col. Colby's? Are not the plans the officers', tho' they do not measure the lines nor draw the maps? Is not the Natural History Portlock's, tho' he does not collect the rocks or plants himself?[303]

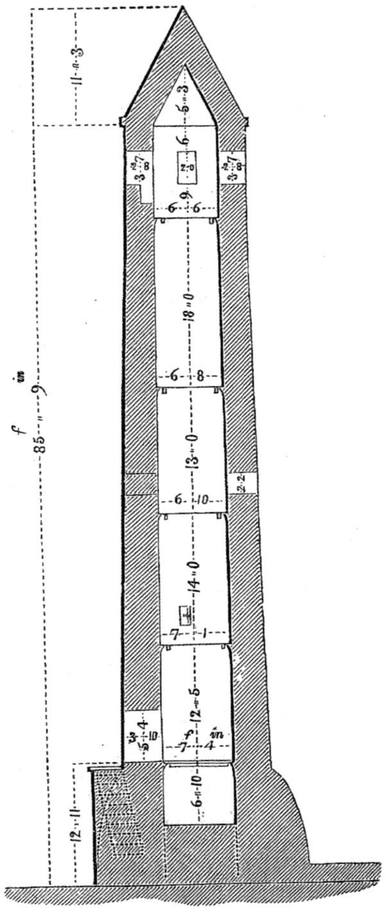

Section of the Round Tower of Clondalkin

However, Larcom was overreacting; in the end, nothing came of Betham's attacks. Incensed at Petrie being awarded a prize for his essay on the Hill of Tara, Betham must have snorted at the prize of £50 and a gold medal awarded Petrie for his essay 'On the Origin and Uses of the Round Towers of Ireland', read on 27 May 1833, which was to lead to the publication of perhaps Petrie's most lasting and valuable contribution to Irish archaeology.

It took Petrie twelve years to prepare his 1833 essay on the round towers of Ireland for publication in the Royal Irish Academy's *Transactions*.[304] The title of the published work was rather wordy: 'The Ecclesiastical Architecture of Ireland anterior to the Anglo-Norman invasion, comprising an essay on the origin and uses of the Round Towers of Ireland'. It was published in 1845. The Academy publishers, Hodges & Smith, also produced that year an edition in a handsome binding with Celtic interlace patterns. The essay, as published, runs to 452 pages in a quarto volume. Petrie set out his arguments carefully. The round towers, the only form of architecture unique to Ireland, follow the distribution pattern of early medieval monasteries, with which they were closely associated. However, as the towers bear almost no marks or carvings that would distinguish them as Christian, many scholars came to the conclusion that they pre-dated the nearby churches, and had been built by Phoenicians or other early settlers in Ireland. To bolster his argument that the round towers and the nearby monastic buildings were from the same period, Petrie included in his book a huge volume of material on stone churches and other ecclesiastical monuments of the period. The question as to what exactly that period might be was a vexed one. Sir James Ware's assertion that no buildings of stone were erected in Ireland prior to the 12th century roused Petrie's nationalist ire, as it indicated Ireland was a backward country. Other antiquaries, including Charles Vallancey, Miss Beaufort and William Betham, and indeed almost the entire South Munster Society of Antiquities, believed that round towers were older, that they were pagan edifices built for fire or sun worship – or as burial towers – possibly by 'Danish' (Viking) invaders. These imaginative antiquarians looked for examples abroad, in the Phoenician monuments of Sardinia, in India or in the ziggurats of the Middle East. Charles Smith posited they may have been built for Christian anchorites, or as penitential prisons.[305] The Cork antiquary John Windele argued that monastic sites such as Kildare were intended for fire worship:

> A site such as that strongly excited the attention of the Christian missionaries and its conversion & appropriation were objects well looked after. The obtainment of such a place was a great triumph of Christianity. No wonder that the place should still be redolent of paganism and abound in heathen remains...[306]

In *Remembrance and Imagination*, published in 1996, Joep Leerssen gives a comprehensive account of these scholarly 'battles' – sometimes humorous, sometimes bitter – fought between the Romantic school of antiquarians, led by Henry O'Brien, Charles Vallancey and others, and the Positivists, represented by Petrie, Dunraven and Margaret Stokes.[307] However, it should be remembered that Petrie was not the first to argue the Christian origins of the towers. In *The Beauties of Ireland*, published in 1825 – a book for which Petrie provided illustrations – James Norris Brewer cited with approval the theories of Colonel Hervé de Montmorencey-Morres, as set out in *An Historical and Critical Inquiry into the Origin and Primitive Uses of the Irish Pillar Tower* (1821), theories which are in broad accord with Petrie's later conclusions.

Petrie set out to establish that while the towers were indeed Christian, they were not built as prisons or penitential cells, but rather to serve as belfries, treasure-houses and look-out towers for monks fearful of Viking predators. All manner of evidence was thrown up by the Romantic school to counter these theories. In 1841, an excavation conducted within the round tower at Cloyne, Co Cork

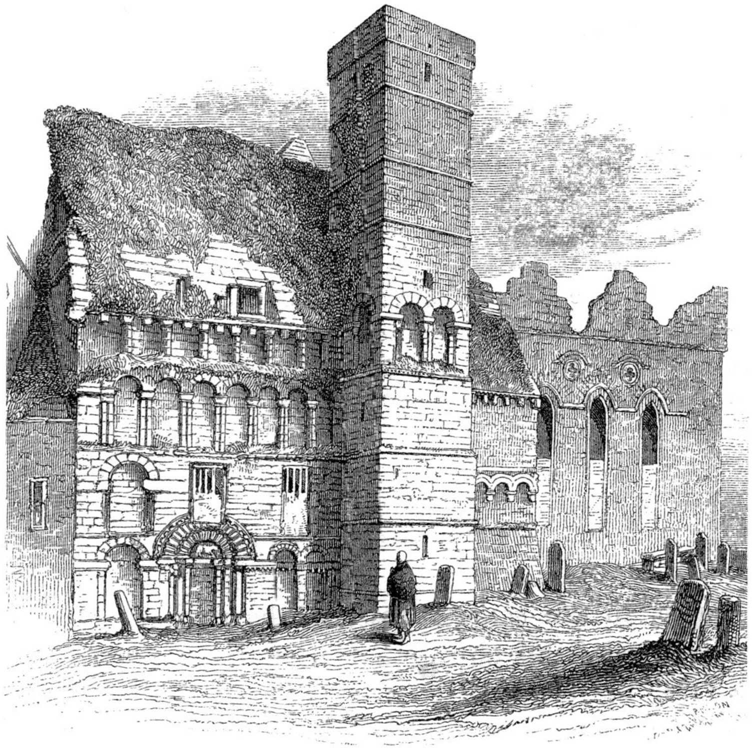

External View of Cormac's Chapel at Cashel (detail)
View of St. Kevin's House at Glendalough
all from G. Petrie, *The Ecclesiastical Architecture of Ireland*, 1845

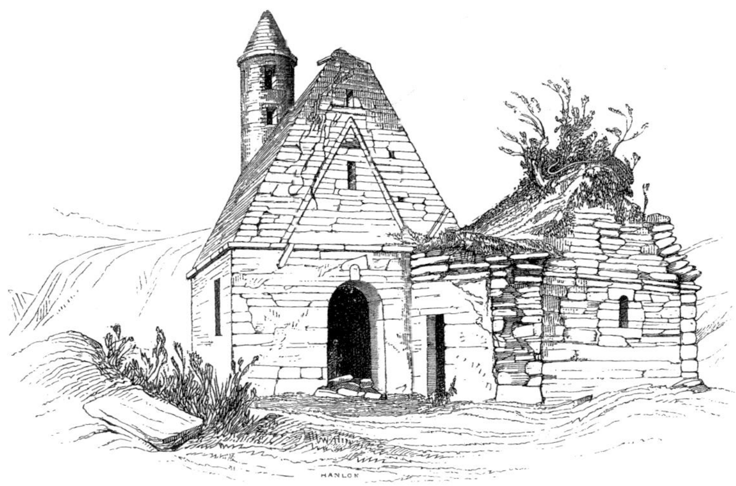

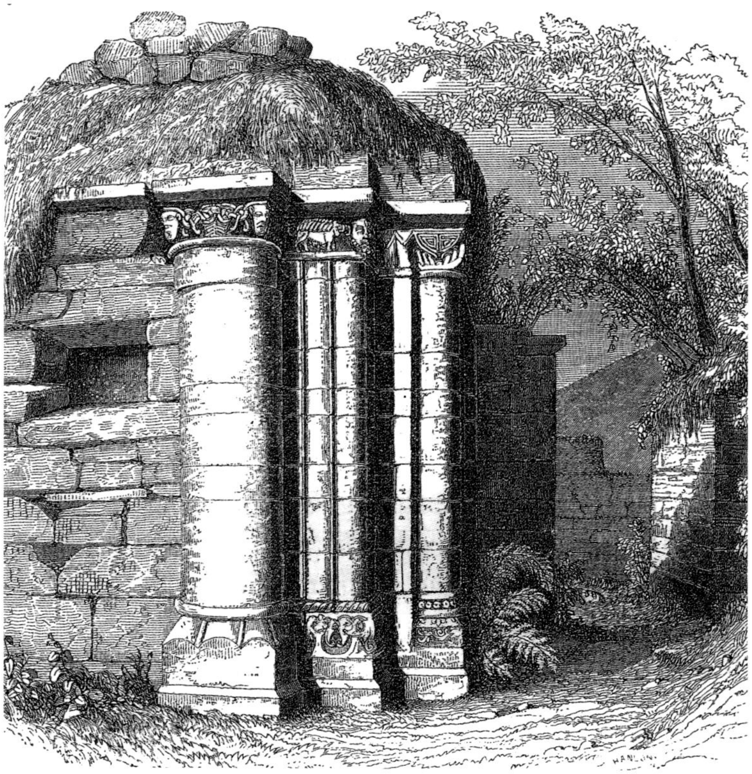

Pilasters of the Chancel-Arch of the Monastery Church at Glendalough (detail)
Inscribed Tomb of Maelfinnia at Clonmacnoise
both from G. Petrie, *The Ecclesiastical Architecture of Ireland*, 1845

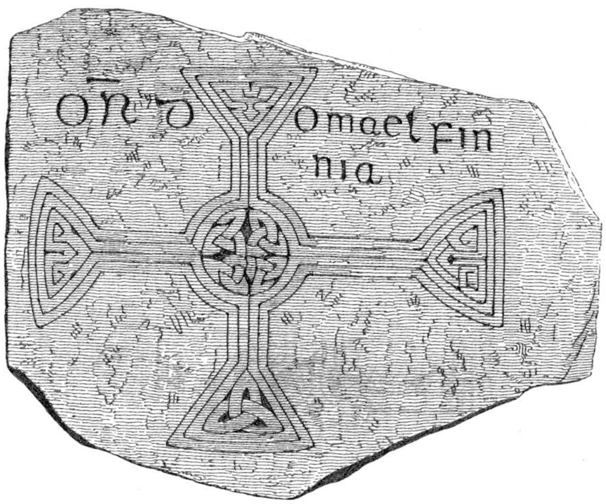

unearthed two skeletons, fuelling the Southern antiquaries' belief that these towers were pagan tombs. Windele sent Petrie a rambling and colourful account of the finds:

> Since then I visited, with others of the ancient craft, the Tower in Question, and I now enclose you a semi official statement of what occurred; I in so doing, it is right, that I should inform you, that the Statement, with regard to fragments of timbering being found, was incorrect. No such remains having been discovered. It is a curious circumstance that many small oyster shells have been taken out from amongst the clay & rubble which cover the skeletons; could these once have been Men? Lord Kames has somewhere said that 'men by inaction degenerate into oysters' and Sir Francis Burdett, in more recent times, when speaking of his Jim Crow propensities, declared he did not know if he should not yet turn into an oyster! We are told of an Indian Bramin who shut himself up into a Tower for 40 years, during which lengthened period, he industriously occupied himself in merely looking at the wall & thinking of – nothing. Who knows but, in these unexpected shells, we may have found some old Indo-Irish Bramin, whose contemplative inaction might have been productive of the ostracism. To the Budhists this, I submit, is worth some consideration...[308]

Windele also wrote to Petrie in May 1842, giving details of a funerary urn said to have been found in the round tower at Abernethy, Scotland, a find which, if true, would have vindicated the pagan theories. However, Windele was anxious also to the record straight, pointing out that only a fragment of an urn had been found. Although Windele continued to defend the pagan and funerary theories, it was not with any great expectation of success:

> But as I expect that we pagans will have a number of heavy blows dealt to us, when you do come out, we are already preparing our minds to see an Abernethy Urn shattered into very small fragments, and tread on as no better than so much very vulgar pottery, and are arranging a run with our small ware, before you come in, to monopolise the whole market. I have communicated a paper on round towers, containing my heathenish sentiments, to S C Hall, which will appear in his 'Ireland' of Fermanagh County, in one or two numbers. My

only present anxiety is to be out of the way previously to the appearance of your long looked-for paper.[309]

Petrie's essay, when published, did indeed deal a heavy blow to Windele, Vallancey and supporters of the 'Heathenish' theories. The essay is divided into two parts, the first setting out different theories of the towers' Viking, Phoenician or other pagan origins, and rejecting these, step by step, as untenable. Petrie also rejects their exclusive use, within a Christian context, as towers for anchorites or penitential prisons, citing the evidence of the buildings themselves, as well as accounts contained in ancient manuscripts. In the second half, again citing historical sources, he gives an account of early Irish ecclesiastical sites, of which the towers were part, devoting individual chapters to describing in detail churches, oratories, belfries, houses, erdamhs, kitchens, cashels and other structures such as wells, tombs and mills. While Petrie himself acknowledged his 'dry facts have too little poetry in them to reach the judgement through the medium of the imagination',[310] his conclusions are still held as accurate, although his dating of the earliest round towers to the 5th century is incorrect. Most of the towers were probably built between the 11th and 12th centuries. The older ones date from the 10th century.[311] Modern scholarship is also less inclined towards the theory of the towers being used as refuges during raids, in spite of the curious feature of the doors being at a height that necessitates a ladder or steps for access. While acknowledging that much of the literary evidence points towards the use of wood in early Christian churches in Ireland, Petrie scoured The Annals of the Four Masters and other manuscripts for evidence of stone churches right back at the time of St Patrick, citing the words such as damhliag, cill, eclais, tempull and regles as indicating stone buildings.[312] However, frustratingly, these churches, at Armagh, Glendalough, Clonmacnoise and other sites, are generally only mentioned by annalists if they were burned during Irish or Viking raids, or, more rarely, when they were hit by lightning. There is virtually no information on them in the earlier centuries. Petrie's assertion that the church at Armagh, erected in 445 by St Patrick, was of stone is unsustainable, as are his attempts to date churches at Killaloe and Iniscealtra to the 7th century.[313] However, Petrie was not always pushing back dates; in the case of Cormac's Chapel, he disagreed with Brewer's tentative 10th century dating, citing the Annals of Innisfallen, where the foundation of the church by Cormac McCarthy in 1134 is recorded.[314] He remained adamant however that there were Romanesque churches in Ireland before the Normans, and even the Vikings, arrived. The engravings are almost all after original drawings by Petrie, although some are based on drawings by Gabriel Beranger, and at least one on a drawing by Frederick William Burton. They show details of doors, windows, 'Cyclopean' stonework, chancel arches and inscribed grave slabs. Some of the best engravings show details of the Church of St Saviour at Glendalough, where Petrie lamented the 'barbarous devastation' whereby the fallen stones of the chancel arch were disappearing from the church: 'I feel it an imperative duty to preserve, so far as is in my power, every memorial of fragments so interesting to the history of art in this country.'[315] The chancel arch, with its elaborately carved stones, was eventually re-erected, in 1875, although the positioning of the stones is somewhat haphazard.

Having visited Clonmacnoise in 1841, Petrie was in a good position to describe its antiquities with accuracy. He uses the plan of Teampull Finghin made by Gabriel Beranger in 1779 for Colonel Conyngham.[316] He admits the heads in the chancel arch are in 'a quite Egyptian style' and in describing the nearby high cross, inscribed with the name of the Abbot Colman, he again berates Ledwich for his 'audacious misrepresentations' in asserting that the cross was late 13th century. (The cross almost certainly dates from 909, and commemorates Abbot Colmán mac Ailella's construction of the *daimhliag mór*, the cathedral). Petrie's method of dating the carved memorial slabs at Clonmacnoise was to link the names on the slabs with those of known abbots. However, this method was highly conjectural and modern scholarship is more cautious in its approach.[317] The year the 'Round Towers' essay was published, Petrie visited Oxford as the guest of the Rev William Sewell of Exeter College. Along with Adare, Henthorn Todd, and William Monsell, Sewell had been one of the original promoters of the new College of St Columba in Dublin. For at least years prior to his Oxford visit, Petrie had been in communication with the Ashmolean Society, sending them information on Irish antiquarian matters.[318] The contrast between the ancient buildings of Oxford, still in use and still maintained, and the ruinous condition of similar buildings in Ireland, did not escape Petrie.[319]

Chapter VIII

Petrie and the Royal Hibernian Academy

After a lifetime of controversy, whether connected with the Royal Irish Academy or the Ordnance Survey, whatever peace of mind Petrie might have hoped to enjoy in later years was overshadowed by a controversy at the Royal Hibernian Academy. A founder member of the Academy in 1826, Petrie exhibited at their annual exhibition regularly. (A complete list of the pictures he exhibited is given in the appendix.) He was elected Librarian in 1830. However, because of the loss of their records, analysis of his involvement in the Academy's affairs is difficult. Fortunately Walter Strickland had culled much material for his 1913 Dictionary of Irish Artists from these sources, some years before the RHA headquarters were destroyed in the Easter Rising of 1916.

The fortunes of the RHA have never been steady, and its history has been marked at every step, it seems, by argument and dissent. In the early 1850s things were probably at a peak of frustration, with the Academy heavily in debt and the attendances falling. The Famine had hit all parts of Ireland hard, but the Academy was slow to recover from the blow. It was stated in the reports of the Academy that, between 1849 and 1854, the income of the RHA had dropped from £771.16.8 to £375.14.2.[320] Petrie, in drafting the report for that year, described them as being in a 'crippled state' – mainly because of the financial embarrassment caused by the Famine. The members of the Academy became divided into two factions: the younger members wanted a clean sweep made of things, the Academy to go back to scratch, as it were, and seek a new charter and increased help from the Government. The older members were more conservative, and realised that the economic conditions that caused these troubles were likely to clear up as the state of the country improved. Internally, things were not good. Strickland relates that the affairs of the Academy were in a deteriorating state, with its rules and regulations being persistently ignored and violated.

When Michelangelo Hayes was elected secretary of the RHA on 5 March 1856, things promised to hot up, for Hayes represented the younger element and he had a strong lobby behind him. At this time, Martin Cregan was the president. Hayes imposed stringent economies on expenditure within the Academy, which involved the salaries of various officials being temporarily suspended. (Even with the Academy deeply in debt, these salaries had been paid directly out of the government grant.) Naturally, these measures were not received with much enthusiasm by the people concerned nor did the older faction think much of them. Petrie had also come in for the particular disapprobation of Hayes, as Strickland relates:

> As Secretary, Hayes had refused to recognise George Petrie as a member of the Academy, or to summon him to its meetings, on the ground that, under the rules, he had forfeited his membership by reason of his not exhibiting for two years.[321]

This was not the only bone of contention between Hayes and Petrie. Inspired by Hayes the members of the Academy had voted against continuing the system that Petrie had introduced of opening the annual exhibitions to the working classes in the evening at a greatly reduced admission fee. In fact, it was this decision that led Petrie to resign as secretary, and Hayes to be elected in his place. Hayes tells of what happened at the meeting in question:

> When the rescinding of the Penny Admission was carried, the three members who dissented left the meeting. As the Secretary (Dr Petrie) was one of those, it was represented to him that whatever the others might do, he, at all events, from

> his official position, was bound to remain; but he persisted in withdrawing, and as but six members were then left, and seven are necessary to constitute a quorum, further business was arrested.[322]

It would be as well, at this stage, to examine briefly some of the issues that had brought matters to this impasse. Petrie had introduced the idea of opening the annual exhibition of the Academy to people who could not afford the high entrance fee, by opening the galleries in the evenings and charging a nominal admission fee. What effect did this have on attendances? Taking the exhibitions of 1848 and 1849; the latter opened to the public on 20 June and it ran until 25 August. The price of admission was one shilling, except in the evenings, when it was reduced to one penny. The daytime exhibition was visited by 3,579 adults and 108 children (there were, in addition, 1000 free tickets given out) and the number of season tickets sold was 352. This was an increase of twenty-six on the previous year. The receipts for the daytime showings were £262.4.6. In 1848 they had been £214.12.0. Of more particular concern are the figures for the cheap evening showings. The admission fee was one penny and the catalogues were fourpence (in the daytime they were sixpence). Although the 1849 exhibition only opened for twenty-four evenings, the attendances were enormous. It is stated in the report that 29,910 tickets were sold in 1849; and that the figure for the preceding year had been 26,433. This means that, on average, over one thousand people saw the exhibition each evening it was open. These phenomenal attendances brought the total receipts for the exhibition of 1849 to £435.11.4; this represented an increase of over £70 on the previous year.[323]

However, as the Academy moved into the second half of the 19th century, in the post-Famine years, balancing the books became increasingly difficult. By 1853 the receipts for the exhibition, both 'Daylight' and 'Gaslight', had decreased to £313.7.10, and in 1854, the Life Drawing School of the RHA had to be closed for want of funds. It was estimated in the accounts that at the end of 1855, the Academy's outstanding debts would have risen to nearly £500, and when a memorial on the state of the Academy was presented to the Lord Lieutenant in 1857, it was stated that the debts of the Academy stood at £823.[324] Michelangelo Hayes' action, on being elected secretary, of cutting the salaries of the officers of the Academy, seems justified in the context of the outgoings of the Academy. In 1853, the officers' salaries and servants' wages amounted to £127, compared to £3 spent on providing living models for the drawing school and a similarly meagre amount expended on books for the library.

The decrease in the receipts for the annual exhibitions was due not to falling attendances, but rather to the fact that so many people who could have afforded to pay the high entrance fee chose instead to come in the evening and only pay a penny. The idea was very successful in attracting people who would not otherwise have come, but the overall result was a reduction in the income of the RHA that could be ill afforded. Each exhibition cost the Academy something in the region of £80 to £100. Hayes was not unsuccessful in his attempts to reverse this trend, as an article in the *Evening Mail* on the 1856 exhibition makes clear:

> The last exhibition opened punctually to the day advertised – a thing unprecedented – and was the best the Academy has had for years. The Penny Admissions were done away with – and at the close of the exhibition, something was realised over and above the expenses, which, considering the former exhibition involved an annual loss of between £80 and £100, was a vast improvement.[325]

Notwithstanding the success of the exhibition – it realised nearly £40 – the other members of the Academy were making things very difficult for Hayes and his supporters. At a General Meeting called for 18 October 1856, only six turned up and Hayes claimed that the others had absented themselves purposely, so that no business could proceed. (A quorum of seven was needed for motions to be carried.) Hayes sent out messengers to those members that were known to be in Dublin, but they ignored the summons. At the next meeting, held on 20 December 1856, Petrie turned up, although he had not been summoned. Hayes held that because he had not attended any meetings for he past ten months and had not contributed any pictures to the last two exhibitions, he had ceased 'ipso facto' to be a member. Petrie rejected this, and a noisy argument broke out amongst the members. Cregan was asked to vacate the president's chair, but refused to do so. An attempt was made to force him to leave the chair, but he remained firm. A second chair was brought forward and Mr Kendrick set up as chairman. Some members walked out of the meeting. Petrie and his friends remained and decided to elect themselves back into the various offices, so there were two sets of executives claiming to represent the Academy. Cregan and Hayes, as president and secretary, had Petrie and Mulrenin claiming to occupy

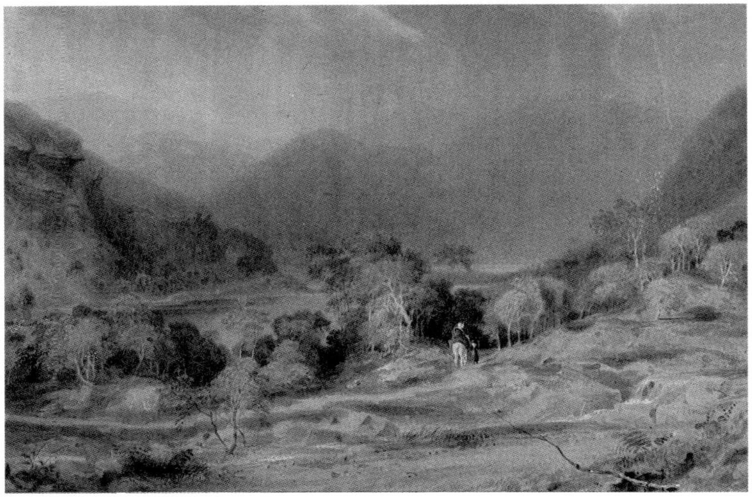

The Knight and the Lady
*c.*1828, watercolour on paper (see colour plate p.21)

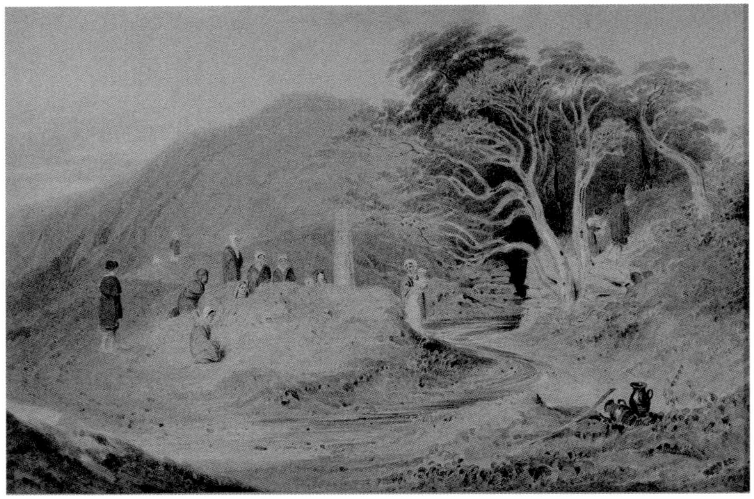

Pilgrims at St. Bridgid's Well, Liscannor, Co. Clare
*c.*1829-30, watercolour on paper, 18.5 x 26 (coll: NGI, cat. no. 2381)

the same posts, and seemingly having a majority of members behind them. Hayes and his friends refused to recognise the validity of the appointments, and he refused to surrender the books and keys held by him. A state of confusion followed, with different meetings being summoned, notices being inserted in the newspapers and contradicted the next day and public notices being torn down and replaced. The treasurer, not knowing what to do, refused to give out any money, and consequently the Academy ceased to function. The servants of the academy were in a terrible state, not knowing whom to obey and being berated at every step.[326]

On 8 April 1857 the 27 year-old Hayes was expelled from the Academy for these stonewalling tactics, but this did not end the confusion. The matter was referred to the Lord Lieutenant and Law Officers, and although no official opinion was given, there was some doubt expressed as to the legality of the meeting which had ousted Cregan and Hayes. Petrie was informed by the Solicitor-General that their case was 'unfavourable to them'.[327] But the schism continued, nonetheless, with neither side giving way, until the next annual meeting, held on 17 October 1857. At this meeting, Petrie was elected president. Strickland is of the opinion that the stance taken up by Hayes was not unjustified, but in the absence of more comprehensive records, the matter will have to rest there. Hayes was later received back into the Academy and again elected secretary. He was involved in a further controversy in 1860, with Catterson Smith. He died in 1877, after falling into the water tank on top of his house in Salem Place.

Whatever about this victory for the old brigade in the RHA, Petrie's days there were numbered, and the 'feather that broke the camel's back', as he put it himself, came not long afterwards. In 1857, a memoir was submitted to the Lord Lieutenant, Lord Naas, asking for an increase in the government grant to the RHA, to set it right. Lord Naas replied, saying that increased government aid could only be given if it was coupled with increased control of the affairs of the Academy. Stokes enumerates some of the proposals made by the government to take the affairs of the Academy in hand. They included government nominees on the committee, a government veto on the election of members, government control of the regulations of the Academy, and many other such restrictions on its independence. Petrie was vehemently opposed to these proposals and he asserted that they would bring the Academy under the control of the Government in a way that would be tolerated by no other such body in the British Empire. In this, however, he was mistaken. George Mulvaney pointed out to him that the Royal Academy in London, although it had no charter, had its constitution granted under George III, and that this constitution stated that all elections of academicians and officers had to have the sanction of the Sovereign in order to be valid.[328] Mulrenin replied to Lord Naas's letter, accepting the conditions laid down, and sparked off another row as he had replied without submitting his letter to a general meeting of the Academy or sealing it in the presence of the members of the Academy, as was required by a bye-law. Petrie was 'astonished' that Mulrenin should have done such a thing without consulting the members first. Petrie had drafted up his own reply to Lord Naas, which was far less agreeable to the Government's line of thinking. He assented to their demand that they have a measure of control in the choosing of 'visitors' to superintend the schools of the Academy, on the grounds that these visitors would receive public money in remuneration, but he was strongly opposed to any controls on the Academy's internal affairs. He felt that for the Government to veto the election of any member would be an insult to the others who had elected him, and that if it was not proposed to exercise this veto, then it should be struck off the charter. He pointed out that the Government that had granted the Academy their last charter had insisted on no such controls.[329] And in the matter of the vetos claimed on the election of all the officers, and on the passing of bye-laws, he felt that these were a tacit recognition of the unfitness of the Academy to run itself.[330]

The Lord Lieutenant was to be present at a meeting of the Academy, and protocol demanded that the address be made by the president of the RHA, but because Petrie did not personally agree with the content of the address as formulated by the Academy, he felt that he had no other option but to resign; this he did immediately, creating some disorder, as a president was needed to make decisions on the future of the Academy.[331] George Mulvaney appealed to Petrie not to leave them in the lurch:

> Disorganised and in serious jeopardy as the Body is, your absence, except from unavoidable cause, would be the signal of further dissension to him & would I fear render the prospect of righting the Academy hopeless and I seriously hope you will reconsider the matter and take your proper place on the occasion of the address. We shall have serious work to reply to MacLeod's report.[332]

(MacLeod had been commissioned by the Government to make an inquiry into the affairs of the RHA.) But Petrie was adamant. In January 1859, when the Academy assented to the proposed charter, Petrie resigned immediately as a member. He wrote to Mulrenin:

> The scene at the Academy the other night was indeed a pitiable one, and in itself enough to disgust, if not drive from the Academy, any men possessing any ordinary self-respect. But it was not the scene that forced me to come to the conclusion that I should resign from an office which I only accepted from a hope that I might be better able to sustain the interests of an important institution and help to avoid its threatened dissolution. That scene was but an item, like the additional feather that broke the camel's back, in convincing me that the indulgence of such a hope was a delusion. When I saw – unmistakably – that it was the gratification of petty objects of personal interest or ambition, and not the general interests of the body, that was uppermost in the minds of so many of the members, and that the very men, whom I had, foolishly, supposed to be my warmest and most disinterested friends, who had persuaded me, or as I may rather say, seduced me against my inclination to accept this office were he very first to abandon me, I felt strongly that I was forfeiting my own self-respect by retaining the office any longer. To a man of feeble constitution, of my age, tranquillity of mind is necessary for preservation of life; and my life is of some value to my children, and should not be sported with, except with a view to the attainment of a worthy object. My resolution is therefore fixed and unalterable.[333]

This weariness at the continual rowing in the Academy seems to be as much responsible for Petrie resigning as his indignation at the new charter.

The latter years of Petrie's life were spent trying to prepare a variety of his works for publication. In 1862 he undertook a tour of the west of Ireland, including the coast of Co Clare, Scattery Island and the Burren, while two years later he visited Co Donegal (for the first time).

Chapter IX

Petrie's Poverty and Eventual Pension

In 1843 Petrie began to feel the pinch of no longer receiving a government income. Although there was no shortage of orders for drawings and paintings by him, he was working hard on his book on the round towers of Ireland and did not wish to leave it aside when it was so near to being ready for publication. Hodges & Smith, the publishers of the work, would not advance him any money – times were bad enough, and with the bills from the wood-cutters of the illustrations for the 'Round Towers' reaching them regularly, they were in no position to start subsidising impecunious authors. Petrie appealed to Adare:

> Now my dear Lord, and best of friends, do not mistake me. I am not going to ask you to lend me money, because though I am persuaded as of my existence that you would befriend me in any way in your power, you have enough to do with your means without having to answer such calls. But if you can *without trouble* procure me the loan of fifty pounds for a few months it will enable me to get on cheerfully, and not as I am now working, with an uneasy mind. I need scarcely say that the payment is certain.[334]

Within two days Adare had responded to this plea by sending off the amount that Petrie had requested, and probably more, for Petrie's gratitude was quite unbounded.[335] However, £50 was not likely to keep him going for long, and he was soon hard-up again. Approaching old age, he was in no position to start trekking around the country again and dashing off watercolours. The few paintings that he did execute are marked by the evident difficulties that attended their execution. He looked to the government for a pension. A friend wrote to him:

> Some way or other these matters are ill-managed in our unfortunate country, that patronage which ought to be held out to students such as you, Curry & O'Donovan is ill distributed – Our parliamentary men would rather exert their influence on behalf of some worthless political zealot, whose services neither advantage nor confer honour on Ireland. I trust it will not be always so, and that I will yet have it in my power to congratulate you on being placed in a position where your talents, genius & industry will have free scope to display themselves, and add further honour to yourself, it that is possible.[336]

Petrie was eventually granted a Civil List pension in 1849, and, according to Stokes, the men who were most prominent in bringing the matter before the government were the Marquis of Kildare, Mr Hamilton and Joseph Napier, Bart.[337] The letter quoted above shows the type of support that Petrie enjoyed, but with Lord Adare to put his case at the highest level, there was little doubt about the outcome – Adare even interested the British Royal Family in Petrie's case. In late June 1849, O'Curry was in London working on a catalogue of the Irish manuscripts in the British Museum when he was invited to breakfast at Buckingham Palace with Adare and Dr Mayer:

> The poor Dr is very wild and very much in want of a few training lessons from you. There was no time that I had the honour and pleasure of a familiar talk with Lord Adare that you did not make a principal part of the subject; and there is no doubt that in him you have a faithful honest friend. You are to have the Queen over there among you shortly, and his Lordship intends to have you brought specially under Prince

> Albert's notice – Indeed I believe the Prince has, or is about to, interest himself with the powers that be, in your favour...[338]

In October of that year, Petrie received a letter from 'Lord C.' stating that 'Lord John' had settled £100 on him and could do no more. But Petrie had been led to believe, from letters written to Todd and Stokes by 'G.A.H.' that Lord John had given a promise that the one hundred was an initial sum and would be increased to two as soon as possible. Petrie said that he would hold his silence on the matter for the moment.[339] A friend of Petrie's called Christopher Moore was acting for him in London in the matter of actually getting the pension. Moore traipsed around from office to office on Petrie's behalf:

> Following up your wish I called on Pennington on Saturday & was sent by him to another office where I paid the fees, £3 11, & £4 for the stamp, total £7 11 to a Mr. Ramsey, who gave me the warrant & sent me to a Mr. Miller in another Dept. of the Treasury & the latter directed me to the Paymaster General's office – where I was told the document should be taken to the Audit Office Somerset House, but it was then too late. Well, this morning I posted off with Her Majesty's warrant – thinking to have it signed and ready for posting off today, but to my great disappointment, after filling up a printed form I had to leave it & was told I cannot have it again before Wednesday or Thursday next! So easy do our officials take these matter; I shall not however lose sight of business.[340]

In the late summer of 1845, after his spring visit to Oxford, Petrie visited Scotland to compare at first hand the round towers of Brechin and Abernethy with those of Ireland. William Wilde accompanied him on this trip.[341] They spent two days in Glasgow and the same time in Edinburgh.[342] The next year, Stokes relates, Petrie visited Scotland again and spent some time on the island of Skye, where he made studies for a picture of *The Valley of Sligachan*, the present whereabouts of which are unknown.

That Petrie did return to painting, as Stokes asserts, as a means of earning a living after the work on the survey had ended, seems to be the case; for in a letter to Petrie in 1845, James Wills of Suirville talks of a painting that Petrie was working on:

> I dreamed the other night that I was getting ready to go out shooting in that last landscape of yours; I suppose I should have been turned off the premises for poaching. It must now be nearly finished, if not wholly. Is its destination fixed?[343]

Frederick William Burton wrote to Petrie at this time and mentioned a painting that Petrie was working on: 'How does your beautiful vision unfold itself? May I soon ask for another glance? For it has rested like a dream not to be forgotten on my memory ever since I saw it.'[344] It is impossible to say with any certainty to which works these two writers refer. Stokes does mention a number of paintings that Petrie worked on after he left the Ordnance Survey: *The Last Round of the Pilgrims at Clonmacnoise* (Plate 30), *Conor's Pass, in the County of Kerry*, *The Fair of Sligachan*, and *The College of St. Brecan in Aran*. However, Stokes' sources are the exhibition catalogues of the Royal Hibernian Academy (see appendix). These catalogues detail only a handful of paintings beyond those Stokes mentions; the most important being *The Home of the Heron*, now in the National Gallery of Ireland. *The Home of the Heron* and *The Last Round of the Pilgrims at Clonmacnoise* are the only two of these later pictures that have been located; both are in the NGI. A recently discovered sketchbook, containing pencil drawings of the ruined castle and round tower at Clonmacnoise, gives precise dates for Petrie's revisiting this site. The drawings are dated between 30 September and 1 October 1842, indicating that he spent several days at Clonmacnoise. The sketches help date the large painting, *The Last Round of the Pilgrims at Clonmacnoise* in the NGI, to that year. It is very unlikely that Petrie painted any pictures, other than those few which he exhibited at the Academy, in this later part of his career. He certainly did not seem too enthusiastic about painting:

> I am now quietly engaged in finishing my picture, which, as well I suppose from want of practice as from bad health, has been a tedious work, but nevertheless I trust it will be my best work of its kind, despite of everything, and the subject is lovely. When I have finished I shall endeavour to get on with my second volume, but it will be slowly, for I must still paint to live.[345]

Through the years, Rothwell had maintained contact with Petrie. In giving his impressions of the Royal Academy exhibition of 1850 (and dissatisfied with the way his own pictures had been hung out of the line), he was not short of praise for his own talents and capabilities:

> ...plenty of room for men who can portray nature in its freshness and this I am resolved to do at all hazards. I am now finishing I think a good picture of some beauty and of a moral effect . . . I have the power to paint in some respects as well as Gainsborough. I can sell my pictures. And I shall enjoy some little nook where I can pour forth my colors in the full comparison of unsophisticated truth. I am thank God in health and now with my mind in full training I shall produce a series of works which will be new to the London gazers.[346]

Rothwell thought William Mulready was the 'first man' of the exhibition, but he thought he had become too conventional and that his elaborate pictures were wanting the 'freshness of first impulse'. Mulready, he said, was 'up to astonish' rather than treating the thing as though it were a reality. Francis Danby, he thought, was singularly deficient in everything; his picture was not worthy of him in any way. Rothwell himself had just had a fourth child, a boy, and he was resolved to return to Ireland with his family as soon as possible:

> I am painting for my loved haunts somewhere above the Dargle where I hope to find a cottage and garden, and where I can see my little children grow up in health, enjoying nature . . . I must, to be happy, have a small garden, a bit of grass to see them tumble on, and a painting room – this I feel must be built. I shall bring many books of Art and all my Art decorations so that I shall have a nook in which my mind may with full devotion kneel at my shrine.[347]

In this same year, Petrie negotiated the purchase of a painting from Danby, for a Francis MacCracken of Belfast, with whom he had much correspondence. MacCracken was afraid to deal directly with Danby, as he had commissioned a picture from him before, which he had been very dissatisfied with when completed. Danby, however, accepted this latest commission from MacCracken, who wanted, as he put it, to possess another specimen of his distinguished countryman's work, 'in his own peculiar and unapproachable walk – say a sunrise or a sunset.' If Danby had anything in this line, MacCracken would fancy it, but after his last experience, he would prefer if Petrie could get Danby to send it to him on approval, and if he did not fancy it he would get Danby a good price for it from the dealers in Belfast. In September 1850, he sent Petrie a cash order for £40, the price that had been agreed upon for Danby's 'little picture'.[348]

POSTSCRIPT

Petrie died of fever on 17 January 1866. He was survived by his daughters Eliza and Mary Ann, his infant son George having died at the age of five.[349] Although in 1847 he had been awarded an honorary LL.D degree by the University of Dublin, the presidency of the Royal Irish Academy eluded him. Twelve years after Petrie's death, in 1878, the two-volume *Christian Inscriptions in the Irish Language* was published by the Royal Historical and Archaeological Association. Edited by William Stokes' daughter Margaret (Maddie), it contained much of the material, including drawings and texts, collected by Petrie during his decades of research and travel. The affection felt for Petrie by his daughters and by the Stokes family is palpable throughout the extant correspondence. The most touching letter of this correspondence was written to Lord Dunraven by Mary Petrie, a year after her father's death. It is preserved amongst the Adare papers now in the library of the University of Limerick.[350]

> May 23rd 1867 — 7 Charlemont Place
>
> My dear Lord Dunraven, I was agreeably surprised by the sight of your handwriting yesterday. I had thought that your promise, and my most unimportant self had alike been packed from your memory amid the glories with which you were surrounded. Your reason for writing now is a very kind one, and I thank you heartily. We have not, however, got the 'the pension', only the half of it, which is a disappointment, as Dr Stokes always led us to suppose we should get the whole, his kind heart made him believe what he so much wished. But though disappointed we are not the less truly grateful to the two or three kind friends whose exertions have been so far successful, knowing full well that but for their zeal, we should have nothing. And more especially to dear Lord Dunraven, who undertook this most unpleasant portion of the business, do we feel more than words can express.
>
> If I grumble it is far less at having an insufficient income, than because I think, in their tardy grant of half what was asked of them, the government have shown a disregard for my father's labours for the benefit of the country which merited a better recognition. Apart from this the part of the disappointment which weighs most on me at present is my inabili-

ty to remain in his house. As the abode of my father in the last years of his life, it is inexpressibly sad for me to leave it and I shall feel in going forth from it, even more lonely than I have felt.

I hope you got the newspaper which contained Dr Stokes 'Afternoon Lecture'. I wish you had heard it – he read it with such expression. The language was most beautiful, and so plain, I think even the butterfly looking young ladies who abounded in the room might have understood it. I am truly glad to hear you are enjoying your tour so much and that you have met with so many things to interest you. I should feel tempted to envy you your wanderings but that I have long since given up any such active feeling with regard to enjoyments which cannot be met with on the banks of the canal or, at least, within the limit of a mile and half. I used to feel ... first in expecting, then hoping, then wishing to see more and newer objects of interest, but as days went by and these feelings were not gratified, they gradually subdued into a sort of pathetic content which does pretty well now. I hope you will not over 'addle' your brains with old churches like poor Maddie Stokes, who has been obliged to go to Scotland to get hers un-addled, they having succumbed beneath the weight of 'opus Hibernicus'.

I suppose I shall never see you again, as before you come to Ireland I shall have retired to some remote or obscure region where you can not look for me. If so, do not quite forget one who will always remember you with fond regard.

Yours most truly
Mary A. Petrie

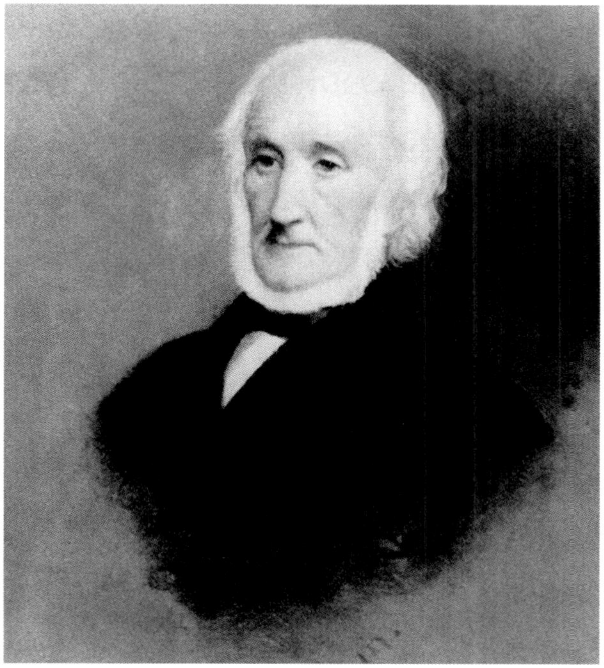

Bernard Mulrenin (1803-68)
George Petrie, artist and archaeologist 1790-1866
oil on panel, 26 x 22 cm (courtesy NGI)

PETER MURRAY is curator of the Crawford Municipal Art Gallery, Cork. He studied History of Art at University College Dublin, and in 1981 was awarded an M.Litt degree by Trinity College for his thesis on the watercolours of George Petrie. He is vice-chairman of the Cultural Relations Committee of the Dept of Foreign Affairs, and was visual arts editor of *The Encyclopaedia of Ireland* (Gill & Macmillan, 2003). He was awarded an honorary MA by University College Cork in 2003.

ABBREVIATIONS

NGI	National Gallery of Ireland
NLI	National Library of Ireland
PRO	Public Records Office, Dublin
RIA	Royal Irish Academy

ENDNOTES

1 William Stokes, *The Life and Labours in Art and Archaeology of George Petrie L.L.D., M.R.I.A.* (Longman Green & Co, London, 1868). Born in Dublin, Dr William Stokes (1804-78) was the son of Whitley Stokes, a religious non-conformist and professor of medicine at the University of Dublin, a post to which William succeeded in 1845. Petrie and James Arthur O'Connor often visited Whitley Stokes' house at Ballinteer. Trained at the College of Surgeons and at Edinburgh, William Stokes worked at the Meath Hospital in Dublin where he introduced the stethoscope and a new system of anatomical diagnosis. He contracted typhus in 1827, working with the poor of Dublin. In addition to his biography of Petrie, he published over one hundred scientific works.

2 Death recorded in the Register of Deaths, Custom House, for the year 1866. The date of Petrie's death is given by Stokes as 17 January, and in the Public Record Office as 18 January, but the Registry of Deaths gives it as 12 January. (The death was uncertified until 30 January.) Letters of Administration were granted to Petrie's daughter, Mary Ann; Administrations 1866, PRO, Dublin.

3 Miss Beaufort, 'The state of architecture and antiquities, previous to the landing of the Anglo-Normans in Ireland', RIA *Transactions*, 15, 1828. His account of the Lia Fail was later refuted by P.W. Joyce. See A.P. Graves, *Irish Literary & Musical Studies,* 1913, p.171 ff.

4 He also contributed articles to the *Dublin Penny Journal* and the *Irish Penny Journal.*

5 Neither of these two journals survived more than a year of publication. For an account of the *Dublin Penny Journal*, see S. Ferguson, *Dublin University Magazine*, 1840.

6 Stokes, p.371

7 Margaret Stokes to Dr Frazer, undated, NLI, MS 3038. Edwin Richard Windham Wyndham-Quin (1812-71), 3rd Earl of Dunraven, MP for Glamorgan (1836-50), and Lieutenant for Co Limerick, was responsible for rebuilding the manor, the village, and several historic churches at Adare. A student of William Rowan Hamilton, he graduated from Trinity College in 1833. Amongst the Adare papers deposited in the University of Limerick are letters from Sir Frederick Burton to Petrie, written between 1827 and 1864, correspondence between Petrie and John O'Donovan (*c.*1830-56), letters from Petrie to Thomas Larcom and Eugene Curry (1836-44), letters from Petrie to the 3rd Earl (1851-65), letters from William and Margaret Stokes to the 3rd Earl (1864-71).

8 Grace Calder, *George Petrie and the Ancient Music of Ireland* (Dolmen Press, Dublin, 1868)

9 NGI, Petrie Portfolio, cat. nos 6660-769. (A full list of watercolours and drawings in the Margaret Stokes bequest is detailed in the catalogue.) As well as assisting her father's work, Margaret Stokes posthumously published Lord Dunraven's work before going on to publish her own *Early Christian Architecture in Ireland* in 1878.

10 *ibid.*; Stokes, p.3

11 M.C. Ferguson, *Sir Samuel Ferguson in the Ireland of his Day*, 2 vols (Wm. Blackwood & Sons, London, 1896) ii, p.114

12 *ibid.*

13 Sir Charles Petrie, *Chapters from Life* (London, 1950) pp.1-3

14 Walter G. Strickland, *A Dictionary of Irish Artists* 2 vols (London and Dublin, 1913) ii, p.243

15 *Portrait of Elizabeth Petrie* by James Petrie, NGI, cat. no. 3032a; *Portrait of George Petrie* by James Petrie, NGI, cat. no. 2231

16 Strickland, *Dictionary*, ii, p.243

17 *ibid.*

18 NLI, PD EMMERO (2) II.

19 Ruan O'Donnell, *Remembering Emmet* (Wordwell, Dublin, 2003); James Petrie, *Portrait of Robert Emmet*, NLI, PD EMME-RO (3) I

20 NLI, EP HOWL-HE (1), Elmes 176, EP REDM-DE (1) II respectively

21 Stokes, p.389, cf. Indian ink portrait of Robert Emmet engraved by J. Heath, after James Petrie, for Barrington's *Historic Memoirs*, and entitled *Taken while on trial for high treason whilst Lord Norbury was charging the jury*

22 Strickland, ii, p.90; Samuel Whyte, *The Shamrock*, or *Hibernian Cresses, a collection of poems, songs, epigrams, &c., Latin as well as English, the original product of Ireland. To which are subjoined, thoughts on the prevailing system of school education respecting young ladies as well as gentlemen, with practical proposals for a reformation* (printed by R Marchbank, Dublin, 1772)

23 Charles Hanlon to (William Stokes?), 1866, recounting his father's recollections of his younger days. NLI, MS 793, no. 555

24 Stokes, p.2

25 H.F. Berry, *A History of the Royal Dublin Society* (Longman Green & Co, London, 1915) p.117. See also John Turpin, *A School of Art in Dublin Since the Eighteenth Century: A History of the National College of Art and Design* (Gill & Macmillan, Dublin, 1995) p.89

26 Terence de Vere White, *The Story of the Royal Dublin Society* (The Kerryman, Tralee, 1955) p.63

27 Turpin, pp.39-42

28 *ibid.* p.65

29 Strickland, ii, p.89

30 Berry, p.122

31 The medal is reproduced in Berry, facing p.119, and the inscription on it reads 'Presented by the Dublin Society to George Petrie for a group of figures, April 4th, 1805'. Stokes says that Petrie received this when he was only fourteen, but going by the birth date given in Strickland, it may be taken that he received the medal when he was but fifteen years and four months of age.

32 Turpin, p.95

33 Turpin, p.148

34 Strickland, ii, p.243. Also PRO, Grants of Probate and Letter of Administration 1863, where Petrie is recorded as having been appointed executor of his stepmother's estate.

35 Eric Adams, *Francis Danby, Varieties of Poetic Landscape* (Yale University Press, New Haven and London, 1973) p.2

36 Letter from Danby to John Gibbons, 2 January 1833, quoted in Francis Greenacre (ed.), *The Bristol School of Artists: Francis Danby and Painting in Bristol 1810-1840* (City Art Gallery, Bristol, 1973) p.33

37 Charles Hanlon's recollections in 1866, NLI, MS 793, no.555

38 Stokes, p.10

39 Stokes, p.6

40 *The Entrance to the Dargle River*, ink on paper, s & d 1807, NGI, cat. no. 6304

41 Peter Harbison, *Guide to the National Monuments of Ireland* (Gill & Macmillan, Dublin, 1970) p.258

42 Stokes, p.5

43 Stokes, p.4

44 Strickland, ii, p.236

45 *Conway Castle*, NGI, cat. no. 6733; *Conway Castle*, NGI, cat. no. 6734

46 Vickery Gibbs, *The Complete Peerage*, vii (London, 1926) p.664. (s.v. 'Glenworth')

47 Stokes, p.7

48 Charles Hanlon's recollections in 1866, NLI, MS 793, no. 555

49 Stokes, pp.3-6; R.M. Leary to William Stokes, 6 April 1866, NLI, MS 795

50 W.F. Wakeman, 'Petrie as a Painter', *Dublin Saturday Magazine*, March 1866, p.634

51 Adams, p.2

52 NGI, cat. nos 6742-46

53 Stokes, p.8

54 'Francis Danby: Obituary', *Art Journal*, 13 February1861

55 Charles Hanlon's recollections, NLI, MS 793, no. 555

56 Stokes, p.8

57 W.F. Wakeman, 'Petrie as a Painter', *Dublin Saturday Magazine*, March 1866

58 James Petrie to George Petrie, undated, quoted in Stokes, p.9

59 W.F. Wakeman, in *Dublin Saturday Magazine*, March 1866, p.364

60 Adams, p.4

61 Francis Danby to John Gibbons, 29 February 1836, quoted in John Hutchinson, *James Arthur O'Connor* (National Gallery of Ireland, Dublin, 1985) p.83

62 W. Justin O'Driscoll, *A Memoir of Daniel Maclise* (Longman Green & Co, London, 1871) p.6

63 Charles Hanlon, NLI, MS 793, no. 555

64 John Henry Brocas sketchbook, NLI, cat. no. 2038

65 Edward Dayes, *Instructions for Drawing and Colouring Landscapes* (1805)

66 William Gilpin, *Three Essays: On Picturesque Beauty; On Picturesque Travel; and On Picturesque Landscape* (London (3rd ed.), 1808)

67 Malcolm Andrews, *The Search for the Picturesque: Landscape Aesthetics and Tourism in Britain 1760-1800* (Scolar Press, London, 1989) p.112

68 Robert Southey, *Letters from England, II*, letter xxx, 1807, pp.12-13; quoted by Patricia Butler in *The Brocas Collection* (NLI, Dublin, 1997)

69 George Barret, *Llanberis with the early morning mists dispersing* (private collection), illustration in Anne Crookshank and the Knight of Glin, *The Painters of Ireland c.1660-1920* (Barrie & Jenkins, London, 1978) p.131

70 Stokes, p.11

71 The resemblance can be uncanny. See Varley's watercolour *Dolbadern Castle*, exhibited Agnews 1999, and reproduced in catalogue (no. 42). For another Varley view of Dolbadern, see C.M. Kauffmann, *John Varley 1778-1842*, exhibition catalogue (V&A, London, 1984) p.34, reproduced p.14

72 See Kathryn Barron, *A Picturesque Tour through Wales 1675 to 1855: watercolours from the Collection of the National Museum of Wales*, exhibition catalogue, (Museum of Fine Arts, Gifu, Japan, 1998) p.117, no. 55, illustrated p.76

73 Thomas Girtin, *Conway Castle, North Wales*, watercolour, exhibited Agnews 2001, cat. no. 35. Samuel Jackson, *The Eagle's Nest, Killarney*, *c*.1825-30, reproduced in Thomas Agnew, *English Watercolours and Drawings* (London, 1999). Painted in pencil and brown ink wash, this work was in the 'grey Eberle Folio', the collection assembled by Alderman J.E. Eberle *c*.1900, comprising only monochrome landscapes by artists of the Bristol School.

74 Richard Wilson, *Llyn Peris and Dolbaddern Castle*, National Gallery of Victoria, New South Wales

75 Caspar David Friedrich, *Ruins of the Oybin Monastery (The Dreamer)*, *c*.1835, Hermitage Museum, St Petersburg

76 *Dublin Saturday Magazine*, March 1866

77 Stokes, p.20

78 Stokes, pp.13-14

79 Strickland, ii, p.237

80 *Glendalough*, private collection; *Glenmalure*, private collection (both illustrated)

81 *Dalkey Castle*, private collection

82 Strickland, ii, p.236

83 H. Levinge to Petrie, 7 October 1826, NLI, MS 791, no. 282

84 O. Bellew to Petrie, 10 July 1827, NLI, MS 789, no. 28

85 O. Bellew to Petrie, 16 July 1827, NLI, MS 789, no. 29

86 *St Lawrence's Gate, Drogheda*, NGI, cat. no. 2374; *View of Kells*, 2369; *Howth Castle*, 2371; *Kildare Cathedral*, 2373; *Clondalkin Round Tower*, 2372

87 *Black Castle, Co. Wicklow*, Ulster Museum

88 *View at Mount Usher*, NGI, cat. no. 2378; *Old Kilcullen Bridge*, 2368; *Slane Castle*, 2367; *Rathmichael Church*, 2370

89 Thomas Kitson Cromwell, *Excursions through Ireland*, 3 vols (Longman, London, 1820)

90 J. Hine to Petrie, undated, NLI, MS 791, no. 241

91 *Puck's Castle in the County of Dublin*, ink wash on paper, private collection

92 Greig, Islington, to Petrie, 17 November 1821, NLI, MS 791, no. 213

93 John Smith to George Petrie, Spring Gardens, Copper House, London, 13 June 1823, NLI, MS 792, no. 341

94 J. Brewer, Pillerton House, Warwickshire, to Petrie, 30 February 1827, NLI, MS 789, no. 74. J.N. Brewer, *The Beauties of Ireland: Being Original Delineations, Topographical, Historical and Biographical of each county [with] engravings by J. and H. S. Storer after original drawings, chiefly by Mr Petrie of Dublin*, 2 vols (Sherwood, London, 1825-26)

95 Brewer to Petrie, 26 August 1826, NLI, MS 789, no. 46

96 *View of Kilmallock*, sepia on paper, 26.7 x 39.7cm, NGI, cat. no. 2375

97 Brewer to Petrie, 8 May 1820, NLI, MS 789, no. 44

98 Brewer to Petrie, 26 March 1820, NLI S 789, no. 43

99 Brewer to Petrie, 8 May 1820, NLI, MS 789, no. 44

100 Brewer to Petrie, 26 August 1826, NLI, MS 789, no. 46

101 Brewer to Petrie, 15 October 1821, NLI, MS 789, no. 54

102 George Petrie to Eliza Petrie, 1 August 1820, quoted in Stokes, p.27

103 Brewer to Petrie, 1 November 1822, NLI, MS 789, no. 64

104 Christopher Bellew to Brewer, undated, quoted in a letter from Brewer to Petrie, 30 April 1823, NLI, MS 789, no. 66

105 Brewer to Petrie, 17 July 1823, NLI, MS 789, no. 67

106 Richard Grenville married Anne Elizabeth, only daughter of the 3rd Duke of Chandos, in 1796, and was created Duke of Buckingham and Chandos in 1822.

107 Brewer to Petrie, 3 January 1824, NLI, MS 789, no. 70

108 Before working on *The Beauties of Ireland*, Storer and his eldest son Henry, who assisted him, had published *The History and Antiquities of the Cathedral Churches of Great Britain* (Sherwood Neely & Jones, London, 1814-19) of which Pugin had said that the engravings were the most accu-

rate views in existence of the cathedrals.

109 Brewer to Petrie, 26 March 1820, NLI, MS 789, no. 43

110 Brewer to Petrie, 3 March 1823, NLI, MS 789, no. 65

111 Brewer to Petrie, 29 August 1821, NLI, MS 789, no. 52

112 *ibid.*, the engravings referred to were in a publication on Edinburgh

113 *ibid.*

114 Brewer to Petrie, 5 March 1822, NLI, MS 789, no. 59

115 Brewer to Petrie, 4 October 1825, NLI, MS 789, no. 73

116 Brewer to Petrie, December 1821, NLI, MS 789, no. 57

117 Brewer to Petrie, 4 October 1825, NLI, MS 789, no. 73

118 George Newham Wright, *Historical Guide to Ancient and Modern Dublin* (London, 1821)

119 George Newham Wright, *Guide to the Lakes of Killarney*; *Guide to the County Wicklow*; *Guide to the Giant's Causeway* (London, 1823), printed as one volume

120 *Drumgoff Barracks*, watercolour on paper, 20.4 x 28.5cm, dated 1822 (private collection, provenance: Whitley Stokes Collection)

121 NGI, cat. no. 6718

122 *The Reeks from Aghadowey*, NGI, cat. no. 6728

123 Thomas Higham, Islington, to Petrie, 27 August 1821, NLI, MS 791, no. 239

124 George Cooke, Hackney, to Petrie, 10 August 1824, NLI, MS 790, no. 128

125 W. Wakeman to Petrie, 5 August 1823, NLI, MS 793, no. 625

126 W. Wakeman, 23 Lr Sackville St, to Petrie, undated (a tentative date of 1821 can be given), NLI, MS 793, no. 622

127 Edward Johnston to Petrie, 8 October 1830, NLI, MS 791, no. 622

128 R. Rothwell to Petrie, 13 August 1828, NLI, MS 793, no. 579

129 *ibid.*

130 R. Rothwell to Petrie, undated, NLI, MS 793, no. 581

131 Fisher, 38 Newgate St, London, to Petrie, 15 August 1828, NLI, MS790, no. 190

132 Fisher to Petrie, 17 September 1828, NLI, MS790, no. 191

133 Fisher to Petrie, 18 September 1828, NLI, MS 790, no. 192

134 *ibid.*

135 Fisher to Petrie, 30 September 1828, NLI, MS 791, no. 193

136 Fisher to Petrie, 24 October 1828, NLI, MS 791, no. 190

137 Fisher to Petrie, 6 October 1828, NLI, MS 791, no. 194

138 Fisher to Petrie, 11 October 1828, NLI, MS 791, no. 195

139 *ibid.*

140 Fisher to Petrie, 24 October 1828, NLI, MS 791, no. 196

141 Fisher to Petrie, 15 November 1828, NLI, MS 791, no. 198

142 Fisher to Petrie, 18 February 1829, NLI, MS 791, no. 199

143 Fisher to Petrie, 4 April 1829, NLI, MS790, no. 189

144 Wright, *Historical Guide to Ancient and Modern Dublin*

145 G.N. Wright, Llanrust, north Wales, to Petrie, 29 September 1828, NLI, MS 794, no. 692

146 NGI, Petrie Portfolio, cat. no. 6708, *View of Howth Lighthouse from Needles*

147 William Millar, Edinburgh, to Wm. Curry & Co, 21 November 1829, NLI, MS 792, no. 340

148 Catalogue of the 1830 RHA exhibition

149 NGI, cat. nos 6700, 6667, 6661, 6841 respectively

150 NGI, cat. nos 6668, 6732, 6663 respectively

151 Ulster Museum, cat. no.839

152 *Dunluce Castle*, private collection

153 *Dunluce Castle*, pencil sketch, NGI, cat. no. 6663

154 Letter from Petrie to his wife, Stokes, p.27

155 Peter Murray, *George Petrie 1790-1866*, M.Litt (Trinity College Dublin, 1980) p.29

156 Brewer to Petrie, 29 August 1821, NLI, MS789, no. 52. This provides confirmation that Petrie's first tour of the west did, in fact, take place in 1821.

157 View of Kilmallock, NGI, cat. no. 2375

158 RIA, MS 12, n.22

159 Stokes, p.18. The present whereabouts of the picture are unknown

160 Brewer to Petrie, December 1821, NLI, MS 789, no. 57

161 RIA, Ms 12, n.4, p.119 (Petrie autograph)

162 *ibid.*, p.121 (another draft of the above)

163 *ibid.*, p.125 (Petrie autograph)

164 *ibid.*, p.205 (Petrie's account of Tuam)

165 Stokes, p.25

166 Stokes, p.26

167 RIA MS 12, n.4, pp.207-11

168 The cross has now been re-erected and stands in the centre of the town, surrounded by a railing. It is thought that the three pieces of which it is composed did not necessarily belong together originally.

169 George Petrie, *The Ecclesiastical Architecture of Ireland*, p.314

170 *ibid.*

171 *ibid.*, p.226

172 Richard Martin (also known as 'Humanity Dick' and 'Hairtrigger Dick') was the former MP for Jamestown , Lanesborough and Co Galway. In 1791 he had obtained damages of £10,000 from one William Petrie (no relation to George, so far as is known), who had eloped with his wife Elizabeth.

173 NGI, cat. nos 6696, 6697 (pencil sketches)

174 NGI, cat. no. 6032 (watercolour)

175 NLI, MS 795 (fragments of Petrie MSS)

176 Stokes, p.34. This passage is not amongst the Petrie MSS as they now stand, but in Stokes that same passage forms the introduction to an extensive description of the village of Cong and its environs, which is contained in the Petrie MSS in the RIA.

177 Stokes, p.34; also RIA, MS 12, n.4, pp.157-69

178 Stokes, p.36

179 Stokes, p.38

180 RIA, MS 12, n.4, p.133: 'Connemara 1822'

181 Stokes, p.281

182 Stokes, p.284

183 Letter from ? to ?, dated 'Clifden, Aug 9, 1822', NLI, MS 795. (If Petrie stayed with Mr Martin at Ballinahinch House in 1822, why is there a letter from Uniacke to Petrie, dated 'Ballinahinch, Feb. 21, 1823', in which he states that he has arranged for Mr Martin of Ballinahinch to take care of Petrie if he comes down to Connemara, and to offer him his house as a headquarters, as if Martin and Petrie were strangers in 1823? See NLI, MS 793, no. 618.

184 RIA, MS 12 n.4, Petrie Papers, undated

185 *ibid.*

186 *Ballinahinch House*, NGI, cat. no. 6840; *Ballinahinch Lake*, 6671, *Ballinahinch Bay*, 6672; *The Home of the Heron*, 6871

187 *Clifden from Road to Castle,* NGI, cat. no. 6681

188 NGI, cat. nos 6670, 6672, 6692

189 Stokes, p.40

190 John Uniacke to Petrie, 21 February 1823, NLI, MS 793, no. 619

191 John Uniacke to Petrie, Ballinahinch, 21 February 1823, NLI, MS 793, no. 618

192 'Our Portrait Gallery, no. iii, George Petrie RHA MRIA', *Dublin University Magazine*, xiv, 1839, p.638

193 Interview with Barry Raftery, Dept of Archaeology, UCD, November 1979

194 Stokes, p.360
195 Petrie, 7 Charlemont Place, to Adare (undated but *c.*1857), Adare Papers, University of Limerick, D3196/I/14/3
196 H. Levinge to Petrie, 7 October 1826, NLI, MS 791, no. 282
197 'Our Portrait Gallery, no. iii, George Petrie RHA MRIA', *Dublin University Magazine*, xiv, 1839, p.638
198 H Levinge to Petrie, 7 October 1826, NLI, MS 791, no. 282
199 J. Bell to Petrie, 26 January 1826, NLI, MS 793, no. 576
200 R.H. Gordon, Bellghly, to Petrie, 2 September 1840, NLI, MS 791, no. 209
201 RIA, MS 12, n.22 (Petrie Papers)
202 Stokes, pp.75-8
203 RIA, MS 12, n.22 (a manuscript history of the RIA in Stokes' handwriting)
204 Mr Underwood, 8 Chancery Lane, to Petrie, 8 March 1856, Adare Papers, Special Collections, University of Limerick, D3196/I/3/40
205 Petrie, *Ecclesiastical Architecture of Ireland*, p.304, illustrated p.310
206 *ibid.*, p.320
207 Dawson, Limavady, to Petrie in Coleraine, 5 August 1833, NLI, MS 790, no. 148
208 There is no doubt that these were the Dean's intentions. R. Anthony relates how the Dean visited his museum at Piltown on 11 September 1840, and spoke to him on the matter. (R. Anthony to Petrie, 24 November 1840, NLI, MS 789, no. 8) Other corroboratory evidence is provided by a letter from Alex Calvill Welsh to Petrie, 19 November 1840, NLI, MS 794, no. 670
209 Stokes, p.80
210 RIA, MS 12, n.22, pp.13, 14
211 Stokes, p.356
212 Worsaae to Petrie, 6 October 1846, NLI, MS 794, no. 688
213 Worsaae to Petrie, 7 November 1846, NLI, MS 794, no. 689
214 Worsaae to Petrie, 11 March 1847, NLI, MS 794, no. 691
215 M. Waldron, Cong, to George Smith, 3 September, 1838, NLI, MS 794, no. 656
216 Charles Ligar to ?, 30 December 1836, NLI, MS 7550, Larcom Papers (private) vol. 1
217 Petrie to Larcom, 20 October 1835, NLI, MS 7550
218 Petrie to Adare, 17 September 1843, NLI, MS 792, no. 443
219 Petrie to Adare, 19 October 1843, NLI, MS 792, no. 445
220 Petrie to Adare, 28 October 1843, NLI, MS 792, no. 447
221 Thomas Tennison to Petrie, 26 April 1859 Adare Papers, University of Limerick, D3196/I/3/44
222 R. Anthony, Piltown, to Petrie, 3 November 1836, NLI, MS 789, no. 4
223 R. Anthony, Piltown, to Petrie, 14 April 1840, NLI, MS789, no. 7
224 W. Wakeman, Listowel, to Petrie, 15 November 1841, NLI, MS 793, no. 636
225 B. Lloyd, the infirmary, Roscommon, to Petrie, 31 May 1840, NLI, MS 791, no. 287
226 Arthur Nugent to Petrie, 13 August 1842, NLI, MS 792, no. 367
227 Stokes, p.81
228 T. Crofton Croker, 3 Gloucester Road, Old Brompton, London, 2 February 1853, to Petrie, Adare Papers, Special Collections, University of Limerick, D3196/I/3/35 (79)
229 RIA, MS 12, n.12, p.17 (Stokes' autograph)
230 Petrie to Adare, undated (first sheet of letter missing), NLI, MS 795. The relationship between Petrie and the 3rd Earl of Dunraven (1812-71), a keen amateur archaeologist, was evidently close. The rebuilding of Adare Manor, begun in 1830, in the Gothic Revival style, shows Dunraven's interest in the medieval. Architects who worked on the project included James Paine, Lewis Nockalls Cottingham and August Welby Pugin. The 3rd Earl, a convert to Roman Catholicism, engaged P.C. Hardwick to complete the house in the Pugin style from 1850-62.
231 J.H. Andrews, *A Paper Landscape* (Clarendon Press, Oxford, 1975) p.14
232 J. Burgoyne, *Memorandum on the history of the O.S.*, NLI, MS 7561, Larcom Papers, vol. 3)
233 Lt. Col. R.E. Colby, to Sir William Gosset, 12 July 1833, NLI, MS 7551, Larcom Papers (private) vol. 2
234 Andrews, p.153
235 NLI, MS, Larcom Letters (supplemental)
236 Stokes, pp.96-7
237 'Our Portrait Gallery: George Petrie', *Dublin University Magazine*, 1839
238 Larcom to Colby, 25 August 1833, NLI, MS 7551
239 Larcom to Petrie, 2 August 1833, NLI, MS 7563 (mem. suppl.) vol. i
240 Larcom to Petrie, 24 January 1834, NLI, MS 7563; also Samuel Ferguson to Petrie, October 1833, RIA, MS 12, n.22, p.17
241 M.C. Ferguson, *Samuel Ferguson*, p.60
242 O'Donovan to Petrie, 18 March 1834, NLI, MS 792, no. 399
243 Larcom to Petrie, 20 February 1834, NLI, MS 7563
244 Larcom to Petrie, 9 September 1836, NLI, MS 7563
245 Larcom to Petrie, 27 September 1836, NLI, MS 7563
246 Larcom to Petrie, 8 October 1836, NLI, MS 7563
247 Larcom to Petrie, 14 October1836, NLI, MS 7563
248 Larcom to Petrie, 20 October 1836, NLI, MS 7563
249 Larcom to Petrie, 27 October 1837, NLI, MS 7563
250 Larcom to Petrie, 21 September 1837, NLI, MS 7563
251 O'Donovan to Petrie, 2 October 1837, NLI, MS 792, no. 401
252 Andrews, p.119
253 O'Donovan to Lord Adare, 1 April 1844, NLI, MS 792, no. 412
254 Larcom to Petrie, 4 July 1837, NLI, MS 7563
255 Larcom to Petrie, 24 August 1837, NLI, MS 7563
256 Larcom to Petrie, 9 December 1837, NLI, MS 7563
257 Andrews, p.158
258 NLI, MS 7553, Larcom Papers, Memoir, vol. 4
259 Petrie to Larcom, 8 April 1840, NLI, MS 7555, Larcom Papers, Memoir, vol. 6
260 NLI, MS 7553
261 Extract from a letter from the Chancellor of the Exchequer to Lord Morpeth, NLI, MS 7553
262 Petrie to Larcom, 1 August 1838, NLI, MS 7553
263 Petrie to Larcom, 5 August 1838 NLI, MS 7550
264 Petrie to Larcom, 20 August 1839, NLI, MS 7550
265 Conleth Manning, 'Clonmacnoise Cathedral', in Heather King (ed.) *Clonmacnoise Studies*, i, seminar papers, 1994 (Dúchas, The Heritage Service, Dublin, 1998) p.83
266 Petrie to Larcom, 24 August 1839, NLI, MS 7550
267 Robert Gavan to Petrie, 28 August 1840, NLI, MS 791
268 Larcom to Petrie, 21 September 1841, NLI, MS 7567
269 William Wakeman to Petrie, 19 November 1841, Adare Papers, Special Collections, University of Limerick, D3196/I/3/13
270 O'Donovan to Petrie, 7 August 1841, RIA, MS 12 n.5
271 Wakeman to Petrie, 8 October 1841, NLI, MS 793, no. 628
272 Wakeman to Petrie, 28 October 1841, NLI, MS 793, no. 631
273 R.C. Walker to Petrie, 30 December 1828, NLI, MS 794, no. 657
274 RIA, MS 12, n.22, Carrowmore draft, 1850 (Petrie autograph)
275 Petrie to Larcom, 10 August 1837, NLI, MS 7550
276 Petrie to Larcom, 11 August 1837, NLI, MS 7550
277 Petrie to Larcom, 13 August 1837, NLI, MS 7550
278 Stokes, pp.243-53

[279] The O'Donovan Letters, printed under the supervision of M.J. O'Flanagan, 1927 (in typescript; only 27 copies printed)
[280] Petrie to Larcom, 15 August 1837, NLI, MS 7550
[281] Petrie to Larcom, 13 August 1837, NLI, MS 7550
[282] Walker to Petrie, 23 July 1836, NLI, MS 794, no. 658
[283] Petrie to Adare, 1843?, NLI, MS 792, no. 448 (first part of letter is missing)
[284] Petrie to Larcom, 31 July 1837, NLI, MS 7550
[285] Petrie to Larcom, 7 August 1837, NLI, MS 7550. Sir William Wilde's home near Cong was named 'Moy Tuire'
[286] Petrie to Larcom, 5 September 1837, Ordnance Survey (Phoenix Park headquarters), MS 1837, Sligo memorandum, pp.80-4
[287] Sir William Wilde, 'The Two Moy Turas', *PRIA* ix, 1866, p.564
[288] Petrie to O'Donovan, 4 September 1837, quoted in Stokes, p.259
[289] Larcom to Petrie, 4 July 1840, NLI, MS 7567
[290] *Freeman's Journal*, 11 March 1844
[291] Colby to Larcom, 26 December 1842, NLI, MS 7553
[292] Andrews, p.165
[293] Colby to Larcom, 7 April 1840, NLI, MS 7555, Larcom Papers, Memoir, vol. 6
[294] Petrie to Larcom, 8 April 1840, NLI, MS 7555
[295] Petrie to Larcaom, 10 April 1840, NLI, MS 7555
[296] Colby to Larcom, 20 June 1843, NLI, MS 7553
[297] Colby to Larcom, 26 December 1842, NLI, MS 7553
[298] Petrie to Larcom, 16 April 1840, NLI, MS 7555
[299] J. Hubard Smith to Petrie, 14 March 1840, NLI, MS 793, no. 597
[300] Henry Petrie, Tower of London, to Petrie, 10 July 1840, NLI, MS 793, no. 561
[301] Larcom to Petrie, 25 May 1840, NLI, MS 7567
[302] Larcom to Petrie, 27 May 1840, NLI, MS 7567
[303] Larcom to Petrie, 29 May 1840, NLI, MS 7567
[304] George Petrie R.S.A., V.P.R.I.A., 'The Ecclesiastical Architecture of Ireland anterior to the Anglo-Norman invasion, comprising an essay on the origin and uses of the Round Towers of Ireland', *The Transactions of the Royal Irish Academy*, xx (Hodges & Smith, Dublin, 1845)
[305] Charles Smith, *Ancient and Present State of the County and City of Cork*, 2 volumes (Cork, 1815)
[306] John Windele to William Hackett, Midleton, 11 October 1844, Adare Papers, Special Collections, University of Limerick, D3196/I/3/24
[307] Joep Leerssen, *Remembrance and Imagination* (University College Cork,1996) pp.109-46
[308] John Windele to Petrie, 29 September 1841, Adare Papers, University of Limerick, D3196/I/3/12
[309] John Windele to Petrie, 2 May 1842, Adare Papers, University of Limerick, D3196/I/3/18
[310] *ibid*, introduction, p.ix
[311] Brian Lalor, *The Irish Round Tower: Origins and Architecture Explored* (Collins Press, Cork, 1999) Lalor posits early 10th-century Rhineland origins for the Irish towers.
[312] Petrie, *The Ecclesiastical Architecture of Ireland*, p.144
[313] *ibid.* pp.278-79
[314] *ibid.* pp.287-88
[315] *ibid.*, p.254
[316] *ibid.* p.264
[317] Raghnall Ó Floinn, 'Clonmacnoise: art and patronage in the Early Medieval Period', in Heather King (ed.) *Clonmacnoise Studies,* i (Dúchas, The Heritage Service, Dublin, 1998) p.87
[318] Mr Lane, Oxford, on behalf of Mr Twiss, to Petrie, 1840, Adare Papers, University of Limerick, D3196/I/3/10
[319] Stokes, p.359
[320] RHA Accounts Abstract, NLI, MS 793, no. 541
[321] Strickland, ii, p.461
[322] Michelangelo Hayes, letter to the *Evening Mail*, Friday, 9 January 1857
[323] Fragmentary draft reports of the RHA, NLI, MS 793, nos 541-48
[324] Article on RHA, *Evening Mail*, 2 January 1857
[325] *ibid.*
[326] Michelangelo Hayes, letter to the *Evening Mail*, 9 January 1857
[327] Petrie to Mulrenin, 8 March 1857, NLI, MS 793, no. 502
[328] G. Mulvaney to Petrie, 10 February 1859, NLI, MS 792, no. 357
[329] Draft letter, Petrie autograph, NLI, MS 793, no. 533
[330] Draft letter, Petrie autograph, NLI, MS 793, no. 537
[331] Petrie to Mulrenin, 22 March 1858, NLI, MS 793, no. 505
[332] G.F. Mulvaney to Petrie, 25 March 1857, NLI, MS 792
[333] Petrie to Mulrenin, undated, NLI, MS 793, no. 520
[334] Petrie to Adare, 26 October 1843, NLI, MS 792, no. 446
[335] Petrie to Adare, 28 October 1843, NLI, MS 792, no. 447
[336] J. Hanna to Petrie, 7 November 1849 NLI, MS 791, no. 227
[337] Stokes, p.358
[338] O'Curry to Petrie, 7 November 1849, NLI, MS 792, no. 379
[339] Petrie to Adare, 10 November 1849, NLI, MS 792, no. 478
[340] C. Moore to Petrie, 7 January 1850, NLI, MS 792, no. 346
[341] T.G. Wilson, *A Victorian Doctor*, being a biography of Sir William Wilde
[342] Stokes, p.354
[343] James Wills to Petrie, 28 December 1845, NLI, MS 794, no. 680
[344] F.W. Burton to Petrie, undated, TCD MS 3562, no. 111. Donal O'Sullivan dates this letter to between 1844 and August 1845, on the basis of the address and some detective work.
[345] Petrie to Adare, 12 October 1845, quoted in Stokes, p.353
[346] R. Rothwell to Petrie, 1850, NLI, MS 793, no. 582s
[347] *ibid.*
[348] F. MacCracken to Petrie, 29 July 1850, NLI, MS 791, no. 293
[349] RIA, Petrie centenary exhibition, 1966, catalogue
[350] Adare Papers, Special Collections, University of Limerick, D3196/I/14/27

BIBLIOGRAPHY

Eric Adams, *Francis Danby, Varieties of Poetic Landscape* (Yale University Press, New Haven and London, 1973)

J.H. Andrews, *A Paper Landscape* (Clarendon Press, Oxford, 1975)

H.F. Berry, *A History of the Royal Dublin Society* (Longman Green & Co, London, 1915)

James Norris Brewer, *The Beauties of Ireland*, 3 vols (Sherwood, Jones & Co, London, 1825)

Hubert Butler, 'Lament for Archaeology' in Roy Foster (ed.), *The Sub-Prefect Should have Held his Tongue* (Allen Lane / Penguin Press, London; Lilliput Press, Dublin, 1990)

Thomas Kitson Cromwell, Excursions through Ireland, 3 vols (Longman, London, 1820)

Myles Dillon, 'George Petrie', *Studies*, Autumn 1967

M.C. Ferguson, *Sir Samuel Ferguson in the Ireland of his Day*, 2 vols (William Blackwood & Sons, London, 1896)

A.P. Graves, 'George Petrie as an Artist and Man of Letters' in *Irish Literary & Musical Studies*, 1913, p.200 ff

Martin Hardie, *Watercolour Painting in Britain*, 3 vols (B.T. Batsford Ltd, London, 1967)

John Hutchinson, *James Arthur O'Connor* (National Gallery of Ireland, Dublin, 1985)

Joep Leerssen, *Remembrance and Imagination: Patterns in the historical and literary representation of Ireland in the nineteenth century* (Cork University Press, 1996)

Desmond F. Moore, 'The Royal Hibernian Academy', *Dublin Historical Record*, March-May 1966, pp.28-37

Peter Murray, 'Trouble at t'Mill: George Petrie and the Royal Hibernian Academy', in Maureen Charleton (ed.), *Martello Arts Review* (Dublin, 1991) pp.14-22

Sir Charles Petrie, *Chapters From Life* (London, 1950)

George Petrie, *Ten Views of the North and North-West* (William Curry Jun. & Co, Dublin, 1830)

Walter G. Strickland, *A Dictionary of Irish Artists*, 2 vols (London and Dublin, 1913)

John Turpin, *A School of Art in Dublin Since the Eighteenth Century: A History of the National College of Art and Design* (Gill & Macmillan, Dublin, 1995)

G.N.Wright, *Historical Guide to Ancient and Modern Dublin* (Baldwin Cradock & Joy, London, 1821)

G.N.Wright, *Tours in Ireland, or Guides to the Lakes of Killarney, the County of Wicklow and the Giant's Causeway.*(Baldwin Cradock & Joy, London, 1823)

G.N.Wright, *Ireland Illustrated from Original Drawings* (Fisher, Son & Jackson, London, 1832)

PUBLICATIONS BY PETRIE

George Petrie, *An Account of an ancient Irish Reliquary called the Domhnac-Argid* (1838)

Margaret Stokes (ed.), *Christian Inscriptions in the Irish Language* (Dublin University Press, 1872-78; originally published by the RSAI in seven parts 1870-77)

George Petrie, 'An Essay on Military Architecture in Ireland Previous to the English Invasion', *Proceedings of the RIA* (Dublin, 1972) pp.153-269

George Petrie, *The Ecclesiastical Architecture of Ireland anterior to the Anglo-Norman Invasion, with an Essay on the Round Towers of Ireland* (Hodges & Smith, Dublin, 1845)

George Petrie, *On the History and Antiquities of Tara Hill* (1839)

George Petrie, *Letter to Sir William R. Hamilton in reply to certain charges against the author by Sir William Betham* (1840)

George Petrie, *The Ancient Music of Ireland, arranged for the piano-forte* (Dublin University Press, 1855). Contains 147 airs, with notes and commentary. A supplementary collection, *Music in Ireland*, was published in 1882.

Charles Villiers Stanford (ed.), *The Complete Collection of Irish Music, as noted by George Petrie, 3 parts in 1* (1902-05. Stanford edited the third part, but it lacks Petrie's notes.

David Cooper (ed.), *The Petrie Collection of the Ancient Music of Ireland* (Cork University Press, 2002). Contains 200 airs, originally published in 1855 and 1882.

ACKNOWLEDGEMENTS

Prof Ann Crookshank
Ann Stewart
John Hutchinson
Prof Tom Dunne
Eamonn De Búrca
Hugh Iremonger
Andrew Bonar Law
Mairead MacParland
Fintan Cullen
Dara McGrath
The late Prof De Valera
Martin Angelsea, Ulster Museum

Siobhan Fitzpatrick, librarian, Royal Irish Academy
Ann Hodge, curator, National Gallery of Ireland
Ken Bergin, librarian, University of Limerick
Anne O'Connor, secretary, Crawford Gallery
Colleen O'Sullivan and Patricia O'Sullivan, Crawford Gallery

Jack Cashman
Michael Purser
Vasco Purser
Dr Vincent Pippet
Dr Barbara O'Hanlon
Andrew O'Hanlon
Helen Skrine

and finally to John O'Regan and Nicola Dearey of Gandon Editions

PHOTOGRAPHIC ACKNOWLEDGEMENTS

National Gallery of Ireland

Ulster Museum

Crawford Municipal Art Gallery
(photographer: Dara McGrath)

APPENDIX

PAINTINGS PETRIE EXHIBITED AT THE ROYAL HIBERNIAN ACADEMY

Year	Title	RHA cat. no.
1826	*Ardfinnan Castle, Co. Tipperary*	277
1827	*Round Tower of Kilbannon, Co. Galway*	252
	Dun Aengus, an Ancient Stone Fortress on the Island of Arran More, Coast of Galway	253
	View of Ardfinnan Castle and Bridge	330
1828	*The Last Circuit of the Pilgrims at Clonmacnoise, King's County, painted for the celebrated Album of a Lady in England*	185
	Derry-Inver Harbour and the mountain Bennabiolae, or the *Twelve Pins: from the hill of Renvylle, Connemara*	316
1829	*The Knight and the Lady – Scene, Coomeen Dubh,* or *The Black Mountain Recess, near Killarney – evening after sunset*	159
	The Ancient Culdean Abbey of Innisnabeo, or 'the Island of the Living,' now commonly called Monainse, or the Bog Island, County Tipperary	245
1830	*Drogheda – a sketch for the Northern Tourist*	163
	Lough Gill – a sketch for the Northern Tourist	200
	Narrow Water Castle – a sketch for the Northern Tourist	210
	Carrick-a-Rede, a sketch for the Northern Tourist	215
	The Long Bridge and Cave-Hill, Belfast, – a sketch for the Northern Tourist	232
	Well-worship, St. Bridget's Well, Co. Clare	233
1831	*The Hill of Doon, Lough Corrib*	211
	View on the Kylemore Road, Connemara	212
	The Llanberris Lakes, North Wales	213
	The Eagle's Nest, Killarney	215
	The Glen of the Horse, Killarney	216
	Knockmoy Abbey and Bridge, Co. Galway	224
	Gougane Barra, the Hermitage of St. Finbar	226
	Windmill at Rathgar Quarry, Co. Dublin	232
	Lough Ina, Connemara	235
1832	*Derry-Inver Harbour and the Twelve Pins, Connemara*	151
	Dolbaddern Castle, and the Upper Lake of Llanberis	235
1833	*Caislan a Kirke, or the Hen's Castle, Lough Corrib, painted for Miss French Lynch's Album*	230
	The Little Killary Harbour, Connemara	235
	Gougane Barra	246
1835	*The Lower Lake of Llanberris – Noon*	229
	Gougane Barra, Co. of Cork – Clearing up after Rain	234
	Lough Ina, Connemara	235
	The Glen of the Horse, Killarney	244
	Dolbaddern Castle and the Upper Lake of Llanberris – Evening	248
1837	Petrie did not exhibit this year (the catalogue records that he had become secretary of the RHA, and that he had donated an edition of *Philipps' Lectures* to the library)	
1840	*The Hen's Castle, Lough Corrib, Shower Passing Off*	254
	Pagan Sepulchral Monument on the Caugh-hill – a Mountain in the parish of Bannagher, county of Londonderry – Twilight	261
1841	*Fall of the Littory River, Ben Littory, Connemara*	333
1843	*Temple Fineen, or MacCarthy's Church and Round Tower, Clonmacnoise*	316
	O'Rourke's Tower, Clonmacnoise – Twilight	317
	Bridge and Castle of Shruel, county of Mayo	324
	Brandon Mountain, from the Pass of Connor Hill, Co. Kerry	328
	Leacht – Finane, the Second Station of Croagh Patrick Mountain, Co. of Mayo	335
1846	*Brandon Mountain, from the Pass of Connor Hill, Co. Kerry – Shower Passing Off*	308
	The Home of the Heron, Lough Atri, looking into Glen Hoghan, Connemara	313
1847	*The Annual Cattle Fair at Sligichan, Isle of Skye*	230
1848	*Ancient Sepulchral stone circle of the Fir Bolg's, or Belgae, at Coolirra, near Sligo – Morning*	173
	Ancient Sepulchral Circle and Cromlech of the Fir Bolg's, or Belgae, at Coolirra, near Sligo – Evening	175
	Sligachan, in the Isle of Skye, on the annual cattle-fair day	176
1849	*A Day among the Pins, Connemara No. 1 – Setting Out, Morning – The Lake and Castle of Ballynahinch*	167

	No. 2 – Ascent of Ben Littory, The lower fall of the Littory River	168
	No. 3 – Ascent of Ben Littory, – The upper fall of the Littory River	169
	No. 4 – Pulling the Boat up the Stream, near Glen Hoghan	170
	No. 5 – Visit to the Pearl Harbour – Bridge on the Old Road	171
	No. 6 – Launching the Boat on Lough Ina	172
	No. 7 – The Rest at Lough Ina	173
	No. 8 – Returning Home – Lough-a-tri, Evening	174
1852	*The Middle Station on Croagh-Patrick Mountain, Co. of Mayo*	181
	The Bridge and Castle of Shruel, County of Mayo (the property of William Stokes, Esq., M.D.)	211
1853	*Brandon Mountain, From the Pass of Connor's Hill, County of Kerry* (lent by Thomas Hutton, Esq., D. L.)	215
	The Last Round of the Pilgrims at Clonmacnoise, King's County (the property of T. Bacon, Esq.)	219
	The Home of the Heron, Lough-a-tri, Connemara, Co. of Galway – immediately after Sunset (lent by Robert Callwell, Esq.)	222
	Sligichan, Isle of Skye, Scotland, on the annual Cattle Fair-day (the property of William Stokes, Esq., M.D.)	232
1858	*Tobar-Kieran, or St. Kieran's Well, Cahermoyle, Co. of Limerick*	300
	The Seven Churches of St. Brecan, in the Island of Arran-More, Bay of Galway – the Connemara Coast, and Joyce-Country	
	Mountains in the distance	304
	Tobar Kieran, or St. Kieran's Well, at Castle Kieran, Co. of Meath	308

1866 THE PETRIE COLLECTION

'The Following Pictures are by the late George Petrie, esq. R.H.A., L.L.D., V.P.R.I.A. Where no Owner's name is given, the works are for sale.' (RHA catalogue, 1866)

RHA cat. no.	Title	Owner
357	*The Fall of the Littora, Connemara*	George Smith
358	*The Great Tower of Clonmacnoise*	Dr. Stokes
359	*The Custom House, Dublin*	R.I.A.
360	*Dolbaddern Castle, North Wales*	Mrs. Hime
361	*Trinity College, Dublin*	R.I.A.
362	*Lying-in Hospital*	R.I.A.
363	*Four Courts*	R.I.A.
364	*The College of Surgeons, as originally designed*	R.I.A.
365	*The Church of Conception, Marlborough Street*	R.I.A.
366	*St. George's Church*	R.I.A.
367	*Llanberis, North Wales*	George Smith
368	*Ardfinnan Castle and Bridge*	Miss Petrie
369	*St. Patrick's Cathedral*	R.I.A.
370	*Coom-a-Dhuv, Killarney*	George Smith
371	*Christ's Church Cathedral in 1627*	R.I.A.
372	*The Royal Exchange*	R.I.A.
373	*Sackville-street, with the Post Office*	R.I.A.
374	*Theatre Royal, as originally designed*	R.I.A.
375	*The Kings Inns, Dublin*	R.I.A.
376	*View of Dublin from the North Side*	R.I.A.
377	*The Chapel at Phibsborough*	Sir William Wilde
378	*Lough Ina, Connemara*	J. Somers
379	*Ruins of Temple Fineen, Clonmacnoise*	G. Smith
380	*Tomb in Dungiven Church, Co. Derry*	
381	*Dunluce Castle, Co. Antrim*	Sir William Wilde
382	*Stone Circle, Carrowmore, Co. Sligo*	Charles Haliday
383	*Druidical Circle, near Londonderry*	Robert Callwell
384	*Tinnahinch, Co. Wicklow*	
385	*Torc Lake, Killarney*	Earl of Dunraven
386	*Mount Bellew, Co. Galway*	
387	*Ross Castle, Co. Kerry*	Dunraven
388	*Slane Castle, Co. Meath*	
389	*Bank of Ireland*	Sir William Wilde
390	*The Post Office, Sackville Street*	Sir William Wilde
391	*Carlow*	
392	*Brendan Head, Co. Kerry*	Mrs. Hutton
393	*Glen-na-Coppaul, Mangerton, Killarney*	J. Somers
394	*Connemara, N.E.View of the Twelve Pins*	J. Somers
395	*Carton, Co. Kildare*	
396	*Trim Castle, Co. Eastmeath*	
397	*Bank of Ireland*	R.I.A.
398	*Old Walls of Londonderry*	Sir Thomas Larcom
399	*The Chapel Royal, Dublin Castle*	R.I.A.
400	*The Last Round of the Pilgrims at Clonmacnoise*	Mrs. Miller
400a	*Connemara, View of the Twelve Pins*	
401	*Fall of the Ess, Glenmalure, Co. Wicklow*	G. Smith
402	*Eagle's Nest, Killarney*	J. Somers
403	*Ruins of Glendalough, Co. Wicklow*	
404	*Station at Croagh Patrick, Co. Mayo*	Earl of Dunraven
405	*Drumgoff Barracks, Glenmalure*	
406	*View at Killarney*	Earl of Dunraven
407	*The Bank of Ireland from College Street*	Sir. Wm. Wilde
408	*Cashel Bell*	Dr. Stokes
409	*Home of the Heron, Lough Atree*	R. Callwell
410	*View in Connemara*	Rt. Hon. Chief Baron
411	*Lough Ina, Connemara*	
412	*Carrickfergus, Co. Antrim*	
413	*MacGillicuady's Reeks, Co. Kerry*	Earl of Dunraven
414	*Stone Circle, Carrowmore, Co. Sligo*	Charles Haliday
415	*Shruel Bridge, Co. Mayo*	Dr. Stokes
416	*Lough Ina, Connemara*	Rt. Hon. Chief Baron
417	*Belfast, Co. Antrim*	
418	*Parsonstown Castle, King's County*	
419	*Sketches in the West of Ireland*	Dr. Stokes

420	*St. Kieran's Well*	Sir. Wm. Wilde
421	*Pulling the Boat up Lough Ina*	Rt. Hon. Chief Baron
422	*Luggela, Co. Wicklow*	
423	*Muckross Abbey, Co. Kerry*	Earl of Dunraven
424	*Kileen Castle, Co. Meath*	
425	*St. Audoen's Church, Dublin*	Sir. Wm. Wilde
426	*St. Kieran's Well, West Meath*	Sir. Wm. Wilde
427	*View in Connemara*	Rt. Hon. Chief Baron
428	*The Windmill, Rathgar*	Dr. Stokes
429	*A Sketch*	Dr. Stokes
430	*Cashel, Co. Tipperary*	
431	*The Hen's Castle, Lough Corrib*	R. Callwell
432	*Aughanore Castle, Co. Galway*	
433	*Kilmallock, Co. Limerick*	Earl of Dunraven
434	*Kilruddery, Co. Wicklow*	
435	*Boyle Abbey; A Sketch from Nature*	
436	*Westport; Llanberis, North Wales;* *Conway Castle and Bridge; Menai Bridge*	
437	*Cattle Fair, in the Valley of Sligichan,* *Island of Skye*	Dr. Stokes
438	*1. Part of the Old Walls of Londonderry* *2. Ancient Tomb, Boncragh, Londonderry* *3. Part of the Old Wall, Londonderry*	Sir Thos. Larcom
439	*1. Doorway of Ancient Church at Maghera* *2. Doorway of Ancient Abbey at Banagher* *3. Part of Ancient Cross at Macosquin,* *Londonderry*	Sir Thos. Larcom
440	*Two Studies from Nature*	
441	*Nelson's Pillar, Sackville Street*	Sir Wm. Wilde
442	*Gougane Barra*	R. Callwell
443	*Dun Aenghus, Island of Arran*	Dr. Stokes
444	*Hore Abbey, Co. Tipperary*	
445	*Ruins and Round Towers, Clonmacnoise*	Dr. Stokes
446	*The Falls of Armoy*	G. Smith
447	*The Twelve Pins, Connemara*	R. Callwell
448	*The Seven Churches of Teampull Brecan,* *Island of Arran*	Earl of Dunraven
449	*The Home of the Heron, Lough Atrie*	Miss Thompson
450	*St. Bridget's Well, Co. Clare*	Dr. Stokes
451	*Dublin from the Phoenix Park*	
452	*Monument on the Boyne, Co. Meath*	

1868 *A Study for Gougane Barra* (RHA cat. no. 307)
(property of Dr J. Moore, Belfast)
This was the last painting by Petrie to be exhibited at the Royal Hibernian Academy.

Towards a National Art?

by Tom Dunne

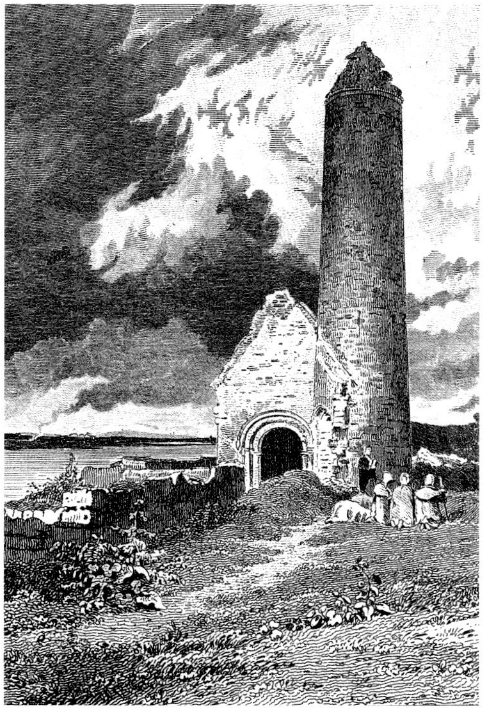

Macarthy's Church & Tower, Clonmacnois, King's County (detail)
engraving after Petrie from T. Cromwell, *Excursions through Ireland*, vol. ii, 1820

Towards a National Art?

George Petrie's two versions of *The Last Circuit of Pilgrims of Clonmacnoise*

TOM DUNNE

'National art is conversant with national subjects. We have Irish artists but no Irish or National art. This ought not to continue.' So wrote Thomas Davis, Ireland's first if rather tentative exponent of a distinctive cultural nationalism, in one of a number of contributions on the subject to *The Nation* newspaper. His appeal to Irish artists focused on history painting and he offered an eccentric list of suitable subjects for their consideration.[1] In this focus he showed a lack of understanding of the contemporary art scene, which had moved away from history painting (never, in any case, a major force in Irish, or indeed English art) and was finding in landscape painting, instead, the visual medium through which 'the nation' was mainly defined or imagined. This was particularly so in England, where Constable's comforting and conservative vision of an unchanged rural idyll competed with Turner's more unsettling, but still highly patriotic romanticism in meeting the needs of a country profoundly disturbed by revolutionary threat, modernisation and change.[2] In Ireland, also, a distinctive landscape art was emerging, though it reflected different political circumstances and needs. And so, among Davis's painter friends, it was landscape artist, George Petrie (1790-1866) who came closest to answering Davis's call, rather than, as Davis hoped, Frederic William Burton, who had designed (anonymously) the frontispiece for the *The Spirit of the Nation* (1845) and exhibited some paintings of the romantic west, full of ethnographic detail and bourgeois sentimentality. By contrast, Petrie's two watercolours of the romantic monastic ruins of Clonmacnoise added significant antiquarian research to the already well established tradition of sentimental identification with the Gaelic past. The first, a small but intense and detailed study of devout pilgrims among the ruins was exhibited at the Royal Hibernian Academy in 1828; the second, nearly four times as large and clearly based on the first was exhibited at the Irish Exhibition in London in 1853. Significant changes in detail, and even more in mood, from an apocalyptic sense of crisis and loss to a calm celebration of identity reflected both contemporary antiquarian debate and changes in the mood of nationalist politics between the Catholic Emancipation campaign and the Repeal movement.

Burton was soon to move to London and become essentially an English painter, following the footsteps of most gifted Irish artists, particularly since the Act of Union of 1800, which significantly reduced artistic patronage in Ireland, and provided a new framework for the centuries-old colonial relationship with England. This involved an acceleration of the process of cultural assimilation, but also of Irish attempts to resist it, particularly by highlighting the distinctive Gaelic element as a badge of identity. Most of those involved in what might loosely be called Irish cultural nationalism in this period, including Davis and Petrie, came from outside the Gaelic tradition and did not know the language (now spoken mainly by the rural poor). Instead, they assimilated an ersatz version of Gaelic culture to dominant English romantic modes, especially through 'translations' of Gaelic poetry, new settings for Irish music and song and the celebration of the ruins of a glorious but lost civilisation in antiquarian and topographical art.

The development of landscape art is often seen nowadays as 'integrally connected with imperialism', and the Irish case tends to confirm this, being an example of an essentially colonial art, its representation of native scenery not only determined by metropolitan conventions, but framed to meet, and please 'the imperial gaze'.[3] While Irish art generally looked to English models, and most Irish landscapes were conventionally picturesque in the English style, it can be argued that a distinctively Irish landscape also emerged in the post-Union period. This reflected the romantic vogue for wild scenery and ruins in the landscape, but, in an Irish context, these resonated with negative concepts, of 'national character', and with conflicted versions of Irish history. A significant stimulus also came from the burgeoning tourist market (mainly British) but even more from the political concerns felt in Britain about Irish lawlessness and poverty, and from the fascination with the Gaelic past, increasingly felt by liberal Irish Protestants, as well as by Catholics. Three elements combined to make a distinctive Irish landscape – romantic (usually wild) scenery, ruins that reflected Ireland's long vanished glories and its violent past, and a picturesque, also stereotypically 'wild' people, portrayed in ways which, as Barrell has shown, were not allowed in contemporary English depictions of their poor, drinking, dancing and fighting.[4] Thus, what might be called the quintessential Irish landscape of this period was Joseph Peacock's massive, *The Pattern, or Festival of St Kevin at the Seven Churches Glendalough* (1817, Ulster Museum) with the towering Wicklow hills framing a scene of peasant drinking, commerce and faction fighting (illustrating why such occasions were anathema to Catholic Church authorities), presided over by that most characteristic of Irish ruins, a round tower, hugely inflated in scale.[5]

Petrie's pictures of Clonmacnoise (which also featured its picturesque setting on the river Shannon near Athlone) were to combine the same three elements, scenery, ruins and the Irish poor to make a more positive and patriotic statement, in effect answering Peacock's presentation of the colonial stereotype, and thus, still determined by it. To what degree can they also be said to be an attempt to answer Davis's call for a 'national art?' In his seminal 1975 article on 'Irish nationalist art 1800-1921,' Cyril Barrett concluded that there was little in Irish art 'designed to arouse or ... capable of arousing nationalist sentiments'. It will be argued here that Petrie's two watercolours go some way to meet Barrett's basic criteria that Nationalist art should have, 'some element of symbolisation' and involve 'subjects [that] not only arouse nationalist and patriotic sentiment, but also define it'.[6] But in doing so, they had virtually no precedents and very few successors, except, arguably, Seán Keating, Paul Henry and (more ambiguously) Jack B. Yeats in the early 20th century.[7] Why Petrie attempted, in these few pictures, to fulfil such a role is best explained, not by his experience as an artist, or even his politics, but by his involvement from very early on in antiquarian research and writing. He was a very complex figure. Best remembered as a romantic landscape artist, like his friends James Arthur O'Connor and Francis Danby, he also produced large numbers of exact topographical pictures and was a leading illustrator of tourist guides. As an antiquarian he was rigorously scientific, was a tough controversialist and has been hailed as the father of archaeology in Ireland. He was also a practical man of affairs, dominating the Antiquities section of the Royal Irish Academy, establishing the basis of the collection of Dublin's National Museum and running the historical section of the Ordnance Survey. Indeed, that work was to take him away from painting when at the height of his artistic powers. Yet, he was also full of self-doubt and often of self-pity, was never fully committed to a career as an artist, and even when president of the Royal Hibernian Academy, for example, did not meet its basic rules that members must paint in oils and exhibit at least every two years. His work with the Ordnance Survey (essentially 1833-39) not only allowed him to indulge his antiquarian interests to the full, it also offered him the only decent and secure income he was to enjoy. When it ended and he accepted, reluctantly, that 'I must still paint to live', his most significant project was to revisit the small painting of pilgrims at the ancient monastic site of Clonmacnoise, done over a decade earlier, and to redo it on a far larger scale, one of the largest indeed of his career.[8] It reflected many elements of that varied experience, as well as his search for identity and a political role.

Not surprisingly, perhaps, some of those who were most prominent in promoting a sense of Irish cultural identity that would combine Gaelic and Anglo-Irish elements – Davis himself, and Lady Morgan, whose fictions are now seen as crucial to the process – had mixed English-Irish parentage. Petrie was less ethnically 'Irish' than either, having four Scottish grandparents and a Scottish mother; his artist father, while born in Dublin, retained strong Scottish links.[9] Yet, in a letter to his friend, Lord Dunraven, just before his death, George Petrie described himself as 'of an Anglo-Norman descent, and an Irishman only by the accident of birth'. This odd 'Anglo-Norman' claim brought him closer to the mainstream of the new cultural movement, and especially to Davis, who had stressed it in his formulation of Ireland's hybrid cultural identity, but had not included the Scottish element. Petrie's accidental Irishness also allowed him to explain his motivation as an artist and antiquarian to Dunraven in a curiously detached way:

> ...it afforded me a deep pleasure to be able to lend even a feeble hand towards the ultimate removal of hostile prejudices

> against the Celtic race amongst whom it was my chance to be cast, whose past sufferings I could not but pity, and whose many noble characteristics of mind and heart as well as their invariable kindness to me as a brother could not but excite, on my part, a deep feeling of gratitude as well as the most affectionate regard.[10]

There was a class bias to this, partly. For Petrie, the peasantry were the real 'Celtic race' and he normally described them as 'poor and barbarous': the peasant was 'disfigured by the vices attendant on degradation yet displaying the virtues that ennoble him'.[11] Even when collecting music in their cabins and shebeens and infatuated by its beauty and variety, he remained an outsider, dependent on others to take down and translate the words. Yet as David Cooper, the modern editor of his *Ancient Music of Ireland* (1855) put it, for Petrie, 'Irish identity was most strongly encoded by the 'purest' melodies, found in the Gaelic language songs of the often dispossessed Catholic peasantry'.[12] Crucial for Petrie was the idea that music reflected 'national character', a constant preoccupation of his generation across Europe, and seen by him in conventional terms as being like Irish skies, 'at one moment bright and sunny, and in the next, flinging their dark shadows over the landscape'. This made Ireland 'the natural home' of 'the poet, the painter and the philanthropist'.[13] Petrie was always, culturally, 'the philanthropist', sharing knowledge, urging reform, but somewhat distant. Yet he also longed intensely to belong, and this was particularly clear in his second Clonmacnoise painting.

Petrie's father, James, was known for his portraits of United Irishmen, Napper Tandy and Robert Emmet, but his access to the latter's body to make a death mask bespoke his military connections rather than political radicalism, for which there is no evidence. His son clearly, was not a nationalist in the sense of wanting Irish independence, and was described by his close friend and biographer William Stokes as 'a liberal in politics ... at once a loyalist and a patriot'.[14] Joep Leerssen has discerned a shift in this period from 18th-century 'patriotism' to 19th-century 'nationalism', but liberal Protestant Unionists who were also Romantics, like Petrie (and his friend and disciple, Samuel Ferguson) complicate the picture, though they frequently used the language of 'nation'.[15] Thus, for Petrie, the Ordnance Survey Memoir was 'a great national work'; the preservation of Irish music, 'so honourable to the national character of my country'; the O'Connell monument he was asked to design was 'a work of such national interest'.[16] The intermediate concept, 'nationality' better describes Petrie's (and, arguably, Davis's) patriotism. A more inclusive and less prescriptive concept, its focus was less political than communal and cultural. Thus, what he hoped to develop in Ireland, Petrie wrote in his introduction to *Ancient Music*, was 'a racy feeling of nationality and cultivation of mind – qualities so honourable to the Scottish character'.[17]

The two Clonmacnoise paintings are among very few by Petrie which feature people in a landscape or topographical study (as opposed to his being forced by engravers or publishers to add them, ' in order to have given it life and bustle').[18] Some of his more conventional paintings can also be seen as contributions to a definition of the 'nation' and deserve a separate study, in particular, *The Twelve Pins, Connemara* (1831), *Gougane Barra with the Hermitage of St. Finbarr* (1831) and *View of Dun Aengus* (exhibited 1866) (all are in the National Gallery of Ireland). But the Clonmacnoise paintings were special, partly because that place uniquely brought into focus all of his antiquarian, artistic and political concerns. After his first visit in 1820 he wrote to his new wife that his two days in 'this wild spot on the banks of the Shannon, where there are the remains of ten or eleven churches and two round towers', had 'put my mind in a greater state of fermentation than I can recollect to have experienced for several years' (including, presumably, his courtship and marriage!). In the entry in his journal (which he had hoped to publish, but never did) his first impressions were antiquarian rather than artistic, and reflected the age-old ambition of Irish writing to challenge the colonial stereotype of pre-conquest Irish barbarism:

> It was not without a considerable feeling of romance that we approached this, the most interesting spot that our island affords; nor without some emotion of awe that we entered its lonely and sacred precincts. Once the chief seat of piety and learning of the Insula Sanctorum, now a place hardly known to the inhabitants of Ireland, yet for ages held the most sacred and venerated; the Iona of Ireland, which her princes embellished, and containing the tombs of her noblest in blood. Journeying thither, we indulged our fancy in such pleasing anticipations that we should find among the ruins of those ancient temples, sufficient evidence that Ireland was not ignorant of architectural art, as practised in Europe during the early ages of Christianity; and that among the tombs we should discover inscriptions which would show her ancient

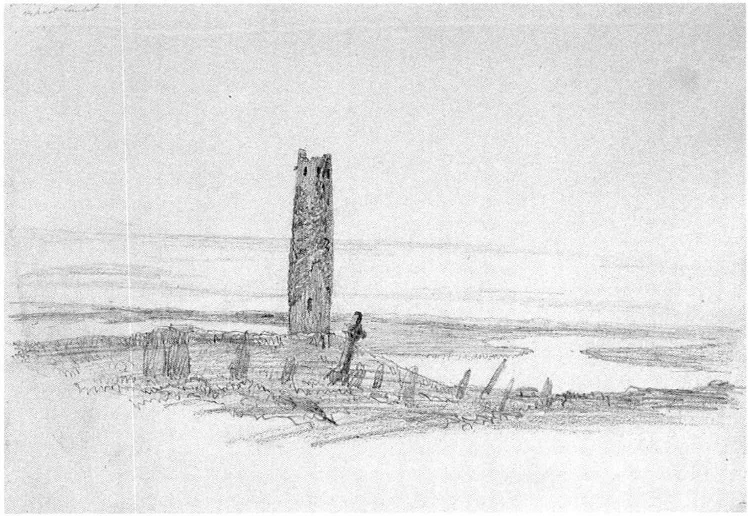

Sketch of round tower and high cross at Clonmacnoise
from the *Robert Callwell Skethbook* (coll: Crawford Gallery)

history was not, as is generally believed a fable. These pleasing hopes were more than realised.

Soon, however, he noticed that: 'The background is everywhere in perfect harmony with the nearer objects of this picture; the chain of bare hills on either side, now sere and wild, but once rich with woodland beauty ... the eye and mind are free to wander with the majestic river in all its graceful windings ... Loneliness and silence ... have here an almost undisturbed reign.'

Then, the third element of the picture he was to do six years later was added: 'The landscape, so striking and harmonious, is rendered still more affecting by the appropriate figures or groups of pilgrims that give at once increased interest and picturesqueness to the scene.'

Finally, 'melancholy reflection' on 'the ancient churches of Clonmacnoise', led him to political musings of a characteristically vague and muted sort:

> Its ruined buildings call forth national associations and ideas. They remind us of the arts and literature, the piety and humanity, which distinguished their time, and are the work of a people who, in a dark age, marched among the foremost on the road to life and civilisation, but who were unfortunately checked and barbarised by those who were journeying in the same course and ought to have cheered them on.[19]

The mood is elegiac rather than exhortatory. Irish civilisation had been destroyed by England, and Ireland was a prisoner of that past, and all that could be done was to achieve greater understanding of what was lost. Years later, describing similar ruins at Monasterboice in his short-lived *Irish Penny Journal* (1840-41), which was dedicated to patriotic antiquarianism, and he believed, 'wholly national' in spirit,[20] he declared that 'if we were desirous to give a stranger a true idea of Ireland', we would show him a 'round tower with its little parent church in some sequestered valley ... and of such a scene we should say emphatically, "This is Ireland".'[21] Note 'is' not 'was': when he painted the ruins of Clonmacnoise, he was painting contemporary Ireland.

In this he was part of a cultural trend. Leerssen has pointed to the political importance of Moore's *Melodies* (1807-34) lying in 'their cultivation of remembrance'; this was 'historical consciousness as cultivated ... for purposes of agitation'.[22] Petrie was profoundly influenced by Moore, both as antiquarian and painter, and quoted his 'Let Erin remember the days of old' in relation to Clonmacnoise, where the Shannon reflected 'the round towers of other days'.[23] The historical section of the Ordnance Survey, which he directed, was also a remarkable attempt to record communal memory, spurred on by the profound cultural loss involved in the rapid erosion of the Irish language. To quote Leerssen again, in its recording of place names especially, 'it turned the entire countryside of Ireland into one vast *lieu de mémoire*'. The Great Famine (1845-49) accelerated the process of cultural erosion and the consciousness of an irreparable breach with the past. In the preface to his *Ancient Music* (1855), Petrie wrote of 'the awful unwonted silence' of the famine years, and the loss of 'the traditions and characteristic peculiarities of feeling that would link them to their remotest ancestors'.[24] But, even on his first visit to Clonmacnoise, thirty-five years earlier, the peasant pilgrims had seemed to him at one with the ruins, 'all equally belonging to other times and other feelings'.[25] In his letter to the Royal Irish Art Union, which commissioned the second Clonmacnoise watercolour he explained what he had attempted to portray.

> It was my wish to produce an Irish picture, somewhat historical in its object, and political in its sentiment – a landscape

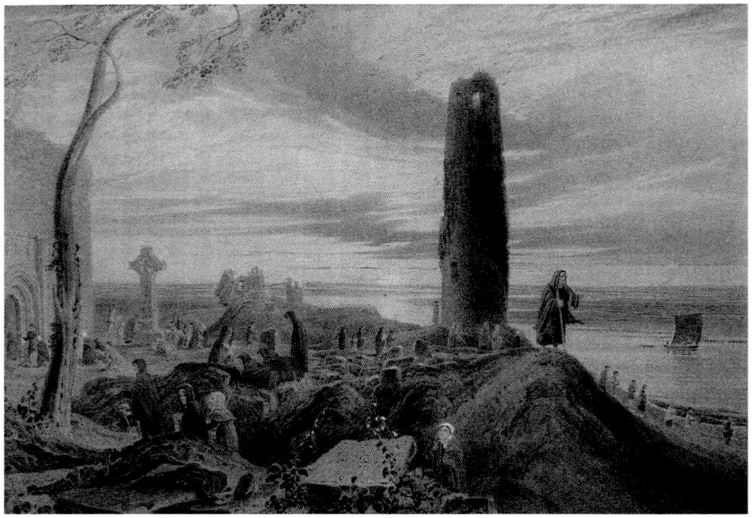

The Last Circuit of the Pilgrims at Clonmacnoise
c.1828, watercolour on paper (coll: Richard Wood collection, University of Limerick)
(see colour plate p.20)

> comprised of several of the monuments characteristic of the past history of our country, and which will soon cease to exist, and to connect with them the expressions of human feelings, equally belonging to our history, and which are destined to a similar extinction.[26]

Round towers, considered to be unique to Ireland, were a particularly visible link between past and present, and had become both symbolic of Ireland's golden age and the centre of intense and bitter debate.[27] When Petrie was elected to the Royal Irish Academy in 1828 (the year his first Clonmacnoise painting was exhibited), the Antiquarian section was virtually moribund and the 18th-century 'patriot' view that the towers were of pre-Christian Phoenician origin (reflecting an advanced ancient civilisation) still held sway. Petrie had long been critical of the mainly Catholic antiquarians who preferred 'romantic legends' to the evidence of 'the historical documents'.[28] As part of his campaign to revitalise antiquarian research, he got the Academy's agreement to a gold medal competition on the origins of round towers in 1830, and three years later was himself awarded the prize for an essay that showed that the towers were, more prosaically, essentially Christian belfries. Controversy raged, culminating in Petrie finally publishing his massively extended and definitive findings in *The Ecclesiastical Architecture of Ireland anterior to the Anglo-Norman invasion, comprising an essay on the origin and uses of the Round Towers of Ireland* (1845). Thus, throughout the period covered by the two Clonmacnoise paintings, Petrie was mainly preoccupied with research into manuscript sources, detailed architectural drawings, and the recording of inscriptions. The romantic elegiast of Clonmacnoise in his journals and paintings, was, at the same time, the improbable leader of a 'newfangled, scientific, pedantic and intolerant factualism' in the Academy.[29] And in his *Ecclesiastical Architecture*, Clonmacnoise again loomed large, its ruins covering almost the entire period of his study and exhibiting many of the characteristics he wanted to highlight, and with its own set of Annals backing up his observations. He also made nearly two hundred detailed drawings of its gravestone inscriptions and ornamentation, later published after his death as *Christian Inscriptions in the Irish chiefly collected and drawn by George Petrie* (1872). Finally, he broke off from a series of detailed drawings and discussions of the doorways of round towers in *Ecclesiastical Architecture* to present a very different kind of drawing of the great tower of Clonmacnoise ('as I have treated so much of this tower in several parts of this work'), which had featured in both watercolours. Underlining the dramatic nature of this sudden shift from the scientific to the romantic, he now described (and drew) it as set 'amid scenery of a solemn and desolate character, which add[s] greatly to its poetical interest'.[30] Mirroring that shift, his earlier paintings had also included important elements of his antiquarian research, and were, in part, restatements in a very different form, of his historical arguments.

The first of these two watercolours was exhibited in 1828, but painted in 1826,[31] 'for the album of Mrs. Haldiman, to which Turner, Danby and others contributed at the same time'.[32] This was the period of his most intense work, producing hundreds of drawings for the illustrated guides of Cromwell, Brewer and Wright.[33] The title of the painting refers to the traditional pilgrimage in June on the feast of St Ciarán, who founded the monastery in AD 548-49, and to the custom of following a particular circuit of the holy places, stopping to pray at various points. Thus, for example, he included in the picture a group he had described in his journal as 'arranged in silent prayer around the rude but gorgeously sculptured stone cross, which they afterwards kiss with the utmost fervency of devotion'. Depicting 'the last circuit' of

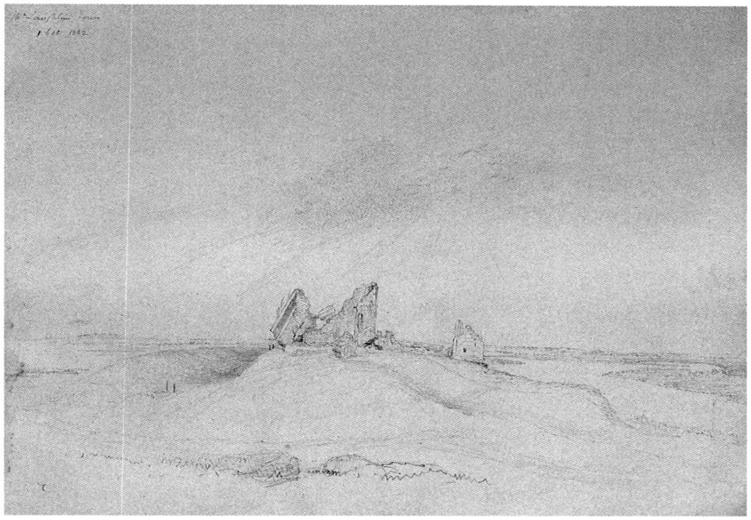

Sketch of ruined castle at Clonmacnoise

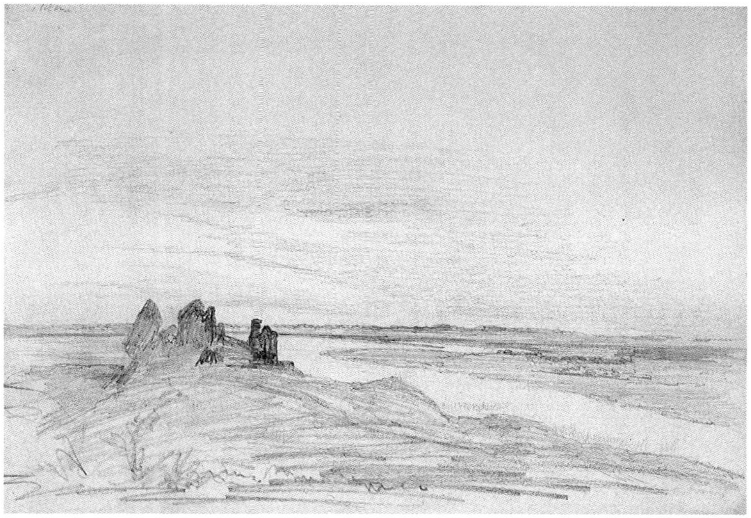

Sketch (heavily shaded) of ruined castle at Clonmacnoise
both from the *Robert Callwell Skethbook* (coll: Crawford Gallery)

the pilgrims as the sun sets on the Shannon river, 'the Irish Ganges' [34] gave the painting an air of romance, but as we've seen, Petrie's initial focus was on the value of the site for antiquarians, like himself, who wanted to establish that early Christian (and pre-Colonial) Ireland had an advanced culture, contrary to the old stereotype (given new life by conservative writers like the Protestant Antiquarian, Edward Ledwich) of barbarism and fable. As well as being 'the most sacred and venerated place', Clonmacnoise offered a potent symbol of Ireland's secular history also, being the burial place of the last High King of Ireland before the Norman invasion, and the target of innumerable lootings and burnings through the Viking and Norman periods, and indeed, right down to 1552, when the Annals of the Four Masters recorded the assault by the Athlone garrison that ensured its final ruinous state.[35] Thus, these ruins symbolised colonial aggression as well as indigenous Christian civilisation and piety.

This little painting neatly encapsulates the argument Petrie was to make in his 1833 essay to the Royal Irish Academy, rearranging key elements of the site a little in order to do so. Dominating it is the great round tower, popularly called O'Rourke's Tower, after the 10th-century King of Connaught, and crucial in his argument that these towers were Christian belfries and not sites of pagan fire worship or other such fantasy. He was to date it, together with the great, decorated Cross of the Scriptures to its left, and the Cathedral, a corner of which appears beside the Cross, to the early 10th century, contrary to the claims of Ledwich and others that they were post-Norman, and thus not proof of Gaelic civilisation. In the middle foreground is an example of one of the several hundred inscribed gravestones he was to copy, and which were to be vital proofs in his argument. This blurred (and damaged) image is possibly a sketch of the tombstone of Suibhne Mac Maelhumai, one of the oldest he found, which echoes designs in manuscripts of the same date, and whose death, *c*.890, is recorded not only in various Irish annals, but in the *Anglo-Saxon Chronicle*.[36] In the middle background, making a point about the secular significance of the site he included the ruins of the Norman castle, built in the early 13th century as part of an attempt to control the Gaelic tribes of the area , and the subject of an earlier watercolour by Petrie, engraved for Cromwell's, *Excursions through Ireland* (1820).[37]

But this antiquarian aspect of the painting is hardly what appealed to Mrs. Haldiman, who was more likely to have enjoyed it as a beguiling example of the picturesque, and especially of the fashion for what Louis Hawes calls 'ruin landscapes'.[38] From his first sight of Clonmacnoise, Petrie too was equally interested in 'the landscapes so striking and harmonious ... [and] the appropriate figures of groups of pilgrims that gave at once increased interest and picturesqueness to the scene'. Indeed, he wrote that he was led to his antiquarian studies by 'an indulgence in my professional taste for the picturesque'.[39] This taste, dominant in British landscape art, reduced nature to influential artistic representations of it, especially the consoling landscapes of Claude Lorrain, and was part of the conservative response to revolutionary upheaval in English romanticism.[40] Its defining feature for one of its most influential proponents, William Gilpin, was a pleasing 'roughness' or 'ruggedness' and an example of this can be seen in Petrie's representation of O'Rourke's tower.[41] In *Ecclesiastical Architecture* he repeatedly stressed its 'beautiful masonry', but also described the effect of its 12th-century restoration, 'the upper portion being of coarse jointed masonry of limestone, while the greater part of the tower below is of close jointed ashlar sandstone'. But, in the picture, 'the greater part of the tower' is rough and uneven, its shape distorted, probably by the ivy that also features in Berenger's more prosaic watercolour, dated by Harbison to the early 1780s.[42] The placing of the tree on the left is also characteristic of the picturesque, a repoussoir figure, establishing depth and scale, but also a romantic feature, doubtless one of those 'lofty ash trees' he describes in his journal, 'that seem of equal antiquity and sanctity' (i.e. to the ruins) and which, 'wave their nearly leafless branches among the silent ruins above the dead'.[43]

Peter Murray has pointed out that Petrie's work for publishers and engravers in the 1820s 'involved selecting views that inclined towards the picturesque rather than the sublime'.[44] As Petrie's collaborator, Brewer, wrote to him in 1820, complaining of the publisher's demands for pictures of the residences of the aristocracy, 'my feelings, as well I believe as your own, would rather incline highly to ruins, interesting from architectural character or picturesque features'.[45] Hawes, in outlining the general vogue for ruins, in poetry as well as art, in the early Romantic period, stressed the special popularity of 'the solitary ruined tower or decayed castle keep, powerfully silhouetted against a luminous sky, and viewed from a low, rather distant vantage point'.[46] Petrie had already produced many such images, particularly for Cromwell's *Excursions through Ireland* (1820), such as *Trim Castle, County Meath* (Royal Irish Academy).[47] The year after Petrie had exhibited his small watercolour of Clonmacnoise, Constable showed his dramatic *Hadleigh Castle* (1829, Tate Britain) at the Royal Academy of Arts in London. Hawes describes it as 'among the most unforgettable ruin images in western art', its power coming from the artist's grief at the death of his wife.[48]

Petrie's painting had a quieter intensity, and its force, reflecting political rather than personal feeling, came from the connection he made – unusual in British and Irish art of this period – between the ruins and the pilgrim poor who prayed among them. 'The enthusiastic painter', he wrote, 'will understand the kind of delight with which I was inspired by those groups of pilgrims, clothed in draperies of the most picturesque form and the most splendid and varied colours'. But what made Clonmacnoise 'altogether lonely, sublime and poetic' was that the pilgrims 'are so identified in character with the ruins, that they may be truly said to belong to each other'.[49] This was intensified by the fact that the pilgrims also represented continuity with the past. In a very early journal, he commented on the tragic fate of the once aristocratic Gaelic families, who were now, 'peasants, to be found in the villain hovels in the wilderness, their rank and inheritance gone and forever'.[50] The pilgrims at Clonmacnoise 'come for the purposes that brought others here for more than a thousand years', in particular, mourning the dead, and he imagines 'the richly adorned figures of princes ... Performing the routine of penances now only the duty of the peasant'.[51] This intimate connection between people and place, between past and present is suggested strongly by the painting. He draws attention to the way that the pilgrims commune with each object of devotion on their circuit by their devout demeanour and by the careful distribution of colourful clothes to every part, especially the 'red they dye with madder', which so excited David Wilkie years later.[52] The dominant figure, exaggerated in scale, is the woman on the knoll to the right of the tower, pointing dramatically to the river, where a ship, more Viking than contemporary in appearance, is passing. Writing of the similar Monasterboice site (in Co Louth) later in *The Irish Penny Journal*, Petrie described witnessing a noble-looking woman singing an Irish lamentation or 'keen' over a grave, and asked the reader to imagine the scene: 'among those lightning scattered ruins and chanted by such a living vocal monument of human woe and desolation'.[53] Richard Wood has described the figure in the painting as 'like a keener at a funeral', but he suggested that the death mourned is Ireland's: 'the sun sinking beyond the river Shannon seems to symbolise the slow agonising death of Celtic Ireland'.[54] Certainly the identification of Ireland with a woman of sadness and prophecy is very old, and in the Jacobite songs still ubiquitously sung by the Irish-speaking poor, she foretold the coming of foreign aid to free Ireland from her colonial masters.[55]

That such an identification may have been made silently by

the artist seems less far-fetched when the figure of the grey-haired man in the group of pilgrims in the left foreground is considered. To the viewer he stands out as the only man in the picture, but a reading of Petrie's journal suggests that for him this figure represented resistance to the historical forces which had created these ruins. He began his account of the various kinds of Clonmacnoise pilgrim he had seen with the figure he was later to paint:

> The aged sinner, supported by his pilgrims staff, barefooted and bareheaded, his large grey coat, the substitute for the forbidden cloak or mantle, sweeping the road, his white hair floating on the disregarded wind.[56]

Clearly, 'the forbidden cloak or mantle' refers to the 16th-century Gaelic *brat* so memorably castigated by Edmund Spenser in 1596 as the main resource of the Irish rebel, while the connection between it and the coat of a latter-day peasant was first made in 1800 by Maria Edgeworth in the first page of *Castle Rackrent*. This further identified the 16th-century Gaelic rebels with those of 1798, reflecting widespread fears that this sense of continuity with the past threatened both Protestant Ascendancy and the colonial land settlement.[57] It can be argued, therefore, that these two figures in Petrie's picture suggest a more subversive, and essentially 'nationalist' politics than he ever articulated in any other way, though their significance was hidden from the viewer. Petrie's identification with the old man, this covert rebel, was strengthened considerably when he came to paint this subject again, but on a much larger scale.

This second painting, now in the National Gallery of Ireland has faded, so that it is difficult to make any comparisons of mood on the basis of colour. The gallery dates it *c*.1838, but Stokes clearly states that it was painted after the break up of the Ordnance Survey in 1839, and it wasn't exhibited until 1853.[58] Petrie's letter to the Royal Irish Art Union, which purchased it for £100 is undated, but a letter of 1845 to a friend, complaining of the 'tedious work' of 'finishing my picture', hoped that 'it will be my best work of its kind ... and the subject is lovely.'[59] Does this refer to Clonmacnoise, which clearly obsessed and delighted him, and to the painting which, in terms of scale and expectations (he hoped it would make a successful engraving), as well as ambition, was a major project? Perhaps so, thus (rather con-

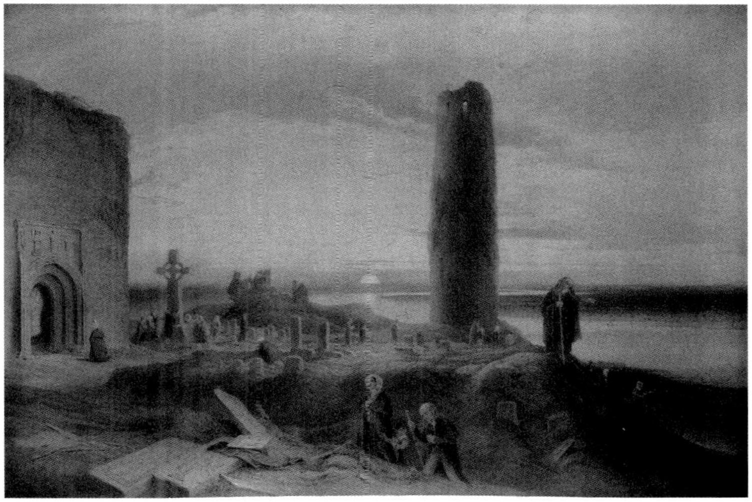

The Last Circuit of the Pilgrims at Clonmacnoise, Co. Offaly
c.1842, watercolour on paper, 67.2 x 98 (coll: NGI, cat. no. 2230)
(see colour plate p.32)

veniently for my argument) dating the painting to the year in which his controversial work on round towers was finally published. (A sketchbook of Petrie's, recently acquired by the Crawford Gallery, includes a series of sketches of Clonmacnoise, dated 30 September 1842. The one closest in vantage point and composition to the watercolours has the added note, '¼ past sunset'.) In any case, the statement in his letter to the Royal Irish Art Union, that he had painted 'an Irish picture ... a landscape comprised of several of the monuments characteristic of the past history of our country and which will soon cease to exist', is echoed in the preface to *The Ecclesiastical Architecture of Ireland*, which claimed that he had been 'actuated solely ... by an ardent desire to rescue the antiquities of my native country from unmerited oblivion'.[60]

He also hoped that the picture would have a value, 'beyond the present time' and connect his name 'with the history of art in Ireland'. And so, 'with this feeling, I did my best to adhere to local as well as general truth'.[61] Yet, as Jeanne Sheehy pointed out, 'individual details and objects are accurate, but he has altered their grouping, and the fall of the ground, to obtain a more picturesque and dramatic effect.'[62] However, the main changes he made from the first version tend rather to reduce the picturesque elements and to accentuate the antiquarian argument. The defining tree has gone, and the north door of the Cathedral is angled more so that its fine carvings can be seen. This draws attention to his emphatic rebuttal in *Ecclesiastical Architecture* of the 'audacious misrepresentations' of Ledwich, who had claimed the doorway was 13th century, whereas 'any person acquainted with the antiquities of this period' could recognise it was a 15th-century restoration of a 10th-century original.[63] Likewise, the addition of a second decorated gravestone (left foreground) pointed up his argument that the Early Christian Irish stood comparison with the ancient Greeks. One of only two of the hundreds he copied that featured what he called 'a parallelogram; a border composed of the gammadion or Greek pattern', its early date was also proof 'that the arts were much cultivated here in the eighth and the beginning of the ninth century'.[64]

There are other interesting differences between the two paintings. Despite its picturesque qualities (and the problems associated with fading colours), the first has a sense of heightened emotion, almost of apocalypse, with its threatening sky and dominant prophetic woman; the second seems more serene, there are fewer pilgrims, the ground has less 'roughness', and the figure of the woman now has its head bowed and seems more accepting. Aesthetically, there are echoes of Burke's distinction between the sublime and the beautiful; politically there may be echoes of the campaign for Catholic Emancipation. The first picture, painted when O'Connell's campaign was entering a more threatening phase, stresses the poetry and decorum of the pilgrims (in contrast to conventional depictions, like Peacock's), but it also seems to echo the sense of unease with which even liberal Protestants, like Petrie, contemplated Emancipation (A literary equivalent is Lady Morgan's last Irish novel, *The O'Briens and the O'Flahertys*, published the year Petrie exhibited his picture.)[65] The second version reflects the calm after the storm; Catholic Emancipation, far from being convulsive, had made Catholicism respectable, just as here the clothes of the pilgrims have been gentrified a little. Petrie's journal also distinguished between two kinds of days at Clonmacnoise, and this may offer a further clue to the differences between the paintings. Some days 'present a scene of wild commotion, when the silent solitude is disturbed by the *ulligaun* or death-cry, raised as some peasant of the country is borne to the grave of his ancestors'. There may be echoes of that mood in his first version of the pilgrims' prayerful circuit. Then there are days of quiet, when 'in all their movements there is an abstracted intensity of feeling that carries the mind back to remote times', and this more reflective mood is captured in the second version.[66]

But the most intriguing change in the second version is the little sketch of the Round Tower lying on a cloak in the left foreground. He had placed two cloaks on the ground, less prominently, but in roughly the same place in the first version. Now, however, the abandoned cloak is clearly connected to the artist himself, and the sketch may even refer back to the first painting. Has the artist, in effect, disappeared *into* the picture? Is this the 'forbidden cloak or mantle' associated with Irish rebellion? Is Petrie now the old man, feeble and in need of support (he was seeking a state pension in the mid 1840s); yet also, by his evocation of this 'national scene' for 'a truly patriotic body', is he also in effect a rebel against the historical forces that created these ruins? More prosaically, he is certainly further emphasising his empathy with Ireland's sad story. His 'Dedication' of his *Ecclesiastical Architecture* to his friends, biographer Stokes and the Earl of Dunraven, suggests an interesting connection in this regard between his writing and his art. It recalled Poussin's

> group of shepherds at an ancient tomb, one of whom deciphers for the rest the simple inscription engraved upon it
>
> Et ego in Arcadia
>
> And it was a natural and grateful desire of the Arcadian shepherd to be remembered in connection with the beloved region in which he had found tranquillity and enjoyment. In like manner I would wish to be remembered...[67]

Petrie is almost certainly referring to Poussin's second, and better known version of *The Arcadian Shepherds* (*c*.1638, Musée du Louvre, Paris), in which three shepherds and a presiding female figure calmly examine an inscription on a tomb set incongruously in their romantic landscape; it reads, 'Et in Arcadia Ego' (Petrie got it wrong). The first version (*c*.1627, Chatsworth) featured a similar but more agitated group who had just discovered the tomb, on which rested a skull.[68] In the second version, according to Panofsky's influential interpretation, 'the Arcadians are not so much warned of an implacable future as they are immersed in mellow meditation on a beautiful past ... We are confronted with a change from thinly veiled moralism to undisguised elegiac sentiment'. Panofsky linked this to a change in the way 'Et in Arcadia Ego' came to be translated. The first version reflects the original and grammatically correct meaning, 'Even in Arcady, there am I' (i.e. death); the second represents what became the widely accepted though ungrammatical version, 'I too lived in Arcady'.[69] Petrie echoed the second meaning in his 'Dedication' (including in his garbling of the Latin) and identified, like the Shepherd, 'with the beloved region in which he had found tranquillity and enjoyment'. Clearly, this involved more than the company of his friends, but came also from his antiquarian researches into, and his artistic depictions of, 'the long faded glories' of Ireland's sad, romantic past. In this, he was representative of his time, like Morgan's fictions and Moore's *Melodies*, and also in sympathy with the essentially nostalgic 'nationality' of Young Ireland. But he was not representative of Irish artists then, or for decades afterwards, or, indeed ever. Few were to follow Davis's advice to depict history subjects, and only Henry O'Neill, best known for his portraits of Repeal leaders, matched Petrie's antiquarian enthusiasm, though his careful record of Irish High Crosses lacked the contemporary resonances of Petrie's Clonmacnoise paintings.[70] Only John Hogan's sculptures, notably, *Hibernia with a bust of Lord Cloncurry* (1844, National Gallery of Ireland) reflected a political and historical sensibility similar to Petrie's Clonmacnoise paintings, and his career did not flourish when he returned from Rome.[71] As Barrett argued, the lack of interest in the market for such subjects may be seen as a mirror of public opinion's general apathy to nationalist rhetoric.[72] Also, as Burton had warned Davis, 'the nationalising of art', and, indeed, 'nationality' itself, could not be produced to order, but could only follow a cultural revolution, led by 'a decided national school of poetry'.[73] But when this happened half a century later, it is difficult to argue that anything as coherent and distinct as a 'national art' emerged, at least in the sense that Davis meant it, except again in public sculpture, mainly in the work of Oliver Sheppard.[74] Petrie's last great painting did not, as he had hoped, connect his name significantly 'with the history of art in Ireland'.[75] It did, however, capture memorably, the political sensibility of that rather muted Irish romanticism that was more a feature of Irish literature and political rhetoric than of Irish art in the first half of the 19th century.[76]

TOM DUNNE is an Emeritus Professor of History at University College Cork. He has published widely on the connections between literature, art and politics. His new book, *Rebellions: memoir, memory and 1798*, has just been published by Lilliput Press.

ENDNOTES

I am grateful to Peter Murray, whose Masters thesis on Petrie was the starting point for my research, whose contributions in a class we taught together sparked off some of the ideas developed here, and whose comments were invaluable.

1 Thomas Davis, 'Art and the Nation', in *Thomas Davis: essays and poems with a centenary memoir 1845-1945* (Gill and Son, Dublin, 1945) pp.113-18. A similar list had been compiled by Joseph Cooper Walker in *Outlines of plan for promoting the art of painting in Ireland, with a list of subjects for painters drawn from the romantic and genuine Histories of Ireland* (Dublin, 1790) pp.1-36

2 See Elizabeth Helsinger, 'Turner and the representation of England', in W.J. Mitchell (ed.), *Landscape and Power* (University of Chicago Press, Chicago and London, 1994) pp.103-45; Tim Barringer, 'The course of empires: landscape and identity in America and Britain 1820-1880', in Andrew Wilton and Tim Barringer (eds), *American Sublime: landscape painting in the United States 1820-1880* (Tate, London, 2002)

3 W.J. Mitchell, 'Imperial landscape', in Mitchell (ed.), *Landscape and Power*, pp.9, 22. Malcolm Andrews, *Landscape and Western Art* (Oxford University Press, 1999), chapter .7

4 John Barrell, *The Dark Side of the Landscape: the rural poor in English painting 1730-1840* (Cambridge University Press, 1980) pp.21-3. Tom Dunne, 'National character and the depiction of the poor in Irish landscape art 1800-1950', in C. O'Halloran, D. Scully and C. Quinlan (eds), *'What ish my nation?': Constructions of Irish identity from medieval to modern* (forthcoming)

5 W.H. Crawford, 'The patron, or festival of St Kevin at the Seven Churches, Glendalough, County Wicklow 1813', in *Ulster Folklore*, vol. 32, 1986, pp.37-47

6 Cyril Barrett, 'Irish nationalism and art 1800-1921', in *Studies*, Winter 1975, pp.393-409

7 S.B. Kennedy, 'An Irish school of art? Depictions of the landscape in a critical period 1880-1930', in Carla King (ed.), *Famine, Land and Culture in Ireland* (University College Dublin Press, 2000) pp.153-68

8 The fullest account of Petrie's life is still that by his friend, the eminent doctor, William Stokes, who included, in the best Victorian tradition, an immense amount of primary material, some of which is now lost. William Stokes, *The Life and Labour in Art and Archaeology of George Petrie L.L.D. M.R.I.A.* (Longman Greene & Co, London, 1868); the quote is from p.347. The best modern assessment is in Peter Murray, *George Petrie 1790-1866*, M.Litt (Trinity College Dublin, 1980). See also Anne Crookshank and the Knight of Glin, *The Watercolours of Ireland: work in pencil, pastel and paint c.1600-1914* (Barrie & Jenkins, London, 1994) pp.162-3.

9 Stokes, p.1. For Morgan, see Tom Dunne, 'Fiction as "the best history of nations": Lady Morgan's Irish novels', in Tom Dunne (ed.), *The Writer as Witness* (Cork University Press, 1987) pp.133-59; Joep Leerssen, *Remembrance and Imagination*

(Cork University Press, 1996) pp.53-67
10 Stokes, pp.404-5, undated. See Thomas Davis, *Essays and Poems*, p.103
11 Stokes, pp.35, 5, 6
12 David Cooper, *The Petrie Collection of the Ancient Music of Ireland* (Cork University Press, 2002) p.11
13 Stokes, pp.71-3, also, pp.315-17, 342-45, 373
14 *ibid*, p.394. See also Ruan O'Donnell, 'Propaganda and iconography: images of Robert Emmet', in *Irish Arts Review*, Spring 2003, pp.108-13
15 Leerssen, p.21 ff
16 George Petrie, 'On the history and antiquities of Tara Hill', in *Proceedings of the Royal Irish Academy*, vol. xviii, 1839, pp.25-232, p.25; *Ancient Music*, p.30; Stokes, *Life*, pp.433-37
17 *Ancient Music*, pp.30-1
18 Murray, p.36
19 Stokes, pp.27-34
20 *ibid*, pp.70-71
21 *ibid*, p.72
22 Leerssen, p.81
23 Stokes, p34
24 *Ancient Music*, p.31
25 Stokes, p32
26 *ibid*, p.32
27 Leerssen, pp.108-43
28 Stokes, pp.23-5. Manuscript journal of 1821. For a discussion of patriot antiquarianism, see Clare O'Halloran, *Golden Ages and Barbarous Nations: antiquarian debate and cultural politics in Ireland, c.1750-1800* (Cork University Press, 2004)
29 Leerssen, p.128
30 George Petrie, *The Ecclesiastical Architecture of Ireland anterior to the Anglo-Norman invasion, comprising an essay on the origins and uses of Round Towers* (Hodges & Smith, Dublin, 1845) pp.411-12. This shows much the same scene as the watercolours, but from a lower angle. It is striking that he made no attempt to show the decoration on the gravestones here as he did in the paintings.
31 Brian P. Kennedy, *Irish Painting* (Dublin, 1993) p.18; Richard Wood, 'The landscape paintings at Fota', *Irish Arts Review*, vol. 1, no. 4, winter 1984, pp.47-55: 53. Measuring only 18.5 x 25.6 cm, it is currently on display at the University of Limerick. It has not been possible to trace either Mrs Haldiman, or the fate of her album.
32 Stokes, pp.14-15
33 Murray, chapter 2. J.K. Cromwell, *Excursions through Ireland*, 3 vols, 1820; J.N. Brewer, *The Beauties of Ireland*, 2 vols, 1825; G.N. Wright, *Ireland, illustrated from original drawings* (1832)
34 Stokes, p.28
35 *ibid*, p.393. Peter Harbison, *Pilgrimage in Ireland: the monuments and the people* (Barrie & Jenkins, London, 1991) pp.111-16; Peter Harbison, *Guide to national and historic monuments of Ireland* (Gill & Macmillan, Dublin (3rd ed.), 1992) pp.276-78.The monastic site had also been a focus of intense rivalry between Gaelic septs before the 12th century, see J. Bradley, 'The Monastic town of Clonmacnoise', in H.A.King, *Clonmacnoise Studies*, i (Dúchas, The Heritage Service, Dublin, 1998) pp 42-55
36 Petrie, *Ecclesiastical Architecture*, pp.326-28, 391-93
37 Murray, *Petrie*, 'Catalogue', no. 55. See Kieran O'Conor and Conleth Manning, 'Clonmacnoise Castle', in H.A.King, *Clonmacnoise Studies*, ii (Dept of the Environment, Heritage and Local Government, 2003) pp.137-65
38 Louise Hawes, *Presences of Nature: British landscapes 1780-1830* Yale University Press, 1982), chapter III
39 Stokes, pp.29, 24
40 See Anne Bermingham, 'System, order and abstraction: the politics of English landscape drawing around 1795', in Mitchell (ed.), *Landscape and Power*, pp.77-101; Mitchell, 'Imperial landscape', p.16; Andrews, *Landscape and Western Art*, pp.129-31
41 William Gilpin, *Three Essays: On Picturesque Beauty; On Picturesque Travel; and On Picturesque Landscape: to which is added a poem on landscape painting* (London, 1784) p.6
42 Stokes, pp.392, 411, 393. P. Harbison, 'Four late Eighteenth Century watercolour drawings of Clonmacnoise antiquities', in *Clonmacnoise Studies*, i, pp34-41
43 Stokes, p.28
44 Murray, p.21
45 *ibid*, p.24
46 Hawes, p.41
47 See Crookshank and the Knight of Glin, p.162
48 Hawes, p.48. Michael Rosenthal, *Constable, the painter and his landscape* (Yale University Press, 1983) pp.214-18
49 Stokes, pp.28-34
50 Murray, p.9
51 Stokes, pp.31-32
52 Fintan Cullen, *Sources in Irish Art: A Reader* (Cork University Press, 2000) p.63
53 Stokes, p.73
54 Wood, 'Landscape paintings', p.53
55 Tom Dunne, '"Tá Gaedhil bhocht cráidhte"': memory, tradition and the politics of the poor in Gaelic poetry and song', in L. Geary (ed.), *Rebellion and remembrance in modern Ireland* (Four Courts Press, Dublin, 2001) pp.93-111
56 Stokes, p.29
57 Tom Dunne, *Maria Edgeworth and the Colonial Mind: the 26th O'Donnell lecture* (National University of Ireland, Dublin, 1984); W.L. Renwick (ed.), *Edmund Spenser: A view of the present state of Ireland* (London, 1934)
58 Marie Bourke and Síghle Bhreathnach-Lynch, *Discover Irish Art at the National Gallery of Ireland* (Dublin, 1999) p.96; Stokes, p.253; Murray, p.121. The painting measures 67.2 x 98 cm
59 Stokes, pp.353-54. Peter Murray also concludes that this is a very late work, *Petrie*, p.121
60 *ibid*, p.15; *Ecclesiastical Architecture*, p.v
61 Stokes, p.15
62 Jeanne Sheehy, *The Rediscovery of Ireland's Past. The Celtic Revival 1830-1930* (Thames & Hudson, London, 1980) p.22
63 Petrie, *Ecclesiastical Architecture*, pp.274-75
64 M. Stokes (ed.), *George Petrie, Christian inscriptions in the Irish language*, 2 vols (Dublin, 1872), i, plate xii, figures 29-30, text, p.23
65 Dunne, 'Morgan's Irish Novels'
66 Stokes, pp.30-34
67 Petrie, *Ecclesiastical Architecture*, 'Dedication'
68 P. Rosenberg and V. Damian, *Nicolas Poussin: Masterpieces 1594-1665* (Cassell, London, 1995) pp.64-68
69 Erwin Panofsky, '*Et in Arcadia Ego*: Poussin and the elegiac tradition', in Panofsky, *Meaning in the Visual Arts* (Penguin Books London, 1970) pp.340-67
70 Walter George Strickland, *A Dictionary of Irish Artists*, 2 vols (Maunsel & Co, Dublin and London, 1913), vol. 11, pp.197-201
71 John Turpin, *John Hogan: Irish neo-classical sculpture in Rome 1800-1858* (Irish Academic Press, Dublin, 1982)
72 Barrett, 'Irish nationalism and art', p.408
73 Charles Gavin Duffy, *Young Ireland: a fragment of Irish History 1840-1850* (London (2nd ed.), 1880) pp.661-63
74 John Turpin, *Oliver Sheppard 1865-1941* (Four Courts Press, Dublin, 2000)
75 Stokes, p.15
76 Tom Dunne, 'Haunted by history: Irish romantic writing 1800-1850', in R. Porter and M. Teich (eds), *Romanticism in National Context* (Cambridge University Press, 1988).

Catalogue of Paintings and Drawings

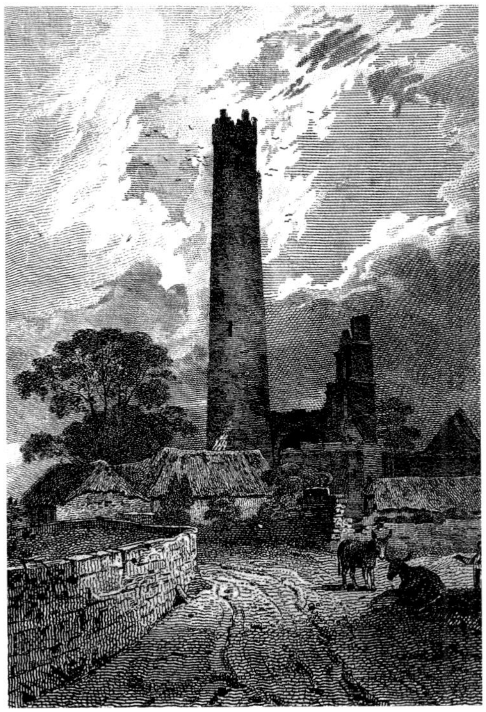

Round Tower, Kildare (detail)
engraving after Petrie from T. Cromwell, *Excursions through Ireland*, vol. iii, 1820

Catalogue of Paintings and Drawings

There are three strands to this catalogue. The first is those paintings and drawings by Petrie that are still extant, in the National Gallery of Ireland (NGI), the Royal Irish Academy (RIA), public museums and private collections. The second strand draws from contemporary accounts, descriptions and exhibition catalogues of the Royal Hibernian Academy (RHA). The published engravings, based on paintings by Petrie, form a third strand, although in many cases the original drawings or paintings, upon which these engravings were based, are now lost. The number of paintings from private collections included in the catalogue is small. The Margaret Stokes bequest of paintings and drawings to the NGI in 1900 gave that gallery the bulk of its Petrie holdings, and over half the paintings from private collections included in this catalogue are still owned by members of that family.

The watercolours and drawings are listed in chronological order where it has been possible to date them with certainty. This is followed by the list of undated works. Measurements are given in centimetres, height before width. Unless otherwise stated, the provenance of works by Petrie in the National Gallery of Ireland is the Margaret Stokes Bequest, 1900. The lists of engravings are compiled from the publications themselves, and from William Stokes' *Life*. As the precise number of engravings included in different editions seems to have varied, the lists may contain more prints than would be found in any one edition.

NOTES ON TECHNIQUE

In his examination of the watercolours and drawings by Petrie in the National Gallery of Ireland, paper conservator Ranson Davey established that most of the sheets were given a very pale brownish wash prior to the drawing, mitigating the somewhat harsh cream colour of the paper. The edge of the wash is visible at the edges of some of the sheets. Petrie has used large sheets of a fine-quality Whatman paper (a heavy handmade wove) cut down to suit his purposes. The watermark 'James Whatman' (as opposed to J Whatman) indicates that he used the 'Antiquarian' size paper. This got its name from the fact that it was a sheet size originally requested by the Royal Society of Antiquaries in order to suit large prints which they published in the late 1800s.

Drawing paper was sold as flat sheets. Some sizes of English handmade papers were indicated by watermarks. Today the Antiquarian size is 53 x 31 inches. However, Tomlinson's *Cyclopedia of Useful Arts* (1854) states that Antiquarian sheets measured 52.5 x 30.5 inches. One ream of Antiquarian paper comprised 480 sheets and weighed 236 pounds.

Abbreviations		
	Coll	Collection
	Prov	Provenance
	Exh	Exhibited
	Lit	Literature
	NGI	National Gallery of Ireland
	RHA	Royal Hibernian Academy
	RIA	Royal Irish Academy
	cat. no.	catalogue number

DRAWINGS AND WATERCOLOURS

GP.1 *The Entrance to the Glen of the Dargle, Co. Wicklow*
Ink on paper, 18.3 x 25.2
Signed and dated: 'Geo Petrie 1807'
Coll: NGI, cat. no. 6304

The Welsh Coast
dated Sunday May 30th 1813
Ink on paper, 14.3 x 26.5
GP.3 Coll: NGI, cat. no. 6742
GP.4 Coll: NGI, cat. no. 6743
GP.5 Coll: NGI, cat. no. 6744
GP.6 Coll: NGI, cat. no. 6745
GP.7 Coll: NGI, cat. no. 6746

GP.17 *The River Vartry at Mount Usher, Co. Wicklow*
*c.*1813, watercolour on paper, 16.1 x 22.7
Signed: 'Geo Petrie 1813'
Coll: NGI, cat. no. 2378
Engraving published in Cromwell's *Excursions* in 1821

GP.3

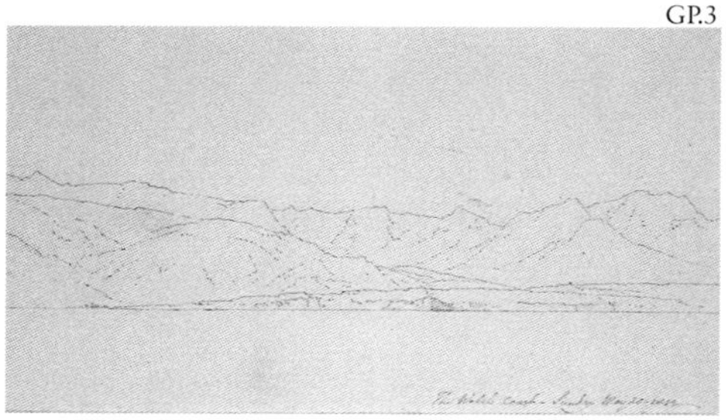

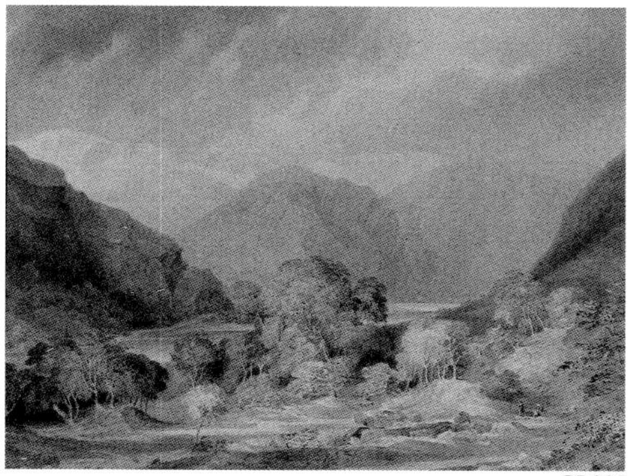

GP.235

GP.235 *The Upper Lake at Glendalough*
watercolour on paper, 28 x 37
(Private collection)
Prov: William Stokes collection
• see colour plate, page 13

GP.8 *Glendalough*
1815, watercolour on paper laid on canvas, 66 x 96.5 (visible size)
Signed: 'G. Petrie Pinx. 1815' bottom left
(Private collection)
Exh: Royal Academy, Somerset House, London, 1816
Lit: Stokes, p.10; Strickland, ii, p.237

Stokes mentions this picture, and that of *Glenmalure* (cat. no. GP.9) as being the property of Lord Whitworth. The painting is also mentioned by Strickland, who adds that it was the only work that Petrie ever exhibited at the Royal Academy.

GP.9 *Glenmalure in the County Wicklow*
1815, watercolour on paper laid on canvas 66 x 96.5 (visible size)
Signed: 'G. Petrie Pinx. 1815' bottom left
(Private collection)
Exh: Royal Academy, Somerset House, London, 1816
Prov: similar to that of *Glendalough* (cat. no. GP.8) of which it is a pair.
• see colour plate, page 14

GP.10 *Crucifixion*
(Present whereabouts unknown)
Lit: Strickland, ii, p.237

According to Strickland, this altarpiece was

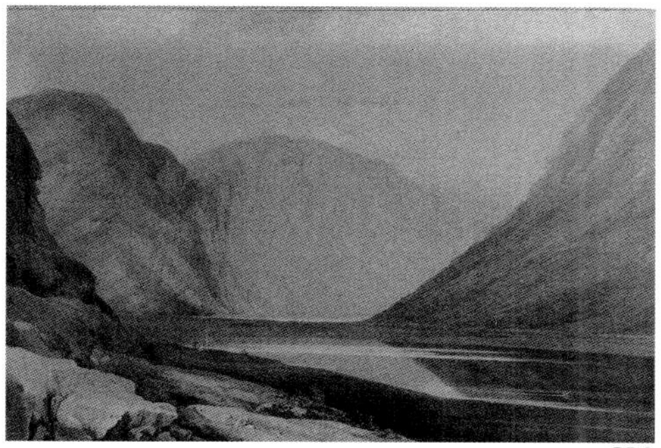

GP.8

painted for the Roman Catholic chapel at Kinnegad in 1815.

GP.11 *Portrait of Lord Manners, Lord Chancellor (5th Duke of Rutland)*
*c.*1815
(Present whereabouts unknown)
Lit: Strickland, ii, p.236.

Strickland notes this painting, one of the few portraits known to have been painted by Petrie, stating it was engraved by Maguire.

GP.12 *Dalkey Castle*
1816, sepia on paper, 17.1 x 23.2
Signed: 'Geo: Petrie, 1816' bottom left
(Private collection)
Prov: Iolo A. Williams, Sabin Galleries 6.3940, Patrick Semple, Stradbally, thence to Robert Goff
Engraving published in Cromwell's *Excursions* in 1819

GP.13 *Luggelaw*
1816, pen and ink and sepia on paper, 18 x 25
Signed: 'Geo: Petrie, 1816' bottom right
(Private collection)

GP.14 *Dolbaddern Castle*
*c.*1818
(Present whereabouts unknown)
Lit: Stokes, p.11

Stokes refers to this painting and states that it was sold as a Wilson. W.F. Wakeman, in an article in the *Dublin Saturday Magazine* in March 1866,

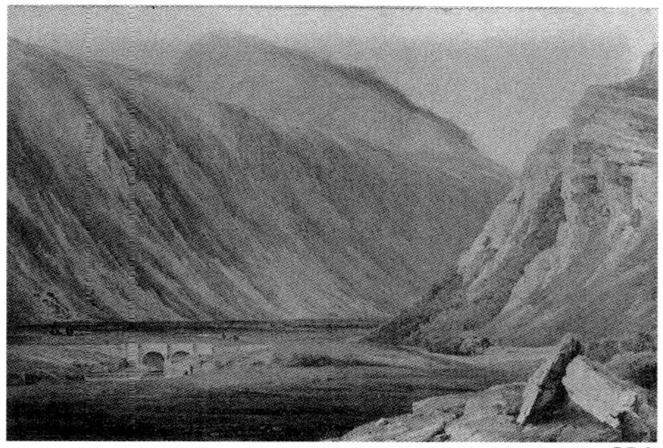

GP.9

implies that this painting was at that time in the possession of Dr Stokes. Petrie visited Dolbadern in Snowdonia on several occasions. A number of sketches of this castle, dated 1842, are in the Robert Callwell sketchbook in the Crawford Gallery collection.

GP.15 *Puck's Castle in the County of Dublin*
*c.*1818, watercolour on paper
(Private collection)
Lit: Stokes, pp.12-13
Engraving published in Cromwell's *Excursions*

The engraving is dated 1 September 1819. William Stokes described the engraving: 'This picture is truly a painted poem. The naked and solitary castle stands in the shade of a passing cloud. Yet all is not gloom, for, looking westward, we see the valley, the mountain, and the sky lit up by the rays of the hidden sun.'

GP.16 *Black Castle, Wicklow*
1819, pencil and wash on white Whatman paper (1819 watermark), 20.3 x 29.7
Signed: 'G. Petrie 1819' bottom left
Coll: Ulster Museum, cat. no. 840
Prov: purchased R.E. Abbott, Barnes, 1957
Engraving published in Cromwell's *Excursions* in 1820

GP.18 *St. Lawrence's Gate, Drogheda*
1819, watercolour on paper, 17.8 x 23.4
Signed: 'Geo. Petrie 1819' bottom left
Coll: NGI, cat. no. 2374
Engraving published in Cromwell's

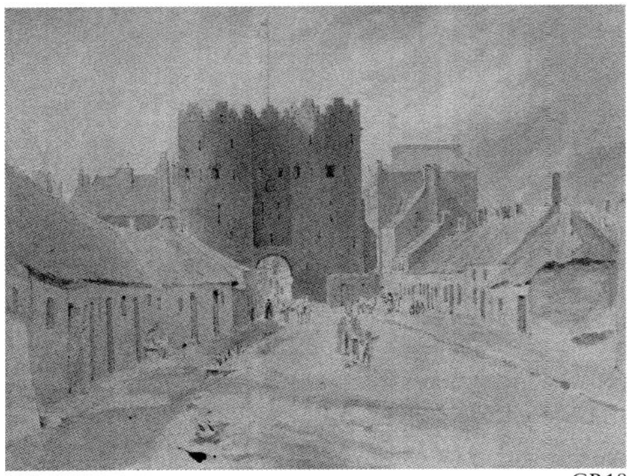

GP.18

Excursions in November 1819
• see colour plate, page 15

Drogheda was originally a walled town with several heavily defended gates, including the West Gate, Sunday's Gate and the East Gate. The only one of these remaining today is the East Gate, also known as St Lawrence's Gate. This defensive fortification, more properly termed a 'barbican', stood several metres in front of the town walls, protecting the actual gate. The upper sections of this barbican are later additions, added by merchants in the 17th century and designed to make the town of Drogheda seem more imposing when seen from ships coming up the River Boyne.

GP.21 *View of Kells, High Street, Co. Meath*
1819, watercolour on paper, 20 x 29 3
Signed: 'Geo. Petrie Delt 1819' bottom right
Coll: NGI, cat. no. 2369
Engraving published in Cromwell's *Excursions* in February 1820

Five surviving high crosses attest to the importance of Kells as a monastic centre in the 10th and 11th centuries. Four of the crosses are situated in the churchyard of St Columba's Church, while the fifth formerly stood at a road junction. The crosses in the churchyard, carved with scenes from the Old Testament, are in varying states of preservation; one is unfinished.

GP.22 *Howth Castle, Co. Dublin, in 1819*
1819, watercolour on paper, 17 x 25
Signed: 'Geo'
Coll: NGI, cat. no. 2371

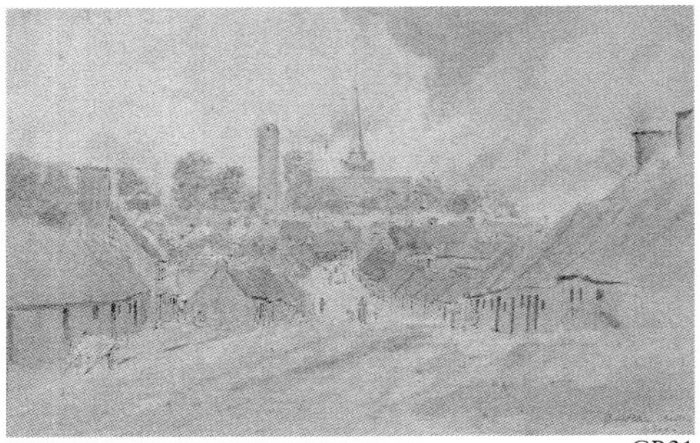

GP.21

Engraving published in Cromwell's *Excursions* in February 1820

GP.23 *Clondalkin Round Tower*
1819, pencil and sepia on paper, 16.1 x 21.5
Signed: 'Geo. Petrie 1819' bottom left
Coll: NGI, cat. no. 2372
Engraving published in Cromwell's *Excursions* in September 1819

GP.24 *Kildare Cathedral, Co Kildare*
1819, watercolour on paper, 18.8 x 27
Signed: 'Geo. Petrie 1819' bottom left
Coll: NGI, cat. no. 2373
Engraving published in Cromwell's *Excursions* in April 1820

GP.19 *Slane Castle, Co. Meath*
*c.*1819, watercolour on paper, 18 x 26.7
Signed: 'Geo. Petrie Delt.' bottom right
Coll: NGI, cat. no. 2367
Engraving published in Cromwell's *Excursions* in September 1820
• see colour plate, page 16

Situated in the Boyne Valley, six miles upstream from the site of the Battle of the Boyne, Slane Castle dates mainly from 1785 when it was rebuilt under the direction of William Burton Conyngham and his nephew, the 1st Marquess Conyngham. Among the architects who worked on the castle were James Gandon, James Wyatt and Francis Johnston. Johnston was also responsible for the gothic gates on the Mill Hill, while the courtyard was designed by Capability Brown. The neoclassical and neo-gothic interiors

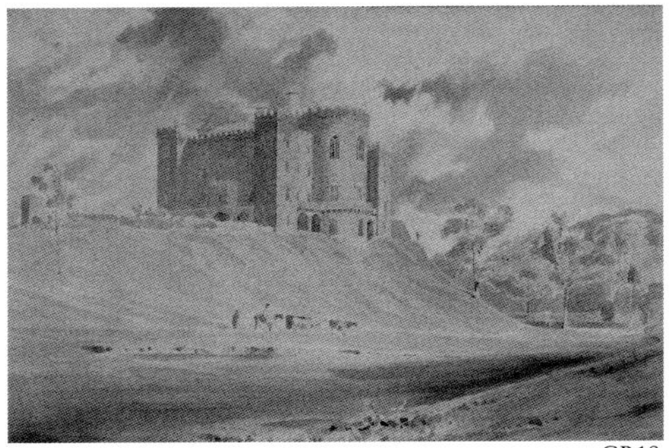

GP.19

are decorated with plasterwork by Robert West and Michael Stapleton. Under the direction of its owner, the Earl of Mount Charles, the house and grounds at Slane have been used as film and rock concert locations. In 1984 it was the location for the recording of *The Unforgettable Fire* by U2. Two years later, over 95,000 people attended a concert by Queen. The Castle was badly damaged by fire in 1991, but has since been restored and was reopened in 2001. In this painting Petrie shows the back of the house, overlooking the River Boyne. The engraving in Brewer's *Beauties of Ireland* (1825-26) is based on a different view, showing the front of the house.

GP.20 *Old Kilcullen Bridge, Co. Kildare*
*c.*1819, watercolour on paper, 14.8 x 22.5
Inscribed (on verso): 'Kilcullen Bridge Co. of Kildare'; also on verso is a sketch of a ruined church
Coll: NGI, cat. no. 2368
Engraving published in Cromwell's *Excursions* in May 1820

GP.20

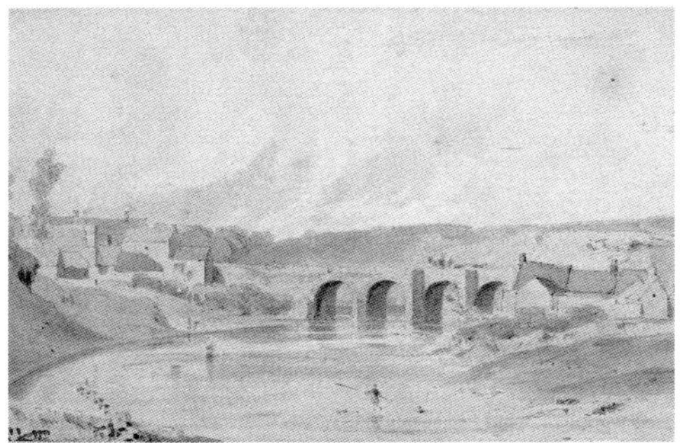

Crossing the Liffey about seven miles south of Naas, Kilcullen Bridge, built in the 14th century, was the site of a battle in 1798, when a company of yeomen under General Dundas and Capt. Robert la Touche exacted revenge for their humiliating defeat at nearby Old Kilcullen. William Makepeace Thackeray described the town in *The Irish Sketchbook* (1845):

> 'The little town, as they call it, of Kilcullen, tumbles down a hill and struggles up another; the two being here picturesquely divided by the Liffey over which goes an antique bridge. It boasts, moreover, of a portion of an abbey wall and a piece of round tower, both on the hill summit, and to be seen (says the Guide-book) for many miles round. Here we saw the first public evidences of the distress of the country. There was no trade in the little place, and but few people to be seen, except a crowd round a meal-shop; Here meal is distributed once a week by the neighbouring gentry. There must have been some hundreds of persons waiting about the doors, women for the most part: some of their children were to be found loitering about the bridge much farther up the street: but it was curious to note, amongst these undeniably starving people, how healthy their looks were.'

GP.25 *Lough Bray*
*c.*1819, atercolour or ink on paper
(Present whereabouts unknown)
Lit: Stokes, p.13, refers to two drawings of Lough Bray
Two engravings of Lough Bray published in Cromwell's *Excursions* in 1819-20

GP.30 *Rathmichael Church*
*c.*1819, watercolour on paper, 23.7 x 34.2
Coll: NGI, cat. no. 2370

GP.26 *The Shattered Ruins of the Castle at Clonmacnoise*
*c.*1819-20, watercolour or ink on paper
(Present whereabouts unknown)
Lit. Stokes, p.13, refers to a painting of the ruined castle at Clonmacnoise being executed around 1820
Engraving published in Cromwell's *Excursions* in November 1820

A preparatory drawing is in the NGI, and there are also sketches of the ruined castle in the Caldwell sketchbook in the Crawford collection.

GP.27 *The Old Church of Deral-Ossary, Co. Wicklow*
*c.*1819-20, watercolour or ink on paper
(Present whereabouts unknown)
Lit: Stokes, p.13, refers to a painting of this title being executed around 1820
Engraving published in Cromwell's *Excursions* in May 1820

GP.28 *The Church of Kilbarrack*
*c.*1819-20, watercolour or ink on paper
(Present whereabouts unknown)
Lit: Stokes, p.13, refers to a painting of this title being executed around 1820
Engraving published in Cromwell's *Excursions* in April 1820

GP.29 *The Church of St. Fechin le Fore*
*c.*1819-20, watercolour or ink on paper
(Present whereabouts unknown)
Lit: Stokes, p.13, refers to a painting of this title being executed around 1820
Engraving published in Cromwell's *Excursions* in November 1820

GP.42 *Trinity College from Westmoreland St.*
1820, Indian ink on paper, 14 x 23.5
Signed: 'G. Petrie 1820' bottom left
Exh: RHA 1866; RIA 1966
Coll: RIA
Prov: presented by the Marquis of Kildare, 1866
Engraving published in Wright's *Guide to Dublin* in 1821

GP.31 *View of the Custom House*
*c.*1820-21, Indian ink on paper, 20 x 27
Exh: RHA 1866; RIA 1966
Coll: RIA
Prov: presented by the Marquis of Kildare, May 1866
Engraving published in Wright's *Guide to Dublin* in 1821

GP.32 *The King's Inns*
*c.*1820-21, Indian ink on paper, 15 x 22.5
Signed: 'G. Petrie' on front barge
Exh: RHA 1866; RIA 1966
Coll: RIA
Prov: presented by the Marquis of Kildare, 1866
Engraving published in Wright's *Guide to Dublin* in 1821

GP.33 *View of Dublin from the North*
*c.*1820-21, Indian ink on paper, 18.5 x 27.5
Exh: RHA 1866; RIA 1966
Coll: RIA
Prov: presented by the Marquis of Kildare, 1866
Engraving published in Wright's *Guide to Dublin* in 1821

GP.34 *View of the Rotunda*
*c.*1820-21, Indian ink on paper, 14 x 25.5
Exh: RHA 1866; RIA 1966
Coll: RIA
Prov: presented by the Marquis of Kildare, 1866

GP.35 *The New Theatre Royal*
*c.*1820-21, Indian ink on paper, 8.5 x 15.5
Signed: 'Geo Petrie' bottom right
Exh: RHA 1866; RIA 1966
Coll: RIA
Prov: presented by the Marquis of Kildare, 1866
Engraving published in Wright's *Guide to Dublin* in 1821

GP.36 *View of the Metropolitan Catholic Church* [Pro-Cathedral]
*c.*1820-21, Indian ink on paper, 10 x 17
Exh: RIA 1966
Coll: RIA
Prov: presented by the Marquis of Kildare, 1866
Engraving published in Wright's *Guide to Dublin* in 1821

GP. 37 *View of the Royal Exchange*
*c.*1820-21, Indian ink on paper, 14 x 21
Signed: 'Geo Petrie Delt 1820' bottom right
Exh: RHA 1866; RIA 1966

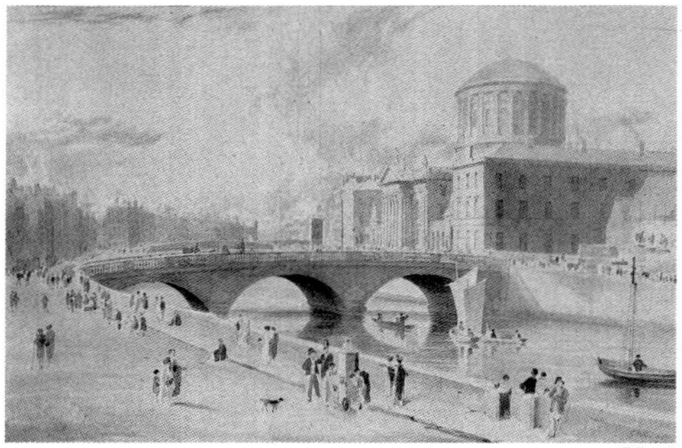

GP.40

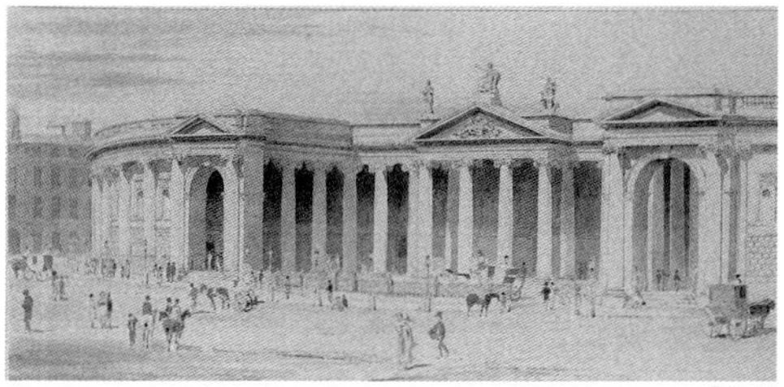

GP.44

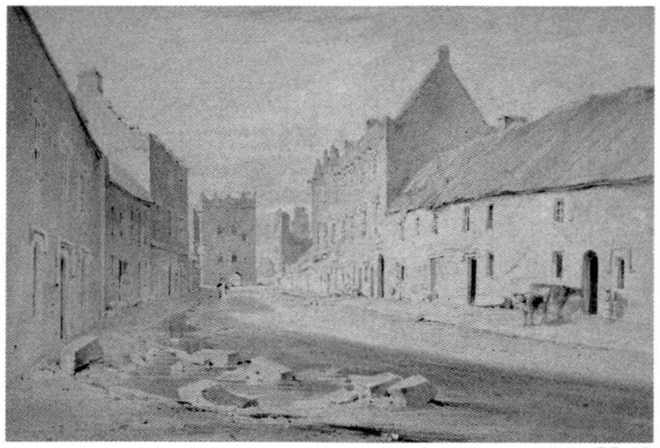

GP.45

Coll: RIA
Prov: presented by the Marquis of Kildare, 1866
Engraving published in Wright's *Guide to Dublin* in 1821

GP.38 *Christ Church Cathedral*
*c.*1820-21, Indian ink on paper, 14.5 x 24
Exh: RHA 1866; RIA 1966
Coll: RIA
Prov: presented by the Marquis of Kildare, 1866
Engraving published in Wright's *Guide to Dublin* in 1821

GP.39 *St. Patrick's Cathedral*
*c.*1820-21, Indian ink and ochre wash on paper, 18.5 x 25
Exh: RHA 1866; RIA 1966
Coll: RIA
Prov: presented by the Marquis of Kildare, 1866
Engraving published in Wright's *Guide to Dublin* in 1821

GP.40 *The Law Courts* [Four Courts]
*c.*1820-21, Indian ink on paper, 16 x 24
Exh: RHA 1866; RIA 1966
Coll: RIA
Prov: presented by the Marquis of Kildare, 1866
Engraving published in Wright's *Guide to Dublin* in 1821

GP.41 *The Castle Chapel and Record Tower*
*c.*1820-21, Indian ink on paper, 16 x 26
Exh: RHA 1866; RIA 1966
Coll: RIA
Prov: presented by the Marquis of Kildare, 1866
Engraving published in Wright's *Guide to Dublin* in 1821

GP.43 *Sackville Street* [now O'Connell Street]
*c.*1820-21, Indian ink on paper, 14 x 22.5
Exh: RHA 1866; RIA 1966
Coll: RIA
Prov: presented by the Marquis of Kildare, 1866
Engraving published in Wright's *Guide to Dublin* in 1821

GP.44 *The Bank of Ireland*
[former Parliament House]
*c.*1820-21, Indian ink on paper, 12 x 24
Exh: RHA 1866; RIA 1966
Coll: RIA
Prov: presented by the Marquis of Kildare, 1866
Engraving published in Wright's *Guide to Dublin* in 1821

GP.45 *Kilmallock High Street, Co. Limerick*
1821, sepia on paper, 26.7 x 39.7
Signed: 'George Petrie Delt 1821' bottom left
Coll: NGI, cat. no. 2375
Engraving published in Brewer's *Beauties of Ireland* in 1824
• see colour plate, page 17

A market town in Co Limerick founded by the Geraldines, Kilmallock received its charter in the reign of Edward III, at which time it was a walled and fortified town entered by four gates. During the reign of Queen Elizabeth it was a military strongpoint, but the fortifications were demolished by Cromwell's army. In addition to the two remaining city gates, the church of SS Peter and Paul has a tower in the north-west corner which is a converted round tower. Petrie's view shows one of the two surviving town gates and several of the fine houses for which the town was noted in its prosperous years.

GP.46 *Drumgoff Barracks*
1822, watercolour on paper, 20.4 x 28.5
Signed: 'Geo: Petrie Delt. 1822'
(Private collection)
Prov: Whitley Stokes collection (label on back of frame); purchased at auction 1970
Engraving published in Wright's *Guide to Wicklow* in 1823.

The engraving is of note in that the bridge depicted in the left middle distance does not feature in the original painting.

GP.47 *Glendalough*
1822, watercolour on paper, 20.4 x 28.5
Signed: 'Geo: Petrie Delt. 1822' bottom right
(Private collection)
Prov: Whitley Stokes collection (label on back); purchased at auction 1970
Engraving published in Wright's *Guide to Wicklow* in 1823
(c.f. NGI sketch, cat. no. 6718)

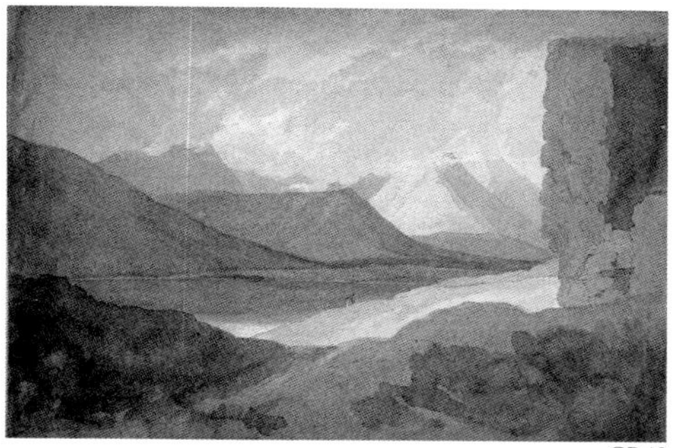

GP.49

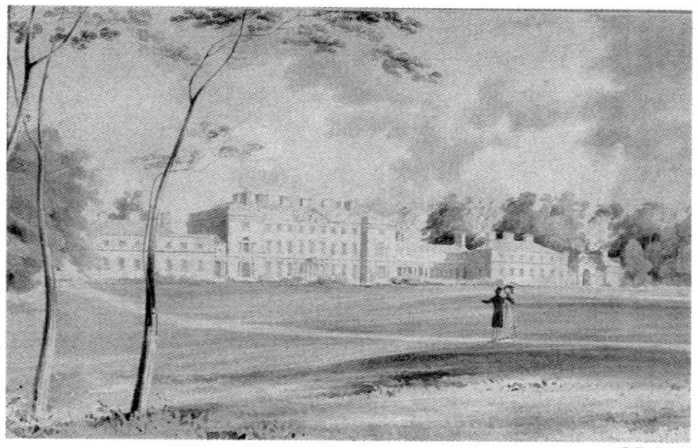

GP.229

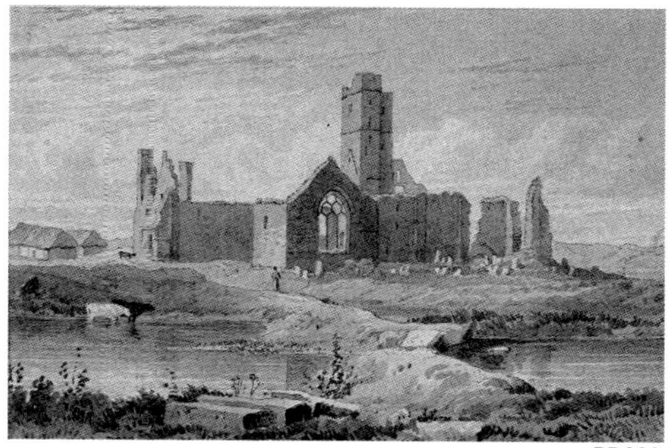

GP.230

GP.48 *Luggelaw 1822*
1822, Indian ink wash on paper,
21.5 x 32.5 (visible size)
Signed: 'Geo. Petrie Delt. 1822' bottom right
(Private collection)

GP.49 *Lough Leane and MacGillycuddy Reeks*
*c.*1822, sepia on paper (watermark 'Whatman 1814')
Coll: NGI, cat. no. 6728
Engraving published in Wright's *Guide to Killarney* in 1823

The base of a round tower and a ruined church survive at the old churchyard at Aghadoe, not far from Killarney town.

GP.229 *View of Carton*
1824-25, Sepia ink on paper, 21 x 30
(Private collection)
• see colour plate, page 18

GP.50 *Ardfinane Castle*
*c.*1825
(Present whereabouts unknown)
Lit: Stokes, p.14

Stokes refers to this as being one of Petrie's largest and finest works, and states that it was exhibited at the RHA in 1826. A preparatory drawing is in the NGI (cat. no. 6762).

GP.230 *Franciscan Abbey at Multifernan, Co. Westmeath*
*c.*1825, sepia ink on paper, 11 x 16
Coll: Crawford Municipal Art Gallery
Prov: Neptune Gallery, Dublin
A preparatory ink drawing for the engraving published in Brewer's *Beauties of Ireland* (1825-26), engraved by Storer

GP.231 *View of an Augustinian Abbey*
[possibly Athassel Priory, Co Tipperary]
*c.*1825, sepia ink on paper, 11 x 16
Coll: Crawford Municipal Art Gallery
Prov: Neptune Gallery, Dublin
Probably a painting done for Brewer's *Beauties of Ireland* (1825-26), but never engraved

GP.51 *The Round Tower of Kilbannon, Co. Galway*
*c.*1827
(Present whereabouts unknown)
Exh: RHA 1827

GP.98 *Dun Aengus Fort, Inismore, Aran Islands*

GP.231

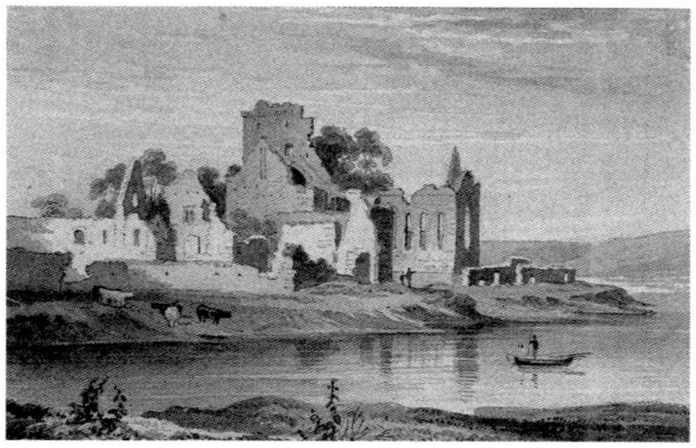

*c.*1827, watercolour on paper, 29.8 x 46.4
Exh: RHA 1827
Coll: NGI, cat. no. 7481
(c.f. pencil sketch in NGI, cat. no. 6695)
Prov: unknown (probably Margaret Stokes)
Lit. Stokes, p.14
• see colour plate, page 19

Situated on a clifftop one hundred metres above the Atlantic Ocean, Dun Aengus promontory fort is one of the most important archaeological sites on the Aran Islands. Dating from the Bronze Age, but substantially built in the Iron Age (perhaps by Iberian settlers), the fort consists of a series of three concentric stone walls with a *chevaux de frise* outer defence of clusters of upright stones set into the ground. It is possible that the fort was originally fully circular in plan, but erosion of the cliffs at some point swept part of the structure into the sea. It is probable that the site was of ceremonial significance, perhaps more so than defensive. Petrie first visited the Aran Islands in 1821 and this watercolour was probably done not

GP.98

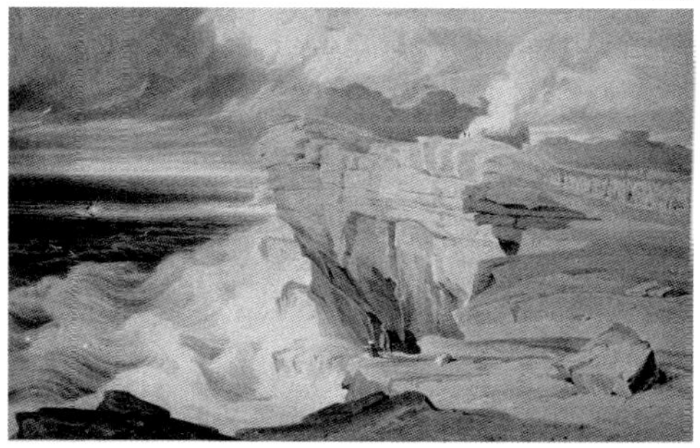

long afterwards, as he exhibited a painting of this title in the RHA in 1827. The watercolour shows the fort prior to its restoration, with the walls in a fragmentary state.

GP.53 *Caernarvon Castle, Wales*
1828, sepia wash on paper, 20.5 x 29.6
Inscribed: 'Caernarvon, Aug. 4th 1828'
Coll: NGI, cat. no. 6753

GP.54 *Llanberis Lake and Llyn Paddern*
1828, sepia wash on paper
Inscribed: 'Llanberis Aug. 1828'
Coll: NGI, cat. no. 6737
(Dolbadarn Castle is visible in the distance, near the shore on the far side of the lake.)

GP.55 *Conway Castle and Suspension Bridge (built 1824-26), Wales*
*c.*1828, sepia wash on paper, 23.3 x 33.5
Coll: NGI, cat. no. 6839
Prov: unknown

Better known as Conwy (or Conway) Castle, Caernarvon Castle forms part of a entire medieval fortified town or 'bastide'. The suspension bridge, built between 1822 and 1826, was designed by Thomas Telford.

GP.56 *The Menai Strait Suspension Bridge*
*c.*1828, sepia on paper, 23.3 x 33.4
Coll: NGI, cat. no. 6838
Prov: unknown

A suspension bridge, 176 metres in length, spanning the Menai Strait from Bangor to the island of Anglesey, the Menai Bridge was completed in1826 to the designs of Thomas Telford. William Makepeace Thackeray describes crossing the bridge on a journey to Ireland in his *Irish Sketchbook* (1845): 'The coach that brings the passenger by wood and mountain, by brawling waterfall and gloomy plain, by the lonely lake of Festiniog and across the swinging world's wonder of a Menai Bridge, through dismal Anglesea to dismal Holyhead – the Birmingham mail manages matters so cleverly, that after 10 hours' ride the traveller is thrust incontinently on board the packet and the steward says there's no use in providing dinner on board, because the passage is so short.'

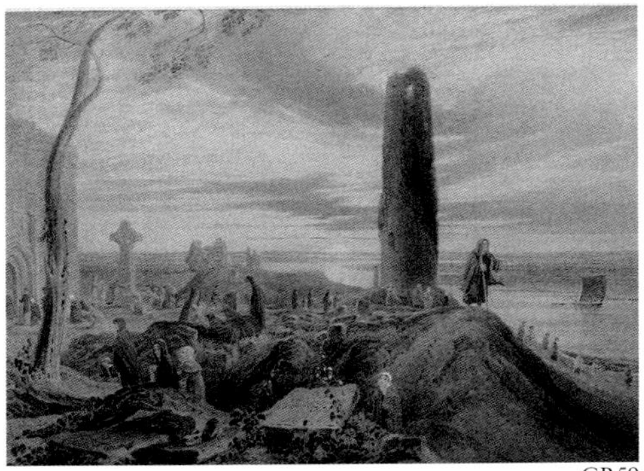

GP.59

GP.57 *Welsh Scenery, Dolbadarn Castle and Llyn Peris*
*c.*1828, sepia on paper, 23.2 x 33.5
Coll: NGI, cat. no. 6845

GP.58 *The Twelve Pins in Connemara*
*c.*1828
(Present whereabouts unknown)
Exh: RHA 1828

GP.59 *The Last Circuit of the Pilgrims at Clonmacnoise*
*c.*1828, watercolour on paper
Coll: Richard Wood collection, Plassey House, University of Limerick
Exh: RHA 1828
Lit: Stokes, p.14
• see colour plate, page 20

Stokes states that this watercolour was painted for the album of Mrs Haldiman in England, to which Turner and Danby also contributed. He states also that Petrie afterwards painted a larger version which was sold to the Art Union for one hundred guineas. This later version, painted around 1843, is in the NGI (cat. no. 2230). A detailed account of both paintings is given in Prof Tom Dunne's essay in this book.

GP.61 *The Knight and the Lady*
*c.*1828, watercolour on paper
(Pivate collection)
Exh: RHA 1829
Lit: Stokes, p.16
• see colour plate, page 21

Stokes describes the 'singular depth of colouring' of this work and gives its location: 'The scene is

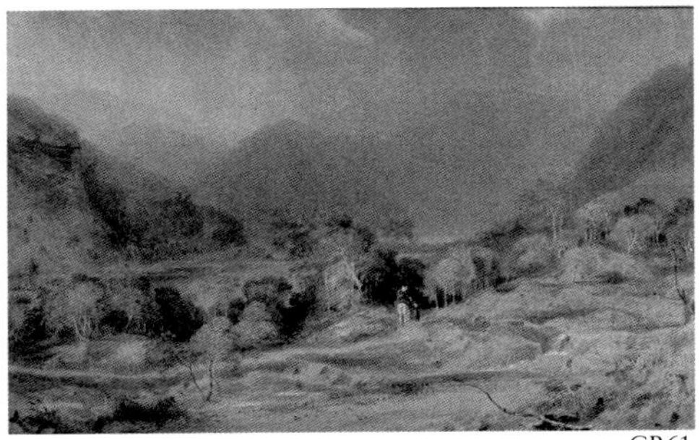

GP.61

laid in the Comeen Dubh, or the Black Valley, in the county of Kerry.'

GP.62 *Ruins of Lord Portlester's Chapel, St. Audeon's Church*
*c.*1828, pencil and wash on paper, 14.3 x 23.1
Coll: NGI, cat. no. 6002
Prov: transferred from the National Museum in 1966
Engraving published in Wright's *Ireland Illustrated* in 1831

GP.60 *Culdean Abbey or Mona Incha Abbey, Co. Tipperary*
1829, watercolour on paper, 23.8 x 36.3
Coll: NGI, cat. no. 2377
Exh: RHA 1829
Lit. Stokes, p.16: 'The second picture is of the Culdean Abbey, in the island of Inisnambeo, or the Island of the Living, in the county of Tipperary.'
• see colour plate, page 22

In their *Early Christian Inscriptions in Munster*, Okasha and Forsythe give the following account of this monastic site:

> Monaincha was once an island in a bog but is now a mound in marshy pasture land. Traditionally it was founded by St Cainnech of Aghaboe in the seventh century and served as a hermit retreat ... It is also associated in the hagiographic sources with St Crónan of Roscrea ... The earliest annalistic reference to the site is the death of Elarius 'anchorite and scribe of Loch Cré' s.a. 806 ... The earliest

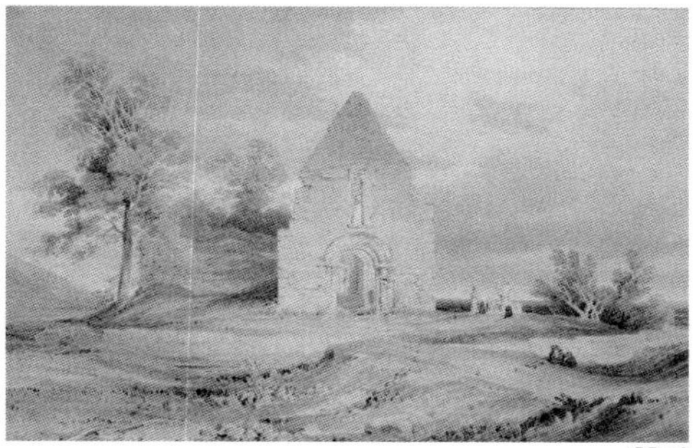

GP.60

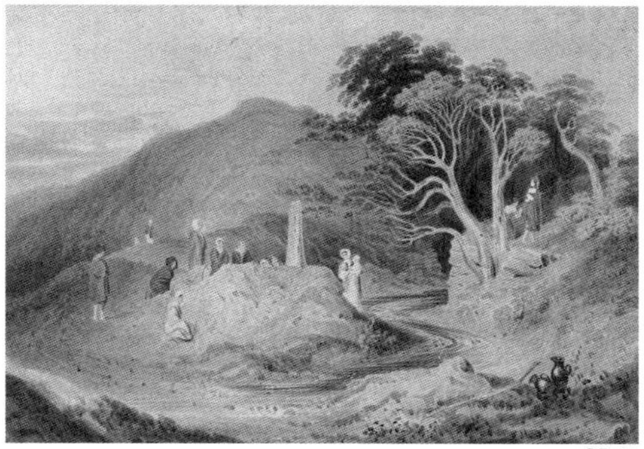

GP.64

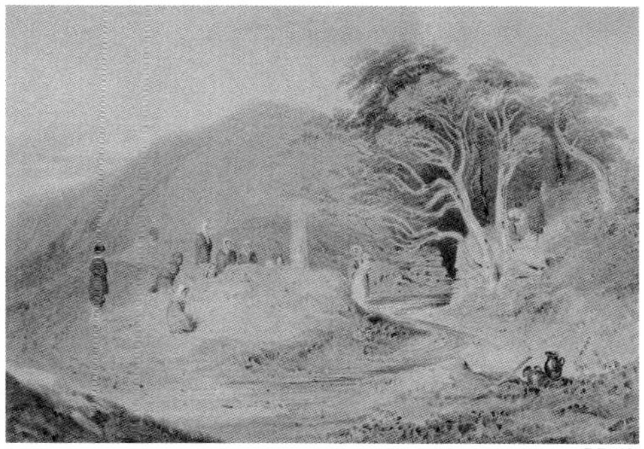

GP.63

building on Monaincha is the ruined but highly ornate Romanesque church; built in the twelfth century, the church had alterations and additions made to it in the thirteenth and fifteenth centuries. Petrie recorded the existence of 'a portion of the shaft of a cross covered with Celtic ornamental design'. This may refer to the 12th-century cross now re-erected to the west of the church ... Crawford also recorded an uninscribed cross-slab then lying north-east of the chancel.

[E.Okasha and K. Forsyth, *Early Christian Inscriptions of Munster: A Corpus of the Inscribed Stones* (Cork University Press, 2001) pp.212-13]

In Margaret Stokes' edition of Petrie's *Christian Inscriptions*, Mona Incha is described:

> MONA-INCHA is situated in the townland of Tighmoney, parish of Corbally, and barony of Ikeran, in the county of Tipperary. The name signifies 'the Bog of the Island', from [Móin Mone], 'a bog' and Incha, 'Island'. A small but deep lake in this bog is all that now remains of Loch Cre, from which the island was formerly called 'Inis locha Cre' ... The remains at Mona-incha now consist of the ruins of a very beautiful church, with richly sculptured western doorway and chancel arch, probably built in the twelfth century, and a portion of the shaft of a cross covered with Celtic ornamental design. Three inscribed stones have been discovered in the church.

[George Petrie, *Christian Inscriptions in the Irish Language*, vol. 2 (1878), M. Stokes (ed.) (Royal Historical and Archaeological Association, Dublin), ii, p.35]

In his description of this painting, William Stokes quotes Geraldus Cambrensis:

> In North Munster is a lake containing two isles; in the greater is a church of the ancient religion, and in the lesser a chapel, whereon a few monks, called Culdees, devoutly serve God. In the greater, no woman, nor any animal of the feminine gender enters, that does not immediately die. This has been proved by many experiments. In the lesser no one can die. This is called Insula Viventium, or the Island of the Living.

Stokes goes on to cite Dr Reeves' dating of the church to the 8th century. [Stokes, p.16]

GP.64 *St. Brigid's Well*

c.1829, watercolour on paper
(Private collection)
Prov: Sir William Wilde had two paintings by Petrie in 1878, both of holy wells. This is most likely one of these works.
Lit: Stokes, p.17
• see colour plate, page 23

Petrie's successor as editor the *Dublin Penny Journal*, Philip Dixon Hardy, was both fascinated and horrified at the excesses of self-mortification that formed an important part of the pilgrimages and patterns associated with holy wells. In 1840 he published a book, *The Holy Wells of Ireland*, in which he dwelt at length on the pre-Christian origins of these customs.

> I have often inquired of your tenants, what they themselves thought of their pilgrimages to the wells of Kil-Archt, Tobbar-Brighde, Tobbar Muire, near Elphin, and Moore, near Castlereagh, where multitudes assembled annually to celebrate what they, in broken English, termed Patterns ('Patron's days); and when I pressed a very old man, Owen Hester, to state what possible advantage he expected to derive from the singular custom of frequenting in particular such wells as were contiguous to an old blasted oak, or an upright unhewn stone, and what the meaning was of the yet more singular custom of sticking rags on the branches of such trees, and spitting on them – his answer, and the answer of the oldest men, was, that their ancestors always did it; that it was a preservative against Geasa-Draoidacht, i.e. the sorceries of Druids; that their cattle were preserved by it from infections and disorders; that the daoini maethe, i.e. the fairies, were kept in good humour by it!

[Philip Dixon Hardy, *The Holy Wells of Ireland, Containing an Authentic Account of Those Various Places of Pilgrimage and Penance Which are still Annually Visited by Thousands of the Roman Catholic Peasantry* (Hardy & Walker, Dublin, 1840)]

GP.63 *Pilgrims at St. Bridgid's Well, Liscannor, Co. Clare*

c.1829-30, watercolour on paper, 18.5 x 26
Exh: RHA 1831
Coll: NGI, cat. no. 2381
Lit: Stokes, p.16

Stokes writes that this painting was intended 'to illustrate the custom of Well-worship so long followed in Ireland', and describes the painting which he had in front of him:

> A rapid rivulet runs round the steep banks of a little promontory, clothed on one side with wild wood. Behind this is the holy well, surrounded by kneeling figures. In the back-ground, their soft and golden hues changing into purple with the fall of the valley, rise the green hills of Clare. A pillar stone, bearing an inscribed cross, crowns the promontory, round which groups of pilgrims, in the old dress of red and purple, are in attitudes of prayer, or standing in meditation. This painting is a gem of colour – a history, not only of days gone by, but of the lasting hold which the early faith has taken on the hearts of the people in the present day. [Stokes, p.16]

Traditionally, pilgrims travelled from Clare and the Aran Islands to St Brigid's Well to take part in the Lughnasa festival on the last Saturday of July. This festival continued into the following day, 'Garland Sunday', in Lahinch. The waters of St Brigid's Well are believed by devotees to have miraculous healing powers. There are also holy wells named after St Brigid in Wexford, Kildare, Westmeath and other counties.

When depicted by Petrie in 1830, St Brigid's Well was in its original location. Twenty-three years later, in 1853, it was moved to a more convenient site under the direction of Cornelius O'Brien, a local landlord and member of parliament. Samuel Lewis mentioned O'Brien in his *Topographical Dictionary* in 1857:

> The residence of Cornelius O'Brien who has much improved his estate and the condition of his tenantry by the erection of neat slated cottages and farm buildings and by other judicious arrangements; a holy well dedicated to St Brigid and much resorted to by the peasantry, which, at Mr. O'Brien's expense, has been surrounded by tasteful plantations and rustic seats.
>
> [Samuel Lewis, *Topographical Dictionary*, 1857]

A memorial column to O'Brien near the well was erected that same year. O'Brien also built roads in the area, making the Cliffs of Moher accessible to tourists.

GP.65 *The Bullring, Drogheda c.1830*
c.1830
(Present whereabouts unknown)
Exh: RHA 1830
A preparatory sketch for this work is in the NGI (cat. no. 6844)
Engraved for the *Northern Tourist* in 1830

GP.66 *Lough Gill*
c.1830
(Present whereabouts unknown)
Exh: RHA 1830
Engraved for the *Northern Tourist* in 1830

GP.67 *Narrow Water Castle*
c.1830
(Present whereabouts unknown)
Exh: RHA 1830
A preparatory sketch for this work is in the NGI (cat. no. 6666)
Engraved for the *Northern Tourist* in 1830

GP.68 *Carrick-a-Rede, County Antrim*
c.1830
(Present whereabouts unknown)
Exh: RHA 1830
A preparatory sketch for this work is in the NGI (cat. no. 6661)
Engraved for the *Northern Tourist* in 1830

GP.69 *The Long Bridge and Cave Hill, Belfast*
c.1830
(Present whereabouts unknown)
Exh: RHA 1830
A preparatory sketch for this work is in the NGI (cat. no. 6841)
Engraved for the *Northern Tourist* in 1830

GP.70 *Dunluce Castle*
c.1830, watercolour on paper, 21 x 30
(Private collection)
A preparatory sketch for this work is in the NGI (cat. no. 6663)
Engraved for the *Northern Tourist* in 1830

Although the rocky promontory at Dunluce in north Antrim has been occupied successively by Neolithic settlers, early Christians and Vikings, the castle, the ruins of which provide a dramatic silhouette on the rocky coastline, was built in the

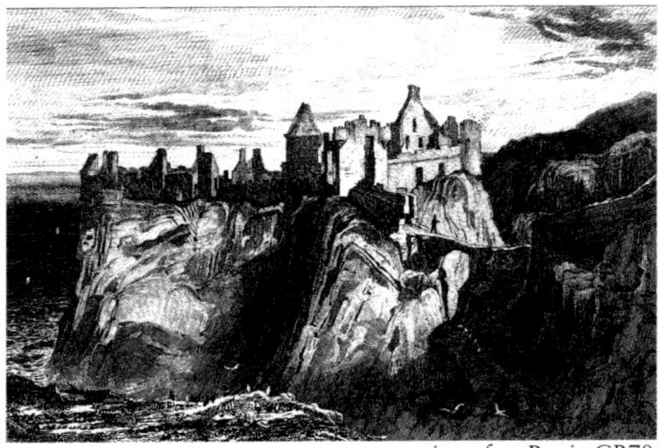

engraving after Petrie GP.70

13th century by the Anglo-Norman Richard de Burgh. Captured by Sorley Boy MacDonnell from the McQuillens in the late 16th century, the castle was renovated and expanded by Randall MacDonnell, becoming a magnificent residence for the Earl and Countess of Antrim. It was probably abandoned because of coastal erosion. At one point in the 17th century the kitchen and domestic quarters collapsed into the sea.

GP.71 *Belfast from Turf Lodge*
c.1830, watercolour on paper, 23.8 x 37.3
Coll: Ulster Museum, cat. no. 839
Prov: purchased J. Douglas, Bangor, 1949
Exh: *Landscapes of Belfast*, Ulster Museum, Belfast, 1977
Engraved for the *Northern Tourist* in 1830

GP.72 *The Hill of Doon, Lough Corrib*
c.1830-31, watercolour
(Present whereabouts unknown; possibly the painting in the NGI titled *Mountain Landscape* (cat. no. 2380))
Exh: RHA 1831

GP.73 *View on the Kylemore Road, Connemara*
c.1830-31, watercolour
(Present whereabouts unknown)
Exh: RHA 1831

GP.74 *The Glen of the Horse, Killarney*
c.1830-31, watercolour
(Present whereabouts unknown. In the NGI there are several sketches of the Glen of the Horse (cat. nos 6726, 6727, 6767))

Exh: RHA 1831
Lit: Stokes, p.17

GP.75 *Knockmoy Abbey and Bridge, Co. Galway*
*c.*1830-31, watercolour
(Present whereabouts unknown)
Exh: RHA 1831

GP.76 *Gougane Barra with the Hermitage of St. Finbarr*
*c.*1830-31, watercolour on paper, 30.9 x 39.7
Signed: 'To my friend R. Callwell by Geo. Petrie R.H.A.' bottom right
Exh: RHA 1831 (Petrie painted at least two versions of this painting)
Coll: NGI, cat. no. 6028
Prov: Miss Annie Callwell Bequest, 1904
Lit: Stokes, p.17; W. Wakeman, *Dublin Saturday Magazine*, March 1866, refers to this painting as being in the possession of R. Callwell of Dublin.

The Hermitage of St Finbarr is located on a small island in the lake of Gougane Barra in the hills of north-west Cork. William Stokes describes this work in his *Life* of Petrie:

> The subject is the hermitage of St. Finbar, situated on a lake between Cork and Bantry. The lake is surrounded by hills, whose apparent height is increased by a shrouding veil of mist while the sky is overcast with dark clouds. There is a partial break in this gloomy canopy overhead through which a single sunray falls perpendicularly on the still waters of the lonely lake, on the ruins, and the wild wood which hangs above them, as if to show that even in its desolation and ruin, and in storm and darkness, some light from heaven still falls on this old scene of Christian worship.

The pilgrimage site was also described by Crofton Croker:

> The scenery of Gougaun lake is bold and rugged, yet will scarcely afford the artist a suitable return for the labour of his journey. Surrounded by rocky and barren mountains, which rise with an air of desolate grandeur above the lake, in its

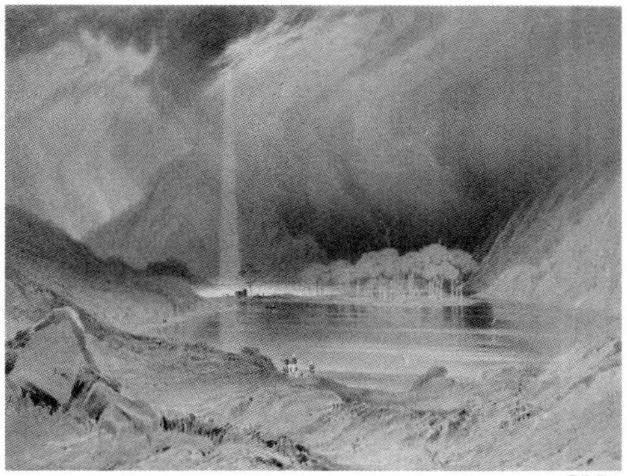

GP.76

> centre is a small and solitary island, connected with the shore by a narrow artificial causeway, constructed to facilitate the rites of religious devotees, who annually flock thither on the 24th of June (St. John's day,) to the celebration of a pious festival ... On a grassy elevation, that appears to have been formerly surrounded by stone steps, stands a wooden pole, the upright remains of a large cross, braced with many pieces of iron. Hundreds of votive rags and bandages are nailed against it, and hung upon it, by those whose faith has made them whole, intended as acknowledgements of their cure ... My first visit to Gougaun was on the 23rd of June, 1813 ... After a walk of about seven Irish miles from the village of Inchegeela, we gained the brow of a mountain, and beheld the lake of Gougaun with its little wooded island beneath us; one spot on its shore, swarming with people, appeared, from our elevated situation, to be a dark mass surrounded by moving specks, which continually merged into it. On our descent we caught the distant and indistinct murmur of the multitude; and as we approached and forded the eastern extremity of the lake, where its waters discharge themselves through a narrow and precipitous channel, an unseemly uproar burst upon us, though at a distance of nearly half a mile from the assembly. It was not without difficulty that we forced our way through the crowd on the shore of the lake, to the wall of the chapels on the island, where we stood amid an immense concourse of people: the interior of the cells were filled with men and women in various acts of devotion, almost all of them on their knees; some with hands uplifted, prayed in loud voices, using considerable gesticulation, and others, in a less noisy manner, rapidly counted the beads of their rosary, or, as it is called by the Irish peasant, their pathereen, with much apparent fervour; or as a substitute for beads, threw from one hand into the other, small pebbles to mark the number of prayers they had repeated; whilst such of them as were not furnished with other means kept their reckoning by cutting a notch on their cudgel, or on a piece of stick provided for the purpose. [Thomas Crofton Croker, *Researches in the South of Ireland, Illustrative of the Scenery, Architectural Remains, and the Manners and Superstitions of the Peasantry, with an Appendix Containing a Private Narrative of the Rebellion of 1798* (London, 1824)]

GP.78 *Old Windmill at Rathgar Quarry, Dublin (now demolished)*
*c.*1830-31, watercolour on paper, 25.5 x 33.2
Exh: RHA 1831
Coll: NGI, cat. no. 2379
Lit: Stokes, p.17.

GP.79 *Lough Ina, Connemara*
*c.*1830-31, watercolour on paper
(Present whereabouts unknown)
Exh: RHA 1831

There are in the NGI several pencil sketches of Lough Ina, or Inagh, one of which is probably a preparatory drawing for this painting (NGI, cat. nos 6685, 6686, 6687).

GP.80 *The Twelve Pins, Connemara, from the north head of Ballinakill Bay*
1831, watercolour on paper, 29.4 x 41.1
Signed: 'Geo. Petrie Pinxit. 1831' bottom right

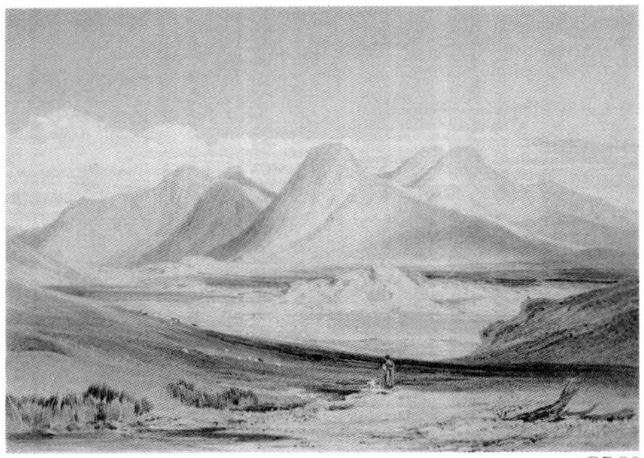

GP.80

Coll: NGI, cat. no. 6027; a preparatory sketch for this work is also in the NGI (cat. no. 6672)
Prov: Miss Annie Callwell Bequest, 1909
• see colour plate, page 24

The Twelve Bens or Twelve Pins is a mountain range that extends from Maam Cross to Kylemore in Connemara, Co Galway. In this view, taken from a vantage point about one kilometre north of Letterfrack, Petrie has smoothed the contours of the mountains and exaggerated their height.

GP.233 *Gougane Barra with the Hermitage of St. Finbarr*
1831, coloured aquatint, 23 x 27
Inscribed: '("Googan Barra") N. Fielding sculpt.'
Published by W.F. Wakeman, *Picturesque Sketches of Ireland* in 1835
(c.f. GP.76, GP.77)

GP.234 *The Twelve Pins, Connemara, Co. of Galway*
1831, coloured aquatint, 23 x 27
Inscribed: 'N. Fielding sculpt.'
Coll: University of Limerick – Norton collection
Published by W.F. Wakeman, *Picturesque Sketches of Ireland* (Dublin, 1835)
(c.f. GP.80, GP.126)

GP.77 *Gougane Barra*
*c.*1831, watercolour on paper, 28 x 38 (visible size)
(Private collection)
• see colour plate, page 25

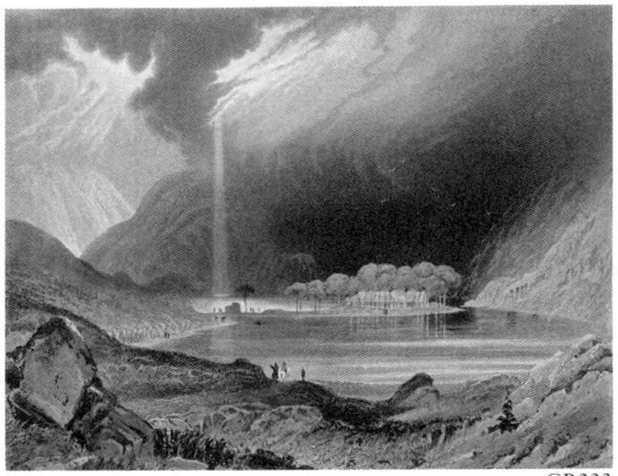

GP.233

GP.81 *Llanberis Lake*
*c.*1831, watercolour on paper
(Present whereabouts unknown)
Exh: RHA 1831
Lit: Stokes, p.17

GP.82 *The Eagle's Nest at Killarney*
*c.*1831, pencil and watercolour on paper, 26.2 x 36.4
Coll: Ulster Museum, cat. no. 1119 (titled *Scene in the West of Ireland*)
Exh: RHA 1831
Prov: purchased from Mrs Mary Clarke, Dublin 1910. William Wakeman refers to this painting as being in the collection of John Somers of Rathmines in 1866.
Lit: W. Wakeman, *Dublin Saturday Magazine,* March 1866
• see colour plate, page 26

Although not high by comparison with other mountains, the Eagle's Nest occupies a dramatic

GP.77

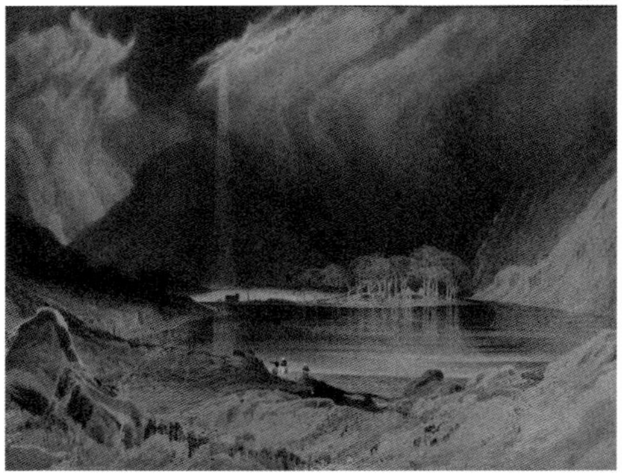

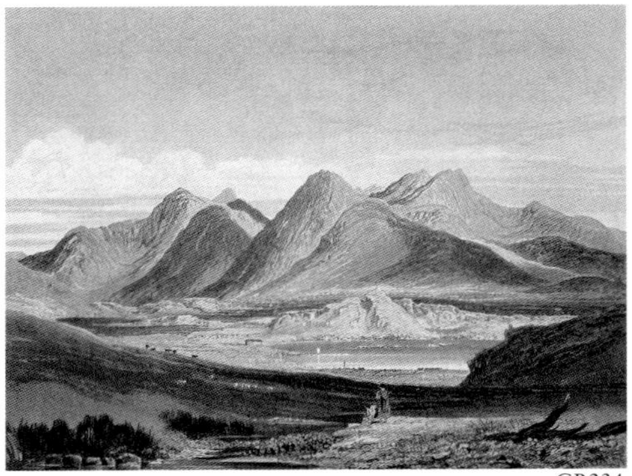

GP.234

site overlooking the channel that connects the Upper and Lower Lakes of Killarney. Long a favourite with artists, including Jonathan Fisher and George Petrie, the Eagle's Nest has been the subject of paintings and engravings since the 18th century. Remarkable echoes are a feature of this area, demonstrated in the 19th century by small cannons being fired, orchestras playing and bugles being blown by boatmen taking tourists across the lakes.

GP.99a *Connemara Mountain Landscape*
[Little Killary Bay]
*c.*1833, watercolour on paper, 15.5 x 22
Coll: NGI, cat. no. 2380

GP.99b *Connemara Mountain Landscape*
[Little Killary Bay]
*c.*1833, watercolour on paper, 15.5 x 22
(Private collection)
• see colour plate, page 27

GP.82

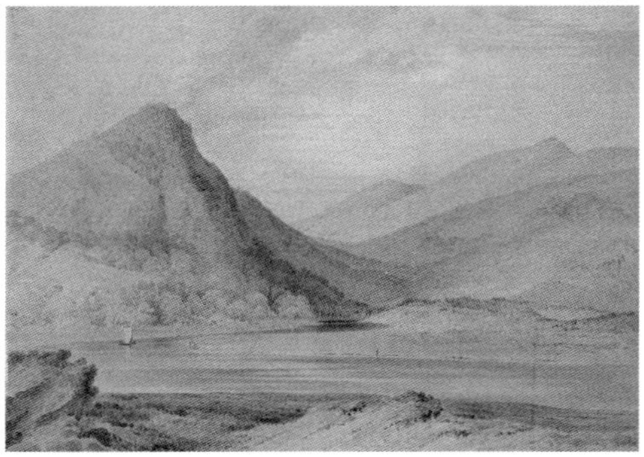

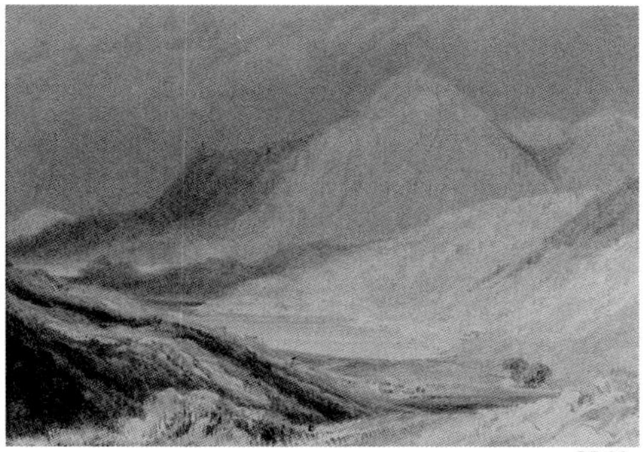
GP.99a

GP.83a *Hen's Castle on Lough Corrib, Co. Galway*
*c.*1833-34, watercolour on paper, 32.5 x 50
Exh: RHA 1834
Coll: NGI, cat. no. 6032 (c.f. sketch in NGI, cat. no. 6697)
Prov: painted for Miss French Lynch's album (RHA cat.); Miss Annie Callwell Bequest 1904
• see colour plate, page 28

Though the Normans failed to capture Connemara, one of their frontier castles, Hen's Castle, survives on Lough Corrib. In medieval times Connemara was ruled by the O'Cadhlas, who were later pushed out by the O'Flahertys, who built a series of castles along the coast, the most famous at Bunowen where Gráinne Uí Mháille (Grainuale) lived for a time when married to Donal O'Flaherty. These were seagoing clans, with castles on Inishbofin and Clare Island and at Renvyle and Ballyinahinch. In his guide to Lough Corrib, Sir William Wilde describes Hen's Castle:

GP.83a
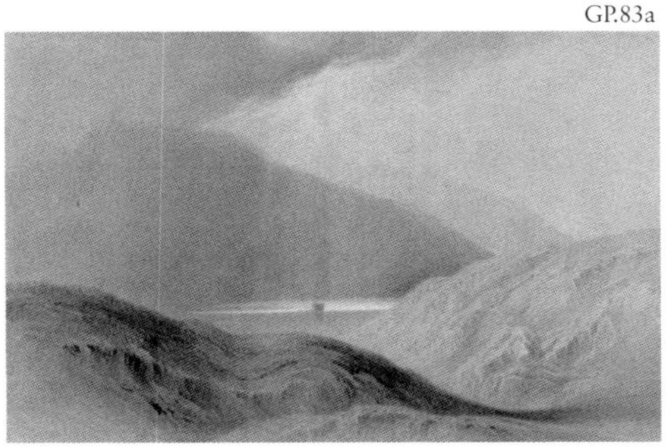

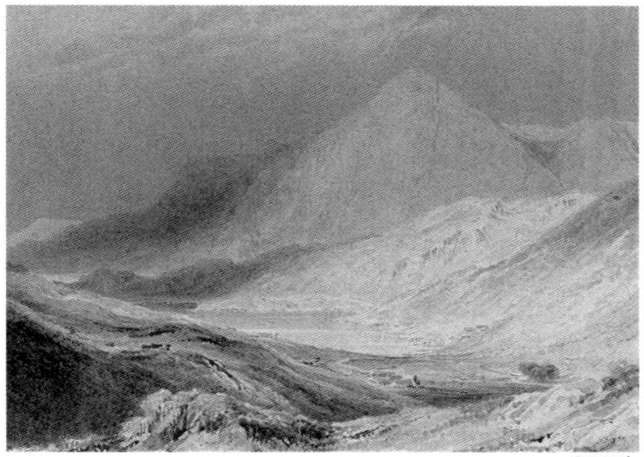
GP.99b

The lake naturally divides itself into four portions: the upper or Conamara and Joyce Country portion, from Mám to Dún, placid, and untenanted by islands, save the bare rock on which the ancient Hen's Castle of the O Conors and O Flahertys stands; the narrow portion along Dubhros and Ceann Eibhir; the broad 'old lake,' crowded with islands, that forms its middle portion the rocky narrow gut that commences below Inis Uí Chuinn, and, turning to the south, by the ferry of Cnoc and Coill Beag landing, opens opposite Port Darach, into the broad expanse of the free lower lake that forms its fourth part, and sends its volume of waters through the Corrib and Mionloch Rivers, and the 'Friars' Cut,' into the Gaillimh, and through it to the ocean.

GP.83b *Hen's Castle, Lough Corrib*
*c.*1833-34, watercolour on paper, 32.5 x 50

GP.83b
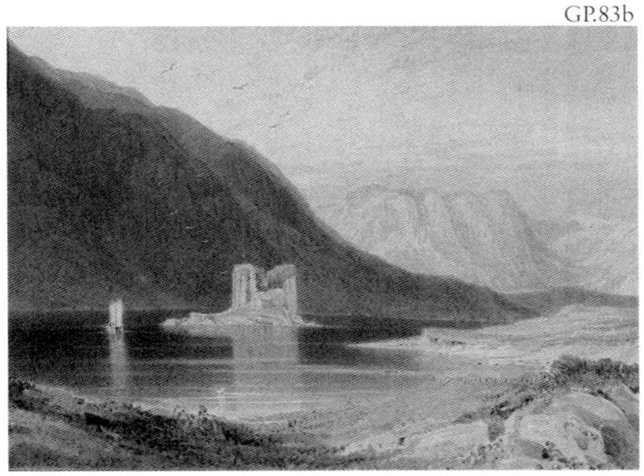

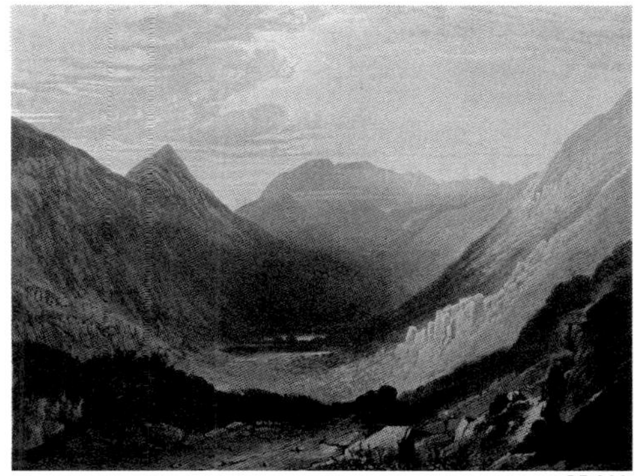
GP.232

(Private collection)
Exh: RHA 1834
• see colour plate, page 29

GP.232 *Comeen Duff or Black Valley, Killarney*
*c.*1835, coloured aquatint, 23 x 27
Signed / inscribed [?]: 'N. Fielding sculpt.'
Coll: University of Limerick – Norton collection
Published by W.F. Wakeman, *Picturesque Sketches of Ireland* in 1835
• see colour plate, page 30

GP.84 *Pagan Sepulchral Monument on the Caugh Hill, a Mountain in the parish of Bannagher, County of Londonderry – Twilight*
or
Stone Circle on Caan Hill, Derry
*c.*1839-40, watercolour on paper, 33.1 x 51.4

GP.84
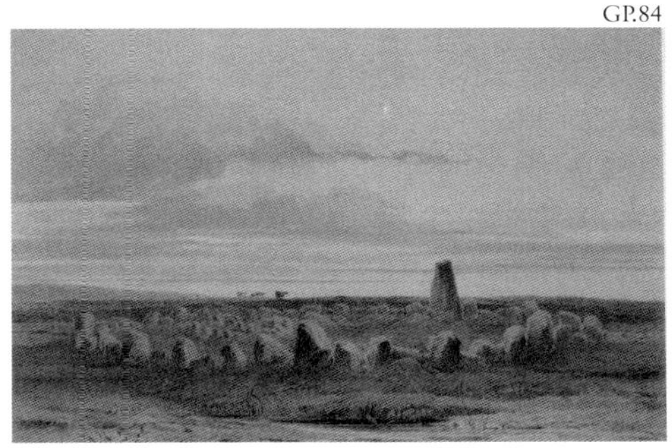

Exh: RHA 1840
Coll: NGI, cat. no. 6033
Prov: Miss Annie Callwell Bequest, 1904
Lit. Stokes, p.20; W. Wakeman, *Dublin Saturday Magazine*, March 1866, refers to a 'Druidical Circle' in the collection of Robert Callwell – almost certainly this painting.
• see colour plate, page 31

Identifying the location of this stone circle in Co Derry is difficult because over the past century several stone circles in the area, such as those at Ballyholly and Letteran, have been destroyed. There is a partial stone circle at Templemoyle Caugh, near Dungiven (map ref. C66330541), with five stones surviving, one of these four-feet tall. The site was overgrown in 2002 and seems to have been virtually forgotten. It is possibly the location of Petrie's watercolour. Stokes describes Petrie's painting as taken on 'Caah Hill', near Dungiven:

> The subject of this picture is one of the Celtic sepulchral monuments of pagan times, commonly called Druidic temples, and which are extremely numerous in many parts of Ireland. The circle is one of several still remaining on the mountain, which, according to the tradition of the peasantry of the district, are the tombs of the chiefs slain in a great battle fought here, and from these the mountain has received its name of Caah or Battle-hill. The tall stones raise their dark forms against the saffron sky, through which the evening star is just appearing and shedding its soft light, while a few cattle stand perfectly motionless on the horizon. The sense of solitude and breathless silence conveyed in this picture, and the deep poetry in the simple treatment of the whole, can be felt only by those who have seen it. [Stokes, p.20]

GP.85 *Fall of the Littory River, Ben Littory, Connemara*
*c.*1840-41, watercolour on paper
(Present whereabouts unknown)
Exh: RHA 1841
(c.f. sketch in the NGI, *Fall of the Littora River, Connemara*, cat. no. 6684)

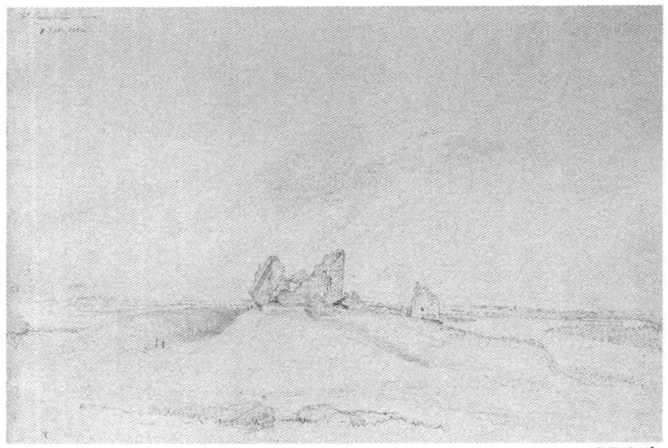
GP.86h

GP.86 *Robert Callwell Sketchbook*
1841-48
Coll: Crawford Municipal Art Gallery

The Robert Callwell Sketchbook contains 25 pages of pencil sketches, mainly of Clonmacnoise and views in Snowdonia. The pencil sketches are all on verso; rectos are blank (with the exception of 86.25). Inside the front cover is inscribed: 'R. Callwell, 25 Herbert Place, Dublin'; also an inscription transcribed from 'Kendal Church, south of the Altar'.

86 a Inscribed: 'measure the ash tree behind the church at Inis Faill, 20ft 11ins circumference Holly tree – do – 9ft 3ins.' Also an indistinct pencil sketch of a mountainside.

86 b Sketch of round tower
Inscribed: 'Rourke's tower, Clonmacnoise'

86 c Sketch of round tower and overgrown church
Inscribed: 'Inis Cealtra 30 Aug 41'

86 d Sketch (heavily shaded) of round tower and ruined church at Inis Cealtra

86 e Inscribed: 'Killick. A small fish found by the shore left by the retreating wave Limerick Harbour chased in by the Sea Gulls which were taking them in great number. Jephart says they are sand eels and are eaten by the inhabitants being taken in great shoals at spring tides here in Dingle Harbour. Dingle 13 Sep 41'
Also inscribed: 'Ballyoughtra Robert Purse 15 Sep 41'

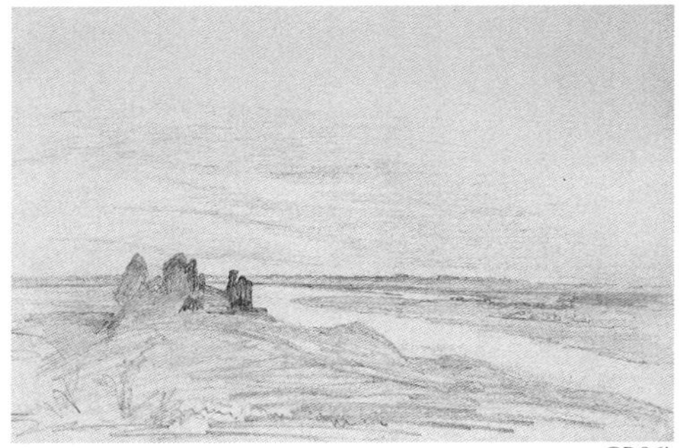
GP.86j

86 f Sketch of Lough Inagh
Inscribed: 'Sep 42. Lough Inagh, Maam Turk, Ben Morrig.'

86 g Sketch of Lough Derryclare
Inscribed: '6 Sep 42. Lough Derryclare, King of the Pins, Lough Inagh.'

86 h Sketch of ruined castle at Clonmacnoise
Inscribed: '30 Sep 42. Clonmacnoise'

86 i Sketch of round tower at Clonmacnoise
Inscribed: '30 Sep 42'

86 j Sketch (heavily shaded) of ruined castle at Clonmacnoise
Inscribed: '30 Sep 42. 1/4 before sunset'

86 k Sketch of round tower and high cross at Clonmacnoise
Inscribed: '30 Feb 42 1/2 past sunset'

86 l Sketch of ruined castle at Clonmacnoise
Inscribed: 'McLoughlin's tower 1 Oct 42'

86 m Sketch of ruined castle at Clonmacnoise
Inscribed: '1 Oct 1842'

86 n Sketch of castle on hillside
Inscribed: '17 July 48 from front window, Bangor'

86 o Sketch of coastal mountains with trees in foreground
Inscribed: '17 July 48. from End Window, Bangor' and 'Great Ormes Head, Pennanback [?], Devy, Penmaenmawr'

86 p Sketch of Dolbadern Castle
Inscribed: 'Dolbadern Castle 18 July 48'

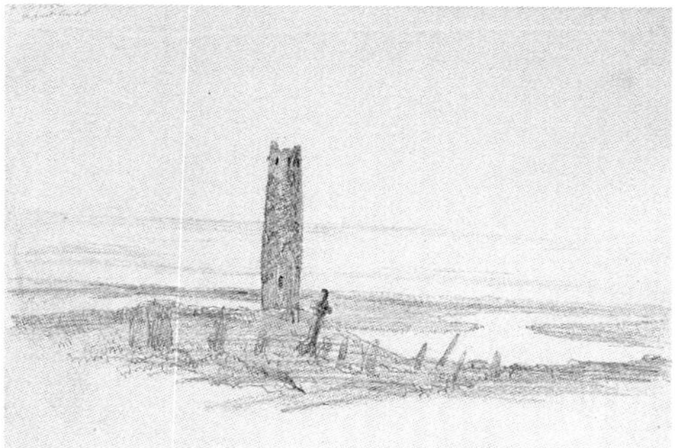

GP.86k

86 q Sketch of Dolbadern Castle
Inscribed: 'Dolbadern Castle 18 July 48'

86 r Inscribed: '19 July 1848 Looking from bedroom window Victoria Hotel, Llanberis, a wet day.'

86 s Inscribed: 'Cumant [?] Mawr, from our parlour window. 19 July 48' and 'Guido's Cottage'

86 t Sketch of three-storey house with flagpole beside, mountains in background Undated (probably in Wales, probable date July 1848).

86 u Sketch of water and mountains
Inscribed: 'Head of Derwent Water 24 July 1848' and 'Grange Hag, Marsden Moor'

86 v Inscribed: 'Gleann Meara, Grange Crag, Castle Crag, Great End, Lord's Hole, Sea Fell Pike, Maedin Moor.'

86 w Verso: pencil sketch of figure sitting under a tree

86 x Verso: pencil sketch of a doorway
Inscribed: 'At a farmhouse on the road to Newlands, about $1^1/_2$ miles from Keswick. 28 July 48'

86 y Recto: pencil sketch
Inscribed: 'Guthmere [?] Haystacks, Hayrocks, High Crag.'

Verso inscribed:
'Sacred to the Memory of the Revd Harry Wellington Star B. A., Curate of All Saint Northampton [?], who perished in frompton [?], while on a tour in North Wales, September 9th 1816, aged 32 years. And whose remains discovered June 1 1847 were interred beneath this stone, June 7 1867. Our only son of a faithful mother, he was unwavering in gratitude and has left a mother and her sisters to mourn for their irreparable loss.
In the midst of life as in death
Be – t – fine reade also
For the Son of Man cometh
At an hour when ye think not.'

86 z Inside back cover:
Sketch of Lough Inagh

GP.87 *The Last Circuit of the Pilgrims at Clonmacnoise, Co. Offaly*
*c.*1842, watercolour on paper, 67.2 x 98
Coll: NGI, cat. no. 2230
Exh: *Irish Exhibition in London*, 1888
(A label on the back of the painting states it was lent by a Mrs Elizabeth Morris of 65 Pembroke Road for this exhibition)
Prov: purchased in Dublin, 1890
• see colour plate, page 32

Of this work, commissioned by the Royal Irish Art Union, probably around 1840, Petrie wrote:

> It was my wish to produce an Irish picture somewhat historical in its object, and poetical in its sentiment – a landscape composed of several of the monuments characteristic of the past history of our country, and which will soon cease to exist, and to connect with them the expression of human feelings equally belonging to our history, and which are destined to similar extinction. [Stokes, p.15]

Petrie's written accounts of Clonmacnoise give a further insight into this painting. He describes how, on his first visit to Clonmacnoise (*c.*1819), he was rewarded with finding among the ruins, evidence that 'Ireland was not ignorant of architectural art, as practised in Europe during the early ages of Christianity'. He describes the round towers, ancient grave stones, ruined churches and high crosses, as well as the pilgrims who came to worship:

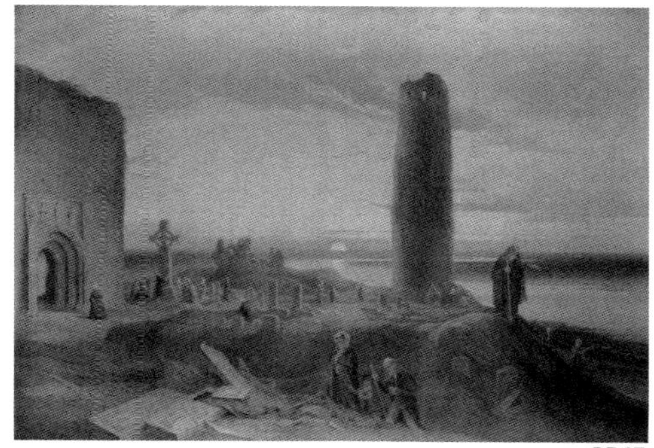

GP.87

> The aged sinner supported by his pilgrim's staff, barefooted and bareheaded, his large grey coat, the substitute for the forbidden cloak or mantle, sweeping the road, his white hair floating on the disregarded wind! [Stokes, p.20]

This figure appears in the painting, and may perhaps be read as representing the artist in his old age. In addition to the churches and graves, Petrie found other attractions at Clonmacnoise:

> ...the young and beautiful girl, with pale face, blue eyes, long black eye-lashes, and dark hair, whose look betrays no conscious guilt, in the midst of her sighing prayers, but rather a feeling of love and devotion; who, notwithstanding her religious duties, is not so entirely unconscious of the power of her beauty, but that she can spare an occasional glance towards the strangers who are endeavouring to fix her figure on their paper or on their memories – a figure, as a friend well observed, that no one but Raphael could draw.

Petrie compared the desolation of the monastery, with its graves of princes of Old Ireland, with that of St Paul's Cathedral in London, at the centre of a bustling metropolis, and went on to describe the different types of pilgrims, and the *ulligaun* or keening, a ritualised form of lamentation. [Petrie, quoted in Stokes, p.30]

In a letter to his new wife, written from Birr and dated 1 August 1820, he dated the inscribed stone slabs at Clonmacnoise to the sixth and seventh centuries [Stokes, p.27], although by the time those same slabs were reproduced in his *Ecclesiastical Architecture of Ireland* twenty-five years later, he had dated the slab that appears in the foreground, inscribed 'A Prayer for Suibine, the Son of Mailae Humai', to the 9th century. Although Petrie dated the slabs at Clonmacnoise by comparing the names on them with those of known abbots, this was highly conjectural. Many of the names were widely used at the time. His dating of the cathedral at Clonmacnoise to the year 909 is considered correct, as is his dating of the Perpendicular style Gothic doorway in the north wall to the mid-15th century.

Situated on what was effectively an island, where a long glacial moraine known as the Esker Riada and the River Shannon meet, Clonmacnoise was founded by St Ciaran in 549. Although the situation is now isolated, at the time this was one of the great crossroads of Ireland. Although the monastic settlement steadily grew to rival Armagh, little is known of the early centuries of the monastery's existence; the historical and archaeological record begins around the mid-8th century, when the monastery became the royal burial place of the Kings of Connaught (enjoying a status within Ireland similar to that of St Denis in Paris). The earliest form of decorated burial slab dates from the mid-7th to the mid-8th century; these consist of a simple Greek cross, often within a square frame. The high crosses at and near Clonmacnoise can be related to examples in Iona and other parts of Scotland, and probably date from the 8th century. In the latter half of the 9th century, when Clonmacnoise came under the control of the Clann Cholmáin kings, notably Máelsechnaill mac Máelruanaid (*c*.846-62), Flann Sinna (*c*.879-916), who built the cathedral in 909, and Máelsechnaill II (980-1002), the monastery enjoyed peaceful times. Prior to this, the monastery had been plundered and burnt on at least nine occasions between 815 and 845. However, only two of these attacks were by Vikings, most of the others represent attempts by the Kings of Munster to gain control in Connaught. The more developed memorial slabs, with fret or spiral design at the cross terminals, date from the time of these Clann Cholmain kings – late 9th to the end of the 10th century. According to the annals the round tower was built in 1120, when the Ua Conchobair kings of Connaught had regained control of the monastery as a royal burial site.

[Raghnall O'Floinn, 'Clonmacnoise: Art and Patronage in the Early Medieval Period', in Heather King (ed.), *Clonmacnoise Studies*, i (Dúchas, The Heritage Service, Dublin, 1998) pp.87-97]

Twelve years after Petrie's death, in 1878, the two-volume *Christian Inscriptions in the Irish Language* was published by the Royal Historical and Archaeological Association. Edited by Margaret Stokes, it contained much of the material, including drawings and texts, collected by Petrie during his decades of research and travel. Stokes also included material collected by the 3rd Earl of Dunraven, including a rubbing made of a stone in the churchyard of Iniscealtra. In *Christian Inscriptions*, Petrie examined 143 carved slabs from Clonmacnoise. Subsequent excavations have revealed the existence of around 700 complete or fragmentary carved stones, making Clonmacnoise by far the most important ecclesiastical site in this regard. (Iona by comparison has just one hundred.) The question as to whom the slabs commemorated has not been decided, but it seems that Petrie's original idea, that many of the slabs commemorated abbots, is not incorrect. The grave slabs are thought to commemorate ecclesiastics as well as laymen who wished to be buried in a holy place.

[Catherine Swift, 'Sculptors and their Customers: A study of Clonmacnoise Grave Slabs' in Heather King (ed.), *Clonmacnoise Studies*, ii, seminar papers 1998 (Dúchas, The Heritage Service, Dublin, 2003) p.120]

GP.88 *Croagh Patrick, Co. Mayo*
c.1842, watercolour on paper,
20 x 30 (visible size)
Coll: NGI, cat. no. 6698
Prov: Petrie exhibited *The Second Station on Croagh Patrick Mountain, Co. Mayo* in the RHA exhibition in 1843, but whether this is the painting at present in the NGI is uncertain

While George Petrie was full of praise for the religious customs he encountered during his tours of Ireland, his successor as editor of the *Dublin Penny Journal*, Philip Dixon Hardy, was less so. Hardy wrote of Croagh Patrick:

> Croagh Patrick is a very high and beautiful mountain in the most western part of the County of Mayo; it rises from the sea in a fine conical or sugar-loaf form. This mountain is considered to be

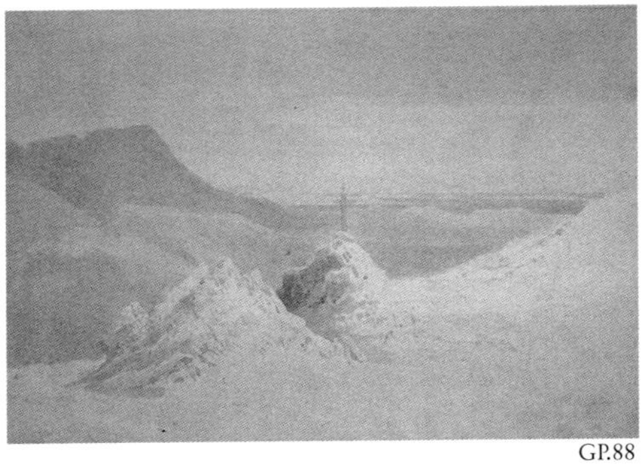

GP.88

> one of the most holy places of pilgrimage in Ireland, it would fill a volume to tell all the fabulous and superstitious stories which are reported and believed about it – but its supposed holiness is derived from its being the place where St. Patrick is said to have driven all the venomous animals, which he banished from Ireland into the sea; a pilgrimage to it is, therefore, supposed to be of powerful efficacy to atone for and wash away sin. The penance done there is thus performed: – They begin their station at the sign of St. Patrick's knee, and there say seven paters, seven aves, and a creed; and go on their knees about the length of four perches, over rocks, until they get to a little altar, where they say fifteen paters, fifteen aves, and a creed; they then return, but still on their knees, and say seven paters, seven aves, and a creed. Thus ends their labour, unless they be married persons who have no children; [the additional rites belonging [54] to such persons we shall not detail;] after which they go down the mountain to the well of glass. There they sit up all night, and bring thither the blind, the halt, and the maimed, presenting them to the saint of the well, and cry to him to deliver them all from their diseases and infirmities. They sit up three nights, to wit, Monday, Wednesday, and Saturday, and next proceed to Aughawale, where they go through a station: and then enter the well, in which are three trouts; they pick up baits and

throw them into the water, and it is the most lucky omen in the world to them if a trout come out and eat the bait, but, if not, they cry out to St. Columbkill to send them out; if they do not appear, there is some misfortune to come upon them, with the loss of friends and relations.

[Philip Dixon Hardy, *The Holy Wells of Ireland*]

GP.89 *Temple Fineen, Clonmacnoise*
*c.*1843, watercolour on paper
(Present whereabouts unknown)
Exh: RHA 1843

It is also known as Teampull Finghin, a 12th-century building at Clonmacnoise. An engraving of *MacCarthy's Church and Tower, Clonmacnoise*, published in Cromwell's *Excursions* in 1820, is possibly based on this painting.

GP.90 *O'Rourke's Tower, Clonmacnoise – Twilight*
*c.*1843, watercolour on paper
(Present whereabouts unknown)
Exh: RHA 1843

GP.92 *Bridge and Castle of Shrule, Co. Mayo*
*c.*1843, watercolour on paper
(Private collection)
Prov: Bay Jellett
Exh: RHA 1843, 1852
see colour plate, page 33

GP.93 *Brandon Mountain, from the Pass of Connor Hill, Co. of Kerry*
*c.*1843, watercolour on paper
(Present whereabouts unknown)
Exh: RHA 1843, 1846
Lit. Stokes, p.353

GP.94 *The Home of the Heron, Lough Atri, Looking into Glen Hoghan, Connemara – Evening*
*c.*1845, watercolour on paper laid on canvas, 67 x 96
Exh: RHA 1846, 1853, 1866
Coll: NGI, cat. no. 6871
(c.f. sketch in NGI, cat. no. 6673, inscribed 'Glen Hoghan')

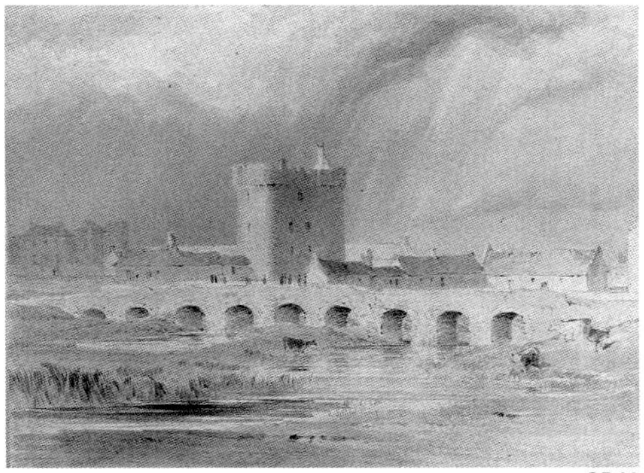

GP.92

Prov: Miss Annie Callwell Bequest, 1904
(Label on back of frame 'Robert Callwell, 25 Herbert Place, Dublin.')
Lit. Stokes, p.19
see colour plate, page 34

William Stokes describes this painting of a characteristic scene in Connemara

The scene is laid in Lough Atree; the view is taken from the southern shore of the lake, looking into one of the deep valleys in the Connemara range, called Glenhoghan, and embraces the little group of islands from which the lake has derived its name. These islands are adorned with trees of native growth now scarcely to be found elsewhere within the barony, and hence the largest of the island of the group has been taken possession of by the herons, which are numerous in the district, and which have been allowed to retain it as a sanctuary and a home. The day has been wet, but towards evening the clouds have dispersed, the sun bursts forth, and the mists, rising as steam from the mountain-sides in this western light, form a rainbow-tinted veil of a most ideal loveliness, softening the rugged outlines of the peaked and barren mountains, and mingling their distant summits with the delicate blue of the heaven above.

GP.95 *The Fair at Sligachan, in Skye*
*c.*1846, watercolour on paper
(Present whereabouts unknown)
Exh: RHA 1848, 1853
Lit: Stokes, p.354

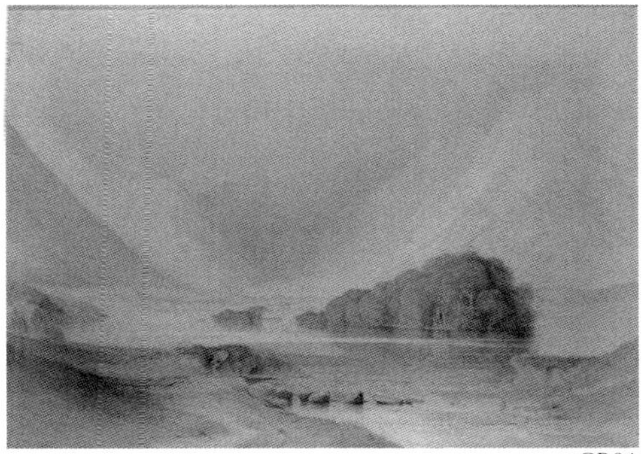

GP.94

Stokes states that Petrie made studies for this painting when he visited Skye in 1846. It was exhibited at the RHA in 1853, and the owner's name was given in the catalogue as being Stokes himself. In the National Gallery of Ireland there is a preparatory sketch for this painting (NGI, cat. no. 6758).

GP.96 *Stone Circle at Coolirra, near Sligo*
*c.*1847-48, watercolour on paper
(Present whereabouts unknown)
Exh: RHA 1848
(Petrie painted two versions of this; one *Morning* and one *Evening*. Both were exhibited in 1848.)

GP.97 *Teampull Breacan, Aran Islands*
*c.*1857, watercolour on paper
(Present whereabouts unknown)
Exh: RHA 1858
Lit. Stokes

Stokes states that Petrie made initial sketches for this painting when he first visited the Aran Islands in 1821, and completed it after his second visit in 1857.

UNDATED WORKS

GP.91 *Vale of Glendalough, Co. Wicklow, with the Round Tower*
watercolour on paper, 32.5 x 43.2
Coll: Victoria & Albert Museum, London (V&A, cat. no. 106-1888)
Lit. Martin Hardy, *V&A Catalogue of Watercolours*, 1926.

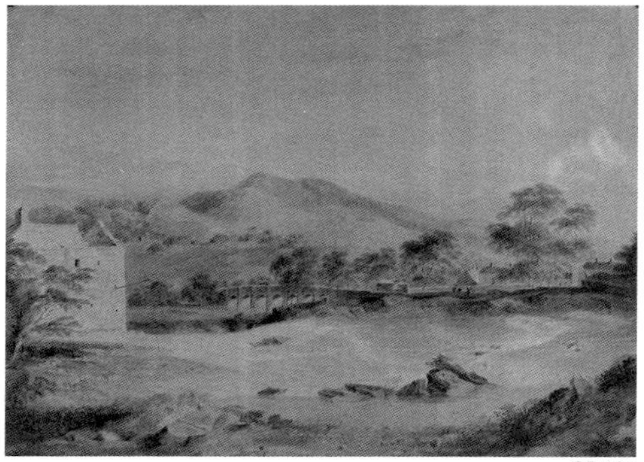

GP.101

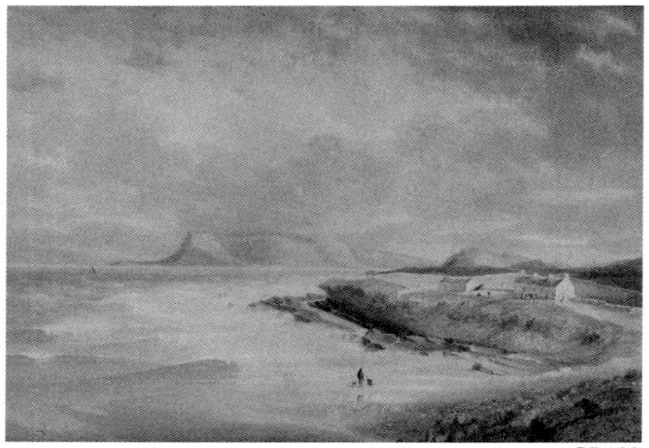

GP.103

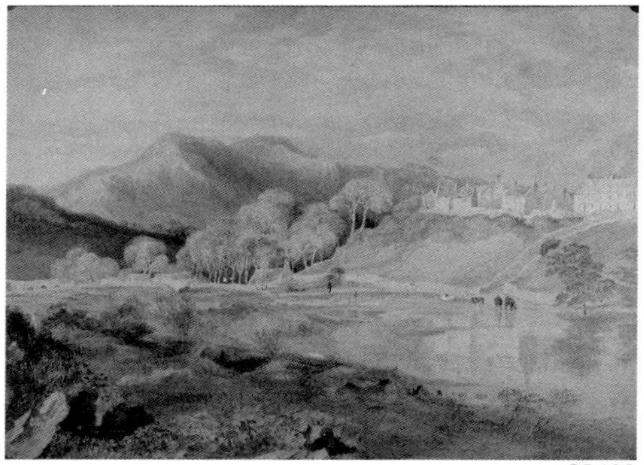

GP.105

GP.100 *The Gap of Dunloe*
Watercolour on paper, 39.5 x 51
Coll: NGI, cat. no. 2502
Prov: purchased from W.B. Pearsall, Dublin, 1902

GP.101 *Bridge and Castle*
Watercolour on paper, 30.5 x 42 (visible size)
(Private collection)
Prov: William Stokes collection

GP.102 *The Upper Lake at Glendalough*
Watercolour on paper, 29 x 37.5 (visible size)
(Private collection)
Prov: William Stokes collection

GP.103 *Achill*
Watercolour on paper, 33.5 x 49 (visible size)
(Private collection)
Prov: William Stokes collection
see colour plate, page 35

GP.104 *The Boyne River near Trim*
Watercolour on paper, 19 x 25.5 (visible size)
(Private collection)
Prov: William Stokes collection

GP.105 *Landscape, The Reeks*
Watercolour on paper, 30.5 x 43
(Private collection)
Prov: William Stokes collection
Lit: Stokes, p.14, refers to a painting of the Reeks at Killarney
see colour plate, page 36

GP.106 *Wicklow Landscape Greystones*
Watercolour on paper, 20.5 x 28 (visible size)
(Private collection)
Prov: purchased at auction

GP.107 *View of the Bay of Dublin from Mount Merrion*
Watercolour on paper
(Present whereabouts unknown)
Lit: Strickland, ii, p.237
Strickland states that this picture was painted for Sir George Hewitt, Commander of the Forces

GP.109 *The Upper Lake at Glendalough*
Watercolour on paper, 28 x 37
(Private collection)
Prov: William Stokes collection

GP.110 *Maam, Connemara*
Watercolour on paper
Coll: Margaret Stokes, Dublin
Prov: William Stokes Collection
There is a preparatory drawing for this in the NGI (cat. no. 6766)

GP.112 *View of O'Connell Street (Sackville Street)*
Oil on panel
Coll: NGI, cat. no. 4130
As this is the only oil painting attributed to Petrie, its attribution must remain doubtful.

GP.113 *View of Swords Castle*
Watercolour on paper
(Private collection)

GP.109

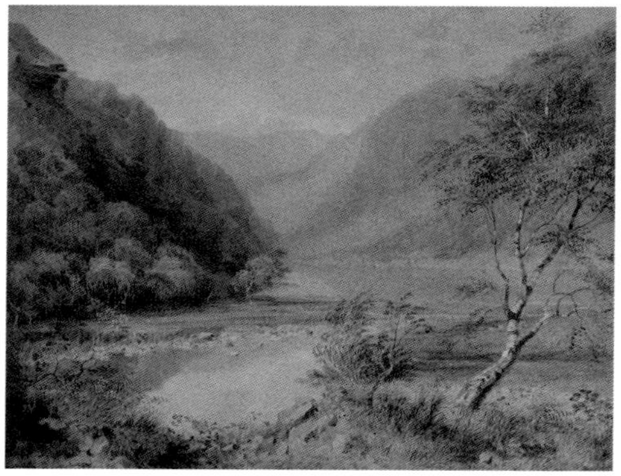

CATALOGUE OF DRAWINGS BY PETRIE

All the following drawings are in the National Gallery of Ireland and form part of the Margaret Stokes Bequest of 1900. All are pencil on paper, unless otherwise stated.

	NGI cat. no.	
	2734	*A Carter Crossing a River*, *c.*1807, 24 x 34.5
	2747	*A Mill*, *c.*1812, 24.1 x 33.6
	3006	*Creagh Castle, Co. Galway* (?), 1821-22, 23.7 x 19.4
	3031	*A Gateway*, 1820s, 22 x 29
GP.114	6660	*A Ruined Castle, Castle Gow*
GP.115	6661	*Carrick a Rede*
GP.116	6662	*Dunluce*
GP.117	6663	*Dunluce Castle*
GP.118	6664	*The Lower Lake, Killarney*
GP.119	6665	*Banagher*
GP.120	6666	*Narrow Water Castle*
GP.121	6667	*Narrow Water Castle, from Carlingford Road*
GP.122	6668	*The Ross Memorial, Rostrevor*
GP.123	6669	*Landscape, Lake Between Hills* (Killarney)
GP.124	6670	*The Pins from Ardbear Bay, Connemara*
GP.125	6671	*Ballinahinch Lake*
GP.126	6672	*Twelve Pins from Head of Ballinakill Bay*
GP.127	6673	*Lough Atri, Looking into Glen Hoghan* (preparatory drawing for *Home of the Heron* NGI, cat. no. 6871)
GP.128	6674	*Delphi, Co. Mayo*
GP.129	6675	*Old Weir Bridge, Killarney*
GP.130	6676	*Lough Corrib*
GP.131	6677	*Mac Gilla Cudha's Reeks from Boriagus Island, Killarney* [*c.*1807]
GP.132	6678	*The Eagle's Nest, Killarney* [*c.*1807]
GP.133	6679	*Connemara Landscape*
GP.134	6680	*Landscape* (probably Connemara)
GP.135	6681	*Clifden from Road to the Castle*, [*c.*1823]
GP.136	6682	*Head of Killary Harbour*
GP.137	6683	*A Waterfall*
GP.138	6684	*Fall of the Littora River, Connemara*
GP.139	6685	*Lough Ina, Connemara* [Lough Inagh]
GP.140	6686	*Lough Ina, Connemara* [Lough Inagh]
GP.141	6687	*Lough Ina, Connemara* [Lough Inagh]
GP.142	6688	*The Little Killary Bay* [*c.*1823] Inscribed: 'The Little Killary Bay' lower right (The view is taken from near Salrock. looking north-west across Little Killary Bay towards Benbury Mountain.)
GP.143	6689	*Renvyle, Connemara* Pencil on paper. Inscribed: 'Renvyle' lower right (The view is taken from a point north of Letterfrack, looking across towards Renvyle House with Mweelray Mountain in the background. Petrie did several sketches at Renvyle, some taken from Tully Cross.)
GP.144	6690	*Renvyle House, Connemara, Co. Galway, from below Tully Mountain*, *c.*1823, 25.5 x 39.5
GP.145	6691	*Near the Pass of Salroc, Connemara, Co Galway*, *c.*1823, 27 x 37.3
GP.146	6692	*The Twelve Pins, Connemara, Co Galway*, *c.*1823, 26.2 x 37 (This view is taken from a different vantage point to NGI cat. no. 6672, which is inscribed 'from the head of Ballinakill Bay'. This present view, which shows Benbaun in the centre of the Twelve Pins (or Bens) is probably taken with Tully Lough in the foreground.)
GP.147	6693	*A Mountain Path, Connemara, Co. Galway*, *c.*1823, 20.3 x 29.4
GP.148	6694	*A Bridge over a stream in Connemara*, *c.*1823, 21.2 x 28.7
GP.149	6695	*Dun Aengus Fort, Inishmore, Aran Islands* *c.*1823, 23.5 x 35.2 (preparatory sketch for NGI Cat.no. 7481)
GP.150	6696	*Hen's Castle, Lough Corrib, Connemara, Co Galway*, *c.*1834, 23.5 x 35.2
GP.151	6697	*Hen's Castle, Lough Corrib, Connemara, Co. Galway*, *c.*1834, 25.1 x 34.8 (preparatory sketch for NGI Cat.No. 6032)
GP.152	6698	*Croagh Patrick* , *Connemara, Co. Mayo*, *c.*1823, 24.8 x 31
GP.153	6699	*Castlepoint, Lough Gill, Sligo*, *c.*1830, paper watermarked 1826, 23.1 x 34
GP.154	6700	*Lough Gill, Co Sligo, from Athamore*, *c.*1830, 20.9 x 33.2
GP.155	6701	*Castlepoint, Lough Gill, Co. Sligo*, *c.*1830, 21.9 x 31.1
GP.156	6702	*Hazlewood House, Lough Gill, Co. Sligo*, *c.*1830, 20.7 x 28.4
GP.157	6703	*Sligo, Co. Sligo*, *c.*1830, 23.9 x 29.8
GP.158	6704	*Dublin from the South*, *c.*1815 (paper watermarked 1813), 21.5 x 30.3
GP.159	6705	*Dublin Bay and the Pigeon House Fort*, *c.*1816, 21.5 x 37
GP.160	6706	*Lambay Island and Howth from across Dublin Bay*, *c.*1816, 22 x 36
GP.161	6707	*Baily Lighthouse, Howth, Co Dublin, built 1814*, *c.*1828, 25.4 x 34.1
GP.162	6708	*Baily Light from the Needles* (preparatory sketch for the title page vignette of Fisher's *Guide to Dublin*. The engravers have exaggerated the forms of the rocks.)
GP.163	6709	*Dublin seen from Howth*, *c.*1828, 24.6 x 36
GP.164	6710	*Killiney Hill and Obelisk, Co. Dublin*, 1820s, 24.5 x 33.5
GP.165	6711	*On the Liffey, beyond Lucan*
GP.166	6712	*Giant's Causeway, Co. Antrim*, 20.2 x 32.1 (illustration for the *Northern Tourist*, 1830)
GP.167	6713	*St. Ciaran's Well, Castle Ciaran, Co Meath*, 1820s, 19.1 x 25.7
GP.168	6714	*The Ruins of Clonmacnois Castle, Co. Offaly*, 1820s, 20.3 x 29.8
GP.169	6715	*A Sailing Boat on the Shore*, 24.8 x 34.5

GP.170 6716 *The Entrance Gates of Kilruddery House, Bray, Co. Wicklow (Lord Meath's Gate)*, *c.*1825, 22.3 x 34.6

GP.171 6717 *St Kevin's, the Cathedral and Round Tower, Glendalough, Co. Wicklow* [1], *c.*1820, 23.2 x 36.1

GP.172 6718 *St Kevin's, the Cathedral and Round Tower, Glendalough, Co. Wicklow* [2], *c.*1822, 20.3 x 29.1

GP.173 6719 *Thomond Bridge (now Rebuilt) Limerick*, *c.*1820s, 20.4 x 34.1

GP.174 6720 *Cathedral and Round Tower, The Rock of Cashel, Co. Tipperary*, 1820s, 22.9 x 35.1

GP.175 6721 *Devil's Punch Bowl, Mangerton Mountain, Killarney, Co. Kerry*, late 1820s, 20.5 x 32

GP.176 6722 *Comeen Dubh Glen, above the Upper Lake, Killarney, Co. Kerry*, *c.*1807, 26.3 x 37.4

GP.177 6723 *The Eagle's Nest, above the Long Range, Killarney, Co Kerry*, *c.*1807, 27.3 x 39.2

GP.178 6724 *The Gap of Dunloe, Killarney*, *c.*1807, 27.8 x 37.8

GP.179 6725 *The Bridge in the Gap of Dunloe, Killarney*, *c.*1807, 27.8 x 37.8
(see after Petrie NGI cat. no. 2502)

GP.180 6726 *In the Glen of the Horse, Mangerton Mountain, Killarney* [1], *c.*1807, 24.8 x 37.6

GP.181 6727 *The Glen of the Horse, Mangerton Mountain, Killarney* [2], *c.*1807, 28.4 x 37.8 (squared for transfer)

GP.182 6728 *Lough Leane and MacGillycuddy's Reeks from Aghadowey* [Aghadoe] *Church, Killarney*, sepia ink on paper 26.8 x 39.2
(engraved for Wright's *Guide to Killarney*, 1823)

GP.183 6729 *The Abbey of Muckross Abbey, Killarney*, *c.*1807, 26.2 x 39.1

GP.184 6730 *Caislan a Kirke (Hen's Castle), Lough Corrib, Co. Galway*, *c.*1823, 22.7 x 28.5

GP.185 6731 *Bride's Glen, Co. Dublin*, *c.*1808, 23.7 x 35.1

GP.186 6732 *Giant's Causeway, Co. Antrim*, 22.9 x 31.8
(illustration for Wright's *The Giant's Causeway*, 1823)

GP.187 6733 *Caernarvon Castle, Wales*, *c.*1810 (watermark 1823), 22.6 x 34.1

GP.188 6734 *Conway Castle, Wales*, 24.7 x 35.9

GP.189 6735 *Dolbadarn Castle above Llyn Peris, Wales*, *c.*1810, 26.6. x 28.9

GP.190 6736 *Llyn Peris and Dolbadarn Castle, Wales*, *c.*1810, 27.1 x 42.3

GP.191 6738 *Llangollen Bridge, Wales*, *c.*1818, 18.9 x 37.2

GP.192 6739 *Llyn Gwynant, Wales*, *c.*1810, with ink and wash, 24.8 x 37

GP.193 6740 *Lyn Gwynant, Wales*, *c.*1810, with ink and wash, 26.7 x 37.4

GP.194 6741 *Baily Lighthouse, Howth, Co. Dublin from the Needles*, 18.1 x 15
(for an engraving, 1829, and frontispiece for Fisher & Jackson's *Ireland Illustrated*, 1831)

GP.195 6747 *Old Weir Bridge, Killarney*, *c.*1807, 17.3 x 23.5

GP.196 6748 *Connemara Mountains*, 24.2 x 19.9

GP.197 6749 *Dolbadarn Castle above Llyn Peris, Wales*, *c.*1818, 22.1 x 25.2

GP.198 6750 *Howth Harbour and Ireland's Eye*, *c.*1828, 23.2 x 26.1

GP.199 6751 *The Baily Lighthouse, Howth, Co Dublin*, *c.*1828, 26.7 x 20.8

GP.200 6752 *The Giant's Causeway, Co Antrim*, *c.*1823, 17.8 x 30.8

GP.201 6754 *The Bride's Glen, Co. Dublin*, *c.*1818, 21.8 x 32

GP.202 6755 *The Archbishop's Castle, Swords, Co. Dublin*, *c.*1828, 21.6 x 29.9

GP.203 6756 *Llyn Peris and Dolbadarn Castle, Wales*, *c.*1810, 20 x 32.3 (penned over)

GP.204 6757 *Howth Village, Co. Dublin*, *c.*1828, 20 x 30.2

GP.205 6758 *A Fair on the Isle of Skye, Scotland*, 20.8 x 34.3
(for a watercolour, 1846)

GP.206 6759 *Menai Bridge*

GP.207 6760 *In the Vale of Glendalough*

GP.208 6761 *The Lower Lake from Ross Island*

GP.209 6762 *Ardfinnan Castle and Bridge, Co. Tipperary*

GP.210 6763 *The Lower Lake from Ross Island, Killarney*

GP.211 6764 *The Lower Lake from Muckross*

GP.212 6765 *On the River Flask, Co. Kerry*

GP.213 6766 *Maam, Connemara, Co. Galway*, 24.4 x 36.2
(for an undated watercolour)

GP.214 6767 *The Glen of the Horse, Mangerton Mountain, Killarney, Co. Kerry* [3], *c.*1807, 26.3 x 37

GP.215 6768 *Llyn Padarn from the Pass of Llanberis, Wales*, 25.5 x 36.8

GP.216 6769 *The Menai Strait Suspension Bridge, Wales*, 25.9 x 37

GP.217 2927 *The North Gate of Trim Castle, Co. Meath*, 1819, 16.5 x 23.5

GP.218 2969 *Aughnanure Castle, Co. Galway*, 1821-22, 23 x 33.4

GP.219 6302 *St. Kevin's Bed*

GP.220 6303 *The New Church at Kilgobbin, Co. Dublin*, *c.*1829, sepia on paper, 16.7 x 10.2, signed: 'Geo Petrie R.H.A. Delt'

GP.221 6305 *The New Church at Simmonscourt Road, Co. Dublin* [St Mary's, Donnybrook], *c.*1829, 16.6 x 10.2, sepia on paper, signed 'Geo Petrie R.H.A. Delt'

GP.222 6840 *Ballinahinch Castle and River, Connemara, Co. Galway*, 1822-23, 27.1 x 38.2

GP.223 6841 *The Long Bridge, Belfast, Co. Antrim*, 26 x 37
(for a watercolour exhibited 1830, and an illustration for the *Northern Tourist*, 1830)

GP.224 6842 *Westport Town, Co Mayo*, 24.9 x 37.5

GP.225 6843 *Drogheda, Co. Louth*, *c.*1830, 27 x 37.3

GP.226 6844 *The Bullring, Drogheda, Co Mayo*, 22.5 x 32.9
(for a watercolour exhibited 1830, and an illustration for Brown's *The Beauties of Ireland*, 1830)

GP.227 6846 *Ballinrobe Bridge, Co. Mayo*, 1820s, 21.1 x 27.6

GP.228 6865 An Album with Notes and 69 Leaves of Celtic, Medieval and Prehistoric Studies, including Three Tombstones from Clonmacnois, Co. Offaly (ill.), *c.*1843, 45.5 x 32

SELECTED ENGRAVINGS

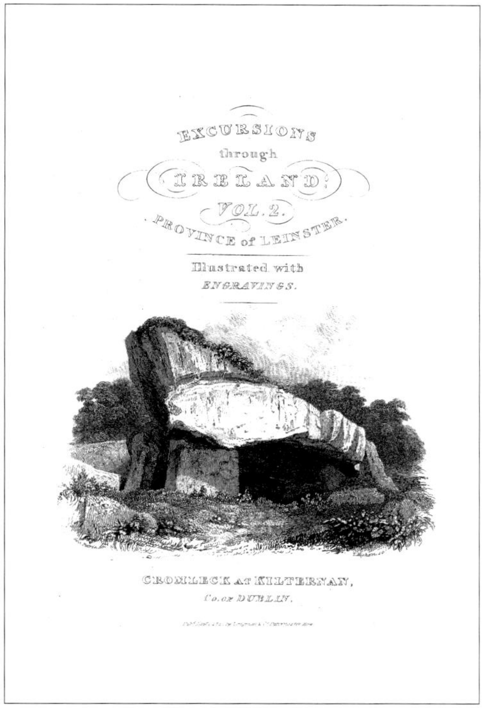

Cromleck at Kilternan, Co. of Dublin
engraving after Petrie from T.K. Cromwell, *Excursions through Ireland*, 1820 (title page, vol.II)

Excursions through Ireland

BY THOMAS KITSON CROMWELL (1820-21)

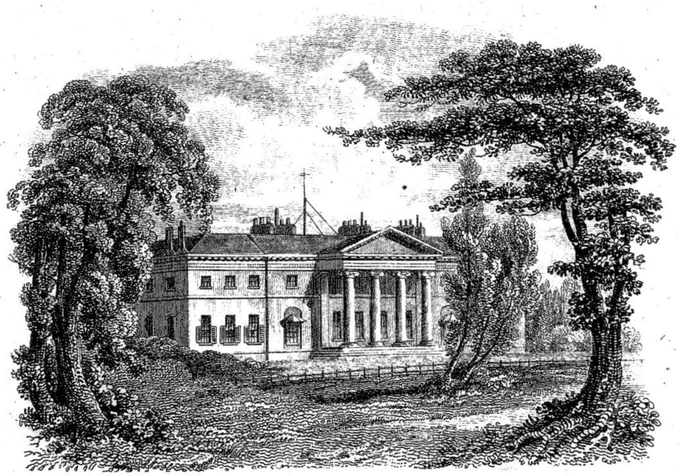

The Lodge, Phoenix Park, Near Dublin, engraving from title page of vol. III

EXCURSIONS
THROUGH
IRELAND:
COMPRISING
TOPOGRAPHICAL AND HISTORICAL DELINEATIONS;
TOGETHER WITH
DESCRIPTIONS OF THE RESIDENCES OF THE NOBILITY AND GENTRY,
Remains of Antiquity,
AND EVERY OTHER OBJECT OF INTEREST OR CURIOSITY.
FORMING A COMPLETE GUIDE
FOR THE
TRAVELLER AND TOURIST.

BY THOMAS CROMWELL.

PROVINCE OF LEINSTER;
Illustrated with
One Hundred and Twenty-One Engravings.

Title page text from vol. I

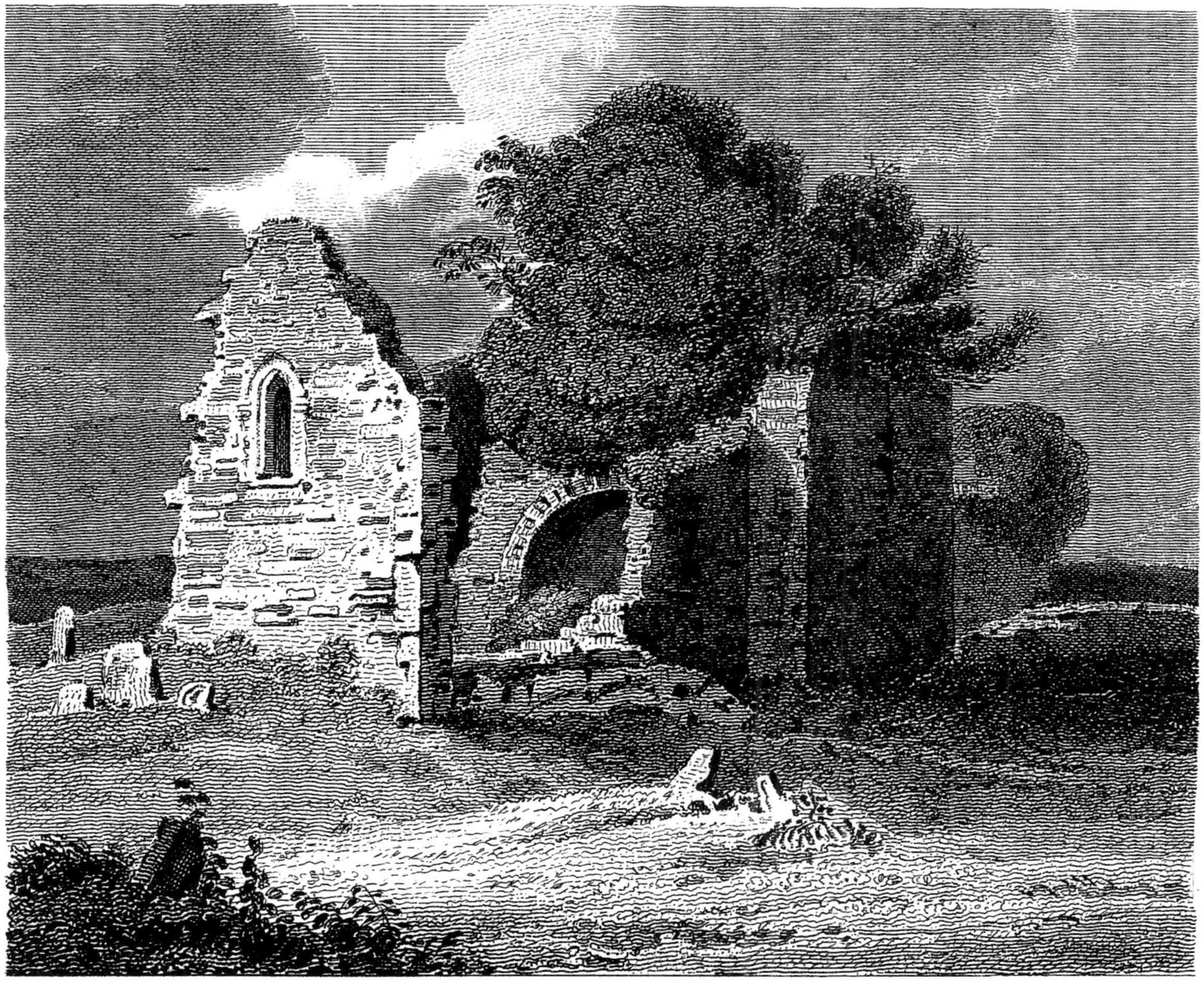

Remains of Rathmichael Church, Co. of Dublin

* additional engravings from a second set of volumes

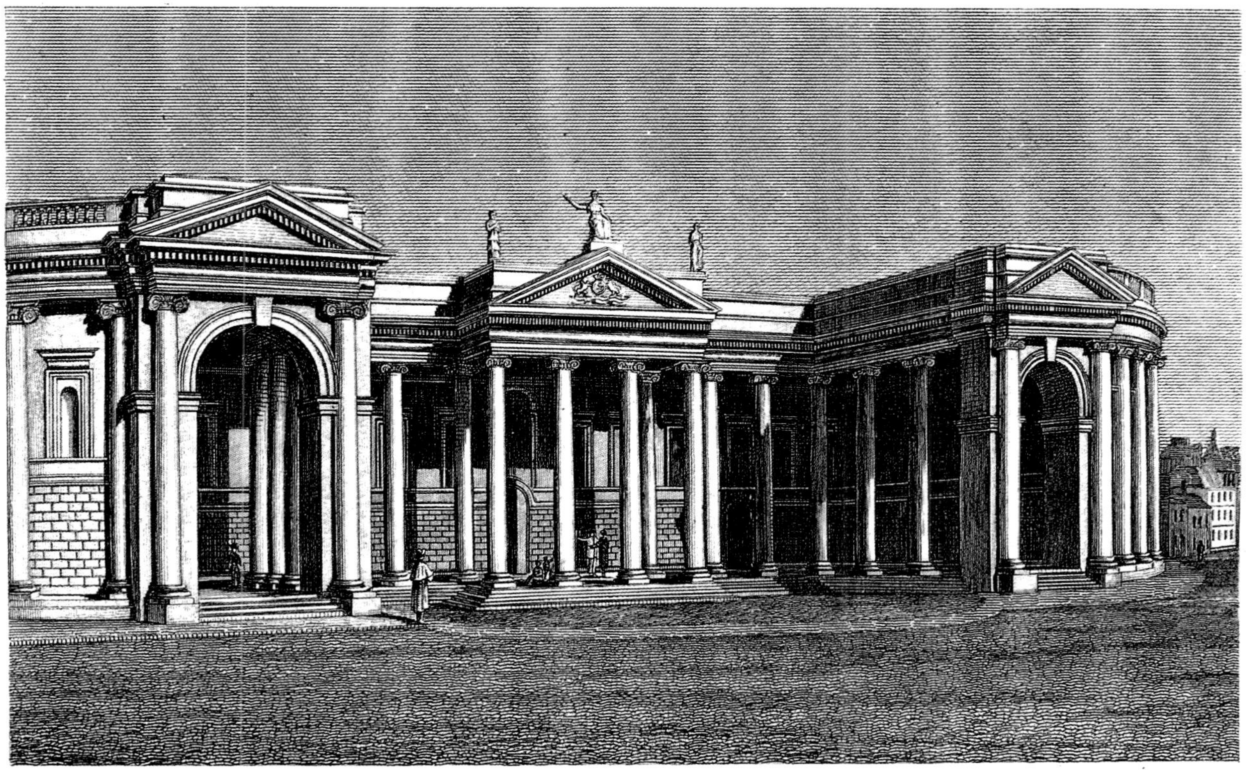

The Bank of Ireland, Dublin

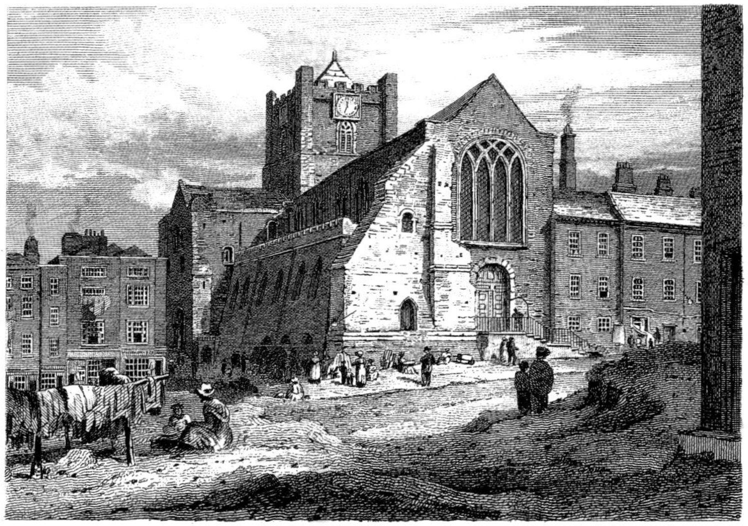

West View of Christ's Cathedral, Dublin

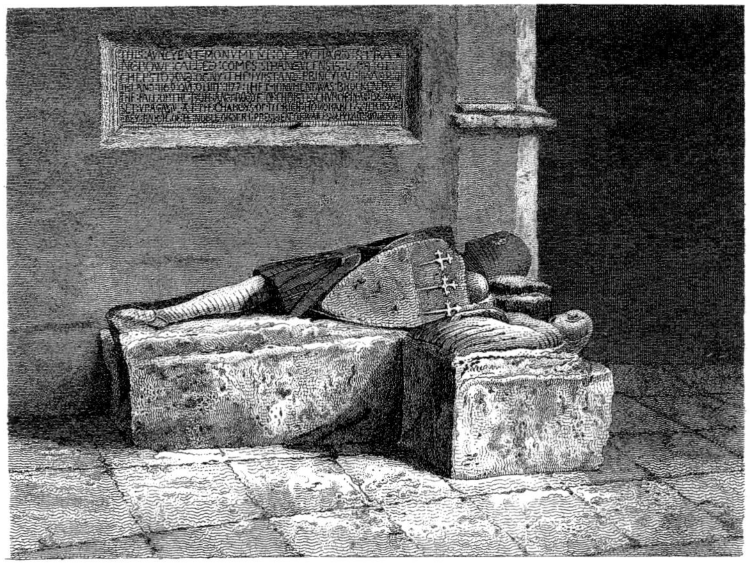

Earl Strongbow's Monument, Christ's Cathedral, Dublin

The Four Courts, Dublin

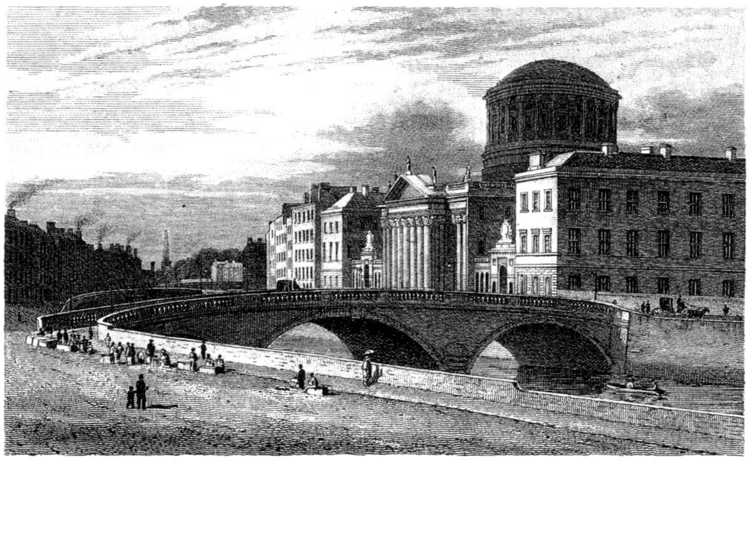

Carlisle Bridge & The Custom House, Dublin

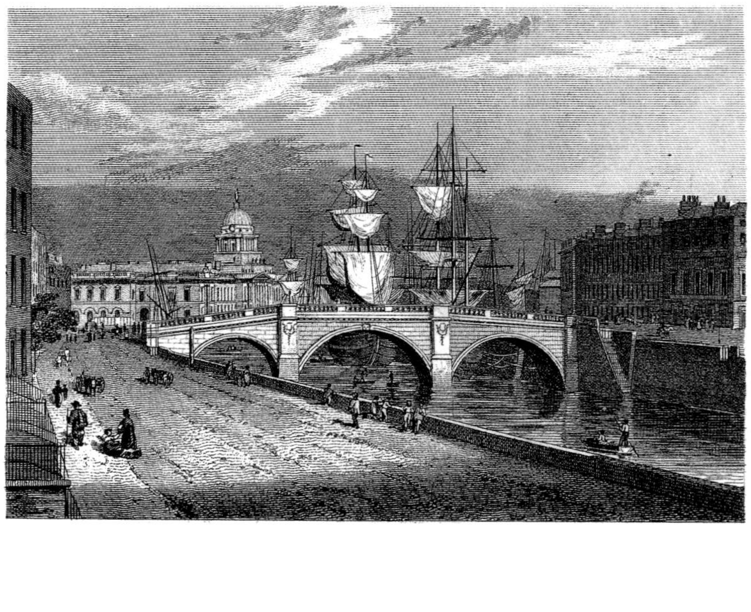

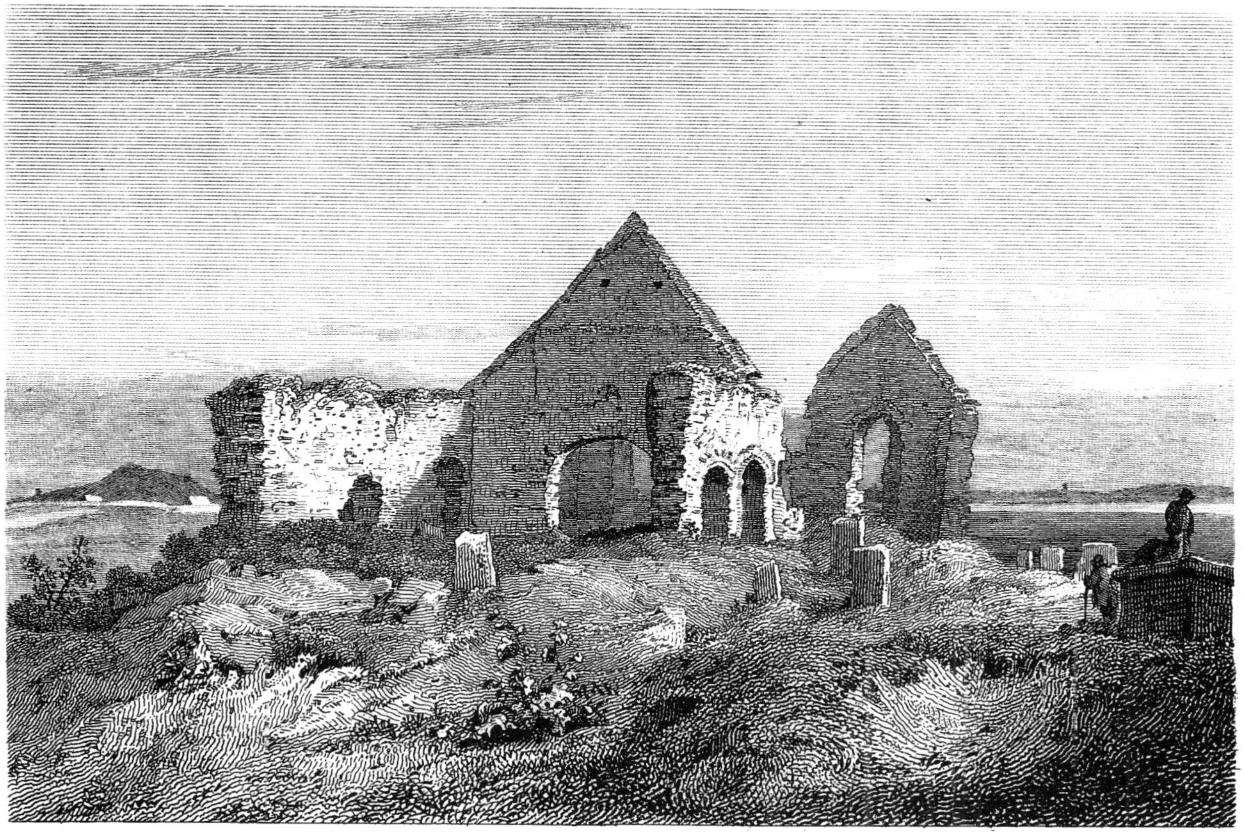

Remains of the Abbey of Kilbarrick, Co. of Dublin

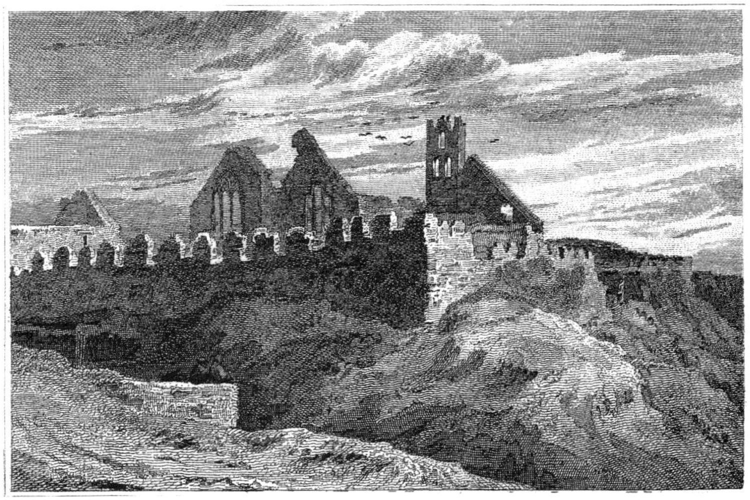

Remains of the College at Howth, Co. of Dublin

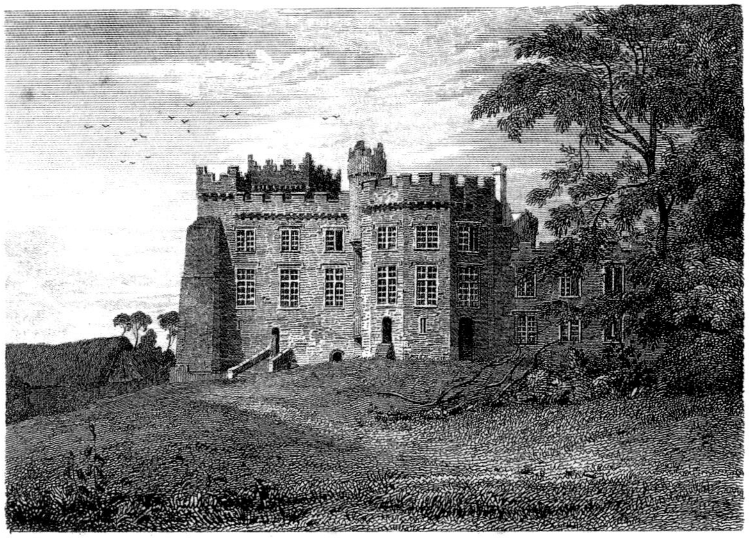

Trimleston Castle, The Seat of Lord Trimleston, Co. of Eastmeath

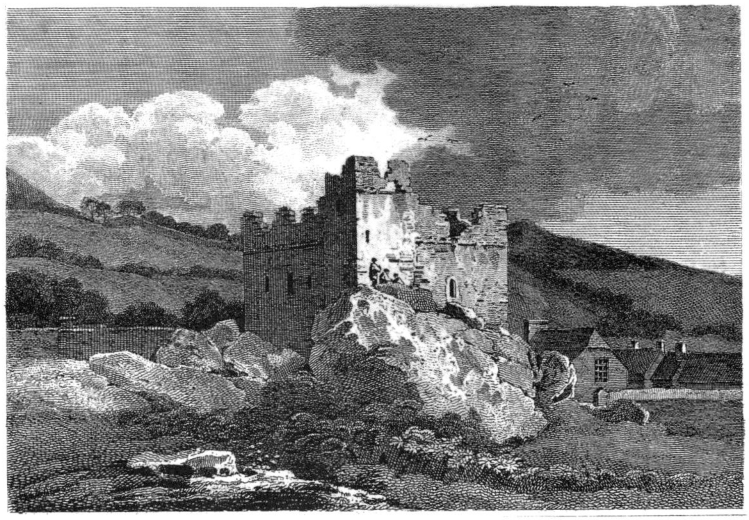

Dalkey, Co. of Dublin

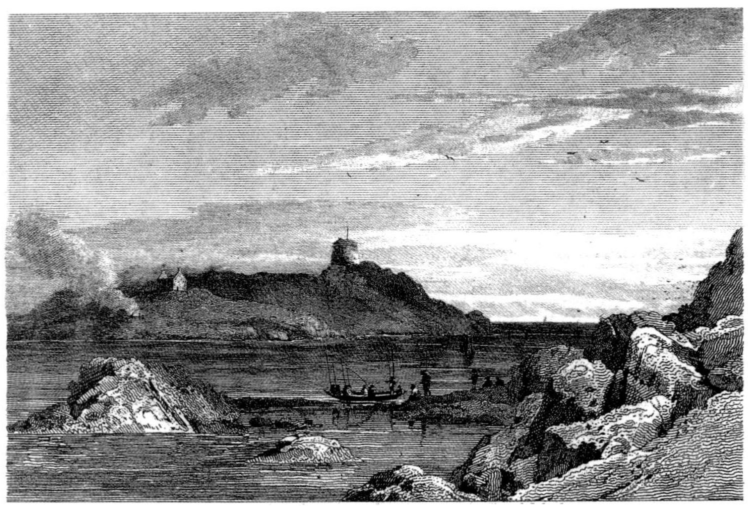

Dalkey Island, Bay of Dublin

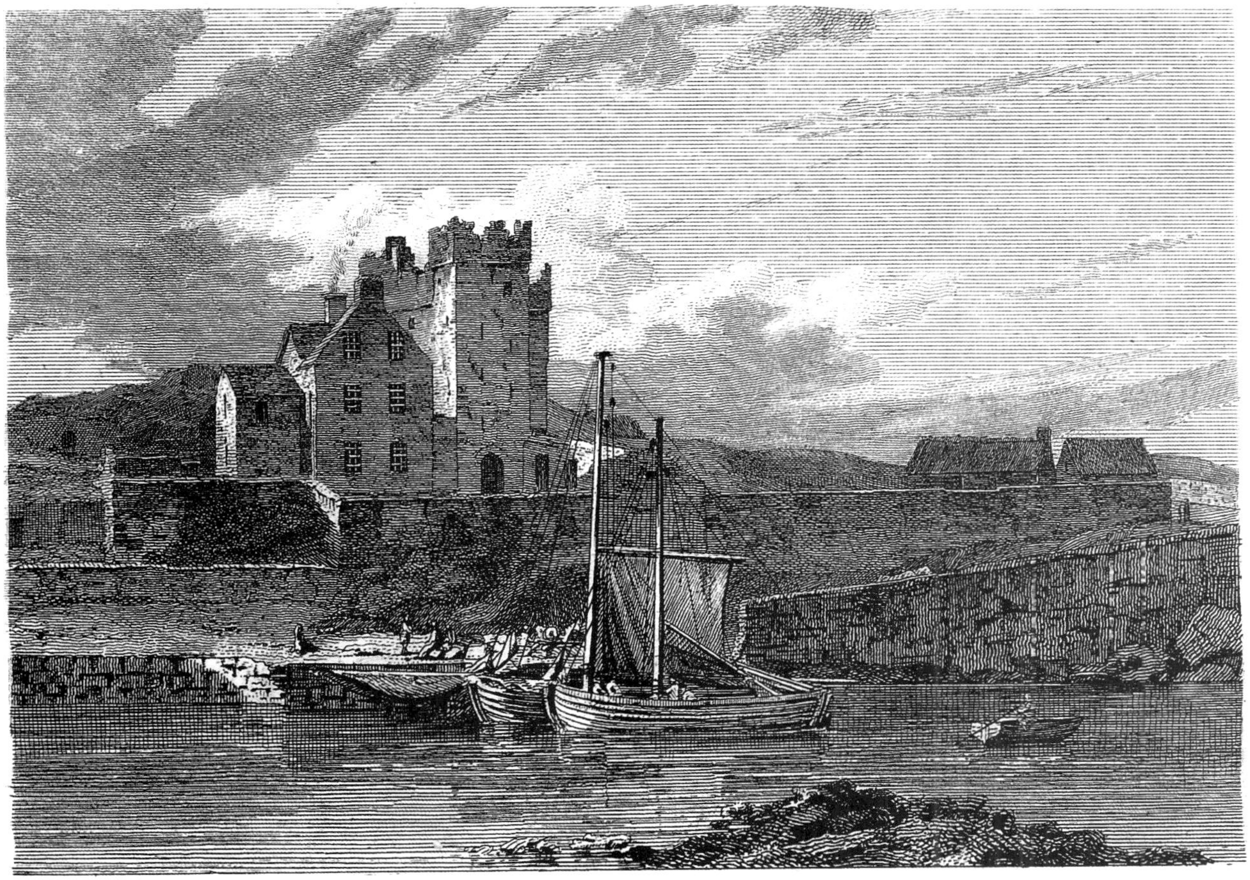

Bullock Castle, Co. of Dublin

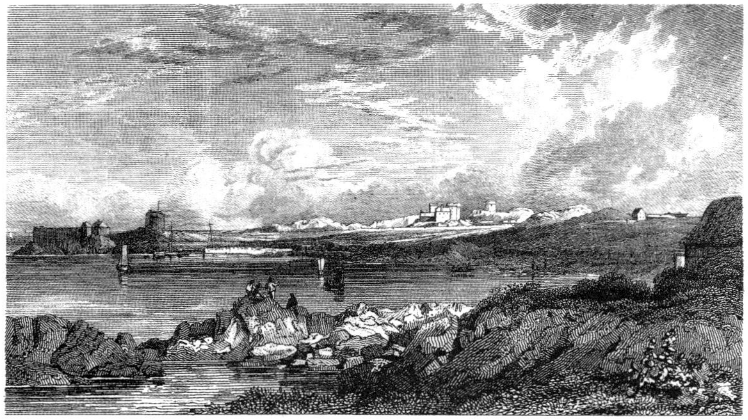

The Coast between Dunleary & Bullock, Co. of Dublin

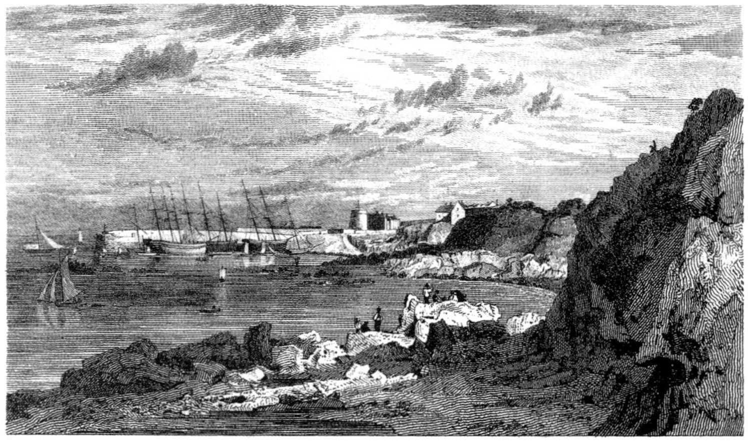

The Old Pier, Dunleary, Co. of Dublin

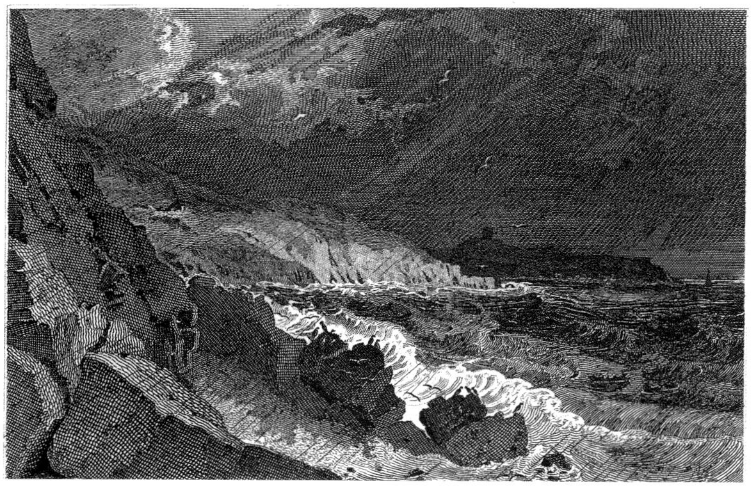

Killiney Bay & Dalkey Island, Co. of Dublin

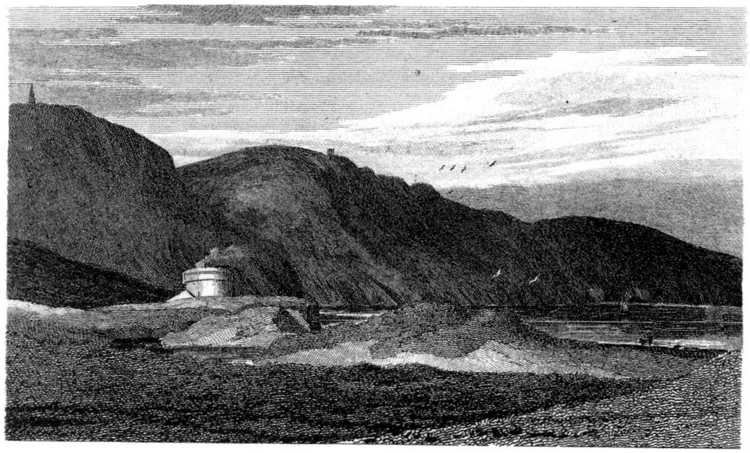

Killiney & Dalkey Hills, Co. of Dublin

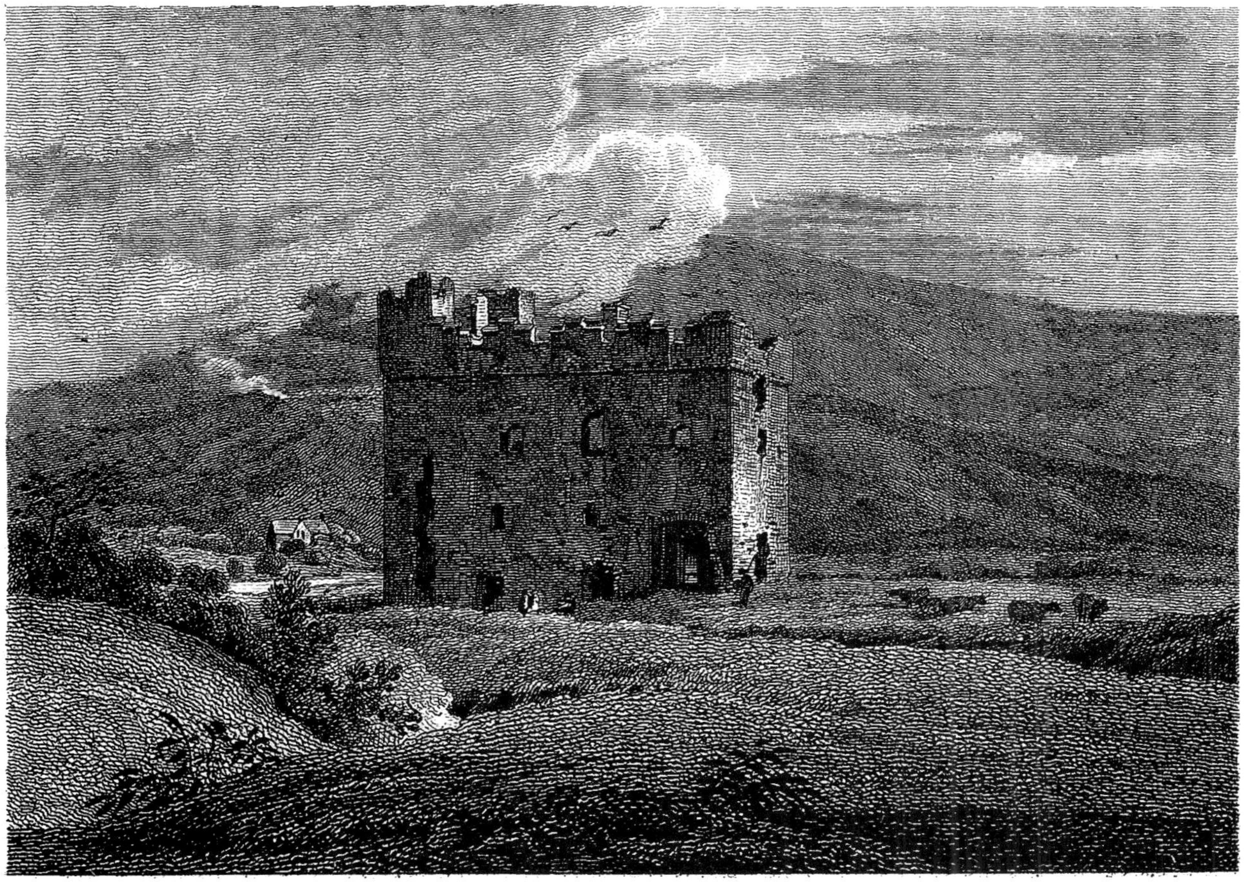

Kilgobbin Castle, Co. of Dublin

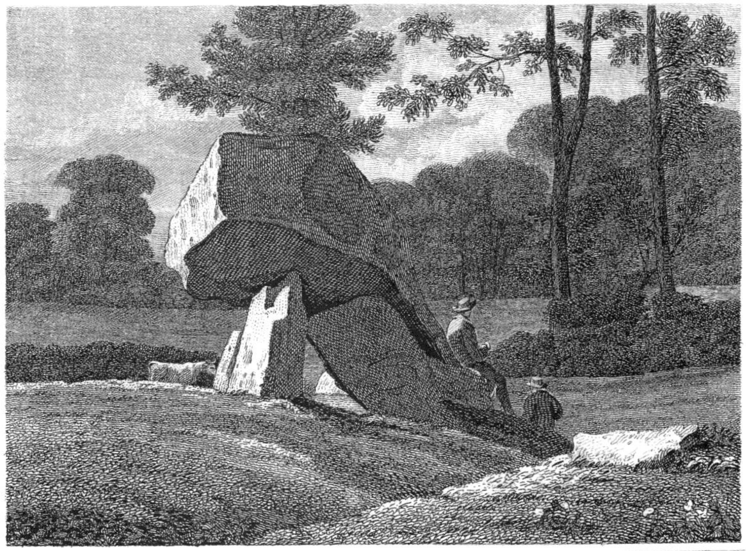

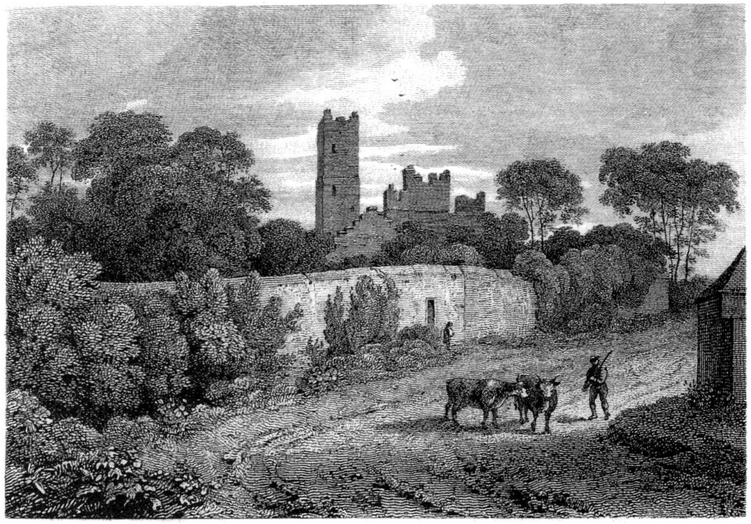

Cromlech at Killiney, Co. of Dublin

Monkstown Castle, Co. of Dublin

Remains of the Castle at Swords, Co. of Dublin

Loughlinstown, Co. of Dublin

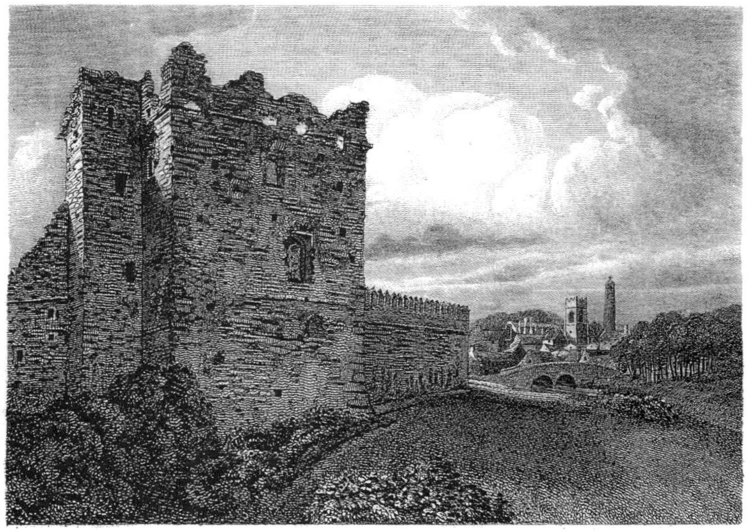

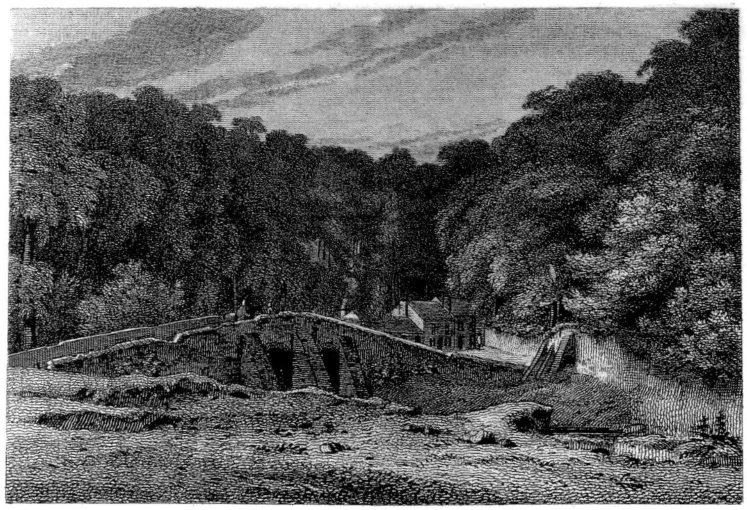

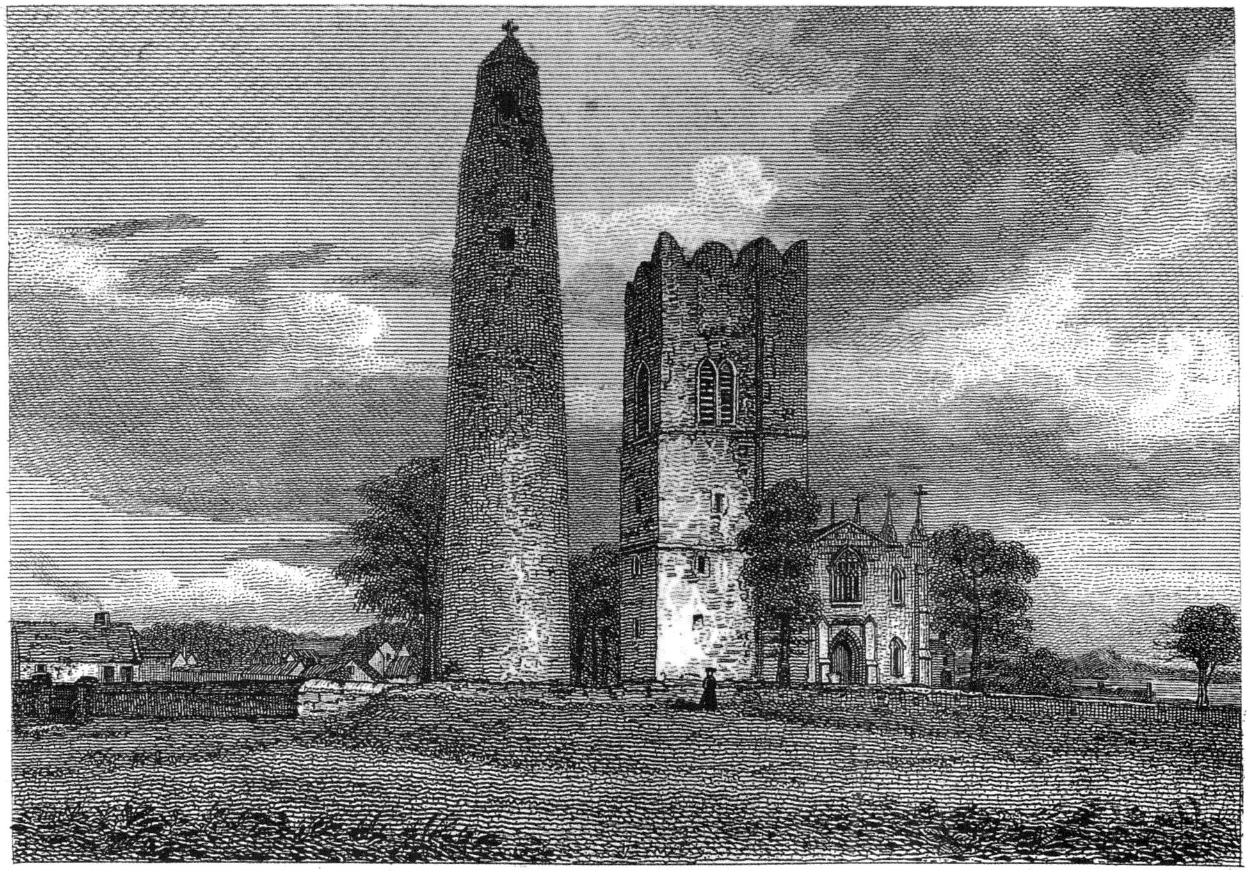

Round Tower, Swords, Co. of Dublin

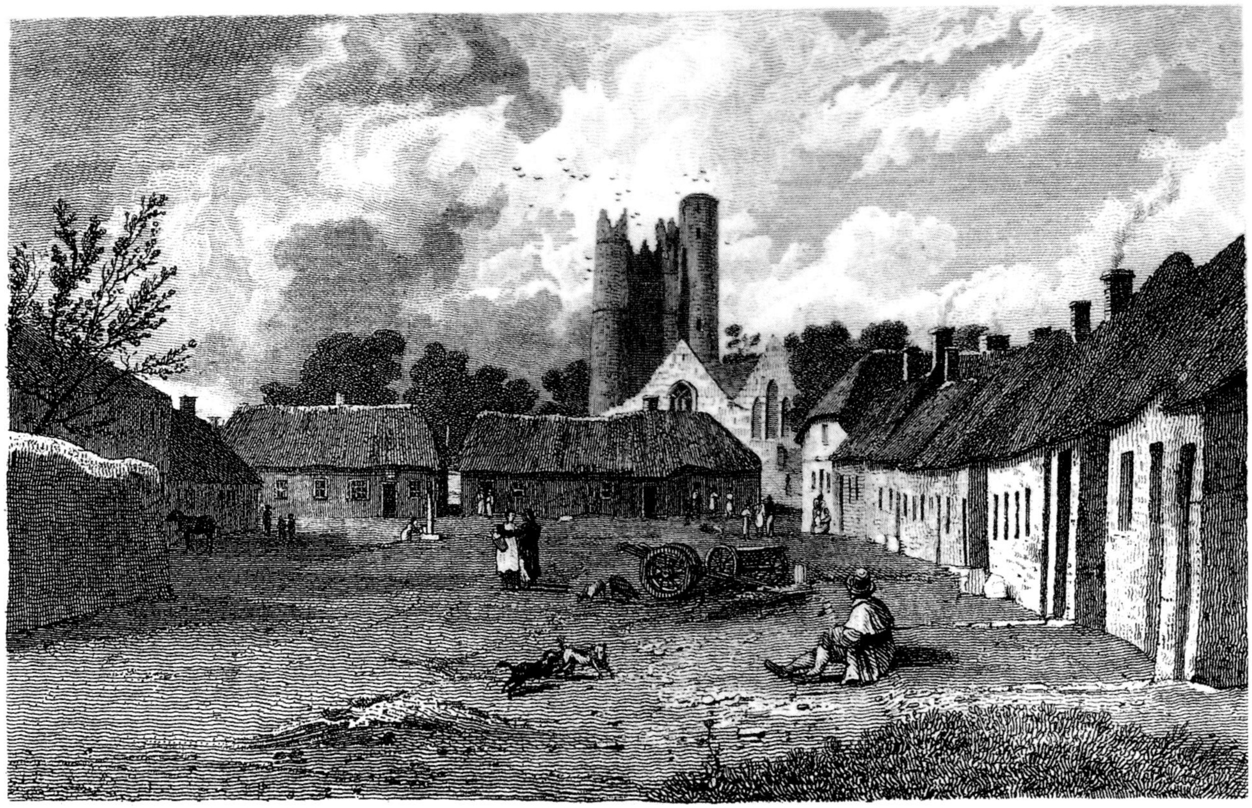

Lusk, Co. of Dublin

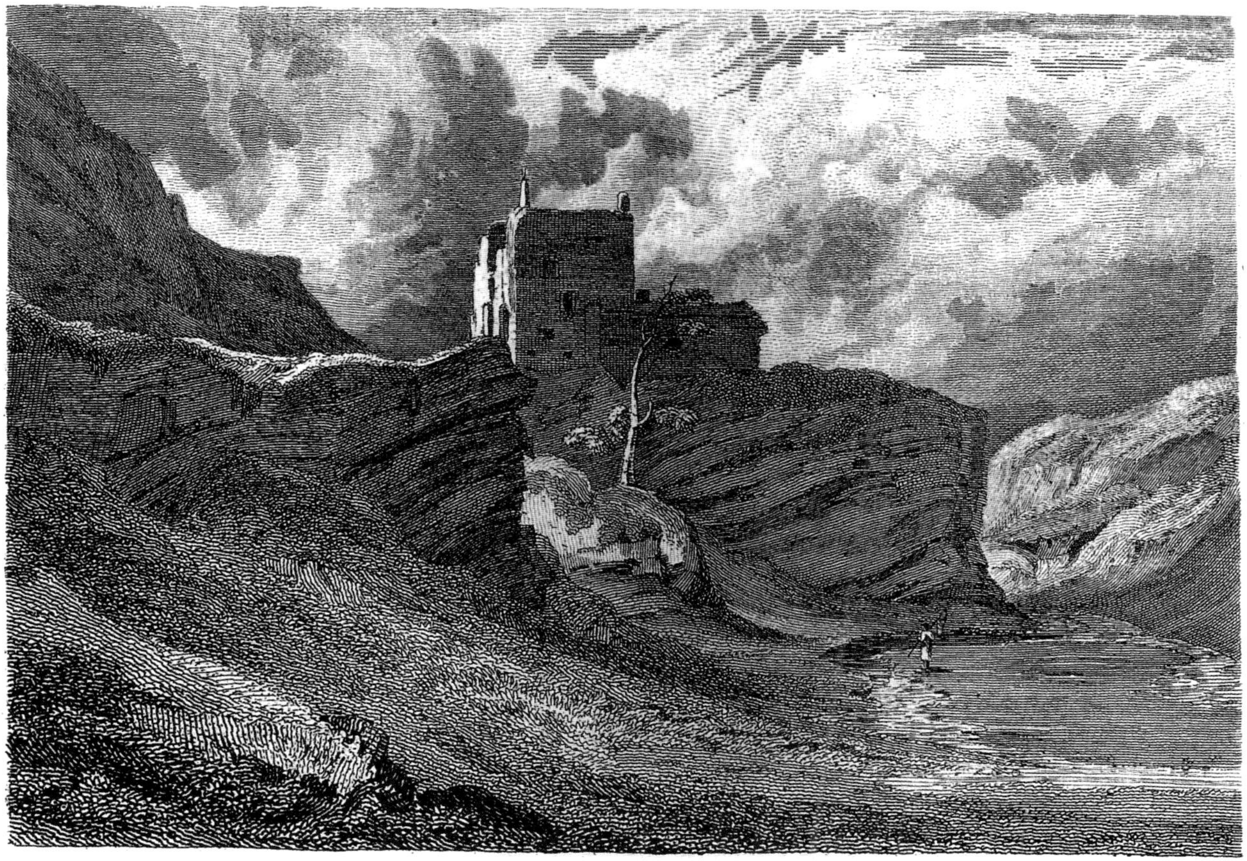

The Black Castle of the Naul, Co. of Dublin

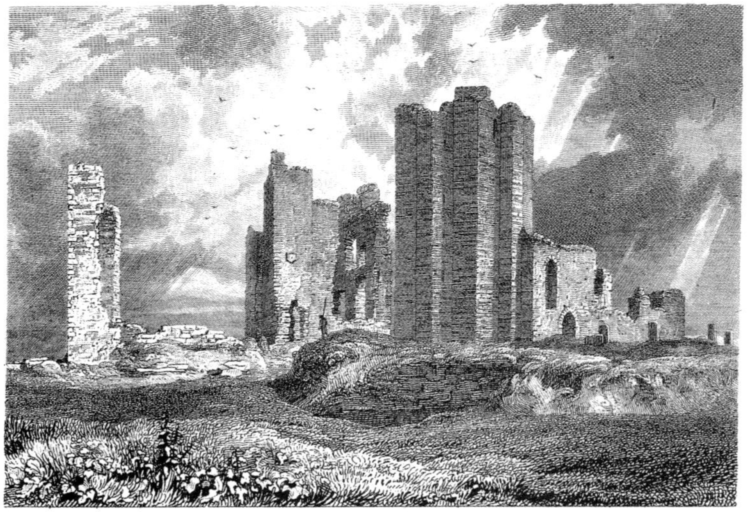

The Church & Castle of Baldongan, Co. of Dublin

The Church of Duleek, Co. of Eastmeath

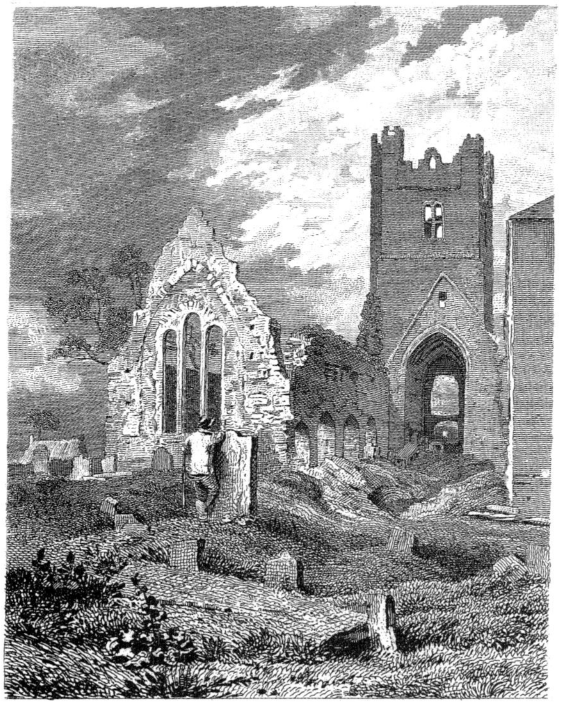

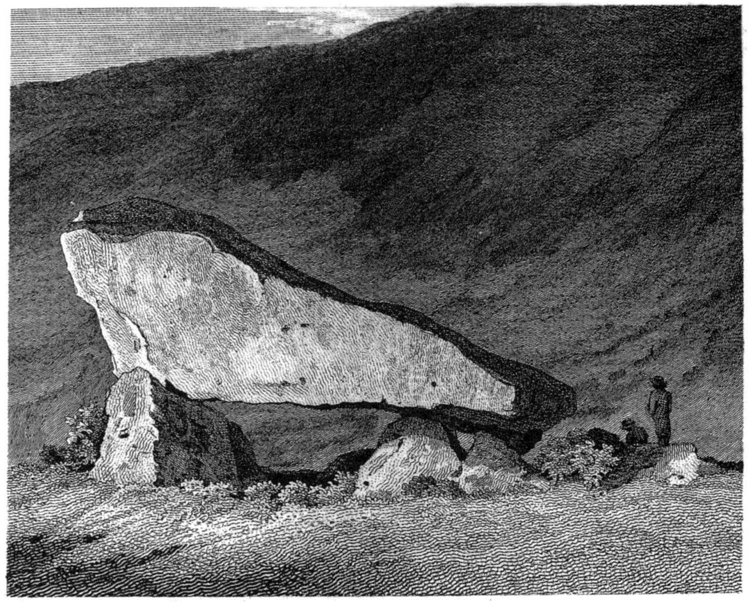

Cromlech at Brennanstown, Co. of Dublin

Tower of the Abbey of St. Mary Magdalen, Drogheda, Co. of Louth

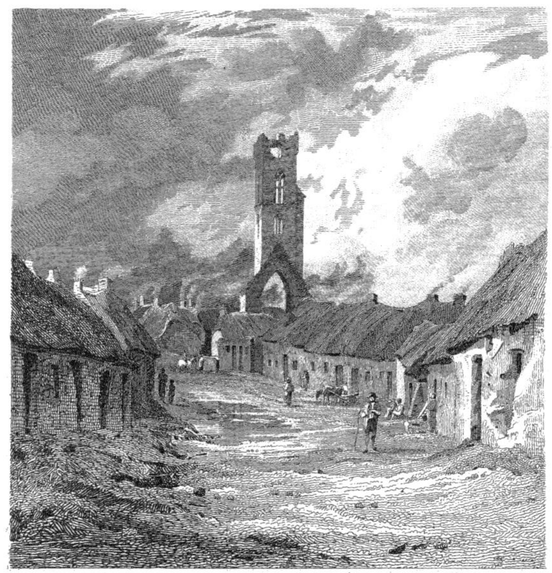

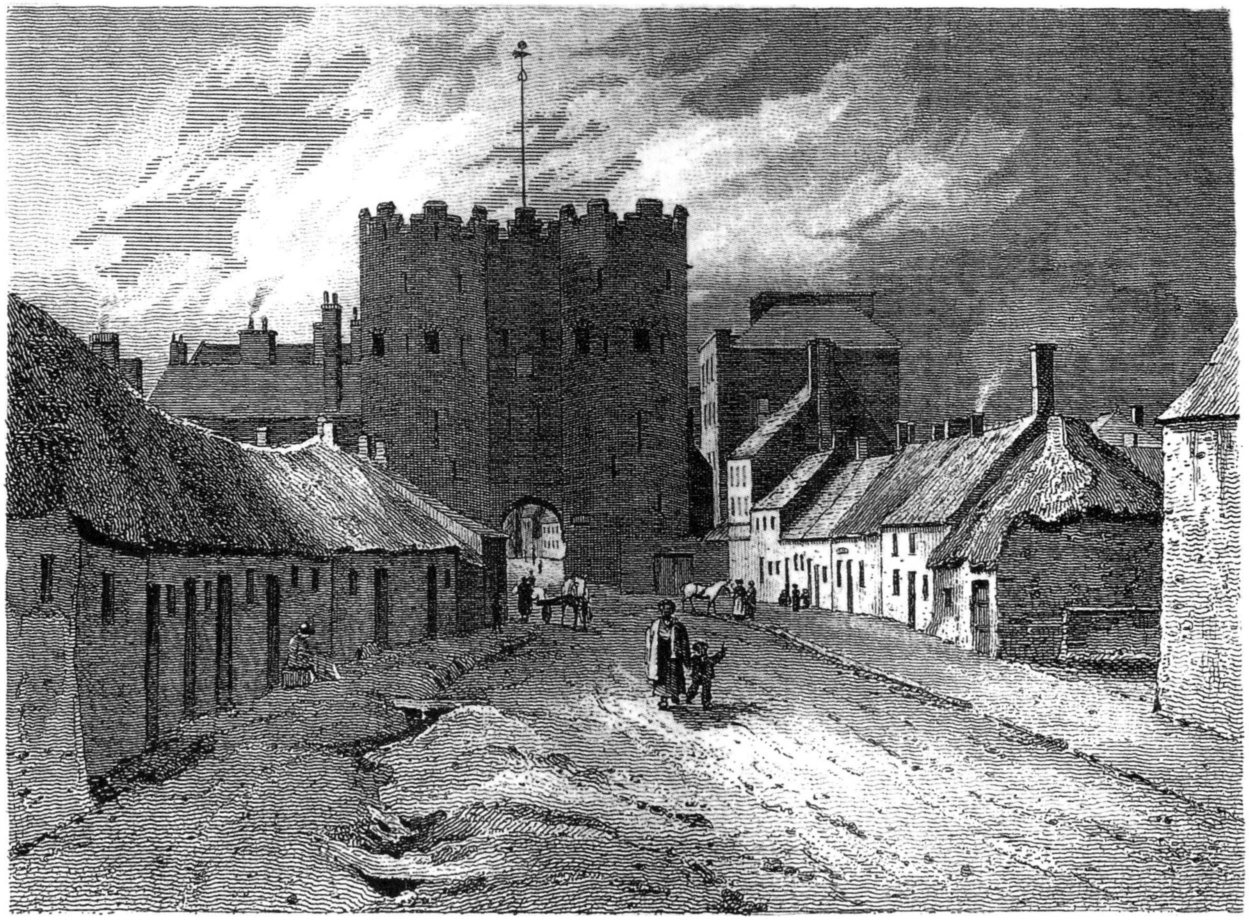

St. Lawrence's Gate, Drogheda, Co. of Louth

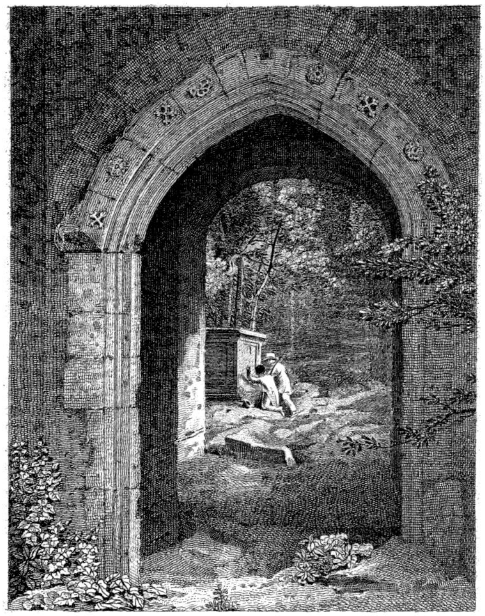

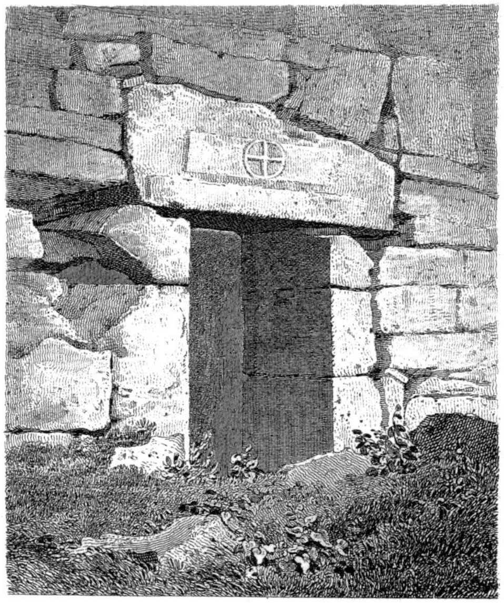

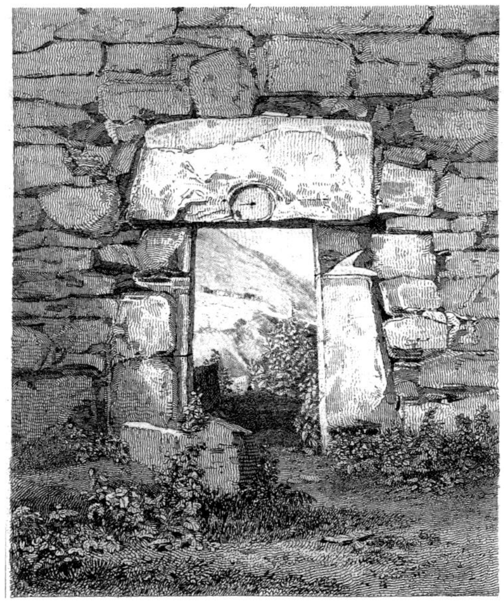

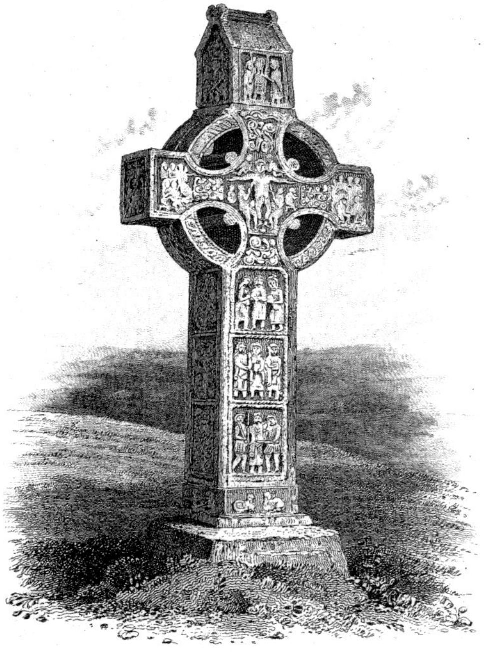

top row

*The Hermitage of St. Eire,
Slane, Co. of Eastmeath*

*The Door of St. Fechin's Church,
Fore, Co. of Westmeath*

*The Door of St. Fechin's Church,
Fore, Co. of Westmeath*

left

*St. Patrick's Cross,
Monasterboice, Co. of Louth*

right

*Stone Cross,
Kells, Eastmeath*

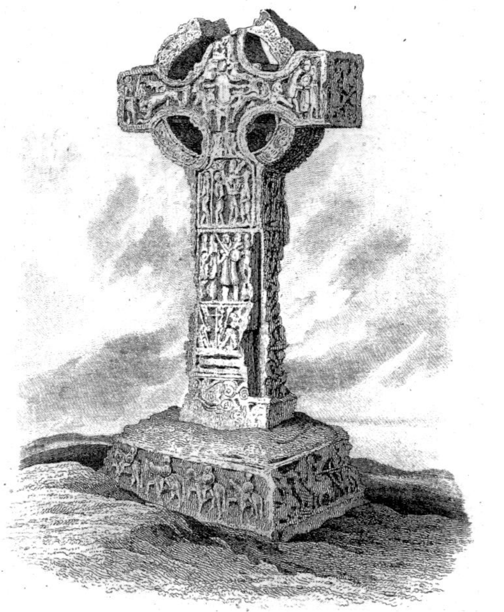

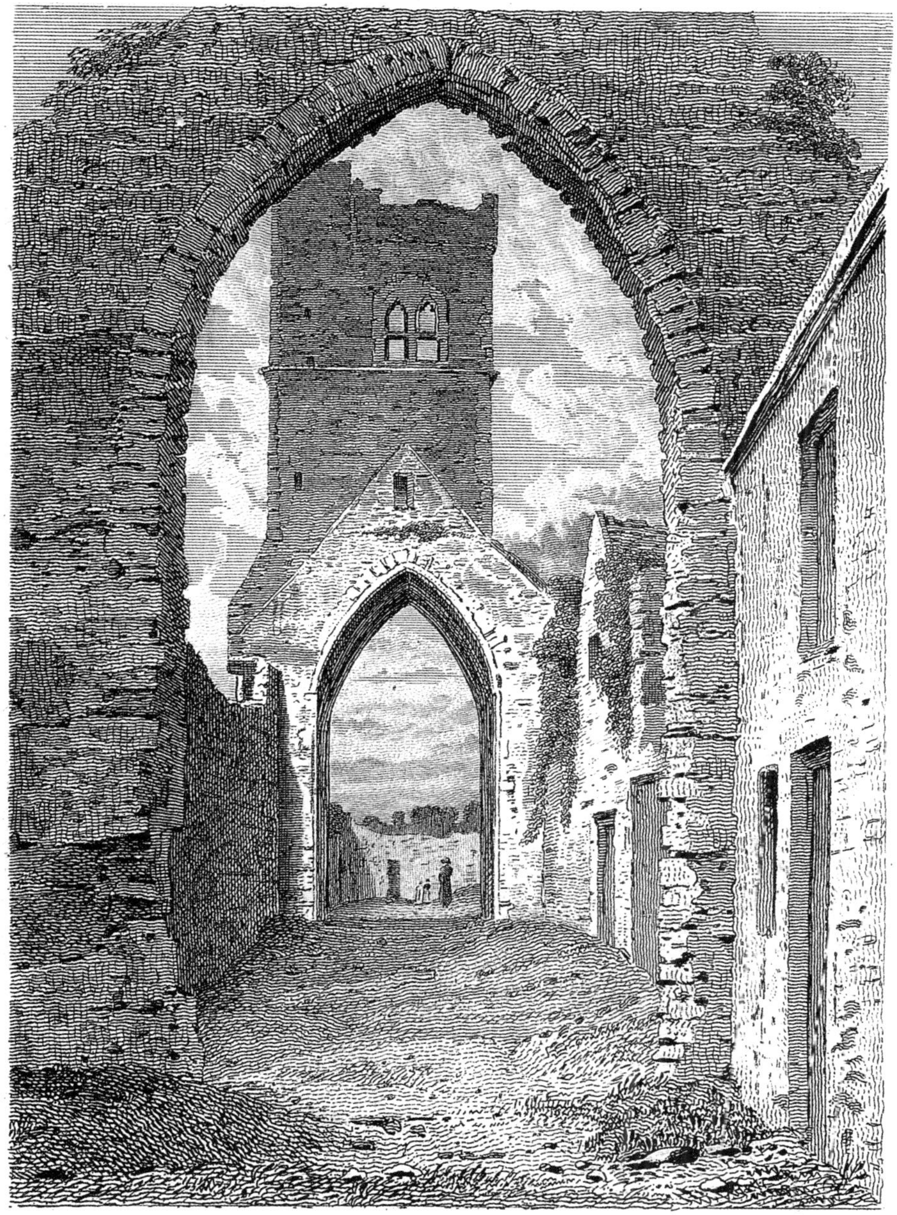

St. Mary's Church, Drogheda, Co. of Louth

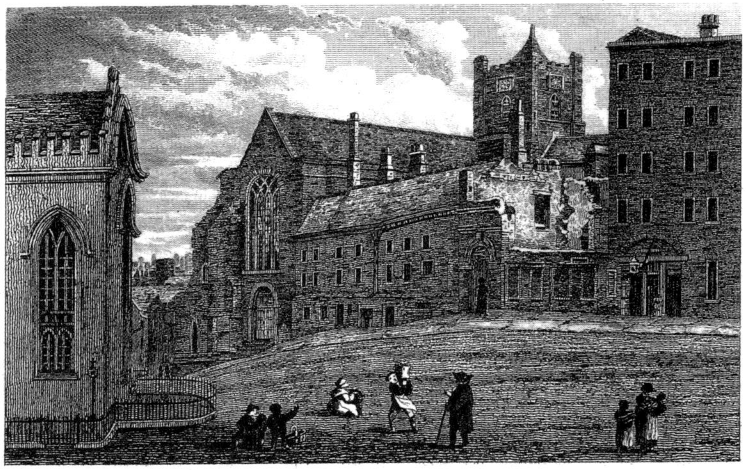

untitled [*South View of Christ's Cathedral, Dublin*]

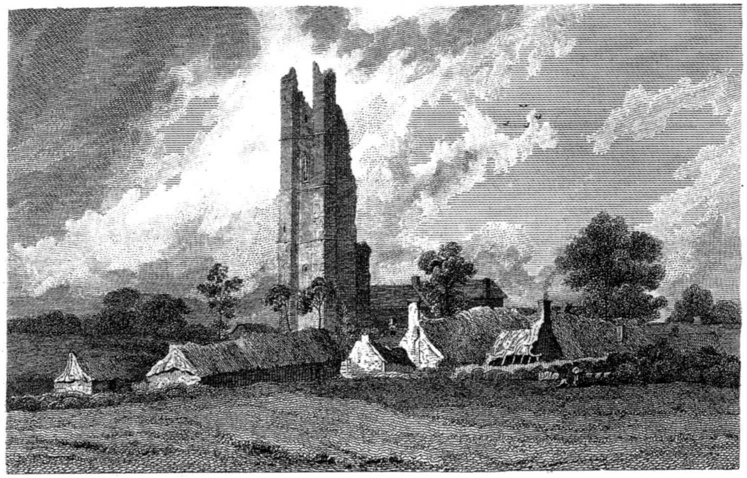

Remains of the Yellow Tower, Trim, Co. of Eastmeath

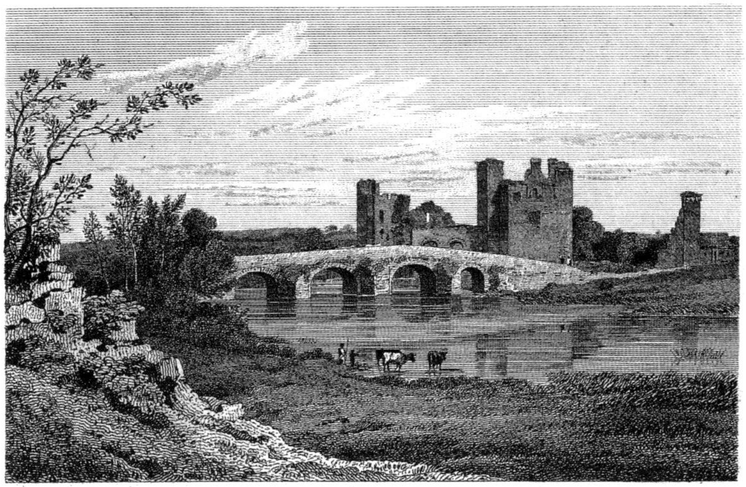

The Bridge and Priory, Newtown, Co. of Eastmeath

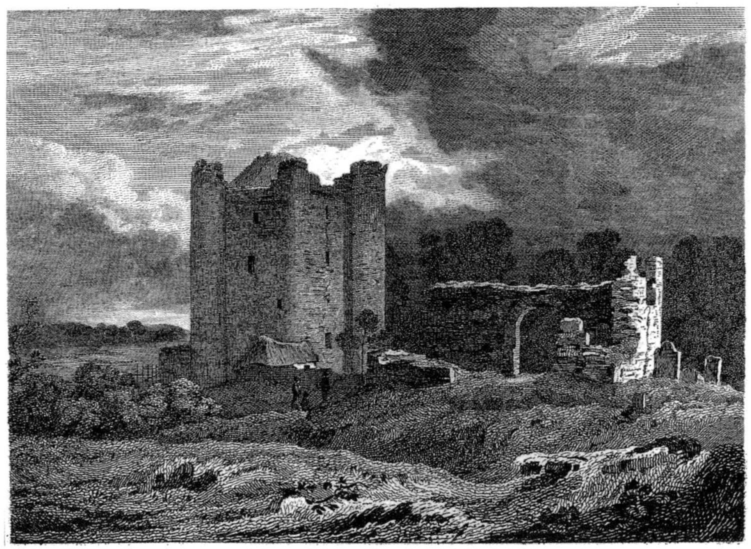

The Church & Castle of Scurlogstown, Co. of Eastmeath

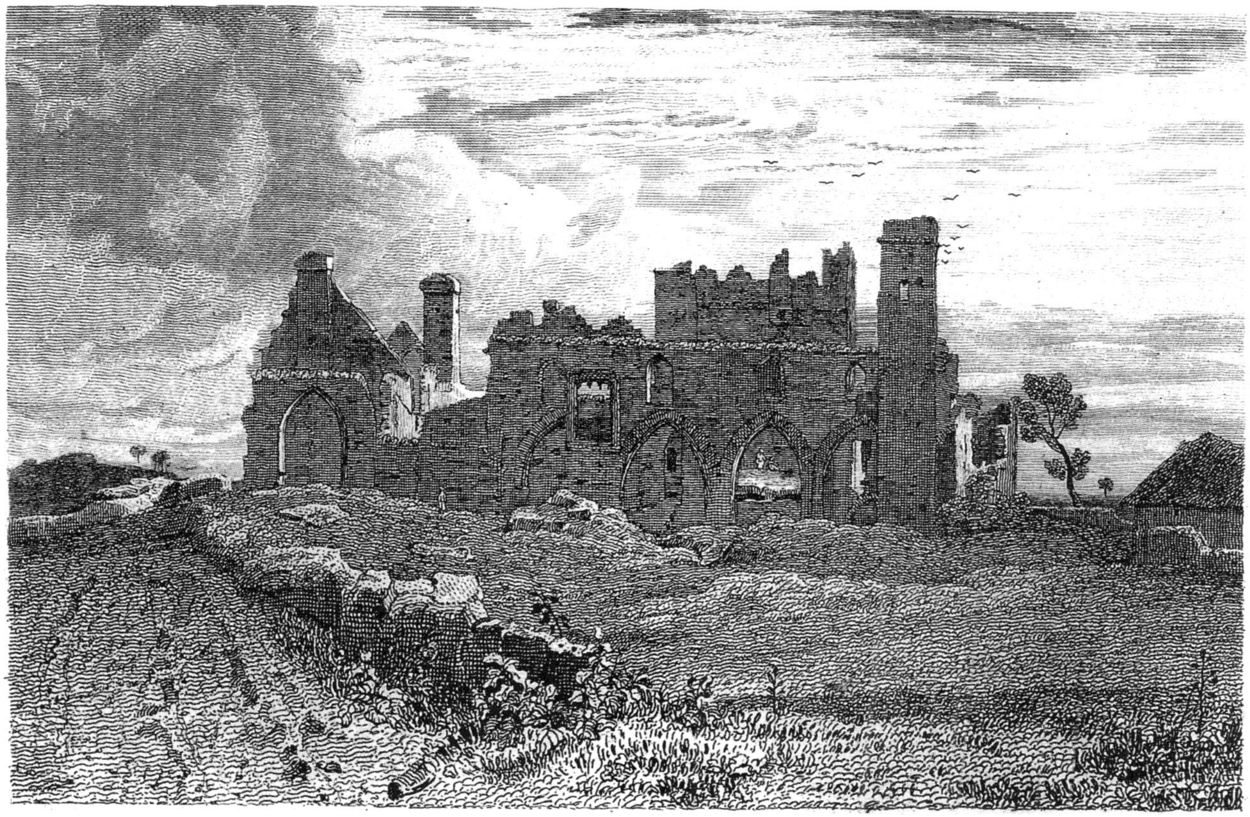

Bective Abbey, Co. *of Eastmeath*

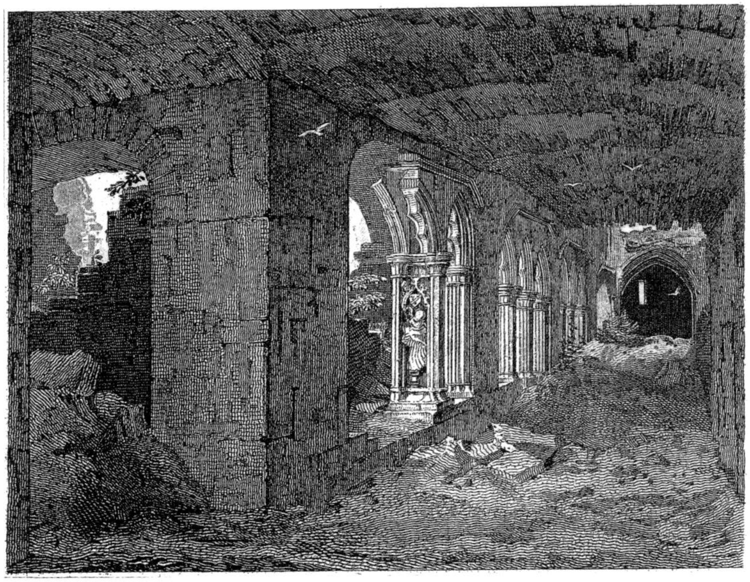

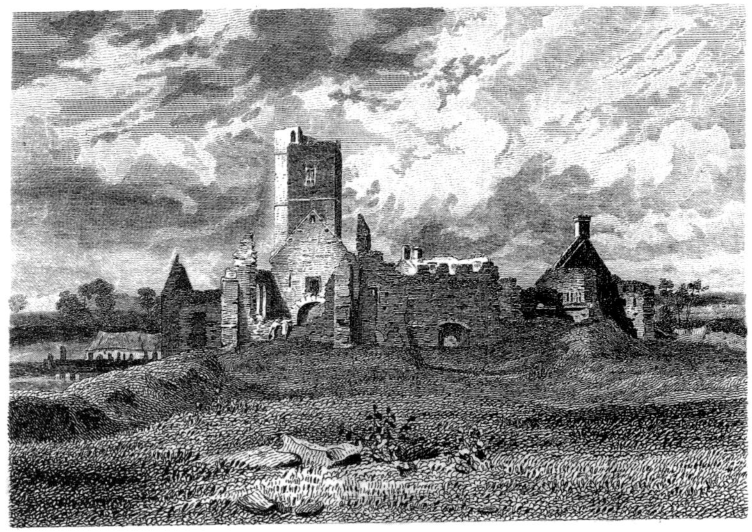

The Abbey of Multifernam, Co. of Eastmeath

The Lady's Finger & Maiden Tower, Co. of Eastmeath

Interior of the Cloisters, Bective Abbey, Co. of Eastmeath

The Castle at Clonmacnois, King's County

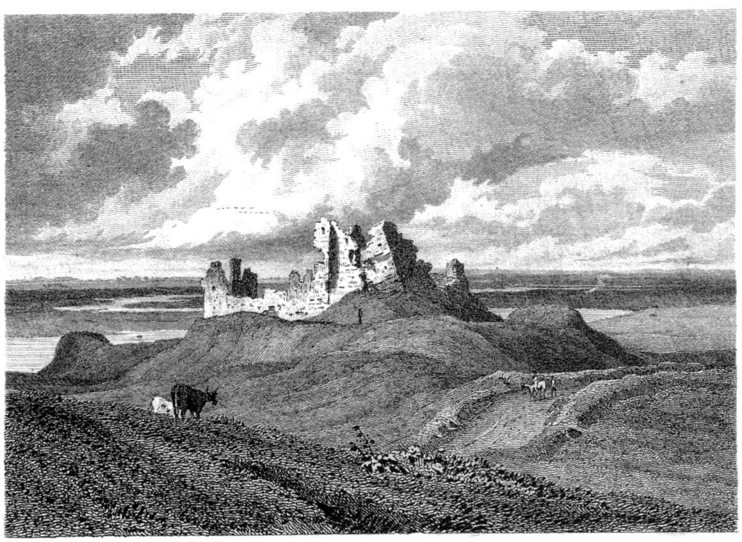

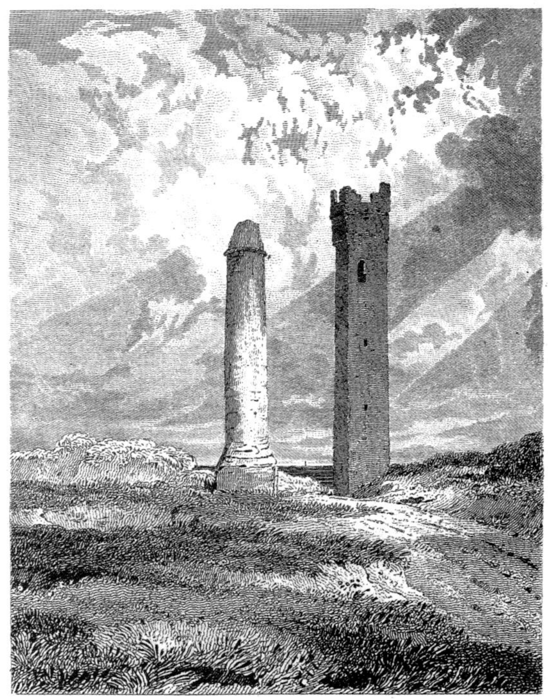

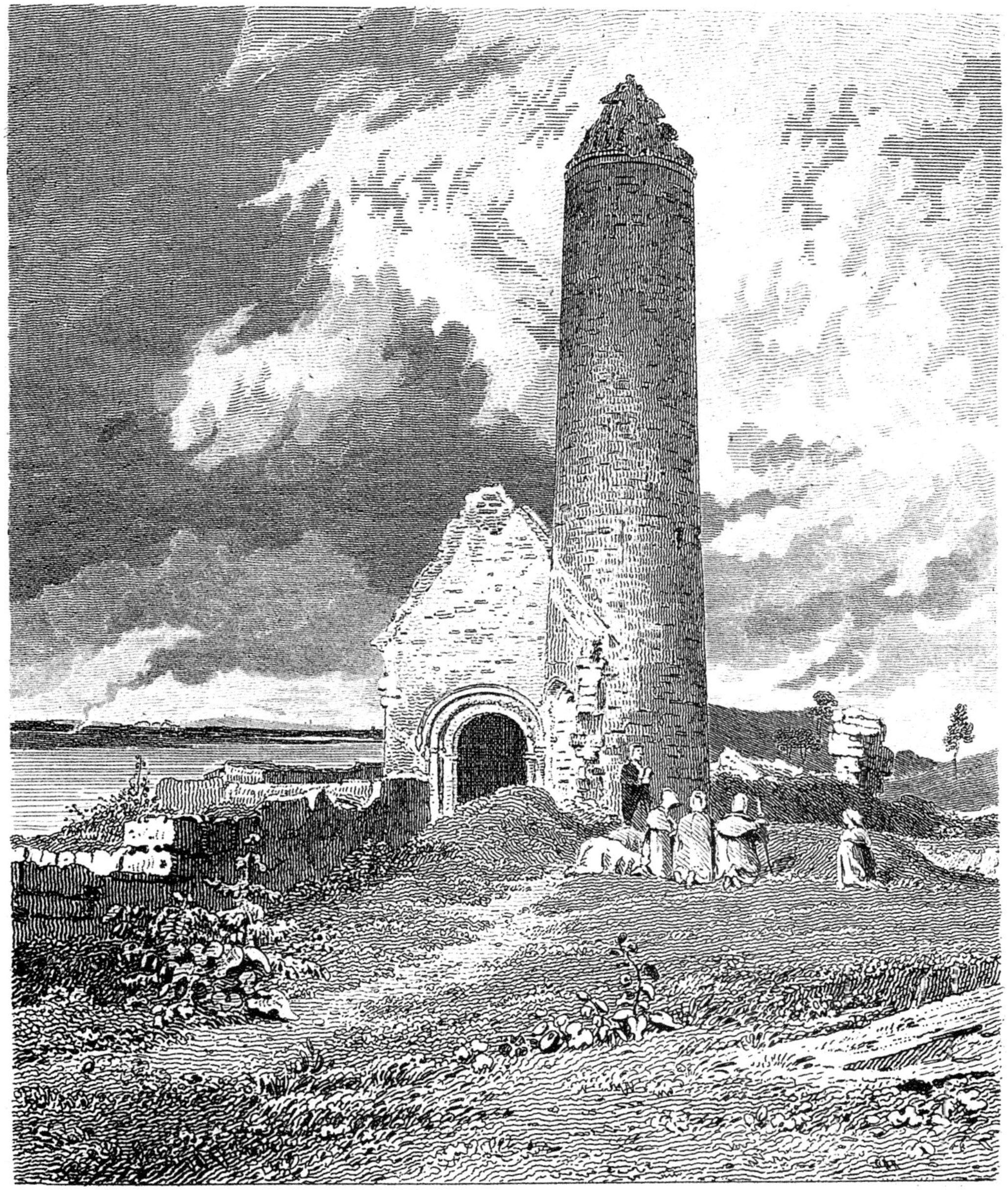

Macarthy's Church & Tower, Clonmacnois, King's County

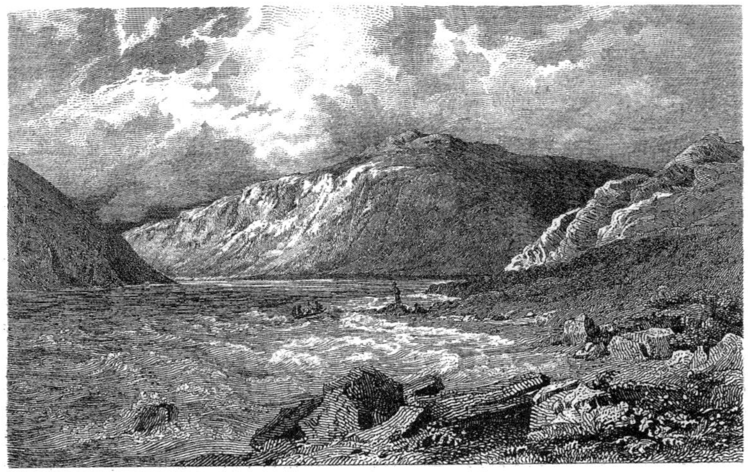

Lough Dan, Co. of Wicklow

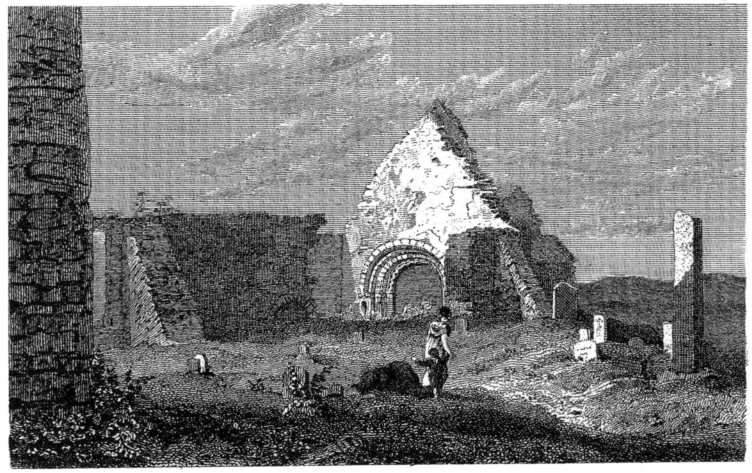

Remains of the Church and Round Tower, Old Kilcullen, Co. of Kildare

The Castle & Abbey of Castledermot, Co. of Kildare

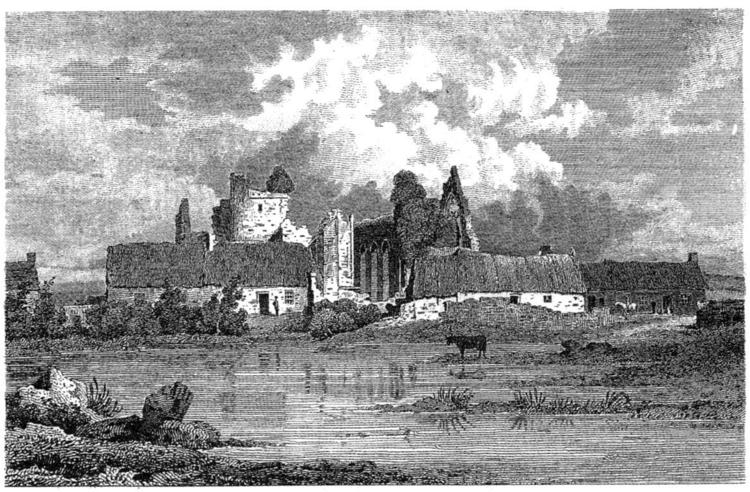

The East Window of the Abbey, Castledermot, Co. of Kildare

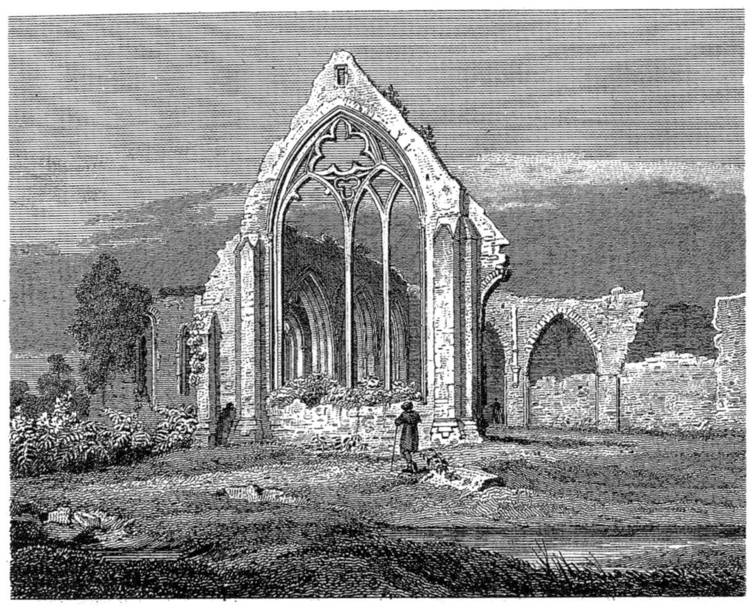

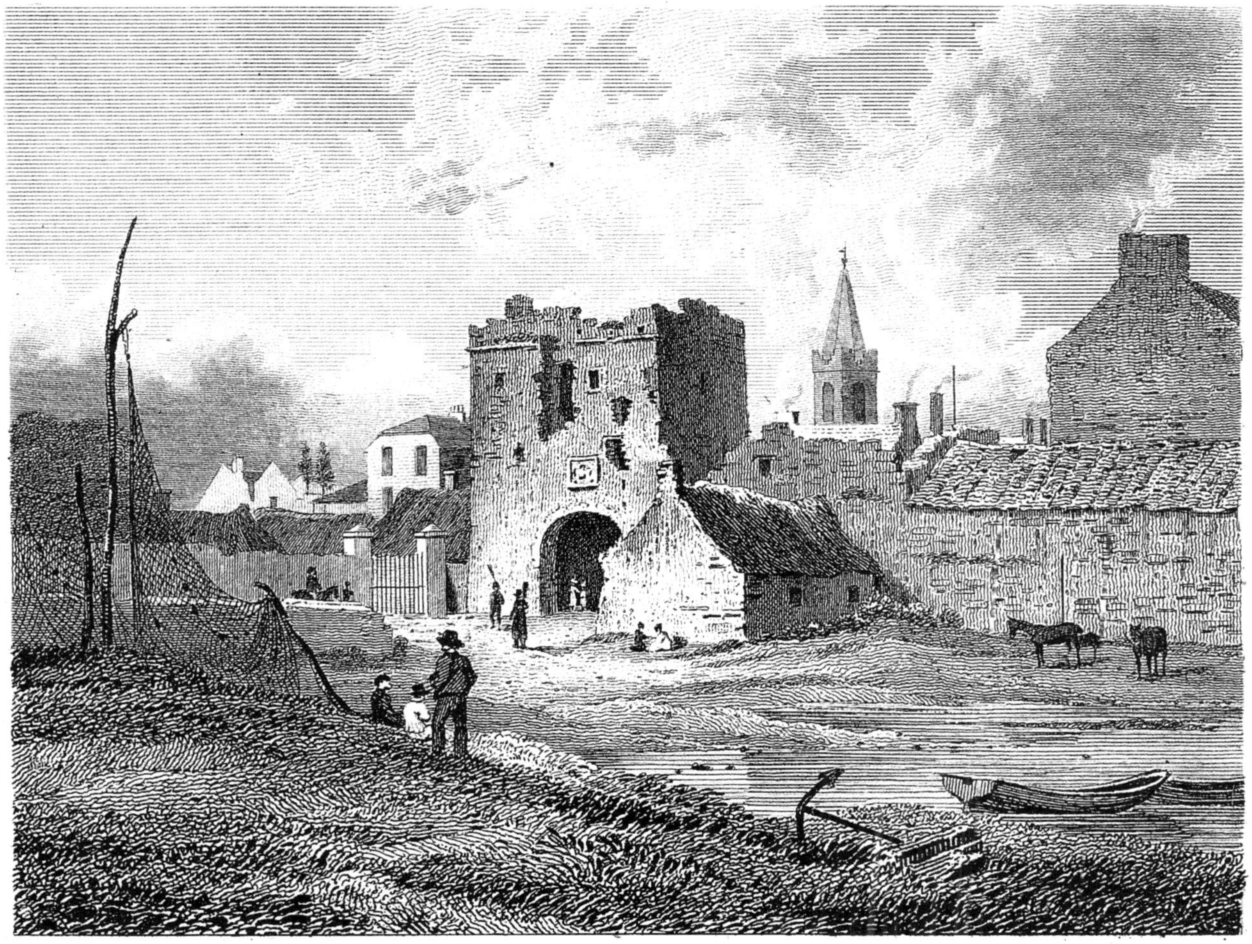

North Gate, Athlone

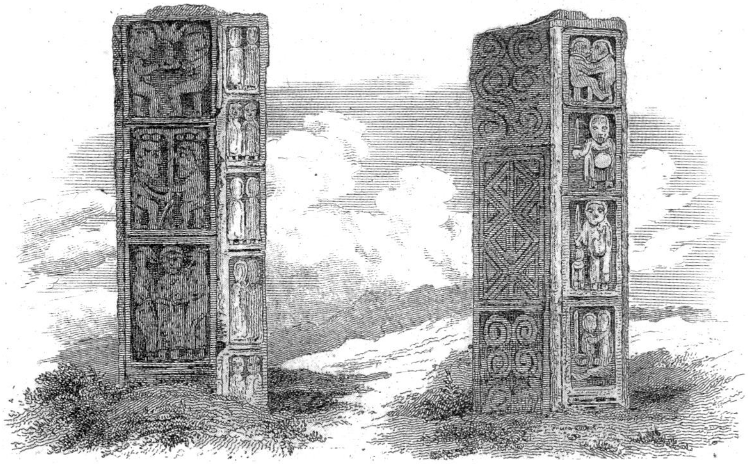

Remains of a Stone Cross, Castledermot, Co. of Kildare

Banagher, King's County

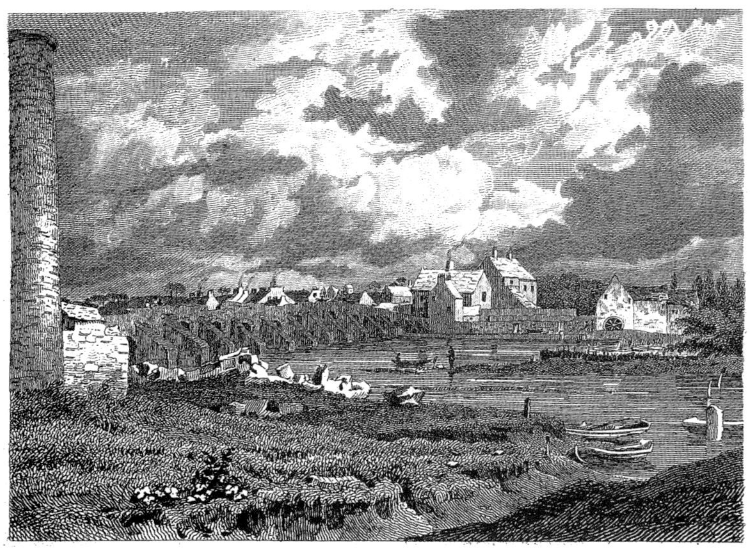

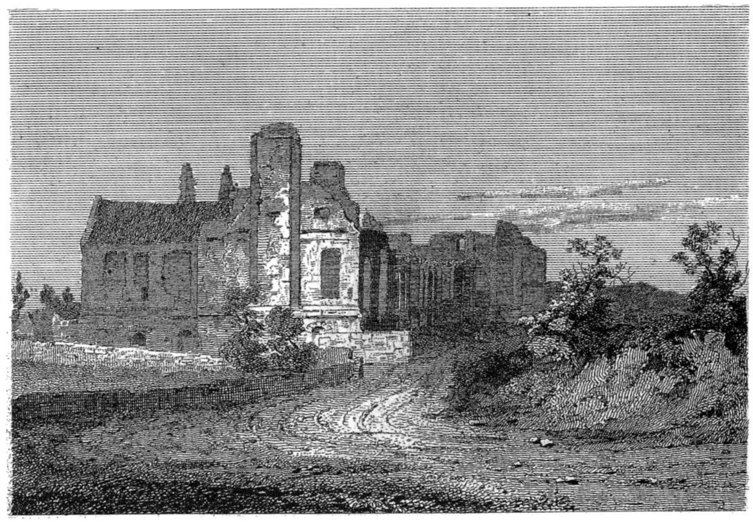

Jigginstown Castle, Co. of Dublin

Poll a Phuca Waterfall, Co. of Dublin

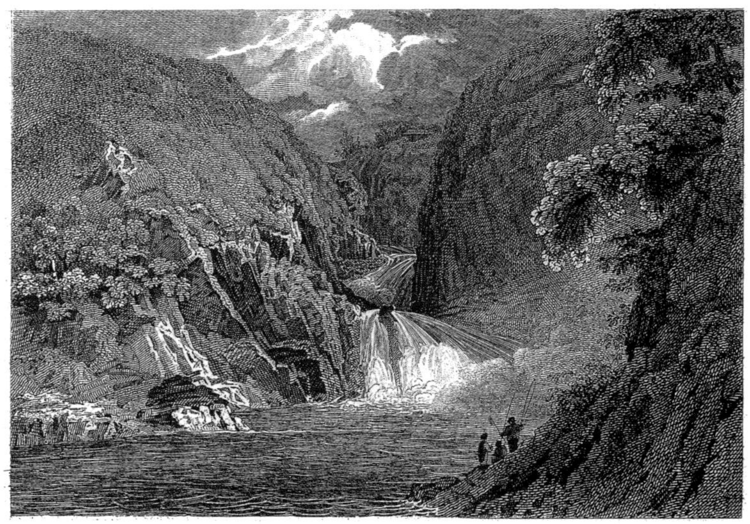

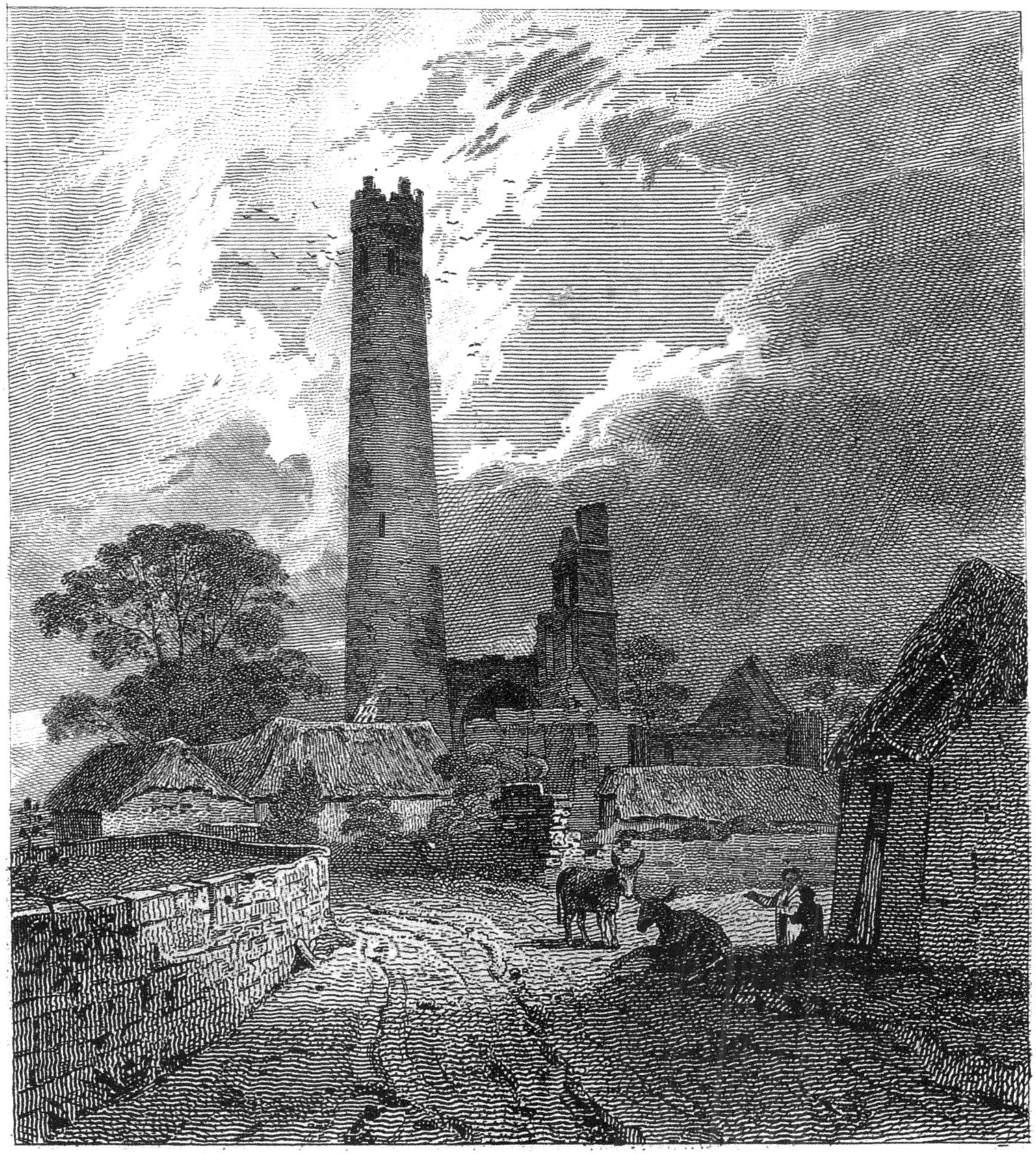

Round Tower, Kildare

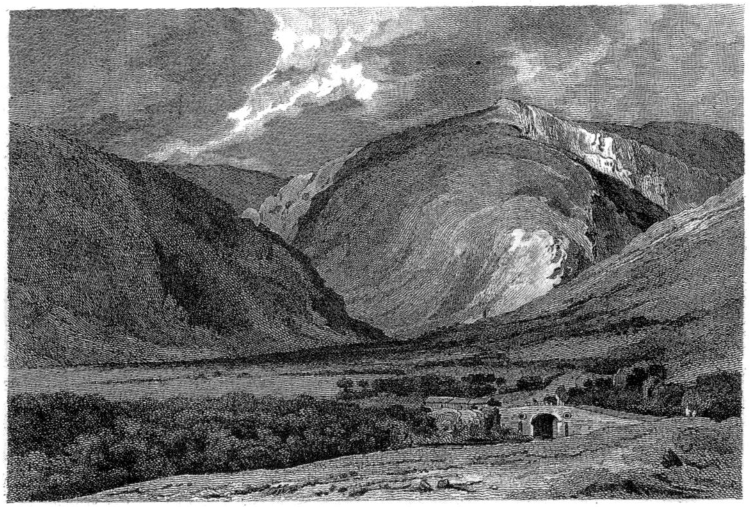

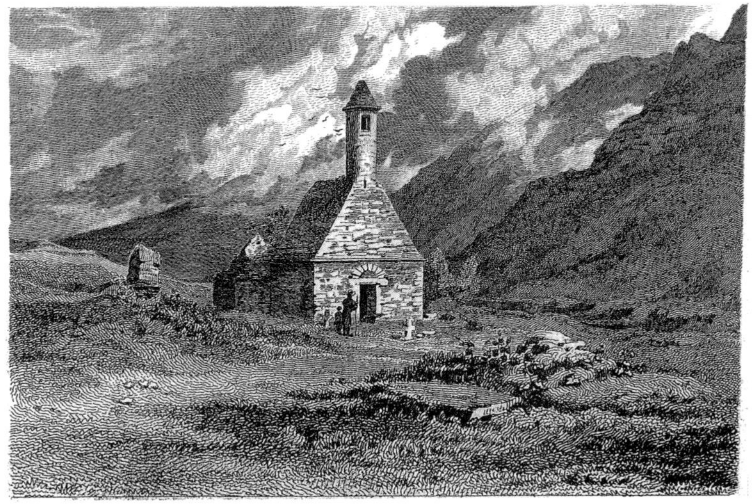

St. Kevin's Kitchen, Glandalough, Co. of Wicklow

Powerscourt Waterfall, Co. of Wicklow

Lara Bridge, entrance to Glandalough, Co. of Wicklow

Our Lady's Church, Glandalough, Co. of Wicklow

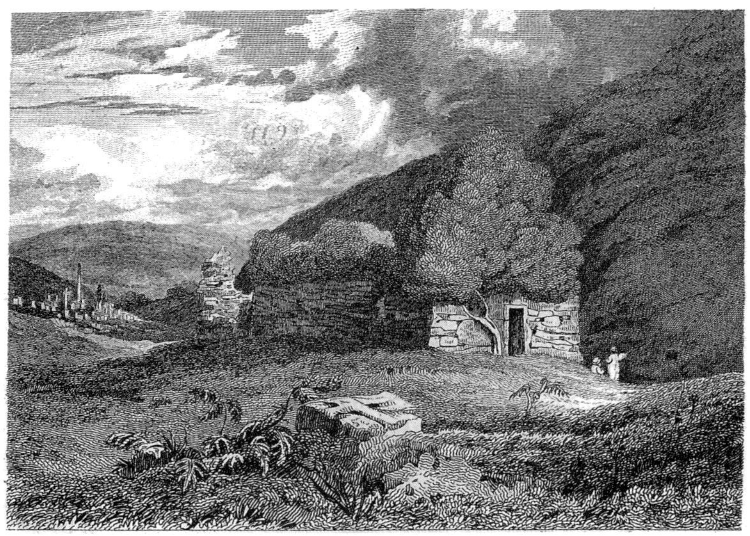

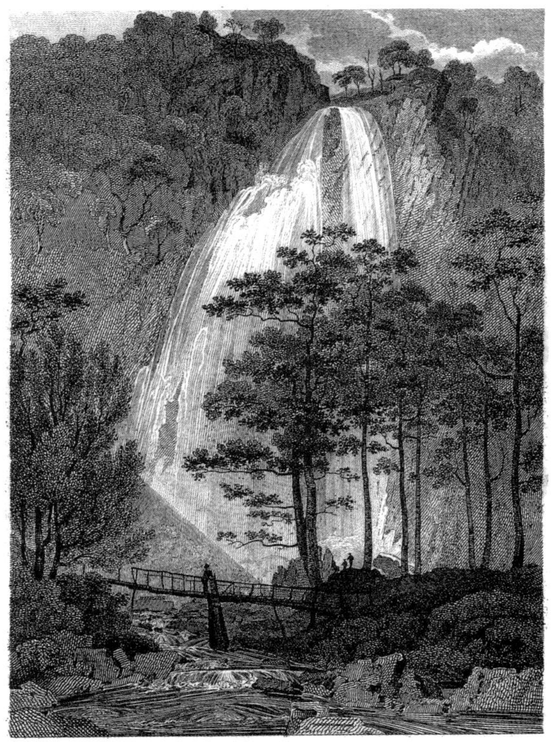

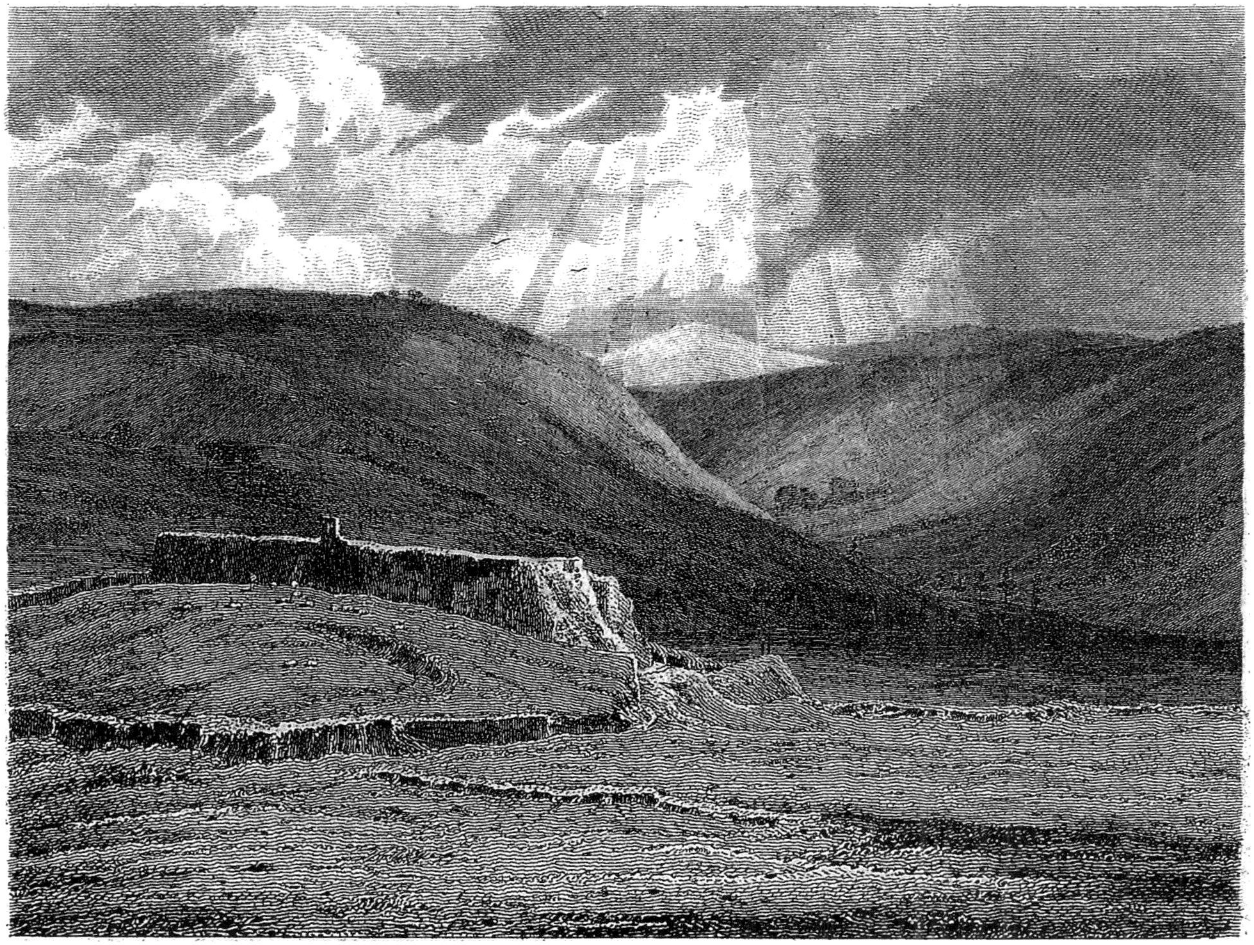

Castle Keivin, Co. of Wicklow

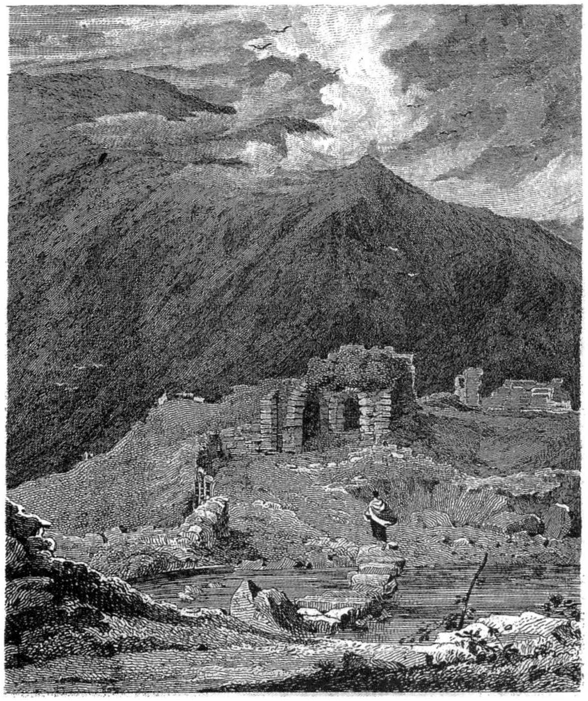

Ancient Archway, Glandalough, Co. of Wicklow

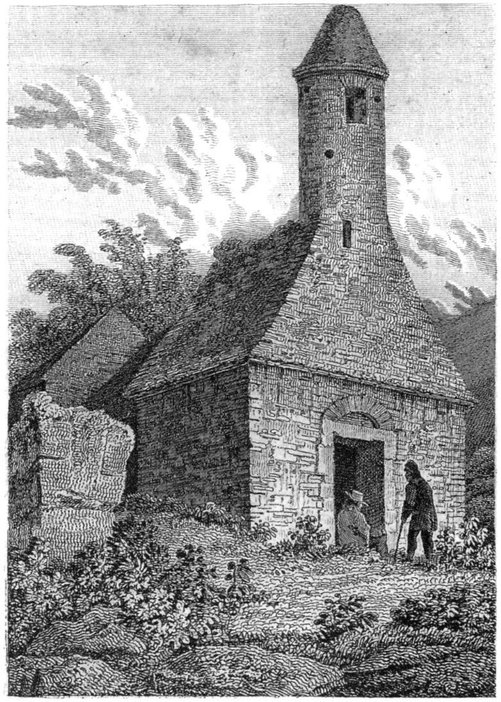

untitled [*St. Kevin's Kitchen, Glandalough, Co. Wicklow*]

View at Mount-Usher, near Newrath Bridge, Co. of Wicklow

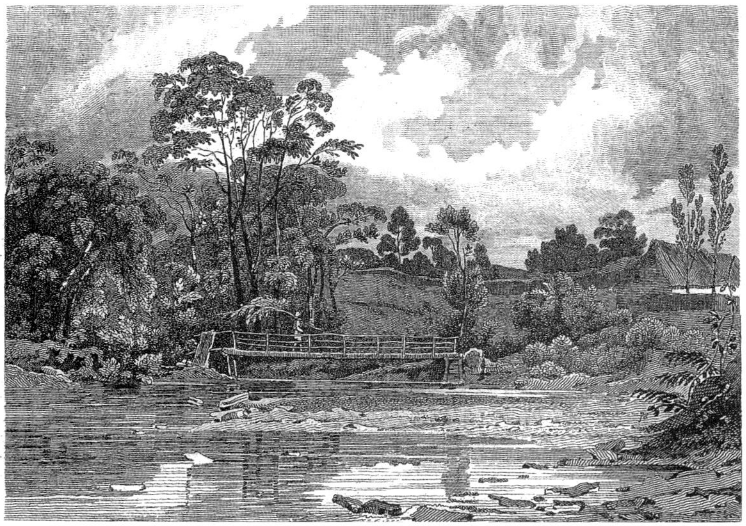

Lough Bray, Co. of Wicklow

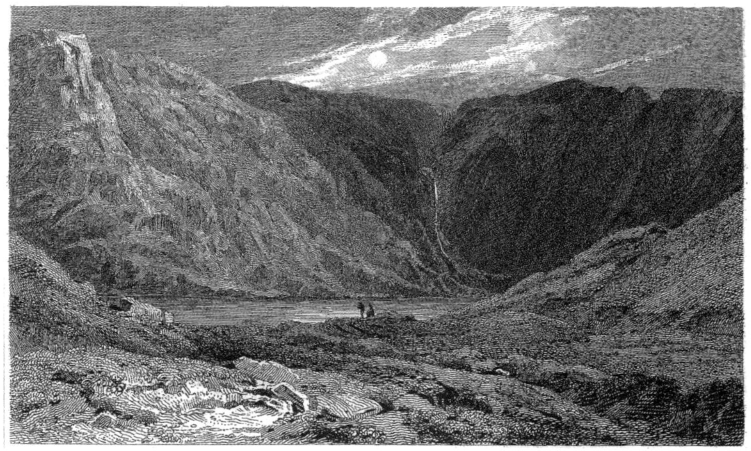

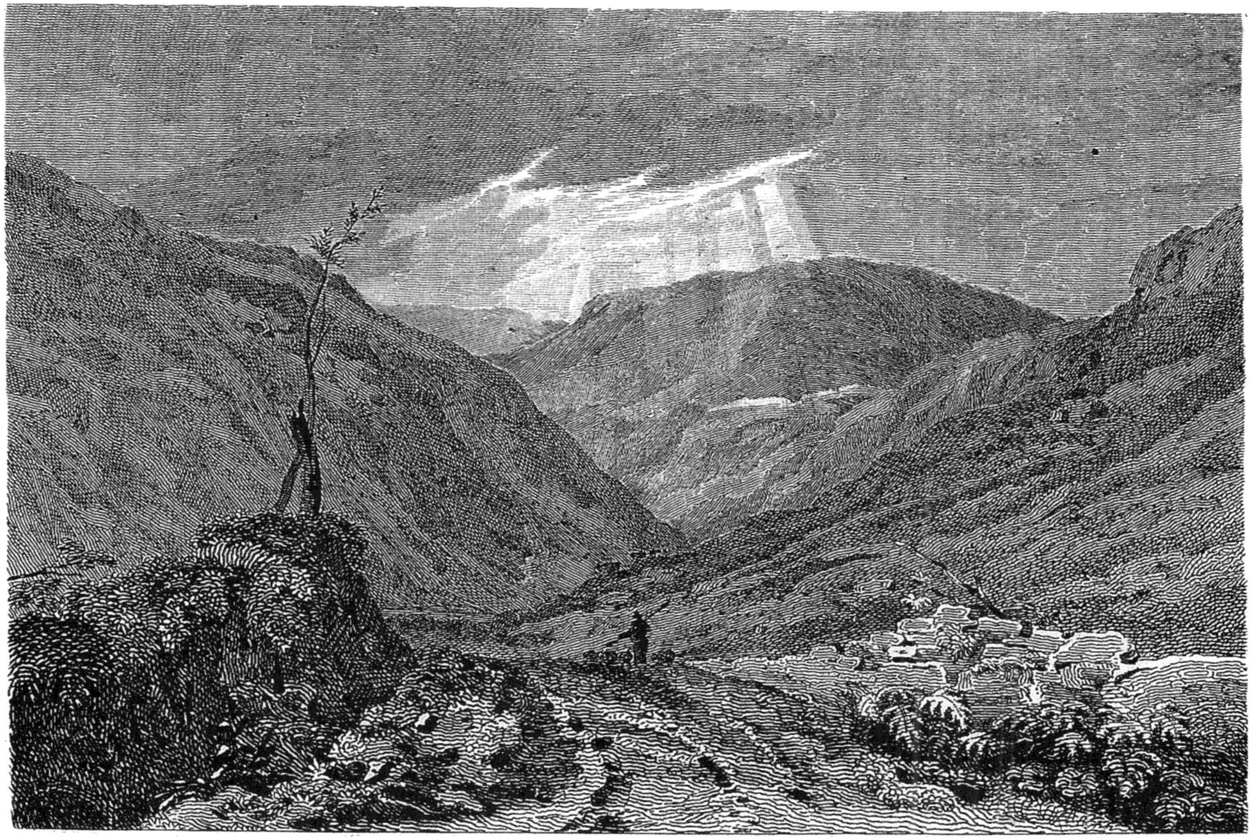

Glen Malure, Co. of Wicklow

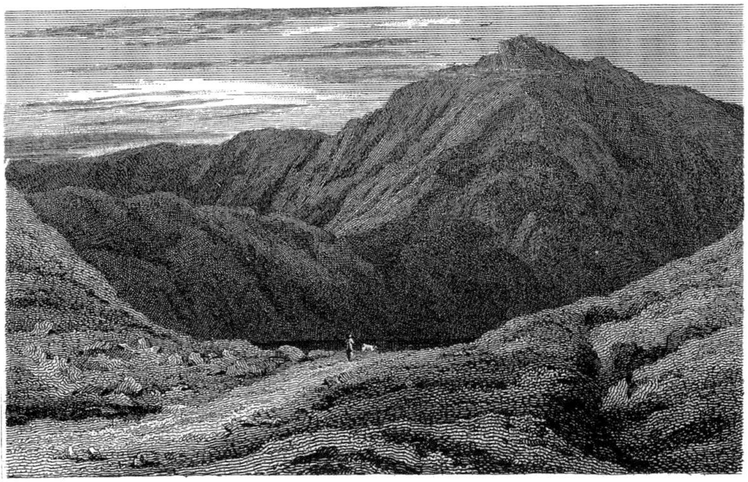

Eagle Rock, Lough Bray, Co. of Wicklow

Howth Castle, The Seat of the Rt. Honble. the Earl of Howth, Co. of Dublin

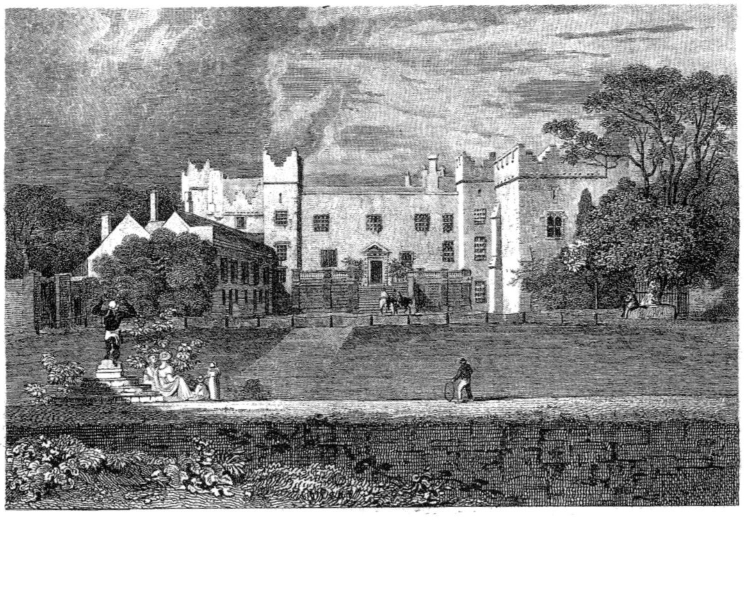

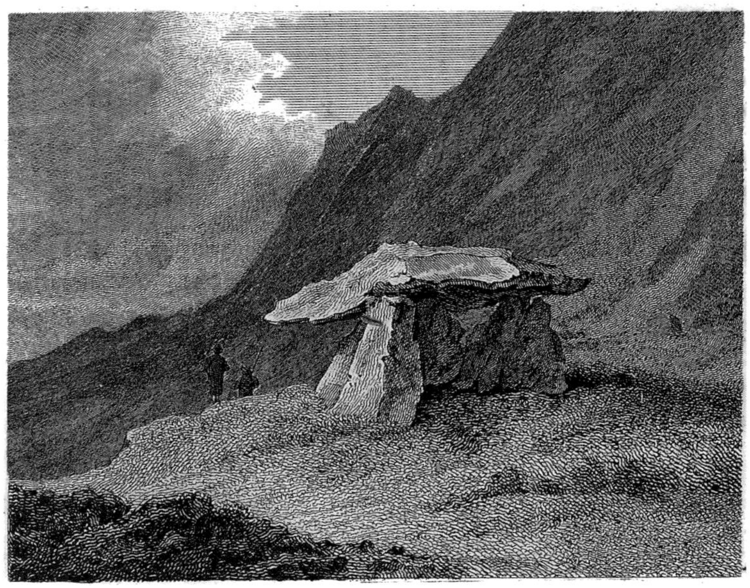

Cromlech on Shankhill, Co. of Dublin

Round Tower, Clondalkin, Co. of Dublin

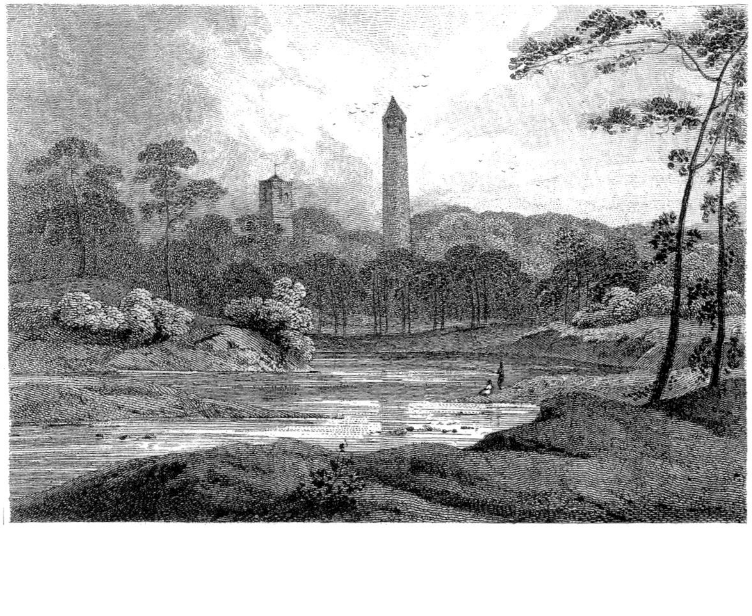

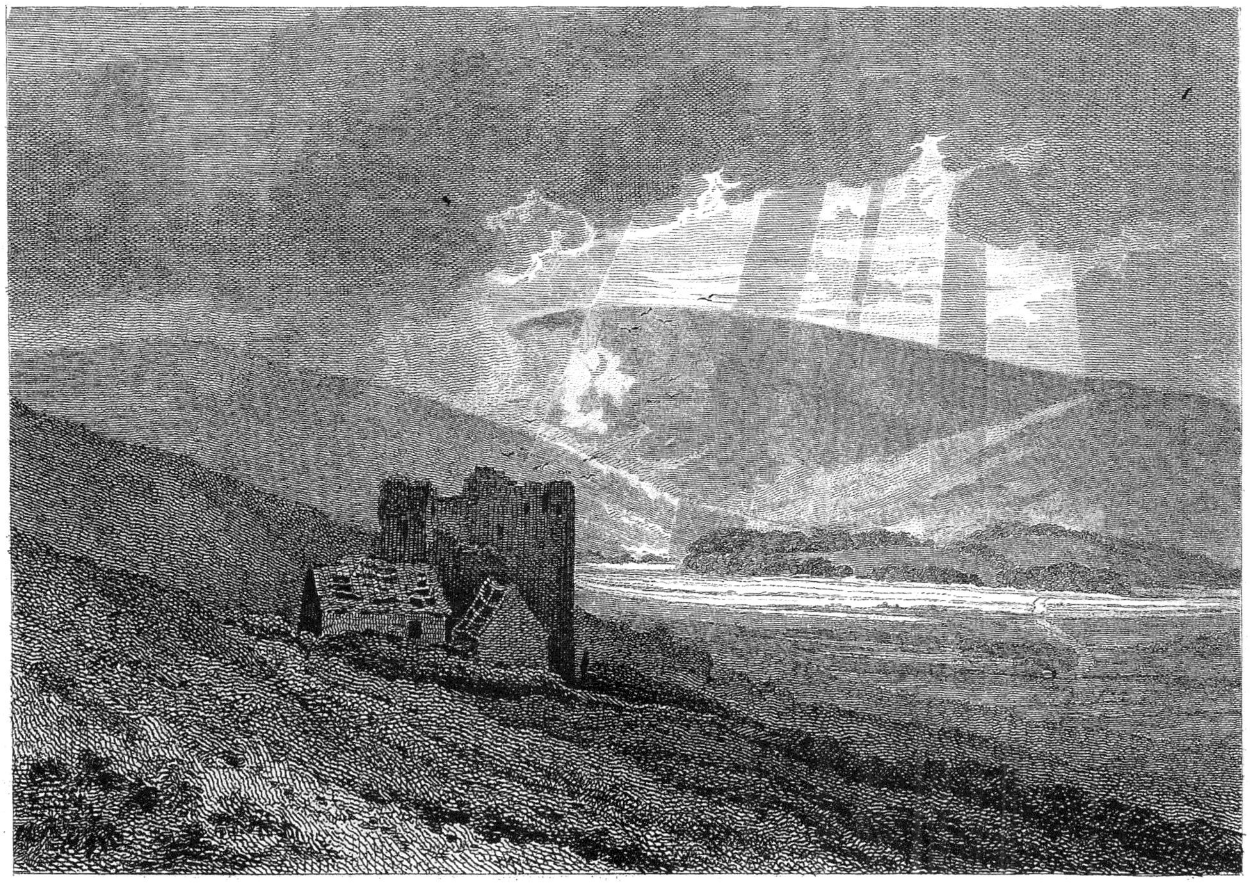

Puck's Castle, Co. of Dublin

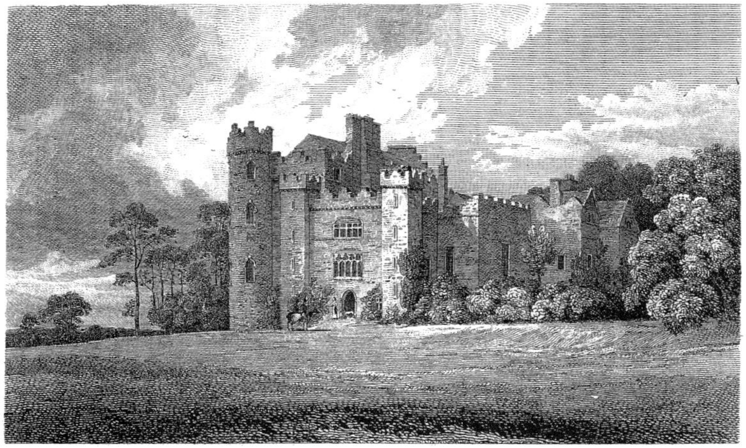

Malahide Castle, The Seat of R.W. Talbot Esq., Co. of Dublin

Garry Castle, King's County

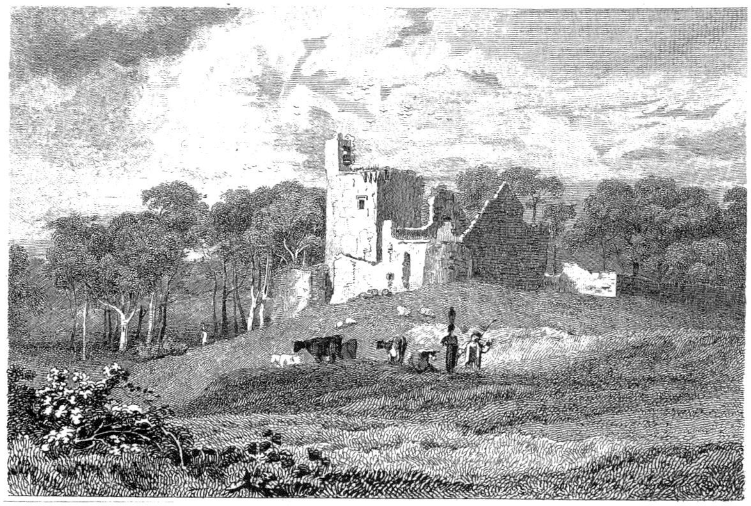

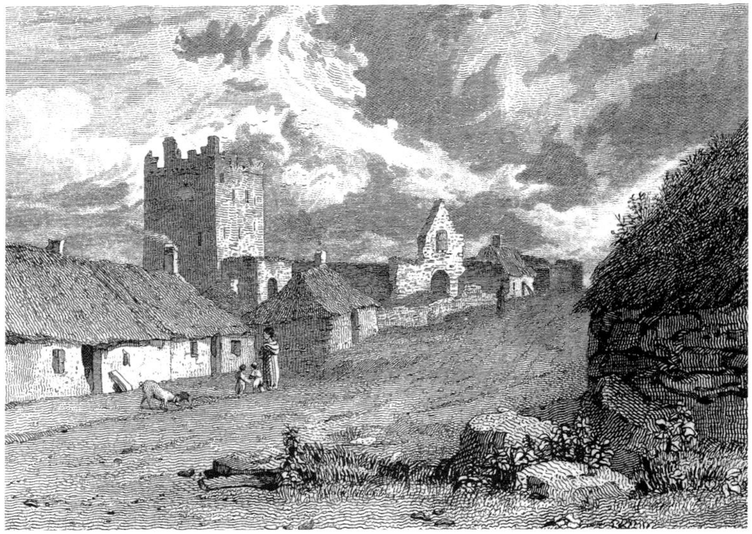

Cloghnony Castle, King's County

Annamo, Co. of Wicklow

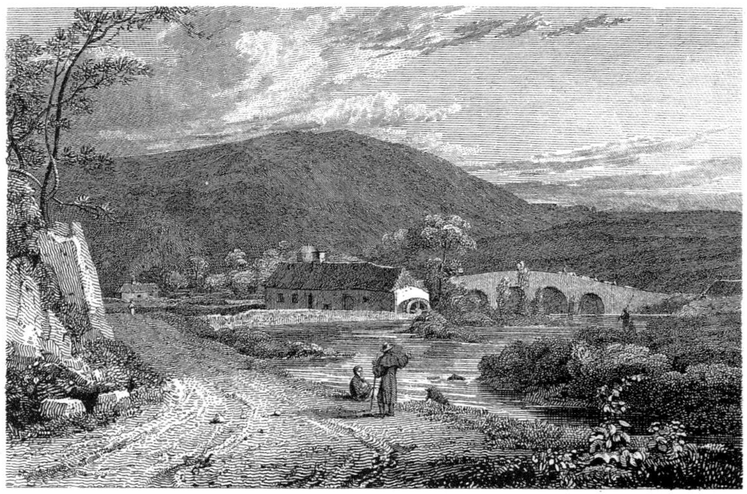

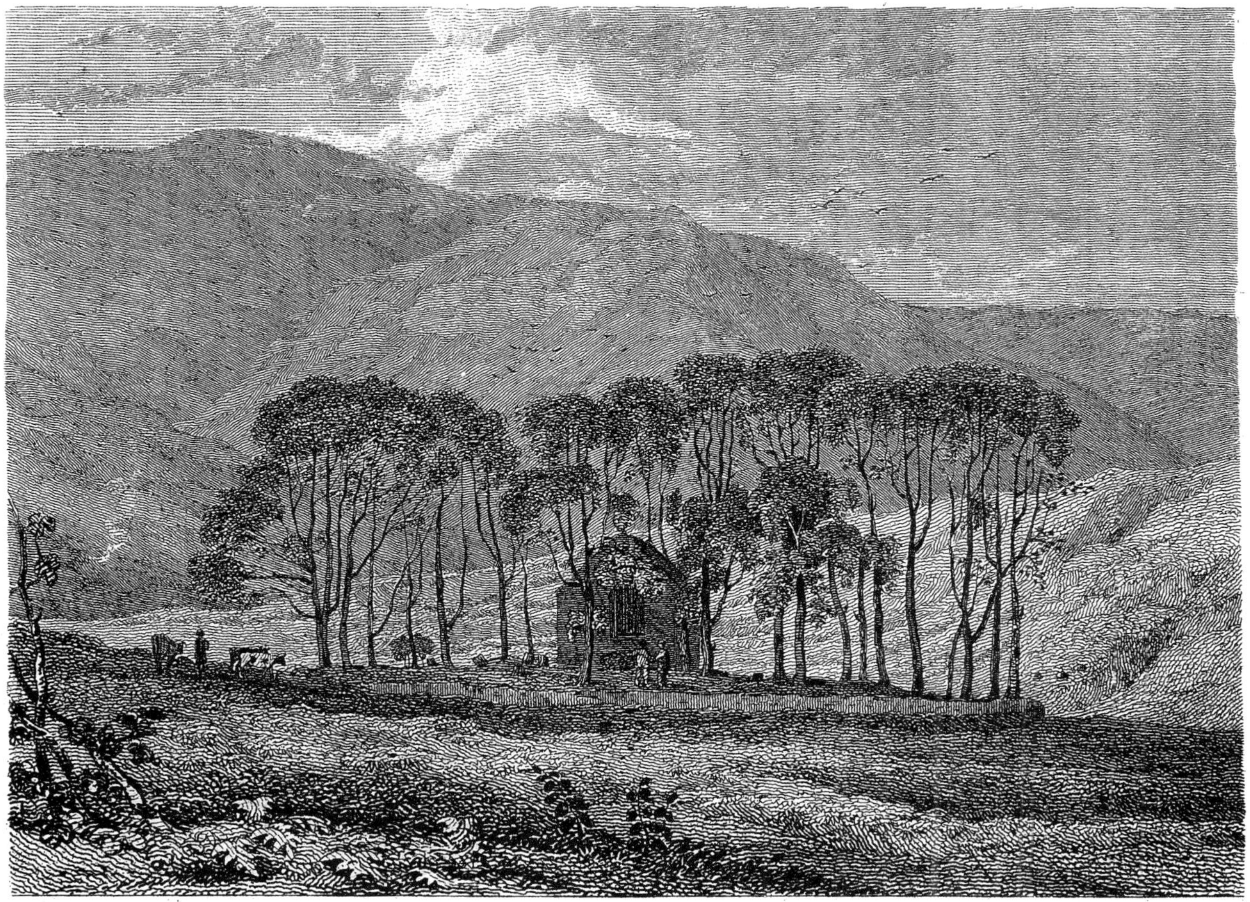

Deralossory Church, Co. of *Wicklow*

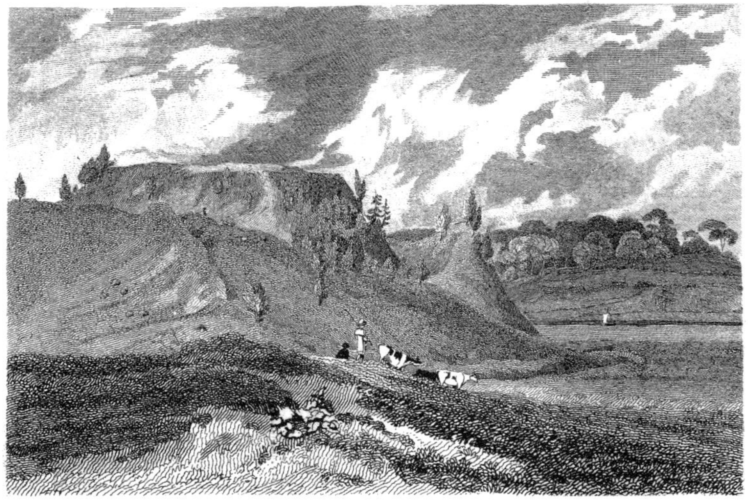

The Rath at Loughlin-Bridge, Co. of Carlow

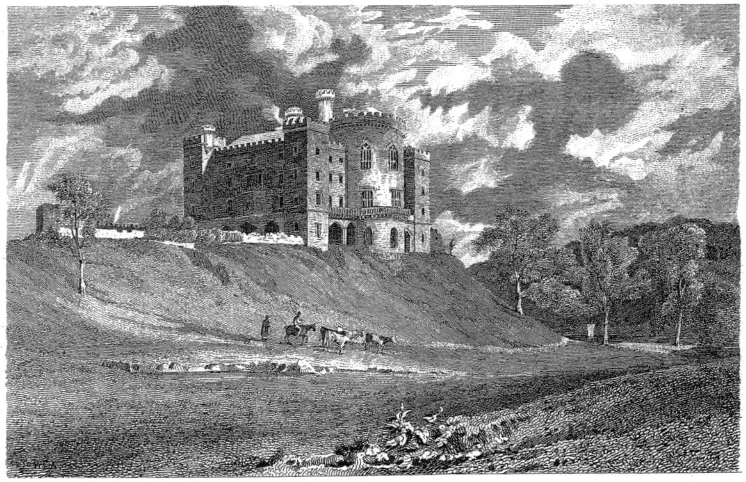

Slane Castle, The Seat of the Marquis of Cunningham, Co. of Eastmeath

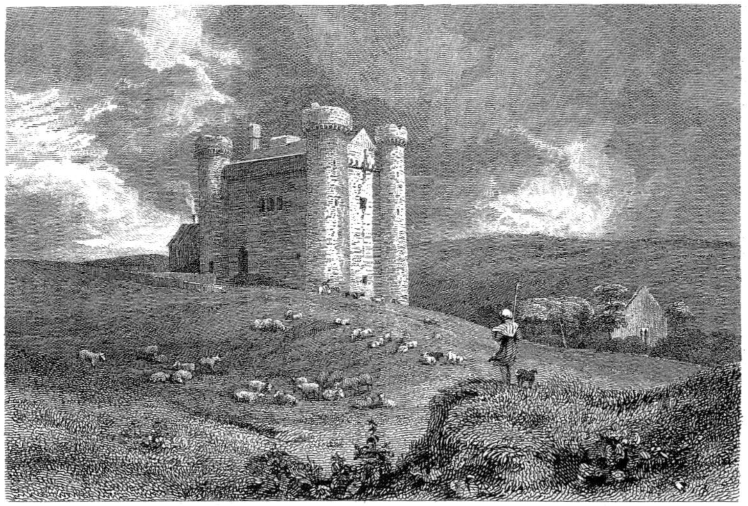

Dunmow Castle, Co. of Eastmeath

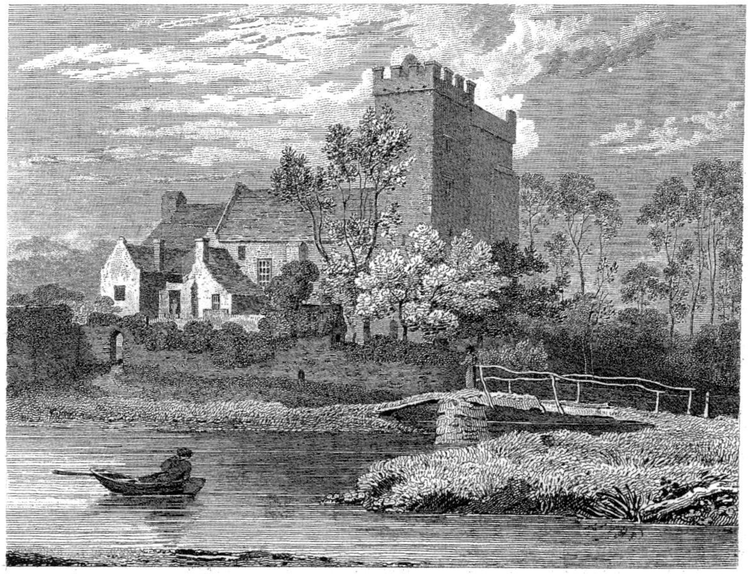

Athcarne Castle, Co. of Eastmeath

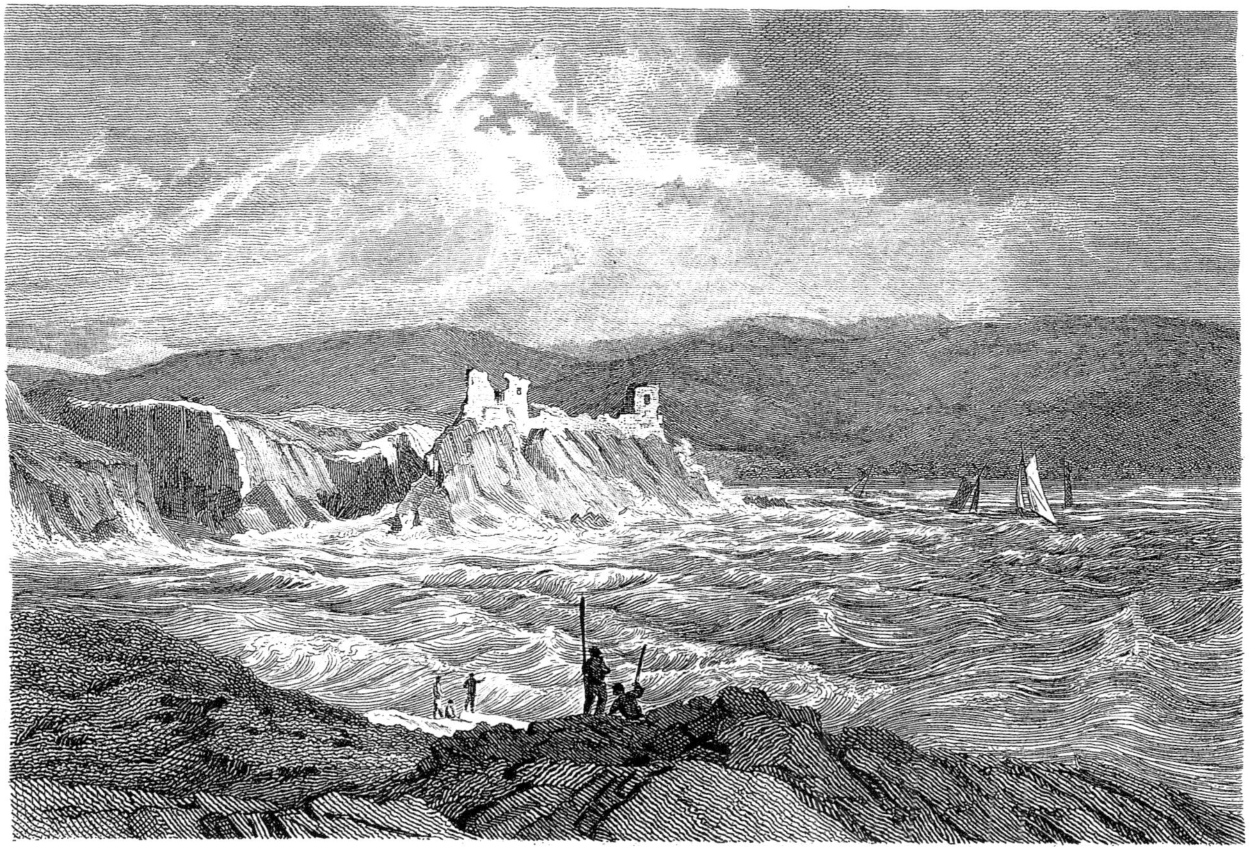

Remains of the Black Castle, Co. of Wicklow

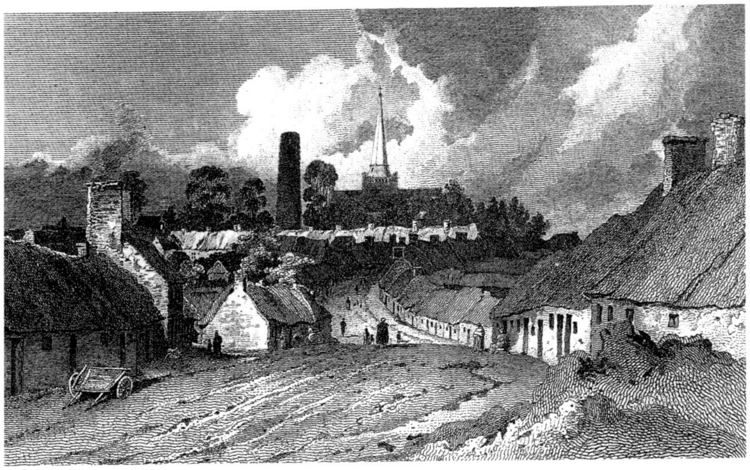

Kells, Co. of Eastmeath

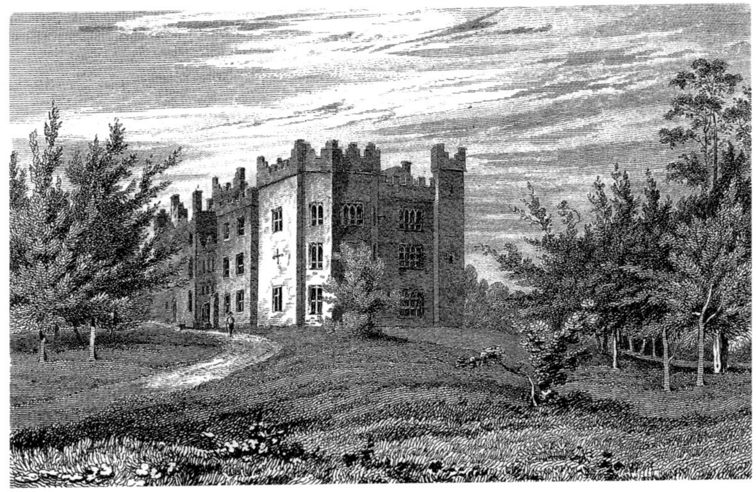

Killeen Castle, The Seat of the Earl of Fingal, Co. of Eastmeath

Dunsany Castle, The Seat of Lord Dunsany, Co. of Eastmeath

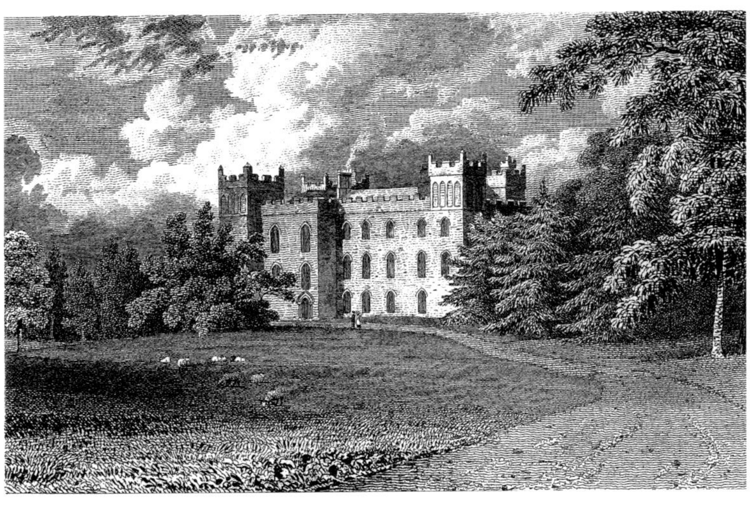

Castletown Delvin, Co. of Eastmeath

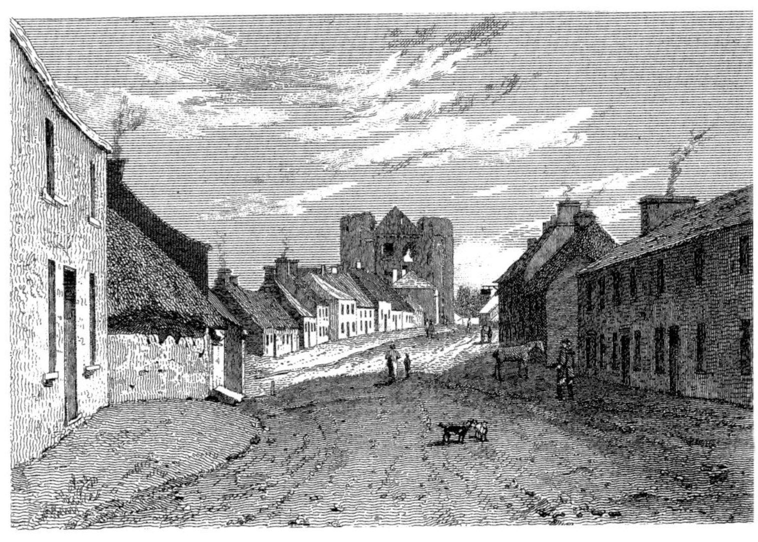

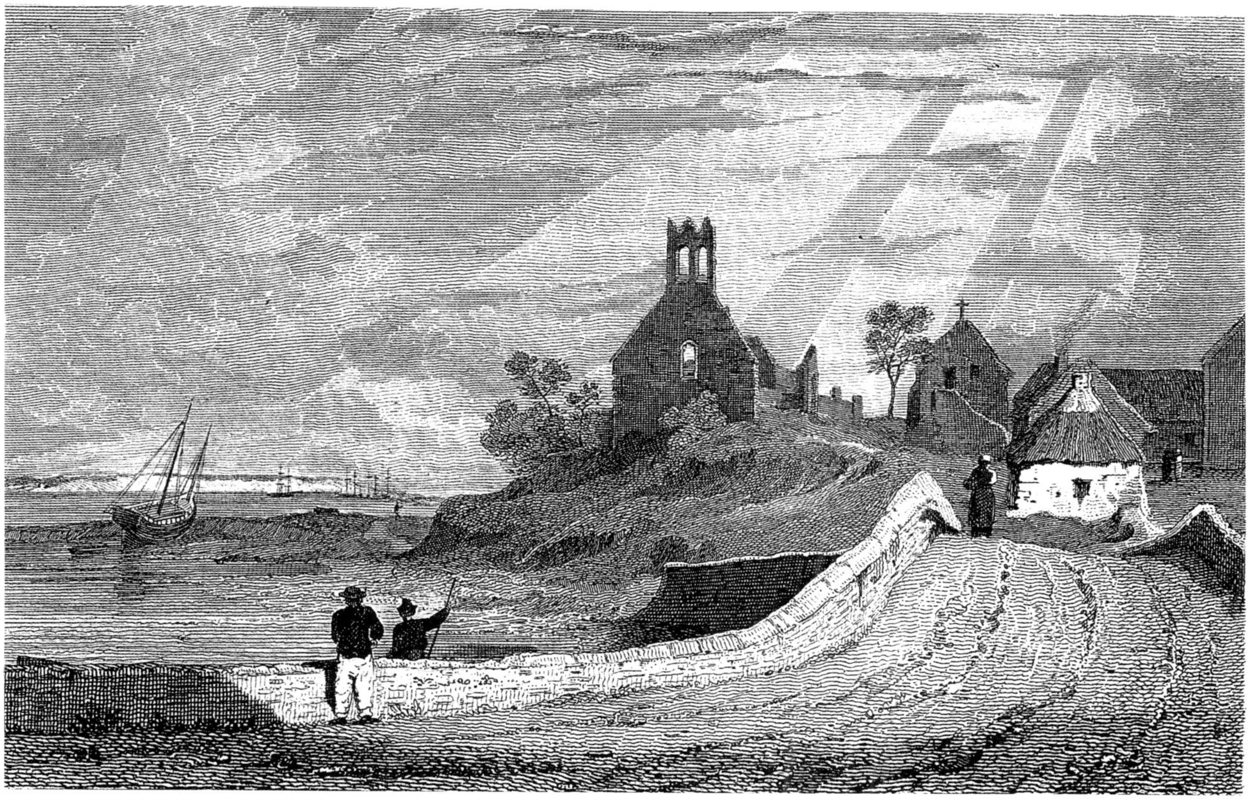

Mornington, Co. of Eastmeath

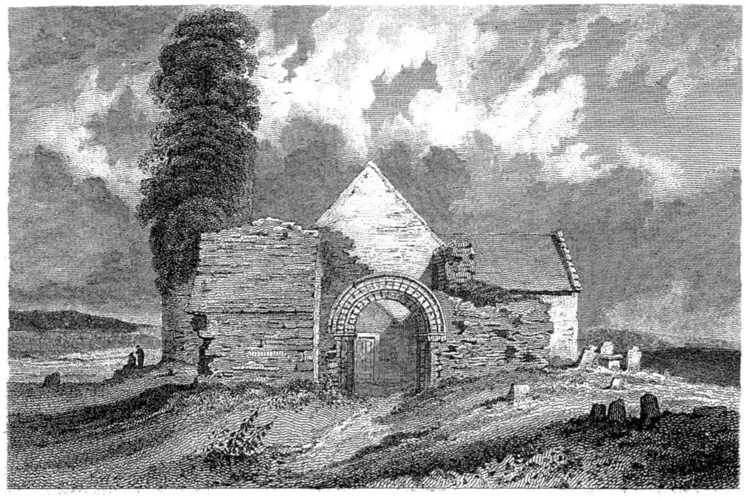

Church & Round Tower, Castledermot, Co. of Kildare

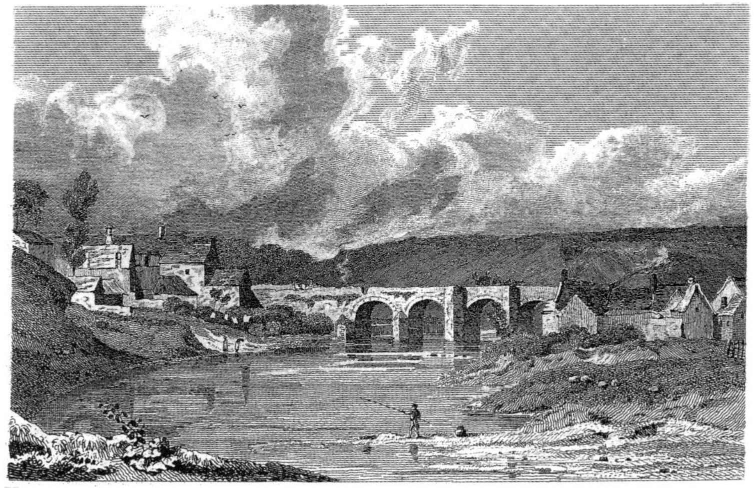

Kilcullen Bridge, Co. of Kildare

The Cathedral, Kildare

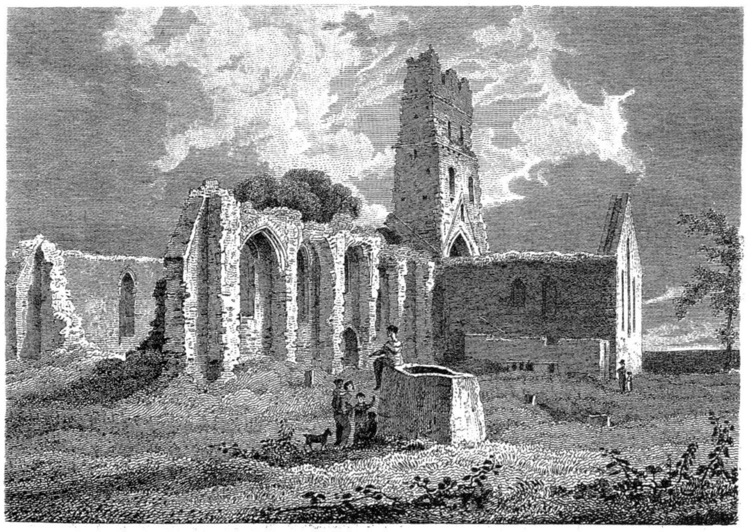

Kilkenny Castle

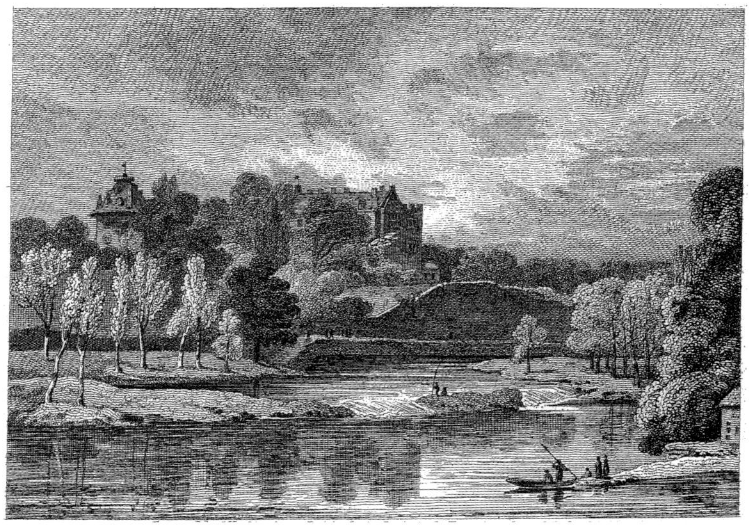

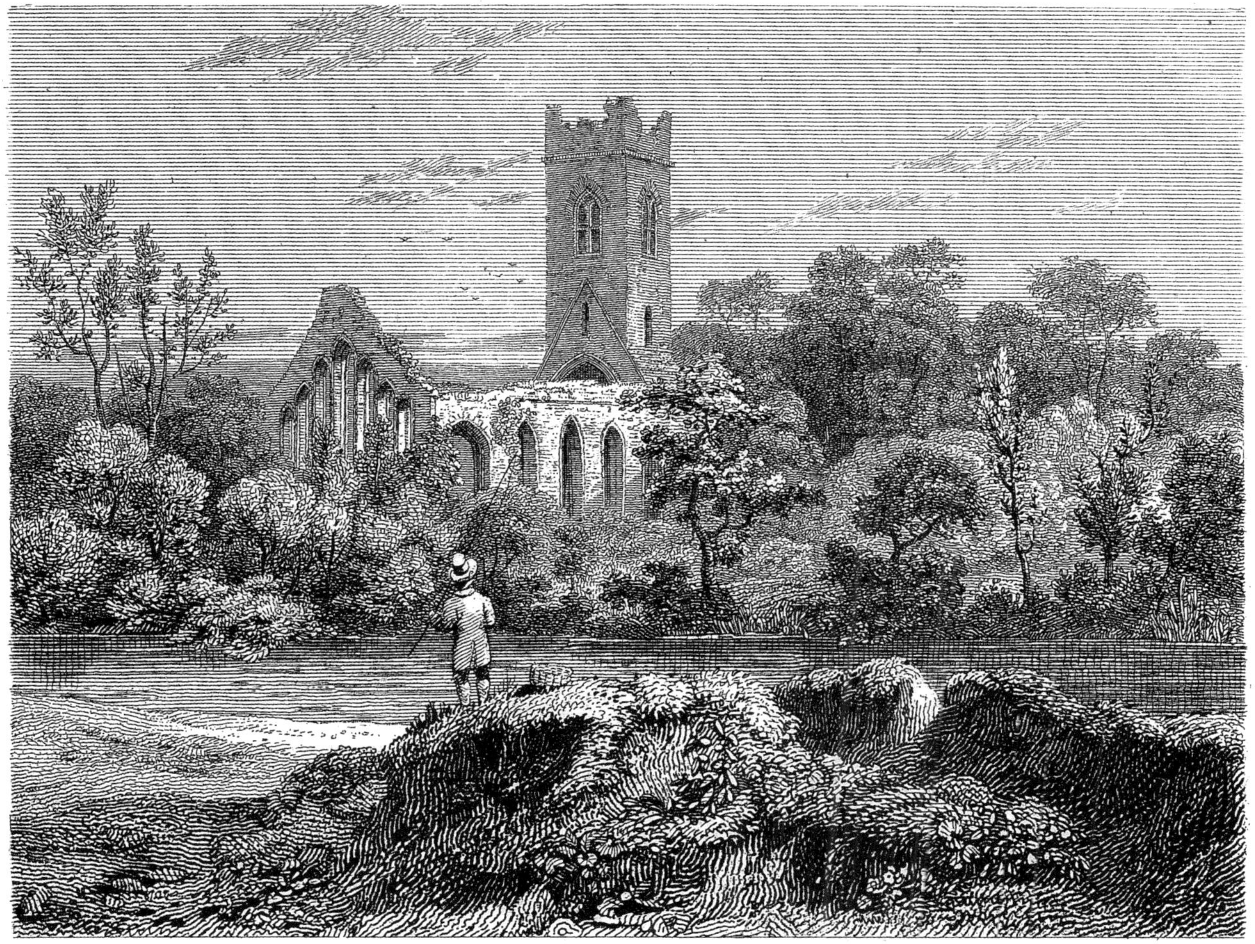

The Franciscan Abbey, Kilkenny

Guides to Ireland

BY REV G.N. WRIGHT (1821-25)

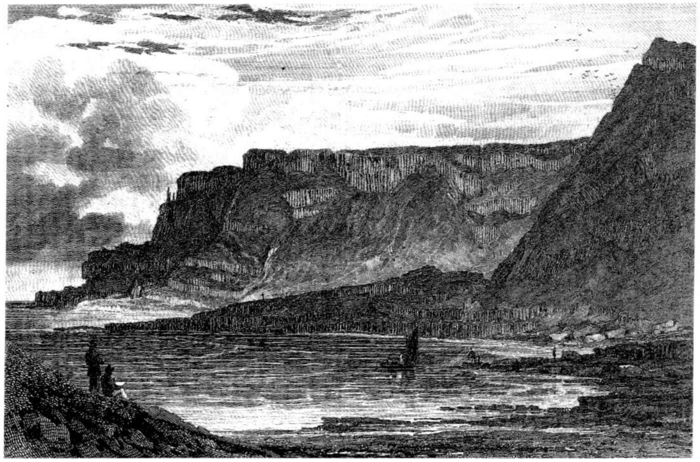

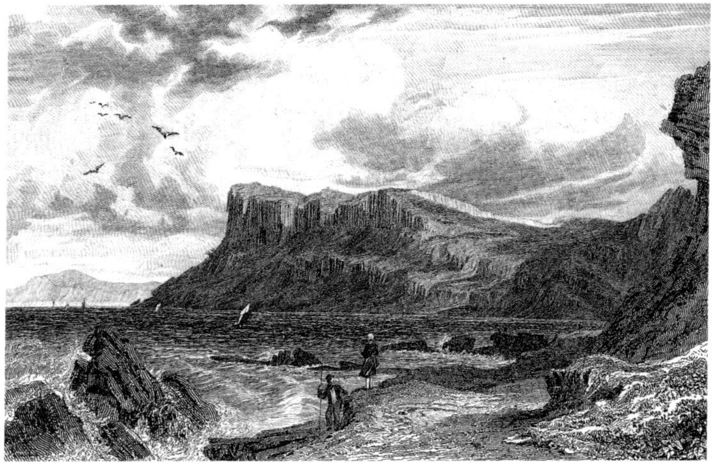

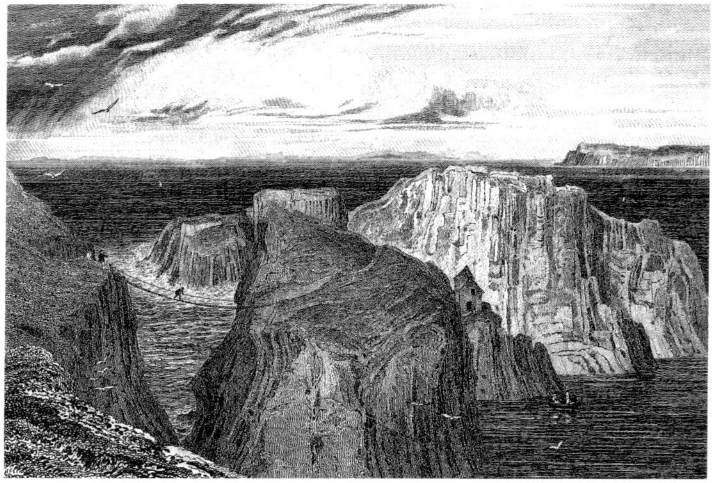

A GUIDE TO THE GIANT'S CAUSEWAY,
AND THE NORTH-EAST COAST OF THE COUNTY OF ANTRIM (1823)

The Giant's Causeway, County of Antrim

Benmore or Fairhead, County of Antrim

Carrick-a-Rede, County of Antrim

Dunluce Castle, County of Antrim

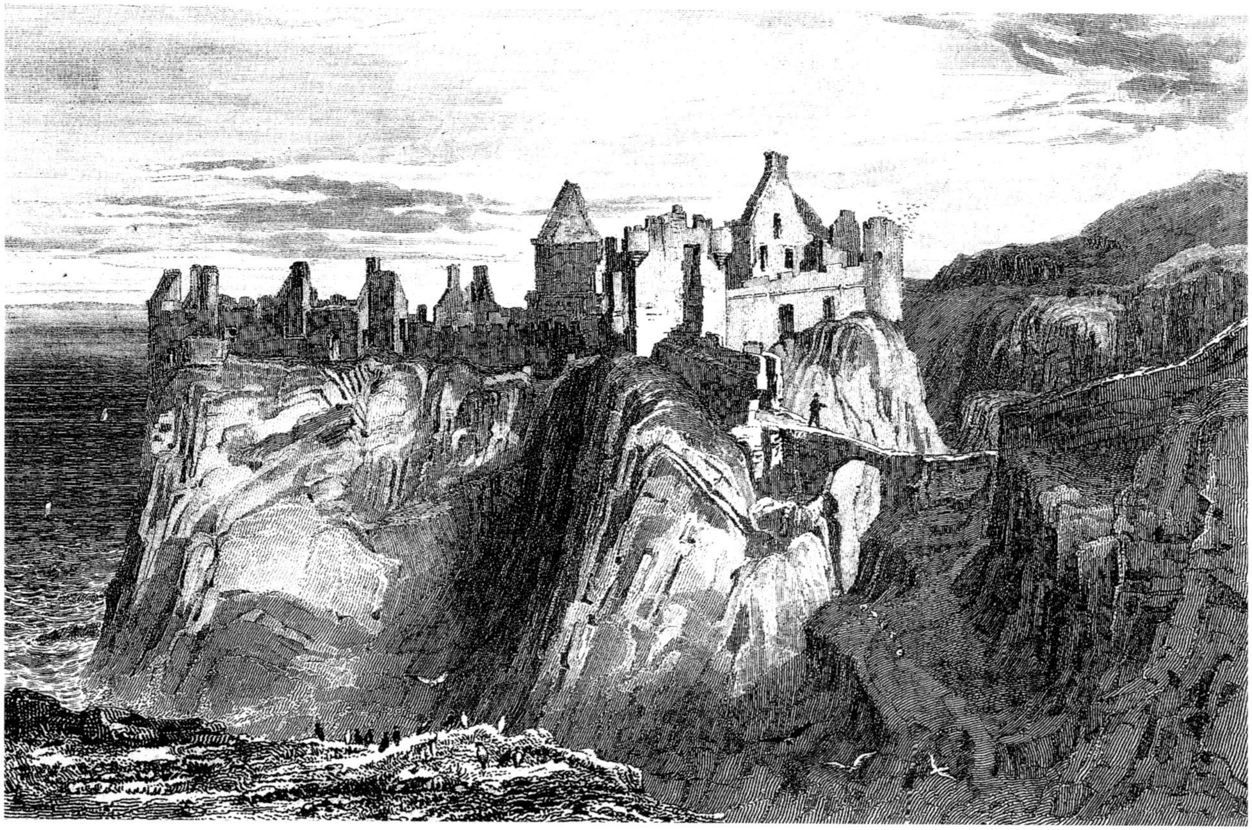

Dunluce Castle, County of Antrim

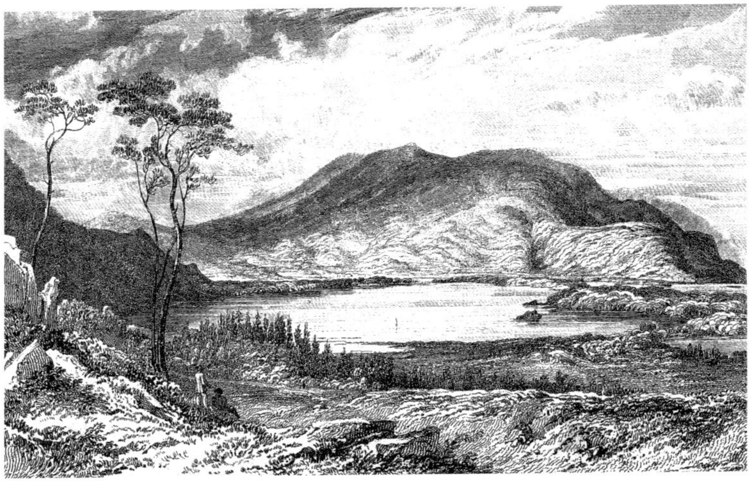

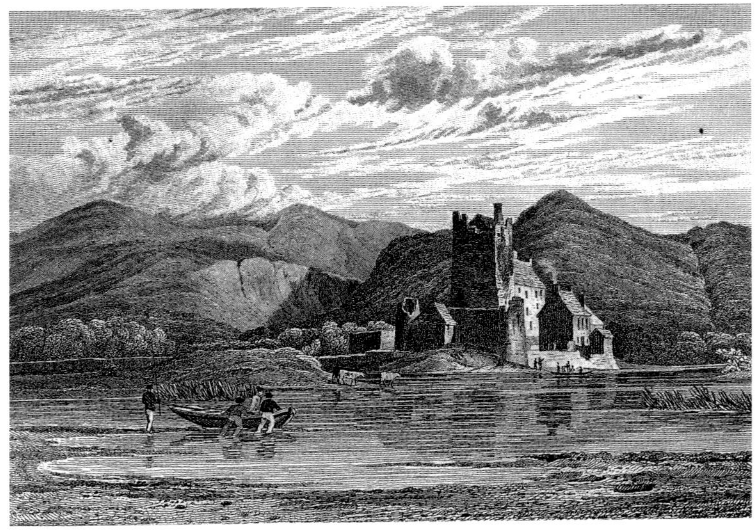

A GUIDE TO THE LAKES OF KILLARNEY (1822)

Turk Lake from the ascent to Mangerton

Ross Castle

The Eagle's Nest

Mac Gilla-Cuddy's Reeks from Aghadoe

Interior of Mucruss Abbey

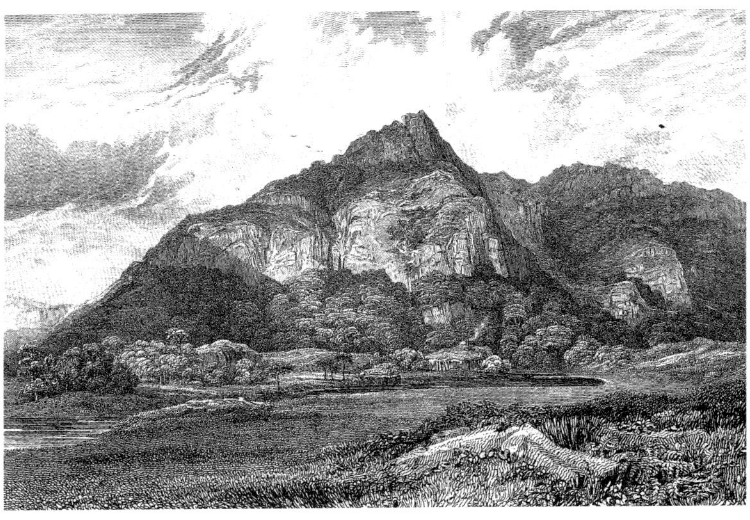

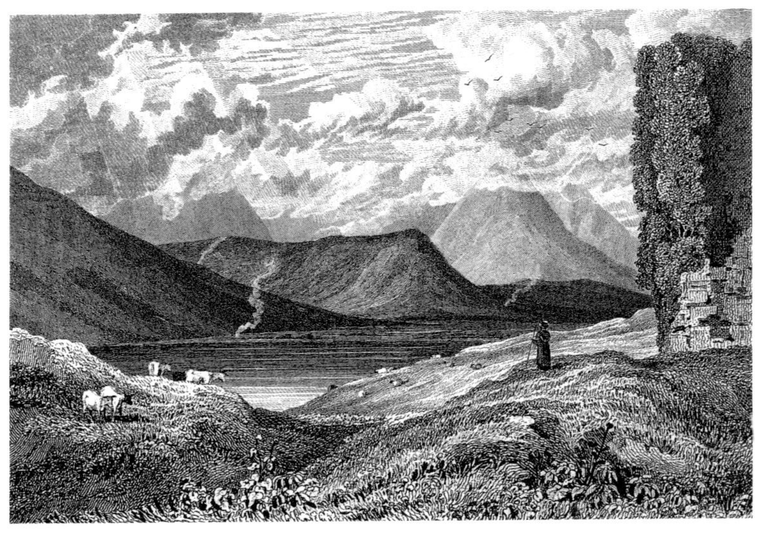

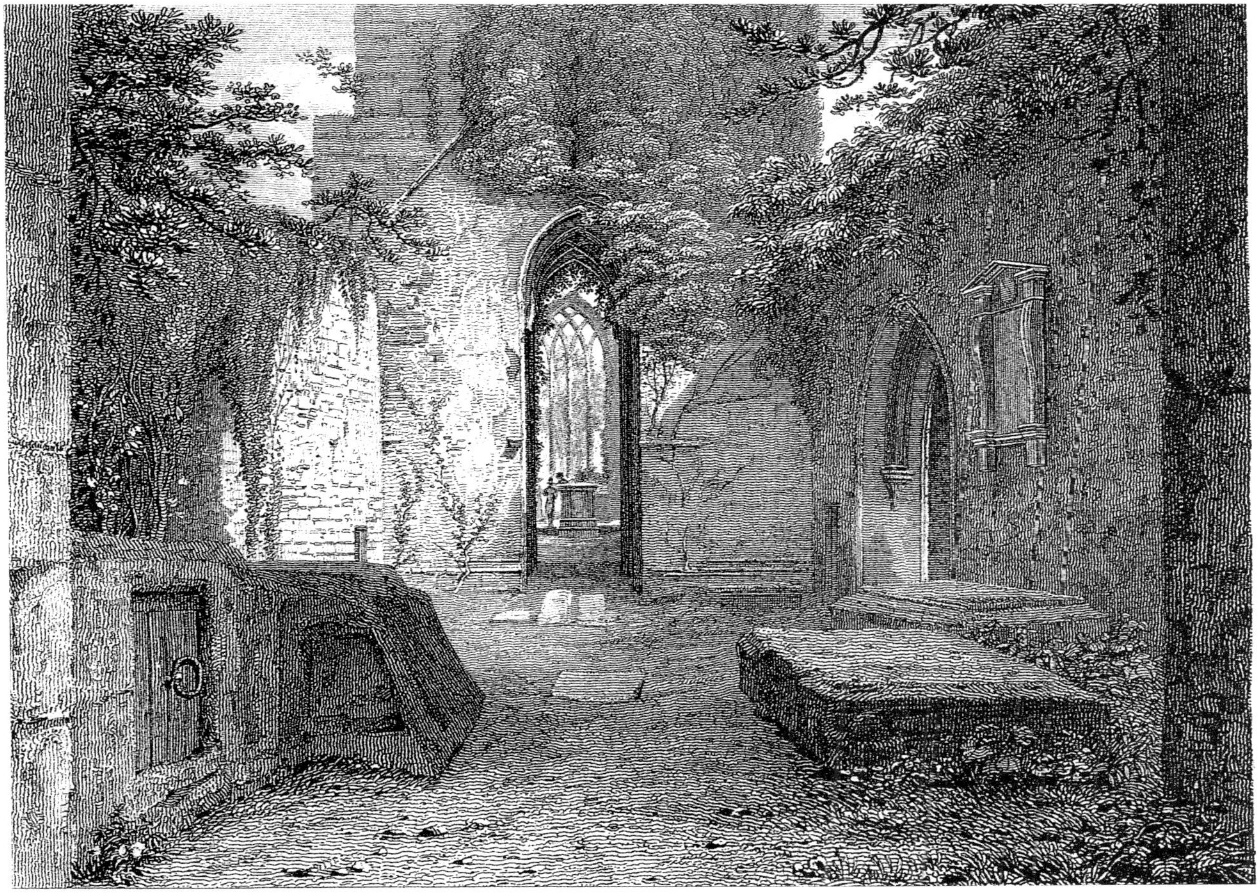

Interior of Mucruss Abbey

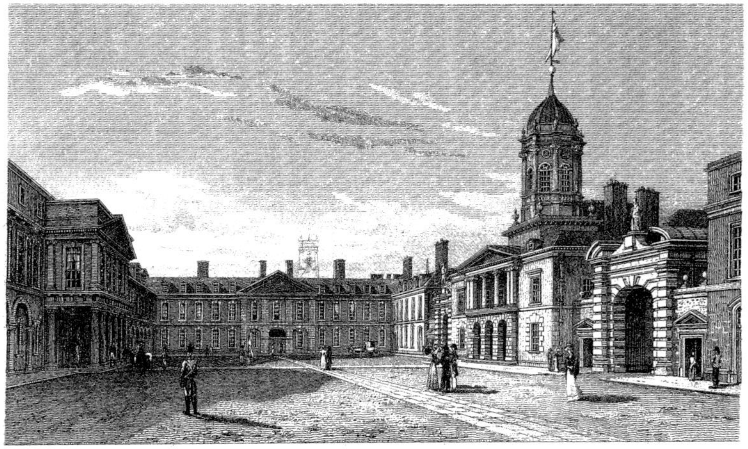

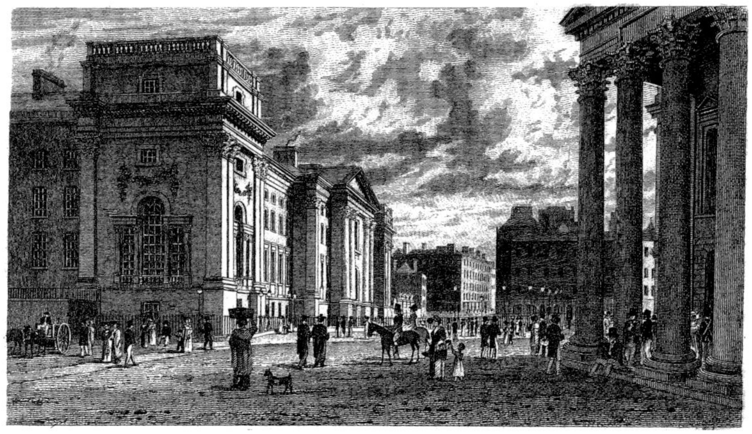

An Historical Guide to Ancient and Modern Dublin (1821)

The Castle
Trinity College
The Bank
St. Patrick's Cathedral
Christ-Church Cathedral
The Metropolitan Catholic Chapel
The Custom House
The Law Courts
The Rotunda & Lying-in Hospital
The New Theatre Royal

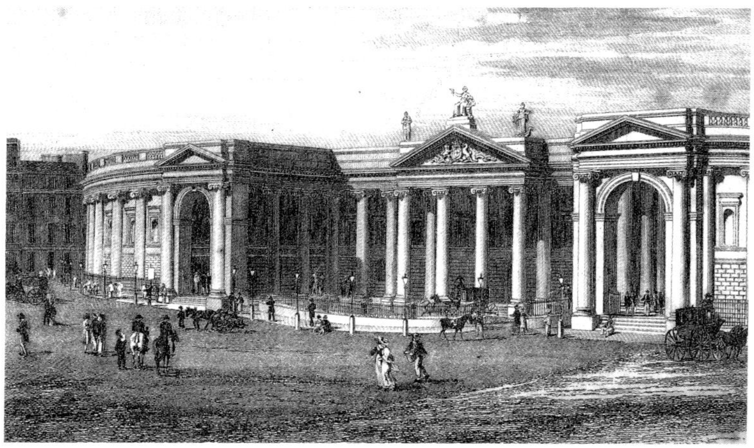

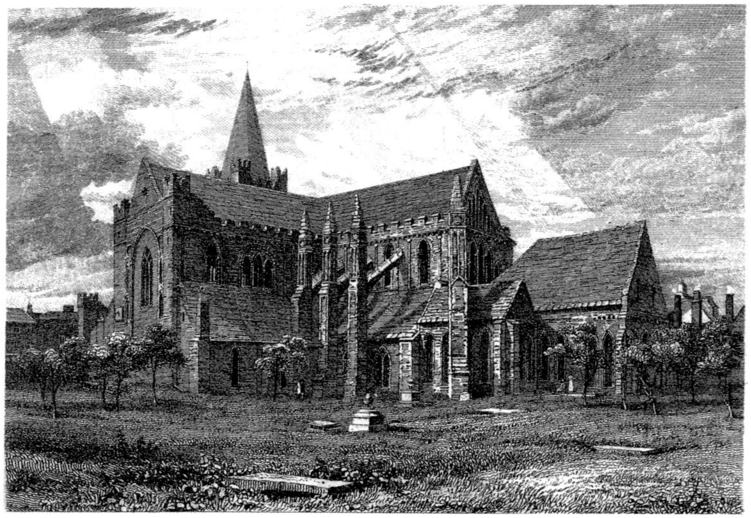

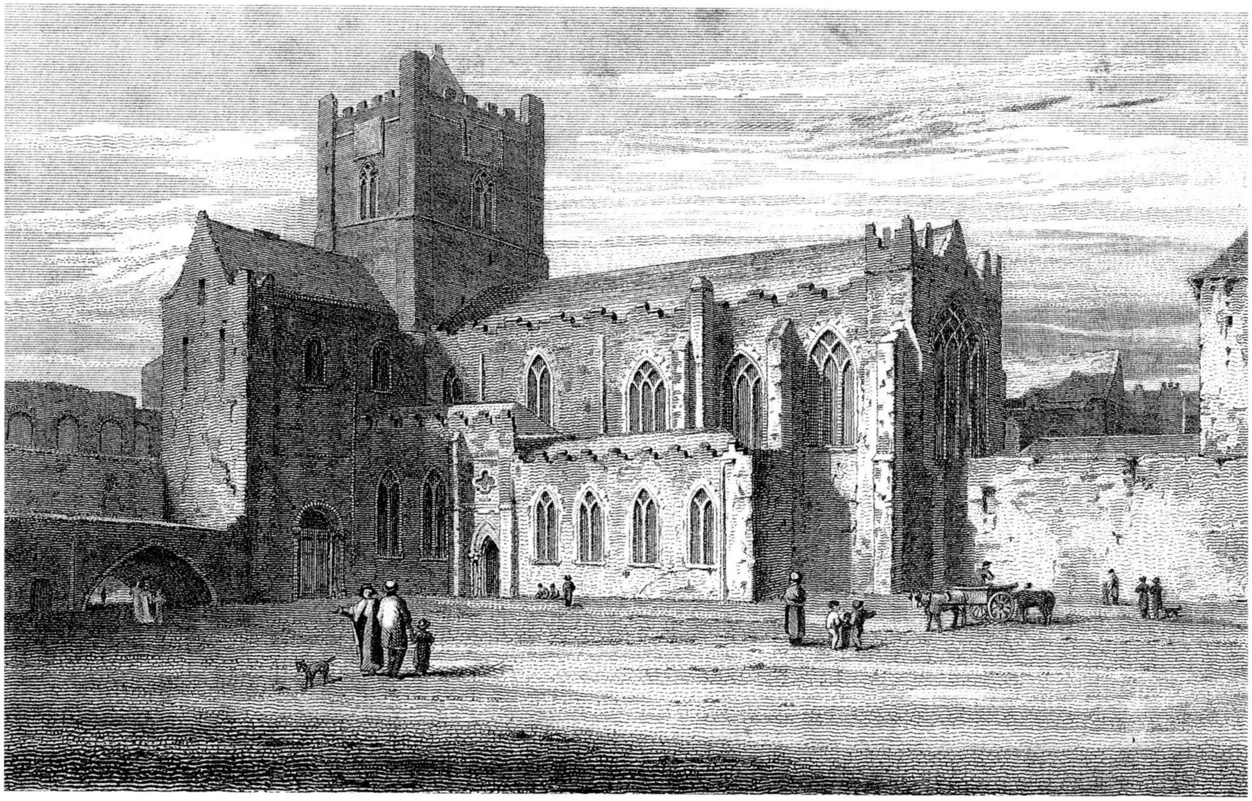

Christ-Church Cathedral

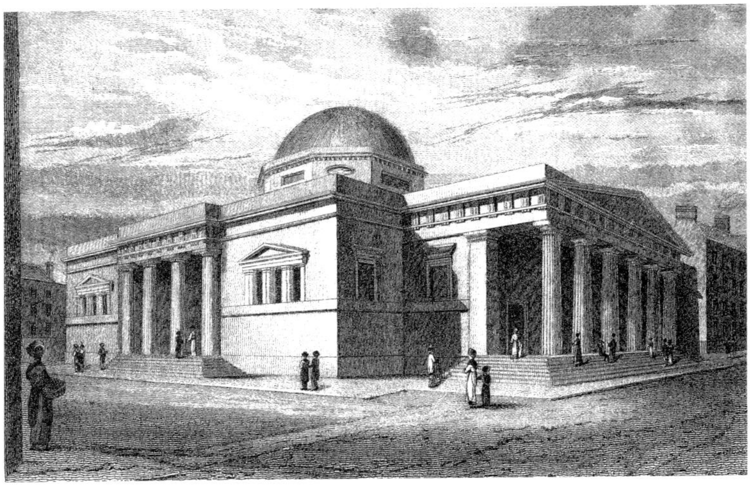

The Metropolitan Catholic Chapel

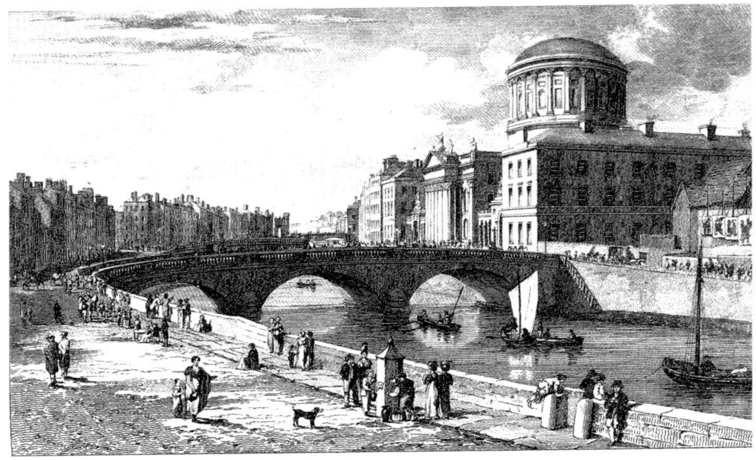

The Law Courts

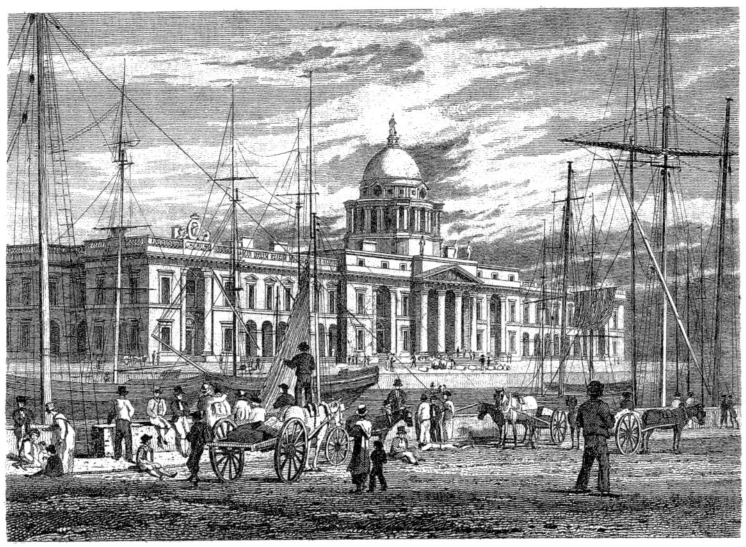

The Custom House

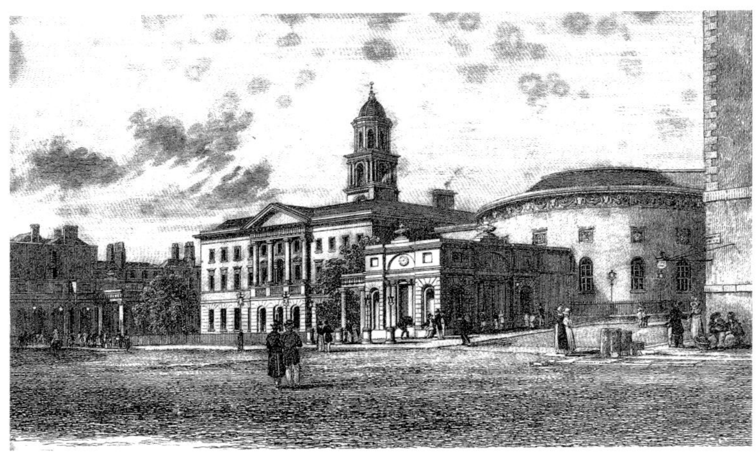

The Rotunda & Lying-in Hospital

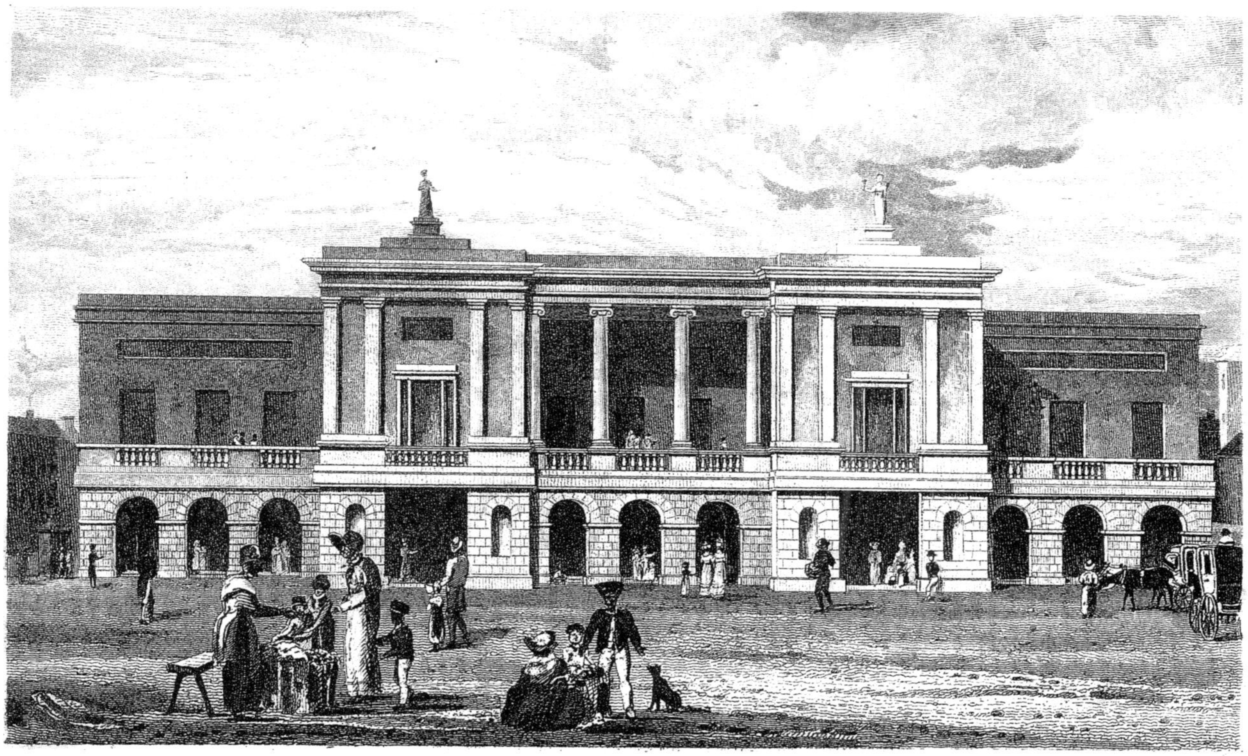

The New Theatre Royal

The Beauties of Ireland

BY J.N. BREWER (1825-26)

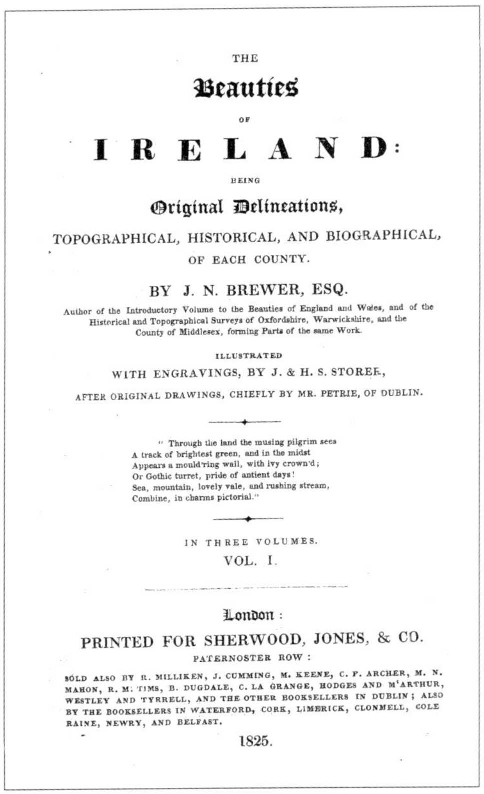

THE
Beauties
OF
IRELAND:
BEING
Original Delineations,
TOPOGRAPHICAL, HISTORICAL, AND BIOGRAPHICAL,
OF EACH COUNTY.

BY J. N. BREWER, ESQ.

Author of the Introductory Volume to the Beauties of England and Wales, and of the Historical and Topographical Surveys of Oxfordshire, Warwickshire, and the County of Middlesex, forming Parts of the same Work.

ILLUSTRATED
WITH ENGRAVINGS, BY J. & H. S. STORER,
AFTER ORIGINAL DRAWINGS, CHIEFLY BY MR. PETRIE, OF DUBLIN.

"Through the land the musing pilgrim sees
A track of brightest green, and in the midst
Appears a mould'ring wall, with ivy crown'd;
Or Gothic turret, pride of antient days!
Sea, mountain, lovely vale, and rushing stream,
Combine, in charms pictorial."

IN THREE VOLUMES.
VOL. I.

London:
PRINTED FOR SHERWOOD, JONES, & CO.
PATERNOSTER ROW:
SOLD ALSO BY R. MILLIKEN, J. CUMMING, M. KEENE, C. P. ARCHER, M. N. MAHON, R. M. TIMS, B. DUGDALE, C. LA GRANGE, HODGES AND M'ARTHUR, WESTLEY AND TYRRELL, AND THE OTHER BOOKSELLERS IN DUBLIN; ALSO BY THE BOOKSELLERS IN WATERFORD, CORK, LIMERICK, CLONMELL, COLE RAINE, NEWRY, AND BELFAST.
1825.

Title page from vol. I

THE BEAUTIES OF IRELAND:
BEING ORIGINAL DELINEATIONS, TOPOGRAPHICAL, HISTORICAL, AND BIOGRAPHICAL, OF EACH COUNTY

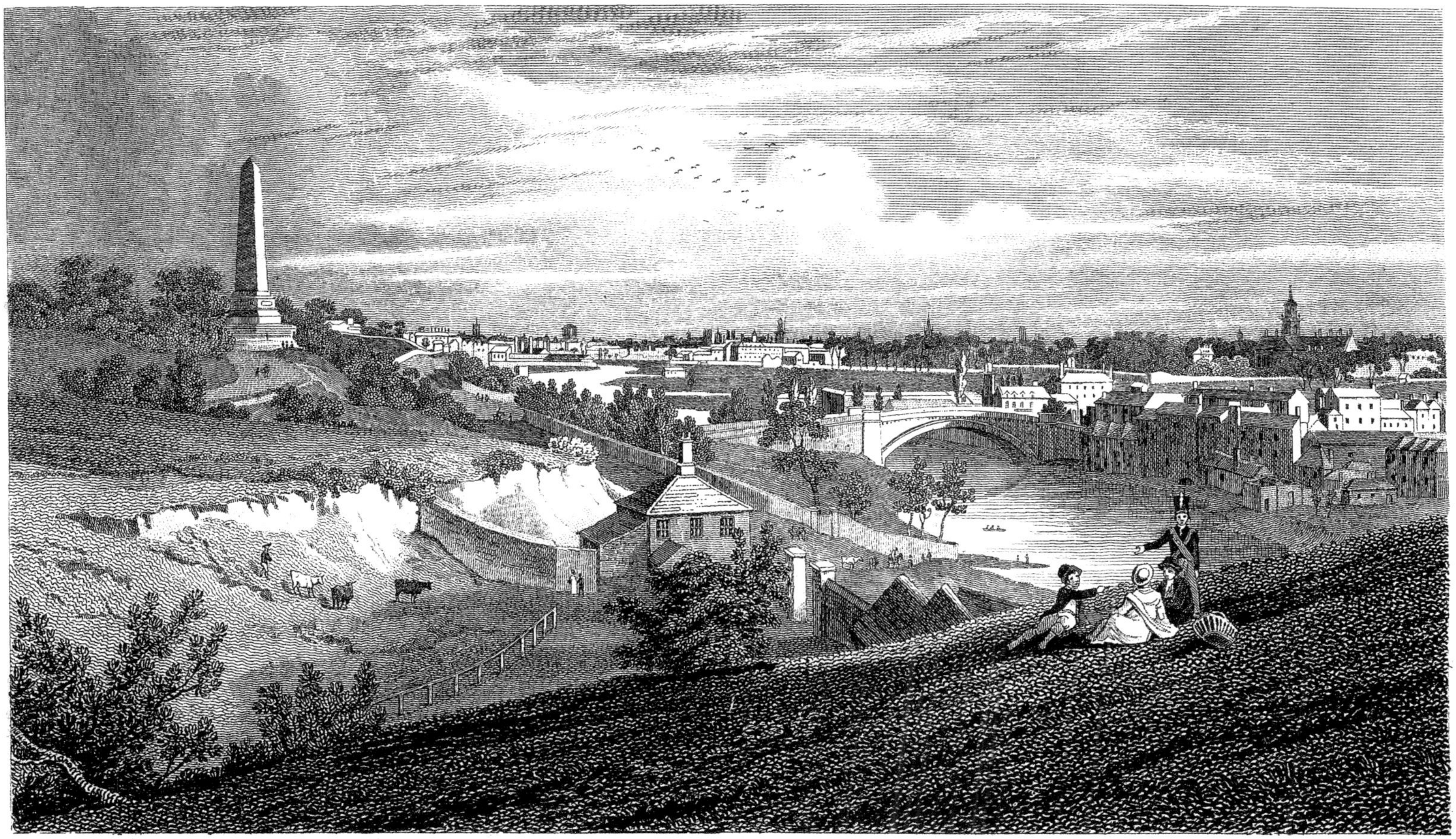

Dublin, from the Phoenix Park

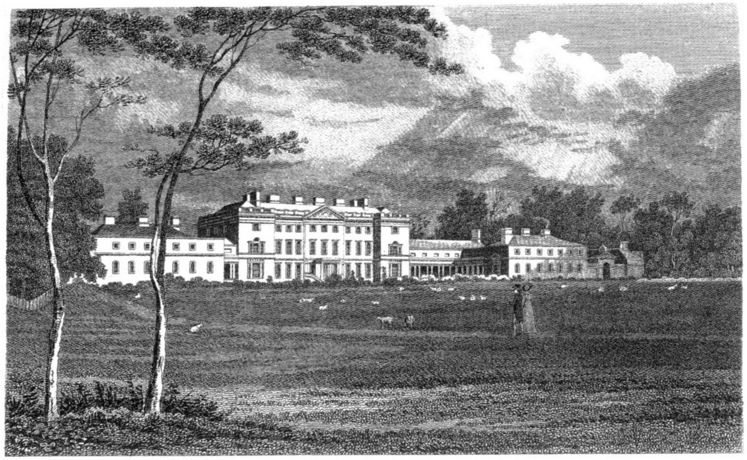

Carton, The Seat of His Grace the Duke of Leinster, Co. of Kildare

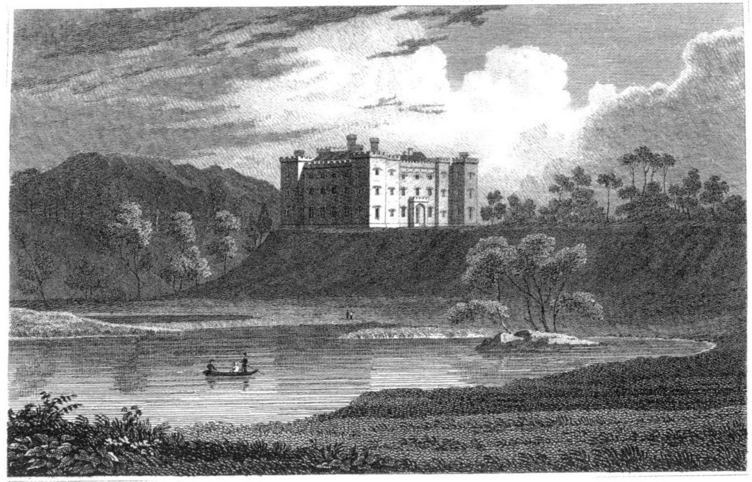

Slane Castle, The Seat of Marquis Conyngham, Co. of Meath

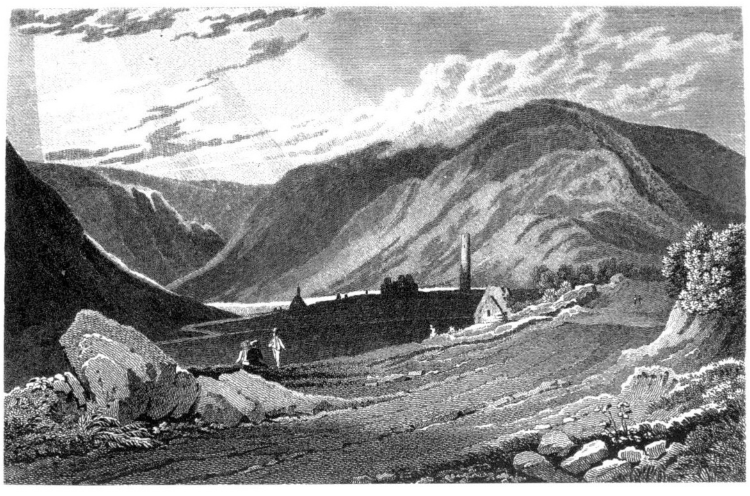

Glendalough, Co. of Wicklow

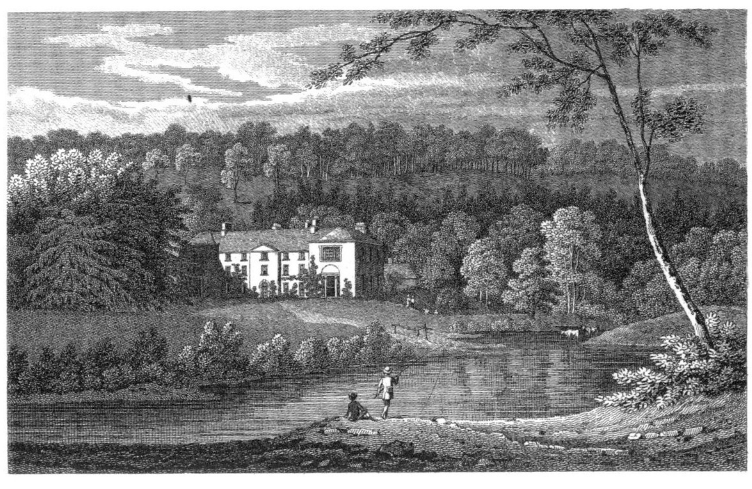

Tinnehinch, The Seat of the late Right Honle Henry Gratton M.P., Co. of Wicklow

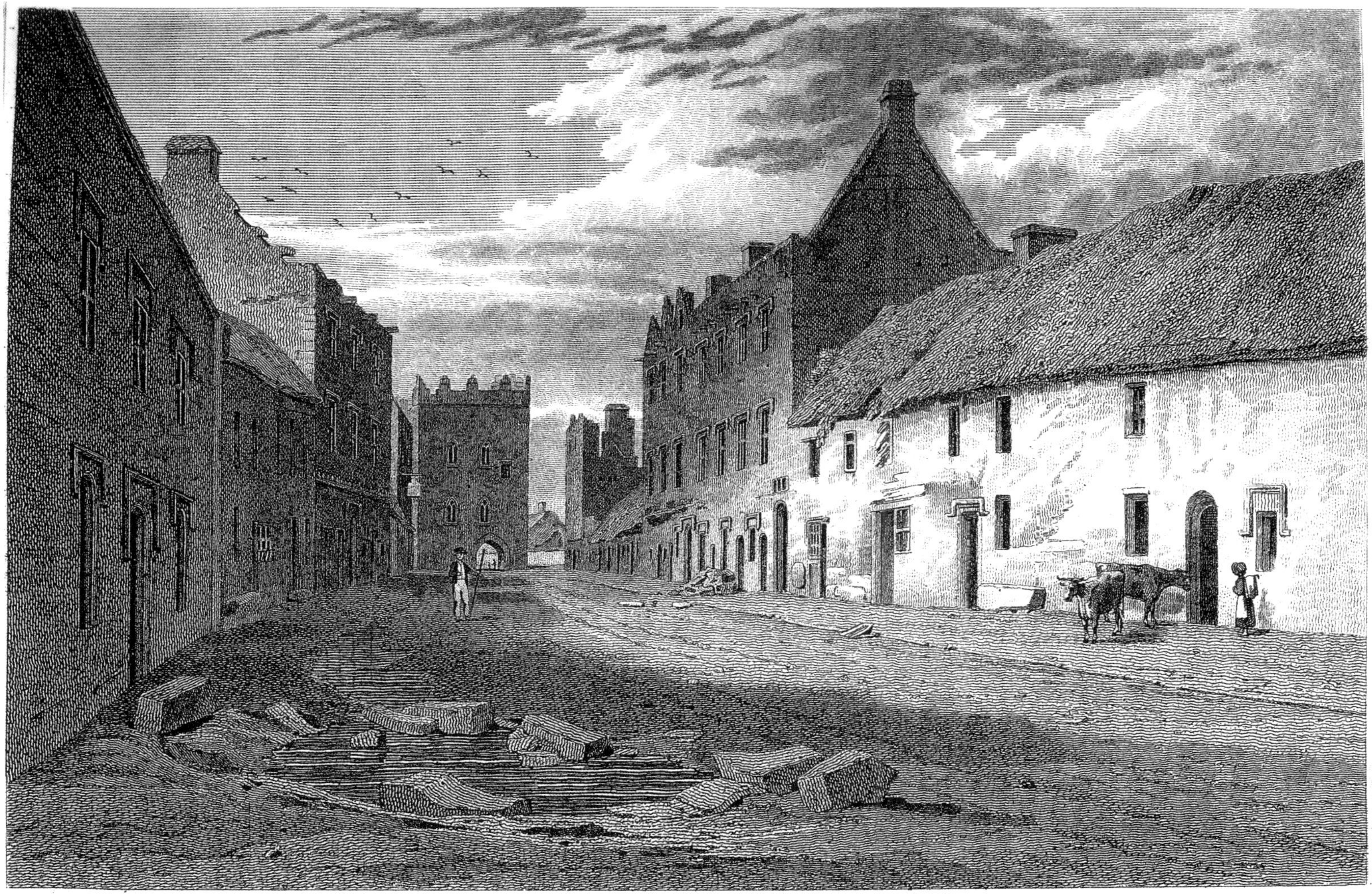

Kilmallock, Co. of Limerick

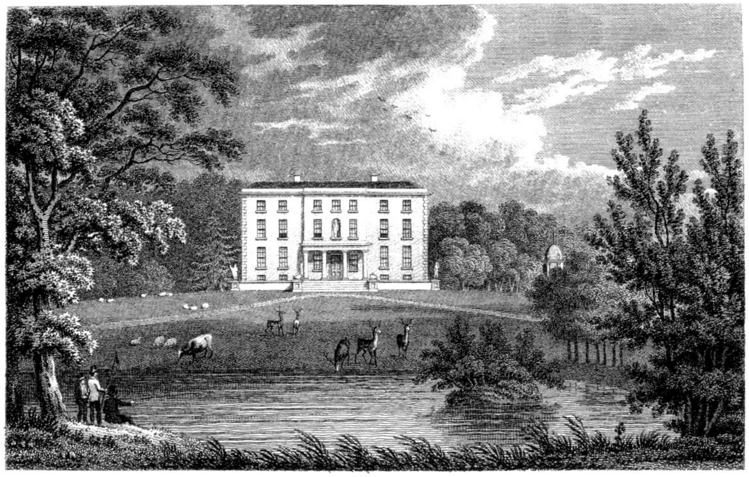

Balynastrag, Seat of Sir Thomas Esmonde, Bart., Co. Wexford

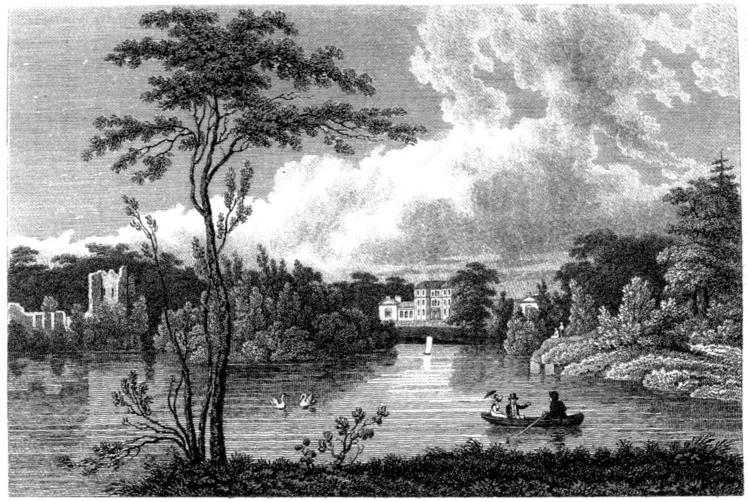

Mount Bellew, Seat of Christopher Dillon Bellow, Esqr., Co. Galway

Ross Castle, Co. of Kerry

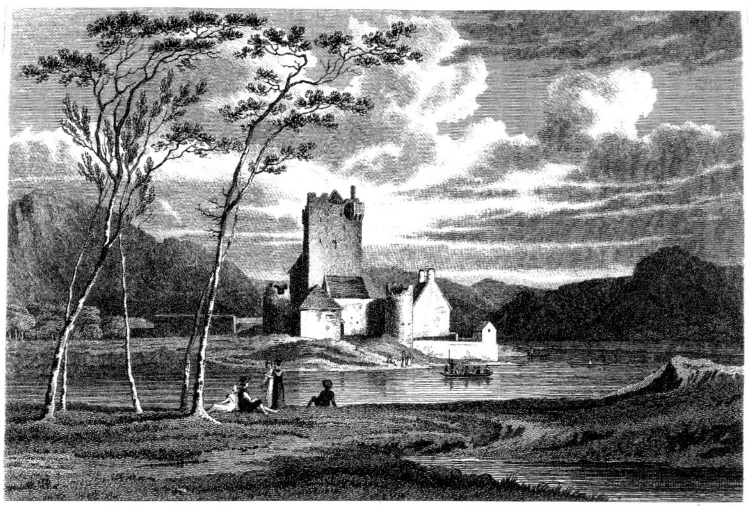

Abbey of Multifernan, Co. of Westmeath

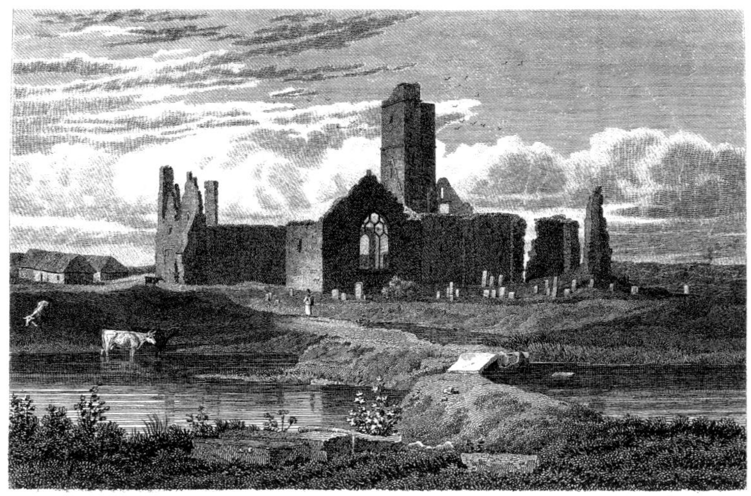

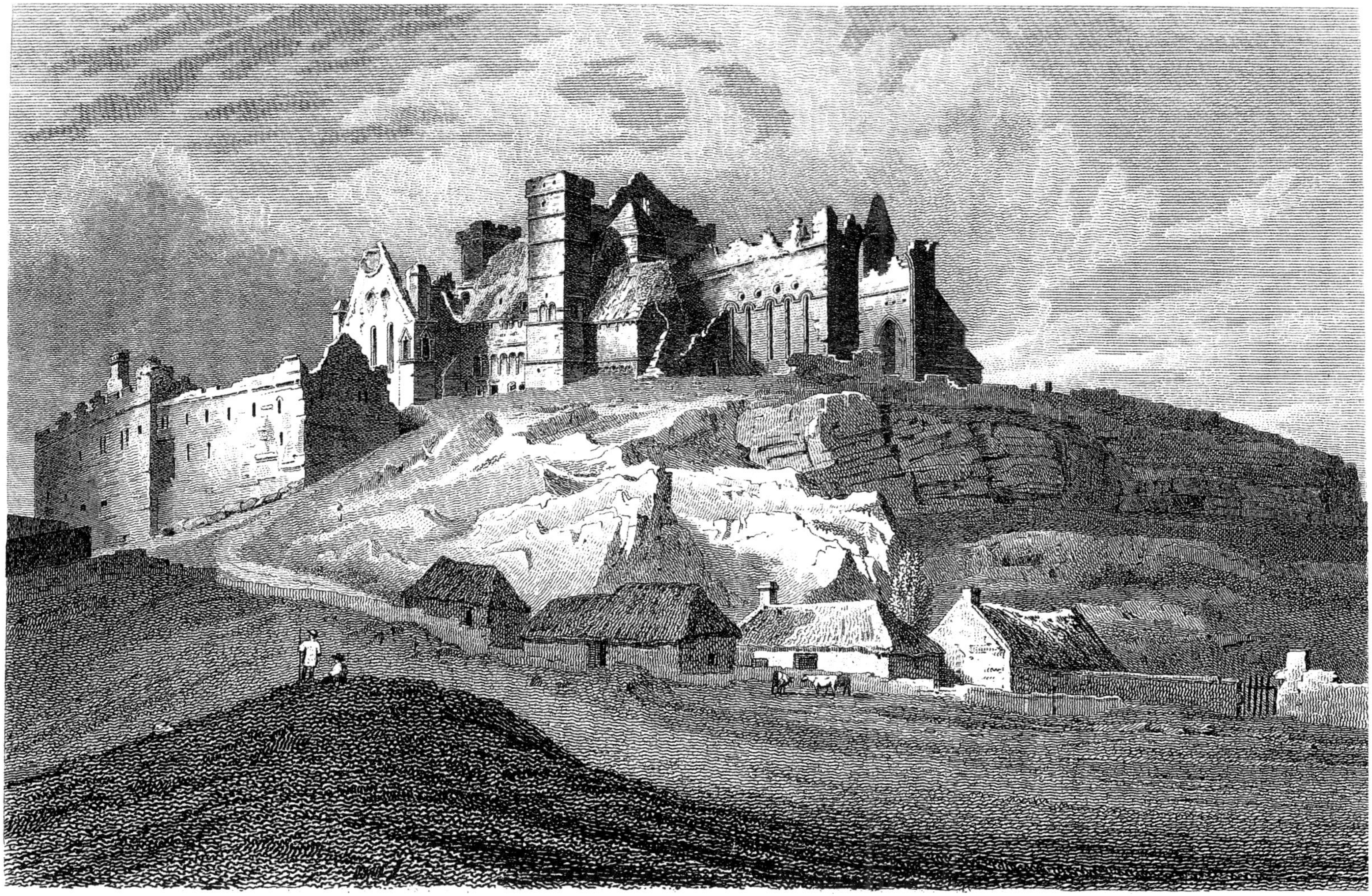

Mount Cashell, Co. of Tipperary

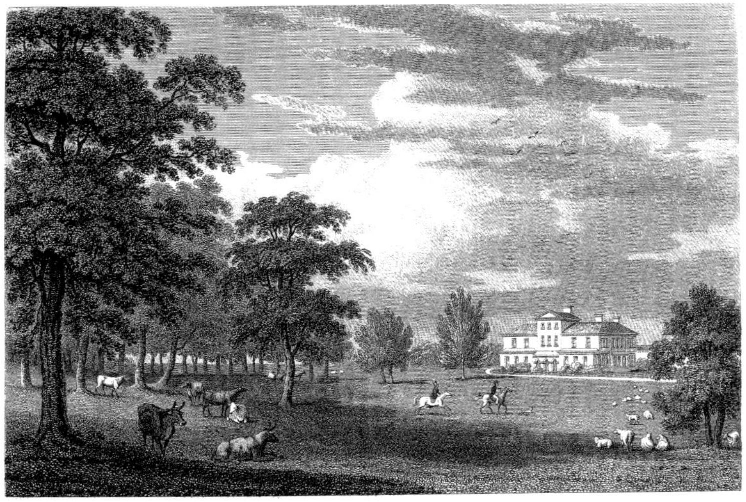

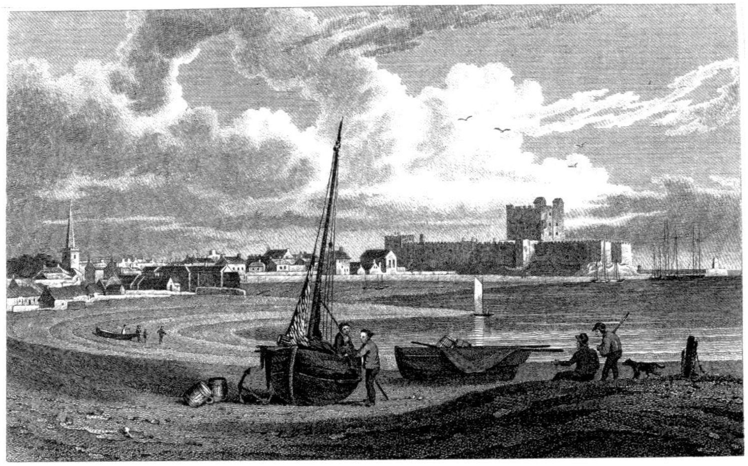

Edgeworth Town, The Seat of Lovell Edgeworth Esq., Co. of Longford

Carrickfergus, Co. of Antrim

Ruins of Clonnacnois, Kings Co.

Antiquities at Mount Cashel, Co. of Tipperary

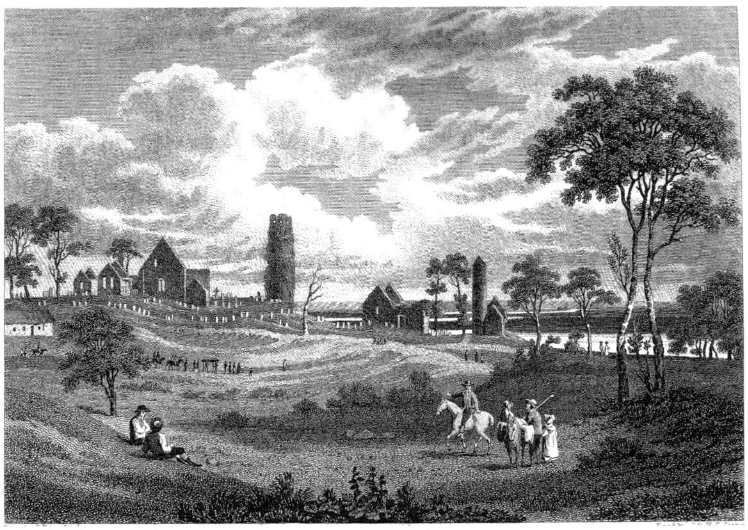

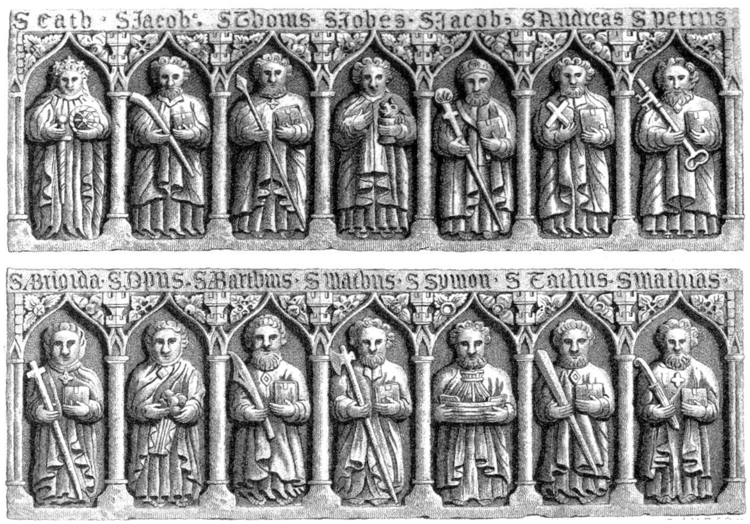

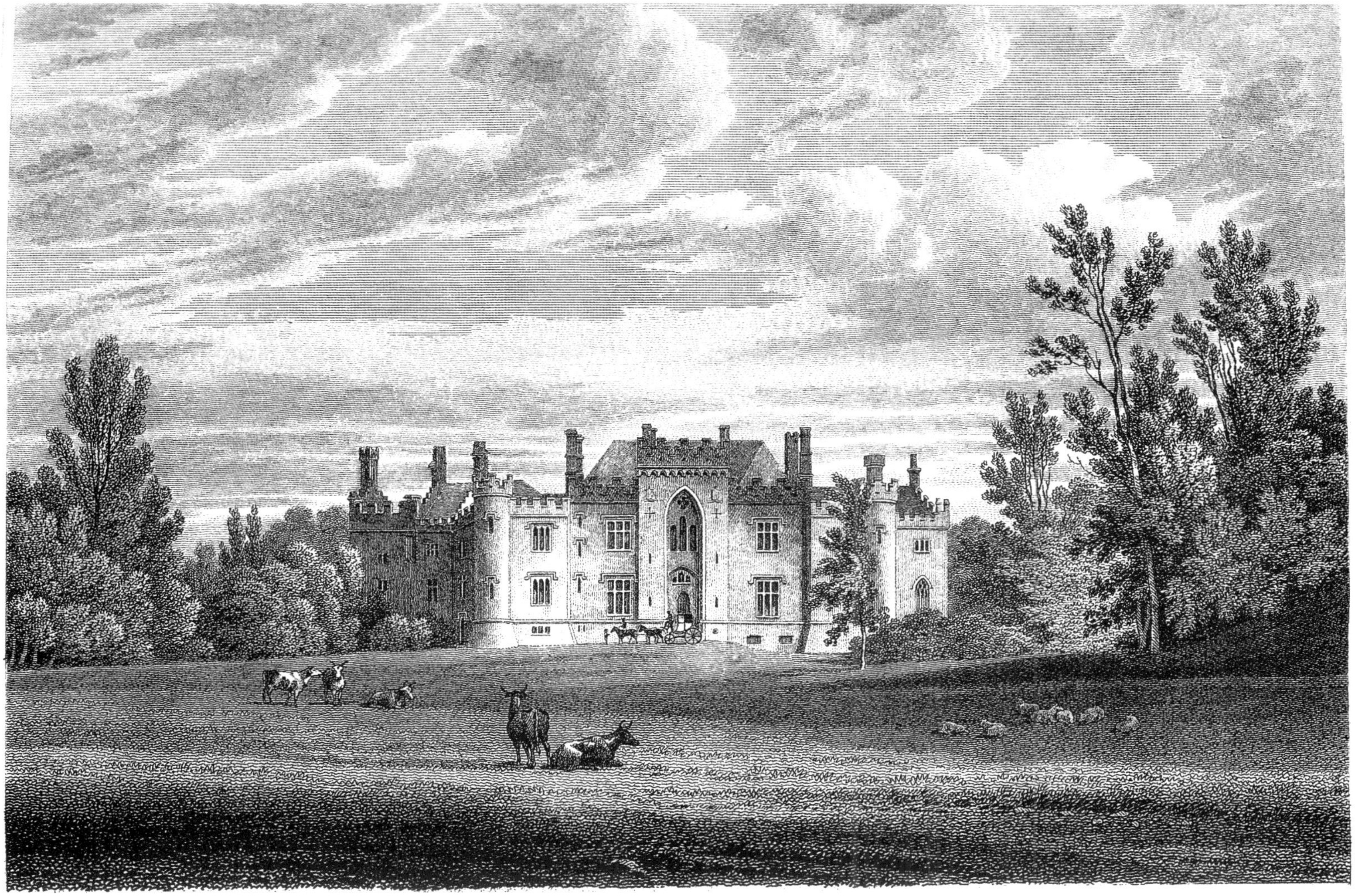

Parson's Town Castle, Seat of the Earl of Ross, Co. of Kings

Ireland Illustrated

BY REV G.N. WRIGHT (1828-39)

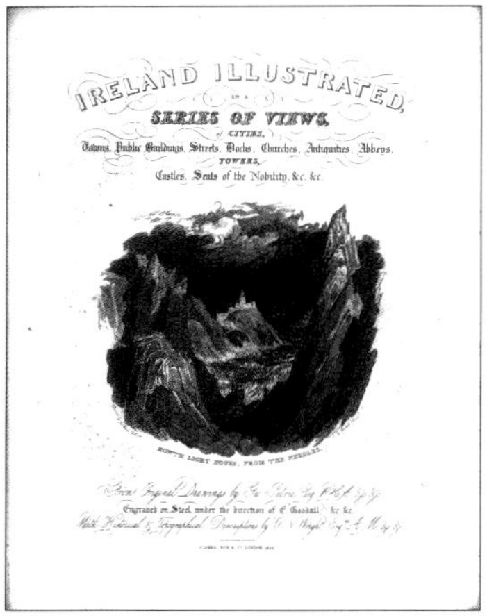

Title page with engraving of *Howth Light House, from the Needles*

Ireland Illustrated, in a series of views of Cities, Towns, Public Buildings, Streets, Docks, Churches, Antiquities, Abbeys, Towers, Castles, Seats of the Nobility, &c. &c. from Original Drawings by G. Petrie, RHA, W.H. Bartlett, & T.M. Baynes, with Descriptions by G.N. Wright, A. M. Esqre

Engravings of Kilkenny Castle, drawn by Robertson and engraved by W. Taylor, show through their coarseness, extremes of contrast and generally more amateur rendering, the high quality of Petrie's work in the preceding pages. Towards the latter half of the book, the engravings after Petrie are far fewer, with Bartlett, T.M. Baynes, and other artists producing views of Cork, Limerick and Belfast.

In his Preface, the editor, referring to himself as 'The Illustrator', praised the work of the artists in supplying pencil sketches for the engravers: 'The Illustrator, unconfined by any definite or preconcerted system, has rambled over subjects without method or restraint – if he has pleased sufficiently, for which he is aware his thanks are to be acknowledged more to the fascinating powers of his coadjutors' pencil, than to the efforts of his pen, the chief object of the Illustrations has been obtained. Like the butterfly, he has winged his desultory course through paths of pleasure adorned with a thousand sweets, passing heedlessly over many of natures's fairest flowers, and gathering only from the blossoms of his choice.' The preface also contains a plug for two similar volumes of English scenery, one illustrating the county of Lancashire; the others the counties of Devon and Cornwall.

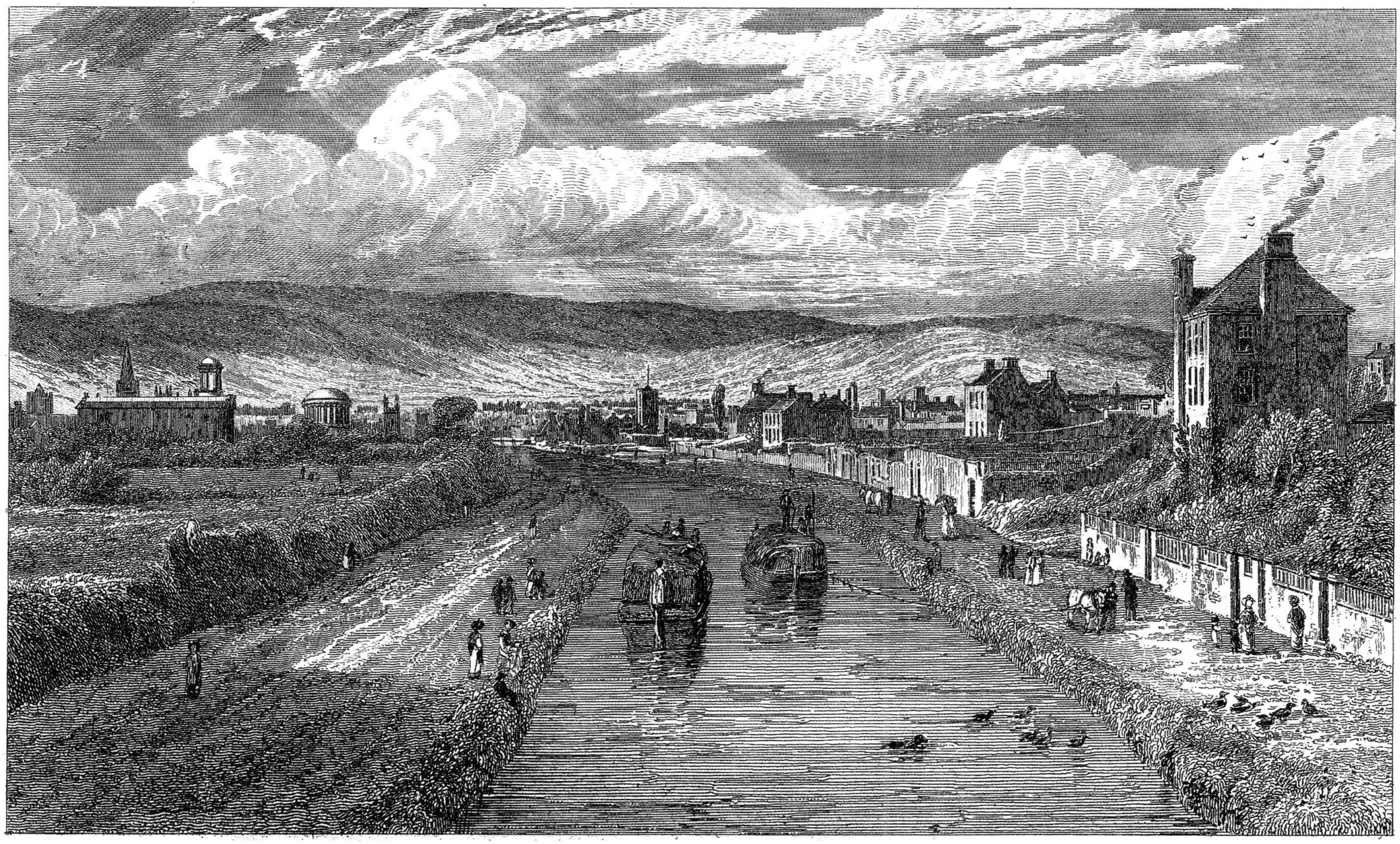

Dublin, from Blaquiere Bridge, Royal Canal

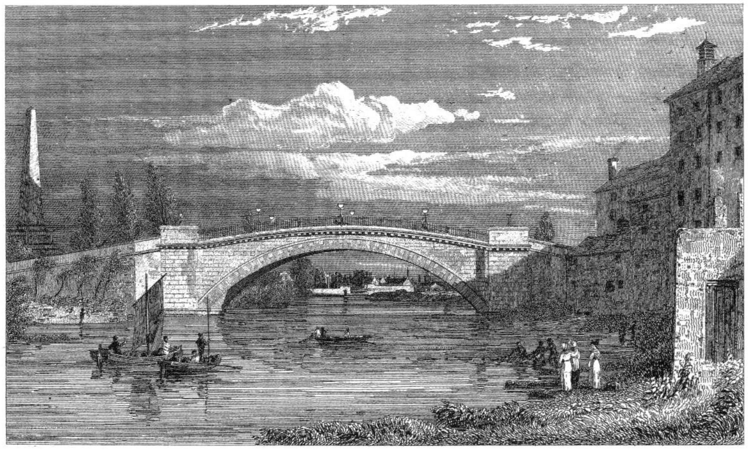

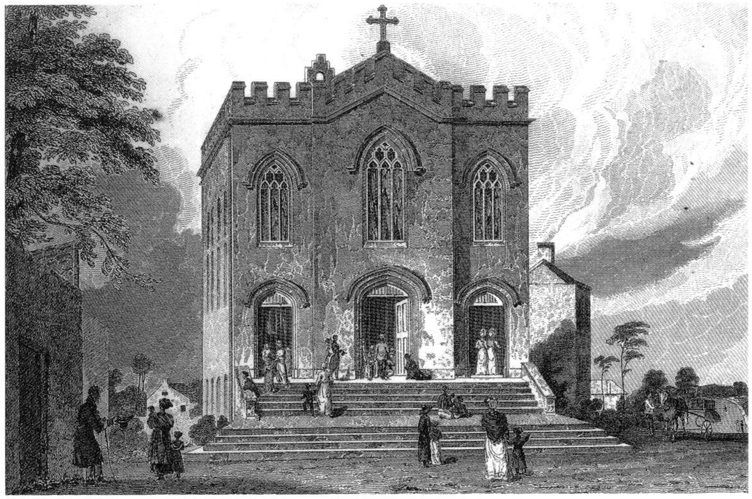

Sarah's Bridge, on the River Anna Liffey

St. Peter's R.C. Chapel & Free Schools, Circular Road, Phibsborough

College Street

opposite
The Wellington Testimonial, Phœnix Park

Post Office, Dublin

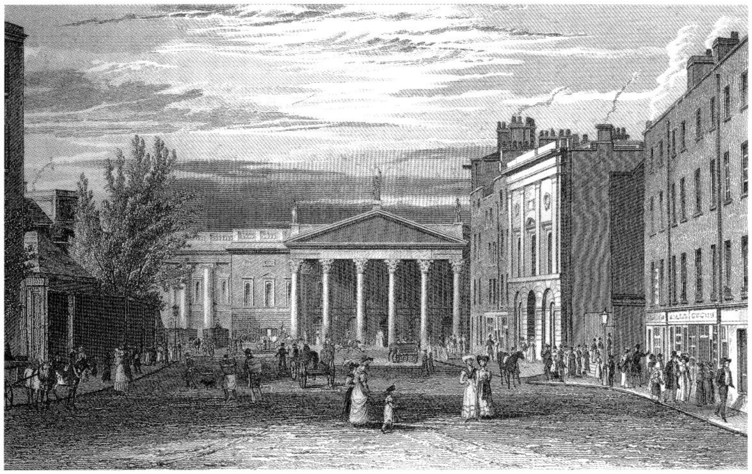

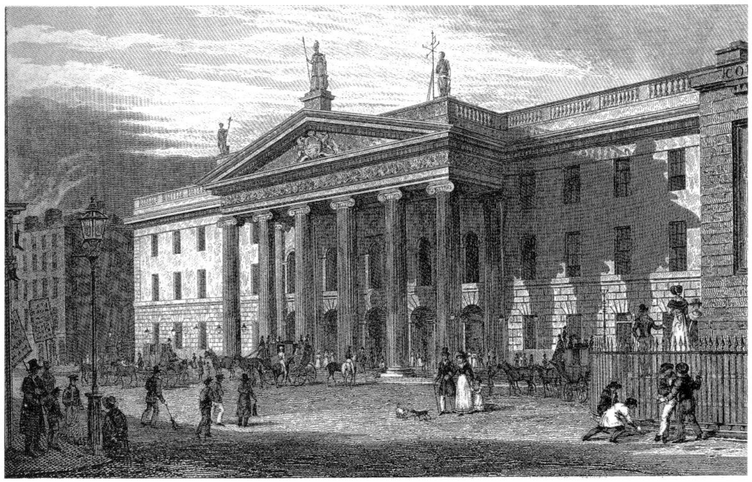

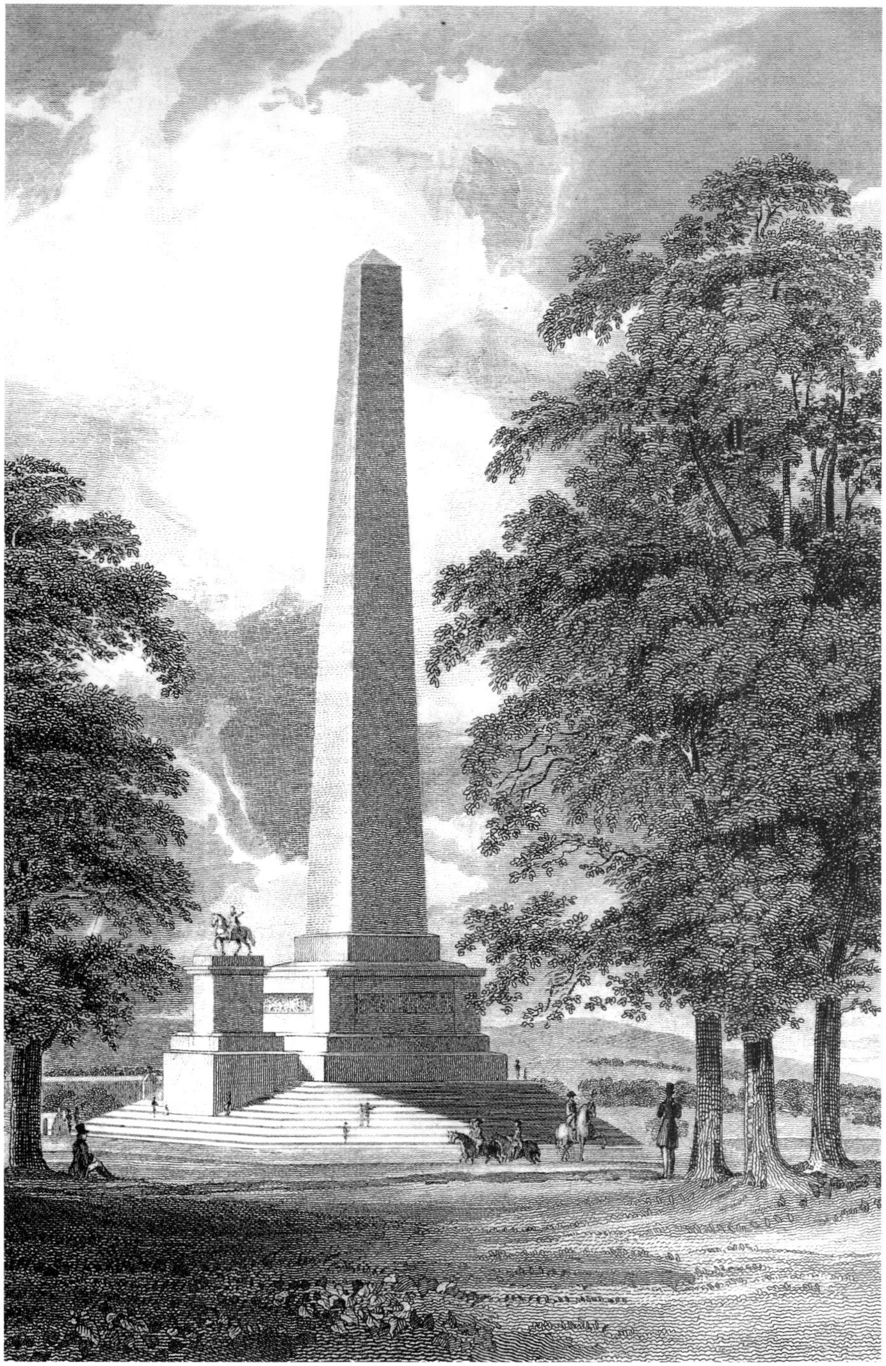

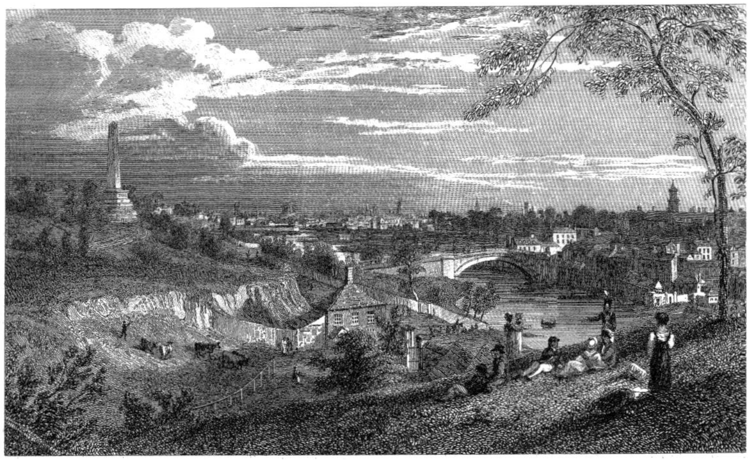

Dublin, from Phœnix Park

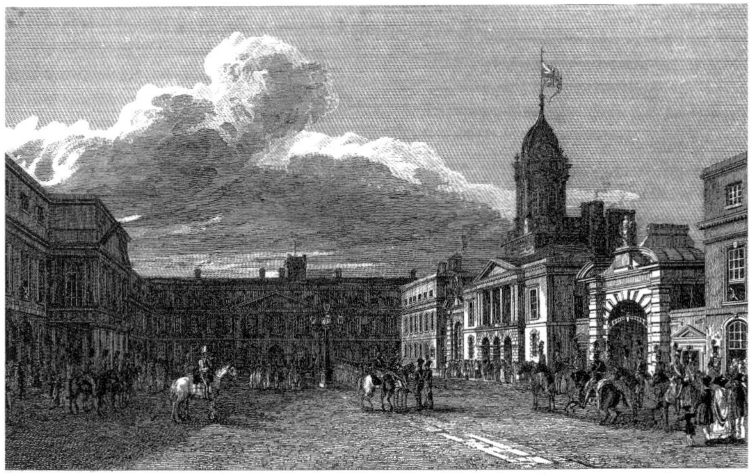

Great Court Yard, Dublin Castle

Memorial of the King's Visit to Ireland, Kingstown

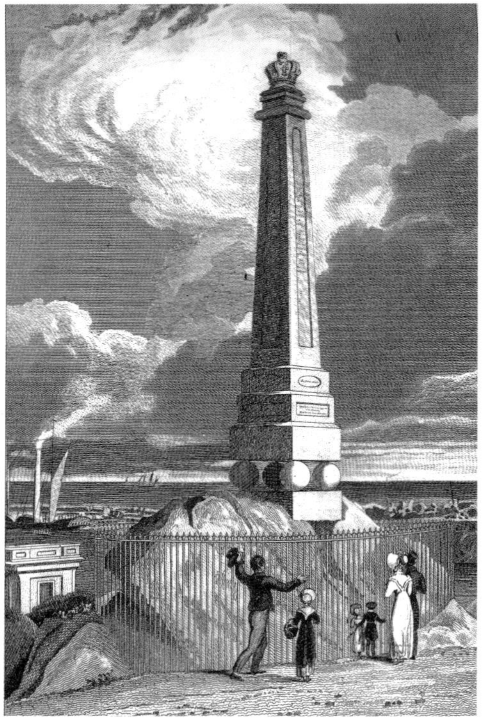

Obelisk, at Newtown-Park, County Dublin

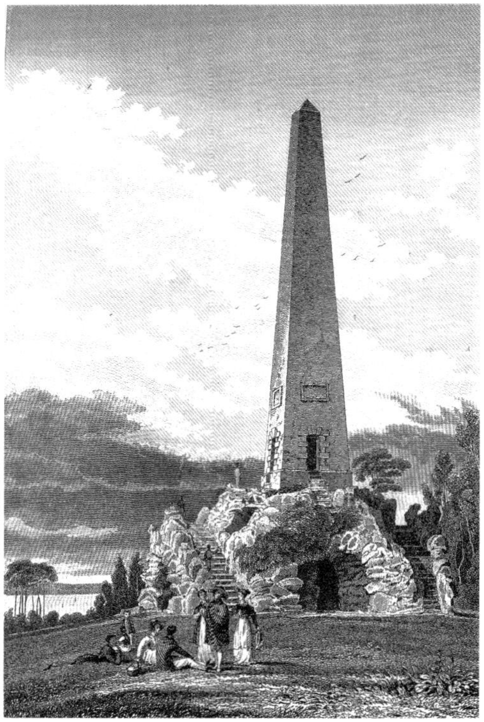

The Phœnix Pillar, Phœnix Park

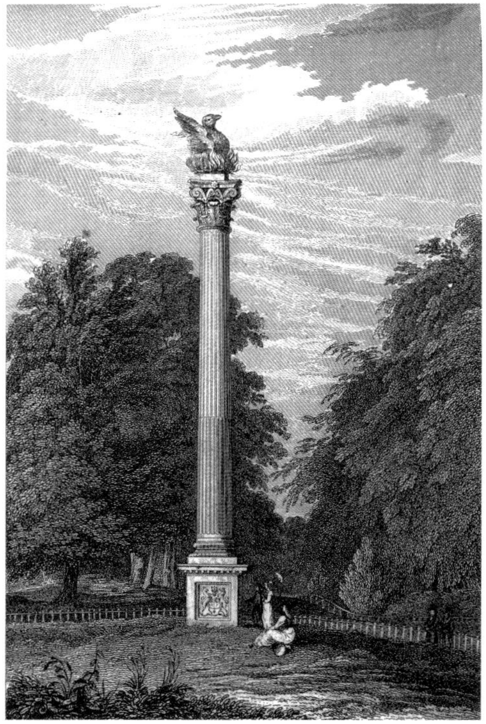

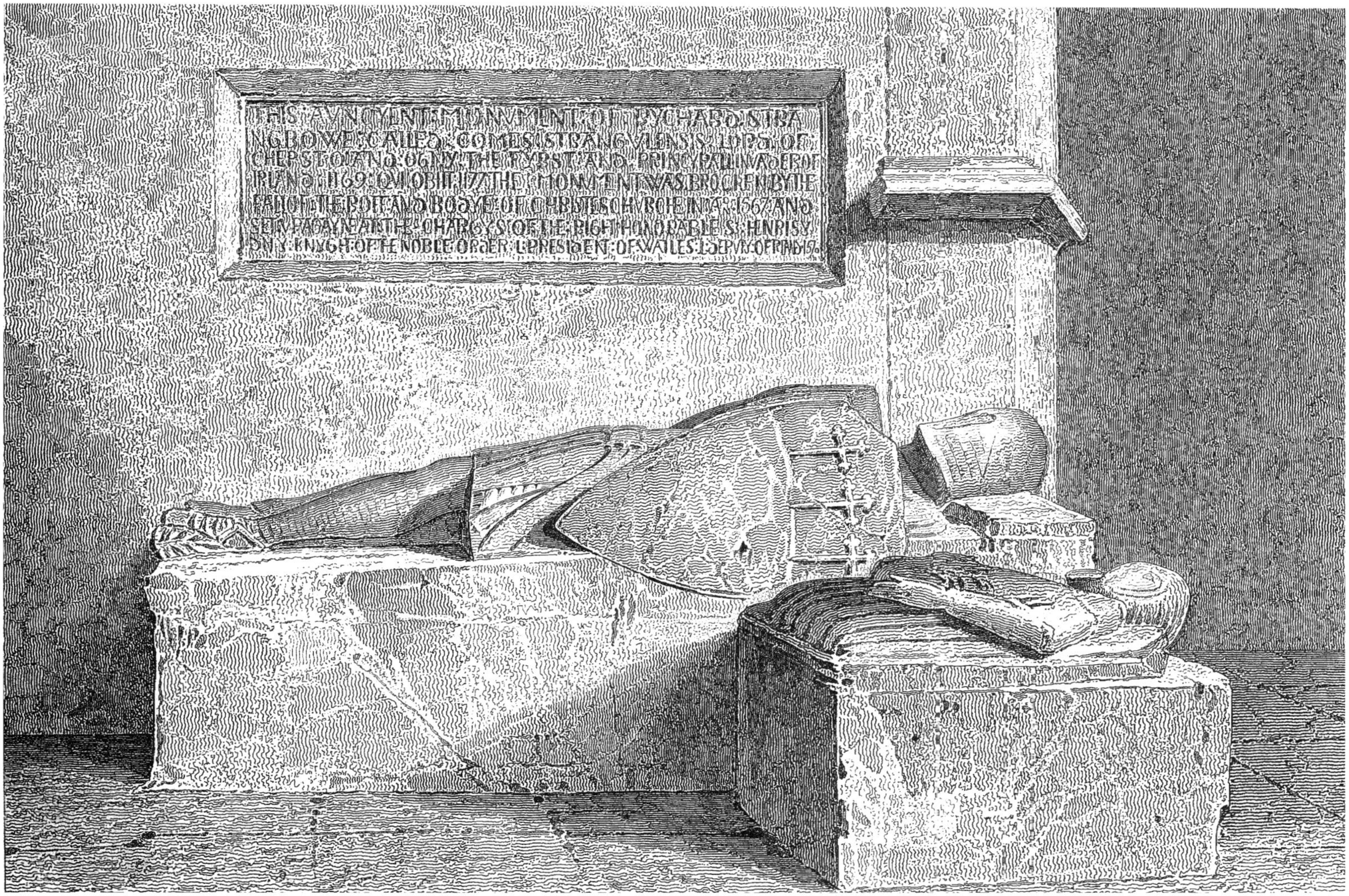

Strongbow's Monument

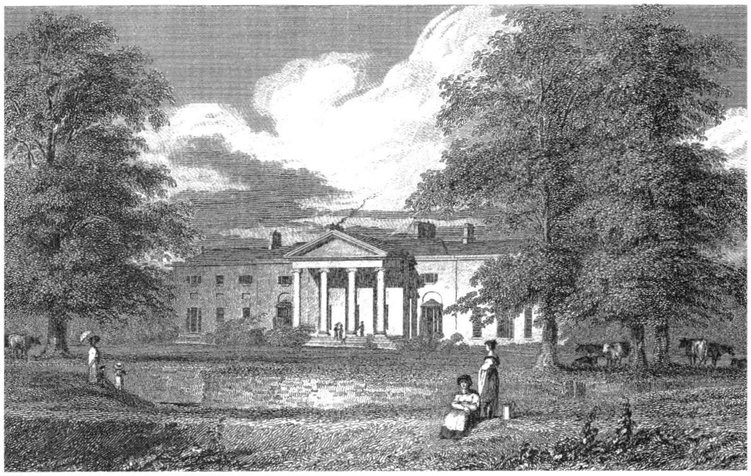

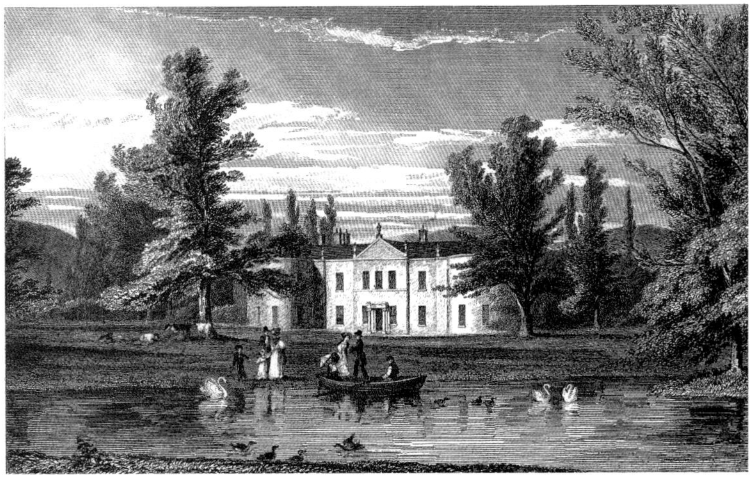

The Vice Regal Lodge, Phœnix Park, Near Dublin

Terenure, Co. Dublin

The King's Bridge, Dublin (West View)

Bank of Ireland, Dublin (South Portico)

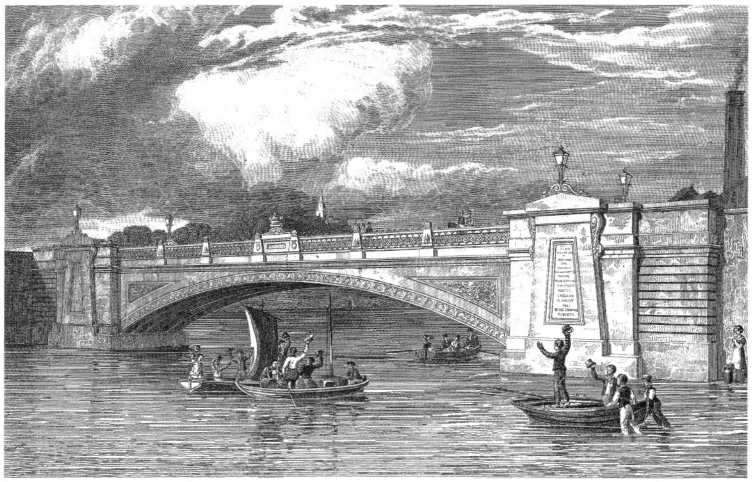

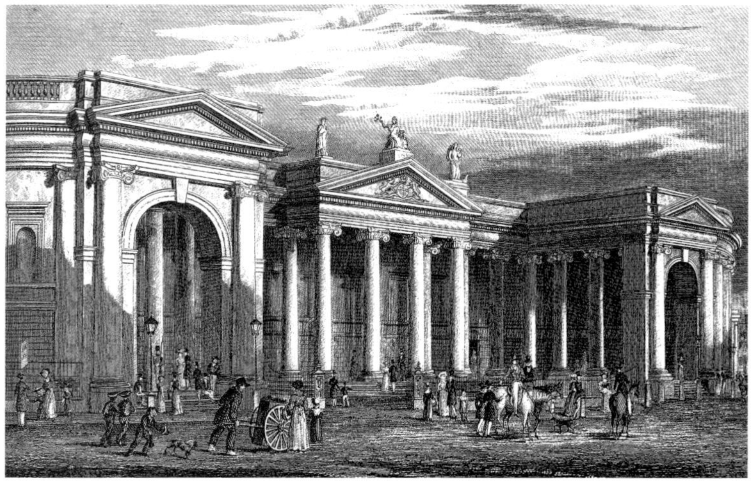

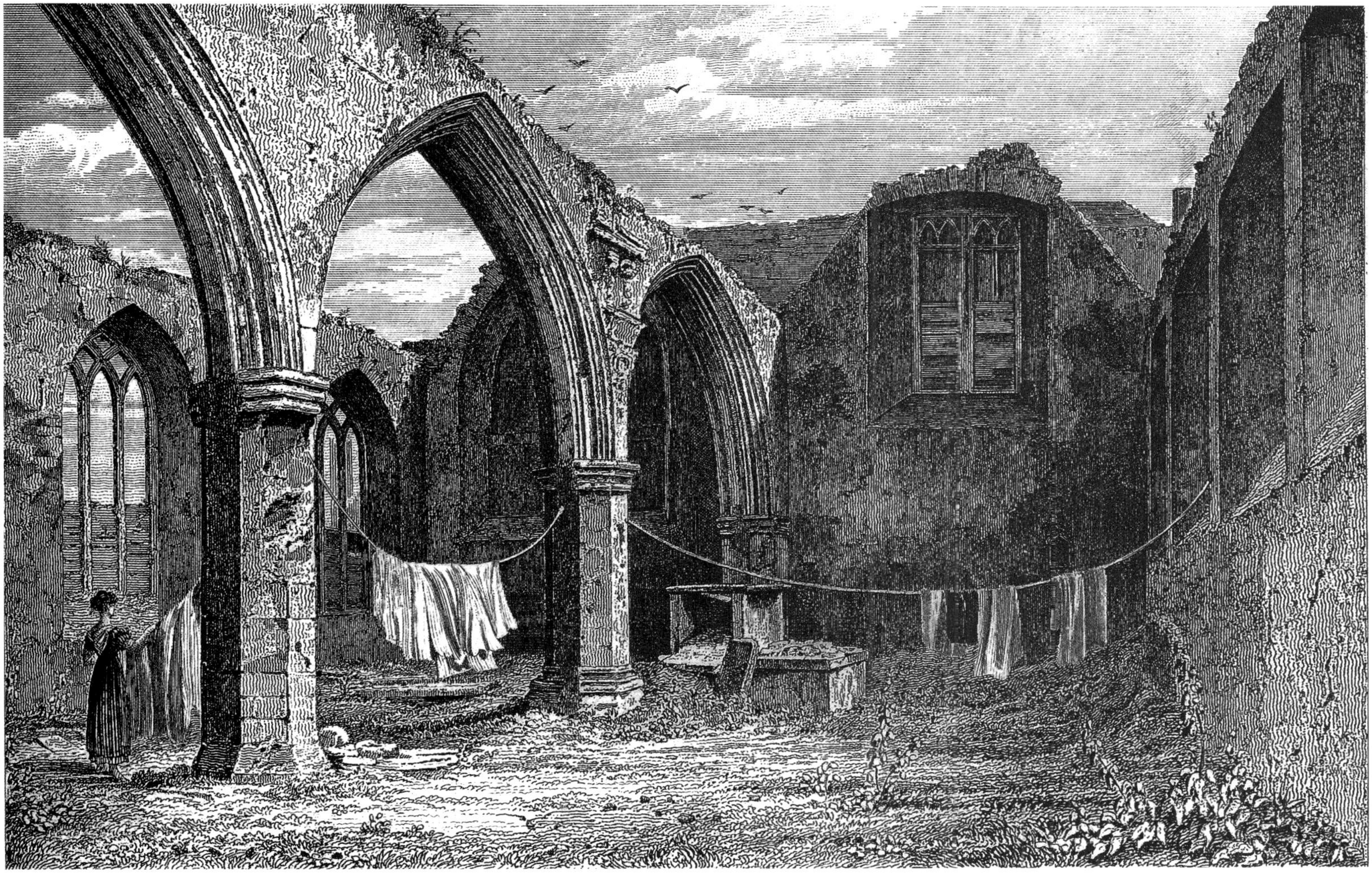

Ruins of Lord Portlester's Chapel, St. Audeon's Church

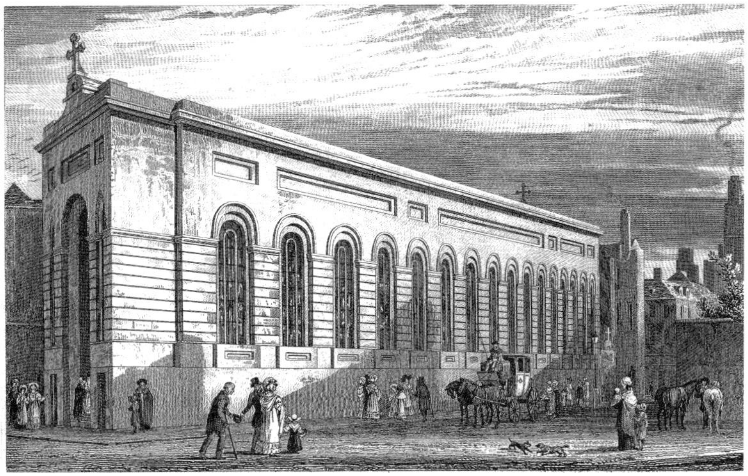

The Church of the Carmelite Friary, York Row

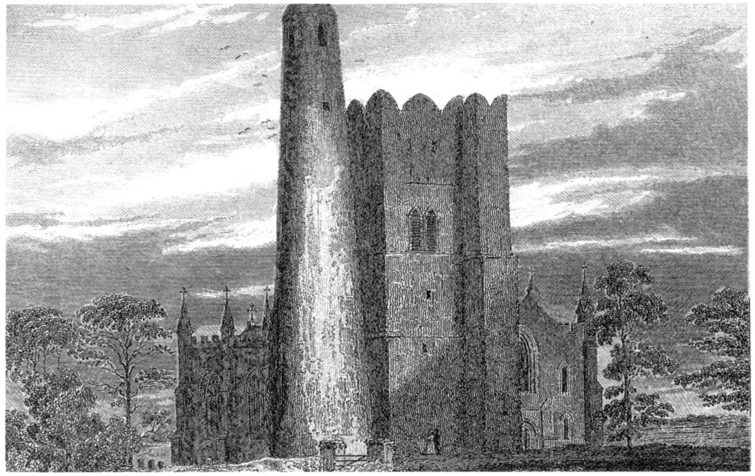

The Round Tower, Belfry & Church of Swords (detail)

Nelson's Pillar, Sackville-Street, Dublin

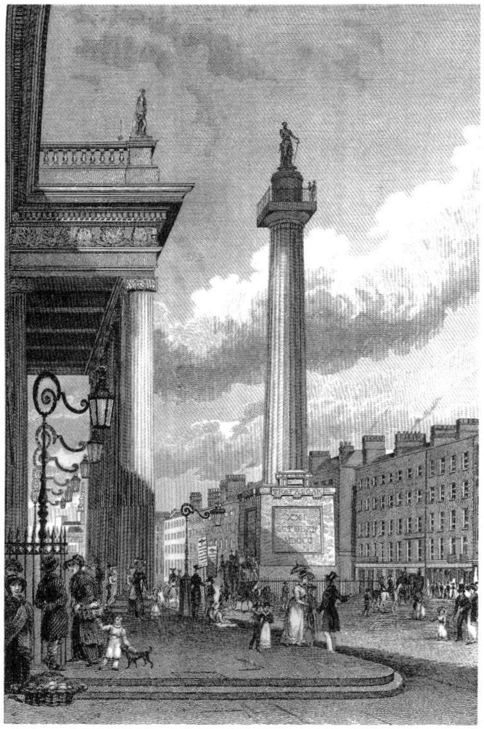

St. George's Church, Dublin

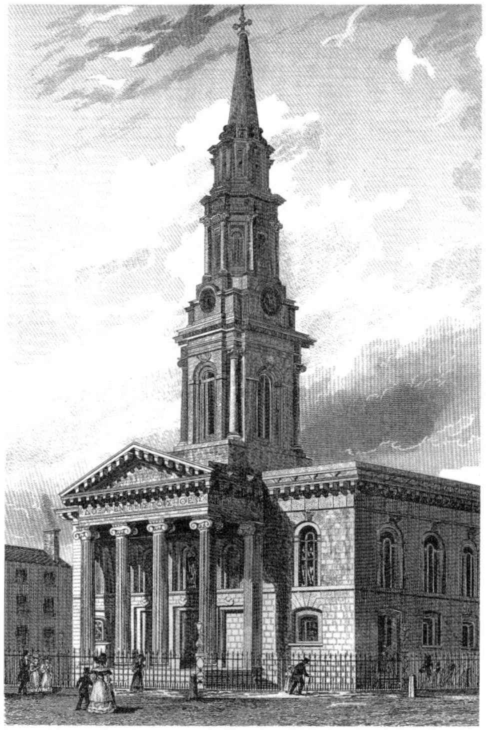

The Round Tower of Clondalkin, Co. Dublin

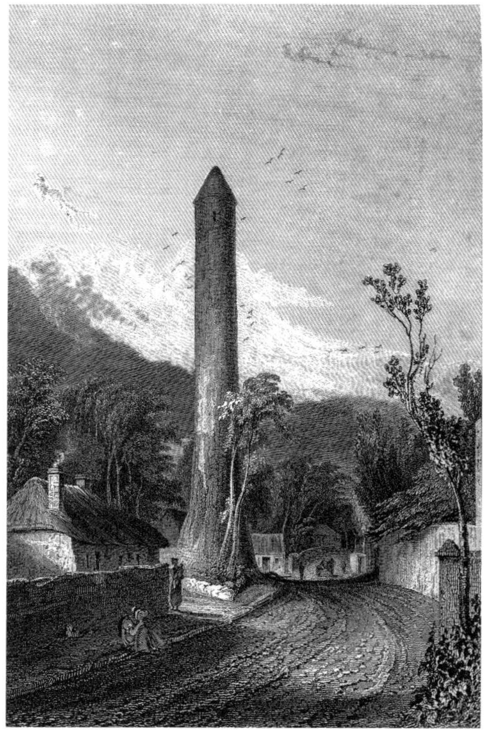

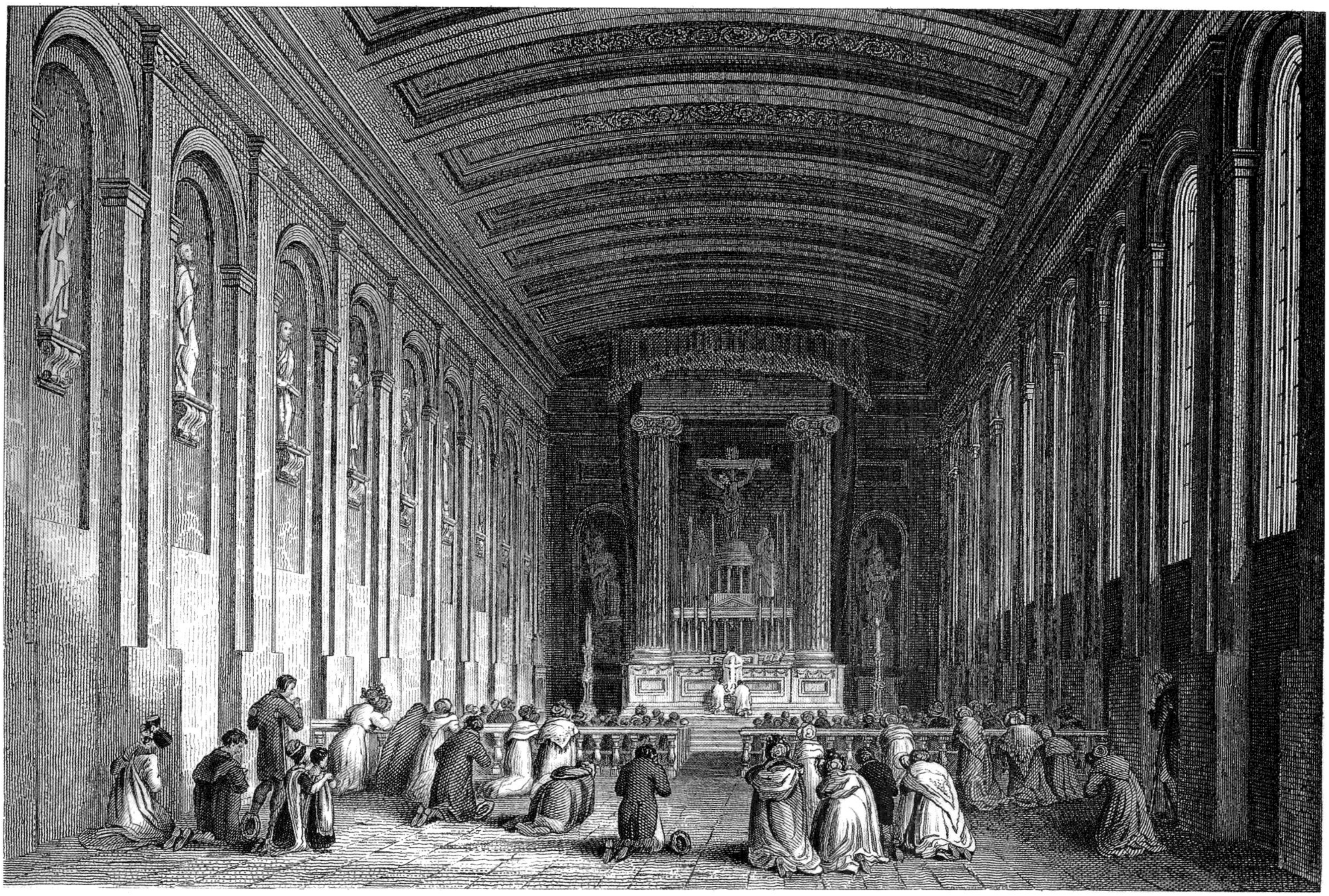

Interior of the Church of the Carmelite Friary

The Ecclesiastical Architecture of Ireland

BY GEORGE PETRIE (1845)

[Note: This is intended as a representative selection of the 256 illustrations in this book]

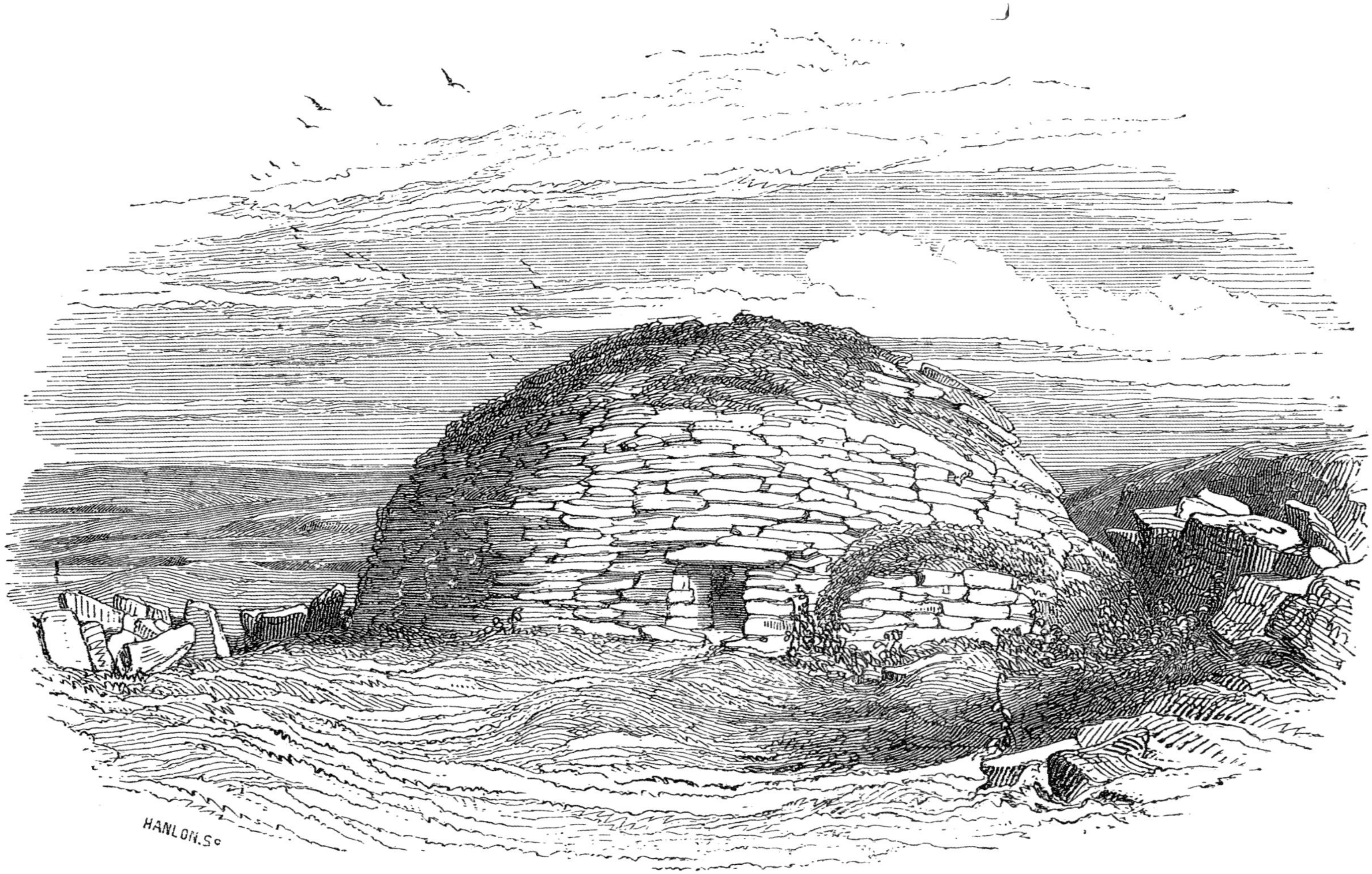

Round Stone-house, called Clochan na Carriage,
on the great Island of Aran, in the Bay of Galway

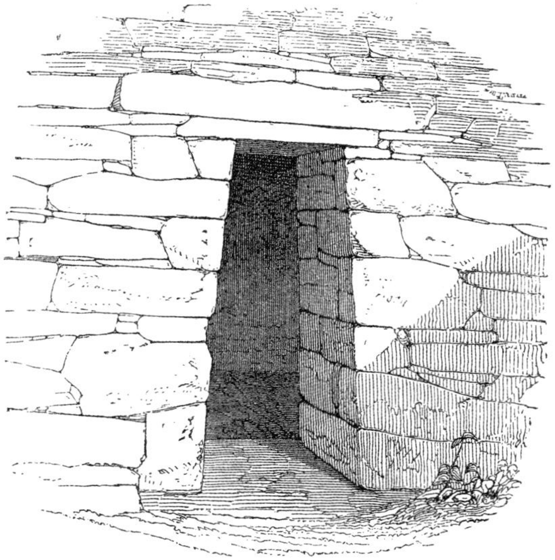

Doorway, in the Cyclopean Style, in the Oratory at Gallerus, in the Co of Kerry

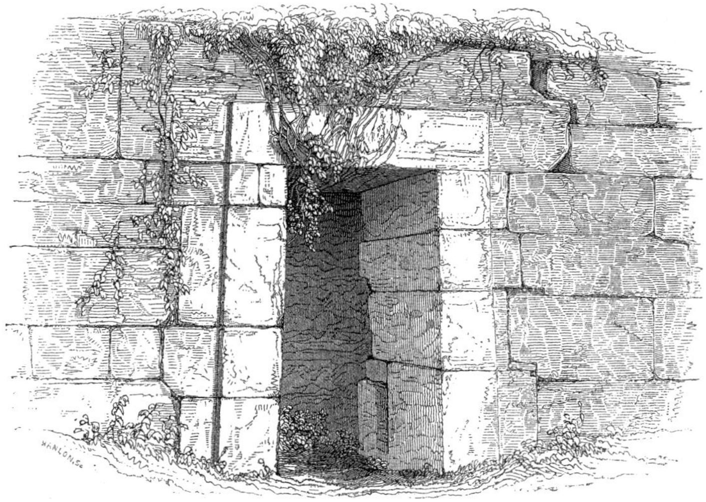

Doorway of the Church of Ratass, near Tralee, in the County of Kerry

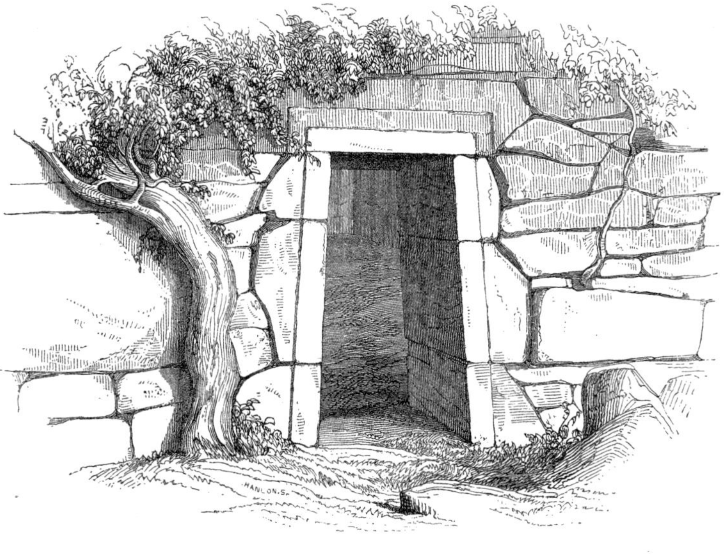

Doorway of Our Lady's Church at Glendalough, in the County of Wicklow

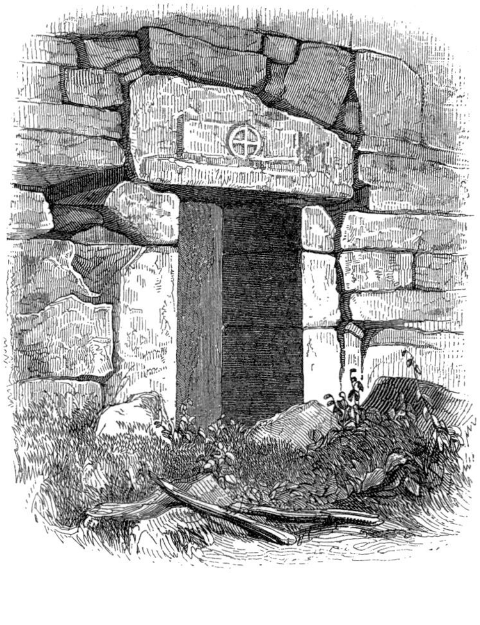

Doorway of St. Fechin's Church at Fore, in the County of Westmeath

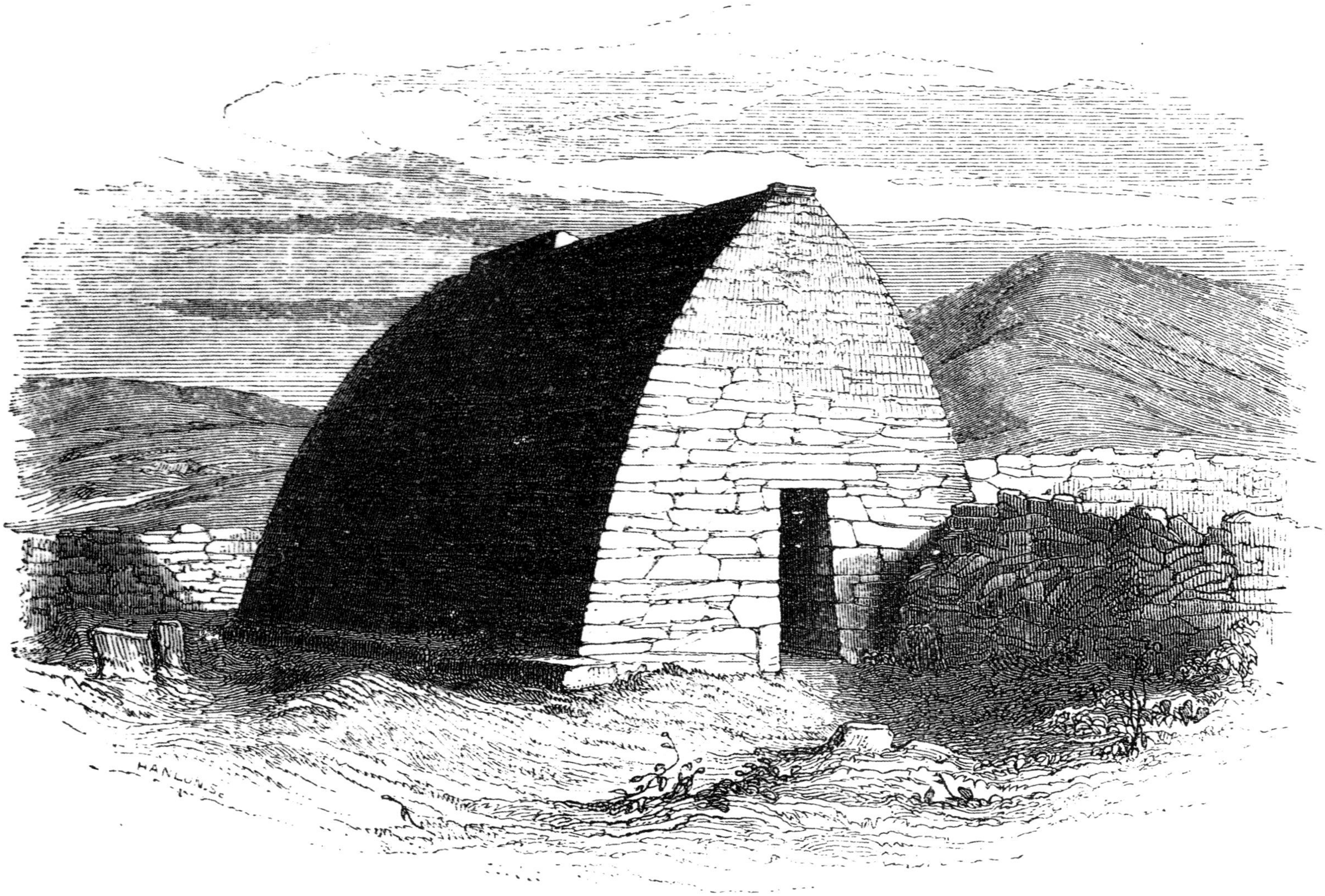

Stone Oratory at Gallerus,
in the Barony of Corcaguiny, in the County of Kerry

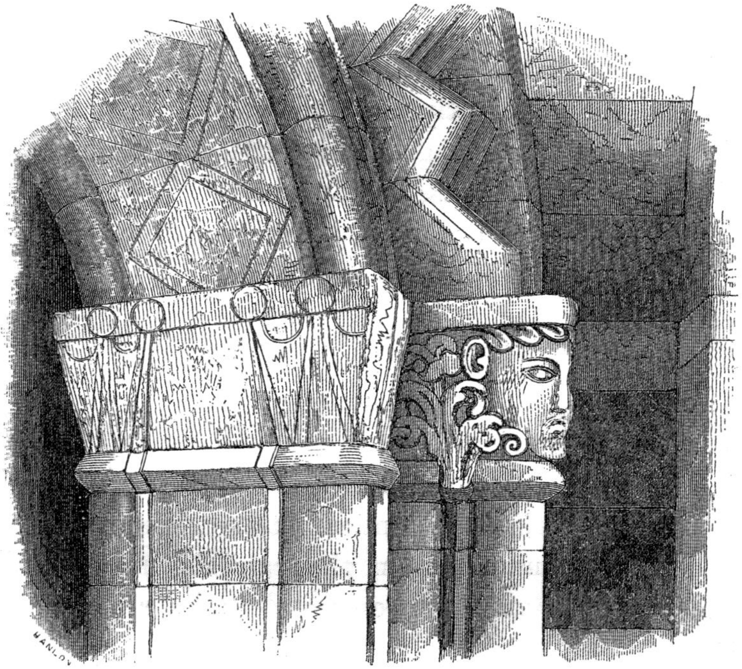

ROUND TOWER OF TIMAHOE, QUEEN'S COUNTY

View of the outer Division of the inner Archway of the Doorway of the Round Tower

Capital at east Side of outer Division of the inner Archway of same

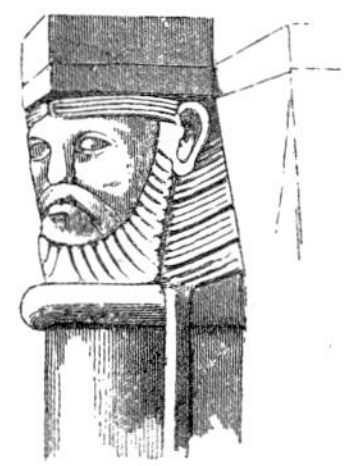

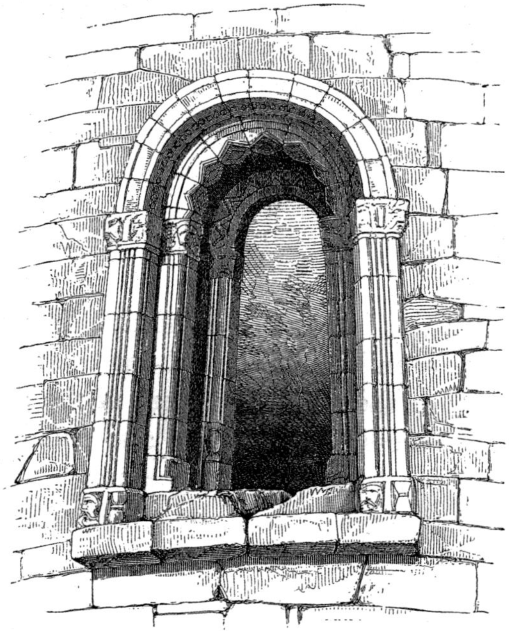

Capitals of the Doorway

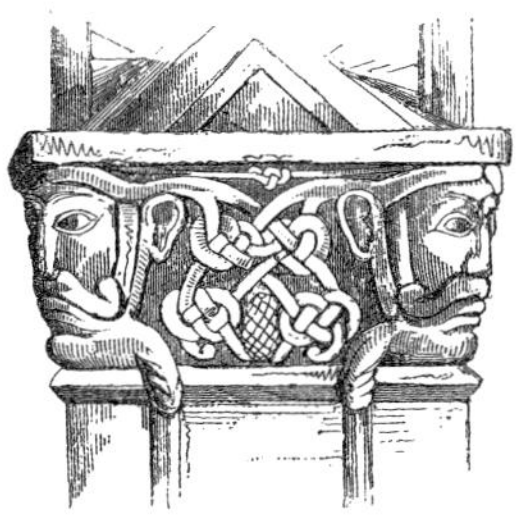

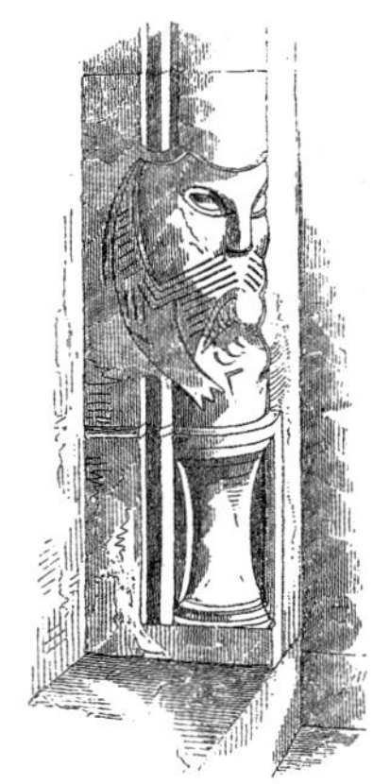

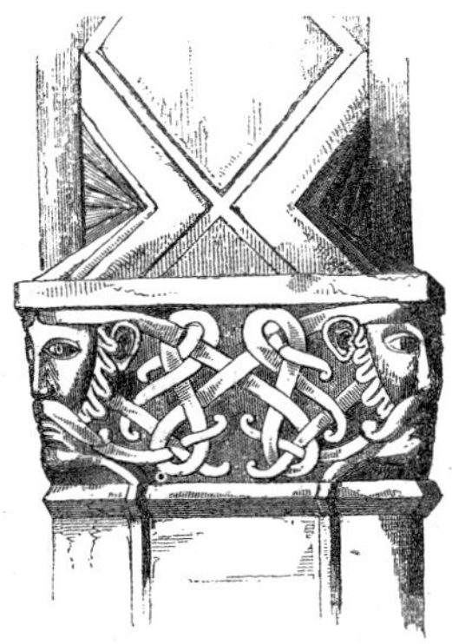

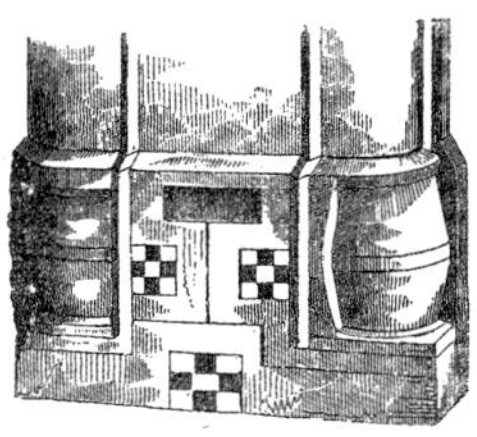

Base of Shaft on west Side of same

Bases of the semicircular Shafts at the Angles of the Archway of the same Doorway, with intermediate Space

right

Doorway of the Round Tower

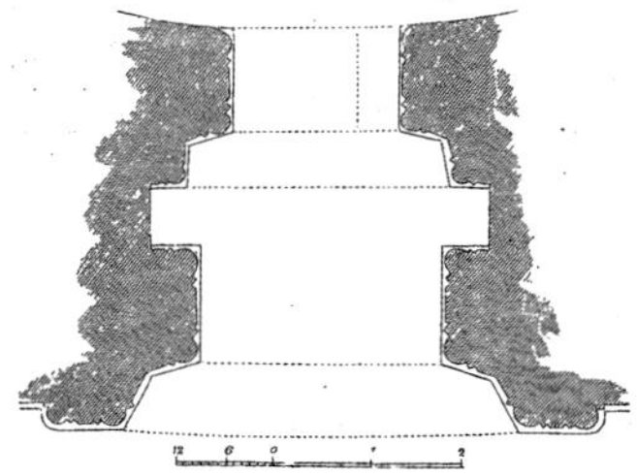

Horizontal and Vertical Sections of the Doorway

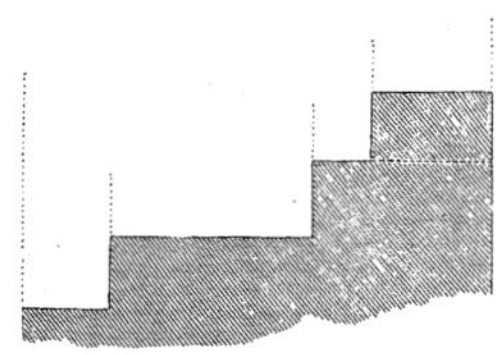

Specimen of Pellet and Bead Moulding on the Soffit of the Arch of the Doorway

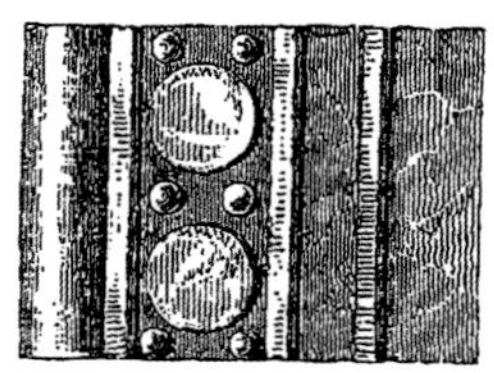

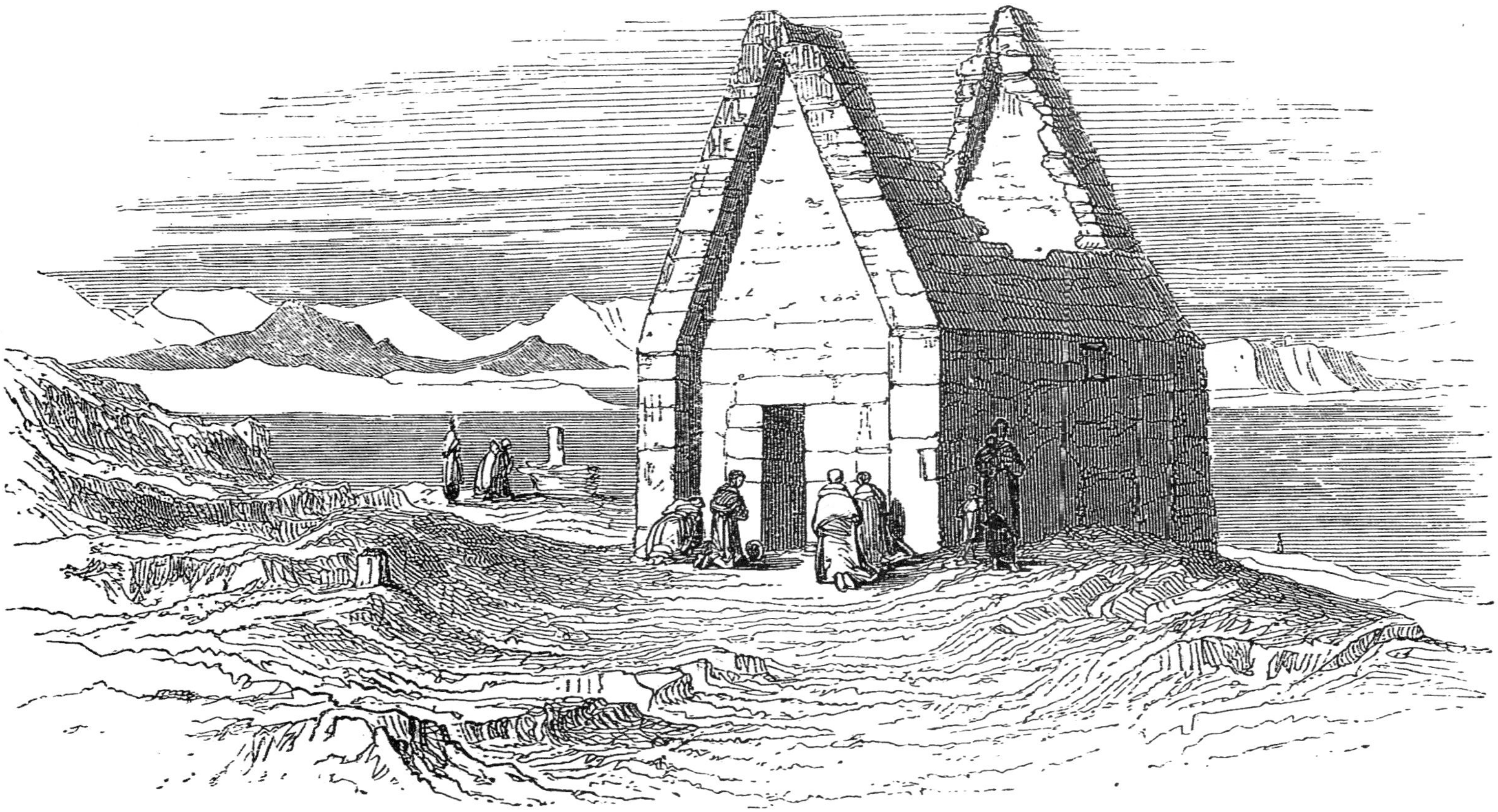

View of the Church of St. Mac Dara,
on the Island of Cruach Mac Dara, off the Coast of the County of Galway

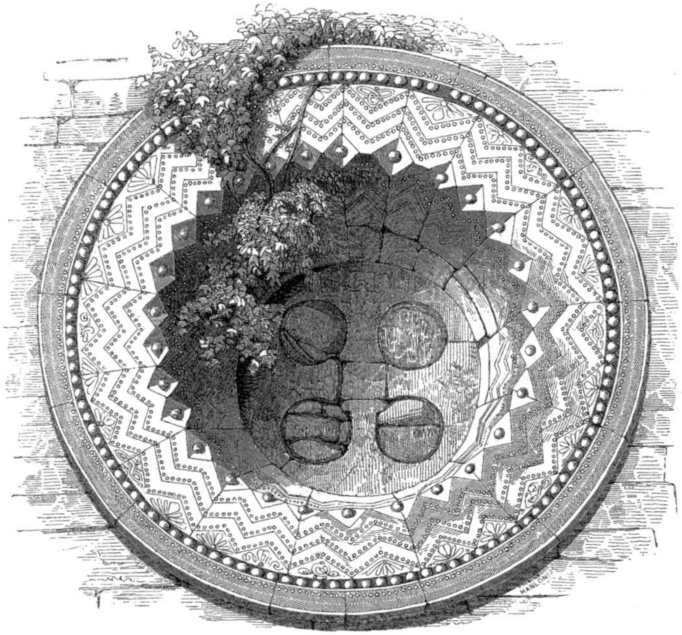

PARISH CHURCH OF RAHIN, IN THE KING'S COUNTY

Round ornamental Window in the Church of Rahin

Ornamental Doorway of the smaller Church of Rahin

right

Columns of the Chancel Arch of the Parish Church of Rahin, in the King's Co.

Capitals of opposite Side of the same

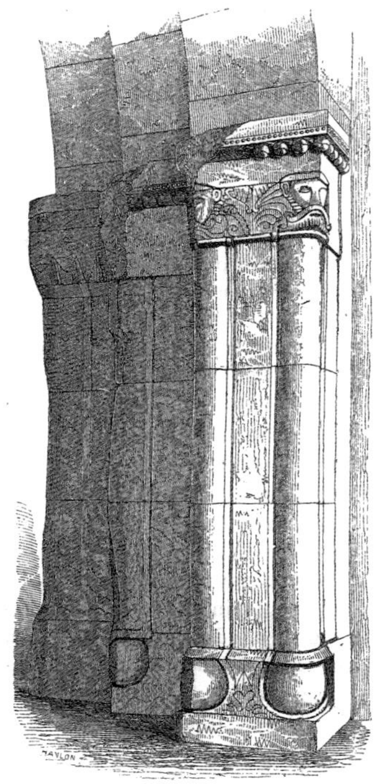

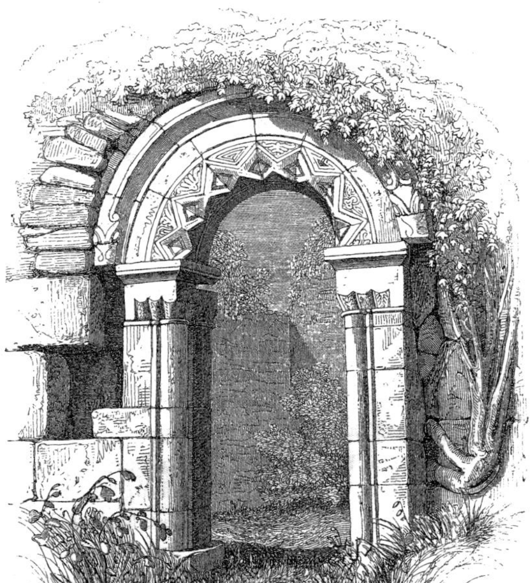

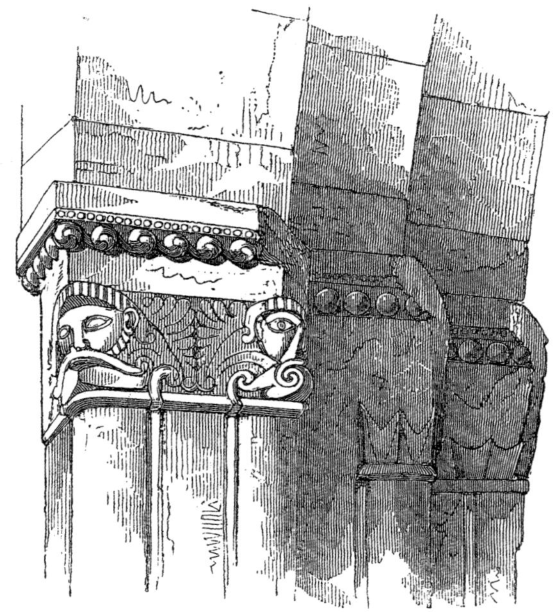

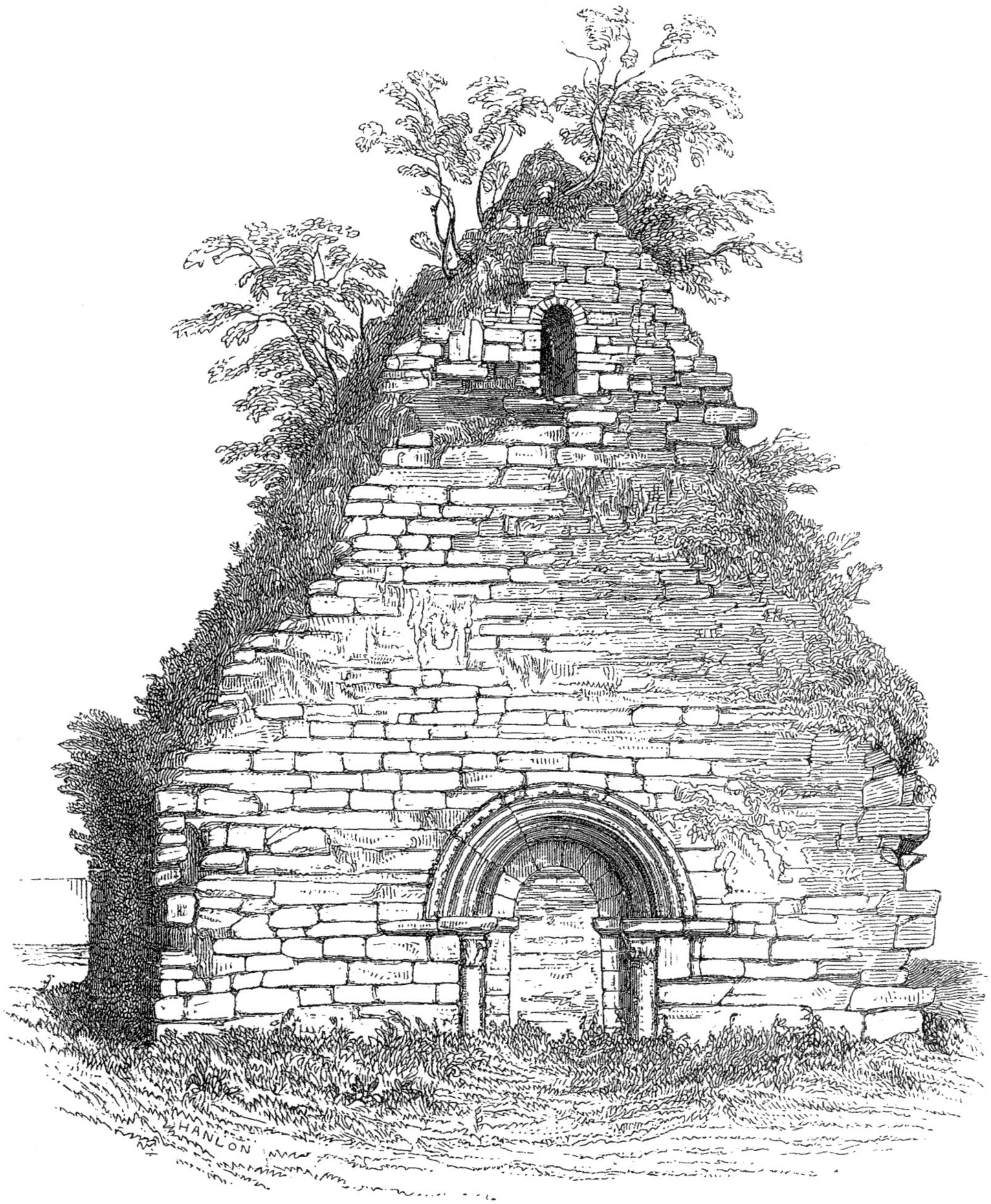

View of the west Gable (containing Doorway and Window) of the Stone-roofed Church at Killaloe

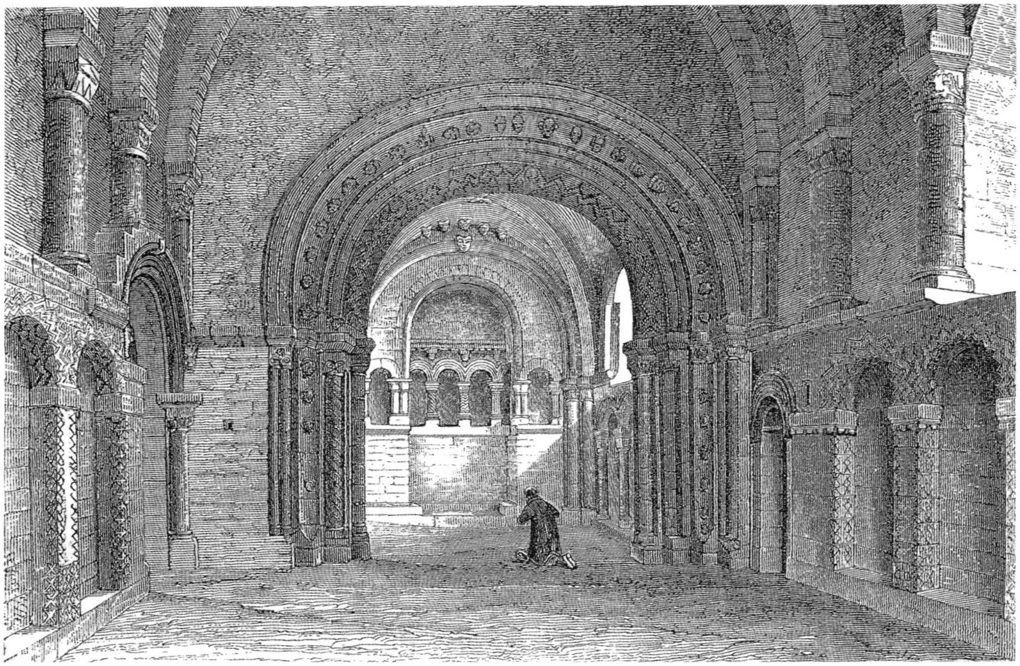

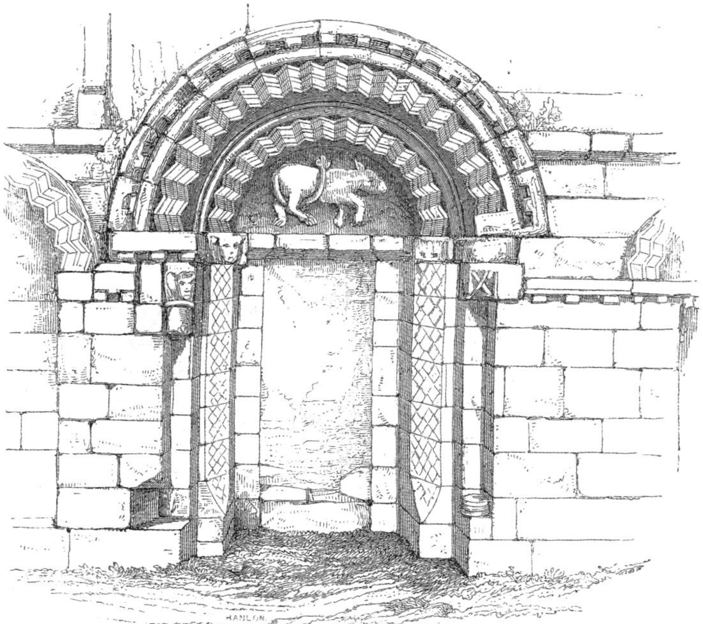

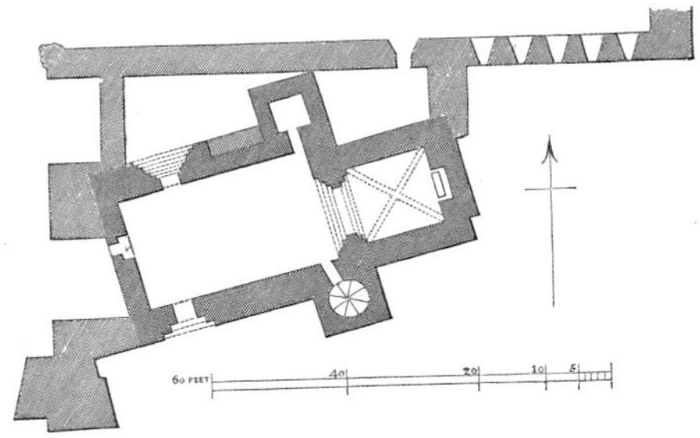

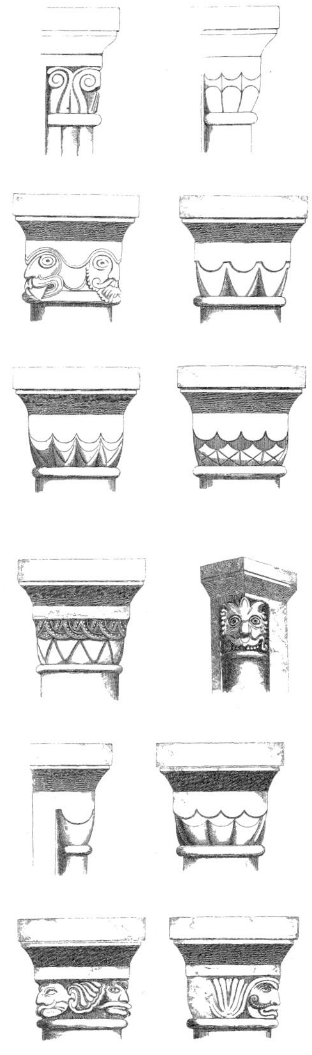

CORMAC'S CHAPEL,
ROCK OF CASHEL

View of the Interior of Cormac's Chapel

South Doorway of Cormac's Chapel

right

Ground-plan of Cormac's Chapel

Capitals of the smaller north Doorway

Capitals of the Semi-Columns which decorate the south Side of the Nave

Capitals of the north Side of the Nave

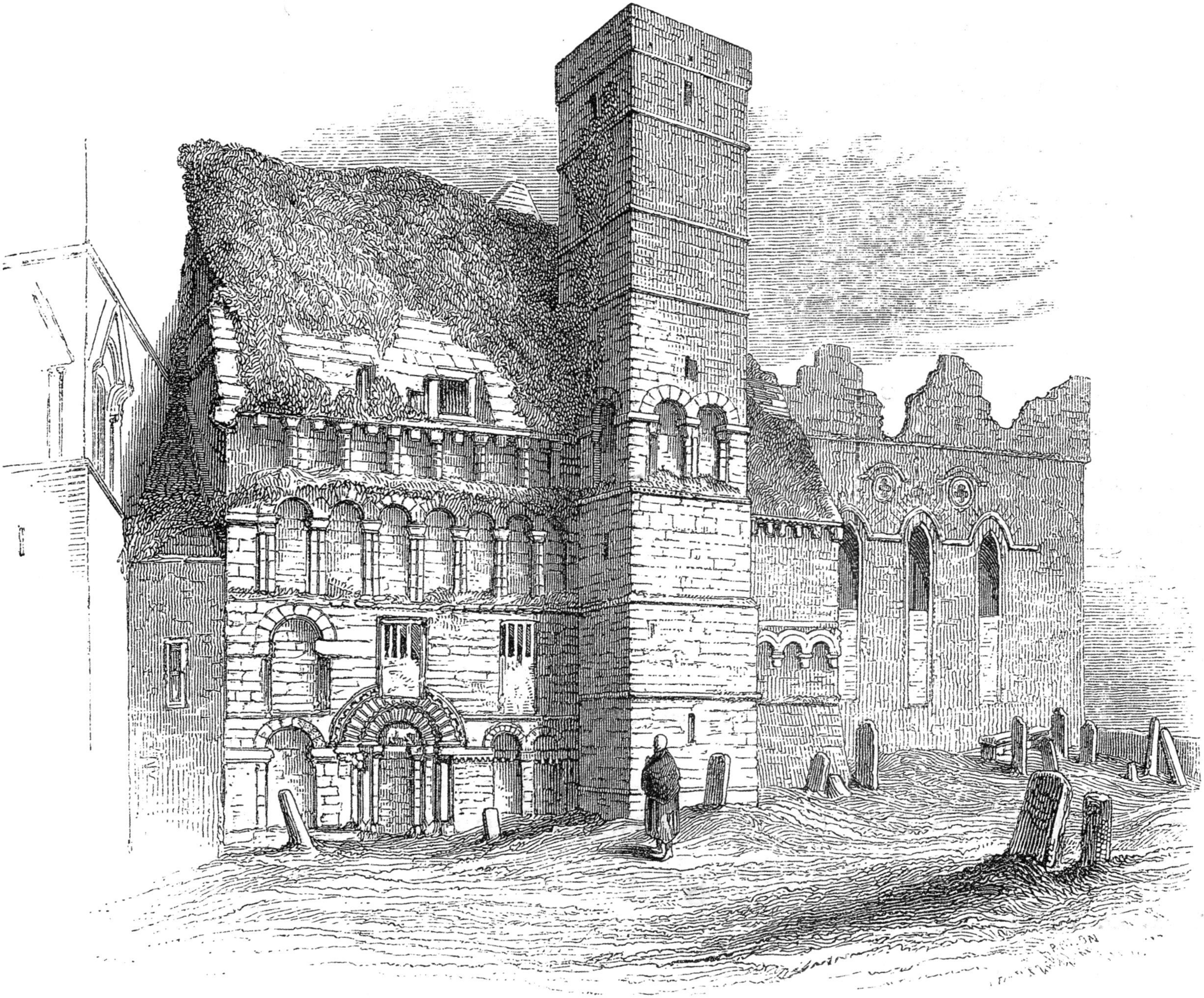

External View of Cormac's Chapel at Cashel

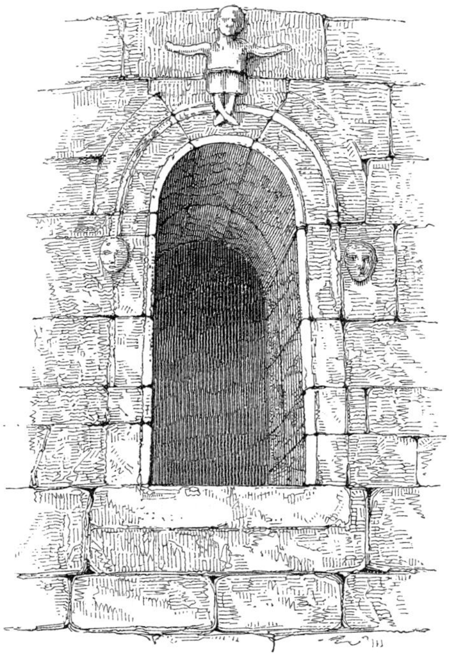

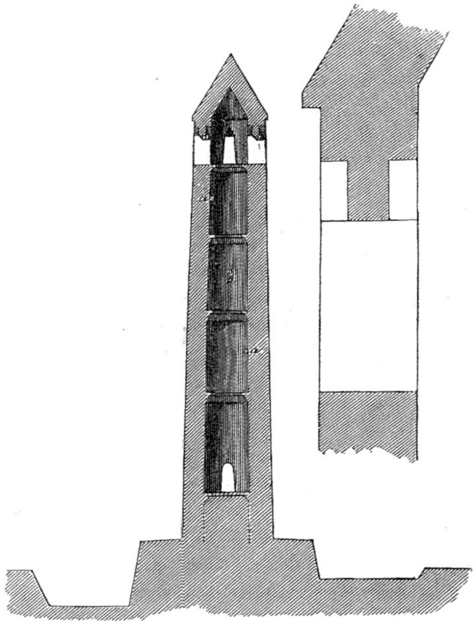

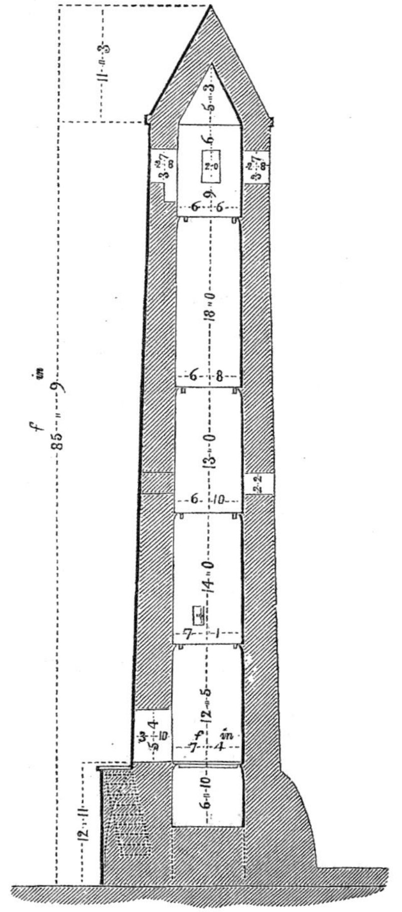

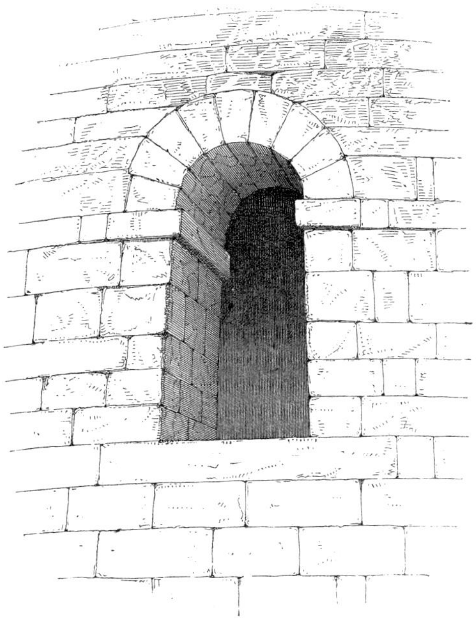

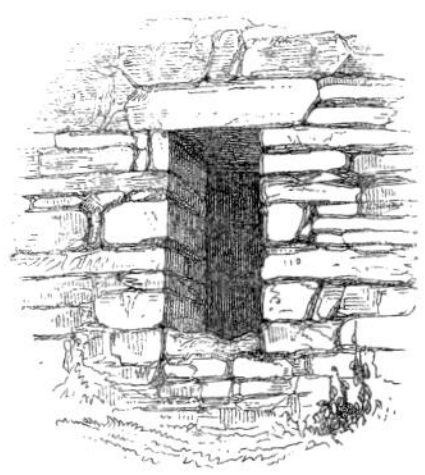

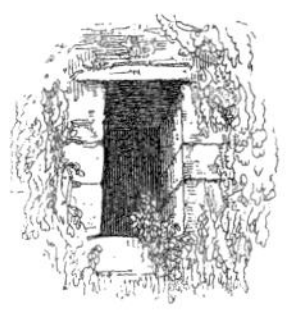

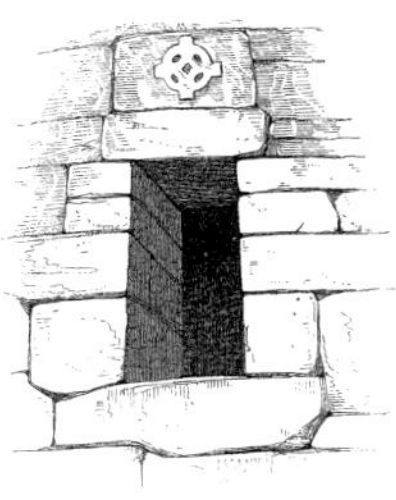

ROUND TOWERS

far left
Doorway of the Round Tower of Donaghmore, County of Meath
Doorway of the greater Tower of Clonmacnoise
top and right
Section of the Round Tower of Clondalkin
left
Lower and Upper Doorways of the Round Tower of Swords
Doorway of the Round Tower of Antrim
right
View of the Round Tower and Church of Teampull Finghin, at Clonmacnoise

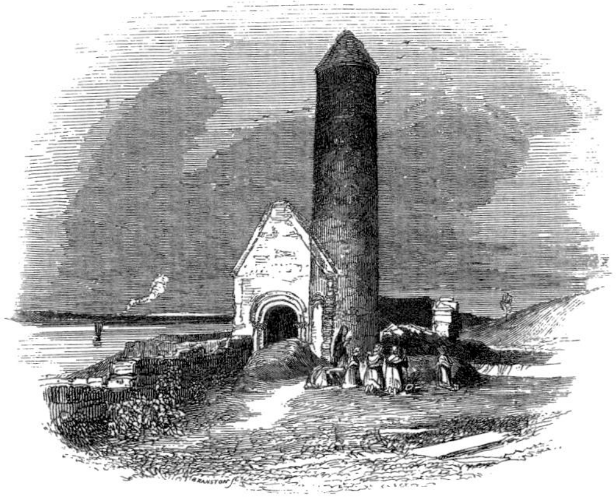

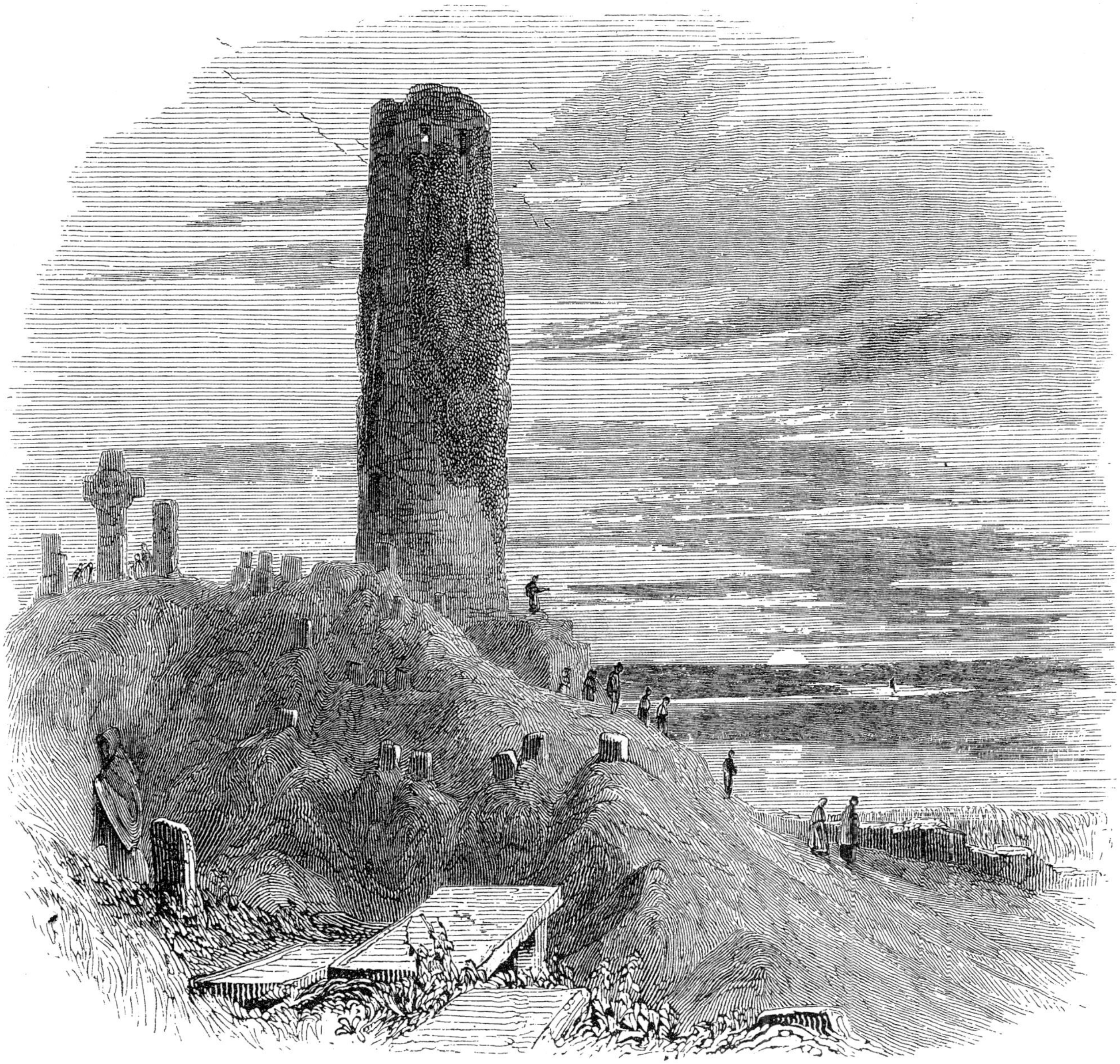

View of the greater Tower of Clonmacnoise

GLENDALOUGH,
CO WICKLOW

Pilasters of the Chancel-Arch of the Monastery Church at Glendalough

View of the Interior of Trinity Church, at Glendalough, showing the Chancel Arch

right

Devices on the Capitals of the south Side of the same

Capitals of the outer Pier of the same

Doorway of the same

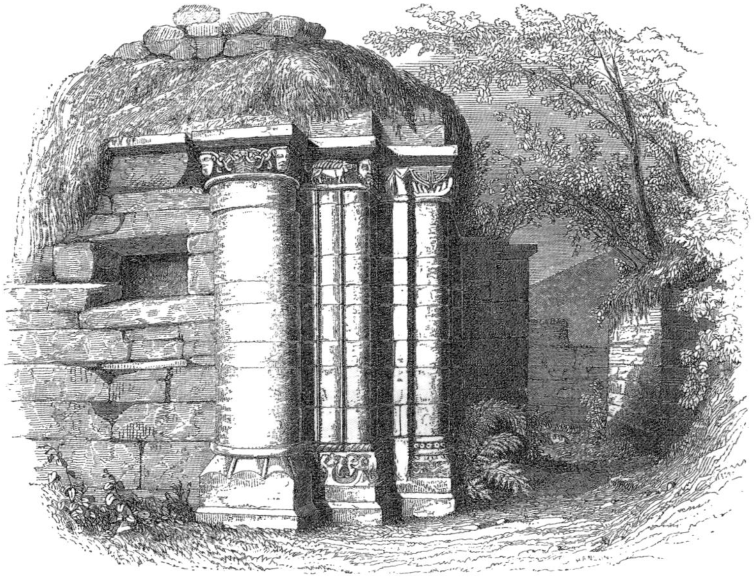

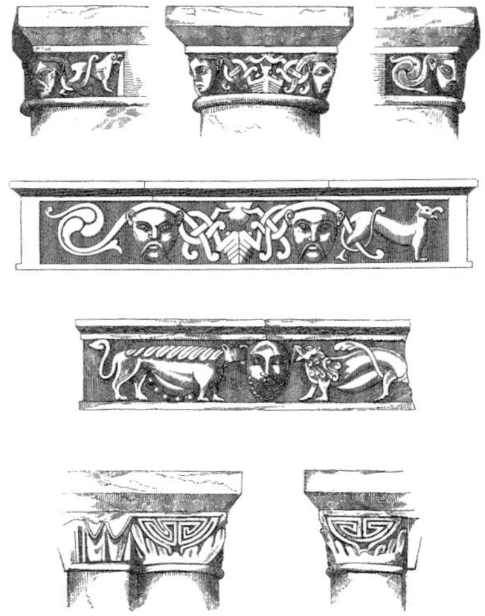

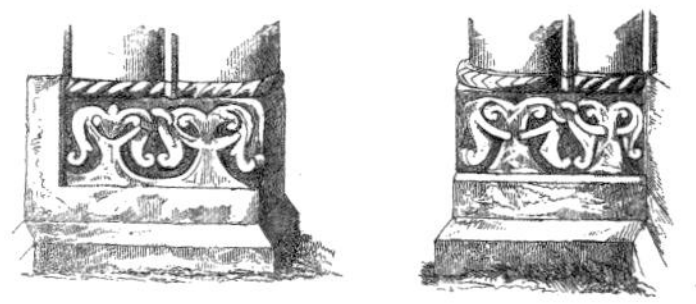

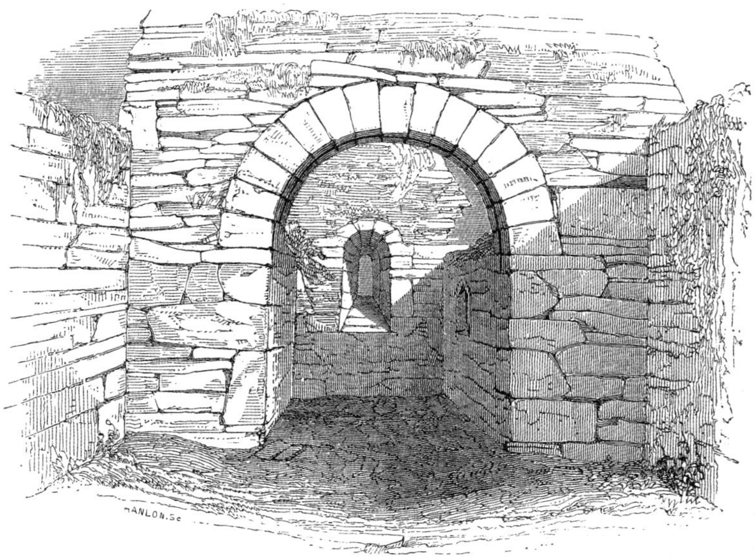

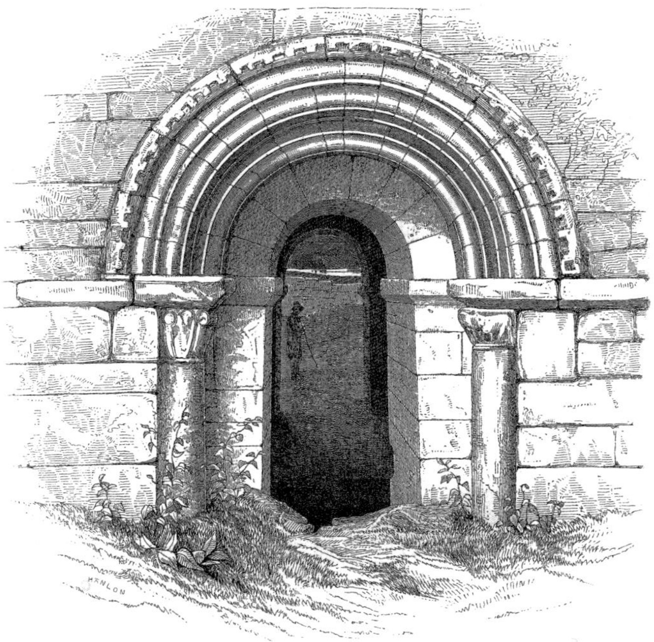

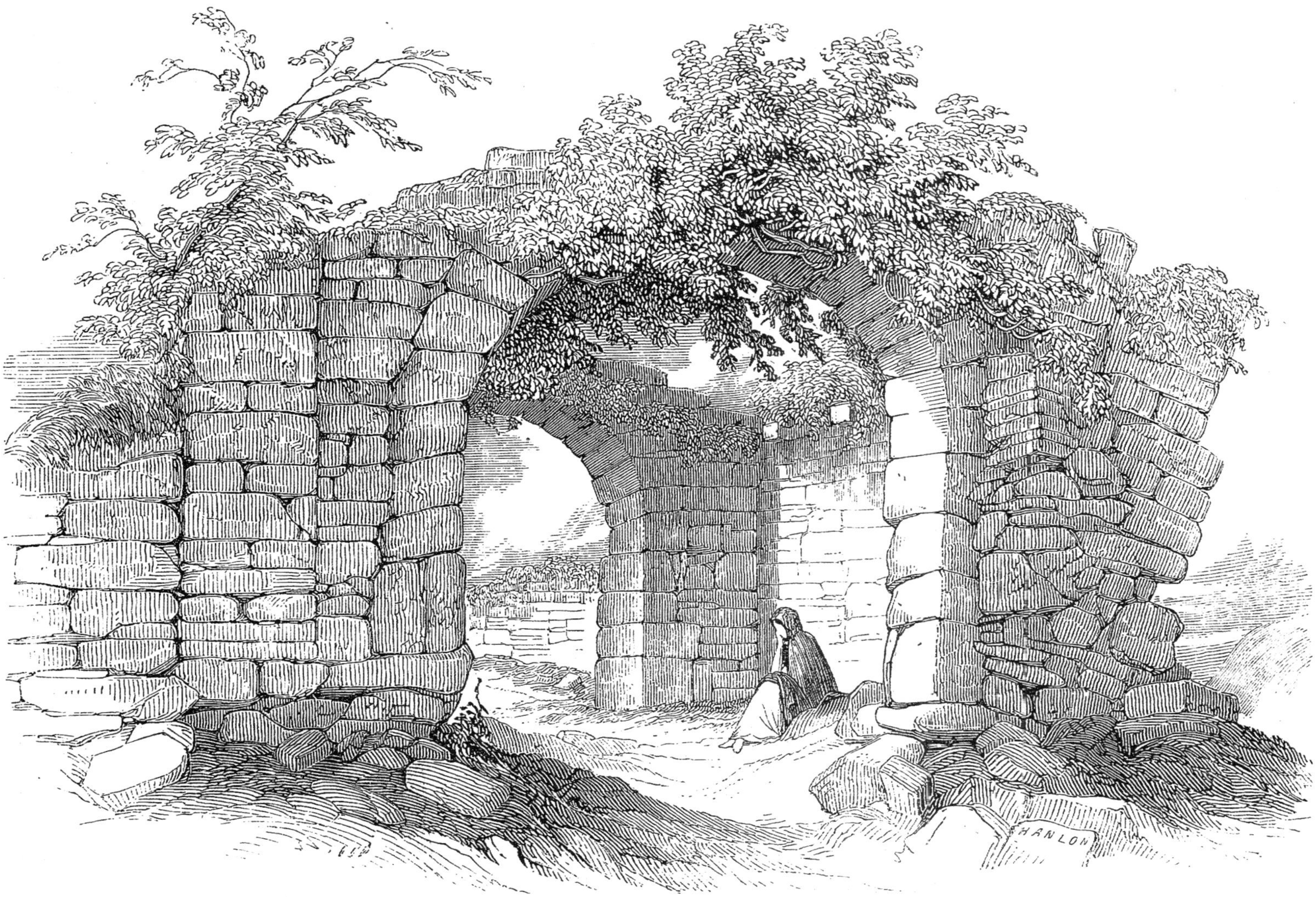

Gateway of the Cashel at Glendalough

INDEXED LIST OF ILLUSTRATIONS

Index ordered alphabetically by county and placename

Titles and spelling of works as found in original books

key [a] aquatint
[d] drawing
[e] engraving
[p] painting
* colour illustration

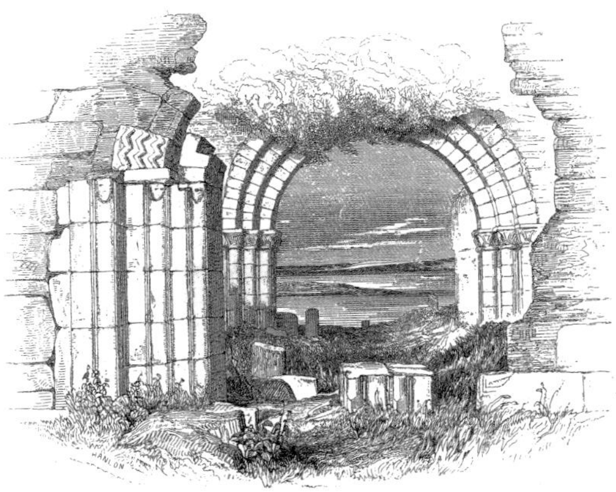

View of the Chancel-Arch and Fragment of the Doorway of St. Caimin's Church in Innishcaltra